# *Making the Team:*
# *A Guide for Managers*

SECOND EDITION

# *Making the Team:*
# *A Guide for Managers*

**Leigh L. Thompson**

*Kellogg School of Management*
*Northwestern University*

Upper Saddle River, NJ 07458

**Library of Congress Cataloging-in-Publication Data**

Thompson, Leigh L.
  Making the team : a guide for managers / Leigh L. Thompson.—2nd ed.
    p. cm.
  Includes bibliographical references and index.
  ISBN 0-13-141658-8 (pbk.)
   1. Teams in the workplace.  2. Performance.  3. Leadership.  4. Organizational
effectiveness.  I. Title.

HD66.T478 2003
658.4'02—dc21

2003048258

**Acquisitions Editor**: David Parker
**VP/Editor-in-Chief**: Jeff Shelstad
**Assistant Editor**: Ashley Keim
**Editorial Assistant**: Melissa Yu
**Media Project Manager**: Jessica Sabloff
**Executive Marketing Manager**: Shannon Moore
**Marketing Assistant**: Patrick Danzuso
**Managing Editor (Production)**: John Roberts
**Production Editor**: Maureen Wilson
**Production Assistant**: Joe DeProspero
**Permissions Supervisor**: Suzanne Grappi
**Manufacturing Buyer**: Michelle Klein
**Cover Design**: Bruce Kenselaar, Robert Weeks
**Cover Illustration/Photo**: Eyewire Collection/Gettyimages
**Full-Service Project Management and Composition**: Pine Tree Composition, Inc.
**Printer/Binder**: Courier Companies, Inc.—Westford, MA

Credits and acknowledgments borrowed from other sources and reproduced, with permission, in this textbook appear on appropriate page within text.

Pearson Education LTD.
Pearson Education Australia PTY, Limited
Pearson Education Singapore, Pte. Ltd
Pearson Education North Asia Ltd
Pearson Education, Canada, Ltd

Pearson Educación de Mexico, S.A. de C.V.
Pearson Education-Japan
Pearson Education Malaysia, Pte. Ltd
Pearson Education Upper Saddle River, New Jersey

10 9 8 7
ISBN 0-13-141658-8

*For my home team:*
*Bob, Sam, Ray, and Anna*

# Brief Contents

# Contents

# *Preface to the New Edition*

When I wrote *Making the Team* in 2000, my intent was to introduce leaders, managers, and executives to practical research on groups and teams. This enterprise required an integration of theory, research, and application. Five professors—Dave Messick, Keith Murnighan, Mark Rittenberg, Brian Uzzi, and I—offer a three-day course for executives in team leadership at the Kellogg School of Management at Northwestern University. Moreover, Kellogg offers a full-term course on teamwork to our MBA students. This book is dedicated to the students of Kellogg's executive program and MBA program.

The title of the book, *Making the Team,* has two audiences: leaders and team members. For the leader, the book directs itself toward how teams can be designed to function optimally; for those people who are members of teams, the book focuses on the skills necessary to be a productive team member.

Since the publication of the first version, many advances have occurred in team and group research. Every chapter has been updated with new information, new research, updated examples, and more. Specifically, I have made three major changes to the revised version of *Making the Team*:

- **New, updated research**: True to the book's defining characteristic—providing managers with the most up-to-date research in a digestible fashion—I have included the latest research on teamwork and group behavior, thus keeping the book up-to-date and true to its strong research focus and theory-driven approach. The updated research also reports on the survey of executives that we have conducted at Kellogg for the past five years. The survey in the first edition reported the responses of 149 managers and executives; the database of this survey has more than tripled, with a current total of 512 responses. In addition, more than 275 new research studies have been cited.

- **More case studies**: I have included more examples and illustrations of effective (as well as ineffective) teamwork. More than 130 new case studies and examples of actual company teams have been added. As before, each chapter opens with an example of a real team. Many of the concepts and techniques in the chapters are supplemented with illustrations and examples from real teams, both contemporary and historical. I do not use these examples to prove a theory; rather, I use them to illustrate how many of the concepts in the book are borne out in real-world situations.

- **Learning and development**: Mostly due to my strong research interests in learning, I have put learning front-and-center in the new edition, with a special focus on how leaders should be in a continuous learning mode. For example, in Chapter 1, I have expanded the team-building skills from two in the 2000 edition (accurate diagnosis and theory-based intervention) to three in the current edition (accurate diagnosis, theory-based intervention, and expert learning).

In addition to the changes discussed, which affect all chapters and sections of the book, several chapters have undergone updates as new theory and research has broken ground and as our world has been shaped by events such as September 11, 2001, and the rash of corporate fraud. For example, Chapter 6 ("Team Decision Making") now has a new section on decision making and ethics. In addition, all of the chapters have undergone a serious facelift. The revision was sparked not only by advances—as well as calamities—in the corporate world, but also even more so by the great scientific research on teamwork that my colleagues have relentlessly contributed to the field of management science in the past three years, since the first edition went to press.

One of the reasons why I love this field is because there are so many wonderful people with whom to collaborate. The following people have had a major impact on my thinking and have brought joy and meaning to the word "collaboration": Cameron Anderson, Linda Babcock, Max Bazerman, Terry Boles, Jeanne Brett, Susan Brodt, John Carroll, Hoon-Seok Choi, Jennifer Crocker, Gary Fine, Craig Fox, Adam Galinsky, Wendi Gardner, Dedre Gentner, Robert Gibbons, Kevin Gibson, James Gillespie, Rich Gonzalez, Deborah Gruenfeld, Reid Hastie, Andy Hoffman, Molly Kern, Peter Kim, Shirli Kopelman, Rod Kramer, Laura Kray, Terri Kurtzburg, John Levine, Allan Lind, George Loewenstein, Jeff Loewenstein, Denise Lewin Loyd, Beta Mannix, Kathleen McGinn, Vicki Medvec, Tanya Menon, Dave Messick, Terry Mitchell, Don Moore, Michael Morris, Keith Murnighan, Janice Nadler, Maggie Neale, Erika Petersen, Kathy Phillips, Robin Pinkley, Mark Rittenberg, Ashleigh Rosette, Ken Savitsky, Elizabeth Seeley, Vanessa Seiden, Marwan Sinaceur, Harris Sondak, Tom Tyler, Leaf Van Boven, Kimberly Wade-Benzoni, Laurie Weingart, and Judith White.

The revision of this book would not have been possible without the dedication, organization, and creativity of Rachel Claff, who created the layout, organized the information, edited the hundreds of drafts, mastered the figures, and researched many of the case studies for this book.

In this book, I talk quite a bit about the "power of the situation" and how strongly the environment shapes behavior. The Kellogg School of Management is one of the most supportive, dynamic environments that I have ever had the pleasure to be a part of. In particular, Dean Dipak Jain and Associate Deans David Besanko and Robert Magee have created an environment in which teaching and research are happily married and very productive. My colleagues across the Kellogg School are uniquely warm, constructive, and generous. Ken Bardach, former dean of Kellogg's Executive Education, was particularly visionary in his development of programs on teamwork. Directing the KTAG (Kellogg Teams and Groups) Center and the Behavioral Laboratory has been a pleasure beyond compare. I am very grateful for the generous grants I have received through the years from the National Science Foundation's Decision, Risk and Management Program, the Kellogg Teams and Groups Center, and its sister, the Dispute Resolution Research Center.

This book is very much a team effort of the people I have mentioned here, whose talents are diverse, broad, and extraordinarily impressive. I am deeply indebted to my colleagues and students, and I feel very grateful that they have touched my life and this book.

# *Preface to the First Edition*

When I first came to the Kellogg Graduate School of Management in 1995, there were only a small number of course offerings on group dynamics and teamwork. Sheer demand for more teamwork led to the development of a three-day team-building program for executives. In this program, leading scholars—Deborah Gruenfeld, Dave Messick, Keith Murnighan, Brian Uzzi, and I—provide the latest team-building and management principles to managers and executives from different industries all over the globe. The participants are always as surprised as we are to see the commonality of concerns and interests regarding their teams. Most of the participants were hungry for a book that would pull together the basic and cutting-edge concepts they learned from the seminar. I searched for a book that would capture and supplement the broad and deep scope that this program reflected. Often, the popular book choices were not theory based and the scholarly books not very practical. I set out to write a book that would do three things:

1. Provide an extremely engaging approach to teamwork by connecting models and theories with actual teams and companies.
2. Maintain a rigorous, cutting-edge research focus—all of the material in the book is produced by leading scholars in the field and represents hard science, in the strict sense of the word.
3. Provide a big-picture view of teamwork by giving the manager and team leader practical advice and solutions to problems.

*Making the Team* separates fact from fiction and outlines in a clear, step-by-step fashion how young managers, as well as seasoned executives, can improve the functioning of their teams. Each chapter opens with a case analysis of a real team. The reader of this book will learn how to diagnose the causes of team failure, conduct a performance evaluation of teams, leverage the team within the organization, determine effective leadership behavior, create opportunity from conflict, deal with global teamwork issues, set the stage for creative, breakthrough thinking in teams, reduce prejudice, and manage meetings and study groups for effective learning and decision making. In short, this book transforms the art of teamwork into a science to be studied and mastered.

I took the perspective of the manager when writing this book; arguably, I should have taken the perspective of the team. However, this choice was for expositional purposes, as all of the messages for the manager of the team apply to the team itself.

The twelve chapters are arranged into a sequence of three major sections: Part I covers the basics (types of teams, facts, and myths); Part II covers internal dynamics of teamwork (building the team, collective intelligence, decision making, conflict, and creativity); and Part III focuses on the external dynamics of teams in organizations (networking, leadership, interteam relations, and information technology).

The first chapter ("Teams in Organizations") lays out the basic concepts of the book and attempts to dispel some common myths about teamwork. It introduces the basic building blocks for analyzing and perfecting teamwork. Chapter 2 ("Performance and Productivity") tackles the question of how we know whether a team is performing well, and if not, what to do about it. Chapter 3 ("Rewarding Teamwork") deals with the question of rewarding teamwork in organizations, the impact of rewards on motivation and behavior, and the choices that organizations have in this regard.

Part II of the book focuses on the internal dynamics—or what is going on inside the team itself. Chapter 4 ("Building the Team") focuses on structuring tasks, selecting people, and fostering team relationships. Chapter 5 ("Sharpening the Team Mind") explores how teams communicate (and the most common reasons for failures), how teams process information, and how they create a collective team intelligence. Chapter 6 ("Team Decision Making") examines the four most common team decision-making pitfalls. It discusses the causes and consequences of conformity and how to deal with it. Chapter 7 ("Conflict in Teams") focuses on how to turn negative conflict into positive conflict for teams. Chapter 8 ("Creativity") examines how to design teams to be maximally creative.

Part III of the book focuses on external dynamics or how the team fits in the organization. Chapter 9 ("Managing the External Environment") takes up the topics of team boundaries, interteam relations, networking, and boundary spanning. Chapter 10 ("Leadership") focuses on the dual tasks of effective leadership: dealing with internal dynamics as well as external dynamics. Chapter 11 ("Interteam Relations") focuses on the issues of conflict and competition between teams in the organization. Chapter 12 ("Teamwork via Information Technology") examines the impact of information technology on global, as well as local, teamwork and some of the choices the manager has for maintaining high productivity.

I also included four appendices that the managers, executives, and students I have worked with told me they wanted to see in this book. Appendix 1 focuses on how to run a meeting. Appendix 2 contains tips for consultants and facilitators of meetings. Appendix 3 focuses on how to build and maintain an effective study group. Appendix 4 contains examples of 360-degree evaluations.

The research and ideas in this book come from an invaluable set of scholars in the fields of social psychology, organizational behavior, sociology, and cognitive psychology. During the past twelve years, my life has been enriched in very important ways by the following people with whom I have collaborated: Linda Babcock, Max Bazerman, Terry Boles, Jeanne Brett, Susan Brodt, Gary Fine, Craig Fox, Dedre Gentner, Robert Gibbons, Kevin Gibson, Rich Gonzalez, Deborah Gruenfeld, Reid Hastie, Peter Kim, Shirli Kopelman, Rod Kramer, Laura Kray, Terri Kurtzburg, John Levine, Allan Lind, Jeff Loewenstein, Beta Mannix, Vicki Medvec, Dave Messick, Terry Mitchell, Don Moore, Michael Morris, Keith Murnighan, Janice Nadler, Robin Pinkley, Vanessa Ruda, Harris Sondak, Tom Tyler, Kathleen Valley, Leaf Van Boven, Kimberly Wade-Benzoni, and Laurie Weingart. In the book, I use the pronoun we because so much of my thinking has been influenced and shaped by this set of eminent scholars.

Fourteen students who were enrolled in an advanced "managing groups" course at the Kellogg School read the book, criticized it, and improved it immensely during the fall of 1998: Diego Lezica Alvear, Pablo Gonzalez Beramendi, Geoffrey Bolan, Elmer Choy, Francesco Dalla Rovere, Read T. DuPriest, Shawna Gwin, Alison Hyman, Jean Johnson, Thomas Lott, Rebecca M. Mayne, Ryan Reis, Pamela L. Skonicki, and Carrie Tower. These people improved the book tremendously and humbled me in the process of doing so.

A number of people read this book in an earlier form and provided very helpful comments: Joan F. Brett, Karen Cates, John A. Drexler Jr., and Jeff Polzer, and our reviewers

Donald Ashbaugh, University of Wisconsin–Madison; Sigal Barsade, Yale University; Theodore Forbes III, University of Virginia; Daniel Gigone, Duke University; Cristina Gibson, University of Southern California; and Judith Gordon, Boston College.

Two other people played an enormously important role in this book: Avi Steinlauf and Greg Grieff. Avi Steinlauf conducted all of the information searches on the examples covered in the book based on real companies. His work was intensive, thorough, and creative, and it made the book really come alive. Greg Grieff was the first-round high-level copy editor for the book. He raised the important questions, reorganized the flow of thoughts, made the logic clear, and provided much of the focus and direction of each chapter.

This book would not have had a chance without the dedication, organization, and editorial skills of Rachel Claff, who created the layout, organized the hundreds of drafts, mastered the figures, and researched its various aspects.

I completed this book while I was at the Kellogg Graduate School of Management, a place whose spirit is motivating, energizing, and inspirational. I feel honored to live and work in the midst of so many great people, and I am indebted to Dean Donald Jacobs and the Kellogg Teams and Groups Center (KTAG) for their generous support of this book and to Ken Bardach for helping to provide the vision for our team executive program. Very important grants from the National Science Foundation's Decision Risk and Management Science Program have made it possible for me to conduct several of the research studies that are discussed.

This book is very much a team effort by the people I have mentioned here, whose talents are diverse, broad, and extraordinarily impressive. I am deeply indebted to my colleagues and students, and I feel very grateful that they have touched my life.

# The Basics of Teamwork

# CHAPTER

# Teams in Organizations:

1

## *Facts and Myths*

*Ten years ago, Standard Motor Products's general manager, Joe Forlenza, was told that "empowerment" could not work in his plant, which contained union contracts. Nonetheless, Forlenza decided to explore self-directed work teams. And now, inside Standard Motor Products's plant, workers say "team" and "empowerment" without snickering. The seven members of the plant's core leadership team rarely dictate or over-rule work teams' decisions. However, the transition to self-empowered teams was not exactly smooth sailing—at first, it was hampered by egos and power struggles. In fact, plant productivity dropped by nearly 25 percent in the first year. However, Forlenza had forecasted this possibility and did not panic. By the end of year two, productivity was back up and improving. At this point in Standard's transition-to-teams process, most of the employees are true believers, and the company continues to grow steadily. Yet, at many other companies (including Standard), about 10 percent of workers do not fit into teams because they simply can't or don't want to work with others. These people often end up leaving the company (Stafford, 2002).*

The transition to teams is not always easy. Virtually everyone who has worked in an organization has been a member of a task-performing group at one time or another. Good teams are not a matter of luck; they result from hard work, careful planning, and commitment from the sponsoring organization. Team design from the inside out is a skill. It requires a thorough understanding of teams to ensure that the team works as designed. Although there are no guarantees, we believe that understanding what makes teams work will naturally lead to better and more effective teams. In this book, we introduce a systematic approach that allows leaders, managers, executives, trainers, and professionals to build and maintain excellent teams in their organizations.

Our systematic approach is based upon scientific principles of learning and change. Implementing change requires that managers audit their own behavior to see where mistakes are being made, consider and implement new techniques and practices, and then examine their effects. Unfortunately, accomplishing these tasks in a typical organizational setting is not easy. This chapter sets the stage for effective learning by first defining what a team is—it's not always clear! Next, we distinguish four types of teams in organizations in terms of their authority and examine why teams are even necessary. We expose some of the most common myths about teamwork and provide some useful observations. Finally, we provide the manager with the results of our survey on how teams are used in organizations and the problems with which managers are most concerned. The problems cited by these managers cut across industries, from doughnut companies to high-tech engineering firms. These problems and concerns are examined in the chapters that follow.

## WHAT IS A TEAM?

According to Sundstrom, DeMeuse, and Futrell (1990), a work team is an interdependent collection of individuals who share responsibility for specific outcomes for their organizations. Not everyone who works together or in close proximity belongs to a team. A team is a group of people who are interdependent with respect to information, resources, and skills and who seek to combine their efforts to achieve a common goal. As is summarized in Box 1-1, teams have five key defining characteristics. First, teams exist to achieve a *shared goal*. Simply put, teams have work to do. Teams produce outcomes for which members have collective responsibility and reap some form of collective reward. Second, team members are interdependent regarding some common goal. Interdependence is the hallmark of teamwork. *Interdependence* means that team members cannot achieve their goals single-handedly, but instead, must rely on each other to meet shared objectives. There are several kinds of interdependencies, as team members must rely on others for information, expertise, resources, and so on. Third, teams are bounded and remain relatively stable over time. *Boundedness* means the team has an identifiable membership; members, as well as nonmembers, know who is on the team. *Stability* refers to the tenure of membership. Most teams work together for a meaningful length of time—long enough to accomplish their goal. Fourth, team members have the *authority* to manage their own work and internal processes. We focus on teams in which individual members can, to some extent, determine how their work gets done. Thus, although a prison chain gang may be a team in some sense, the prisoners have little authority in terms of managing their own work. Finally, teams operate in a larger social system context. Teams are not islands unto themselves. They do their work in a larger organization, often alongside other teams. Furthermore, teams often need to draw upon resources from outside the team and vice versa—something we discuss in Part III of this book.

A *working group,* by contrast, consists of people who learn from one another and share ideas, but are not interdependent in an important fashion and are not working toward a shared goal. Working groups share information, perspectives, and insights, make decisions, and help people do their jobs better, but the focus is on individual

---

**BOX 1-1**

### Five Key Characteristics of Teams
### (Alderfer, 1977; Hackman, 1990)

- Teams exist to achieve a shared goal.
- Team members are interdependent regarding some common goal.
- Teams are bounded and stable over time.
- Team members have the authority to manage their own work and internal processes.
- Teams operate in a social system context.

goals and accountability. For example, consider the "superintendent's club" created by AKAM Associates, Inc., one of New York City's premiere residential management companies. The club is a fellowship among the seventy-five superintendents and resident managers that serve the AKAM portfolio of luxury and middle-income condominiums and cooperatives. The club is designed as a "think tank," a place where supers can meet, exchange ideas and experiences, and learn from each other. Whereas the club does not meet the definitions of a team, there is a solidarity among the supers. For example, when one of the luxury condos had a major basement flood, club members arrived with wet-vacs, mops and buckets—all voluntarily (Kaminoff, 2002).

## WHY SHOULD ORGANIZATIONS HAVE TEAMS?

Teams and teamwork are not novel concepts. In fact, teams and team thinking have been around for years at companies such as Procter & Gamble and Boeing. In the 1980s, the manufacturing and auto industries strongly embraced a new, team-oriented approach when U.S. firms retooled to compete with Japanese companies that were quickly gaining market share (Nahavandi & Aranda, 1994). During collaboration on the B-2 stealth bomber between the U.S. Air Force, Northrop, and some four thousand subcontractors and suppliers in the early 1980s, various teams were employed to handle different parts of the project. "As new developments occurred or new problems were encountered during the program, the Air Force/Northrop team formed ad hoc teams made up of [their] own experts and specialists from other companies and scientific institutions" (Kresa, 1991).

Managers discovered the large body of research indicating that teams can be more effective than the traditional corporate hierarchical structure for making decisions quickly and efficiently. Even simple changes such as encouraging input and feedback from workers on the line can make a dramatic improvement. For instance, quality control (QC) circles and employee involvement groups are often vehicles for employee participation (Cole, 1982). It is a mark of these programs' success that this kind of thinking is considered conventional wisdom nowadays. But, although these QC teams were worthy efforts at fostering the use of teams in organizations, the teams needed for the restructuring and reengineering processes of the future may be quite different (Nahavandi & Aranda, 1994). This point is brought home even more clearly in light of A. T. Kearney's findings (1995) that nearly seven out of 10 teams fail to produce the desired results. ("The Trouble with Teams," 1995).

At least four challenges suggest that building and maintaining effective teams is of paramount importance.

### Customer Service Focus

The first challenge has to do with *customer service*. Businesses and companies all over the world have moved from a transactional, economic view of customers and clients to a relational view of customers. Transactional models of teamwork are characterized by discrete exchanges, are short-term in nature, and contain little interaction between the customer and the vendor. In contrast, relational models of teamwork occur over time, are more intense, and are built upon a relationship between the people involved. There is good reason to care about the customer from a relational point of view given that 85 percent of customers who stop buying from a company do so because they believe the company does not care about them or their business (Carder & Gunter, 2001). Moreover, acquiring new customers costs five to 10 times more than keeping existing customers happy. To the extent that teams are positioned to care about the customer from a relational perspective, this can add tremendous value for the organization. For example, a company's profits can increase by as much as 85 percent if it can lower the percentage of customers who stop buying by as little as 5 percent (reported in Carder & Gunter, 2001).

## Competition

The second challenge has to do with *competition.* In today's economy, a few large companies are emerging as dominant players in the biggest markets. These industry leaders often enjoy vast economies of scale and earn tremendous profits. The losers are often left with little in the way of a market—let alone a marketable product (Frank & Cook, 1995). Think, for example, of Microsoft's Windows operating system and Office Products market share dominance. The division that develops the Office Products software—which includes Word, Excel, PowerPoint, Outlook, and Access—employs thousands of people. Those products share a lot of code with each other, and so teamwork is critical to coordinate the activities of the various component groups that make up the Office Products Division (Anonymous, 1996). With so much at stake, companies are aggressively competing in a winner-take-all battle for market share. Thus, bringing out the best in teams within the company has become even more important. This means that people can be expected to specialize more and more in their areas of expertise, and these areas of expertise will get ever more narrow and interdependent. Both companies and people have to increasingly rely on others to get access to their expertise. This is the core structure of a team-based approach to work.

## Information Age

A third factor is the *emergence of the information age.* In the knowledge era, employees are knowledge workers and teams are knowledge integrators. Information techology was the catalyst for the knowledge economy. For example, Garry Embleton, a business-development manager at Rhodia (formerly part of Rhone-Poulenc) needed to reduce the time it took to transfer technology to plants in Canada. "We used to think a year was normal for this type of project," said Embleton, who tried something new by letting his global team use software that would let him see all of the speed bumps that were slowing them down. In one case, a teleconference was held using project software, and the problem was solved in one day (Warner, 2002). The role of managers has shifted accordingly; they are no longer primarily responsible for gathering information from employees working below them in the organizational hierarchy and then making command decisions based on this information. Their new role is to identify the key resources that will best implement the team's objectives and then to facilitate the coordination of those resources for the company's purposes.

The jobs of the team members have also changed significantly. This can be viewed as a threat or a challenge. Millions of jobs have been altered dramatically or have disappeared completely since the advent of computers. For example, in 2001, the New York Stock Exchange (NYSE) laid off 150 floor reporters whose positions were no longer needed due to automation (Ceron, 2001). Decisions may now be made far from their traditional location; indeed, sometimes even by contractors who are not employees of the company. This dramatic change in structure requires an equally dramatic reappraisal of how companies structure the work environment.

## Globalization

The fourth challenge is *globalization.* An increasingly global and fast-paced economy requires people with specialized expertise, yet the specialists within a company need to work together. Moreover, as acquisitions, restructurings, outsourcing, and other structural changes take place, the need for coordination becomes all the more salient. Changes in corporate structure and increases in specialization imply that there will be new boundaries among the members of an organization. Boundaries both separate and link teams within an organization (Alderfer, 1977; Friedlander, 1987), although the boundaries are not always obvious. These new relationships require team members to learn how to work with others to achieve their goals. Team members must integrate through coordination and synchronization with suppliers, managers, peers, and customers. Teams of people are required to work with one another and rarely (and, in some cases, never) interact in a face-to-face fashion. With the ever-improving ability to communicate with others anywhere on the planet (and beyond!), people and resources that were once remote can now be reached quickly, easily, and inexpensively. This has facilitated the development of the virtual team—groups linked by technology so effectively that it is as if they were in the same building. Technology also gives managers options they never had before, in terms of which resources they choose to employ on any particular project. Furthermore, cultural differences, both profound and nuanced, can threaten the ability of teams to accomplish shared objectives.

## TYPES OF TEAMS IN ORGANIZATIONS

Organizations have come to rely on team-based arrangements to improve quality, productivity, customer service, and the experience of work for their employees. Yet not all teams are alike. Teams differ greatly in their degree of autonomy and control vis-à-vis the organization. Specifically, how is authority distributed in the organization? Who has responsibility for the routine monitoring and management of group performance processes? Who has responsibility for creating and fine-tuning the design of the group (Hackman, 1987)? Consider the four levels of control depicted in Figure 1-1.

### Manager-Led Teams

The most traditional type of team is the **manager-led team.** In the manager-led team, the manager acts as the team leader and is responsible for defining the goals, methods, and functioning of the team. The teams themselves have responsibility only for the actual execution of their assigned work. Management is responsible for monitoring and managing performance processes, overseeing design, selecting members, and interfacing with the organization. Examples of manager-led work teams include automobile assembly teams, surgery teams, sports teams, and military teams. A manager-led team typically has a dedicated, full-time, higher-ranking supervisor, as in a coal-mining crew.

Manager-led teams provide the greatest amount of control over team members and the work they perform; they allow the leader to have control over the process and products of the team. In addition, they can be efficient, in the sense that the manager does the

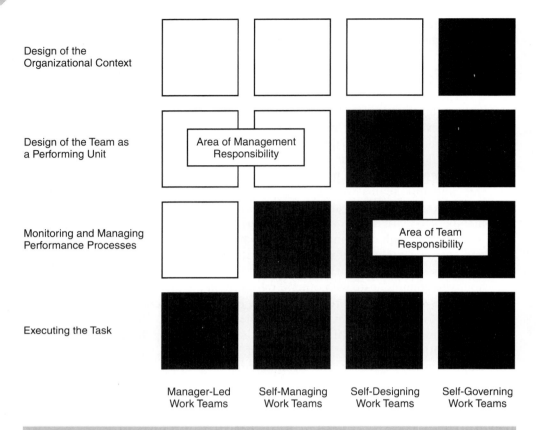

Design of the
Organizational Context

Design of the Team as
a Performing Unit

Area of Management
Responsibility

Monitoring and Managing
Performance Processes

Area of Team
Responsibility

Executing the Task

| Manager-Led | Self-Managing | Self-Designing | Self-Governing |
| Work Teams | Work Teams | Work Teams | Work Teams |

**FIGURE 1-1** Authority of Four Illustrative Types of Work Teams
*Source:* Hackman, J. R. 1987. "The Design of Work Teams." In J. W. Lorsch (Ed.). *Handbook of Organizational Behavior.* Upper Saddle River, NJ: Prentice Hall.

work of setting the goals and outlining the work to be done. In manager-led teams, managers don't have to sit by and watch the team make the same mistakes they did. Manager-led teams also have relatively low start-up costs. However, there can be some key disadvantages, such as diffusion of responsibility and conformity to the leader. In short, members have less autonomy and empowerment. Manager-led teams may be ideally suited for simple tasks in which there is a clear overriding goal, such as task forces or fact-finding teams. Other examples include military squads, flight crews, and stage crews.

## Self-Managing Teams

In **self-managing** or **self-regulating teams,** a manager or leader determines the overall purpose or goal of the team, but the team is at liberty to manage the methods by which to achieve that goal. Self-managed teams are increasingly common in organizations. Examples include executive search committees and managerial task forces. Self-managing teams improve productivity, quality, savings, and employee morale, as well as contribute to reductions in absenteeism and turnover (Stewart & Manz, 1995). These benefits have been observed in both manufacturing and service settings.

At Whole Foods Markets, the largest natural-foods grocer in the United States, the culture is premised on decentralized teamwork. The team, not the hierarchy, is the defining unit of activity (Fishman, 1996). Teams of eight to 10 people manage different parts of each of the 133 stores throughout the country—produce, grocery, prepared foods, and so on. Each team is given the authority to hire, discipline, and motivate each person within the team (Kelley & Lavandara, 2001). Similarly, Chevron's Western Production Business Unit established 11 self-managing work teams among its 80 employees (Attaran & Nguyen, 1999). The five to eight member teams are balanced for technical expertise, as well as social and leadership skills. The goal of each team is clear: improvements are the core focus.

Chris Capossela is a team leader at Microsoft Project, which evolved into a culture of self-managing teams. Says Capossela, "You know the guy who comes into your office with a crappy project schedule and says, 'This is the way the project is going to run'? That guy used to be me" (Warner, 2002b, p. 48). After encountering resistance, Capossela decided to give team members more of a say in the process by mapping out a rough calendar for his project team, but he resisted putting in all the details. He sent the rough draft to the team members who would be doing the work. Then, instead of insisting that the team route its e-mail comments and suggestions back to him, Capossela had the team's feedback entered into a central project database that was then used to fill out the project plan automatically (Warner, 2002b).

Self-managing teams build commitment, offer increased autonomy, and often enhance morale. The disadvantage is that the manager has much less control over the process and products, making it difficult to assess progress. Self-managing teams can also be more time-consuming.

## Self-Directing Teams

**Self-directing** or **self-designing teams** determine their own objectives and the methods by which to achieve them. Management has responsibility only for the team's organizational context. Self-directed teams offer the most potential for innovation, enhance goal commitment and motivation, and provide opportunity for organizational learning and change. However, self-directed or self-designing teams are extremely time-consuming, have the greatest potential for conflict, and can be very costly to build. (For a step-by-step guide to setting up self-designing teams, see Orsburn, Moran, Musselwhite, & Zenger, 1990.) Furthermore, it can be extremely difficult (or impossible) to monitor their progress. Other disadvantages include marginalization of the team and lack of team legitimacy. However, self-directed teams are often capable of great accomplishments (see Sidebar 1-1 for an example).

Self-designing teams may be ideally suited for complex, ill-defined, or ambiguous problems and next-generation planning. At the Harley-Davidson Motor Company, there is a "commitment to making the company a high-performance work organization, where the people closest to a job have the authority and responsibility to do it the best way they can. Part of the company's management approach is freedom and teamwork—it encourages each plant to solve its problems in its own way" (Imperato, 1997, p. 104). According to former CEO Rich Teerlink, "The issues are always the same . . . quality, productivity, participation, flexibility, and cash flow. But each plant deals with them in a different way. We don't have cookbooks because there isn't a cookbook.

## Sidebar 1-1. An Example of a Self-Directing Team

It's Wednesday evening at Carnegie Hall. The air is charged with the excitement generated when people know that they are about to experience an event that will stimulate their senses and challenge their minds. As the Orpheus Chamber Orchestra takes the stage to warm applause, the musicians exude confidence. There's something different about this orchestra: There is no conductor. Founded in 1972 by cellist Julian Fifer, Orpheus gives every person great power to direct great music. Orpheus is designed to rely on the skills, abilities, and passionate commitment of the members, rather than on the monolithic leadership of a conductor. The decision to give power to the musicians—a radical innovation in the orchestra world—required a structural model that was fundamentally different from the rigid command-and-control hierarchy universally employed by traditional orchestras. The original members of Orpheus found their inspiration in chamber music, a world grounded in democratic values, where small ensembles (generally fewer than ten musicians) function as self-directing teams, and where power, responsibility, leadership, and motivation rest entirely with the team (Seifter & Economy, 2001).

We're on a journey that never ends. And the day we think we've got it made, that's the day we'd better start worrying about going out of business" (p. 104).

At the GE/Durham plant that assembles engines for the Boeing 777, there are nine teams, each with only one directive: they are told the date by which their next engine must be loaded (Fishman, 1999; Maccoby, 2000). Self-directing teams decide who does which work; they schedule training, vacations, and overtime, and they monitor their own performance issues, such as lack of productivity or lack of work ethic. However, this is seldom a problem. Even though there are no incentives other than promotion on the basis of skills, technicians are motivated by the work itself, the drive for perfection, and pride in supplying one of the highest-thrust engines in the industry. The leader of these teams is responsible for listening, informing, and focusing on costs.

### Self-Governing Teams

**Self-governing teams** and boards of directors are usually responsible for executing a task, managing their own performance processes, designing the group, and designing the organizational context. They are the extreme in terms of control and responsibility. In many companies, the president or chief operating officer has been replaced with an executive, self-governing team (Ancona & Nadler, 1989). Examples of this approach include John Reed's structuring of Citicorp's senior management when he succeeded Walter Wriston, and Walter Shipley's creation of the "three president" structure at Chemical Bank in the 1980s. When British Steel developed a unique, patented steel-skinned concrete panel system called the bi-steel system, it did so with the use of "a semi-autonomous team within a giant conglomerate not widely credited for encouraging innovative virtually self-governing teams" (Greek, 1997, p. 19).

In certain cases, companies want to set up a self-governing (autonomous) team, similar to the independent counsel's office, to investigate serious problems such as the sexual harassment case at Mitsubishi (e.g., the team headed up by Lynn Martin;

Holland, 1996). The way the military has handled problems with sexual harassment stands in sharp contrast, not only in terms of the kinds of teams set up to examine the problems, but also in terms of the results they have achieved. In other cases, these kinds of teams could be disastrous, such as a committee composed of boards of directors—employees could be intimidated by the authority of these individuals and, therefore, unwilling or unable to provide a critical perspective on the status quo.

There are trade-offs involved with each of these four types of teams. Self-governing and self-directed teams provide the greatest potential in terms of commitment and participation, but are also at the greatest risk of misdirection. When decisions are pushed down in organizations, team goals and interests may be at odds with organizational interests. Unless everyone in the organization is aware of the company's interests and goals, poor decisions (often with the best of intentions) may be made. An organization that chooses a manager-led group is betting that a manager can run things more effectively than a team can. If it is believed that the team can do the job better, a self-governing or self-designing team may be appropriate. One implication of this is that the manager's traditional role as a collector of information is less and less important. If shared control over the performance situation and processes is preferred, a self-managing group is chosen.

# SOME OBSERVATIONS ABOUT TEAMS AND TEAMWORK

There is a lot of folklore and unfounded intuition when it comes to teams and teamwork. We want to set the record straight by exposing some of the observations that managers find most useful. This is not an exhaustive list, obviously, but we believe the factors on this list have the most value for leaders when it comes to understanding how teams perform, change, and grow.

## Teams Are Not Always the Answer

When companies are in trouble, they often restructure into teams. However, putting people into teams does not solve problems; if not done thoughtfully, this may even cause more problems. For every case of team success, there is an equally compelling case of team failure. Teams can outperform the best member of the group, but there are no guarantees. Admitting the inefficiency of teams is hard, especially when most of us would like to believe the Gestalt principle that the whole is greater than the sum of its parts! As we discuss in later chapters, teams can suffer from many drawbacks, such as too much emphasis on harmony or individualism, which causes a feeling of powerlessness and creates discord (Griffith, 1997). Teams are not a panacea for organizations; they often fail and are frequently overused or poorly designed. In the best circumstances, teams provide insight, creativity, and cross-fertilization of knowledge in a way that a person working independently cannot. In the wrong circumstances, teamwork can lead to confusion, delay, and poor decision making.

## Managers Fault the Wrong Causes for Team Failure

Imagine yourself in the following situation: The wonderful team that you put together last year has collapsed into lethargy. The new product line is not forthcoming, conflict has erupted, and there is high turnover. What has gone wrong? If you are like most managers, you place the blame on one of two things: (1) external, uncontrollable forces (i.e., a bad economy) or (2) the people on the team (e.g., difficult personalities). Conveniently for the manager, both of these problems do not directly implicate poor leadership. However, according to most research investigations, neither of these causes is the actual culprit. Most team problems are not explained by external problems or personality problems. According to Charan and Useem (2002), most companies fail for one simple reason: managerial error.

The **misattribution error** is the tendency for managers to attribute the causes of team failure to forces beyond their personal control. Leaders may blame individual team members, the lack of resources, or a competitive environment. By pointing to a problem team member, the team's problems can be neatly and clearly understood as emanating from one source. This protects the leader's ego (and in some cases the manager's job), but stifles learning and destroys morale. It is more likely that the team's poor performance is due to a structural, rather than personal, cause. Furthermore, it is likely that several things are at work, not just one.

## Managers Fail to Recognize Their Team-Building Responsibilities

Many new managers conceive of their role as building the most effective relationships they can with each individual subordinate; they erroneously equate managing their team with managing the individual people on the team (Hill, 1982). These managers rarely rely on group-based forums for problem solving and diagnosis. Instead, they spend their time in one-on-one meetings. Teamwork is expected to be a natural consequence. As a result, many decisions are based upon limited information, and decision outcomes can backfire in unexpected and negative ways (see Sidebar 1-2).

## Experimenting with Failures Leads to Better Teams

It may seem ironic, but one of the most effective ways to learn is to experience failure. Evidence of this is provided by the fallout that accompanied the Los Angeles Police Department's (LAPD) handling of the riots that broke out following the Rodney King beating verdict in 1992. A *Los Angeles Times* editorial following the incident stated that "successful policing is a team effort; likewise, unsuccessful policing of the magnitude that occurred the night the riots broke out is a team failure" (*Los Angeles Times,* 1992, p. B4). The aftermath of the criticisms levied upon the LAPD and the people who ran the department caused an overhaul within the management ranks of the department. A failed team effort should be viewed as a critical source of information from which to learn. The problem is that failure is hard to embrace: our defense systems go into overdrive at the mere inkling that something we do is not above average. The true mark of a valued team member is a willingness to learn from mistakes. However, this learning can only come when people take personal responsibility for their actions.

The truth is, teams have a flatter learning curve than do most individuals; it takes teams longer to "get on their feet." However, teams have greater potential than do individuals. We discuss this further in Chapter 2.

## Conflict among Team Members Is Not Always a Bad Thing

Many leaders naively boast that their teams are successful because they never have conflict. However, it is a fallacy to believe that conflict is detrimental to effective teamwork. In fact, conflict may be necessary for effective decision making in teams.

## Sidebar 1-2. Team-Building Responsibilities

Steve Miller, managing director of the Royal Dutch/Shell Group of Companies, develops exercises that allow teams to assess their performance as a group and the impact a leader has on the group. For example, one of his exercises involves giving each team a video camera. Each team has 90 minutes to come up with a 5- or 6-minute video that illustrates the old culture of the company and the new culture of the company. This exercise instigated a major change in the Austrian business offices of Royal Dutch/Shell.

In the first program involving the video camera exercise, the Austrian team was clearly lagging behind all the other teams in terms of motivation, participation, and enjoyment. What's more, it was obvious to the Austrians as well as the other teams that they were not performing well. Needless to say, their morale was suffering, and Miller was uncertain how to help the struggling team turn things around.

At one point during the week, the team leader for the Austrian group was called away suddenly and was not present for the video exercise. At first, this seemed to be the worst thing that could happen to the Austrian team—they were leaderless and facing a real out-of-the-box problem.

The Austrian team surprised everyone by coming up with a powerful and humorous video. The video showed a man who needs to use the bathroom very urgently. The "old Shell" video depicts the man walking around in great discomfort, looking for a toilet. The doors are locked; there is all kinds of bureaucratic paperwork to complete and needless rubber-stamping. The clip ends with the man nearly collapsing in the men's room. That was the Austrian's idea of the "old Shell."

The next clip depicted the "new Shell" culture. The same man immediately finds the men's room, is greeted by a hospitable attendant, and is offered personal toilet paper and amenities. The video concludes with the service attendant trying to zip up the man's fly.

Everyone watching the video was completely stunned by the creativity and humor of the video. Clearly, the Austrians had won this competition, which turned out to be the beginning of a dramatic shift in their motivation, performance, and participation in the entire event. When the Austrian leader returned, he began to realize how capable and motivated his team really was. This single event was a turning point in how the team and the leader worked together; the team went on to dramatically improve their business in Austria (Pascale, 1998).

Conflict among team members can foment accuracy, insight, understanding, and development of trust and innovation. Just as there are two kinds of cholesterol, "good" and "bad," there are two kinds of conflict in teams. "Good" conflict (which we discuss in greater detail in Chapter 7) is conflict about issues, and is divorced from evaluations of people's character. "Bad" conflict is conflict that is personalized and, therefore, highly threatening and damaging for team relationships.

## Strong Leadership Is Not Always Necessary for Strong Teams

A common myth is that to function effectively, teams need a strong, powerful, and charismatic leader. In general, leaders who control all the details, manage all the key relationships in the team, have all the good ideas, and use the team to execute their "vision" are usually overworked and underproductive. Teams with strong leaders may succumb to flawed and disastrous decision making.

As we discuss in Chapter 10, a leader has two main functions: a *design* function, meaning that the leader structures the team environment (working conditions, access to information, incentives, training, and education), and a *coaching* function, meaning that the leader has direct interaction with the team (Hackman, 1996).

## Good Teams Can Still Fail under the Wrong Circumstances

Teams are often depicted as mavericks: bucking authority, striking out on their own, and asking for permission only after the fact. Such cases do occur, but they are rare and tend to be one-shot successes. Most managers want consistently successful teams. This is particularly important in industries where considerable tooling up is required for team members.

To be successful in the long run, teams need ongoing resources and support. By resources, we mean more than just money. Teams need information and education. In too many cases, teams tackle a problem that has already been solved by someone else in the company, but a lack of communication prevents this critical knowledge from reaching the current task force.

To lay the best groundwork for teams before the problems begin, it is important to consider such factors as the goals and resources of the team: Are the team's goals well defined? Does everyone know them? Are the goals consistent with the objectives of other members of the organization? If not, how will the inevitable conflict be managed? Does everyone on the team have access to the resources necessary to successfully achieve the goal? Is the organizational hierarchy set up to give team members access to these resources efficiently? If not, it might be necessary to reconsider the governance structure within which the team must operate. What are the rights of the team members in pursuing their duties, who can they contact, and what information can they command? It is also important to assess the incentive structure existing for team members and for those outside the team with whom team members must interact. Does everyone have the right incentives (to do the things they are supposed to do)? Are team members' incentives aligned with those of the group and the organization, for instance, to cooperate with one another and to fully share information and resources? There is no cookie-cutter solution to team structure. For instance, it may be appropriate for team members to compete with one another (in which case, cooperation may not be an achievable feature of the group dynamic). Choosing the structure of the group and the incentives that motivate the individuals inside it are essential factors contributing to the success of any team.

## Retreats Will Not Fix All the Conflicts between Team Members

Teams often get into trouble. Members may fight, slack off, or simply be unable to keep up with their responsibilities, potentially resulting in angry or dissatisfied customers. When conflict arises, people search for a solution to the team problem. A common strategy is to have a "team-building retreat," "corporate love-in," or "ropes and boulders course" where team members try to address underlying concerns and build trust by engaging in activities—like rock climbing—that are not part of what they ordinarily do as a team. Perhaps this is why one review of the Fish! Movement, posted on

Amazon.com, says of such retreats, "What's sad is that companies actually think that throwing fish around is something that should be done. [The company] I worked for had a fish throw . . . an actual afternoon dedicated to throwing dead fish at each other. . . . I was burned out on the philosophy after two days of training and I voluntarily left the company two months after being hired" (Walker, 2002, pp. 87–88).

A team retreat is a popular way for team members to build mutual trust and commitment. A retreat may involve team members spending a weekend camping and engaging in cooperative, shared, structured activities. This usually results in a good time had by all. However, unless retreats address the structural and design problems that plague the team on a day-to-day basis in the work environment, they may fail. Design problems are best addressed by examining the team in its own environment while team members are engaged in actual work. For this reason, it is important to take a more comprehensive approach to analyzing team problems. Retreats are often insufficient because they encourage managers to blame team failures on interpersonal dynamics, rather than examining and changing deeper, more systemic issues.

## WHAT LEADERS TELL US ABOUT THEIR TEAMS

To gain a more accurate picture of the challenges leaders face in their organizations when designing, leading, and motivating teams, we conducted a survey, spanning six years, of 515 executives and managers from a variety of industries.[1] Here are some highlights of what they told us.

### Most Common Type of Team

By far, the most common teams are cross-functional project groups, followed by service, operations, and marketing teams (see also Katzenbach & Smith, 1993). Cross-functional teams epitomize the new challenges outlined earlier in this chapter. They represent the greatest potential, in terms of integrating talent, skills, and ideas, but because of their diversity of training and responsibility, they provide fertile ground for conflict.

### Team Size

Team size varies dramatically, from 2 to 80 members, with an average of 15.4. However, the modal team size is 5. These numbers can be compared with the optimum team size. As we discuss later in the book, teams should generally have fewer than 10 members—more like 5 or 6.

### Team Autonomy versus Manager Control

Most of the managers in our survey were in self-managing teams, followed by manager-led teams, with self-directing teams distinctly less common (see Figure 1-2). There is an inevitable tension between the degree of manager control in a team and the ability of team members to guide and manage their own actions. As a general principle,

[1] Survey results are based on the responses from executives in attendance at the Kellogg Leading High Impact Teams program, 1997–2003, $N = 515$.

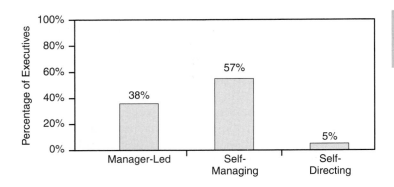

FIGURE 1-2 Team Autonomy versus Manager Control

manager-led teams provide more control, but less innovation than stems from autonomy. We do not suggest that all teams should be self-directing. Rather, it is important to understand the trade-offs and what is required for each type of team to function effectively.

## Team Longevity

The teams in our survey varied a great deal in terms of how long they had been working together. On average, teams had been in existence for one to two years (see Figure 1-3).

## The Most Frustrating Aspect of Teamwork

Managers considered several possible sources of frustration in managing teams. The most frequently cited cause of frustration and challenge in teams was developing and sustaining high motivation, followed by minimizing confusion and coordination problems (see Figure 1-4). We discuss issues of motivation in Chapter 2, as well as in a special chapter that focuses on team compensation and incentives (Chapter 3). We address creativity in Chapter 8 and look at conflict (and ways to effectively manage it within a team) in Chapter 7.

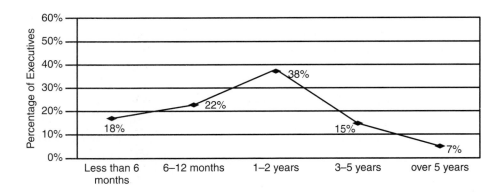

FIGURE 1-3 Team Longevity

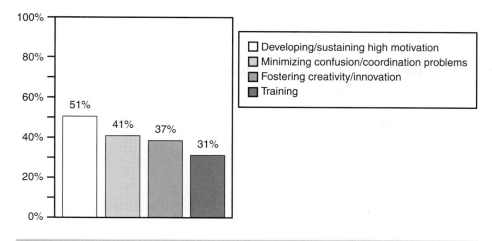

FIGURE 1-4  The Most Frustrating Aspects of Teamwork

Not surprisingly, among the skills on the most-wanted list for managerial education are developing and sustaining high motivation, managing conflict productively, providing leadership and direction, fostering creativity and innovation, and minimizing confusion and coordination problems. Consequently, we designed this book to prepare managers and reeducate executives in how to effectively deal with each of these concerns.

## DEVELOPING YOUR TEAM-BUILDING SKILLS

This book focuses on three skills: accurate diagnosis of team problems, theory-based intervention, and expert learning.

### Skill 1: Accurate Diagnosis of Team Problems

One of the biggest shortcomings of managerial effectiveness is an inability to accurately diagnose situations; for instance, is a team performing well or poorly? It is very rare to identify a simple, obvious measure of team functioning because effectiveness is hard to define. For example, perhaps your organization beat the competition in winning a large contract, but the contract was ultimately not very profitable. Was this a victory or a failure? What will be the implications for future competition?

Many people make the mistake of looking for causes *after* they find effects. In the scientific literature, this is known as **sampling on the dependent variable.** For example, if your goal is to identify the determinants of a successful team, it may appear useful to look for effective teams in your organization and then try to determine what is common among them. This sounds logical, until you realize that there may be many common factors that have nothing to do with making a team successful, like the fact that everyone wears clothes! Or there may be common features that interfere with good teamwork, but are nonetheless difficult to detect—perhaps precisely because they are common to all the teams, successful or not. One important example of this is the institutional background of the company, for example, taking certain established practices for granted, such as operating procedures, information sources, and even contractual relationships. In this case, the team may be effective, but not as effective as it might otherwise be. A more serious problem is that a manager who is also entrenched in the institutional framework of the company may perceive a team as effective, while overlooking its shortcomings. Thus, it is essential to be as independent and critical as possible when analyzing team effectiveness.

How do you avoid the trap of sampling on the dependent variable? From a methodological point of view, you can do one of two things: (1) identify a baseline group—that is, a comparison group (in this case, unsuccessful teams)—and look for differences between the two; or (2) do an experiment in which you provide different information, education, communication, and so on to one group (randomly assigned) but not the other. Then look for differences. Unfortunately, most executives do not have the time or resources to do either of these things. This book provides insights based upon research that has done these things before drawing conclusions. However, nothing can substitute for a thoughtful understanding of the environment in which the team operates, the incentives facing team members, and so on. We discuss these factors throughout this book.

Another problem is called **hindsight bias** (Fischhoff, 1975), or the "I knew it all along" fallacy. This is the tendency to believe that something seems obvious, even inevitable, *after* you learn about it when you have not predicted (or cannot predict) what will happen in advance. This can result in an unfortunate form of overconfidence: Managers think they know everything, when in fact they actually don't. We often see managers engage in post hoc justification rather than careful reasoning. The best way to avoid this trap is to read actively to learn about other possibilities, critically examine your own assumptions, and be open to a change of mind once you have the facts. As you read this book, some things will surprise you, but much will seem obvious. As a general principle, do not rely on your intuition; rather, test your assumptions.

## Skill 2: Theory-Based Intervention

"A business person once stated 'there is nothing as practical as a good theory'" (Lewin, 1943, p. 35). Once a problem or area of improvement has been identified, a manager still needs to deal effectively with it. This involves identifying reasons and remedies, such as finding ways to change the motivational structure of the task, the composition of the group, and so on. Mechanisms for transferring information from those who have it to those who need it must be developed, as well as a means to manage power, politics, and conflict involving the group. All this is much easier said than done, of course. For every managerial problem, there are a dozen purported solutions and quick fixes. How can a manager knowledgeably choose among them?

The interventions presented in this book have a key quality going for them: They are all theory based and empirically sound. This means that they are not based on naive, intuitive perceptions; rather, they have been scientifically examined. This book was written to provide managers with up-to-date, scientifically based information about how best to manage their teams.

## Skill 3: Expert Learning

Effective managers make mistakes, but they don't make the same mistakes twice. Expert learning involves the ability to continuously learn from experience. One of the great fallacies about learning is that people reach a point where they have acquired all the knowledge they need; in contrast, great leaders are always learning. In this book, we use a model that we call **expert learning** to refer to how managers can continuously benefit, even from the most mundane experiences. We strongly endorse Chris Argyris's (1977a) distinction between single-loop versus double-loop learning. According to Argyris, **single-loop learning** is learning that is primarily one-dimensional. For example, a leader may believe that she has nothing to learn from a subordinate, but that the subordinate can learn from her. Therefore, the interactions between the leader and the subordinate will be primarily one-directional, or single-loop. In contrast, Argyris argues that effective leaders engage in **double-loop learning** processes, which involve a reciprocal interchange between leaders and teams. This means, of course, that leaders coach and direct and instruct their teams, but that teams also help their leaders to learn.

Another important aspect of learning is the use of examples to illustrate and convey concepts. Since 1996, I have conducted research with Dedre Gentner and Jeff Loewenstein on knowledge transfer. Our research program is centered upon a single, guiding question: Do managers and executives actually use the principles and skills they learn in the MBA and executive classroom? Setting aside the fact that many of our colleagues thought this was heretical, the most important insights to come out of our intensive investigations of over 500 managers, executives, and consultants revealed an important key to whether knowledge is actually used or remains inert—what Whitehead, over seventy years ago, called the **inert knowledge problem** (Whitehead, 1929). The key to unlocking the pervasive inert knowledge problem lies in how the manager processes the information, and we found time and time again that more examples, all making the same point, result in better-learned knowledge and more "portable" knowledge than only a single example (Thompson, Loewenstein, & Gentner, 2000). However, it is not enough to have several examples; rather, the manager needs to compare the examples and pull out their commonalities. Thus, in this book, we attempt to provide several ways of looking at the same problem via a combination of theory, research, and real business practices.

---

## A WARNING

We believe that teamwork, like other interdependent social behaviors, is best perfected in an active, experimental, and dynamic environment. Thus, to fully benefit from this book, it is necessary for you to actively engage in teamwork and examine your own behavior. It may seem somewhat heretical to make the point in a textbook that team-building skills cannot be learned exclusively from a textbook, but we do so anyway.

We strongly urge you to work through the models and ideas presented here in the context of your own experience. We can think of no better way to do this than in a classroom setting that offers the opportunity for on-line, applied, experiential learning. It is easy to watch, analyze, and critique other teams, but much more challenging to engage in effective team behavior yourself. We hope that what you gain from this book, and the work you do on your own through team-building exercises, is the knowledge of how to be an effective team member, team leader, and team designer. In the long run, we hope this book will help you in developing your own experience, expertise, and models of how you can best function with teams.

## CONCLUSIONS

There is no magic scientific formula for designing and maintaining an effective team. If there were, it would have been discovered by now. In some ways, a team is like the human body: No one really knows an exact regimen for staying healthy over time. However, we have some very good information about the benefits of a lean diet, exercise, stress reduction, wellness maintenance, and early detection of disease. The same goes for teamwork. Just as we rely on science to cure disease and to advance health, this book takes an unabashedly scientific approach to the study and improvement of teamwork in organizations. This is extraordinarily important because there is a lot of misperception about teams and teamwork. Intuition and luck can only take us so far; in fact, if misapplied, they may get us into trouble. In the next chapter, we undertake a performance analysis of teamwork, asking these questions: How do we know a healthy and productive team when we see it? What are the biggest "killers" and "diseases" of teams? And, more important, what do we need to do to keep a team functioning effectively over time? In Chapter 3, we deal with the question of incentives and rewards for good teamwork. Part II focuses on internal team dynamics, and Part III focuses on the bigger picture—the team in the organization.

# CHAPTER

# Performance and Productivity:

2

## *Team Performance Criteria and Threats to Productivity*

*Of the 56 active mines in Pennsylvania, 34 are located beside abandoned mines, many of which have since become filled with groundwater. Miner Mark Popernack's maps showed that he was at least 300 feet from a potentially dangerous, abandoned mine. The map was wrong. At nine P.M. on July 24, 2002, he was running his mining machine against a wall of coal in the Quecreek Mine in Lincoln, Pennsylvania. He and crew leader Randall Fogle first knew something was wrong when they heard running water. When there is only a weak wall between you and 60 million gallons of water—the equivalent of 70 Olympic-size swimming pools, an underground tsunami—you have only seconds to escape. Fogle's crew paddled through chest-high dirty water to find a way out. But the water rushed ahead of them and blocked every escape route. The team of nine made their way a few hundred yards uphill to the highest point of the mine—70 feet long, 18 feet wide, about 4.5 feet high—at the end of the tunnel. The water started to rise. From the outset, the men agreed to work as a team and tied themselves together so they would be found as a team if they lived—or if they drowned. During this time, things got so desperate that they wrote their last messages to family members. Then, the water stopped rising. They sat in the dark to preserve their headlights and talked. As a team, they kept each other warm by sitting back-to-back and snuggling together. They also took turns encouraging each other when someone became downcast. They rationed three gallons of distilled water and each man was allowed one bite of a single corned-beef sandwich. The men worked together in a fight for their lives, and, after 77 hours in the flooded mine, all nine were rescued (AP/Canadian Press, July 28, 2002; Watson & Leinwand, 2002).*

The team of men in Pennsylvania surmounted a series of threats to their ability to achieve their clear and elevating goal: to stay alive, each and every one of them. A careful examination of the dynamics involved reveal leadership, trust, cooperation, and problem solving. Most teams do not have to operate under such intense, omnipresent, life-threatening circumstances, but they do have to work together in a productive fashion for their companies to survive. Ideally, teams could benefit from a model or set of guidelines that would tell them how to organize and how to deal with inevitable threats to their goal achievement. Such a model would serve two purposes: **description,** or the interpretation of events so that managers can come up with an accu-

21

rate analysis of the situation, and **prescription,** or a recommendation on what to do to fix the situation.

In this chapter, we introduce a model of team performance. The model tells us the conditions that have to be in place for teams to function effectively and how to address problems with performance. The remainder of the chapter focuses on different parts of the model and provides choices to enact change.

## AN INTEGRATED MODEL OF SUCCESSFUL TEAM PERFORMANCE

The best models of teamwork put the team in the context of the organization—that is, they deal with internal processes of teams, as well as how the team works with other units (see Hackman, 1987, 1990; Hill, 1995). Figure 2-1 is a descriptive-prescriptive model of team performance. It tells us what to expect in terms of team performance and suggests ways to improve the functioning of teams. As promised in Chapter 1, the model in Figure 2-1 is based upon empirical research. This chapter steps through each piece of the model.

The message of the model is actually quite simple. It asserts that the context of the team (referring to its internal processes and external constraints and opportunities) affects the team's ability to do three essential things: perform effectively, build and sustain motivation, and coordinate people. These essential conditions are the causal determinants of the team's performance—that is, whether it succeeds or fails. The remainder of the chapter is divided into three key sections corresponding to the three pieces of the model: team context, essential conditions, and team performance. We begin with the team context.

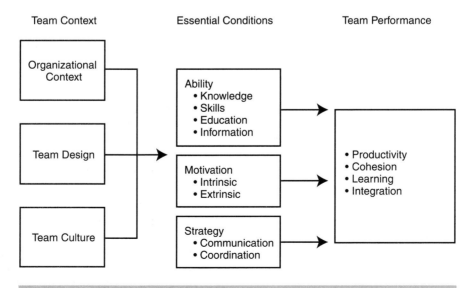

**FIGURE 2-1** Integrated Model of Teamwork

## Team Context

The **team context** includes the larger organizational setting within which the team does its work, the design of the team in terms of its internal functioning, and the culture of the team. High performance teams are not created exactly the same way across organizations. Moreover, there is no single best method for achieving team success. In part, this means that the team relies on the organization to provide resources, funding, individuals for membership, and so on. In Chapter 1, we stated that teams operate in a social context which shapes and confines behavior. As we discuss in Parts II and III, the team leader must not only think about the internal functioning of the team (i.e., ability, motivation, and coordination among team members), but also the external functioning of the team, including the organizational context, team design, and group norms.

### Organizational Context

The organizational context includes the basic structure of the organization (e.g., lateral, hierarchical), the information system, the education system, and the reward system. It includes organizational policy and material and physical resources required to accomplish group tasks. Even if a team possesses spectacular skills, motivation, and coordination, lack of critical organizational infrastructure such as information, tools, equipment, space, raw materials, money, and human resources will hurt team performance. Teams ideally need a supportive organizational context—one that recognizes and welcomes their existence; responds to their requests for information, resources, and action; legitimizes the team's task and how they are achieving it; and expects the team to succeed (Bushe, 1984).

### Team Design

Team design refers to the observable structure of the team (e.g., manager-led or self-managing). It refers to the leadership style within the team, functional roles, communication patterns, composition of the team, and training of members. We examine team design in Part II of the book. In contrast to the team's culture, which we describe next, the team design is the deliberate aspect of teamwork. Although the team's culture evolves and grows and is not under the direct control of a manager, the design of a team is a deliberate decision or choice made by managers; even though it is true that some managers may not realize that by not making a choice or leaving teamwork up to natural forces, they are, in fact, designing their team. We urge the leaders and managers of teams to carefully think through their options when it comes to team design.

### Team Culture

Culture is the set of shared meanings held by team members that make teamwork possible. In contrast to team design, which is often deliberate and explicit, team culture includes the unstated, implicit aspects of the team that are not discussed in a formal fashion, but nevertheless shape behavior. Member roles, norms, and patterns of behaving and thinking arise from team design and the structure and system of the organization in which the team operates. One way in which teams develop their culture is by imposing ways of thinking and acting that are considered acceptable. A **norm** is a generally agreed upon set of rules that guides behavior of team members. Norms differ from organizational policies in that they are informal and unwritten. Often, norms are so subtle that team members are not consciously aware of them. Team norms regulate key behaviors such as honesty, manner of dress, punctuality, and emotional expression. Norms can either be **prescriptive,** dictating what should be done, or **proscriptive,** dictating behaviors that should be avoided.

Norms that favor innovation (Cummings & Mohrman, 1987) or incorporate shared expectations of success (Shea & Guzzo, 1987) may foster team effectiveness. Companies that report success in applying work teams have had similar cultures, often guided by philosophies of top managers (Galagan, 1986; Poza & Marcus, 1980; Walton, 1977). Often, culture is more a property of work units than the entire organization. This means that certain norms may exist in teams but not the larger organization. For example, two teams in the Western Electric Company's Hawthorne Works developed highly different norms, even though they were in the same shop. One group spent much time in conversation and debate, played games involving small bets, and maintained uniformly high output. In contrast, the other group traded jobs (a prohibited activity), engaged in joking, and maintained uniformly low output (Homans, 1950).

Norms develop as a consequence of precedent. Whatever behaviors emerge at a team's first meeting will usually define how the team operates—just look at the consistency of seating arrangements in business meetings. Norms also develop because of carryovers from other situations or in response to an explicit statement by a superior or coworker. They may also result from critical events in the team's history. Robert Henderson capitalized on the absence of norms when he started a team to build the most powerful commercial jet engine in history. Henderson says, "My outlook was, 'let's push the envelope as far as we can at the start, because it's the only chance we'll get to do that. What you establish is what gets perpetuated. Starting a culture is so much easier than changing a culture'" (Fishman, 1999, p. 188). We cover norms in greater detail in Part II of the book.

## Essential Conditions for Successful Team Performance

Obviously, there are a number of factors that must be in place for a team to be successful (Hackman, 1987; Steiner, 1972). The team members must

1. Bring adequate *knowledge and skill* to bear on the task.
2. Exert sufficient *motivation and effort* to accomplish the task at an acceptable level of performance.
3. *Coordinate* their activities and communication.

Next, we discuss each of these essential conditions in greater detail.

*Knowledge and Skill*

For teams to perform effectively, members must have the requisite ability, knowledge, and skill to perform the task. This requires that the manager appropriately match people with the right skills to the tasks at hand and to the organizational human resource structure itself.

**Team Member Skills**    One consistent predictor of team effectiveness is team members' average cognitive ability. For example, the average of team members' cognitive abilities in military tank crews (Tziner & Eden, 1985), assembly and maintenance teams (Barrick, Stewart, Neubert, & Mount, 1998), and service teams (Neuman & Wright, 1999) directly predicts effectiveness. Conscientiousness, as a trait, also predicts effective team performance in assembly and maintenance teams (Barrick et al., 1998) and service teams (Neuman, Wagner, & Christiansen, 1999; Neuman & Wright, 1999).

Moreover, an effective team needs people not only with the technical skills necessary to perform the work, but also with interpersonal skills, decision-making skills, and problem-solving skills. Broadly thought of as emotional intelligence, interpersonal skills are critical for effective management (Goleman, 1995). Perhaps this is because executives spend 78 percent of their working time interacting with others, and as much as 50 percent of that time in interactions with subordinates (Mintzberg, 1973). Peter Grazier of Teambuilding Inc. says, "Teams have told us that if they had to do it over again, they would have more of the people skills up front. They don't struggle with the technical stuff. They tend to struggle with the people skills" (Strozniak, 2000).

Subordinates reporting good relationships with superiors are better performers, assume more responsibility, and contribute more to their units than those reporting poor relationships (Liden & Graen, 1980). In their book, *First, Break All the Rules,* Buckingham and Coffman (1999) report on the results of a blockbuster survey analysis of more than five thousand managers. The key determinant of whether people stay in their jobs can be strongly predicted by whether they believe that their managers care about them. Thus, building and nurturing relationships is an important skill for leading highly effective teams.

Moreover, there appears to be an intimate connection between social behavior and intelligence. For example, people who view themselves as independent, or not attached to a team or group, actually show significant deficiencies in intelligent thought, including IQ and standardized test performance (Baumeister, Twenge, & Nuss, 2002).

How do you know whether you have an effective working relationship with someone? As a start, you can consider where your relationship stands on each of the dimensions listed in Table 2-1. If the majority of the dimensions of your relationship are listed on the right-hand side, this means that an effective relationship has developed.

Anyone who is a member of a team fully understands that not all of the work of teams is accomplished in the physical presence of the other group members. Teams constantly make decisions about what will be done as a team, or alone. It is important to understand what types of work are best performed as a team, in the presence of a team, or independently. As a general principle (that we discuss in detail in Chapter 8), teams are superior to individuals in terms of analyzing information, convergent thinking, and assimilating information. However, teams are worse than individuals in terms of divergent thinking.

Moreover, as an entity, teams can create performance pressure and performance anxiety that can hinder the performance of well-intentioned team members. For experts, the physical presence of the team can be a great benefit, because the presence of others increases motivation to perform and the expert knows the skill sets required. However, for people who are not quite experts, the presence of others can hinder performance. For example, Barb Linquist, a swimmer at the U.S. Open, "choked" when she heard the announcer reciting the accomplishments of her competitors. "I was next to a swimmer that I had read about. I got really flustered by hearing her accomplishments. . . . I didn't concentrate on my race and . . . I finished last" (Hudepohl, 2001). **Choking under pressure** occurs when a person's performance declines despite incentives for optimal performance (Baumeister, 1984).

**Learning Curves and Expertise**    The physical presence of other people is stimulating at a very primitive, innate level. We are born with the tendency to become aroused in the presence of others; it is part of our genetic inheritance. This greater arousal or

**TABLE 2-1** Summary of Dyadic Dimensions along Which Relationships Develop

| From | To |
| --- | --- |
| ***Openness and Self Disclosure***[a, b, c, d, f] | |
| Limited to "safe," socially acceptable topics | Disclosure goes beyond safe areas to include personally sensitive, private, and controversial topics and aspects of self |
| ***Knowledge of Each Other***[b, d, e, f] | |
| Surface, "biographic" knowledge: Impressionistic in nature | Knowledge is multifaceted and extends to core aspects of personality, needs, and style |
| ***Predictability of Other's Reactions and Responses***[b, d, e, f] | |
| Limited to socially expected or role-related responses, and those based on first impressions or repeated surface encounters | Predictability of the other's reactions extends beyond stereotypical exchange and includes a knowledge of the contingencies affecting the other's reactions |
| ***Uniqueness of Interaction***[a, b, e] | |
| Exchanges are stereotypical, guided by prevailing social norms or role expectations | Exchanges are idiosyncratic to the two people, guided by norms that are unique to the relationship |
| ***Multimodality of Communication***[a, b] | |
| Largely limited to verbal channels of communication and stereotypical or unintended nonverbal channels | Includes multiple modalities of communication, including nonverbal and verbal "short-hands" specific to the relationship or the individuals involved; less restrictiveness of nonverbal |
| ***Substitutability of Communication***[a, b] | |
| Little substitution among alternative modes of communication | Possession of and ability to use alternative modes of communication to convey the same message |
| ***Capacity for Conflict and Evaluation***[a, b, c, e] | |
| Limited capacity for conflict; use of conflict-avoidance techniques; reluctance to criticize | Readiness and ability to express conflict and make positive or negative evaluations |
| ***Spontaneity of Exchange***[a, b, c] | |
| Interactions tend to be formal or "comfortably informal" as prescribed by prevailing social norms | Greater informality and ease of interaction; movement across topical areas occurs readily and without hesitation or formality; communication flows and changes direction easily |

stimulation acts as a motivator on behavior. Whatever we might be doing, we do with more "gusto" when in the presence of other people, especially our team. However, there is a catch: The presence of other people enhances performance for well-learned behaviors or behaviors that are almost second nature. Thus, greater arousal or stimulation enhances our performance on tasks that are well-learned, but hinders our performance on novel tasks. The presence of other people triggers one of two responses: challenge (if someone is an expert) or threat (if someone is not an expert). Moreover, the cardiovascular responses of people while they perform a well-learned task in the presence of others provide physiological evidence that experts feel challenged—increased cardiac response and decreased vascular resistance (Blascovich, Mendes, Hunter, & Salomon, 1999). However, if people are performing an unlearned task in the presence of others, they go into "threat mode"—increased cardiac response and increased vas-

**TABLE 2-1**   Summary of Dyadic Dimensions along Which Relationships Develop *(continued)*

| From | To |
| --- | --- |
| ***Synchronization and Pacing[a, b]*** | |
| Except for stereotyped modes of response, limited dyadic synchrony occurs | Speech and nonverbal responses become synchronized; flow of interaction is smooth; cues are quickly and accurately interpreted |
| ***Efficiency of Communication[a, b]*** | |
| Communication of intended meanings sometimes requires extensive discussion; misunderstandings occur unless statements are qualified or elaborated | Intended meanings are transmitted and understood rapidly, accurately, and with sensitivity to nuance |
| ***Mutual Investment[b, g]*** | |
| Little investment in the other except in areas of role-related or situation interdependencies | Extensive investment in other's well-being and efficacy |

[a]Altman & Taylor, 1973, pp. 129–136.
[b]Levinger & Snoek, 1972; Levinger & Rausch, 1977, pp. 100–109.
[c]Jourard, 1971.
[d]Hinde, 1979, pp. 133–134.
[e]Swensen, 1973, pp. 105–106, 230–237, 455.
[f]Triandis, 1977, pp. 191–193.
[g]Secord & Backman, 1964.

*Sources:* Galegher, J., Kraut, R. E., & Egido, C. 1990. *Intellectual Teamwork: Social and Technological Foundations of Cooperative Work.* Mahwah, NJ: Lawrence Erlbaum & Associates.
Altman, I., & Taylor, D. A. 1973. *Social Penetration: The Development of Interpersonal Relationships.* New York: Holt, Rinehart & Winston.
Hinde, R. A. 1979. *Non-Verbal Communication.* Cambridge, England: Cambridge University Press.
Jourard, S. M. 1971. *Self-Disclosure: An Experimental Analysis of the Transparent Self.* New York: John Wiley & Sons.
Levinger, G. K., & Rausch, H. L. 1977. *Close Relationships: Perspectives on the Meaning of Intimacy.* Amherst, MA: University of Massachusetts Press.
Levinger, G. K., & Snoek, J. D. 1972. *Attraction in Relationship: A New Look at Interpersonal Attraction.* Morristown, NJ: General Learning Press.
Secord, P. F., & Backman, C. W. 1964. *Social Psychology.* New York: McGraw-Hill.
Swensen, C. H. 1973. *Introduction to Interpersonal Relations.* Glenview, IL: Scott Foreman.
Triandis, H. C. 1977. "Cross-Cultural Social and Personality Psychology." *Personality & Social Psychology Bulletin,* 3(2), 143–158.

cular resistance. Consider, for example, what happens to pool players when they are observed by others in pool halls (Michaels, Brommel, Brocato, Linkous, & Rowe, 1982). Novice players perform worse when someone is watching. In contrast, expert players' games improve dramatically when they are observed. Similarly, joggers speed up on paths when someone is watching them and slow down when no one appears to be in sight (Worringham & Messick, 1983). Additionally, people giving impromptu speeches perform worse in the presence of others than when alone.

**Social Facilitation versus Social Inhibition**   **Social facilitation** is the predictable enhancement in performance that occurs when people are in the presence of others. **Social inhibition** occurs when people are the center of attention and they are concerned with discrepancies between their performance and standards of excellence. Thus, team leaders will actually make the performance of their team suffer if they apply performance pressure to people who are not yet expert.

The key question for team players is how to ensure that their behavior is the optimal response. There are two routes. *Expertise* is one way: experts are trained to focus on what matters most. *Practice and rehearsal* is another strategy: it modifies the behavioral response hierarchy, so that the desired response becomes second nature. However, being an expert does not completely protect people from choking. Just look at professional players on sports teams. In the championship series in professional baseball and basketball, the home team is significantly more likely to lose the decisive game than it is to lose earlier home games in the series (Baumeister & Steinhilber, 1984). Why? Remember that expertise is the result of overlearning. The pressure to perform well causes people to focus their attention on the process of performing—the focus of attention turns inward. The more pressure, the more inwardly focused people become. The problem is that when people focus on what are overlearned or automated responses, this actually interferes with performance (Lewis & Linder, 1997). As an example, consider shoelace tying. Most adults are experts at tying their own shoes. This comes from years of practice. Most people can carry on conversations without thinking about the process of shoelace tying when they are engaged in the act. Now, suppose that you had to tie your shoes onstage in front of an audience that was watching and timing you. You might become so preoccupied with the process that you would actually perform worse than if you were not under pressure. In short, hyper-self-awareness interferes with the ability to perform.

It is best to avoid trying to learn difficult material or perform complex tasks in groups, because peer pressure will obstruct performance. However, if team members are experts, they will likely flourish under this kind of pressure. Practice not only makes perfect, but it also makes performance hold up under pressure. Not all teamwork needs to be done in a team setting; sometimes it is beneficial to allow team members to complete work on their own and bring it back to the group.

**Flow: Between Boredom and Choking**    At a precise point in between boredom with a task and intense pressure is a state that psychologist Mihaly Csikszentmihalyi calls *flow*. According to Csikszentmihalyi, flow is a psychological state in which a person is highly engaged in a task—so interested, in fact, that the person loses track of time and the process of engaging the task is its own reinforcement. In his book, *Finding Flow: The Psychology of Engagement with Everyday Life* (1997), Csikszentmihalyi gives lots of examples of people in flow states, ranging from marathon runners to everyday gardeners. The flow concept also applies to teamwork. According to Jean Lipman-Blumen and Harold J. Leavitt, coauthors of *Hot Groups* (1999), people on "hot teams" don't view their work as work, they view it as fun. They're addicted to it. They don't think about anything else. They want to talk about it, think about it, and do it all day long—and they want to be around people who feel the same way.

**Stress versus Challenge**    As anyone on a team knows, there is a fine line between challenge and stress. For example, people who strive to accomplish difficult goals may perceive their goal as a challenge, rather than a threat, and perform quite well. Stressful tasks may be challenging or threatening. Challenge is experienced when there is an opportunity for self-growth with available coping strategies, whereas threat is experienced when the situation is perceived as leading to failure with no available strategies for coping. For example, in one investigation, people evaluated companies' stocks and had to make decisions quickly and accurately (Drach-Zahavy & Erez, 2002). The same level of goal difficulty impairs performance and adaptation to change when people appraise the situation as a threat, but improves adapation to change when participants appraise the situation as a challenge (Drach-Zahavy & Erez, 2002).

*Motivation and Effort*

It is not enough for members of a team to be skilled, they also must be motivated to use their knowledge and skills to achieve shared goals. Contrary to popular opinion, motivation is not strictly based on external factors, such as reward and compensation. Motivation comes both from within a person and from external factors. People by nature are goal directed, but a poorly designed team or organizational environment can threaten team dedication and persistence. At certain times, members of a team can develop a defeatist attitude: They may feel that their actions do not matter, that something always goes wrong to mess things up (e.g., a sports team on a losing streak), or that their input is not listened to. This can also happen if team members feel they are unable to affect their environment or cannot rely on others. (As a case in point, consider Sidebar 2-1). The belief that the group has in themselves, also known as group

## Sidebar 2-1. Game of Envelopes and Money

Consider the "envelopes and money" game (Murnighan, 1992). In this game, an envelope is passed around a room, and team members can choose to donate money to the envelope. The instructor (or leader) states that if a certain amount of money is collected, all group members will be given a bonus of $10, but that their original donation will not be returned, as it is anonymous. Theoretically, it is possible for all group members to make a positive profit, but this requires trust on the part of members that all others will contribute. Inevitably, the group donations fall short of what is needed to gain bonuses.

potency, is a significant predictor of actual performance (Shea & Guzzo, 1987). For example, in one investigation, officer cadets completed a task in teams. Group potency, or "thinking we can," contributed to group performance over and above pure measures of cognitive ability (Hecht, Allen, Klammer, & Kelly, 2002).

**Social Loafing**   A French agricultural engineer named Max Ringelmann was interested in the relative efficiency of farm labor supplied by horses, oxen, machines, and men. In particular, he was curious about their relative abilities to pull a load horizontally, such as in a tug-of-war. In one of his experiments, he had groups of fourteen men pull a load and measured the amount of force they generated; he also measured the force that each man could pull independently. There was a linear decline in the average pull per member as the size of the rope-pulling team increased. One person pulling on a rope alone exerted an average of 63 kilograms of force. However, in groups of three, the per-person force dropped to 53 kilograms, and in groups of eight, it plummeted to only 31 kilograms per person—less than half of the effort exerted by people working alone (Ringelmann, 1913; summarized by Kravitz & Martin, 1986). This detailed observation revealed a fundamental principle of teamwork: People in groups often do not work as hard as they do when alone. This is known as **social loafing.**

Team performance increases with team size, but the rate of increase is negatively accelerated; the addition of new members to the team has diminishing returns on productivity. Similar results are obtained when teams work on intellectual puzzles (Taylor & Faust, 1952), creativity tasks (Gibb, 1951), perceptual judgments, and complex reasoning (Ziller, 1957). Social loafing has been demonstrated in many different cultures,

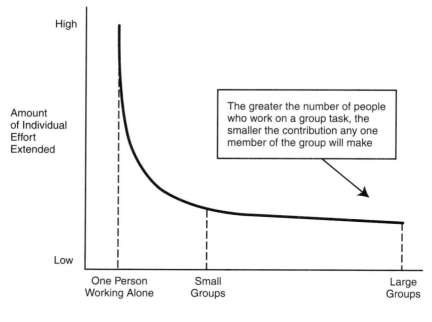

High

Amount
of Individual
Effort
Extended

The greater the number of people
who work on a group task, the
smaller the contribution any one
member of the group will make

Low

One Person
Working Alone

Small
Groups

Large
Groups

Number of People Working

**FIGURE 2-2**  The Social Loafing Effect
*Source:* Greenberg, J. 1996. *Managing Behavior in Organizations.* Upper Saddle River,
NJ: Prentice Hall. (p. 189)

including India (Werner, Ember, & Ember, 1981), Japan (Williams & Williams, 1984),
and Taiwan (Gabrenya, Latané, & Wang, 1983). The general form of the social loafing
effect is portrayed in Figure 2-2.

**Free Riders**   Many team leaders have asked: Is my team working as hard as it can?
Their suspicions may be correct: People's motivations often diminish in a team. Also,
the larger the team, the less likely it is that any given person will work hard. For many
team tasks, there is a possibility that others can and will do most or all of the work necessary for the team to succeed. This means that free riders benefit from the efforts of
others while contributing little or nothing themselves. Team members are sensitive to
how important their efforts are perceived to be. When they think their contributions
are not going to have much impact on the outcome, they are less likely to exert themselves on the team's behalf. How do teams react once a free rider has been detected?
As a general principle, people abhor free riders. Team members want equitable working arrangements. Indeed, a strong work ethic holds in most teams, with greater
rewards coming to those who work harder. If someone is not working as hard, the
other team members might attempt to reduce that person's reward (e.g., not allow
someone to put his name on the group report if he has not contributed) or reduce their
own inputs (i.e., the other members of the group might stop working hard). Obviously,
this kind of behavior by one person can undermine the effectiveness of the team on
several dimensions. However, the company itself bears the greatest cost from this kind

of behavior. When everyone stops working hard in retaliation against someone else's bad conduct, ultimately, the work does not get done or done well. Perhaps this is why some companies charge people $10 per minute for every minute they are late to a meeting. Perhaps this is also why some companies endow each person with gold Krugerrands that they can "toss" to someone in a meeting when a team member contributes something really important. These types of whimsical, but meaningful, behaviors emphasize the team's core values: showing up and contributing. The leaders of these teams correctly recognize that free riding and social loafing, if unchecked, can be a serious threat to team productivity.

**Three Main Causes of Free-riding**    Why do people loaf and free ride? Three reasons: diffusion of responsibility, a reduced sense of self-efficacy, and the "sucker effect."

***Diffusion of Responsibility***    In a team, a person's effort and contributions are less identifiable than when that person works independently. This is because everyone's efforts are pooled into the team enterprise and the return is a function of everyone's contribution. It is difficult (or impossible) to distinguish one person's contribution from another. At an extreme, this can lead to **deindividuation**—a psychological state in which a person does not feel individual responsibility. As a result, the person is less likely to perform or contribute. Consider, for example, a dramatic, real-world illustration. A woman named Kitty Genovese was on her way home from work late one evening in New York (based upon Latané & Darley, 1968). She was attacked by a man and stabbed to death. Thirty-eight of her neighbors in the apartment building where she lived witnessed the attacker approach and slay her; however, not a single person so much as called the police.

Upon hearing this story, most people are horrified and attribute the neighbors' lack of assistance to social and moral decay. We might look at this, however, from another perspective: People are more likely to free ride as the number of others in the group increases. Perhaps this is one reason why many people employed by companies that regularly committed accounting fraud did not blow the whistle. Observers in Kitty Genovese's apartment building who knew that others were also watching felt less responsible and so less inclined to intervene. In effect, they told themselves, "Someone else has probably already called for help." Why inconvenience yourself when it is likely the woman will receive help from someone else? Of course, if everyone thinks this way, the probability that the victim eventually gets help decreases dramatically.

***Dispensability of Effort***    In some cases, it is not diffusion of responsibility that hinders people from contributing to a team effort, but rather the feeling that our contributions will not be as valuable, efficacious, or worthwhile as they might be in a smaller group. In short, we believe our contributions will not be sufficient to justify the effort. Consider, for example, the problem of voting. Most everyone agrees that voting is a good practice. Why then did only 51 percent of the eligible U.S. population turn out to vote during the presidential election of 2000? People may feel that their vote has such a small impact on the outcome that voting is not worthwhile. Similarly, team members may feel they lack the ability to positively influence a team's outcome. Indeed, when the least capable member of a team feels particularly indispensable for group success, the group actually experiences a sort of "social striving" effect—that is, working harder to achieve their goals (Hertel, Kerr, & Messe, 2000).

*Sucker Aversion*   A common concern held by team members is whether someone will be left doing all of the work and getting little or no credit (Kerr, 1983). Because everyone wants to avoid being taken advantage of, team members hedge their efforts and wait to see what others will do. The problem is that when everyone does this, no one contributes. When people see others not contributing, it confirms their worst fears. The sucker effect becomes a self-fulfilling prophesy.

**Suggestions for Enhancing Successful Team Performance**   Suppose you are managing a team that processes insurance claims. Prior to the formation of teams, you measure average claim processing time and find it to be three days. After forming the teams, you find the average has increased to about nine days. Has your team fallen victim to social loafing? Your upper-division manager advises you to immediately dismantle the teams. Someone else tells you that the company's incentive system needs to be overhauled. What do *you* think?

Before you dismantle the teams or completely restructure the company's entire pay structure, consider the following strategies:

*Increase Identifiability*   When each member's contribution to a task is displayed where it can be seen by others (e.g., weekly sales figures posted on a bulletin board or e-mail), people are less likely to loaf, or slack off, than when only overall group (or companywide) performance is made available (Kerr & Bruun, 1981; Williams, Harkins, & Latané, 1981). Whole Foods subscribes to this line of thinking by collecting and distributing vast amounts of performance data throughout all levels of the organization. Sensitive figures on store sales, team sales, profit margins, and even salaries are available to every person in every location. It collects and distributes information to an extent that would be unimaginable almost anywhere else. In fact, the company shares so much information so widely that the Securities and Exchange Commission (SEC) has designated all six thousand five hundred employees "insiders" for stock-trading purposes (Fishman, 1996). However, the key is not identifiability per se, but rather, the evaluation that identifiability makes possible (Harkins & Jackson, 1985; Harkins & Szymanski, 1987).

*Promote Involvement*   Social loafing may be eliminated if the task is sufficiently involving (Brickner, Harkins, & Ostrom, 1986), attractive (Zaccaro, 1984), or intrinsically interesting (Petty, Cacioppo, & Kasmer, 1985). When the task is challenging and interesting, people feel more motivated to perform. Generally, when tasks are highly specialized and routinized, monotony sets in; in contrast, when team members are responsible for all pieces of a work product or service, they feel more responsibility for the work. This is perhaps why many companies, such as IBM Credit Corporation, restructured into teams that handle all aspects of a credit application. The walk-through time in IBM Credit Corporation for a single credit application decreased from nine days to two days. This is largely because teams of individuals feel personally responsible for a particular client in a way that they did not feel before the restructuring. According to Jeff McHenry, director of Executive Development at Microsoft, "The single most important factor is that effective teams have a clear goal. They work toward something. And everybody understands what the goal is. We tend to hire people who are achievement-oriented and results-driven. When they don't have a goal, they tend to flounder because they have nothing to work toward. When they do have a goal, their achievement orientation takes over — and great things happen" (Anonymous, 1996).

Challenging tasks may be particularly important for teams composed of people who are good at what they do or who believe that they are superior. It is a well-known psychological fact that most people regard themselves to be superior on a number of intellective and social tasks. For example, the majority of people regard themselves to be better-than-average drivers (Svenson, 1981); they also believe that they are more likely to have a better job, and so on (Taylor & Brown, 1988). Known as the *positive illusion bias,* unwarranted beliefs in one's own superiority can wreak havoc in teams. Huguet, Charbonnier, and Monteil (1999) theorized that work teams composed of people with strong motives to view themselves as distinctly more talented than others are likely to suffer from social loafing when the task is unchallenging. In particular, Huguet et al. suggest that men and people from individualistic cultures are most likely to have such motives. People who see themselves as above average would be the most likely to engage in social loafing, because they have a false sense of the value of their contributions. Indeed, people who feel uniquely superior expend less effort when working collectively on easy tasks. However, they actually work harder when the task is challenging.

***Reward Team Members for Performance***    Team members should recognize and reward contributions by individuals. For example, in many MBA programs, students do as much as 50 percent of their work in teams and groups, thereby building essential teamwork skills. In such courses, groups receive a group grade, which might encourage social loafing. However, in many courses, students are also given 100 points to allocate among team members to reflect the contributions made by others. As one professor tells her students, "I don't give Cs in this course, but you do!"

Rewarding team members need not mean large financial incentives: Symbolic rewards are often more powerful than money. Sales managers may strategically use symbolic rewards, such as high-performer sales clubs or plaques and ceremonies honoring exemplary service, to deliver messages to the sales force. These can be used to underscore the values of the sales organization and help shape salesperson behavior.

It is important for team members to feel appreciated and acknowledged by the members of their team, as well as the organization. There can be serious consequences if people feel they are not valued and respected, so much so that people are more likely to cheat and steal from the organization when they feel they have been unfairly treated (Greenberg, 1988). For example, when people feel that they are respected by their superiors, they are more likely to contribute to the group's welfare (De Cremer, 2002). Feeling respected is most important for members who feel least included (i.e., peripheral members).

***Strengthen Team Cohesion***    People worry a lot about being a sucker, especially when the norms of a team are created early on and people get labeled. Leaders can demonstrate trust by putting themselves in a vulnerable position. By showing vulnerability and requiring trust, leaders show they trust the team and set that expectation. Cohesive teams are less inclined to loaf (Williams, 1981).

***Increase Personal Responsibility***    The buck stops with the team. When teams set their own performance goals, they are less likely to loaf (Brickner, Harkins, & Ostrom, 1986).

***Use Team Contracts***   Ideally, at the outset of teamwork, members should develop a written statement of objectives and practices. This should be written, posted, and perhaps most important, revisited. According to Katzenbach and Smith (1993), the best teams in their extensive study invest a tremendous amount of time and effort exploring, shaping, and agreeing on a purpose that belongs to them collectively and individually. This "purposing" activity continues through the life of the team. In contrast, failed teams rarely develop a common purpose. The best teams also translate their common purpose into specific performance goals.

***Provide Team Performance Reviews and Feedback***   Oftentimes, people don't realize that they are not doing their fair share. It is common practice for people to receive regular performance feedback from their supervisors. Why shouldn't we do the same for teams? As we noted in Chapter 1, team leaders often fail to manage their team as an entity, preferring to manage the individual relationships with each team member. We believe that team leaders should meet with the entire team on a regular basis to talk about how the team is performing. And the communication should be double-loop, such that the team leader is asking questions in addition to providing feedback.

***Maintain the "Right" Staffing Level***   As the team gets larger and larger, personal contributions to the team become less important to the team's chances of success (Kerr, 1989; Olson, 1965). In short, as team size increases, feelings of anonymity increase.

Suppose that you implement the preceding steps, and your team's performance is still less than what you think is possible. What should you do? Consider the third source of threats to productivity: coordination problems.

### Coordination Strategies

Ability and motivation are essential and desirable, but insufficient for effective team functioning. A team needs to *coordinate* the skills, efforts, and actions of its members so as to effectively enact team strategy. For example, distributed.net is a coordinated team of computer programmers and enthusiasts. Armed with tens of thousands of computers linked over the Internet, distributed.net solved the Data Encryption Standard (DES) Challenge II sponsored by RSA Data Security, Inc. The goal of the challenge was to break the fifty-six-bit security code provided by the government's DES and recover the secret key used to encrypt messages. As the *PR Newswire* reported on February 26, 1998:

> The distributed.net team met the challenge in 39 days, less than half the 90 days of computing time it took the original challenge to be solved by a university team. The distributed.net organization utilized the idle time of computers throughout the world to solve particularly arduous computing tasks. For the DES Challenge II, the team managed to coordinate the efforts of 22,000 participants throughout the world, linking together over 50,000 computers to power through 72 quadrillion possible keys. One by one, the computers crunched through all possible combinations until the winning key was found to decode the message encrypted with the DES algorithm.

This feat was possible because the team was highly coordinated.

Coordination problems must be surmounted for a team to be effective. Team members may be individually good at what they do, but unless they coordinate their activities, they will not meet their team objectives.

**Coordination** is the combined synchronization of the strategies of all members. Teams vary in terms of their coordination or synchrony. Consider a football team—the slightest misunderstanding about a play can lose the game. Another example is a rowing team or a dance troupe—unless everyone is synchronized, they cannot achieve their performance goals, no matter how skilled and motivated the individuals. This is why teams often sing or chant to synchronize their movements and actions. Sir Adrian Cadbury, former chairman of Cadbury Schweppes, rowed in the 1952 Olympics. "Sir Adrian took more than the lesson of timing from the world of rowing when he entered corporate life. 'What has always been important to me is the team—rowing taught me that. More importantly, trust.' Rowing is certainly a sport that places more emphasis on team harmony than others—there's less scope for those with individual flare to shine. 'The beauty of racing in a crew is that you learn that any victory is the combined effort of everyone. In the same way company results reflect the performance of the whole firm.'" (Phelps, 1996, p. 110).

Coordination problems increase with team size and do so in an accelerating manner. The number of ways in which a team can organize itself (e.g., divide responsibilities, combine contributions, coordinate efforts) increases rapidly as the team gets larger (Kelley, 1962).

Most of the threats to team productivity are attributable to coordination problems, but most managers, used to thinking in terms of ability and motivation, fail to realize this—an example of the misattribution problem discussed in Chapter 1.

Most people take coordination and communication in teams for granted. In other words, they do not anticipate that their handwriting will be misread by a teammate or that a fax won't transmit. People have a biased sense about the clarity of their own messages and intentions. They may not be as clear as they think they are. The problems in communication and coordination are compounded when the medium of communication is less rich, such as in e-mail, fax, and videoconferencing (a topic discussed in Part III on global teamwork).

What are some practical steps to ensure better coordination of efforts within teams?

**Use Single-Digit Teams**    Most teams are too large. As the number of people on a team increases, it is that much harder to schedule meetings, move paperwork, and converge on ideas. The incidence of unanticipated failure increases. As a rule of thumb, teams should have fewer than ten members and just enough to cover all needed skill areas.

**Have an Agenda**    Members need a clear sense of where they are going and how they will get there. If the team does not know where it is going, its efforts will be fragmented and members will waste time and energy.

**Train Team Members Together**    Team members who train together, as opposed to separately, work more effectively. This is because they have an opportunity to coordinate their strategies. A side benefit of training team members together is that training provides the opportunity to build trust.

**Practice**   Teams are low on the learning curve when the team members begin to work with one another. A team might be motivated and highly skilled, but naive in terms of communicating with one another in a highly synchronized and coordinated fashion. Teams require more practice than do individuals.

**Minimize Links in Communication**   For most tasks, it is better for team members to directly communicate rather than going through others (gatekeeping).

**Set Clear Performance Standards**   Every team needs clear performance standards. In the absence of performance standards, it is impossible to evaluate the effectiveness of a team. The most common means by which people are evaluated by organizations is through a performance appraisal, which we discuss in detail in the next chapter. Many performance appraisals are routine and occur on a regular basis. In the best of circumstances, they are objective, based upon hard facts and deliverables. People receive clear and informative feedback about what they are doing well and what they need to work on. We've argued that performance appraisals should be used when evaluating team performance.

How does a manager know whether a team is performing effectively? If this question is hard to answer, then it will be difficult to pull together a high-performance team and diagnose problems before they threaten team performance. Furthermore, even if you happen to be in the fortunate position of working on a successful team, unless you understand what makes your team effective, you may make the wrong choices or be indecisive at inopportune times.

Team performance evaluation is more difficult than individual performance evaluation. Teams are harder to track, and higher turnover can blur the relationship between the actions that people take and the results achieved by the team. Nevertheless, it is still possible to do a rigorous performance evaluation on teams, just as it is with individual employees. In this chapter, we consider *what* factors are important to consider in assessing team performance. In the next chapter, we deal with the thornier issue of *how* to measure performance and structure the incentive system.

## Performance Criteria

What are the criteria by which we should evaluate team effectiveness? By performance criteria, we mean those factors used to evaluate the success or failure of a team effort. Hackman (1987) identified three key criteria in his model of group effectiveness: productivity, cohesion, and learning. To this, we add a fourth criterion, integration, suggested by Gruenfeld (1998).

### Productivity

*Productivity* is arguably the most important measure of team success. Did the team achieve its goals? According to LaFasto and Larson (2001), the single most important determinant of team success is whether the team has a clear and elevating goal. Team productivity requires that the team have a clear goal and adapt accordingly as new information arrives, goals change, and organizational priorities shift. This also holds true for changes in the marketplace—for example, the entrance or exit of a competitor or a stock market plunge. There are many different dimensions to productivity: What was the team's output? How does the output correspond to the team's original goals?

How quickly or timely were results achieved? How effective was the outcome? What is the correspondence between the team output and a measurable accomplishment (such as improved market share, new product development, etc.) by the organization? Efficiency is also important. If the team's goals were accomplished, at what cost did this happen? Was it worth it? The productivity of a team is highly correlated with its goals, as well as the ability of the team to adapt, change, and accommodate the goals in the face of new information, changing organizational priorities, and the changing marketplace.

The productivity criterion asks whether the team's output meets the standards of those who have to use it—that is, the end user. It is not enough that the team is satisfied with the output or even that it meets some objective performance measure. If the team's output is unacceptable to those who have to use it, the team is not effective.

For these reasons, it is important to identify the legitimate clients of the team. The various end users who depend on the team's output may focus on different performance standards (e.g., quantity, quality, cutting costs, innovation, and timeliness). For the world-famous Mayo Clinic, the goal is the patient and everyone knows this: "The best interest of the patient is the only interest to be considered" (Roberts, 1999a, p. 148).

Despite what teams would like to believe, perceptions of productivity do not always mirror reality. For example, Gladstein (1984) asked members of telecommunication sales teams to rate their teams' performance and aggregated their scores to get a measure of the team's perception of their performance. Aggregated member ratings did not correlate with an objective indicator of group performance—sales revenues. For many people, the buck stops here; anything else is inconsequential. We disagree.

### Cohesion

A second major criterion on team performance is *team cohesion*. The word cohesion derives from the Latin word *cohaesus,* meaning to cleave or stick together. In physics and chemistry, cohesion refers to the force(s) binding molecules of a substance together. For teams, cohesion refers to the processes that keep members of a team (e.g., military unit, work group, etc.) together and united (Dion, 2000). Did the team work together well and are its members better able to work together in the future as a result of this experience? Are team members' needs more satisfied than frustrated by the group experience (Sundstrom et al., 1990), and "is the capacity of members to work together on subsequent group tasks enhanced or maintained"? (Hackman & Oldham, 1980, p. 170). Consistent with most managers' intuitions, cohesion is a consistent predictor of team performance within project teams (Gillespie & Birnbaum-More, 1980; Greene, 1989; Keller, 1986), but not necessarily service teams (for a review, see Sundstrom, McIntyre, Halfhill, & Richards, 2000). Sometimes, teams meet their goals, but relationships suffer and are not dealt with in a way that allows members to work productively together in the future. "Mutual antagonism could become so high that members would choose to accept collective failure rather than to share knowledge and information with one another" (Hackman, 1990, p. 6). In an effectively functioning team, the capability of members to work together on future projects is maintained and strengthened.

It is worthwhile to ask why team cohesion is important, as opposed to being just a nice side benefit. For example, if a team successfully puts a person on the moon, is this not a success regardless of whether the team was cohesive? The main reason has to do with the future of the team or project. If the team effort really and truly is a one-time effort, then maximizing team cohesion may not be necessary. However, most of us want to build teams that will last for some meaningful length of time. If team members do not enjoy working on a team, performance will suffer. A manager in Societé Generale, a French investment bank and corporate finance institution, summed it up by saying, "I ask myself whether I want to work with these people again. If the answer is yes, then the team was successful. If the answer is no, the team was not successful."

Successful teamwork means that the team accommodates to changes in membership due to additions, growth, and turnover. A prime example of this kind of teamwork is evident at Whole Foods Market Inc. Everyone who joins Whole Foods quickly grasps the primacy of teamwork. That's because teams—and only teams—have the power to approve new hires for full-time jobs. Store leaders screen candidates and recommend them for a job on a specific team. But it takes a two-thirds vote of the team, after what is usually a 30-day trial period, for the candidate to become a full-time employee. Successful teamwork means that team members may need to routinely reject candidates. According to CEO and cofounder John Mackey, teams do not become effective until they have rejected someone: "They're saying, 'This person isn't good enough to be on our team.' They're standing up to the leader, taking ownership of their team, saying, 'Go back and try again' " (Fishman, 1996, p. 103).

### Learning

In addition to the functioning of the team as a whole, *learning* is also important. As anyone who has attended an executive education course can testify, cohesion may be present, but learning may be absent. Simply stated, teams should represent growth and development opportunities for the individual needs of the members. Human beings have a need for growth, development, and fulfillment. Some teams operate in ways that block the development of individual members and satisfaction of personal needs. In short, members' needs should be more satisfied than frustrated by the team experience. Teams should be sensitive to members and provide opportunities for members to develop new skills. This does not mean that teams, or for that matter, organizations, exist to serve individual needs; rather, successful organizations create opportunities that challenge individual members. At United Parcel Service (UPS), learning is considered to be so important that high-level managers routinely spot-quiz supervisors about their new employees—"What are his hobbies?" "Where is she going to school?" (Hammonds, 2002, p. 103). Supervisors are taught to demonstrate an interest in their workers as individuals. Why? Jennifer Shroeger, a UPS executive, knows that people are going to leave. But, instead of worrying about them leaving, she takes an interest in their future. And UPS executives put their money where their mouth is—they help pay college tuition bills and offer Saturday classes for computer skill development and career-planning discussions.

### Integration

Another perspective is that of the larger organization. Thus, a fourth criterion of team performance is *integration*. Does the organization benefit from the team? In many instances, the team becomes so self-serving and egocentrically focused that it loses sight of the organization's larger goals. (This is most likely the case with teams that have greater autonomy.) This can occur when the team's goals are incompatible with those of other departments or areas. If, for instance, a company's sales force dramatically improves sales over a short period of time, this does the company no good. In fact, it could even hurt the company if the manufacturing group cannot fulfill the promises made by the sales force or if the technical support group cannot handle the new customer calls. This is an example where the sales strategy backfires at the organizational level.

In other cases, different teams in the organization may reinvent things already developed by the organization because they are not able to learn from outside their group. It is important for teams to understand the organization's goals in order to work effectively toward them. Teams need to integrate with other units in the organization. Practically, this means that teams must disseminate information, results, status reports, failures, expertise, and ideas in a timely and efficient manner. Achieving integration

---

**BOX 2-1**

## Team Performance Analysis

Conduct a performance analysis of your team using the following four criteria as a baseline. Remember, you don't have to wait until the team is finished with its task to begin an evaluation. It is actually best to continually assess performance as the team is working toward its goal.

### PRODUCTIVITY

- Does the team have a clear goal?
- What objective performance measures will be used to evaluate results?
- Who are the legitimate clients of the team?
- Does the team's output (e.g., decisions, products, services) meet the standards of those who have to use it?
- Under what conditions should the goal change?
- What sources of information should the team consider to assess whether the initial goal should be changed?

### COHESION

- Do the team members enjoy working together?
- What conditions could lead to feelings of resentment?

- What conditions could prevent team members from working together in the future?
- How are team members expected to accommodate to changes, such as additions to the team, growth, and turnover?

### LEARNING

- How can team members best learn from one another?
- Do the individual team members grow and develop as a result of the team experience?
- Do team members have a chance to improve their skills or affirm themselves?
- What factors and conditions could block personal growth?
- Are individuals' growth needs understood and shared by group members?

### INTEGRATION

- How does the team benefit the larger organization?
- Are the team's goals consistent with those of the larger organization?
- What other groups, departments, and units are affected by the team?
- What steps has the team taken to integrate its activities with those of others?

requires solid planning and coordination with the rest of the company. Box 2-1 is an executive summary of our team performance analysis, which can be performed by team members or team leaders. The relative importance of each of the four criteria vary across circumstances, and there is no single best set of conditions for optimizing performance. There are many ways a team can perform work well and, unfortunately, more ways for it to be ineffective. Teams are governed by the principle of equifinality (Katz & Kahn, 1978)—a team can reach the same outcome from various initial conditions and by a variety of means.

Having presented the four major criteria in our team performance review, it is important to point out that this is not a magic list, or even a standard list. We think it is important for every team leader to think about which criteria are important when evaluating teamwork and to specify those in an *a priori* fashion.

## THE TEAM PERFORMANCE EQUATION

Now that we have discussed the four critical measures of team performance and the three key ingredients for team success, we can put them together in a single equation for the leader to use when assessing team performance (Steiner, 1972):

$$AP = PP + S - T$$

Where  AP = Actual Productivity
       PP = Potential Productivity
       S  = Synergy
       T  = Performance Threats

The actual productivity of a team is a function of three key factors: The potential productivity of the team, synergy, and threats. The first factor, the **potential productivity** of a team, depends on three subfactors: task demands, the resources available to the team, and the team process.

**Task demands** are the requirements imposed on the team by the task itself and the rules governing task performance. Task demands determine the resources needed for optimal performance and how to combine resources. **Resources** are the relevant abilities, skills, and tools possessed by people attempting to perform the task. **Process** concerns the way teams use resources to meet task demands. *Team process* describes the steps taken by the team when attempting the task and includes nonproductive as well as productive actions. The task demands reveal the kinds of resources needed; the resources determine the team's potential productivity; and the process determines the degree of potential realized.

**Synergy** refers to everything that can and does go better in a team compared with individuals working independently (Collins & Guetzkow, 1964). **Performance threats** refer to everything that can go wrong in a team. Unfortunately, teams often fall below their potential; there is considerable **process loss,** or underperformance, due to coordination problems and motivational problems (Davis, 1969; Laughlin, 1980; Steiner, 1972). As a general principle, managers can more easily control threats than synergies. Synergies can emerge, but they usually take more time than anyone expects. Therefore, the manager's job is to set the stage for synergies by attempting to minimize all possible threats.

# CONCLUSIONS

Unless a team has a clear goal, it will be impossible to achieve success. However, having a clear goal in no sense guarantees successful team performance. Successful team performance is a multidimensional concept. To be sure, managers want their teams to satisfy the end user or client, but they also need to make sure that teamwork is satisfying and rewarding for the members. If the team does not enjoy working together, sustaining long-term productivity will be impossible. Moreover, managing a team successfully must include managing and investing in the individual team members. Thus, teamwork ultimately needs to be a growthful and rewarding experience for team members. Finally, as organizations move toward flatter structures and greater team empowerment, the possibility arises that team goals may become superordinate to those of the larger organization. A successful team is integrated with the larger organization. Putting teams on a course to achieve these four markers of success requires a combination of managing the internal dynamics of teams (ability, motivation, and coordination), as well as the external relations of teams within the larger organization. One of the most effective things a manager can do to ensure team success is to take a proactive approach and undertake an analysis of the essential conditions affecting team performance. One of the biggest managerial shortcomings in terms of teamwork is a failure to account for threats to team performance. This is unfortunate because managers can more easily control threats than synergies.

# CHAPTER

# Rewarding Teamwork:

## 3

## *Compensation and Performance Appraisals*

*In 1992, Michael Dettmers, cofounder of Dettmers Industries in Stuart, Florida, decided to restructure his $3 million company, which makes seating and table products for private aircraft. Dettmers made an unusual proposition to his employees: Teams would be paid 25 percent of sales of the specific product that they made, and they would distribute those revenues among their teammates as they saw fit. Teams would be responsible for scheduling, customer service, quality, and even their own cash flow. That first year, 1992, Dettmers tried the system on just one team, promising employees that they wouldn't earn less than they had the previous year, and it turned out that average annual wages increased from $32,000 to $45,000. Says Dettmers, "Once people began to see that if they worked more effectively as a team they would make more money, they had enthusiasm for working in this new way, and they made a commitment to learning" (Fenn, 1996). The following year, four more teams were organized similarly (Fenn, 1996).*

The move to self-managing teams begs the question of reward and compensation in teams because hierarchical pay plans centered on individuals may not make sense in the context of teams and may, in fact, be detrimental (Lawler, 2000). If pay plans reward the individual but the corporate message is teams, then teamwork may be undermined. Perhaps it is for this reason that 76 percent of businesses with self-directed teams tie team members' compensation partly to team performance (Lawler, Mohrman, & Ledford, 1995). This does not mean, however, that team members should all be paid equally. People in teams know that there is variable performance among members.

Team compensation is not as simple as it might seem. For example, rewarding team performance could set up a system where teams compete viciously with other teams in their same company (see, e.g., Sidebar 3-1). Even though teams may be perfectly capable of allocating pay or rewards to individuals in the team, this may sometimes mean that superstars are not rewarded unless other teammates forgo part of their own profit sharing.

Even if a compensation system can be set up that appropriately rewards team effort, some team members may be unwilling to determine their coworkers' pay. For example, teams in the Dallas office of New York Life Insurance Company conducted "peer reviews" to assess members' contributions to a team's performance, but team

## Sidebar 3-1. When Team Pay Backfires

The Levi Strauss Corporation moved from a piecemeal system to a team system, in which workers were no longer paid by how much they produced personally, but rather by the performance of the team (King, 1998). Levi Strauss did this for seemingly good reasons—to give employees more variety in their work, making it more interesting and less likely that employees would be injured due to repetitive stress disorders, and so on. But the results were disastrous. Workers with more skills resented those with fewer skills because they ended up with less pay than before, even though the average pay increased across the board. The conflict among team members was fierce. Yet given the structure that was set up, conflict almost seemed inevitable, and there was little that employees could do to change the situation. In fact, highly skilled workers provoked the antagonism of less capable workers, including those with injuries, to get them to quit (and thus increase the average productivity of the group).

   Consider also what happened at Solar Press in Naperville, Illinois (Garfield, 1992). Employees were assigned to specific machines and divided into work teams with four or five members. The more a team produced during a given month, the bigger the bonus for each of its members. Teams competed for additional dollars. The bonus plan, put in place in the spring of 1984, had an immediate effect: Packaging machines ran faster than ever and production rates doubled. But there were also problems. Because of the pressure to produce, teams put off routine maintenance, so machines broke down more often. Employees who found more efficient ways of working hoarded the information to prevent others from winning their bonuses. Moreover, the plan did not take into account unfair distributions of work assignments, or the fact that some jobs demanded more work than others. According to Sue Smith, the Solar Press scheduling manager, the "system totally dismantled any feeling of team work or company-wide spirit" (Garfield, 1992, p. 252).

members were not comfortable deciding the size and recipients of the resulting incentive awards. So, management decided for them (Lawler, Mohrman, & Ledford, 1995). Other companies, such as Johnsonville Foods, address the problem by creating more objective standards to evaluate team members' performance. For example, three Southwest-region Johnsonville teams prepare a detailed weekly scoreboard to set and track specific activity, such as the number of sales calls. As we discuss in this chapter, team members feel more comfortable when performance criteria are based on objective standards.

   This chapter examines the types of team pay and the choices companies have for rewarding their teams. We discuss the advantages and disadvantages of each method. In the second section of the chapter, we take up the question of performance appraisals: What are they? What should be measured? Who should do the measuring? We examine 360-degree evaluations in detail. In the third section of the chapter, we examine the types of biases that can play havoc on performance appraisals and discuss what to do about these biases. We conclude the chapter by providing a step-by-step guide for implementing a variable team-based pay structure.

## TYPES OF TEAM PAY

There is no all-purpose team compensation plan. In this section, we consider four types of team pay or reward: incentive pay, recognition, profit sharing, and gainsharing (see Table 3-1). Pay, in a large measure, is a communication device. According to Gross (1995), pay is one of the loudest and clearest ways a company can send a message to an employee. People tend to behave according to the way they are evaluated and paid. Therefore, if the organization values teamwork, team members must be ultimately recognized and compensated for teaming. First and foremost, employees must understand how the incentive system works in their company. Generally, the simpler, the better.

**TABLE 3-1** Team-Based Pay

| Type | Description/Types | Advantages/Applications | Disadvantages |
|---|---|---|---|
| **Incentive pay** | A team of employees receives money based on increased performance against predetermined targets | • Can combine a focus on individual and team performance <br> • Team can be given opportunity to allocate | • Employees averse to thinking of selves as team members <br> • Risky if base pay is reduced <br> • Guided by upper management and corporate initiative |
| **Recognition** | One-time award for a limited number of employees or groups for performing well beyond expectations or for completing a project, program, or product | • Easy to implement <br> • Distributed at the local (team level) <br> • Introduced easily, quickly, and inexpensively without layers of approval <br> • Comparatively simple | • Employees concerned they won't be recognized for own contributions <br> • Risky if base pay is reduced <br> • Carry less front-end motivation |
| **Profit sharing** | A share of corporate profits is distributed in cash on a current basis to all employees, (driven by financial factors) | • Serves communication purpose by signaling that rewards are in balance across the organization <br> • Informs and educates employees about financial well-being of organization | • Far removed from workers' control to affect performance |
| **Gainsharing** | A percentage of the value of increased productivity is given to workers under prearranged formula (driven by operational factors [e.g., quality, productivity, customer satisfaction]) | • Geared toward production-oriented workers <br> • Add-on to compensation, so easily accepted by employees | • Far removed from workers' control to affect performance |

For example, burying incentives and recognition for team membership in the company's basic compensation package can dampen the intended motivating effect on individuals. Second, an incentive system should be comprehensive enough that people feel fairly treated. Employees compare their pay with that of others. An incentive system that appears unfair can result in trouble (see Sidebar 3-2 for an example).

### Sidebar 3-2. Women Are Still Paid Less Than Men for the Same Work

It is well known that women earn significantly less money for doing the same work as men. Women presently comprise almost 45 percent of the paid labor force, and 64.3 percent of married mothers with children younger than the age of six are now employed (U.S. Department of Labor, 2001a). Yet despite a number of gains, women's annual earnings remain at 72 percent of men's (U.S. Department of Labor, 2001b).

In the traditional model of compensation, base pay was designed to attract and retain employees. Incentives and bonuses were reserved for managers, salespeople, and higher executives. Now, many companies are moving to align pay systems with business strategies (Gross, 1995). Individual incentives, commissions, profit sharing, and gainsharing are different methods of variable pay that are offered to motivate and reward performance. However, they are not designed to motivate and reward teams. Rather, the two most common practices for rewarding and motivating team performance are team incentives and recognition.

### Incentive Pay

In terms of salary and pay, **base pay** is how companies determine an individual's base salary. This is an integration of internal equity (based on job evaluation) and external equity (based on market data). The second issue in pay is **variable pay.** One type of variable pay is incentive pay. In general, variable pay should not be more than 15 to 20 percent for individuals in the lowest levels of the company. As employees move up the organizational chart, the proportion of variable pay should increase—along with their amount of control over the situation.

Many organizations have incentive-based pay plans based on individual performance. Because the focus of this book is on teams, we deal with team-based pay. When teams are an organization's choice approach to job design, it often makes little sense for the organization to use systems that reward individual performance. Particularly destructive are performance appraisal systems for individuals that require a fixed number of positive and negative rations or provide fixed pots of budget money that need to be divided up differentially among individuals in a group; these practices put team members in competition for rewards (Lawler, 1992).

Incentive strategies can combine a focus on individual performance and team performance to reflect the degree to which a job calls for individual work and teamwork. For example, a bonus pool may be created based on the performance of the overall team. The bonus pool can be divided among the individuals who are members of the team based on how well the individuals performed. (For an example of the implementation of bonus pay, see Sidebar 3-3.) To ensure that team members do not compete in

**Sidebar 3-3. Team Bonus Pay**

One large national retail corporation with more than eight hundred outlets was exploring ways to increase sales (see Shea & Guzzo, 1987). Management believed that increasing group incentives to sell would increase sales and service by increasing salespeople's customer orientation and cooperativeness. Consequently, the salesforce went from being paid an hourly wage to being paid an hourly wage plus a group bonus. The bonus depended on sales gains in the current calendar month over sales for that month in the preceding year. The bonuses were distributed noncompetitively; each person could earn an hourly bonus that ranged from a few cents to over a dollar for each hour worked in a month, depending on the size of the team's sales. No financial penalties existed for sales losses. Posting the weekly sales figures meant that groups received continual feedback regarding their opportunity to earn bonus money. During the seven-month period of this study, sales gains corporationwide averaged approximately 28 percent. At the work group level, outcome interdependence increased significantly, and marked changes occurred in the patterns for work interaction among group members. Rewarding entire groups for focusing on sales was associated with an increase in mutual assistance and a decrease in members' blocking or hindering each other's work.

a destructive fashion, a 360-degree feedback method can be used (which we discuss in detail in the next section). Another alternative is to have two separate reward systems operating in tandem. One system provides bonuses to teams based on their performance; the second rewards individuals, based on how well they have performed. These systems can be based on separate budgets so that they do not compete.

A critical question is whether to reward behavior or to reward results. Traditional thinking may lead managers to link team performance to their results. Bob Gore, the CEO of W. L. Gore & Associates who developed the revolutionary fabric Gore-Tex, believes in effort—even when a project is abandoned, employees may be taken out for drinks to congratulate them for their work and efforts in a lost cause (*Sunday Times–London,* March 24, 2002). For goals such as cost reduction, this is easy to quantify, but for other areas, this is much more difficult. For example, Motorola's David Goodall, corporate director of compensation, argues that "[i]t's unfair to reward cross-functional teams solely on the basis of results, because they are often put into positions to move organizations forward by taking risks. Sometimes the risks they take might not be successful. The worst thing to do would be to rap their knuckles" (Pascarella, 1997, p. 16). One solution is to redefine or broaden the meaning of success—much as the previous chapter reviewed the four measures of team productivity (productivity, cohesion, learning, and integration). Thus, many managers reward competencies rather than results—for example, does the person display participative behavior? Does the person empower others? Does the person listen in a team environment?

Consider the incentive program at InterDigital Communications Corp., which develops advanced wireless technologies. Employees who come up with a patentable invention get more than two thousand options: one-third vest when the patent is filed, two-thirds when it is granted. There's also an Investors' Dinner for those who've filed for or have been awarded patents that year. The dinner recognizes, with cash awards, the team or individual names as inventor on the most patents. The program was created to encourage an atmosphere of competition. In 2001, InterDigital applied for 256 patents, five times the number it applied for in 1999 (Singer & Buchanan, 2002).

Companies are more likely to add incentives to support team activity when a person is assigned full time to a project. At TRW Inc.'s Cleveland-based automotive group, Project ELITE (Earnings Leadership In Tomorrow's Environment), a number of people are temporarily assigned to a team effort, and it is expected that they will return to their units or to a full-time permanent position sometime in the future. A significant portion of their pay is tied to the accomplishment of their goals and the organization's goals, which are clearly articulated.

Although team incentives offer significant advantages, there are some potential drawbacks (see DeMatteo, Eby, & Sundstrom, 1998). Most important, the use of team-based rewards may create the potential for motivational loss (i.e., social loafing and free riding). This may result from perceptions of inequity when other team members are perceived as free riders, but rewards are nevertheless allocated based on equality. Moreover, team rewards may not foster cooperation in teams (Wageman, 1995). In fact, team rewards may foster competition between teams, leading to suboptimization of the organizational goals (Mohrman, Lawler, & Mohrman, 1992).

## Recognition

The power of positive recognition often is severely underestimated. According to Bob Nelson, author of *1001 Ways to Reward Employees* and *1001 Ways to Energize Employees,* "Most employees today say the only time they hear from their boss is when they make a mistake. And that's a big mistake" (Robinson, 2001). Making sure that employees are happy and feel that they are appreciated builds loyalty and productivity. Leaders should not approach this passively. Bob Beyster, CEO of Science Applications International Corp., will stalk those worthy employees: "If somebody does something good and I don't know who did it, that bugs me. I ferret down and try to find out who did it" (Lindquist, 2002). Furthermore, it can cost virtually nothing—just a little time, energy, and forethought. According to Gross (1995), "One of the smartest things companies can do is to develop a systematic program of recognition of team results" (p. 129). Recognition, rewards, spot cash awards, or "celebrations of success" reward contributions after the fact, when performance is known.

The idea behind team recognition is that money is not everything. There are infinite sources of nonmonetary recognition—plaques, trophies, small gifts, vacations, and dinners with company officers. The most important feature of any of these is to give the gift respectfully, personally, and sincerely. First and foremost, this means that people and teams are singled out—if everyone gets the same recognition, it doesn't work. This is why Bob Nelson does not like "employee of the month" programs—because everyone is going to get it eventually (Robinson, 2001). The reward should be chosen with the people in mind. Not everyone likes sporting events or ballet, for example. It is important to clearly tie the recognition to team performance; it will lose its effect if the organization waits two months to reward the team. Bernie Nagle, principal consultant at PriceWaterhouseCoopers, advises management to recognize and celebrate the team. Also, team members should be encouraged to speak to management and explain how they achieved their objectives. (For some general guidelines for implementing recognition awards, consult Table 3-2.)

**TABLE 3-2** Implementing Recognition Awards: A Guide

*To have maximum possible impact, recognition awards should have the following features:*

| | |
|---|---|
| **Purpose/objective** | The program should clearly recognize what has been accomplished by the team and how that effort is linked to the company's values. |
| **Eligibility** | Companies must clearly determine whether teams or individuals will be recognized; lower, middle, and upper management; and how frequently employees are eligible for awards. |
| **Program award levels** | Use a few levels to recognize different accomplishments and different degrees of contributions: (a) application noncash awards (up to $250); (b) awards for significant financial contribution ($250–$2,500) for team members whose efforts significantly exceed expectations, support the unit's efforts, and produce measurable results; (c) awards for "extraordinary financial results" ($2,500–$10,000) for team members whose efforts have exceptional bottom-line impact. |
| **Benefit implications** | Recognition awards are not considered benefit bearing. |
| **Funding** | Recognition programs are typically funded out of the expense budget of the business unit and department, and are often stated as a percentage of the payroll. |
| **Types of awards** | (Noncash versus cash) |
| **Nomination procedures** | For appreciation award level, nomination procedure should be as simple as possible; for companywide rewards, nomination procedures may be much more elaborate with peers, customers, and supervisors all having opportunity for input. |
| **Timing** | All awards should be given as close to the event as possible to reinforce the actions that led to the event. |
| **Award presentation** | This should be a positive experience, that makes the winner(s) feel proud; comments should be personalized and refer to details of the achievement; the connection between the accomplishment and the company's business strategy should be made clear; never present the award in passing; publicize the award (e.g., via memo, e-mail, bulletin board, or newsletter). |
| **Program evaluation** | Annually, a rewards and recognition committee should be chartered to evaluate the program in terms of its effectiveness. |

*Source:* Adapted from Gross, S. E. 1995. *Compensation for Teams: How to Design and Implement Team-Based Reward Programs.* New York: AMACOM.

### Cash and Noncash

Spot awards (also known as lightning bolts) can either be cash or noncash. Noncash awards, which are the most common, are given out for a job well done and are usually of nominal value. Cash awards can be far more substantial, although usually they are small bonuses. There is a lesson to be learned about cash and noncash recognition awards: "To recognize efforts and activities above expectations, give non-cash awards. To get results, pay cash" (Gross, 1995, p. 130).

Recognition awards are regarded to be effective, according to the 1994 Hay survey of 86 large U.S. corporations represented in the Business Roundtable, an association of 200 chief executives of the largest U.S. companies. The size of recognition awards varies significantly, from $100 to $15,000, with the average much closer to the low end. Cash awards need to be significant enough to merit being awarded. This usually means over $250. Gross (1995) uses the "VCR test" as a rule of thumb: if someone can't buy a VCR with the award, it is probably not enough.

There are an infinite variety of noncash rewards that companies can give to teams to recognize contributions, ranging from thank-you notes to time off to lavish, all-expenses-paid trips for two to exotic places. For example, at CISCO Systems, Inc., all employees are invited to a 90-minute "birthday breakfast" in the month of their birth (Byrne, 1998). Such rewards often reinforce the company image and strengthen the connection between the employer and the employee. Satyam Computers gives "suggestions mileage cards" to their employees—the more suggestions an employee makes, the more points she earns—and just like any other card, attractive rewards can be redeemed, depending on the number of points that have been accumulated (Misra & Misra, 2002). To be effective, recognition needs to be clearly focused on the team whose achievements are being celebrated, rather than on a general self-congratulatory party for the entire unit or organization.

An especially thorny issue is whether recognition awards to teams should equally recognize all team members. (For an example of how recognition could backfire, see Sidebar 3-4.)

## Sidebar 3-4. When Recognition Backfires

Recognition can invite complaints. Motorola's Goodall cites the case of an international team made up of six people representing different businesses from different regions. When they successfully completed their project, the organization decided it would give each individual a $1,000 aftertax bonus. Three of the six members felt the money was unnecessary: "We've already had the satisfaction of being on the team, having the recognition of being able to report back to the senior staff." These team members were further disturbed by the fact that, irrespective of the level they were in the organization, each received the same dollar amount: "We want to be rewarded for the effort we put in as individuals" (Pascarella, 1997). Team members may say to themselves, "We saved the company millions and they only give me a thousand."

James A. Tompkins, president of Tompkins Associates Inc., a Raleigh, N.C., consultancy, warns that management needs to be careful about anything that may be viewed as "buying" the team. He gives the following example: "If I'm stuck on the side of the road and you stop and help me change a flat tire, and I give you $10, you are insulted. But if I send your wife a bouquet of flowers, you are complimented" (Pascarella, 1997, p. 16). The gesture must be customized for the team. For example, giving team members tickets to an evening ball game in reward for putting in long hours on a project may be deflating to team members with families.

Many consultants believe that teams should be given a role in distributing recognition awards—letting the team decide which members get how much. This practice is consistent with the whole idea of self-managing teams: autonomy and self-management (see Box 3-1).

According to the 1994 Hay Compensation Conference Survey, recognition awards are more widely used by companies (38 percent) than are special pay programs for

### Seven Ways to Praise Teams

Bob Nelson, author of *1001 Ways to Reward Employees* (1994), suggests these seven methods of recognizing the accomplishments of a team, as well as the achievements of individual team members:

1. Have managers pop in at the first meeting of a special project team and express their appreciation for the members' involvement.

2. When a group presents an idea or suggestion, managers should thank members for their initiative.

3. Encourage a lunch meeting with project teams once they've made interim findings. Have managers express their appreciation.

Encourage continued energy. Provide the lunch.

4. Promote writing letters to every team member at the conclusion of a project thanking them for their contribution.

5. Encourage creative symbols of a team's work, such as T-shirts or coffee cups with a motto or logo.

6. Have managers ask the boss to attend a meeting with the employees during which individuals and groups are thanked for their specific contributions.

7. Suggest catered lunches or breakfasts for high-performing groups.

teams (12 percent). Two types of incentive pay systems that are not designed specifically for teams but are popular in participative management companies and are consistent with many team-based approaches are profit sharing and gainsharing. They can be tailored for teams.

### Profit Sharing

Many companies use profit sharing schemes, wherein a portion of the bottom-line economic profits is given to employees. These internally distributed profits may be apportioned according to equality or equity. In the typical profit sharing plan, profit sharing bonuses are put into retirement plans. This makes it more difficult to clearly relate rewards to controllable performance. Thus, most profit sharing plans have little impact on the motivation and behavior of employees (Lawler, 2000).

Profit sharing plans serve an important communication purpose by signaling to everyone that rewards are in balance across the organization. Second, they inform and educate employees about the financial health of the organization. Finally, profit sharing makes the labor costs of an organization variable, thus adjusting them to the organization's ability to pay (Weitzman, 1984).

### Gainsharing

Gainsharing involves a measurement of productivity, combined with the calculation of a bonus, designed to offer employees a mutual share of any increases in total organizational productivity. In gainsharing plans, an organization uses a formula to share financial gains with all employees in a single plant or location. The organization establishes a historical base period of performance and uses this to determine whether gains in performance have occurred. Typically, only controllable costs are measured for the purpose of computing gain. Unless a major change takes place in the company's products or technology, the historical base stays the same during the entire history of the plan. Thus, the organization's performance is always compared with the time period before it started the gainsharing plan. When the organization's performance is better than it was in the base period, the plan funds a bonus pool. When its performance falls short, no bonus pool is created; when performance is met or exceeded, the typical plan pays about half of the bonus pool to employees and the rest is kept by the company. Payments are usually made on a monthly basis, with all employees receiving the same percentage of their regular base pay. A trend of large corporations that have their own gainsharing plans has led more companies to adopt gainsharing.

Gainsharing plans appear to work. Gainsharing enhances coordination and information sharing among teams, instigates attitude change, raises performance standards, and enhances idea generation and flexibility (Lawler, 2000). (For an in-depth discussion of gainsharing, see Lawler, 2000, Chapter 10.) Gainsharing plans are more than just pay incentive plans; they are a way of managing and a technology for organizational development. For gainsharing to work successfully, it should be developed in collaboration with the people it will affect. It is important that employees understand and know how to influence the formula, that the standards seem credible, that bonuses be timely, and that some mechanism exists for change. A company needs a participative management system for the plan to work because it requires employees to take ownership of the success of the company (Blinder, 1990; Lawler, 2000).

Profit sharing plans are typically less effective than gainsharing plans in influencing employee motivation and changing culture than are gainsharing plans (Blinder, 1990; Lawler, 2000). This lack of effectiveness is largely attributable to the disconnection between individual performance and corporate profits—even with high-level involvement. This depends on how salient profit sharing benefits are made to the workers. Consider the company that boldly posts its stock value for all employees to view in public areas—people see the value literally.

These four systems for rewarding employees—incentive pay, recognition, profit sharing, and gainsharing—should not be looked at as competing approaches, but rather as compatible systems that accomplish different, important objectives. For example, the combination of gainsharing and profit sharing deals directly with an organization's need to have variable labor costs and helps to educate the workforce about financial information. There is no surefire plan or formula that works for most teams. It depends on the organization. We offer these differing plans to increase the possibilities.

## TEAMS AND PAY FOR PERFORMANCE

According to Lawler (2000), in order for teams to be optimally effective, a reward system should be attuned to the behaviors and skills that are needed for team success. Lawler distinguishes four types of teams: parallel teams, production and service teams, project teams, and management teams. Table 3-3 suggests the best possible pay for performance schemes, according to each type of team.

**TABLE 3-3**    Pay Strategies for Four Types of Teams

| Type of Team | Work Focus | Pay for Performance |
|---|---|---|
| **Parallel** | Supplement regular organizational structure and perform problem-solving and work-improvement tasks (e.g., problem-solving teams, quality circles, employee participation teams) | Gainsharing or other business unit plan to reward savings<br><br>Recognition rewards |
| **Production and Service** | Responsible for producing a project or service and are self-contained, identifiable work units (e.g., manufacturing teams, assembly teams, tactical teams, customer sales or service teams) | Team bonuses or business unit bonuses if teams are interdependent<br><br>Use individual bonuses that are based on peer evaluations |
| **Project** | Often involve diverse group of knowledge workers, such as design engineers, process engineers, programmers (e.g., new project development teams) | Use bonuses based on project success<br><br>Profit sharing and stock plans |
| **Management** | Composed of well-trained managers; often have stable membership; teams usually permanent; expected to provide integration, leadership and direction to organization | Team or business unit bonuses<br><br>Profit-sharing and stock-based options |

*Source:* Adapted from Lawler, E. E. 2000. *Rewarding Excellence: Pay Strategies for The New Economy,* p. 217. San Francisco, CA: Jossey-Bass.

# TEAM PERFORMANCE APPRAISAL

Individual performance appraisal is an evaluation of a person's behaviors and accomplishments in terms of the person's work in an organization. Performance appraisals are a source of feedback, a basis for personal development, and a determination of pay. The rise of teams presents special challenges for performance appraisal. It is difficult for a supervisor to conduct a traditional performance appraisal of an individual who is serving at least part time on a team. When the individual is part of a self-managed, self-directing, or self-governing team, it is virtually impossible, because supervisors are rarely close enough to the teams to evaluate them. The catch-22 is that if they were, they might hinder the performance of the team. We saw in Chapter 2 that it is useful for teams and managers to focus on four measures of team productivity. According to Meyer (1994), the overarching purpose of a measurement system should be to help a team, rather than to employ top management to gauge its progress. Moreover, a truly empowered team should play a lead role in designing its own measurement system. Here, we deal with the question of exactly how performance should be measured and by whom.

## What Is Measured?

A change in traditional performance appraisals, precipitated by the rise of teams, concerns what is measured in performance reviews. In many traditional control-oriented organizations, the major determinant of employees' pay is the type of work they do or their seniority. The major alternative is competency-based pay. Companies are increasingly recognizing that dynamic factors, such as competencies and skills, may be a better way to measure success than static measures, such as experience and education. In the following paragraphs, we review job-based pay, skill-based pay, and competency-based pay.

### *Job-Based Pay*

Job-based pay is determined by a job evaluation system, which frequently takes a point factor approach to evaluating jobs (Lawler, 2000). The point factor approach begins with a written job description that is scored in terms of duties. The point scores are then translated into salary levels. A key advantage of job-based pay systems is that organizations can determine what other companies are paying and can assess whether they are paying more or less than their competitors. Another advantage of job evaluation systems is that they allow for centralized control of an organization's pay system.

### *Skill-Based Pay*

To design a skill-based pay system, a company must identify those tasks that need to be performed in the organization. Next, the organization identifies skills that are needed to perform the tasks and develops tests or measures to determine whether a person has learned these skills. For this reason, it is important to specify the skills that an individual can learn in a company. Employees need to be told what they can learn given their position in the organization and how learning skills will affect their pay. People are typically paid only for those skills that they currently can and are willing to perform. Many skill-based plans give people pay increases when they learn a new skill. One system of skill-based pay is a technical ladder, in which individuals are paid for the depth of skill they have in a particular technical specialty. Procter & Gamble started using skill-based pay in the late 1960s to support the development of work teams. In the P&G system, production employees are paid for horizontal skills and, in some cases, upwardly vertical skills. In a few cases, they are also paid for learning downwardly vertical skills, such as cleaning and routine production tasks. (For an example of how one skill-based pay plan failed to work, see Sidebar 3-5.)

### *Competency-Based Pay*

Competency-based pay differs from skill-based pay in that employees prove they can use their skills. After all, it is possible for people to attain skills (e.g., training and mentoring programs) but never use them—or be ineffective when using them. For example, Volvo gives every employee in a work area a pay increase when the employees in that area prove they can operate without a supervisor (Lawler, 1992). It is important for organizations to focus on demonstrated competencies, rather than accumulated accreditations.

Competency-based pay is regarded as a much more sensible and ultimately profitable approach to use in a team-based organization. First, competency-based pay systems promote flexibility in employees: When employees can perform multiple tasks,

**Sidebar 3-5. When Skill-Based Pay Doesn't Work**

John Powenski, the HR manager at Frito Lay in Kirkwood, New York, helped to orchestrate a performance and productivity improvement at the eight hundred-employee facility, with initially strong results. A leadership team, composed of manufacturing, distribution, planning, technical, and HR managers, challenged the plant to become more customer-focused, team-based, and owner-driven. Teams trained together, met to discuss production plans, and give each other 360-degree feedback. However, "'All hell broke loose when we linked pay to performance,' Powenski says. It was a radical departure, and employees had not been included in development of the new compensation structure. 'They didn't like a peer affecting their pay and had concerns about the integrity of the whole system,' Powenski notes. 'We had not included the technicians in the pay restructuring, and that was a big mistake.' Recognizing that the change had not been accepted, the Leadership Team returned to the previous system" (Novak, 1997).

organizations gain tremendous flexibility in using their workforce. This, of course, is the concept of cross-training. In addition to the benefits of cross-training, individuals who have several skills have an advantage in terms of developing an accurate perspective on organizational problems and challenges. When employees have an overview of the entire company, they are more committed. When they are broadly knowledgeable about the operations of an organization, they can increase their self-managing, coordinate with others, utilize organizational resources, and communicate more effectively.

However, competency-based pay systems are not perfect. An organization using a competency-based pay system typically commits to giving everyone the opportunity to learn multiple skills and then to demonstrate them; thus, the organization has to make a large investment in training and evaluation. There is a trade-off between getting the work done and skill acquisition and demonstration.

### Who Does the Measuring?

The standard is the employee's supervisor, or some set of top-level persons. With the increasing use of teams, peer review is becoming more common and more necessary in organizations. Popularly known as **360-degree** or **multirater feedback** methods, the peer review procedure involves getting feedback about an employee from all sides: top (supervisors), bottom (subordinates), coworkers, suppliers, and end-user customers or clients (see Figure 3-1). Typically, several people (ideally five to 10) participate in the evaluation, compared with a traditional review where only one person, usually a supervisor, provides feedback. For example, at W. L. Gore and Associates, teams of 10 people anonymously rank their peers according to the amount they contribute to the group (*Sunday Times–London,* March 24, 2002). The highest paid should be the highest ranked when the results are plotted on a graph. Anonymity is the key to building a nonbiased feedback system, especially for peers and subordinates. Otherwise, the entire system is compromised. General Electric's former CEO, Jack Welch, explains how his company does it: "Every employee is graded on a 1–5 scale by his manager, his peers, and all his subordinates in areas such as team-building, quality focus and vision.

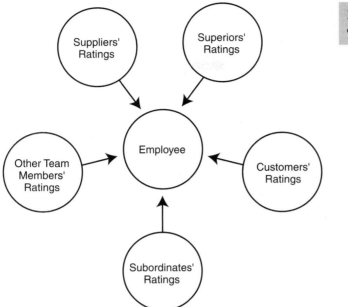

**FIGURE 3-1** 360-Degree or Multirater Feedback

Some people think it's bureaucratic. But it embodies our values (which come out of years of discussions with employees). And the subordinates clearly provide the best input. Peers are a little more careful, and the boss is always a little more cautious" (Hillkirk, 1993, p. 5B).

A big disadvantage of the top-down performance review is evaluation bias. The multiple data points and aggregate responses provided by 360-degree feedback make the bias of a single person less of a problem.

A second major disadvantage of single-source evaluation is that it is easy to dismiss the information. "If my boss tells me something, I can easily ignore it," says Mark Edwards of Teams, Inc. With multiple sources, the information becomes more credible and is more difficult to discount. As Jarman (1998) puts it, "If in the course of a day you meet a disagreeable person, chances are you've met a disagreeable person. But if in the course of a day you meet five disagreeable people, chances are you're the disagreeable person" (p. D1).

As an example of how companies put 360-degree feedback in place, consider the Long Term Credit Bank of Japan, or LTCB, which bases its annual bonuses for managers in part on evaluations by their subordinates. LTCB, which previously adopted a skill-based pay system, is trying to increase the transparency of its performance evaluation methods by inviting the rank and file to grade bosses. In the system, managers select a group of up to 20 subordinates, colleagues, and supervisors to grade their job performance. Of the group, as many as nine employees, including two or three who work directly under the manager, evaluate their boss. Managerial employees receive a monthly base pay plus two bonuses; over 30 percent of their bonus is based on the evaluations (*Dow Jones News Service,* April 14, 1998).

At Phelps Dodge, 360-degree evaluations were first administered to the company's top 180 executives worldwide, including chairperson Douglas Yearley. The company developed a set of core competencies, such as demonstrating sound business judgment, driving for results, fostering teamwork, and creating an ownership philosophy among employees, and evaluated executives on these dimensions. Because the core competencies used to evaluate employees are part of the company's or department's mission statement, the 360-degree process helps bring performance of individual employees in line with company goals and values. In fact, companies beginning to develop 360-degree evaluations are encouraged to start with their mission statement.

In theory, the 360-degree process provides a multifaceted view of the team member. However, putting it into practice can be difficult: If the number of feedback sources is limited, raters are not guaranteed anonymity and may fear retaliation. The system is subject to abuse if members make side deals to rate one another favorably. Many people going into it are against the idea, and it takes time to make several evaluations.

However, despite its difficulties, 360-degree or multirater feedback is usually regarded to be a more fair assessment of performance than is top-down review (for an argument of how information systems [IS] can benefit from 360-degree feedback, see Sidebar 3-6). Although team members are often best qualified to rate each other, there are some weaknesses to this approach. Team members unpopular for reasons other than performance can suffer. Team members do not always grasp the big picture in terms of organizational goals. As raters, peers can suffer from evaluation biases.

### Sidebar 3-6. Why Information Systems (IS) Need 360s

Michael Schrage jokes that "whenever managers talk about 360-degree job reviews, I think of that joke about the nattering egomaniac at the cocktail party: 'But enough about me; let's talk about you. What do you think about me?'" (Schrage, 1998, p. 33).

Schrage quite seriously goes on to argue that the key reason why IS should passionately embrace 360s is that these reviews represent the best way to promote better communication of expectations. Basically, 360s force technical people and businesspeople to communicate about something other than the tasks, specs, and deadlines at hand. Properly managed, 360s hold the promise of creating new networks of interactions around the challenge of creating productive relationships.

### Developing a 360-Degree Program

It is impossible to develop a 360-degree evaluation program overnight. Most teams are not ready to base all of their pay on multisource performance management, especially when teams are relatively new. Most teams are hesitant to have all of their pay tied to team member evaluations; at the same time, they scoff at individual pay performance systems. The key is to set up a system of feedback that is anonymous and private and slowly build into an open feedback, public knowledge system. Often, team members will let companies know when they are ready to have pay based on their individual performance as evaluated by relevant others.

There is no standard method for 360-degree implementation. Some companies administer and develop the whole system. Some allow outside consultants to prepare and analyze feedback to ensure anonymity. For example, Groupe Schneider, an international firm, invites its managers to participate in 360-degree evaluations by choosing nine people to provide confidential evaluations. The entire evaluation is carried out by an outside consulting firm that collects and prepares all the results, which are completely confidential. Often, the survey used to evaluate employees is developed by a cross-sectional team of company employees. In addition to specifying evaluation criteria, the group also determines the makeup of the evaluation teams and how they will be selected. This team also makes decisions on who will get to see the results of the evaluations and devises a follow-up program to ensure that employees take action on the feedback they receive.

As a start for developing 360-degree evaluation systems, consider the steps outlined in Box 3-2 (see Hoffman, 1995; Milliman, Zawacki, Norman, Powell, & Kirksey, 1994).

The answers to the questions in Box 3-2 will be different for every organization. Duplicating systems used by world-class companies is not necessarily the best approach. Each organization should develop the 360-degree system that will optimize effectiveness within its organizational design. Companies should first use a test 360-degree program that is not tied to compensation and is not public. In the beginning stages, only the employee sees all of the feedback; gradually, the supervisor is brought into the loop. Eventually, it is important to tie employee compensation to the 360-degree evaluation. Yet there is considerable variation on this. For example, at Phelps Dodge, 360-degree feedback is used as a development and training tool and not the basis for performance evaluation and pay. In contrast, Farm Credit Services Southwest uses 360-degree reviews to evaluate the performances of its employees and determine their compensation levels.

---

**BOX 3-2**

### Things to Think about before Developing a 360-Degree Program in Your Company

Companies should ask themselves the following questions before undertaking 360-degree evaluation programs (Hoffman, 1995; Milliman, Zawacki, Norman, Powell, & Kirksey, 1994):

- Should only the 360-degree feedback be used or should the process be combined with other appraisal systems?

- Should an outside consultant be used?

- Can a program be purchased off the shelf or should the process be customized for the organization?

- Is a computer-based or paper and pencil form best for the organization?

- How many raters should be used? (The ideal is five to 10; fewer than five limits perspectives; more than 10 makes the system too complex and time-consuming.)

- Who should do the rating?

- Who selects the raters?

- How does the organization define *peer, internal customer, supervisor, subordinate,* and so on?

- How many questions/items should be included on the form?

- Should the feedback be anonymous?

- How should employees be trained on giving and receiving constructive feedback and the nature of 360-degree feedback?

At Johnson & Johnson Advanced Behavioral Technology, which has many teams but still retains traditional hierarchical reporting relationships, ratees develop a list of key internal and external customers with whom they interact and then recommend five to 10 people to serve as raters. The supervisor has the ultimate responsibility for the appraisal. In contrast, at Digital Equipment, the ratee has the primary responsibility for selecting the raters. The Digital ratee works with the team leader to select a panel consisting of a coach and three other employees to be objective advocates. Raters are then selected at random from the ratee's team by a computer-generated system and notified by e-mail to participate in the appraisal. The random system ensures that a fair distribution of raters is created (Milliman, Zawacki, Norman, Powell, ad Kirksey, 1994).

As companies begin to challenge old assumptions about performance appraisals, they need to be careful not to cross the line of legal liability (see Box 3-3). If people other than management are involved in the appraisal process, then they must be trained on the legal issues involved with discrimination law, the Americans with Disabilities Act, and other relevant legislation. Stated more eloquently:

> The use of multiple raters is becoming more popular as many firms move toward team-based management systems. Use of multiple raters reduces the influence of idiosyncratic rating policies on personnel decisions. However, sharing ratings to arrive at a consensus is not an acceptable way of offsetting the bias of a single rater (*Loiseau v. Department of Human Resources*, 1983). An important caution in the use of multiple raters as illustrated in the

---

**BOX 3-3**

## Prescriptions for Legally Defensible Appraisal Systems
### (Adapted from Bernardin & Cascio, 1988)

1. Job analysis to identify important duties and tasks should precede development of a performance appraisal system.

2. The performance appraisal system should be standardized and formal.

3. Specific performance standards should be communicated to employees in advance of the appraisal period.

4. Objectives and uncontaminated data should be used whenever possible.

5. Ratings on traits such as dependability, drive, or attitude should be avoided.

6. Employees should be evaluated on specific work dimensions rather than on a single, global, or overall measure.

7. If work behaviors rather than outcomes are to be evaluated, evaluators should have ample opportunity to observe ratee performance.

8. To increase the reliability of ratings, more than one independent evaluator should be used whenever possible.

9. Behavioral documentation should be prepared for ratings.

10. Employees should be given an opportunity to review their appraisals.

11. A formal system of appeal should be available for appraisal disagreements.

12. Raters should be trained to prevent discrimination and to evaluate performance consistently.

13. Appraisals should be frequent, offered at least annually.

Hopkins case, is that illegal bias on the part of one or two raters can taint the entire process with legal discrimination. (Austin, Villanova, & Hindman, 1996, p. 283; reference to *Price Waterhouse v. Hopkins*, 1989, which involved gender bias in a consensus promotion decision made by PW partners)

For a detailed look at actual items used in 360-degree evaluations, consult Appendix 4.

## RATER BIAS

Peers are often best qualified to evaluate a team member's performance. Empirical research indicates that peer assessment is a valid and reliable evaluation procedure (Huber, Neale, & Northcraft, 1987). In addition, the team's supervisor and the team's customers or clients (either internal or external, if available) are also valuable sources of input. These information sources are valuable, but can also be biased. Raters are not perfect; below we discuss several serious biases that can threaten the quality of peer evaluation.

### Inflation Bias

Candid performance evaluation and feedback is essential for team members because it allows them to adjust their behavior and motivation and to seek training (Ashford & Cummings, 1983). However, raters frequently positively distort performance ratings when they anticipate giving feedback to ratees (Antonioni, 1994). Inflation appears to stem from two sources: empathic buffering and fear of conflct. Stated simply: People are generally reluctant to transmit bad news to a poorly performing employee (Tesser & Rosen, 1975). And, when doing so, they feel bad themselves (Longnecker, Sims, & Gioia, 1987). A second reason is that raters want to avoid interpersonal conflict, particularly with someone they expect to respond defensively to criticism (Bond & Anderson, 1987).

### Extrinsic Incentives Bias

Most managers believe that employees are primarily motivated by extrinsic incentives (e.g., job security and pay) and less motivated by intrinsic incentives (e.g., learning new things). For example, Douglas McGregor (1960) explicitly acknowledged this tendency when he described a social fault line between managers who inferred motivations incorrectly and those who inferred them correctly. He bemoaned the commonness of *Theory X* managers (who believe that employees dislike work, wish to avoid responsibility, and desire security above all) and the scarcity of *Theory Y* managers (who believe that employees like work, wish to develop their skills, and desire to participate in tasks that advance worthy organizational goals). Consider a survey of 486 prospective lawyers who were questioned by Kaplan Educational Centers during a preparation course for the Law School Admissions Test (Lawler, Mohrman, & Ledford, 1995). The prospective lawyers were asked to describe their own motivations for pursuing a legal career and then those of their peers. Although 64 percent said that they were pursuing a legal career because it was intellectually appealing or because they had always been interested in the law, only 12 percent thought this about their peers. Instead, 62 percent thought that their peers were pursuing a legal career because of the financial rewards. Indeed, most of us have claimed that "they're only in it for the money" many more times than we have claimed "I'm only in it for the money" (Heath, 1999).

According to Frederick Taylor, "What workers want most from their employers beyond anything else is high wages" (Taylor, 1911). In contrast, McGregor (1960) and other members of the human relations school of management argued that intrinsic features motivated employees.

The extrinsic incentives bias states that people believe that others are more motivated than themselves by situational or extrinsic factors, and less motivated than themselves by dispositional or intrinsic factors (Heath, 1999). For example, in one survey, 74 MBA students ranked the importance of eight different motivations (benefits, pay, job security, learning new skills, praise from manager, developing skills, accomplishing something worthwhile, and feeling good about oneself) for themselves and predicted the rank order that would be provided by their classmates and by actual managers and employees (customer service representatives at Citibank; Heath, 1999). The MBA students overestimated how highly the Citibank managers would rank extrinsic incentives. They predicted that the top four incentives would be primarily extrinsic (pay, security, benefits, and praise); however, the actual Citibank employees listed only one extrinsic incentive in their top four (benefits).

If managers falsely assume that others' motives are less noble than their own, then they may fail to communicate the importance and relevance of the organization's goals (Bennis & Nanus, 1985). Corporate managers may spend too little time highlighting the satisfaction of solving customer problems; nonprofit managers may spend more time describing the joys of charity balls than the pleasures of community service. When managers fall prey to the extrinsic incentives bias, they may overlook the importance of feedback, neglect opportunities to make jobs more interesting, and underestimate the employee's desire to participate in team and organizational decisions. Managers could substantially improve their ability to understand the motivations of others if they would assume that others are motivated exactly as they are (Heath, 1999).

People work hard for a lot of different reasons. It is a mistake to think that the only thing that drives performance is monetary incentives and that people hoard effort until incentives justify greater contributions. Many managers incorrectly believe that people are primarily motivated by monetary reward. However, they view themselves as having loftier reasons. For example, most people overestimate the impact that financial reward exerts on their peers' willingness to donate blood (Miller & Ratner, 1998).

In sum, evolutionary biology, neoclassical economics, behaviorism, and psychoanalytic theory all assume that people actively and single-mindedly pursue their self-interest (Schwartz, 1986). However, organizational science research tells a different story. People often care more about the fairness of procedures they are subjected to than the material outcomes these procedures yield (Tyler, 1990); they often care more about a group's collective outcomes than about their personal outcomes (Dawes, Orbell, & van de Kragt, 1988); and their attitudes toward public policies are often shaped more by values and ideologies than the impact they have on material well-being (Sears & Funk, 1990, 1991).

## Homogeneity Bias

Generally, appraisers rate appraisees who are similar to themselves more favorably than those who are different from them. This means that in general, white male superiors tend to favor white male subordinates over females and minority supervisees (cf. Kraiger & Ford, 1985).

## Halo Bias

Once we know one positive (or negative) fact about someone, we tend to perceive all other information we learn about them in line with our initial perceptions. This has several serious implications, the most obvious of which is the fact that physically attractive people are evaluated more positively than are less attractive people—even when holding constant their skills and competencies.

## Fundamental Attribution Error

We tend to perceive people's behaviors as reflecting their personality rather than temporary, situational factors. This can obviously be a good thing for someone who seems to be doing well, but very problematic for a person who seems to be performing under par.

## Communication Medium

Performance appraisers give poor performers substantially higher ratings when they have to give face-to-face feedback as opposed to anonymous written feedback. In one investigation, managers were asked to give feedback to a poorly performing employee, either in a face-to face mode or via tape-recorded message (Waung & Highhouse, 1997). In all cases, the objective information about the poorly performing employee was identical. However, managers using direct, face-to-face communication gave more positive performance feedback than managers who used the indirect mode (the tape recorder).

## Experience Effect

Experienced appraisers tend to render higher quality appraisals, and training and practice can reduce error in ratings (Klimoski & Inks, 1990).

## Reciprocity Bias

People feel a strong social obligation to return favors. Thus, a potential flaw of 360-degree programs is that they are subject to collusion: "I'll give you a good rating if you give me one." Providing for anonymous rating may reduce both biases. However, this is difficult to achieve when team size is relatively small.

## Bandwagon Bias

People want to "jump on the bandwagon," meaning that they will want to hold the same opinion of someone as does the rest of the group. Consider, for example, the question of how a team leader might react if he were to learn that his opinion of a team member differed from that of another member. In one investigation, people with organizational supervisory experience made an initial performance judgment about a profiled employee (Makiney & Levy, 1998). These leaders then received additional information that was discrepant from their initial judgment (either positive or negative) from one of two sources (the profiled employee himself or one of his peers). Leaders were more likely to use discrepant information to alter their performance judgments in a consistent direction when the source was a peer (but not the profiled employee; Makiney & Levy, 1998).

### Primacy and Recency Bias

People tend to be overly affected by their first impression of someone (primacy) or their most recent interaction with this person (recency).

There is no simple solution to overcoming these biases. Awareness is an important first step. We suggest that everyone in the business of providing performance evaluations be made aware of these biases. Employees in companies probably do receive some form of training on conducting performance appraisals, but hardly anyone receives training on the biases that afflict ratings. As a second step, we suggest that only objective behavior and productivity measures be used—they are less susceptible to biases than are traits and attitudes. As a rule of thumb—if you can't observe it directly, then don't measure it.

## RATEE BIAS

In addition to the rater biases discussed earlier, the quality of a 360-degree process can be compromised by the ratees themselves. Although countless articles and books have dealt with sources of rater bias, virtually no attention has been paid to the biases that ratees might have—as if feedback, once delivered, is perfectly received by the recipient. In fact, that is not the case. The more managers know about ratee bias, the better able they will be to anticipate the impact of a performance review on the employee.

### Egocentric Bias

Most people feel underrecognized for the work they do and the value they bring to their company. This feeling is largely attributable to the human cognitive system, which is primarily egocentric in nature. In short, people give themselves greater credit than do others. This means that in a typical 360-degree evaluation, no matter how positive it may be, people will feel underappreciated by others. There is no perfect solution to dealing with this. Our suggestion is that the supervisor (or person providing the feedback) should present as many facts as possible to justify the ratings and feedback. It is important to focus on behaviors rather than attitudes when assessing others, because it is more difficult to misinterpret objective information (e.g., "you've been late 18 out of the last 20 days").

### Intrinsic Interest

As we noted earlier, people are strongly motivated by intrinsic interest, rather than extrinsic rewards. However, this is not to say that people don't care about extrinsic rewards. Furthermore, this does not mean that intrinsic interest will always flourish. In fact, even positive feedback, if not carefully administered, may undermine intrinsic interest (Freedman, Cunningham, & Krismer, 1992). That is, employees may do something for purely intrinsic reasons, such as the joy of learning new things or expressing themselves; however, if a supervisor or a person of obvious importance praises the work and administers large extrinsic rewards for the work, this may lead the employees to believe that they are doing the work for the money (or other extrinsic rewards). In some cases, external reward may undermine intrinsic interest. For example, Kohn (1993) argues that incentive or pay-for-performance systems tend to make people less enthusiastic about their work.

We are not suggesting that companies should never offer extrinsic (e.g., pay-based) rewards to their employees. Rather, the manager should emphasize, when providing the reward, what is valued about the work and how the company views the employee. The research evidence supports this: When high effort is rewarded, people are more industrious. Just as people can be reinforced for working hard, they can be reinforced for creativity (Eisenberger & Selbst, 1994). Thus, for fabulous work effort, a supervisor or company may give the team a special cash reward or noncash recognition and clearly communicate to the team that the company values their inspiring motivation, creativity, and attention to detail. It is important to clearly indicate what is being rewarded.

## Social Comparison

Ideally, raters' evaluations should be objective, and associated with objectivity is the belief that ratings are based on some absolute or externally defined standard. However, teams and leaders often make comparative rather than absolute performance judgments (Ilgen & Feldman, 1983). Perhaps this is because people have a basic drive to compare themselves with others. This is why students feel less value in receiving an A if they find out that everyone has received an A. Thus, supervisors must anticipate that team members will talk and compare notes, one way or another, about the feedback they receive. It is often these comparisons that drive how employees interpret feedback. Saavedra and Kwun (1993) examined how a rater's relative performance affects their ratings of peers. Self-evaluations were higher than ratings given to the self by one's peers, and high performers were the most likely to be discriminating. Below-average and average contributors tended to make external attributions for their low performance (Saavedra & Kwun, 1993).

Supervisors should anticipate that social comparison will occur, and be frank about feedback to employees and team members. For example, it would be wrong to imply that an employee was the only stellar performer if, in fact, over 60 percent performed at the same level. (For this reason, it may be useful to provide information about averages and standard deviations to employees.)

## Fairness

People evaluate the quality of their organizational experiences by how fair they regard them to be. Whether the ultimate outcome is positive or negative, people are more likely to accept the outcome if they think the procedure has been fair. The fairness of procedures is determined by the extent to which the employee has a voice in the system, among other things (Lind & Tyler, 1988). Supervisors should actively involve the employee in the performance review, because people who are invited to participate regard procedures and systems to be fairer than those who are not invited. For example, superiors may ask employees to anticipate the feedback they will receive and to suggest how to best act upon it.

Although there is no surefire way to eliminate the biases on the part of the ratee, awareness of the bias is key. A second step is to recognize that many ratee biases are driven by a need to maintain or enhance self-esteem. Put evaluations in a positive light and help employees view them as opportunities to grow, rather than marks of failure. A third step is to involve employees actively in the evaluation procedure before they receive their results. For this reason, an early planning meeting months ahead of the evaluation can be an ideal opportunity for teams and leaders to work together to identify and clarify goals. Finally, recognize that performance appraisals, in any form, tend to be stressful for all involved. However, they provide an opportunity for everyone to gain feedback about what otherwise might be an "undiscussable problem." Tools such as 360-degree evaluations have the power to break down the barriers of fear in the organization. However, this can only be effective if managers are trained and skilled at using the information to break down barriers instead of building new ones.

## GUIDING PRINCIPLES

An organization that wants to institute some kind of variable team-based pay structure needs to follow a step-by-step approach. However, even before that, the organization needs to adhere to some basic guiding principles (Gross, 1995).

### Principle 1: Goals Should Cover Areas That Team Members Can Directly Affect

"Otherwise, the team is disempowered. Compensation won't motivate employees unless there is a direct line of sight between performance and results. For example, when incentives are tied only to the final profit of a company or group, which can be affected by all sorts of market forces, the connection between performance and reward is weakened. At the same time, pay should bear some kind of relationship to the company's bottom line. If the company is in the red, team rewards appear nonsensical—unless management is confident that ultimately the team's superior productivity and quality will help turn the company around." (Gross, 1995, p. 20)

In effective programs, rewards are contingent upon performance. This is in perfect contrast to a Las Vegas slot machine, in which payouts are contingent upon luck. Furthermore, a system that always pays out is ineffective. The key is to devise a system that equitably spreads the risk between the team and the company, offers a potential gain that makes the risk worth taking, and gives employees a fair shot at making more by working harder, more intelligently, and in a more coordinated fashion.

### Principle 2: Balance the Mix of Individual and Team-Based Pay

For many teams, a thoughtful balance of individual and group incentives may be most appropriate. A good rule of thumb is to balance this proportion in line with the amount of individual and team-based work an employee is expected to do or the percentage of control and responsibility the individual and the team have.

### Principle 3: Consult with the Team Members Who Will Be Affected

The process by which an organization introduces a program is more important than the program itself. The programs with the greatest likelihood of success are those that have input from all levels of the organization, including members of the team, teams that support or interface with the team, those who will administer the plan, management, and customers. The feasibility of the team pay program is determined through a full understanding of the business, the wants and needs of the management and employees, the impact of the current compensation program, and the company's ambitions for the new plan.

If people remain ignorant or uninformed about a process, they are more likely to reject it out of hand when they see it—even if it is perfectly compatible with their interests. In short, people want to be involved. The team members who are affected will have greater buy-in to the program if they had a hand in shaping it, and they can be valuable sources of information. In addition, employees need to feel that nothing is set in stone—if something does not work, employees will feel better knowing it can be changed. (For an example of how this can be effectively done, see Box 3-4.)

## Principle 4: Avoid Organizational Myopia

Many programs fail not because they are inherently flawed, but rather because they create problems with other teams, groups, and units within the organization. Managers often are myopic about their own team issues; good leaders are able to ask the question of how the particular team compensation system fits into the larger organization. This is the heart of what we referred to in the last chapter as "integration."

## Principle 5: Determine Eligibility (Who Qualifies for the Plan)

Every member of the team should be eligible for the plan, and the plan should indicate when someone becomes eligible or loses eligibility. (Another complication concerns full- and part-time membership.)

## Principle 6: Determine Equity Method

There are two basic variations: same *dollar* amount (wherein each team or each member is given the same amount of pay) and same *percentage* amount (wherein each team or each member is given the same percentage of pay).

## Principle 7: Quantify the Criteria Used to Determine Payout

There are two main ways to measure team results: financial and operational. *Financial* measures tend to be "bigger," encompassing profit and loss (measured either companywide or in terms of the teams' contribution) or revenues. *Operational* measures are typically productivity based (e.g., cycle time). There are several drawbacks to financial measures that primarily stem from the inability of team members to control the corporate-level decisions that will affect their microfinances. Operational measures are more firmly within the team's grasp.

## Principle 8: Determine How Target Levels of Performance Are Established and Updated

Goals can either be based on past performance or projected performance. There are advantages and disadvantages to each. The most immediate advantage of the historical approach is that people can readily accept it. However, many managers like to set stretch goals. One popular compromise is **raising the bar,** in which the baseline is increased and employees are given a one-time payment to compensate them for lost incentive opportunity. However, there is likely to be conflict over the amount of the

BOX 3-4

## Honeywell's Participative Pay Team

Honeywell's Commercial Avionics Division charged a group of employees to align compensation with business goals (Caudron, 1996). The team's decision to link workers' pay to division profitability got better buy-in because it was employee driven. In their plan, a percentage of each employee's yearly pay is based on the achievement of annual company objectives. In many cases, employees are resistant to this kind of risk-sharing plan because if results fall short of expectations, then paychecks are cut. But, Honeywell's incentive program met with little resistance because it was the employees themselves, through a group of twenty-five volunteers called the Participative Pay Team, who decided how the plan would work.

The first step in this plan was for human resources (HR) to teach the members of the team, which included secretaries, machine shop workers, engineers, and department managers, the principles of compensation in a 2.5-day training workshop. Armed with this basic knowledge, the team members then were assigned to do additional research on their own. The HR department provided no guidelines as to how the plan should work; it was up to team members to make recommendations to the company's executive leadership.

The end result of the team effort was a self-funded gainsharing program in which a percentage of each employee's pay is at risk, pending the achievement of business goals linked to Honeywell's profitability. Second, employees also have the opportunity to earn more than their annual salary when the company has an exceptionally good year.

The biggest challenge was explaining the program to employees. Honeywell realized it had to educate its workforce on business fundamentals, so it developed a course called Business Basics to provide information on how to calculate the three measures used to determine company performance: profit, working capital, and economic value added. Conducted by the participative pay team members, the course participants get a big picture of their work in the company. The communication effort to support the plan was supported by HR, which produced two publications about the plan: a comic book depicting two employees having a dialogue about the new pay system, and a typical HR document distributed in an orientation course. The plan embodies key principles:

- Emphasizing the direct stake all employees have in the continued success of the business
- Emphasizing the importance of executives and employees working toward similar business goals
- Recognizing and rewarding employees' impact on major improvement opportunities
- Improving employee understanding of the division's financial performance
- Supporting the culture of teamwork, employee involvement, and participation

Now that the plan is in place, the focus of the participative pay teams has shifted: It works with the finance department to monitor the books. The crux of their role is to provide a "trust" message to the workforce—to validate what is being reported by management.

payout. The **rolling average** method sets the baseline against which performance is measured as an average of some relevant period of time. (For a detailed discussion of payment options, see Gross, 1995.)

### Principle 9: Develop a Budget for the Plan

All plans should pay for themselves, with the exception of safety plans. This means that the improvements must be quantifiable.

### Principle 10: Determine Timing of Measurements and Payments

Shorter measurement periods and faster payouts motivate employees more and—particularly when pay is at risk—are fairer. However, there are a number of disadvantages with a short turnaround system that include administrative overhead and manipulation of results.

### Principle 11: Communicate with Those Involved

As stated earlier in the chapter, it is important for companies to be completely straightforward about what counts and how things are going. For example, Richard Semler, co-managing director of Semler Brossy Consulting Group and CEO of Semco, states:

> Nothing matters more than those vital statistics—short, frank, frequent reports on how the company is doing. Complete transparency. No hocus-pocus, no hanky-panky, no simplifications. On the contrary, all Semco employees attend classes to learn how to read and understand the numbers, and it is one of their unions that teaches the course. Every month, each employee gets a balance sheet, a profit and loss analysis, and a cash flow statement for his or her division. Everybody knows the price of the product. Everybody knows the cost. Everybody has the monthly balance sheet that says exactly what each of them makes, how much bronze is costing us, how much overtime we paid, all of it. And the employees know that 23 percent of the after-tax profit is theirs. (Garfield, 1992, p. 253)

### Principle 12: Plan for the Future

As teaming becomes more developed and the organization experiences shifts in culture or focus, a new mix of rewards needs to be defined to keep the organization in alignment.

## CONCLUSIONS

Many organizations promote and value teamwork, yet pay people based upon individual accomplishments. Individuals operating under this system feel the tension. Just as college basketball players who feed their teammates instead of shooting will not compile impressive scoring statistics and are less likely to be drafted by the pros, managers who devote energy to organizational goals will often not enhance their own career.

Viewed in this sense, it is rational for team members to think of themselves first and the team second. The organization that wants otherwise had better align their incentive system with the stated goals. This chapter does not provide easy answers to team compensation problems because there are none. However, there are some fundamental questions to think about, and there exist choices for managers and organizations when it comes to rewarding teams. Lawler (2000) perhaps sums it up best. First, he emphasizes paying the individual instead of the job. And, second, he asserts that pay for performance should focus on collective performance move than individual performance. These two guiding principles encourage team members to learn the right skills to make teams effective and, more importantly, motivate the right type of performance focus.

# PART

# II

# Internal Dynamics

# CHAPTER 4

# Building the Team:

## *Tasks, People, and Relationships*

*Jacqui Lopez, a producer with Industrial Light and Magic, leads what Cheryl Dahle (1999) calls an "extreme" team—where ordinary people are called upon to achieve extraordinary results. According to Lopez, "The trickiest part of the job is when you're on your 18th straight day of work, when you've been at it for 14 hours a day, when the director is screaming at you and the studio is up in arms—and you have to keep all the stress from filtering down to your crew. In film, we can't miss our deadline, but if I start pressuring artists about time and budget, then creativity suffers" (Dahle, 1999, p. 310). Her team uses parallel processing to achieve great results. Meetings are a series of entrances and exits; no one sits through an entire session. Animators leave as soon as their shots are critiqued; production assistants leave when they get new assignments; model-makers exit after they give their opinions on the logistics for a new scene. "When there's work to be done, keeping people in a meeting longer than they need to be there is pointless and aggravating" (p. 312). The leaders of this team have created an environment in which people can perform at a high level and not be burned out when they are done. This is critical because everyone knows that three months later, they will all be working as a team on another project.*

Seasoned managers recognize that their success in large part depends on how effectively they can build and maintain a well-functioning team, and how they can sustain high performance over time. Managing an effective team involves two sets of responsibilities: (1) managing the internal dynamics of the team itself—that is, specifying the task, selecting the members, and facilitating the team process; and (2) managing the external dynamics of the team—navigating the organizational environment and managing relationships with those on whom the team is interdependent (Ancona, 1990). We refer to these dual processes as "internal team management" and "external team management." Beginning with this chapter in Part II, we focus on internal team dynamics. The starting point presumes that the manager has determined that teams are necessary to do the work required. For expositional purposes, we take the point of view of the manager when we discuss building the team. However, we do not presume a manager-led team; all of our messages can be extended to the team as its own manager (i.e., as in the case of self-managing and self-designing teams). This chapter takes you through the steps involved in building a team and keeping it running smoothly. The goal of this chapter is to create a tool kit for the busy manager to use in developing and maintaining teams. In Part III, we focus on external team dynamics.

# BUILDING THE TEAM

In a 1995 survey distributed to 134 separate project teams in 88 companies in the United States, respondents indicated that "despite positive indications on some of the key team building elements, overall results show companies are generally doing a poor job of team building. Lack of effective rewards, inadequate individual and team performance feedback mechanisms, lack of project management skills, and inadequate individual and team goal-setting are all weak areas" (Tippett & Peters, 1995, p. 29). (For an example of poor team design that was eventually turned around, see Sidebar 4-1.)

## Sidebar 4-1. Turning Poor Team Design Around

When Rexam Custom in Matthews, North Carolina, a division of Rexam PLC, first employed teams, the outcome was a failure. Why? The team was too large, which made meetings impossible for anything other than information sharing and updating; there was a lack of goals or objectives, which led to members attending meetings with the sense that anything was fair game. Thus, they addressed everything from capital improvements to pay and benefits. The resulting frustrations often led to extended gripe sessions. Teams were poorly structured, and, as a result, members often had different and competing interests. Members did not share information, and meetings became a competition between conflicting priorities. Consequently, meetings rarely resulted in any action steps or outcomes. After identifying and correcting these key problems, Rexam was able to successfully implement their team-based approach (Pope, 1996).

Any team, whether it is manager-led, self-managing, self-directing, or self-governing, can be better understood and improved by examining its internal dynamics. Contrary to popular thought, it is more important to have a well-designed team than a team with a good leader. For example, in an intensive study of customer service teams at Xerox with team sizes ranging from three to 12 persons, well-designed teams were more successful on a number of key organizational effectiveness criteria—assuming collective responsibility, monitoring their own performance, managing their own task strategies, and customer approval—than were poorly designed teams (Wageman, 1997). Poorly designed teams, even under good leadership, were significantly less effective. In the case of Xerox, team effectiveness was judged by supervisors as well as customers, thus providing a comprehensive view of team effectiveness.

It may be more important to have excellent team members than to have an excellent leader to achieve success. Perhaps this is why many leaders prefer to hire people smarter than they are.

Once it is determined that a team is desirable for the work and viable within the organization, then the manager must focus intently on three key aspects of building a team: the *task*, the *people*, and the *relationships* among team members. These three critical internal dynamics are illustrated in Figure 4-1. Phase 1 concerns the **task** facing the team. Does it call for creativity or problem solving? Is it purely cooperative or do members compete with one another? Phase 2 concerns the **people** on the team. How should team members be selected? What level of diversity is best? Phase 3 involves the **relationships** among the group members in terms of how they do their work together.

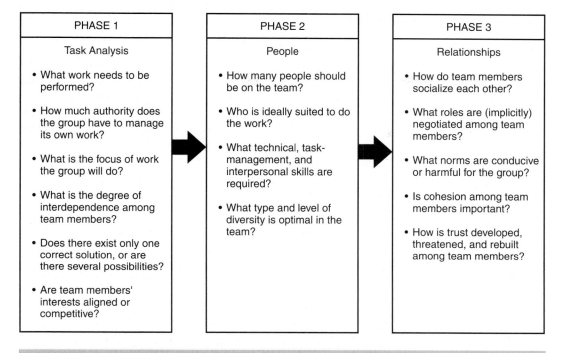

| PHASE 1 | PHASE 2 | PHASE 3 |
|---|---|---|
| Task Analysis | People | Relationships |
| • What work needs to be performed? | • How many people should be on the team? | • How do team members socialize each other? |
| • How much authority does the group have to manage its own work? | • Who is ideally suited to do the work? | • What roles are (implicitly) negotiated among team members? |
| • What is the focus of work the group will do? | • What technical, task-management, and interpersonal skills are required? | • What norms are conducive or harmful for the group? |
| • What is the degree of interdependence among team members? | • What type and level of diversity is optimal in the team? | • Is cohesion among team members important? |
| • Does there exist only one correct solution, or are there several possibilities? | | • How is trust developed, threatened, and rebuilt among team members? |
| • Are team members' interests aligned or competitive? | | |

FIGURE 4-1  Internal Dynamics: Key Questions to Ask When Building the Team

Is there a norm of challenging one another? Do members feel cohesive? Do team members trust one another?

These three factors—tasks, people, and relationships—form the basic, internal system of teamwork. Just like Rome, the building and maintenance of a team is not something that is accomplished in a day. We begin by discussing the task, then we move to the people, and we conclude by discussing the relationships.

## THE TASK: WHAT WORK NEEDS TO BE DONE?

What practices and structures need to be put into place to achieve highly functioning teams? To a great extent, this is determined by the nature of the work that groups are doing. For example, some teams make products, some teams provide services, other teams make decisions, and still others provide advice and consultation. The nature of the work sets constraints on design. However, there is much variation in team design, even among companies doing very similar types of work—and sometimes even large variation among teams within the same company!

Obviously, there is no single recipe for optimal team design—it depends on the type of work the team is doing, the structure of the organization, and so on. However, managers often do not think carefully about team design, leaving it up to the team to work out on their own or falling back on traditional, functional practices. If left to their own devices, teams rarely explicitly plan or develop performance strategies (Hackman, Brousseau, & Weiss, 1976; Weingart, 1992). Those that do, however, usually perform better, especially when the appropriate performance strategy is not obvious (Hackman et al., 1976). It is useful to distinguish **preplanning** (before actually performing the task) and **on-line planning** (during the task itself; Weingart, 1992). Teams permitted to plan between periods of task completion perform better than those that plan only during periods of task completion or do not have opportunities to discuss and develop plans (Shure, Rogers, Larsen, & Tasson, 1962).

In keeping with our goal of providing choices for managers, we raise some critical team design issues in the following sections. We suggest that managers and team designers work through each of these issues when thinking about team design and redesign.

## How Much Authority Does the Team Have to Manage Its Own Work?

In short, what is the ratio of team governance to managerial governance? This issue was raised in Chapter 1, where we presented four types of teams: manager-led, self-managing, self-directing, and self-governing. There is an inherent trade-off here. The more authority team members have to manage their own work, the more likely they are to be motivated and highly involved in the work. However, this comes at a loss of control for the manager. Furthermore, when teams set and carry out their own objectives, they may not be aligned with those of the larger organization.

## What Is the Focus of the Work the Team Will Do?

Obviously, the possibilities are endless. However, it is helpful to distinguish three types of tasks that teams do: tactical, problem solving, and creative. Table 4-1 describes tactical, problem solving, and creative teams and the disadvantages and advantages of each.

**Tactical teams** are those in which the key objective is to execute a well-defined plan. For tactical teams to be successful, there must be a high degree of task clarity and

**TABLE 4-1** Types of Work That Teams Do

| Broad Objective | Dominant Feature | Process Emphasis | Threats |
|---|---|---|---|
| Tactical | Clarity | • Directive, highly focused tasks<br>• Role clarity<br>• Well-defined operational standards<br>• Accuracy | • Role ambiguity<br>• Lack of training<br>• Communication barriers |
| Problem solving | Trust | • Focus on issues<br>• Separate people from problem<br>• Consider facts, not opinions<br>• Conduct thorough investigation<br>• Suspend judgment | • Failure to stick to facts<br>• Fixate on solutions<br>• Succumb to political pressures<br>• Confirmatory information search |
| Creative | Autonomy | • Explore possibilities and alternatives | • Production blocking<br>• "Lumpy" participation |

*Source:* Adapted from Larson, C. E., & LaFasto, F. M. 1989. *Teamwork: What Must Go Right/What Can Go Wrong.* Newbury Park, CA: Sage.

unambiguous role definition. Some examples of tactical teams include cardiac surgery teams, military teams, many sports teams, and other teams that are tightly organized (see LaFasto & Larson, 2001).

**Problem-solving teams** are those that attempt to resolve problems, usually on an ongoing basis. To be effective, each member of the team must expect and believe that interactions among members will be truthful and of high integrity. Thus, a key feature of problem-solving teams involves trust and respect. Some examples of problem-solving teams include the Mayo Clinic oncology group, the Centers for Disease Control, Sandia Laboratory's nuclear weapons team, and other teams that are focused on solving a problem (see LaFasto & Larson, 2001).

**Creative teams** are those in which the key objective is to create something, think out of the box, and question assumptions. The process focus of creative teams is that of exploring possibilities and alternatives. We discuss creative teams in much more depth in the last chapter of Part II. Some examples of creative teams include the IDEO design teams, Hallmark's creative advisory group, and the teams responsible for HBO's original programming.

In fact, teams usually contain some blend of all three elements. Usually, however, there is a dominant focus. Sometimes, teams are mischaracterized—for example, a team that is supposed to be creative uses a problem-solving perspective, or a team that really requires problem solving is organized as a tactical team. This may happen when the goals of the team are not clear. This can also happen when teams are not apprised of the organization's objectives. Managers must take a hard look at the type of team they need and guide members' understanding of the relationship between the goal and the design of the team.

## What Is the Degree of Task Interdependence among Team Members?

By definition, team members are interdependent. However, there are many types of task interdependence that affect the way teams get their work done (Thompson, 1967, see Figure 4-2). Consider three types of task interdependence:

- **Pooled interdependence** means that group members work independently and then pool their work. For example, a furniture department within a department store is comprised of several salespeople, each of whom is compensated based on sales performance. On an interdepartmental level, however, the sales of each salesperson are added together and compared across departments, so that cosmetics, furniture, and men's accessories can all be compared and added together to determine overall store profit. Throughout this process, each salesperson is independent. Another analogy would be a team of sprinters, each running as fast as they can; the team's output is simply the average time.

- **Sequential interdependence** is the classic assembly line or division of labor; each member of the team has a particular skill or task to perform. Members are more interdependent, with those further down the line more dependent on others. For example, as a new car proceeds through the factory at the Ford Taurus manufacturing plant in Atlanta, pieces are added to it at certain stages of the process that could not have been added prior to that stage. An analogy would be a relay race in which each runner needs to "hand off" to the other team member.

- **Reciprocal interdependence** is the highest form of interdependence. Every member is dependent on others at all levels—not just in a simple linear fashion, as in sequential interdependence. An analogy would be a rowing team in which members need to coordinate

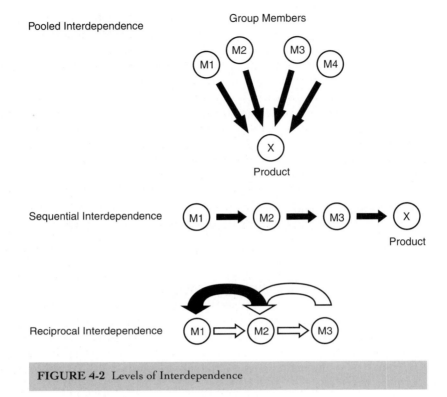

**FIGURE 4-2** Levels of Interdependence

and synchronize their work. For example, when software developers are writing code, each person must have a high degree of familiarity with the other pieces of the program, otherwise the likelihood of bugs increases significantly. Charles Parnell of the Miller Brewing Company epitomizes the complexities of reciprocal interdependence. During a speech delivered at Marquette University, Parnell gave an example of teamwork at Miller: "If Marketing wants to launch a group of new products, they will set up a task force and call in someone from Finance, Human Resources and Operations. The Operations people will explain to the Marketing Group the realities of brewing, packaging and shipping more than 40 brands of beer in more than 2,800 different can, bottle, keg, package and label configurations. This means that if Marketing had been thinking about introducing 10 new brands next year, they will understand that's a virtual impossibility for the Operations people and they will know why" (Parnell, 1998).

Recent studies of team performance reveal that high levels of task interdependence, which require interactions among group members to obtain crucial resources (such as in the Miller Brewing Company), consistently enhance performance (Fan & Gruenfeld, 1998). Highly dependent members come up with solutions faster, complete more tasks, and perform better than teams whose members are not highly dependent upon one another.

The degree of interdependence has design implications for teamwork. To the extent that tasks are easily divisible and threats to performance (Chapter 2) have been adequately ironed out, pooled interdependence may be very effective for groups. For example, in a customer service call center, members do roughly the same type of work.

However, pooled interdependence often cannot work for teams because completing the tasks requires specialization and division of labor. Thus, sequential or reciprocal interdependence is necessary. For example, in a Saturn assembly line, members' tasks are highly differentiated and specialized. To a large degree, greater specialization means greater interdependence, because team members must rely on others to complete their portion of the work. The start-up times for reciprocal interdependence may seem daunting, but it may be especially important for highly complex tasks that require high levels of customer satisfaction. Another advantage of reciprocal interdependence is that all team members know the overall objectives of the team and may feel more accountable (thus reducing the motivational problems discussed in Chapter 2).

### Is There a Correct Solution That Can Be Readily Demonstrated and Communicated to Members?

Some tasks have one correct solution; other tasks have several possible solutions. Contrast, for example, a team assembling a house, in which each component (the framework, the windows, the insulation, etc.) has to conform to a specified blueprint, versus a consulting team outlining a strategy proposal for a company. In the case of the construction team, the blueprint is the criterion by which the team will be judged. This kind of team task is known as a **demonstrable** task (Steiner, 1972).

In contrast, no single best answer exists for the consulting team. This kind of team task is known as a **nondemonstrable** task. In nondemonstrable tasks, it is important for team members to discuss the indices they will use to assess their performance as a team. Otherwise, there could be considerable disagreement after the work is completed—not only among team members but also between the team and the client!

### Are Team Members' Interests Perfectly Aligned (Cooperative), Opposing (Competitive), or Mixed in Nature?

In many team-based organizations, reward structures are constructed so that some portion of team members' pay is contingent on the performance of the team as a whole, to promote cooperation and reduce the incentive for competition among team members.

It is important to determine the extent to which members have an incentive to work with one another or compete with other group members for monetary gain (such as might exist within some sales teams), promotion, and so on. For example, IBM's manufacturing and marketing/sales departments have very closely aligned interests. Teams that are rewarded for a mix of both individual and team performance outperform teams whose rewards are purely individual or purely group based (Fan & Gruenfeld, 1998).

### How Big Should the Team Be?

One final issue about task design concerns how many people to put on the team. Obviously, this depends on the nature of the work to be done and the level and overlap of skills among team members. Generally, teams should be fewer than 10 in number. In fact, it is wise to compose teams using the smallest number of people who can do the task (Hackman, 1987). Unfortunately, there is a pervasive tendency for managers to err on the side of making teams too large. There are many reasons for this—it is easier to include others than to exclude them to the fact. Unfortunately, managers seriously underestimate how coordination problems can geometrically increase as team members are added. This is an example of how managers inadvertently focus on individuals, rather than the team.

Teams that are overgrown can have a number of negative effects on performance (Nieva, Myers, & Glickman, 1979). Larger teams are less cohesive (McGrath, 1984), and members of large teams can be less satisfied with team membership, participate less often in team activities, and are less likely to cooperate with one another (Kerr, 1989; Markham, Dansereau, & Alutto, 1982). People are more likely to behave in negative and socially unacceptable ways in larger teams, perhaps because team members feel more anonymous or are less self-aware (Latané, 1981; Prentice-Dunn & Rogers, 1989).

As team size increases, the frivolity of conversation increases and people tend to avoid serious subjects. One reason is that people tend to become aroused in the presence of others and, therefore, are more self-conscious and concerned about projecting the right image. It is safer for people to avoid serious topics.

A big problem of large teams has to do with the equality of member participation. For example, in a team of two to three, one person may do more of the talking, but all may participate. As the size of the team grows, more and more people do less talking relative to others. Sometimes, a few members say and do nothing.

In contrast, there are advantages to smaller, even understaffed teams. Members of understaffed teams work harder, engage in a wider variety of tasks, assume more responsibility for the team's performance, and feel more involved in the team (Arnold & Greenberg, 1980; Perkins, 1982; Petty & Wicker, 1974; Wicker, Kermeyer, Hanson, & Alexander, 1976; Wicker & Mehler, 1971).

If smaller teams are more advantageous, why are they relatively rare? The problem is that managers of teams appear to have an overstaffing bias. When team leaders are asked whether their teams could ever become too small or too large, 87 percent believe that understaffing is possible, but only 62 percent agree overstaffing is possible (Cini, Moreland, & Levine, 1993).

Once managers have some idea of the task design issues facing them, they are ready to turn to the people part of team building—how to best select members for their team. Obviously, the freedom to select team members is constrained in many ways: Managers may be limited to selecting members from a particular department, of a particular status, and so on. In other cases, managers may go outside the organization to recruit. At the opposite extreme, some managers do not have a choice about who is on their team; existing departmental structures determine team membership. Many teams are built by accretion and swapping members, not just created from scratch. Whatever their position is in terms of selection opportunity, managers need to know some basic facts about team composition.

## THE PEOPLE: WHO IS IDEALLY SUITED TO DO THE WORK?

What manager has not wrestled with the question of who to put on the team? As ill-advised as it may sound, many managers form their team without too much thought and, subsequently, attempt to figure out how to capitalize upon and match up people's skills. A much better approach is to carefully think about the task in terms of the work to be done, and then choose people on the basis of their skills relevant to that work. For example, consider the three basic purposes of teamwork described earlier: tactical, problem solving, and creative. Obviously, creative types are not as well suited for tactical teams as are highly organized, results-driven people, and vice versa.

As a manager faced with the opportunity to build a team, how do you begin? The more you know about the task, the better you can suit people to the task. The following skills are important to think about when forming any team:

- *Technical or functional expertise:* If the task calls for open-heart surgery, a chemist or a lawyer will not suffice, no matter how great they are at what they do. Team members must have demonstrated competence to perform what they need to do for the team to accomplish its goals. In most team tasks, it is necessary to recruit members with diverse skills. In an age of increasing specialization, it is rare for one person to be knowledgeable in all aspects of a complex task.
- *Task-management skills:* It is not enough for team members to simply perform their functional area of expertise. They need to coordinate the efforts of the team, set goals, carry out plans, and so on. Task-management skills involve planning the work, monitoring performance, dealing with disappointments and unknowns, and dealing with coordination problems. The list of key task-management skills is potentially endless, but for starters, see Table 4-2. The left-hand side focuses on task-management skills; the right-hand side focuses on interpersonal skills.
- *Interpersonal skills:* People on teams are not just automatons who simply carry out their tasks according to some predetermined plan. Because members of teams are people first—with their own issues, problems, and agendas—and team members second, the people side of teams is always present and a powerful influence on productivity. Interpersonal skills include attributes such as the ability to give constructive criticism, objectivity, ability to give recognition, ability to learn from others, and so on. Consult the right-hand side of Table 4-2 for examples of interpersonal skills in groups.

The type and blend of skills needed on a team depend largely on the task the team does. For example, problem-solving tasks often require more interpersonal skills; tactical teams require more organizational skills. Unfortunately, there is no simple paper and pencil test that neatly measures and classifies people. However, by drawing upon the following sources of information, the manager can go a long way toward making thoughtful and accurate assessments of skills:

- *Self-report:* What do employees regard to be their key strengths (and weaknesses)?
- *Past accomplishments:* What projects have employees been involved with that called for these skills?
- *360-degree reports:* What do employees' peers, supervisors, and subordinates regard to be their key strengths and weaknesses vis-à-vis these tasks?

The well-rounded team member, who possesses exquisite technical, task-management, and interpersonal skills, is a statistical rarity. More often, team members excel in one area. Thus, a key task of the manager is not to search for "Jacks and Jills of all team skills," but rather to focus on the task of *diversifying* the team so as to meet and exceed performance objectives. This is a harder goal, because it requires the manager to think in terms of multiple dimensions and blends of team members, rather than evaluating team members solely on their individual merits.

**TABLE 4-2** Task-Management and Interpersonal Skills

| Task-Management Skills | Interpersonal Skills |
|---|---|
| • **Initiating:** Suggesting new goals or ideas<br>• **Informating seeking:** Clarifying key issues<br>• **Opinion seeking:** Clarifying attitudes, values, and feelings<br>• **Elaborating:** Giving additional information—examples, rephrasing, implications—about points made by others<br>• **Energizing:** Stimulating the team to continue working when progress wanes<br>• **Coordinating:** Pulling together ideas and suggestions<br>• **Orienting:** Keeping the team headed toward its stated goals<br>• **Detailing:** Caring for operational details<br>• **Recording:** Performing a "team memory" function by documenting discussion and outcomes<br>• **Challenging:** Questioning the quality of the team's methods, logic, and results | • **Encouraging:** Fostering team solidarity by reinforcing others<br>• **Harmonizing:** Mediating conflicts<br>• **Compromising:** Shifting one's own position on an issue to reduce conflict in the team<br>• **Gatekeeping:** Encouraging all team members to participate<br>• **Reflecting:** Pointing out the positive and negative aspects of the team's dynamics and calling for change if necessary<br>• **Following:** Accepting the ideas offered by others and serving as an audience for the team<br>• **Standard setting:** Expressing, or calling for discussion of, standards for evaluating the quality of the team process |

*Source:* Adapted from Benne, K. D., & Sheats, P. 1948. "Functional Roles of Group Members." *Journal of Social Issues, 4,* 41–49.

At the heart of this issue is *diversity* in team membership. This being said, how do managers best optimize the diversity of their teams?

## Diversity

Diversity is a hot topic in organizations for a lot of reasons. First, it is the correct thing to do. It is illegal to discriminate on the basis of gender, race, sexual orientation, or disability status. However, diversity goes beyond gender and race issues. Diversity is also valuable in terms of functional skills. Diversity in and of itself is an extremely important tool for the team, the manager, and the organization as a whole.

Left to their own instincts, most leaders and most teams opt for homogeneity, not diversity. In a large-scale study, spanning 33 project groups over four years, work partner choice was biased toward others of the same race (Hinds, Carley, Krackhardt, & Wholey, 2000). When people in actual workgroups had an opportunity to select future group members, their choices were biased toward those who were from the same racial group as themselves, but also those who had a reputation for being competent and hardworking, and those with whom they had developed strong working relationships. According to Hinds et al. (2000), people strive for predictability when choosing future work group members. Joe Watson, founder and CEO of StrategicHire.com (an executive search firm), puts it this way: "[P]eople are scared to death about the steps necessary to [diversify their teams]. If you told them that Howard University is having a job fair and they need to drive a car through Washington, D.C., park on the street in a predominantly African-American neighborhood, and walk into a room filled with

African-Americans, let's be honest: That would make a lot of people uncomfortable. They haven't done it before" (Salter, 2002, p. 44).

What are the key advantages of having teams composed of diverse members? There are several compelling reasons.

- **Expanded talent pool:** First and foremost, the company that does not tolerate or promote diversity has access to a smaller amount of corporate talent—the less diversity, the less likelihood of recruiting and maintaining talented individuals.

- **Multiple viewpoints:** Diverse (or heterogeneous) teams are more likely to come up with creative solutions and solve problems more accurately than are homogeneous teams—a topic we take up in Chapter 8 (creativity). Heterogeneous groups are more effective than are homogeneous groups at solving complex problems (for a review, see Shaw, 1981). Groups whose charter members are ethnically diverse socialize newcomers more readily than groups with all Anglo founders (Arrow, 1998).

- **Better decision making:** Diverse decision-making teams make better decisions than teams that lack diversity. For example, all-male or male-dominated teams make decisions that are overaggressive (LePine, Hollenbeck, Ilgen, Colquitt, & Ellis, 2002).

- **Competitive advantage:** The key reason why diversity is so advantageous is that by sampling from a larger pool of potential team members, teams increase their competitive advantage. That is, nondiverse teams have a smaller talent pool to recruit from, which can only hurt their performance.

### Challenges of Diversity

Diversity is not without its challenges, however. The following are some key challenges in creating and managing diversity within a team:

**Diversify on What?**    Just exactly what should team leaders diversify? The number of possibilities, such as demographics (age, race, sex, nationality, ethnicity, socioeconomic status), task-related knowledge, values, beliefs and attitudes, personality and cognitive style, or status in the organization, is infinite. Jehn (1999) distinguishes three types of diversity in work teams: social category diversity, informational diversity, and value diversity. *Social category diversity* refers primarily to visible demographic characteristics, such as age, sex, and race. *Informational diversity* refers to differences related to education, work experience, and organizational tenure. *Value diversity* refers to differences in underlying work values and goals. Teams that focus on informational diversity (work experiences, education, training, functional expertise, etc.) debate constructively, whereas teams that focus on differences in gender, race, and age are more likely to stereotype and interpret things in a personal manner that is often destructive. Teams that hold similar values are less likely to engage in destructive conflict. Above all, the organization should focus on companywide values. According to Chatman, Polzer, Barsade, and Neale (1998), the benefits of demographic diversity are more likely to emerge in organizations that make organizational membership salient and encourage people to regard one another as having the organization's interests in common, rather than focusing on individualism and distinctiveness among members.

**How Much Diversity?**    The question of how much diversity to strive for is not always clear. A team that is so diverse that it has little or no overlap in terms of interpersonal style or disciplinary or strategic background and training will have a difficult time getting anything done. As a general principle, however, managers tend to err in the direction of not diversifying enough. We suggest that managers should specify those skills they see as necessary to perform the job and then sample from *all* persons who meet those requirements. The optimal degree of diversity may depend on "interpersonal congruence"—the degree to which we see ourselves as others see us. A longitudinal study of eighty-three work groups revealed that diversity improved performance on creative tasks—provided that interpersonal congruence was high (Polzer, Milton, & Swann, 2002). Yet, diversity undermined the performance of groups with low interpersonal congruence.

**Conflict**    Diverse teams will often (but not always) experience more conflict than will homogeneous groups, as individuals attempt to reconcile one another's views or simply decide upon a single course of action. According to Pelled, Eisenhardt, and Xin's (1999) investigation of 45 teams from the electronics divisions of three major corporations, functional background diversity drives task conflict, but multiple types of diversity drive emotional conflict. Race and tenure diversity are positively associated with emotional conflict, whereas age diversity is negatively associated with emotional conflict. Similarly, in an investigation of 92 work teams in a household goods moving company, three types of team diversity were explored: social category diversity (e.g., gender, race), value diversity, and informational diversity (Jehn, Northcraft, & Neale, 1999). Informational diversity positively influenced group performance; social category diversity positively increased team morale; and value diversity decreased satisfaction, intent to remain, and commitment to the group. In a study of top-management teams in bank holding companies, heterogeneity with respect to age and experience outside the industry was positively related to turnover rates (Jackson, Brett, Sessa, Cooper, Julin, & Peyronnin, 1991). If improperly managed, culturally diverse groups may not perform up to their potential. In a study of culturally diverse work groups over a 15-week period (Watson, Kumar, & Michaelsen, 1993), homogeneous groups reported more process effectiveness than did heterogeneous groups during the early period (the first few weeks). The diverse groups (composed of one Caucasian-American, one African-American, one Hispanic-American, and one foreign national) reported more difficulty in agreeing on what was important and in working together, and they frequently had members who tried to be too controlling. The result was lower total task performance for the culturally diverse groups over the first nine weeks. However, at nine weeks, the diverse and homogeneous groups performed about the same. Diverse groups improved at generating ideas, but homogeneous groups remained superior in overall task performance. "It would seem unwise to expect newly formed groups with a substantial degree of cultural diversity to be able to solve problems very effectively" (Watson et al., p. 598).

**Bias in Performance Reviews**    One of the most important responsibilities of a team leader or any manager is to give performance reviews. Obviously, overly harsh performance reviews should be avoided. However, failing to give team members honest, straightforward feedback is another problem. We noted earlier that learning is a key goal for most team pursuits and in the absence of clear, straightforward, thoughtful feedback, it is not possible for people to change. The leader of diverse teams faces a particular challenge: how to provide constructive, critical feedback along racial and other demographic divides. According to Harber (1998), this task is anything but easy. For example, Harber's investigation of job performance feedback revealed that the feedback Caucasian-Americans offer to African-Americans is significantly less critical than when evaluating the identical performance by a Caucasian-American. Moreover, the tendency toward what Harber (1998) called a "positive bias" became even more pronounced as the task grew increasingly subjective—for example, evaluations of the "content" of written essays led to more positive bias than evaluations of the "mechanics" of essays. Whereas the more positive feedback may trace to a norm to be kind (Hastorf, Northcraft, & Picciotto, 1979) or sympathy motives (Jones, Farina, Hastorf, Markus, Miller, & Scott, 1984), the recipients of such "kindness" may, in fact, be robbed of important learning opportunities. Inflated praise and insufficient criticism may dissuade minority team members from striving toward greater achievement levels and may misrepresent the level of effort and mastery that professional advancement in the organization actually entails (Massey, Scott, & Dornbusch, 1975). Biased feedback may deprive minority team members of the mental challenge that educators have cited as critical for intellectual growth (Sommers, 1982). What's more, African-Americans are wary of praise from a Caucasian supervisor, so much so that the receipt of it can actually depress their self-esteem (Crocker, Voelkl, Testa, & Major, 1991).

What is the best approach that team leaders should follow? The key lies in the delivery of the feedback. In particular, when African-Americans receive "unbuffered" critical feedback, they respond less favorably to the feedback than do Caucasian-Americans who receive identical feedback, both in terms of how they evaluate the person delivering the feedback and how motivated they feel about the task (Cohen, Steele, & Ross, 1999). However, when the critical feedback is accompanied by an invocation of high standards, and by an assurance of that person's capacity to reach those standards, African-Americans respond as positively as Caucasian-Americans and both groups show more identification with their skills and their careers.

**Solo Status**    Individuals experience solo status when they are the only member of their social category (e.g., gender or race) present in a group. As a general principle, the smaller the number of other (disadvantaged, minority) group members present, the more negative the experience for the individual. According to Kanter (1977), solos are more visible in a group and are more likely to be isolated and experience role entrapment. The increased visibility pressures create performance pressure on the "token." Because they are more likely to be stereotyped according to their group membership, they experience isolation and are essentially trapped into whatever role is expected of them. For example, an investigation comparing men's and women's job performance ratings revealed that women's performance evaluations worsened as their proportion in the work group declined, whereas men's performance evaluations were independent of their relative numbers in the work group (Sackett, DuBois, & Wiggins-Noe, 1991). And, in a testing situation, solos performed more poorly during an oral examination (Sekaquaptewa & Thompson, 2002). Moreover, men, particularly solos and nonsolos, appear to merit positive evaluations simply by being men (Williams, 1992). When women are active in groups, they may overcome the solo stigma (Fuegen & Biernat, 2002).

### Creating Diverse Teams

Fortunately, there are several opportunities—almost more than ever—to capitalize on diversity. Changing workforce demographics mean that work teams can be diversified in terms of gender, race, ethnicity, national origin, area of expertise, and organizational affiliation on an increasing level. In California, racial diversity is fast approaching the point at which no single group will represent a majority. Although the proportion of African-Americans has remained relatively stable, their employment patterns have shifted considerably, resulting in higher degrees of racial integration in clerical, technical, and skilled craft jobs (Tuch & Martin, 1991).

Women are entering the labor force in growing numbers. By the year 2008, women are expected to make up approximately 48 percent of the civilian workforce. Furthermore, gender-based segregation in the workforce is declining. Although they are still seldom seen in corporate boardrooms, women currently represent more than 46 percent of the administrative and managerial workforce (International Labour Organization, 1997).

In terms of age and diversity, the shrinking rate of growth in the labor pool is pushing employers to hire at both extremes of the age distributions, with the result that both student interns and former retirees are being hired to fill vacant positions (Hopkins, Nestleroth, & Bolick, 1991). Variability in age may create conflict, because team members with different training and experience are more likely to have different perspectives about their jobs (Pfeffer, 1983). Also, teams whose members vary more widely in age have greater turnover (Wagner, Pfeffer, & O'Reilly, 1984).

Diversity may raise challenges for the managers, but these are not insurmountable problems. In contrast, the problems associated with a *lack* of diversity may be insurmountable. A properly managed workplace meets these challenges, and it is worth the effort that it will take to address these problems because a diverse workforce greatly benefits the firm and the team. However, it would be inaccurate to imply that once diverse teams are created, everything is fine. Managing diversity is an ongoing process. We outline here a four-pronged plan.

**Publicly Commit to Valuing Diversity**   An important first step is for companies to publicly commit themselves to valuing diversity. For example, the diversity (or lack thereof) in recruiting teams sent out to business schools is a public statement about diversity. Ideally, this statement should not be forced upon the company (although it may have to be); rather, it should be something that the company regards to be part of its own mission. (For examples of companies that use their Web sites to promote diversity, refer to Sidebar 4-2.)

**Solicit Ideas and Best Practices from Employees on How to Diversify**   Managers should pay attention to what team members say, and implement at least some of these ideas. Part of this plan also includes asking team members to suggest ways to deal with conflict before it erupts. It is less useful to ask members how to deal with conflict after it erupts because once embroiled in conflict, people are less objective and more ego-centric in their suggestions. Along these lines, asking members to identify the causes of conflict will inevitably lead to finger-pointing or blame-finding attributions.

**Educate Members on the Advantages of Diversity**   Rather than just stating the advantages of diversity, managers should explain in hard numbers the facts. Instead of preaching to the team (e.g., "you should diversify because it is the right thing to do"), managers should explain why diversity is in members' best interests.

---

### Sidebar 4-2. Commitment to Diversity

Evidence of commitment to diversity is sometimes provided by visiting the corporate recruiting Web sites of many global companies.

- **Intel's** Web site contains an entire section dedicated to diversity (it boasts a global workforce of more than 80,000 employees from over 45 nations), including sections on "Women in the Workforce" and "Multicultural Training": http://www.intel.com/jobs/diversity/

- **British Telecom's** Web site contains an area dedicated to valuing diversity: http://www.btplc.com/Betterworld/Employees/Equalityanddiversity/Equalityanddiversity.htm

- **Exxon Mobil Corp.** has a supplemental area of its Web site which details "Global Diversity—Highlights of Initiatives and Progress": http://www.exxonmobil.com/news/publications/c_diversity_01/c_index.html (for their 2001 report). It also contains a "Minority and Women-Oriented Community Activities" section: http://www2.exxonmobil.com/Corporate/About/CommunityPartnerships/Corp_CP_Ed_WomenMinorities.asp

- **S.C. Johnson Wax** promotes diversity by mentioning that they were nominated as one of the best companies for working mothers: http://www.scjohnsonwax.com/family/fam_pre_pre_news.asp?art_id=27

---

**Diversify at All Levels**    Joe Watson of StrategicHire.com advises companies that they need to hire diverse people for all areas, particularly middle management, where the majority of hiring is done (Salter, 2002). It is probably not enough for organizations to simply hire more diverse people and hope they interact. Thus, in addition to diversity at the individual level, the organization must commit to and work toward diversity at the team level and the governing level.

Now that we have talked about diversity in detail and proposed an action plan for creating and maintaining diversity, we need to consider the other issues that face the manager when designing the internal dynamics of teams.

## RELATIONSHIPS: HOW DO TEAM MEMBERS SOCIALIZE EACH OTHER?

Someone could get the idea from reading this chapter that teams are built from scratch and that, once built, the manager's work is largely done. This assertion, of course, is false. Teams are not built from scratch. Instead, a member or two is added to a team that is changing its direction; members leave teams for natural (and other) reasons. In short, members of teams are continuously entering and exiting; as a consequence, the team itself is constantly forming and reconfiguring itself. Group socialization is the process of how individuals enter into and then (at some point) leave teams. The process is disruptive, to be sure, yet it need not be traumatic or ill-advised.

When people begin to work together as a team, they immediately begin a process of socialization, such that members of the team mutually shape each other's behavior. More often, teams may undergo changes in membership, such that some members may leave and new ones may enter. The process of socialization is essential for team members to be able to work together and coordinate their efforts. We begin by describing the basic processes involved in team socialization. Then, we discuss the process of role negotiation, norm development and maintenance, cohesion, and trust.

## Group Socialization

Group socialization is the process by which a person becomes a member of a group. Most people think of socialization as a one-way process, wherein the team socializes the individual member—usually a newcomer—in the norms and roles of the team. However, this is an overly narrow and inaccurate view. As any leader can attest, the introduction of a new team member is a process of joint socialization.

Think about a time when you joined an existing team. Perhaps you joined a study group that had been previously formed, took a summer internship with a company that had ongoing teams already in place, or moved to a different unit within your organization. In all of these instances, you went through a process of group socialization (Moreland & Levine, 2000a). Three critical things go on during group socialization that can affect the productivity of teams: evaluation, commitment, and role transition.

### Evaluation

Teams evaluate individual members, and individual members evaluate teams. In short, the individuals on the team "size each other up." Basically, people do a primitive sort of cost-benefit analysis when it comes to appraising teams. For example, if team members receive (or expect to receive) relatively high returns from team membership while enduring few costs, they probably like their team. Teams, too, evaluate a member positively who makes many contributions to the collective while exacting few costs (Kelley & Thibaut, 1978; Thibaut & Kelley, 1959). In addition to this direct cost-benefit analysis, some people are simply attracted to teams, whereas others are not. For example, people with either little prior experience or negative experiences in teams often avoid working in groups (Bohrnstedt & Fisher, 1986; Gold & Yanof, 1985; Hanks & Eckland, 1978; Ickes, 1983; Ickes & Turner, 1983).

### Commitment

Commitment is a person's "enduring adherence" to the team and the team's adherence to its members (Kelley, 1983). The key factor that affects commitment is the alternatives that are available to the individual and the team. For example, if a team has its choice of several, highly qualified candidates, its level of commitment to any one candidate is less than if a team does not have as many alternatives.

### Role Transition

A person usually moves through a progression of membership in the team, going from nonmember to quasi-member to full member (see Figure 4-3). One key to gaining full member status is to be evaluated positively by the team and to gain the team's commitment. This can often (but not always) be achieved by learning through direct experience with the team, and also through observations of others in the team. Indeed, newcomers in teams feel a strong need to obtain information about what is expected of them (Louis, 1980; Van Maanen, 1977; Wanous, 1980); simultaneously, teams communicate this knowledge through formal and informal indoctrination sessions (Gauron & Rawlings, 1975; Jacobs & Campbell, 1961; Zurcher, 1965, 1970). However, newcomers may not learn crucial information they need to perform their jobs, such as information about the preferences of supervisors or administrative procedures, until they are

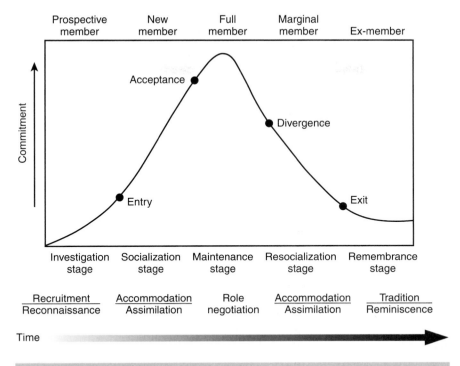

**FIGURE 4-3** Role Transition in Groups
*Source:* Moreland, R. L., & Levine, J. M. 1982. "Socialization in Small Groups: Temporal Changes in Individual-Group Relations." In L. Berkowitz (Ed.), *Advances in Experimental Social Psychology* (Vol. 15, pp. 137–192). New York: Academic Press.

trusted by their coworkers (Feldman, 1977). According to Swann, Milton, and Polzer (2000), people who join groups can either engage in self-verification or what they call appraisal effects. *Self-verification* occurs when group members persuade others in the team to see them as they see themselves. In contrast, *appraisal* occurs when groups persuade members to see themselves as the group sees them. Of the two, self-verification is more prevalent than is appraisal. When team members get their group to see them the way they see themselves, this heightens the feelings of connection to the team, lessens A-type (unhealthy) conflict, and improves performance on creative tasks. In contrast, when groups beseech individuals to see themselves as the group sees them, this improves performance on computational tasks (e.g., tasks that have a single, correct answer).

What are some best practices that managers and team leaders can use to increase the likelihood of a favorable match between an individual and a team? The following strategies are especially useful for integrating new members into teams.

*Upper Management and Leaders: Make It Clear Why*
*the New Member Is Joining the Team*
Many times, the introduction of a new team member is threatening for individuals, when it need not be. The manager should not assume that everyone is fully aware of

why the newcomer is joining the team. Simple, clear, straightforward statements about how upper management sees the relationship between the individual and the team are needed early on before an unnecessary cycle of paranoia is set in motion.

### Existing Team Members: Explain What You Regard to Be the Strengths and Weaknesses of the Team

It can be very revealing for existing team members to talk about their strengths and weaknesses when a new member joins. The new member can "see" the team through the eyes of each team member.

### New Members: Understand the Team's Goals and Processes

Existing members often expect newcomers to be anxious, passive, dependent, and conforming. Further, new members who take on those characteristics are more likely to be accepted by old-timers (Moreland & Levine, 1989). What newcomers may not realize, however, is that they inevitably pose some threat to the team. This is often because newcomers have a fresh and relatively objective view of the team, which causes them to ask questions or express opinions that are unsettling. New members can take initiative by demonstrating an interest in learning about the team. Remember that the team may be hypersensitive about past failures. Therefore, it is often a good idea to deflect defensive reactions by noting the team's positive qualities.

## Role Negotiation

In all teams, task-management and people-management skills are required. *Task-related roles* focus on getting the work done and accomplishing the task at hand; *interpersonal roles* focus on how the work gets done and satisfying the emotional needs of team members. However, unlike traditional functional roles, such as finance, sales, and manufacturing, the roles of task management and people management are not necessarily played by one particular person. That is, these roles are more fluid and dynamic than are functional roles.

We do not discuss leadership until Chapter 10, but here we distinguish two different kinds of leadership: *task* versus *people*. In virtually all teams, a person or set of persons will take on the role of managing the team in terms of getting the work done. This person is often called the leader. Another role in most teams is that of managing the people aspects of the team—this role may be taken on by the task leader, but not necessarily. In manager-led teams, the manager or supervisor often takes on these roles in some form. However, even in manager-led groups, there can be implicit role renegotiation, whereby team members attempt to demonstrate skill in these areas.

Over time, through the process of role negotiation, various roles emerge (Bettenhausen & Murnighan, 1985). Most often these roles and the negotiations for them are not talked about in an explicit fashion; rather, people engage in actions designed to take on that role, which are either accepted or rejected by other members of the team. What should the manager expect in terms of role negotiation?

First, there is no one set of ideal roles for any particular team. In fact, roles are unique to each team. However, some roles are more common than others. An **action plan** might be to ask the team members, either at the outset or after a few meetings, what roles are helpful to have in the team. (Provide them the list in Table 4-2 as a starting point.)

Second, few people can simultaneously fulfill both the task and interpersonal needs of the team (Bales, 1955, 1958; Parsons, Bales, & Shils, 1953). When taskmasters move troops toward their goals, they often appear domineering, controlling, and unsympathetic. These actions may be conducive to goal attainment, but team members may react negatively. Because team members believe the task specialist is the source of the tension, someone other than the task leader must often assume a role aimed at reducing interpersonal hostilities and frustrations (Burke, 1967). The diplomat who intervenes to restore harmony and cohesion is the *socioemotional master.* An example of this interplay on a corporate scale is provided by the management styles of the former and current chairman and CEO of AMR Corp. (parent of American Airlines), Robert Crandall and Donald Carty, respectively. Although they each assumed the same task-related role as chairman and CEO, their management styles allowed them to play very different socioemotional roles. Crandall was known for his often abrasive and formal demeanor, whereas Carty is known as a soft-spoken, casual leader. Crandall's socioemotional role may have been to push for results from his employees; Carty takes a more coaxing role.

Third, role negotiation may take the form of **status competition** within the team. Status competition is the process by which people acquire the authority and legitimacy to be the taskmaster or the relationship coordinator of the team. Even in teams with established status roles, status competition can emerge as certain members attempt to compete with the leader. How does status competition work in a team and what can the manager do to capitalize on the process so as to improve overall team functioning?

Team members intuitively take note of one another's personal qualities they think are indicative of ability or prestige (years on the job, relevant connections, etc.). People take two types of cues or information into consideration: Real status characteristics and pseudostatus characteristics. **Real status** characteristics are qualities that are relevant to the task at hand (e.g., previous experience with the decision domain). **Pseudostatus** characteristics include factors such as sex, age, ethnicity, status in other groups, and cultural background. Typically, pseudostatus characteristics are those that are highly visible. Pseudostatus characteristics, of course, have little to do with ability but people act as if they do.

Status systems develop very quickly, often within minutes after most teams are formed (Barchas & Fisek, 1984). Soon after meeting one another, team members form expectations about each person's probable contributions to the achievement of the team's goals (Berger, Rosenholtz, & Zelditch, 1980). These expectations are based on personal characteristics that people purposely reveal to one another (real status characteristics such as intelligence, background, and education) or that are readily apparent (pseudostatus characteristics such as sex, age, race, demeanor, size, musculature, and facial expression; Mazur, 1985). Personal characteristics that are more relevant to the achievement of team goals have more impact on expectations, but even irrelevant factors are evaluated. People who possess more valuable characteristics evoke more positive expectations and are thus assigned higher status in the team. An **action plan** for a manager who suspects that pseudostatus characteristics may supplant more relevant qualifications would be to provide clear information to team members about others' qualifications well in advance of the team meeting (e.g., circulating members' resumes). In addition to this, the leader should structure the first meeting of the team so as to ensure that relevant factors are made known to all members (e.g., a round-robin discussion in which members review their experiences).

## Team Norms: Development and Enforcement

Just as role negotiation and status competition occur early on in the development of groups, so do *norms,* or the ideas and expectations that guide appropriate behavior for members. Norms differ from formal rules in that they are not written down. Norms are critical for team and organizational performance. Because norms are expectations about appropriate behavior, they embody information about what people should do under various conditions. This makes it easier for people to respond appropriately under new or stressful conditions and helps ensure that everyone is working toward the same goal. Thus, norms reduce threats to productivity and, in particular, they reduce coordination problems. Precious time is not lost while staff members brainstorm about what to do. For example, at Nordstrom, it is well known by employees as well as shoppers that customer service is the number one priority. In the case of any uncertainty about what needs to be done, the customer service dictum provides direction.

Many norms develop within the first few minutes of a team's first meeting—such as whether it is appropriate to come a few minutes late, seating arrangements, and so on (Bettenhausen & Murnighan, 1985; Gersick, 1988; Schein, 1988). As a general principle, however, this is not a very desirable state of affairs. When norms are left strictly to natural processes and interaction patterns among members, those individuals who are most disruptive and least self-conscious may set unfavorable norms. This is because people who are the most outspoken and the least self-conscious do the most talking. What is the best way to counteract these undesirable norms? One of the best mechanisms is to introduce some kind of structure to the team early on (see Appendix 1 on meeting management); structure is the opposite of free-form interaction, where anything goes.

Adding structure to a team can mean that the team makes a commitment to do what the members value. For example, at Intel Corporation, there is a norm of constructive confrontation, which advocates that people challenge others in a productive fashion, rather than stand idly by and agree just to avoid conflict or hurt feelings. Still other norms may focus on improving group cohesion (e.g., team members regularly arriving with specialty coffee and breakfast items to share with others, technical engineers bringing their dogs to work at companies in Silicon Valley, office birthday parties, and casual Fridays).

Although some level of agreement is necessary for an expectation to be a norm, this does not mean that norms may not be in conflict. For example, in one hospital, nurses might think that the amount of work administrators expect the nurses to do is about right, whereas in another, nurses might think administrators expect the nurses to do too much paperwork (Argote, 1989). It may be that the norm within one department of a company is to allow its employees to take time during the workday to handle personal matters, as long as the time is made up later, but this may not be considered acceptable behavior in another department within the same company.

Like rules, norms may often be broken. What are the consequences of norm violation in a team? Contrary to naive intuition, the first response of a team to a norm violator is not exclusion, but rather to persuade that person to change. When regularity is interrupted, or violated, the "injured" parties frequently attempt to regain regularity by appealing to the norm (e.g., "Why didn't you circulate the report—we always do that!"). When a team member repeatedly violates a norm, there are serious repercussions, even if the behavior in question is useful for the organization. Consider, for example, the studies conducted at the Hawthorne Plant in the 1940s. Strong norms developed among work group members concerning the rate of acceptable productivity. That is, members in a particular work group developed a pace at which to work, that was just enough to produce the desired output requested by the supervisor, but not enough to overly tax group members. Consequently, when members of the work group failed to produce at the level displayed by their peers, they were sharply reprimanded. Furthermore, when members of the group overproduced (worked harder than other members of the group), they were harshly punished. In the Hawthorne Plant, a behavior called "binging" was observed, in which the "rate buster" (i.e., the overproducer) was given a sharp blow to the arm so as to reprimand the employee and decrease the level of output.

Certainly, not all cases of norm violation in organizational work groups are met with physical aggression. The first response of a team is usually to attempt to correct the misbehavior with some reminding. Teams will often persist in this kind of corrective activity for a long period of time before they move to more drastic measures. Indeed, there are other forms of punishment and aggression that are perhaps even more detrimental to individual and organizational well-being, such as **ostracism,** in which people are excluded from certain social or professional activities (Williams, 1997). Ostracism can have negative repercussions for the company as well if the isolated individual is not given sufficient information to effectively do the job.

Once established, norms are not easily changed. Norms are often maintained over several "generations" during which old members gradually leave the team and new members join (Jacobs & Campbell, 1961; Weick & Gilfillan, 1971). Teams' efforts to transmit their norms are particularly strong when newcomers are involved (Levine & Moreland, 1991; Moreland & Levine, 1989). Teams are highly motivated to provide newcomers with the knowledge, ability, and motivation they will need to play the role of a full member. Consequently, newcomers are usually receptive to these influence attempts because they feel a strong need to learn what is expected of them (Louis, 1980; Van Maanen, 1977).

### Cohesion: Team Bonding

Most people who have been a part of a team will claim that there is a critical quality of teams that is difficult to capture, but yet is ever-present and very powerful, that goes beyond norms. When asked to describe this quality, managers will use words such as *camaraderie, fellow-feeling, energy, rapport, we-feeling,* and *team spirit.* Intuitively, people on teams seem to know when these positive feelings are present and also when they are absent.

**Cohesion**—or solidarity, morale, community, and fellow-feeling—is the binding material of teams. Cohesion makes people feel better, and it is a crucial ingredient for team viability.

What does a cohesive team look like? Members of cohesive teams sit closer together, focus more attention on one another, show signs of mutual affection, and display coordinated patterns of behavior. Furthermore, members of cohesive teams who have a close relationship are more likely to give due credit to their partners. In contrast, those who do not have a close relationship are more likely to take credit for successes and blame others for failure (Sedekides, Campbell, Reeder, & Elliot, 1998). Cohesive groups are easier to maintain. Members of cohesive teams are more likely to participate in team activities, stay on the team and convince others to join, and resist attempts to disrupt the team (Brawley, Carron, & Widmeyer, 1988; Carron, Widmeyer, & Brawley, 1988). Cohesion increases conformity to team norms (O'Reilly & Caldwell, 1985; Rutkowski, Gruder, & Romer, 1983). This effect can be helpful when deviance endangers the team or harmful when innovation is required. Cohesive teams are more likely to serve team rather than individual interests (Thompson, Kray, & Lind, 1998). Most important, members of cohesive teams are more productive on a variety of tasks than are members of noncohesive groups (Dion & Evans, 1992; Michel & Hambrick, 1992).

However, *the relationship between team cohesion and performance is primarily correlational rather than causal.* Stated simply, cohesive teams are more productive than are less cohesive teams, but it could very well be that (1) more productive teams become more cohesive, (2) something other than cohesion is responsible for increased productivity, or (3) both. The link of cohesion with performance may depend on team norms: Cohesion amplifies norms favoring both high and low production (Stogdill, 1972). There are many ways to promote cohesion (see Sidebar 4-3 for some interesting examples).

## Sidebar 4-3. Notes from the Field

There are two companies based in Boulder, Colorado, that advocate writing poetry or banging on drums to help teams build cohesion. According to a participant in one of Kandome Percussion Workshop's sessions, "It builds a rhythm through the company." A brochure for CorPoet asserts that its method "reveals and anthologizes the heart and soul of your business" (LeJeune, 1997).

*Building Cohesion in Groups*
Building cohesion is often easier than we think.

- *Help the team build identity.* Simply assembling people into a team is enough to produce some cohesion (Hogg, 1987), and the more time people spend together (in a face-to-face fashion), the more cohesive they become (Manning & Fullerton, 1988). When team members think about their identity (i.e., what they stand for) and what they have in common, they become more cohesive (Prentice, Miller, & Lightdale, 1994).

- *Make it easy for the team to be close together.* Physical proximity and real or perceived similarity strengthen team cohesion (e.g., Ruder & Gill, 1982; Stokes, 1983; Sundstrom & Sundstrom, 1986).

- *Focus on similarities among team members.* Team members feel more cohesive when they focus on their similarities, rather than their differences.

- *Put a positive spin on the team's performance.* Teams are more cohesive when they succeed rather than fail, though some teams can preserve (if not strengthen) cohesion even when they fail (Brawley et al., 1988).

- *Challenge the team.* External pressure (Glickman et al., 1987) and rewards for team performance also increase team cohesion (Shea & Guzzo, 1987).

*Warning:* Many of the factors that produce greater cohesion in teams are in contradiction to those that promote diversity. We suggest that the manager first consider strategies for building diversity, and then focus on building cohesion within the diverse team.

## Trust

**Trust** is the confidence one person places in another that the other will honor all commitments, including those that are difficult to define or specify in advance, especially when it is difficult to monitor or otherwise observe the other person's behavior after the fact. Trust is built on previous experience, on an understanding of the other party's interests, motives, and ideas, as well as more subtle factors, such as a willingness to believe a commitment. Thus, trust is two-sided, depending partly on the believability of the other party and partly on the willingness to believe. Many things can affect either of these, and abridgments to either can compromise teamwork.

Robert Nagle and Ian Adamson, the founders of Team EcoInternet, an adventure racing team, base their entire team strategy on mutual trust. The team can move only as fast as its weakest member. And because each race stretches over a series of exhausting days, every person on the team will be the weakest member at one point or another. Says Nagle, "If one of us stumbles for the second time in 10 minutes, there's no question about what needs to be done: Somebody reaches into that person's pack and takes out some weight, and then we all just move on" (Dahle, 1999, p. 310). The team members sum it up this way: "You're not the hero for taking on extra weight or the schmoe for needing help. You know that, three hours from now, the guy carrying all your stuff may need you to carry his stuff" (Dahle, 1999, p. 310).

### Trust or Faith?

Business is built on relationships of all sorts and almost nothing is truly guaranteed in writing. No contract can be so complete as to specify, for instance, what an employee must actually do at a given time on a given day in a particular instance, especially since at some level, just about every situation is unique. Faith in other team members' integrity to do things that cannot be specified in a contract or monitored after the fact is an essential feature of a successful team—or for that matter, any business relationship. It is the integrity of the individual team members, and the members' trust in this integrity, that allows for successful teamwork.

The absence of a positive, trusting relationship can undermine any team activity, and so fostering trust is one of the most important tasks of a manager. Contractual relationships (such as when a consulting firm is hired for a project) come with the understanding that they will be evaluated, at least in part, by how fairly they used their time, that is, basically, how trustworthy they are in their billing practices. However, this is not a normal part of the relationship between coworkers, who are presumed to be working toward the same common goal. Moreover, what to do in cases when it seems like coworkers are furthering their own interests at the expense of the team is less certain than it is with an outside contractor who, at the least, can be excluded from further work with the company.

Many other forms of trust are also essential inside the organization, such as trust in the abilities or knowledge of other workers. Moreover, the absence of trust need not be associated with anything malicious; a lack of trust can stem, for instance, from a lack of experience working with others, such as when a cross-functional team is put together to establish organizational policy or to hire key executives to lead the company. The next few sections elaborate on the issue of trust—how to get a better understanding of it and its role in working relationships and, most important, where and when to find it.

### Incentive-Based Trust

*Incentive-based* or *calculated trust* involves designing incentives to minimize breaches of trust. When an arrangement, such as a contract, is made on favorable terms for the other party, it is easier to trust that they will fulfill their end of the deal. Companies often pay bonuses, in fact, to ensure just this kind of outcome. For instance, contracts often include provisions for bonuses depending on when a job gets done. The idea is that by providing incentives to the other party to do things that match your objectives, you can trust that they will be more likely to get things done the way that you want them done. Bonuses are only one mechanism that can be used to ensure this alignment. (As we noted in Chapter 2, free riding is a frequent problem for teams and a major threat to team performance. For an example of free riding in teams, see Sidebar 4-4.)

### Trust Based on Familiarity

As people become more familiar with one another, they are more likely to trust each other. For this reason, group turnover presents special challenges for trust within the team. For example, Moreland and Levine (2002b) argue that distrust of new members places extra burdens on full members who must work harder to make sure that the team's expectations are clear and that new members' behaviors are monitored.

### Trust Based on Similarity

Oftentimes, trust can develop based on commonalities, such as being alumni of the same school, belonging to the same religious institution, or having kids who play on the same Little League team. People who are similar to one another in beliefs, attitudes, and interests tend to like each other more. It seems natural that we are attracted to those who are similar to us, and we are more likely to help and trust them. This principle explains why successful salespeople are trained immediately to find common ground with others: "Hi, Mrs. Jones! I have the same aluminum siding as you! Would you like to change your long-distance service?" Of course, the dark side of this is that people have lower trust in people who are less similar (more diverse).

### Trust Based on Social Networks

Trusting relationships in organizations are often based upon social networks. *Social embeddedness* refers to the idea that transactions and opportunities take place as a result of social relationships that exist between organizational actors (Uzzi, 1997). This is conducive to organizational teamwork in that trust and shared norms of reciprocal compliance have beneficial governance properties for the people involved. In short, embedding commercial exchange in social attachments creates a basis for trust that, if accepted and returned, crystallizes through reciprocal coinvestment and self-enforcement for use in future transactions. Trust based on social networks offers several advantages (Uzzi, 1997). According to Uzzi, "embedded ties" reduce the time needed to reach and enforce agreements. Second, the expectations and trust associated with embedded ties increases risk taking and coinvestments in advanced technology. Third, the transfer of proprietary information through embedded ties leads to more

## Sidebar 4-4. Free Riding in Teams

An example of free riding in teams can be easily constructed. Imagine that the efforts of each individual on a five-person team consist of choosing a dollar amount to contribute to a joint investment. The investment returns a certain 5 percent; so, for each dollar contributed, the investment returns $1.05. To make this a team story, let's set up the problem this way. Every person contributes anonymously to a team account (so no one can observe whether or how much any one person contributes—all that can be observed is the net amount of funds collected), and the returns from the investment are distributed to all team members equally. Thus, if all five people contribute $1 apiece, they each receive $1.05 back in return; if four people contribute $1 and one person contributes $6, they each receive $2.10. The decision problem faced by individual team members is how much to contribute. Clearly, everyone is better off the higher the total contribution. However, payoffs cannot be separated based on individual contributions, so each team member receives only 21 cents in return directly as a consequence of their contribution (do you see why this is true?). Hence, from an individual point of view, a contribution costs more than it returns. On the other hand, everyone receives a share of the total pie regardless of whether they contribute. If four people contribute $1 and the fifth person contributes nothing, they each get back 84 cents. This is bad for the four people who pitched in, but great for the person who put in nothing. What will team members do in this instance? If their objective is to maximize return, they will each contribute nothing. Thus, despite the fact that high contribution levels are good for the team as a whole (total contributions are a public good), the free-riding effect prevents anyone from contributing, and so the worst outcome is achieved.

The problem in this example is that individual contributions cannot be monitored. Hence, people can hide behind the anonymity offered by the team structure to mask their lack of effort. If there were a way to remove anonymity, for instance, by having a taxing structure that collected $1 from everyone, or by somehow installing a monitoring system that could directly observe contributions, this would prevent the free-riding problem, because everyone could get back their fair share attributable to their efforts.

*(A final note: Don't get caught up in the artificial details of this example. The structure of the example is meant to capture the fact that putting effort into teamwork is costly and difficult to monitor and that results from teamwork are generally attributed to the entire group, not allocated according to individual efforts.)*

win-win types of arrangements. Finally, embedded ties promote cooperation, even when groups will not work together very long.

### Implicit Trust

Sometimes, we put our trust in others even in the absence of any rational reason or obvious similarity. We might trust someone on the basis of a short interaction. Trust, in this sense, is based upon highly superficial cues. In every social interaction, there are subtle signals that we attend to even though we are not aware of their influence. They operate below our conscious awareness. Some examples follow.

**Instant Attitudes**    These are near-immediate, intense likes or dislikes for a novel object based on a first encounter with it (Greenwald & Banaji, 1995).

**Mere Exposure: "He Grew on Me"**    The more we see someone, the more we like them (Zajonc, 1968). This even goes for people that we initially do not like. However, most people do not realize that their liking for people is driven by how often they see them. This **mere exposure** principle is the cornerstone of advertising and sales.

**Schmoozing: "Let's Have Lunch Sometime"**    Small talk might not appear to be relevant to accomplishing a work task. The exchange of pleasantries about the weather or our favorite basketball team seems to be purposeless, except for conforming to social etiquette. However, on a *preconscious* level, schmoozing has a dramatic impact on our liking and trust of others. For example, even a short exchange can lead people to develop considerably more trust in others than in the absence of interaction.

**Mirroring**    People involved in a face-to-face interaction tend to mirror one another in posture, facial expression, tone of voice, and mannerisms. This phenomenon, known as **social contagion,** is the basis for the development of rapport between people (Drolet, Larrick, & Morris, 1998). On the surface, it might seem that mimicking others would be extremely annoying—almost like a form of mocking. However, the type of mimicry that is involved in everyday social encounters is quite subtle, but definitely powerful. When two people are mimicking one another, their movements are like a choreographed dance. In this sense, people's behavior becomes synchronized. To the extent that our behaviors are synchronized with those of others, we feel more rapport, and this increases our trust in them.

**"Flattery Can Get You Anywhere"**    We like people who appreciate us and admire us. This means that we will tend to trust people more who like us. Many people believe that for flattery to be effective in engendering trust, it must be perceived as genuine. However, even if people suspect that the flatterer has ulterior motives, this can still increase liking and trust under some conditions (Jones, Stires, Shaver, & Harris, 1968).

**Face-to-Face Contact**    We are more likely to trust other people in a face-to-face encounter than when communicating via another medium, such as phone or fax machine. Perhaps this is why people often choose to travel thousands of miles for a short, face-to-face meeting when it would be more efficient to communicate via phone, fax, or mail.

## Turnover and Reorganizations

One of the most frequently occurring but daunting challenges for teams is personnel turnover, defined as the entry of new members and/or the exit of old members (Levine, Choi, & Moreland, 2003). Turnover represents a change in team composition that can have profound consequences for team performance, because it alters the technical knowledge of the team, as well as the interpersonal dynamics. As might be expected, turnover disrupts group performance, especially when group members are reciprocally interdependent (Naylor & Briggs, 1965); when the group has high, rather than low structure (Devadas & Argote, 1995); and when the task is complex rather than simple (Argote, Insko, Yovetich, & Romero, 1995).

*Newcomer Innovation*

A quite different view of turnover is suggested by Levine, Choi, and Moreland (2003), who suggest that, contrary to popular opinion, turnover might benefit a group—through the exit of "oldtimers" who lack the skills or motivation to help the group attain its goals and the entry of newcomers who possess needed skills. Three factors determine the extent to which newcomers can introduce change: (1) their commitment to the team; (2) their belief that they can develop good ideas for solving team problems; and (3) their belief that they will be rewarded. The bottom line is that for turnover to have positive effects, it must outweigh the substantial benefits that group members derive from working together (Argote & Kane, in press; Hollenbeck, Ilgen, LePine, Colquitt, & Hedlund, 1998). In one investigation of turnover, teams worked on an air surveillance task over two days (Levine & Choi, in press). On both days, specialists monitored changing plane information (e.g., airspeed, altitude) and transmitted it to the commander, who integrated this information and assigned threat values to the planes. At the beginning of day 2, there was turnover: In some teams, one of the specialists was replaced with a specialist from another team; in other teams, the commander was replaced with a commander from another team. Teams performed better when newcomers had high rather than low ability; this was particularly pronounced when newcomers had high status (commander) rather than low status (specialist).

Moreover, there are several different "newcomer" roles (Arrow & McGrath, 1995): visitors, transfers, replacements, and consultants. *Visitors* are people who are expected to remain on the team for a short time and are not viewed as instrumental to attaining long-term goals. Because they are viewed as lacking in commitment, their ability to change the team is muted (Gruenfeld & Fan, 1999; Gruenfeld, Martorana, & Fan, 2000). *Transfers* have recently belonged to a similar team and have expertise. *Replacements* take the place of former members. *Consultants* join the team to observe its work practices and to suggest improvements.

## CONCLUSIONS

We have focused on some of the important dimensions of creating and managing teams in a direct fashion. Much planning needs to precede the construction of teams, and, once constructed, teams need fairly continuous maintenance. To the extent that the teams are manager-led, this work is the purview of the leader or manager; the more self-directing the team becomes, the more the team must do this for itself. When the team is built—in terms of the task, the people, and their relationships—the leader's work does not stop. During this time, the leader needs to also assess the physical, material, economic, and staffing resources necessary for performing the work to be done. The focus of the leader should not be to presume that everything is fine, but rather to coach the team to work through the issues of task, people, and relationships systematically.

# CHAPTER

## Sharpening the Team Mind:

### *Communication and Collective Intelligence*

*Having access to multiple databases and the Geographic Information System's (GIS) mapping expertise was vital to the New York City teams of rescuers, medical staff, and cleanup crews after September 11, 2001, when its new, high-tech emergency operations center was destroyed along with the World Trade Center towers (Brown, 2002). Working nonstop for over 72 hours after the terrorist strike, managers and technicians from a host of agencies and contractor firms teamed up on Pier 92 at 52nd Street along the Hudson River. There, they patched together an operations and mapping center. The center's big color plotters cranked out fresh maps every day, superimposing an aerial photo of the rubble at Ground Zero that highlighted all kinds of features that rescue workers needed to know about—hazards such as fuel tanks and elevator shafts; hot spots where buried fires burned most intensely; locations of electric cables, gas pipes, water mains, and sewers; and routes cleared for trucks hauling heavy loads of twisted steel beams from the area. The teams' technique of laying data and looking for patterns within them is an information management strategy that dates back at least as far as 1854, when central London was in the grip of a lethal cholera outbreak. By plotting the locations of deaths and the location of the public-drinking water pumps, pioneering epidemiologist Dr. John Snow observed that the cholera cases clustered around one of the 11 water pumps in the area. Officials removed the pump's handle to protect the rest of the population from the cholera-tainted well (Brown, 2002).*

Disaster management may be a step removed from the collective intelligence challenges faced by teams in a typical company, but as teamwork grows more specialized, teams and their leaders must deal with communication obstacles and knowledge integration. Namely, how to collect and assimilate the right data, sift through it and transform it into knowledge, and collaborate with other teams and groups are skills that are often left to intuition rather than science. The *knowledge economy,* in which symbols, rather than raw materials, are the means by which organizations create value (Toffler, 1991) and where attention is the scarcest resource (Simon, 1973), poses special challenges for teams. Whether organizations make fighter airplanes or cookies, effective decision making and behavior rely upon effective communication and common understanding. Thus, to be effective, teams must not only transmit and receive ideas from other group members accurately; they must also have a shared understanding of what the information means. This is especially critical in teams because members rely on the judgments of others to make important decisions.

This chapter examines how members of teams communicate and develop team intelligence. We begin by discussing communication within teams and the possible problems that can occur and how to effectively treat them. Then, we describe the information-dependence problem—the fact that team members are dependent on one another for critical information. After this, we build a model of team-level collective intelligence. We suggest that teams implicitly develop mental models, which are causal structures that spell out how a team solves problems and does its work together. We then explore the team mind in depth and the nature of transactive memory systems, which are the ways in which teams encode, store, and retrieve critical information necessary for doing their work. Next, we undertake a case analysis of the effects of different types of training on transactive memory systems. Finally, we make some recommendations for team development and review some evidence pointing to the effects of group longevity, particularly in creative teams.

## TEAM COMMUNICATION

Most people take communication for granted in their interactions with team members. However, the tragic events described in Box 5-1 suggest this can be a mistake. Communication among people and between teams is subject to biases that afflict even the most rational of human beings with the best of intentions.

---

BOX 5-1

### Colossal Communication Failures

In 1988, Iran Air Flight 665 took off from Bandar Abbas Airport and headed across the Persian Gulf en route to Dubai. Seven minutes into the flight, Captain William Rogers of the USS *Vincennes,* judging the airliner to be a hostile fighter plane, destroyed it with two missiles. Captain Rogers had approximately three minutes in which to process information from several of his support staff and make the decision as to whether to shoot the (misidentified) Iranian airbus and protect his crew. Although the decision was militarily correct, 290 civilians died and questions were raised regarding the inadequacy of our scientific knowledge concerning team decision making and decision support systems in this setting.

In 1989, an Avianca Airlines flight crashed in New York while awaiting clearance for landing, critically low on fuel. Ground control misinterpreted the Colombian pilot's urgent message regarding his fuel shortage and assumed that a fuel emergency had not been reached. More than 270 people died.

In 1990, Martin Marietta deployed a satellite into the wrong orbit when engineers instructed the computer programmers to open the bay door to the hatch containing the satellite. The programmers opened the "wrong door," although they had followed the instructions correctly (Associated Press, 1990). Today, $150 million sits dead in orbit around the earth. The total cost of the miscommunication: $500 million.

In a perfect communication system, a sender transmits or sends a message that is accurately received by a recipient. There are at least three points of possible error: The sender may fail to send a message; the message may be sent, but is inaccurate or distorted; or, an accurate message is sent, but it is distorted or not received by the recipient. In a team environment, the complexity grows when teams of senders transmit messages and teams of recipients receive them. Here, we examine some of these biases and then take up the question of how to effectively deal with their existence.

### Message Tuning

There are infinite possibilities of how to send any one message. **Message tuning** refers to how senders tailor messages for specific recipients. People who send messages (e.g., "I have no fuel"; "I did not receive the attached file") will convey their messages in a way that they think best suits the recipient. For example, people give longer and more elaborate street directions and instructions to people whom they presume to be nonnatives or unfamiliar with a city (Krauss & Fussell, 1991). Also, senders capitalize on the knowledge that they believe the recipient to already hold (e.g., "Turn right when you see that big tree that the city pruned last week"). For this reason, team members may send shorter, less complete messages to one another because they believe that they can capitalize on an existing shared knowledge base. However, team members often overestimate the commonality of information they share with others. Consequently, the messages they send become less clear (e.g., in the previous example, the other person may not know the location of the tree that was pruned by the city last week).

Often, in a team or group situation, a person needs to communicate a message to someone in the group in a way that others cannot understand. For example, when a client visits a product development team, members of the product development team may need to communicate with each other in the presence of the client, but do not want the client to understand their communications. Fleming and Darley (1991) refer to this as the **multiple audience problem.** In such situations, team members try to convey certain information to one person (or team) while simultaneously concealing it from one another. People are quite good at this. For example, in one investigation, one person acted like a "studious nerd" in the presence of one person (e.g., a supervisor); the same person acted like a "fun-loving party animal" with another person (e.g., a coworker; van Boven, Kruger, Savitsky, & Gilovich, 2000). The same person interacted with the supervisor and the coworker at the same time and was actually able to preserve the two different identities (the supervisor continued to view the person as studious and the coworker continued to view the same person as a party animal). The only cautionary note is that people believe that they are better at dealing with the multiple audience problem than they actually are—in short, they are overly confident (van Boven et al., 2000).

### Message Distortion

Message senders have a bias to present information that they believe will be favorably received by the recipient and will, therefore, distort messages (Higgins, 1999). For example, when people present a message to an audience whom they believe has either a pro- or anti- stance on a particular topic, they err in the direction of adopting the audience's point of view. It is as if they know that the messenger who brings unwelcome news is endangered—so one way of dealing with this to modify the news. A former senior executive at Xerox says, "I was never allowed to present to the board unless things were perfect. [I] could only go in with good news. Everything was prettied up" (Charan & Useem, 2002, p. 50). Unfortunately, message distortion can wreak havoc on effective teamwork.

## Biased Interpretation

Senders are not the only ones who distort messages. Recipients often hear what they want to hear when receiving messages, especially ambiguous ones. For example, when people are given neutral information about a product, they tend to interpret it in a way that is favorable toward their own position. Furthermore, they selectively pay attention to information in a report that favors their initial point of view and ignore or misinterpret information that contradicts their position.

## Perspective-Taking Failures

People are remarkably poor at taking the perspective of others. For example, people who are privy to information and knowledge that they know others are not aware of still tend to act as if others are aware of it, even though it would be impossible for the receiver to have this knowledge (Keysar, 1998). This problem is known as the **curse of knowledge** (Camerer, Loewenstein, & Weber, 1989). For example, in a simulation, traders who possessed privileged information that could have been used to their advantage behaved as if their trading partners also had access to the privileged information. Perspective-taking deficiencies also explain why some instructors who understand an idea perfectly are unable to teach students the same idea. They are unable to put themselves in their students' shoes to explain the idea in a way the students can understand. Perspective-taking deficiencies explain why teams fail, even though every team member really wants to succeed. It is as if people are saying after the fact, "I thought I was clear" or "I thought you knew that." Thus, we overestimate the commonality or overlap between our own knowledge base and that of others. (For an example of how an executive training company has been formulated to address the tendency for leaders to fail to take the perspective of others, see Sidebar 5-1.)

### Sidebar 5-1. A Real Lesson in Perspective Taking

Teams who attend Peter Leffkowitz's Tall Pony Ranch in Parkville, Missouri, chop wood, muck out stalls, stack hay, and feed horses. Much like Tom Sawyer, Leffkowitz may be the only person who can get companies to pay anywhere from $25,000–$50,000 to clean out his own barn. At Tall Pony, senior-level executives get to see whether their team members can adapt to new tasks—like rounding up stray "dogies." And, if somebody dares to free ride and not cut their share of firewood, everyone gets really cold in about 15 minutes. However, it is not always easy to get high-powered executives to step out of themselves and see how they affect their team. On one occasion, Leffkowitz saddled up a particularly arrogant sales manager atop a mule and sent him down the steepest, most gnarly trail on the premises. The manager was mad as a hornet, but "he sure found out how his team would feel if he mounted them on a program that they weren't prepared to ride" (Balf, 2000, p. 86).

## Transparency Illusion

People believe that their thoughts, attitudes, and reasons are much more transparent—that is, obvious to others—than is actually the case (Gilovich, Savitsky, & Medvec, 1998). For example, members of teams often have no idea what their leaders are thinking, but the leaders believe they are being perfectly clear. Part of the reason for the transparency illusion is that people find it impossible to put themselves in the position of the receiver. For example, when people are told to "tap out with their fingers" famous songs such as "Happy Birthday," they significantly overestimate the likelihood that a listener will understand which song they are tapping—but the listeners hardly ever do! (Griffin & Ross, 1991). Perhaps it is for this reason that most communicators overestimate their effectiveness. In short, people expect others to understand them more often than others actually do (Keysar & Henly, 2002).

## Indirect Speech Acts

Each statement one person makes to another has an intended meaning that is couched in casual conversation. **Indirect speech acts** are the ways in which people ask others to do things—but in indirect ways. For example, consider the various ways of requesting that a person shut a door (see Table 5-1). Each statement can serve as a request to perform that act although (except for "close the door") the sentence forms are not requests but assertions and questions. Thus, statements 2 through 9 are indirect speech acts; a listener's understanding of the intention behind a communicator's intention requires an extra cognitive step or two—and can often fail, especially in cases of stress.

Indirect speech acts are a function of the magnitude of the request being made (i.e., trivial requests, such as asking someone for the time of day, are easy to accommodate; asking someone if you can have a job is much more difficult to accommodate), the power the recipient has over the sender, and the social distance in the culture (Brown & Levinson, 1987). Thus, as the magnitude of requests increases, the power distance increases, and the social distance increases, requests made by team members will become more indirect. Of course, indirectness can be disastrous for effective communication.

**TABLE 5-1** Different Ways to Make a Request that Require Progressively More Inferences and Assumed Common Knowledge on the Part of the Receiver

1. Close the door.
2. Can you close the door?
3. Would you close the door?
4. It might help to close the door.
5. Would you mind awfully if I asked you to close the door?
6. Did you forget the door?
7. How about a little less breeze?
8. It's getting cold in here.
9. I really don't want the cats to get out of the house.

*Sources:* Adapted from Krauss, R. M., & Fussell, S. R. 1996. "Social Psychological Models of Interpersonal Communication." In E. T. Higgins, & A. W. Kruglanski (Eds.), *Social Psychology: Handbook of Basic Principles* (pp. 655–701). New York: Guilford; Levinson, S. C. 1983. *Pragmatics* (p. 264). Cambridge, England: Cambridge University Press.

### Uneven Communication

The **uneven communication problem** refers to the fact that in virtually any group, a handful of people do the majority of the talking. For example, in a typical 4-person group, two people do over 70 percent of the talking; in a 6-person group, three people do over 86 percent of the talking; and in a group of eight, three people do 77 percent of the talking. This would not ordinarily be a problem, except for the fact that the people who do the majority of the talking may not be the people who are the most informed about the problem. Figure 5-1 plots the percentage of communication attributed to each member in groups of four, six, and eight members; in all cases, communication is uneven and skewed.

## INTELLECTUAL BANDWIDTH

A team's **intellectual bandwidth** is an upper boundary on their ability to solve problems and achieve their goals. To create value, teams must search for knowledge, share it, and bring it to bear on their goals. Consider Figure 5-2, in which the process of understanding transitions through levels of abstraction (Bellinger, Castro, & Mills, 2000; Nunamaker, Romano, & Briggs, 2002).

- *Data: Understanding symbols.* In understanding data, team members need to understand the meaning of symbols in a particular context, as data have no meaning outside the context.

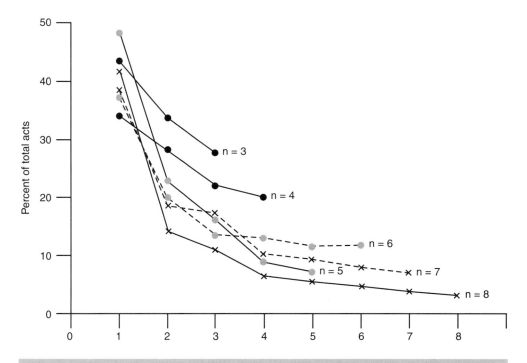

**FIGURE 5-1**  Distribution of Participation As a Function of Group Size
*Source:* Shaw, M. E. 1981. *Group Dynamics: The Psychology of Small Group Behavior* (3rd ed., pp. 170). New York: McGraw-Hill. Reprinted with permission.

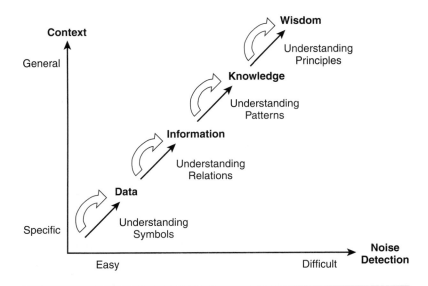

**FIGURE 5-2** The Hierarchy of Understanding
*Source:* Nunamaker, J. F., Jr., Romano, N. C., & Briggs, R. O. 2002. "Increasing
Intellectual Bandwidth: Generating Value from Intellectual Capital with
Information Technology." *Group Decision and Negotiation, 11,* 69–86.

- ***Information: Understanding relationships among symbols.*** In understanding information, team members understand relationships between data items.
- ***Knowledge: Understanding patterns in information.*** In understanding knowledge, team members must understand the patterns that emerge in information. Patterns are not relationships among data; they exist separately from information.
- ***Wisdom: Understanding principles.*** Wisdom entails understanding the cases and consequences in patterns.

To create value for the organization, teams must be able to share their intellectual capital. A team's intellectual bandwidth, therefore, is a function of its capacity to transform data into wisdom, but also its ability to collaborate (Nunamaker, Romano, & Briggs, 2002).

## THE INFORMATION DEPENDENCE PROBLEM

Teams presumably have access to a broader range of decision-making resources and, hence, should be better equipped to make high-quality decisions than any single person could alone. By pooling their different backgrounds, training, and experience, team members have the potential to work in a more informed fashion than would be the case if the decision were relegated to any single person. The fact that team members are dependent on one another for information is the **information dependence problem.** As an example of information dependence in groups and the dire consequences it can have, consider the case in Box 5-2.

When the team consists of members who come from different functional areas—with different areas of expertise, different information, different priorities, and differ-

---

BOX 5-2

## Information Dependence

"In 1955, the Centers for Disease Control took the responsibility of evaluating the polio vaccine developed by Jonas Salk. In late 1954, six vaccine manufacturers met with the Division of Biological Standards, with Jonas Salk, and others. Some of them had been having problems with inactivation of the virus during the process of vaccine manufacture. While one of the manufacturers was explaining that his company had been more efficient and successful at inactivating the virus, a representative from one of the other manufacturers had a telephone call, left the room, and came back after the discussion. Within two weeks after the beginning of the nationwide vaccination program in April 1955, CDC began to get reports of polio. What was significant was that these children had received the vaccine 6–8 days earlier and had developed polio, almost invariably in the arm or leg where they received the shot. Of the six reported cases, the vaccine contaminated with the live virus was manufactured by the laboratory whose representative took the phone call during the discussion on inactivating the virus" (Larson & LaFasto, 1989, p. 46).

---

ent perceptions of problems and opportunities—the information dependence problem is even more pronounced. The challenge is finding a way to quickly and efficiently pool all the relevant information in a coordinated fashion. Thus, a central issue facing any group charged with making a collective decision is how to get the ideas, information, and expertise in each person's head onto the table for all to see.

## The Common Information Effect

Pooling unique information in a team is valuable. Rehashing commonly known information or "stating the obvious" is largely a waste of time. Unfortunately, unique information does not readily emerge in team interaction; rather, teams tend to discuss what everyone already knows. This team fallacy is known as the **common information effect** (Gigone & Hastie, 1997). Consider a typical group decision-making task in the ABC Company. A three-member top-executive committee, Allen, Booz, and Catz, is charged with the task of hiring a new manager for an important division within the ABC firm. The company has determined that six pieces of information are critical to evaluate in a candidate for this position:

- Previous experience (A)
- Academic grades (B)
- Standardized test scores (C)
- Performance in round 1 interview (D)
- Cultural and international experience (E)
- Letters of recommendation (F)

Allen, Booz, and Catz have narrowed the competition down to three candidates: Kate, Ken, and Kerry. As is standard practice in the company, members of the hiring committee specialize in obtaining partial information about each candidate. Stated another way, each member of the hiring committee has some of the facts about each candidate, but not all of the facts. Thus, Allen, Booz, and Catz are information dependent on one another.

What will happen when they discuss various candidates for the job? Consider three possible distributions of information (see Figure 5-3):

- *Nonoverlapping case:* Each partner, Allen, Booz, and Catz, has unique information about each candidate.
- *Distributed, partial overlap:* Each partner knows something about each candidate that others also know (common information), but also knows some unique information.
- *Fully shared case:* Each partner knows full information about each candidate. In this sense, the partners are **informational clones** of one another.

The only difference among these three cases is the **information redundancy,** or how equally the information is distributed among decision makers. The collective intel-

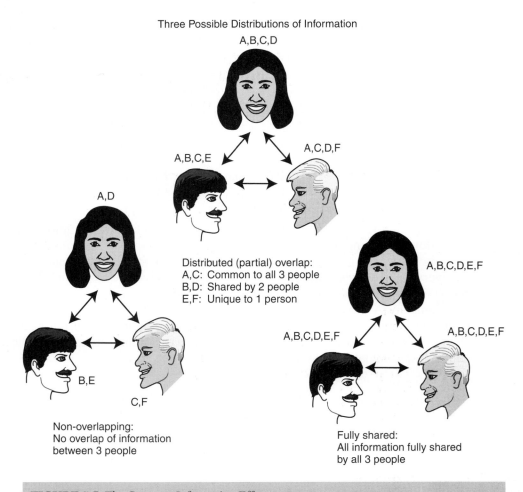

Three Possible Distributions of Information

Distributed (partial) overlap:
A,C: Common to all 3 people
B,D: Shared by 2 people
E,F: Unique to 1 person

Non-overlapping:
No overlap of information
between 3 people

Fully shared:
All information fully shared
by all 3 people

**FIGURE 5-3** The Common Information Effect

ligence of the partners is identical in all three cases. Does the distribution of information affect the way the partners make decisions? In a rational world, it should not, but in real teams, it does.

The impact of information on the aggregate decision of the team is directly related to the number of members of the team who know the information prior to making a group decision. Stated simply, *information held by more members before team discussion has more influence on team judgments than information held by fewer members, independent of the validity of the information.*

This means that even though (in an objective sense) the six pieces of information are really equally important, the top management group will tend to overemphasize information (such as A and C in the distributed case) more than is warranted.

The common information effect has several important consequences. First, team members are more likely to discuss information that everyone knows, as opposed to unique information that each may have. As a consequence, decisions will be biased in the direction of whatever information happens to be commonly shared. This often means that technical information (which is often not fully shared) is not given the weight that experts believe it should have. Information that people have in common is not only more likely to be discussed, but it also gets discussed for a longer period of time, and this too can exert a significant bias on the integrity of decision making.

The bottom line is that teams often fail to make the decision that would be supported if all the team members had full information about the choices.

## Hidden Profile

A **hidden profile** is a superior decision alternative, but its superiority is hidden from group members because each member has only a portion of the information that supports this superior alternative (Stasser, 1988). Stated another way, the information held in common by group members favors a particular choice, whereas the unshared information contradicts the choice.

Let's consider an executive meeting, in which three different candidates (Alva, Jane, and Bill) are up for promotion to partner in the organization—obviously, an extremely important decision. Each of the three potential candidates has been with the company for some number of years; each has made a different number and type of accomplishments. The executive group can only promote one person for the position at this time.

In theory, the executive group can benefit the organization by pooling individual members' information so as to gain a complete picture of the qualifications of each candidate. This is particularly important when individual members of the decision-making team are biased by virtue of their own agendas.

However, free-style discussion may be an ineffective way of disseminating information, because information that is known to only one or a few members will often be omitted from discussion (Stasser & Titus, 1985). Team members are not only more likely to mention information if it was known to all before discussion, but are also more likely to bring it up repeatedly and dwell on it throughout the discussion. Thus, the team decision will often reflect the common knowledge shared by members before discussion rather than the diverse knowledge emanating from their unique perspectives and experiences.

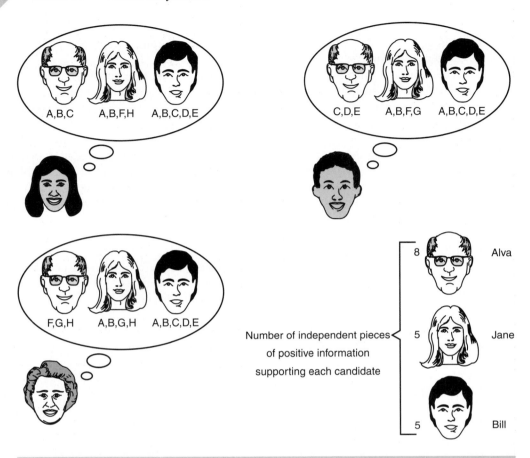

**FIGURE 5-4** Hidden Profiles

Consider the scenario in Figure 5-4. In this situation, the initial bias favors Bill. At the outset of the meeting, each team member has more information about him (five pieces of information). The information the team has about Bill is fully shared, meaning that all team members are apprised of this candidate's qualifications prior to the meeting. Obviously, Bill has done an excellent job of marketing his own achievements within the organization!

However, consider Alva, who has a combined total of eight pieces of favorable information supporting his candidacy for the partnership. However, each member of the executive team is privy only to three pieces of information about this candidate, and the information is not redundant. In an objective sense, Alva is by far the most qualified; yet his accomplishments are not fully shared among the top-management team—a factor that will not be corrected with discussion (at least unstructured discussion).

If this team were immune to the common information effect, and optimally combined and pooled their unique information, a hidden profile would emerge. *A hidden profile is a conclusion that is only apparent after team members have fully shared information.* In this case, Alva would prevail.

Common information also affects people's memory for team discussions. People recall fewer unshared arguments from team discussion (Stasser & Titus, 1985, 1987). Moreover, analysis of tape-recorded discussions reveals that unshared arguments are less likely to be expressed (Stasser, Taylor, & Hanna, 1989).

The reliance on previously shared information is not an optimal use of team resources because uniquely held or previously unshared information may be most enlightening for the team as a whole. Unstructured, free-style discussion, even among trained professionals who have every motivation to make an accurate diagnosis, is insufficient for ensuring the quality of outcomes. (For an illustration of the inability of professionals to share relevant information, see Box 5-3.)

---

## BOX 5-3

### Hidden Profiles in Medical Diagnosis

Professional teams are created for a number of important reasons. For example, in medicine, the use of teaching rounds, interdisciplinary consults, and case conferences serves both clinical and educational functions. Collaborative efforts of this sort are designed to ensure that relevant information is brought to bear on important clinical decisions, to facilitate the coordinated action of experts toward appropriate treatment goals, and to train novices. Consider how clinical teams composed of a resident, intern, and third-year medical student arrive at patient diagnoses on the basis of case information (Christensen, Larson, Abbott, Ardolino, Franz, & Pfeiffer, 1998). (For example, the management of a seriously ill geriatric patient may require input from specialties and subspecialties such as internal medicine, pulmonology, and oncology, as well as from nurses and nutritionists.) Prior to discussion, team members may individually review different versions of a videotaped interview with a patient actor. Each videotape contains some information that is present in all three versions (shared information) and some that is present in only that version (unique information). In addition, some patient case profiles are constructed so that unique information that appeared in only one tape was crucial for a correct diagnosis (i.e., "hidden profile" situation). After viewing the tapes, the team members meet to discuss the case and develop a differential diagnosis for the patient.

These medical specialists were not immune to the common information effect. Shared information about the patient was mentioned more often (67 percent) than was unique information (46 percent). More disconcerting, teams offered incorrect diagnoses substantially more often for the "hidden profile" patient case than for the "standard" patient cases: Overall, 17 of the 24 hidden profile cases were diagnosed correctly (a hit rate of about 70 percent), whereas all of the shared information cases were correctly diagnosed. Clearly, the medical teams' overreliance on previously shared information and the inability to appropriately utilize unique information were detrimental when a correct diagnosis demanded the inclusion of such information.

## Practices to Put in Place

There are ways to avoid the biases induced by the common information effect and hidden profiles. We want to point out first, however, some "obvious" solutions that do not work, either because they actually reinforce the problem or do not address the problem adequately.

### *Things That Don't Work*

**Increasing the Amount of Discussion**   It would seem that, if teams had more time to discuss a matter or issue, they would eventually discuss what they do not have in common. However, even when teams are explicitly told to spend more time discussing information, they still fall prey to the common information effect (Parks & Cowlin, 1996).

**Separating Review and Decisions**   It would seem reasonable to structure the group discussion by dividing deliberations into two parts: Review the information available in the first phase and then, making decisions and judgments in the second phase. However, this is not effective; teams simply discuss what they already know during the first phase. For example, in one investigation, team members were given instructions intended to curb the common information effect (Stasser et al., 1989). Team members avoided stating their initial preferences and were encouraged to review all relevant facts. These instructions did increase the *amount* of discussion that occurred, but the discussion primarily favored those facts initially shared by team members (67 percent of all shared facts were discussed in contrast to 23 percent of unshared facts).

**Increasing the Size of the Team**   As team size increases, but the distribution of information stays the same, the tendency to discuss common information increases. For example, the bias is more pronounced in 6-person groups than 3-person groups. In a typical 3-person group, 46 percent of shared information is mentioned, in contrast to only 18 percent of unshared information. This difference is even larger for 6-person groups (Stasser et al., 1989). Moreover, if unique information is held by racially diverse members, even less information is being shared (Sawyer, Houlette, & Muzzy, 2002).

**Increasing Information Load**   If members of the team are given additional information, but the relative distribution of information remains the same, the common information effect still plagues the team (Stasser, 1992; Stasser & Titus, 1987). In fact, the bias to discuss shared information is most likely to occur when there is a large number of "shared" facts to discuss.

**Accountability**   Accountability refers to the extent to which people and teams feel responsible for their actions and decisions. Surprisingly, accountable teams are less likely to focus on unshared information than groups that are not held accountable (Stewart, Billings, & Stasser, 1998). For example, the medical teams described in Box 5-3 were videotaped and told to come up with a correct diagnosis that would be evaluated; yet they still overrelied on previously shared information and, consequently, misdiagnosed the case. Why doesn't accountability help? The problem is that accountable teams focus on the wrong thing—shared information.

**Prediscussion Polling**   One of the most common strategies for beginning a discussion is polling the group. In a sense, group members want to know where everyone stands. However, this strategy can have extremely negative effects on the quality of the discussion that follows if the initial preferences of the team members are based on insufficient information. If the group is unanimous, it is inevitably concluded that there is little or no need for discussion. Furthermore, the very act of polling triggers conformity pressure, such that lower-status group members, anxious to secure their position in the organization, may agree with the majority. Kelly and Karau's (1999) investigation of teams in a management simulation deciding which of two cholesterol-reducing drugs to market revealed that initial preferences were the major determinants of the group's final decision.

### Effective Interventions

Fortunately, there are ways to successfully combat the common information effect. They have one thing in common: They put the team leader in the position of an **information manager.** In fact, having a leader in the team can be an advantage in itself: Team leaders are consistently more likely than are other members to ask questions and repeat unshared (as well as shared) information (Larson, Christensen, Franz, & Abbott, 1998). Leaders can play an important information management role during team discussion by focusing the team's attention, facilitating communication, stimulating member contributions, and ensuring that critical information brought out during discussion is "kept alive" and factored into the team's final decision. The type of leader is also important. Directive leaders are more likely than participative leaders to repeat unshared information and, consequently, identify the best options (Larson, Foster-Fishman, & Franz, 1998). Leaders with more experience are also more effective (Wittenbaum, 1998). The common information effect can be substantially reduced when the leader actively does the following:

**Redirects and Maintains the Focus of the Discussion to Unshared (Unique) Information**    The leader should be aware that some information is common to all members, whereas other information is not. The leader should be persistent in directing the focus of the discussion to unique information. The leader must work against the natural tendency of the team to retreat to the comfortable by discussing and rehashing facts they already know. Furthermore, the leader must reintroduce noncommon information after it has been dismissed. The longer the delay in mentioning unique items of information, the lower the team's performance (Kim, 1997).

**Labels the Task As a "Problem" to Be Solved, Not a "Judgment" to Be Made**    Subtle differences in wording of the team's goal dramatically affect the way people think and process information. Leaders can take a proactive role in this process by labeling the task as a "problem" to be solved with "demonstrable evidence" and explicitly state that they are not interested in personal opinion and judgment. Teams are less prone to overlook unshared information if they believe that their task has a demonstrably correct answer (Laughlin, 1980; Stasser & Stewart, 1992).

As an example, consider the instructions given to a panel of jurors. Members of the jury are explicitly told to pay attention to the facts and evidence of the case. They are cautioned that the lawyers representing the parties in the case are not witnesses but rather are attempting to sway members of the jury to adopt a particular belief. It is precisely for this reason that trial lawyers have an opportunity to dismiss potential jurors who are regarded as unable to consider the facts because their mind is already made up—that is, they enter the courtroom with a particular bias or belief.

**Ranks Rather Than Chooses** When teams are instructed to "rank" candidates or alternatives, they are more likely to make the best decision than when they are simply told to "choose" (Hollingshead, 1996b). The reason is that when teams are asked to choose, people make comparisons among candidates, and if the best candidate is a hidden profile, teams are likely to choose the wrong candidate. If teams can move away from choosing among candidates to estimating or predicting the performance of each individual candidate, an accurate, or data-based, choice is more likely (Gigone & Hastie, 1997).

**Considers the Decision Alternatives One at a Time** Leaders should make sure their team discusses one alternative fully before turning to the next (Larson, Foster-Fishman, & Keys, 1994). Otherwise, hidden profile alternatives may be prematurely rejected.

**Heightens Team Members' Awareness of the Types of Information Likely to Be Possessed by Different Individuals** When team members are publicly identified, the likelihood that unshared clues will be mentioned during discussion increases (Stasser, Stewart, & Wittenbaum, 1995). For example, when team members know who has expertise in specific knowledge domains, the amount of unshared information discussed increases significantly (Stasser, 1988; Stasser, Stewart, & Wittenbaum, 1995). This creates important metaknowledge for the team (Larson & Christensen, 1993). However, the metaknowledge must be accurate.

**Suspends Initial Judgment** Probably one of the most effective strategies for avoiding the common information effect is to caution team members against arriving at a judgment prior to the team discussion of the candidates. Indeed, the common information effect is a direct result of the biases that people bring to discussion, not the team discussion itself (Gigone & Hastie, 1993). The more group members choose the same alternative prior to the group discussion, the more strongly the group prefers information supporting that alternative (Schulz-Hardt, Frey, Lüthgens, & Moscovici, 2000).

**Builds Trust and Familiarity among Team Members** Although it seems obvious, the practical implications are profound. Teams that trust one another more are more likely to make use of nonredundant types of information. Team members who are familiar with one another are less likely to make poor decisions resulting from the common information effect than are teams whose members are unacquainted (Gruenfeld, Mannix, Williams, & Neale, 1996). However, groups that have both task and team experience show a greater propensity toward discussing common information (Kim, 1997).

**Communicates Confidence** The communication of confidence is a subjective measure of how sure team members are about what they are saying. Teams whose members are encouraged to express confidence about their decisions and judgments perform more effectively and learn significantly more from their interaction than do teams whose ability to communicate confidence during interaction is reduced (Bloomfield, Libby, & Nelson, 1996).

**Minimizes Status Differences** In one investigation, groups contained either equal-status members or unequal-status members (Hollingshead, 1996a). In some of these groups, the critical information required to make the best decision was given only to the low-status member. As compared with equal-status groups, mixed-status groups made poorer decisions and made fewer references to the critical information than the equal-status groups.

## COLLECTIVE INTELLIGENCE

### Team Mental Models

**Mental models** are mental representations of the world that allow people to understand, predict, and solve problems in a given situation (Gentner & Gentner, 1983; Johnson-Laird, 1980; Rouse & Morris, 1986). Mental models reflect people's experiences and expectations and guide their behaviors in different situations. Mental models organize information and knowledge about a problem and influence how people interpret information. Mental models can represent many different problems and systems. They can be models of a simple physical system, such as the trajectory of a thrown object; on the other hand, mental models can represent a complex social system, such as an organization or financial system. Mental models are not always accurate. Yet, mental models influence the process by which people and teams go about solving particular problems—what information they seek, how they combine it, how they formulate plans, and how they enact them.

A **team mental model** is a common understanding that members of a group or team share about how something works (Klimoski & Mohammed, 1997). From this, members form expectations about what others will do in a given situation. Team members do not come equipped with hardwired mental models; they are acquired by learning and experience. Team members not only have mental models about the work they do, they also have mental models about the the operation of their team. Consider, for example, the mental models that team members might have for how their team functions:

- *Manufactured product model:* Some people understand teams as manufactured products, such that well-made ones "last" and "work" and poorly constructed ones "fall apart" and "break."
- *Journey:* Some people reason that teamwork is like an ongoing journey in which team members "travel" through good times and bad times.
- *Sports model:* Some people understand teamwork to be a sport such that they need to practice, compete, score, and win.
- *Marriage model:* Some people understand teamwork to be like a marriage vow, in which they make commitments to one another that last through time.

These different models of teamwork are neither right nor wrong; the important point is that they can influence how team members try to deal with problems in the team, conflict, and a host of other internal dynamics. If team members have different (and perhaps conflicting) mental models about their team, this can lead to conflict.

There are two key considerations in terms of the mental models that members have about their actual work: the *accuracy* of the model and the degree of *correspondence* (or noncorrespondence) between members' models.

#### Accuracy

As an illustration of what we mean by accuracy, suppose that you are asked to explain how the thermostat in your house operates (Kempton, 1986, 1987). According to one (erroneous) model, the "valve" model, the thermostat works much like the accelerator in a car. People who hold a valve mental model of a thermostat reason that just as greater depression of the accelerator causes the car's speed to increase at a faster rate, turning the thermostat setting to high temperatures causes the room temperature to increase at a faster rate.

A different (and correct) mental model is the "threshold" model, in which the heat is either on or off and the thermostat setting determines the duration for which the heat is on. The greater the discrepancy between the current room temperature and the thermostat setting, the longer the heat will be on. These two models have different implications for how people set the thermostat in their homes. People with valve models will continuously adjust their thermostat setting in an effort to reach a comfortable room temperature. In contrast, those with threshold models will determine at what temperature they are comfortable and set the thermostat to only one or two settings per day, a nighttime setting and a daytime setting. Indeed, after interviewing people to determine the mental models they use to understand the operation of a thermostat, Kempton revisited thermostat records and showed that people's models of how thermostats operate predicted the stability of their actual thermostat settings.

This simple analogy illustrates an important aspect of the use of mental models in problem solving: The use of an incorrect mental model can result in inefficient or undesirable outcomes. People with an incorrect mental representation of a thermostat as a valve will spend greater time and effort adjusting the thermostat setting. In addition, they will be perpetually uncomfortable because they will either be too warm or too cold.

There are several implications for teamwork. If team members hold erroneous mental models concerning the task at hand (either because they lack technical training or communicate poorly), their well-intentioned behaviors could produce disastrous results.

*Correspondence*

Let's now turn to the question of correspondence between members' models. Effective teams are able to adapt to external demands and anticipate other members' information needs because of shared or compatible knowledge structures or team mental models. For example, when novel or unexpected events are encountered (such as when an airplane enters another's airspace), teams that cannot strategize overtly must rely on preexisting knowledge and expectations about how the team must perform in order to cope with task demands. The greater the overlap or commonality among team members' mental models, the greater the likelihood that team members will predict the needs of the task and team, adapt to changing demands, and coordinate activity with one another successfully (Cannon-Bowers, Salas, & Converse, 1993; Cannon-Bowers, Tannenbaum, Salas, & Converse, 1991). For example, the negative effects of fatigue on air crew performance can be overcome when crews develop interaction patterns over time (Foushee, Lauber, Baetge, & Comb, 1986). And, an investigation of 69 software development teams revealed that "expertise coordination"—the shared knowledge of who knows what—was a key predictor of team performance over and above expertise and administrative coordination (Faraj & Sproull, 2000).

The following example, taken from Perrow's (1984) book on normal accidents, illustrates the concepts of accuracy and correspondence:

On a beautiful night in October, 1978, in the Chesapeake Bay, two vessels sighted one another visually and on radar. On one of them, the Coast Guard cutter training vessel *Cuyahoga,* the captain (a chief warrant officer) saw the other ship up ahead as a small object on the radar, and visually he saw two lights, indicating that it was proceeding in the same direction as his own ship. He thought it possibly was a fishing vessel. The first mate saw the lights, but saw three, and estimated (correctly) that it was a ship proceeding toward them. He had no responsibility to inform the captain, nor did he think he needed to. Since the two ships drew together so rapidly, the captain decided that it must be a very slow fishing boat that he was about to overtake. This reinforced his incorrect interpretation. The lookout knew the captain was aware of the ship, so did not comment further as it got quite close and seemed to be nearly on a collision course. Since both ships were traveling full speed, the closing came fast. The other ship, a large cargo ship, did not establish any bridge-to-bridge communication, because the passing was routine. But at the last moment, the captain of the *Cuyahoga* realized that in overtaking the supposed fishing boat, which he assumed was on a near parallel course, he would cut off that boat's ability to turn as both of them approached the Potomac River. So he ordered a turn to the port. (p. 215)

The two ships collided, killing eleven sailors on the Coast Guard vessel. Clearly, the captain's mental model was incorrect. In addition, there was a lack of correspondence between the captain and the first mate's mental models.

## The Team Mind: Transactive Memory Systems

As capable as the human information-processing system is, it is insufficient for most organizational work. For this reason, people rely on others for the information they need. Thus, many people supplement their own memories, which are known to be highly limited and unreliable, with various external aids. For example, objects such as address or appointment books allow us to store and retrieve important information externally rather than in our own long-term memory. Similarly, other people (e.g., friends, family, coworkers, and teammates) also function as external memory aids.

A **transactive memory system (TMS)** is a group-level information-processing system that is an extension of the human information-processing system: A shared system for attending to, encoding, storing, processing, and retrieving information (Wegner, 1986; Wegner, Giuliano, & Hertel, 1995). Think of transactive memory systems as a division of mental labor. The key to an effective TMS is a shared knowledge base. In short, when each person learns in some general way what the other persons on the team may know in detail, team members can share detailed memories. In essence, each team member cultivates the other members as external memory and, in doing so, they become part of a larger system. A TMS develops implicitly in many teams to ensure that important information is not forgotten. A TMS is a combination of two things: *knowledge* possessed by particular team members and *awareness* of who knows what. In this way, a TMS serves as an external storage device, such as a library or computer that can be visited to retrieve otherwise unavailable information. Teams that have a TMS have access to more and better information than any single group member does alone.

To see how a TMS might work within a team, consider a team composed of a finance, marketing, and production manager. The team members would expect that the person from finance would remember details concerning costs or profitability; the person from marketing would remember the results of a study concerning how customers responded to test marketing; and the production person would remember details about the mechanics of making the product. In other words, the other members of the team instinctively expect that the "experts" on the team will remember the details most closely associated with their area of expertise. Even when the experts are not so clearly defined, people still seem to specialize in remembering certain kinds of information, and it is generally understood by all members of the team (although often implicitly) which person is to remember what. This way of processing information provides an advantage to teams because they can collectively remember and utilize more information than can individuals acting on their own—even the same number of individuals considered separately.

The main disadvantage is that team members are dependent on one another for knowledge and information. Teams who have been working together for years find it nearly impossible to reconstruct interactions with clients and other shared experiences without the other team members present.

What does a TMS do for teams? How does it affect productivity in terms of the key dimensions of performance criteria? More important, how can the manager best capitalize on the strengths of a TMS while minimizing the liabilities?

### Tacit Coordination

Tacit coordination is the synchronization of members' actions based on assumptions about what others on the team are likely to do. This is important because task-oriented groups rarely discuss plans for how to perform their tasks unless they are explicitly instructed to do so (Hackman & Morris, 1975). Team members' attempts to coordinate tacitly begin prior to interaction. Evaluating the competence of other team members can be difficult, however. Claims of personal competence by coworkers cannot always be trusted, because they may reflect members' desires to impress one another (Gardner, 1992). Accepting coworkers' evaluations of one another's competence can be risky as well because these secondhand evaluations are often based on limited information (Gilovich, 1987) and may reflect impression-management efforts by the people who provide them (Cialdini, 1989). Knowing who is good at what is valuable for a team because it can improve the team's performance in several ways. For instance, it becomes easier to plan activities so that the people most suited for a particular task actually become responsible for that task. Similarly, coordinating actions and dealing with unexpected problems is easier when team members know who is good at what.

### The TMS and Team Performance

Teams that have a TMS generally perform better than teams that do not in tasks that require memory and retrieval of information. The TMS eliminates a lot of the coordination loss that can plague team effectiveness (Moreland, Argote, & Krishnan, 1998). Teams that have a transactive memory structure because its members are familiar with one another are less likely to fall prey to the common information effect as compared with teams composed of previously unacquainted persons (Gruenfeld et al., 1996). Thus, the key question for the manager is how to ensure that teams develop an accurate TMS.

Probably the most straightforward way is to simply ask members of the team to indicate what knowledge bases the other members of the group possess. If there is high intrateam agreement, the TMS is higher than if there is low agreement about who knows what.

Consider, for example, how submarines are developed. In the past, the U.S. Navy used what were conventional, industrial-age techniques: Engineers would use pencil, paper, and wood models and then "throw the plans over the wall" to the shipbuilder. In the development of newer model submarines, such as the Virginia-class submarine, the Navy used a more collaborative process (Rosenfeld, 2000). The Electric Boat Corporation, primary contractor for the Navy's nuclear fast-attack submarine, reconstituted its departmental structure into 11 cross-functional teams, each one corresponding to a vertical slice of the submarine: stern, engine room, reactor component, and so on. Moreover, the flight crews, who actually drive the machine, were made part of each team. The old model of teaming gave way to a new model in which collective responsibility and collective intelligence could flourish. Information gathering and collective knowledge were such important priorities that Captain Paul Sullivan started what came to be known as the "Good Ideas Database." He sent out a call for ideas to the entire fleet and collected 1,200 ideas (Rosenfeld, 2000).

### Developing a TMS in Teams

As TMS naturally seems to develop when a team works together over time. However, it may take quite a bit of time for a team to realize each member's strengths and to learn how to capitalize on those strengths in a coordinated fashion. Training is one of the most effective ways of ensuring that groups quickly and accurately develop a TMS.

The development of a team TMS begins with training. Training is widely used in organizations. The American Society for Training and Development (ASTD) reports that employers continued to spend more on training between 2000 and 2001, despite economic downturn and layoffs. Training expenditures (averaged across 376 companies) were $704 per employee in 2000, up 4 percent from $677 in 1999, according to the 2002 ASTD State of the Industry Report (*HR Focus,* 2002). These figures are likely to increase as a result of changes in the nature of work and characteristics of the workforce (Goldstein, 1989; "Labor Letter," 1992; Webb & Smith, 1991). A fundamental question that companies face is whether to train individuals independently or as part of a team. As a guiding principle, there should be a high degree of correspondence between workers' experiences during training and their experiences on the job. The key reason is that similar conditions will facilitate the transfer of knowledge learned in training to how individuals actually carry out their job. This type of state-dependent learning can be a strength of teamwork. Too often, learning is decontextualized from the work teams are doing.

People perform their work differently when they are working in teams than when they are alone. This means that individuals require different kinds of training when they work in teams than when they work alone or apart. People that will work together as a team should train together, because (among other reasons) even during training, a TMS will ensure that the right structure of information sharing and responsibility will develop. Training can be specifically geared toward developing specific TMS structures. For example, teams can plan who will be responsible for what types of information;

they can also make explicit efforts to discern expertise and then make that information known to members. Transactive memory training may be especially important when team members will only work together for a single project or when the team interacts with several other teams across the organization. It is important to align the unit of work—for example, individual, small team, large group—with the unit that is being trained. Therefore, when small teams will be working together, they should be trained together; when large groups will be working together, they should train together; when individuals will be working alone, it may be best to train them as individuals. ₋rgote (2002) studied surgery teams in a hospital and found that teams who had worked together performed more successful hip and knee surgeries, as compared with teams whose members were equally competent, but had not worked together.

Recall that in the last chapter, we reviewed three types of competencies for team members: technical skills, task-related skills, and interpersonal skills. If a company has limited resources for training, it is far better to ensure that employees who will work together receive their technical training together. If that is not feasible, the training that they do undergo together should be directly connected to the work they will do together. Merely having workers undergo interpersonal skills training together (that is largely divorced from the real work they will do together) can undermine performance.

A reasonable counterargument may be that even if people do not train together (and therefore do not develop a TMS and underperform initially), after working together for a while, they will inevitably develop a TMS. However, it should be recalled that the key to effective learning in most situations is the receipt of timely and effective feedback, so that workers can best recalibrate how they are doing their work. With some notable exceptions, clear feedback is not necessarily forthcoming to all newly minted teams. In fact, core teams may be pulled together for a single project that might last for several months; ideally, they should do some training together at the outset so as to better prepare them for the work they will do together in the future.

### *Example of Training in Work Groups*

As an illustration of the effect of a TMS on performance, simulated work groups were asked to assemble AM radios as part of a training experience (Moreland, Argote, & Krishnan, 1996). There were two ways in which the training was organized: (1) individually based training (as is common in many companies), and (2) group training, in which groups of three people worked together. In the training phase, all individuals and groups received identical information. Groups were not given any instructions in terms of how they should organize themselves. The *only* difference was whether people were trained alone or as part of a group.

Exactly one week later, the participants were asked to assemble the radios again. This was more difficult, because no written instructions were provided, as had been the case in the training phase. In this part of the investigation, everyone was placed into a three-person team, given the parts of the radio, and asked to assemble it from memory. This meant that some of the groups were composed of people who had trained individually and others were composed of people who had trained with a team. Thus, any difference in performance between the two types of groups would be attributable to the differences in training.

Not surprisingly, the groups that had trained together did dramatically better. They were more likely to successfully complete the assembly and did so with fewer errors. The intact groups performed better than did the ad hoc groups because they were able to tap into the TMS that had spontaneously developed during training.

A TMS and an emphasis on team training are most relevant to tactical teams (i.e., teams that carry out a procedure) as opposed to creative or problem-solving teams. Thus, if a team is assembling radio parts, operating machinery in a coal mine, flying a jetliner, or doing heart surgery, it helps a lot for the members to have trained together on the job. However, as we saw in the last chapter, teams do more than perform routinized procedures; sometimes teams need to solve problems or create things. For example, consider a company like Johnson and Johnson, dealing with a public relations nightmare: Someone has tampered with a bottle of Tylenol and people have died. Many things have to take place quickly, both to ensure the health and safety of customers, as well as to preserve the company's image and reputation as a quality firm concerned with the well-being of its customers. Obviously, this team cannot take the time to train together, but it probably does help if the people on the emergency task force have worked together and have a sense of each other's competence in particular areas. (See Box 5-4 for a case analysis of training effectiveness.)

*Recommendations for Team Development*

What are the ways to maximize team performance through a TMS? We present five fundamentals.

**Work Planning**    Teams whose members will work together should plan their work. Teams spend a disproportionate amount of their time together doing the task, rather than deciding how it should be done. Team tasks, unlike individual tasks, require coordination of effort and planning. There is a strong bias in teams to get down to work immediately and to get busy, if for no other reason than to signal to relevant organizational authorities that they are hard at work. Team members often wish they would have spent more time thinking about how they should do their work together before jumping into it.

**Optimizing Human Resources**    Teams should assess relevant areas of expertise among team members. Teams perform better when their members know who is good at what (Stasser et al., 1995). For example, when bank loan officers review the financial profiles of various companies and predict whether each company will go bankrupt, diversity in expertise and the ability of groups to recognize expertise lead to more accurate predictions (Libby, Trotman, & Zimmer, 1987). Unexpected problems can be solved more quickly and easily when members know who is good at what (Moreland & Levine, 1992). Such knowledge allows team members to match problems with the people most likely to solve them. People learn and recall more information in their own area of expertise when their partner has different, rather than similar, work-related expertise (Hollingshead, 2000).

**Anticipation in Addition to Reaction**    Teams should learn to anticipate problems, not just react to them. They are better able to do this if they know one another's strengths and weaknesses.

BOX 5-4

## Case Analysis of Different Types of Training Effectiveness

### PRELIMINARY INVESTIGATION

At a certain factory that assembles radios, a consultant was called in to assess variations in performance. To create healthy within-company competition, workers were organized into self-managing teams. There were four such teams in the plant, but performance varied dramatically across the four teams. What was the problem?

The consultant began her investigation by asking for information about how the different teams were trained. She uncovered four distinct training programs used by each of the teams. Upon interviewing each team in the plant, she found that each team was convinced that its method was the best one. When the consultant confronted teams with the evidence pointing to clear differences in performance, the team pointed to a number of countervailing factors that could have affected their performance. The managers were particularly concerned because the company was about to hire and train four new plant teams and they did not know which method would be best. The consultant devised the following test using the radio assembly task previously described (based upon Liang, Moreland, & Argote, 1995). Everyone in the entire plant received identical technical training and ultimately performed in a three-person group. However, certain aspects of the training were systematically varied. The consultant tracked the following teams:

- **Red team:** Members of the red team were trained individually for 1 day.
- **Blue team:** Members of the blue team were given individual training for one day and then, the entire team participated in a two-day team-building workshop, designed to improve cohesion and communication.

- **Yellow team:** Members of the yellow team were given group training for one day but were reassigned to different teams on the test day.
- **Green team:** Members of the green team were given group training for one day and remained in the same team on test day.

### TEST DAY

On test day, the consultant wanted to capture the four key measures of team performance outlined in Chapter 2. Whereas the hiring organization seemed primarily interested in productivity—as measured by number of units successfully completed—the consultant was also interested in assessing other signs of team performance, such as cohesion, learning, and integration.

The consultant first asked each team to recall as much as they could about the training. In short, each team was asked to reconstruct the assembly instructions from memory. The consultant used this as a measure of organizational memory.

The consultant then asked each team to assemble the radios without the benefit of any kind of written instructions. Thus, each team was forced to rely on the training principles they had learned and (hopefully) remembered. Results were timed so that each team could be evaluated with respect to both efficiency and how accurately they met specifications.

Then, the consultant asked each team member to evaluate other team members in terms of their task expertise. This was a measure of the tendency to specialize in remembering distinct aspects of the task, as well as who was regarded by all team members as having a certain, relevant skill. The consultant videotaped each team during the critical test phase and documented how smoothly members worked together in terms of the principles of coordination (discussed in Chapter 2). Specifically, did members drop things unintentionally on the floor? Lose parts? Bump elbows? Have to repeat questions and directions? Question each others' expertise and knowledge? Or, alternatively, did the team work together seamlessly?

The tapes revealed the level of team motivation and also allowed the consultant to document things like how close members of the team sat to one another and the tone of their conversation. Finally, the consultant recorded the "we-to-I" ratio, or the number of times team members said "we" versus "I"—an implicit measure of team identity and cohesion. What do you think happened?

## OUTCOME

The green team outperformed all of the other teams in terms of accuracy of completion.

## DEBRIEFING WITH MANAGERS

One of the managers found it difficult to believe that team training received by the blue team in the area of cohesion and interpersonal skills did not make an appreciable difference. "We spend a lot of money every year trying to build trust and cohesion in our teams. Is this going to waste?" The consultant then shared the information in Figure 5-5.

The results in Figure 5-5 directly compare teams with a total of six weeks of working intensively with one another on cohesion-building (non-technical-skill building) tasks with teams who are virtual strangers, with the exception of having trained together. As you can see, the fewest number of errors were made by groups who trained with one another and then worked with one another; having special training in cohesion on top of that does not seem to matter much.

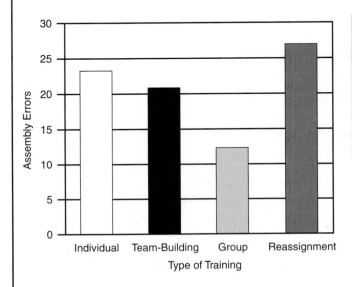

**FIGURE 5-5** Effects of Various Training Methods on Assembly Errors
*Source:* Moreland, R. L., Argote, L., & Krishnan, R. 1996. "Socially Shared Cognition at Work." In J. L. Nye & A. M. Brower (Eds.). In *What's Social about Social Cognition?* Thousand Oaks, CA: Sage. Reprinted by permission.

**Teams That Will Work Together Should Train Together**    Most organizations emphasize individual learning in their training programs. Participants in these programs work on their own, under the guidance of instructors, to learn how various tasks should be performed. The fact that they may later perform those tasks in teams is largely ignored. Some training programs include team activities, of course, but these often focus on general topics (Oddou, 1987; Silberman, 1990; Tetrault, Schriescheim, & Neider, 1988). Teams whose members work and train together perform better than teams whose members are equally skilled but do not train together (Hollingshead, 1998; Littlepage, Robison, & Reddington, 1997). Team training increases performance by facilitating recognition and utilization of member expertise.

Some organizations train team members together; for example, General Motors, at its Saturn automobile manufacturing plant, or the U.S. Army unit personnel replacement system (Griffith, 1989). Airlines often provide team training for cockpit crews (Oberle, 1990). The importance of work group familiarity vis-à-vis training is hard to overestimate. For example, archival analysis of coal mine accidents and fatalities reveals that familiarity among team members is associated with fewer accidents among pairs of crew members working closely together (e.g., roof bolters and bolter helpers; Goodman & Garber, 1988). Although familiarity with the terrain has somewhat more impact than personnel similarity, the latter factor is clearly important, especially when teams work in less familiar terrain. Familiarity is associated with higher levels of crew productivity, even after labor, technology, and environment factors are taken into account (Goodman & Leyden, 1991).

**Plan for Turnover**    At some point, teams dissolve; a member leaves or is transferred and the team is left to find a replacement. Sometimes turnover is planned; other times it is unanticipated. Turnover can be a disruptive factor in teams, largely because newcomers and old-timers are unfamiliar with one another. However, much of the potential damage of turnover can be averted by strengthening team structure, such as assigning roles to members and prescribing work procedures (Devadas & Argote, 1995).

# TEAM LONGEVITY: ROUTINIZATION VERSUS INNOVATION TRADE-OFFS

Teams whose members work together for longer periods of time are more likely to develop a TMS and will, therefore, be more productive. However, there is a countervailing force at work in teams that have been together for long periods of time, namely, routinization. That is, because a TMS is basically a set of expectations, certain working relationships may become entrenched over time. For example, Joe always handles the design aspects, so the team can (implicitly) trust him to ensure the product will look good; Sally always handles the technical aspects, so the team can trust that she will make sure the product works; likewise for the channeling of information, and so on. This suggests that when delegation is optional (which a TMS does not ensure), and in a world in which the team's expectations about what is needed (e.g., consumer demand) are accurate, then more TMS should basically lead to more routinization of the task and, hence, to a more efficient channeling of efforts by team members (because there will be less coordination loss involved in understanding each team member's role). Such expectations would seem to be best when there is little need for innovation. Thus, there is a precarious trade-off of sorts between *routinization* and *innovation.*

For much of the work that organizations do, routinization is a good thing; however, for a large part of what organizations do, innovation is desirable and necessary to meet the competitive challenges we outlined in Chapter 1. Thus, a well-defined TMS could hinder the team's ability to be adaptive.

For these reasons, there may be significant problems associated with extended team longevity. As a case in point, let's examine an R&D facility of a large American corporation (Katz, 1982). The division, which included 345 engineers and scientific professionals, was geographically isolated from the rest of the organization. Katz examined 50 project groups in this division that varied greatly in terms of their longevity—that is, how long members of one group had worked with one another.

To keep informed about relevant developments outside the organization as well as new requirements within the organization, project groups must collect and process information from a variety of outside sources. The preferred means for obtaining such information for engineering professionals is interpersonal communication, rather than technical reports, publications, or other written documentation.

Therefore, for a period of 15 weeks, professionals kept records of their work-related communication; any time that a group member consulted or spoke with others, whether at the water cooler or in the parking lot, this was recorded.

As a final step, the department managers (a total of seven) and the two lab directors evaluated the performance of each project produced by each group with which they were technically familiar. Criteria that the managers considered included schedule, budget and cost performance, innovation, adaptability, and ability to cooperate. A consultant then computed a correlation between the longevity of teams and their performance. The results were startling.

As may be seen in Figure 5-6, the performance of these groups increased as they gained longevity, but only up to a point. After five years of working together, team project performance declined steeply, as well as intraproject communication, organizational communication, and external professional communication—basically all the types of communication that serve to bring fresh ideas to the group.

Four behavioral changes took place in groups that worked together for over five years:

- **Behavioral stability:** Project members interacting over a long time develop standard work patterns that are familiar and comfortable. This can happen very rapidly—for instance, the way people in a group tend to sit in the same places in meeting after meeting, even when there may be no logical reason for doing so. Over time, this behavioral stability leads to isolation from the outside. The group can grow increasingly complacent, ceasing to question the practices that shape their behavior.
- **Selective exposure:** There is a tendency for group members to communicate only with people whose ideas agree with their own. It is related to the homogeneity bias—the tendency to select new members who are like members in the existing group. Over time, project members learn to interact selectively to avoid messages and information that conflict with their established practices and disposition.
- **Group homogeneity:** Groups that are separated from the influence of others in the organization develop a homogeneous set of understandings about the group and its environment.

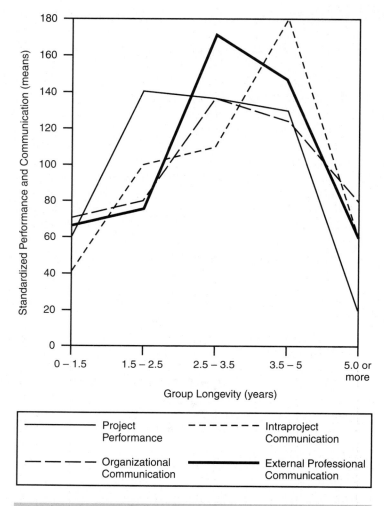

**FIGURE 5-6** Group Longevity
*Source:* Katz, R. 1982. "The Effects of Group Longevity on Project Communication and Performance." *Administrative Science Quarterly, 27,* 81–104.

The members of the group act as reinforcing agents for behaviors and practices of the group.

- ***Role differentiation:*** As we have seen in the analysis of the TMS groups, as groups work and train together, they become increasingly specialized in project competencies and roles. This results in greater role differentiation, which in turn results in less interaction among group members because the roles and expectations held by each are so well entrenched. Consequently, they lose access to much of the internal talent, and their ability to learn new ideas from one another is diminished.

Thus, in terms of actual task performance, as team longevity increases, certain social processes conspire to lower levels of project communication, which in turn decrease project performance. Project groups become increasingly isolated from key information sources both within and outside their organizations with increasing stability in their membership. Reductions in project communication adversely affect the technical performance of project groups. Variations in communication activities are more associated with the tenure composition of the project group than with the project tenures of the individual engineers. Stated another way, it is not the age of the employee that is of critical importance, but the age of the team. Furthermore, individual competence does not account for differences in performance. Thus, it is not the case that the older, less skilled members were working in teams that were of greater longevity. Furthermore, the longevity of project groups does not appear to be part of the mental models of the managers—virtually no one was aware of the tenure demographics of their project groups.

What does all of this mean for team longevity? A certain amount of familiarity is necessary for teams to work together in a productive fashion. The effect of working together tends to make team members grow more familiar with each other's relevant knowledge base, and, hence, a TMS can develop. A TMS can be helpful in tasks where coordination losses need to be reduced and tactical precision is key. Although a certain amount of routinization is desirable in any team, the overly routinized team hinders communication and obstructs innovation. Unfortunately, we don't have a precise answer as to how long teams should work together on a particular task; it simply depends too much on the nature of the task and the membership of the team.

Looking at this question from a team design standpoint might offer some insights. It may be desirable, for example, to design some teams whose primary objective is to act as innovation experts for the creation and transfer of the organization's best practices. According to Kane and Argote (2002), groups are more likely to benefit from the knowledge and ideas brought by a newcomer when they share a superordinate identity with one another. Moreover, when members sit in an integrated fashion (versus sitting on opposite sides of a table), a superordinate identity is more likely to be established.

## CONCLUSIONS

For teams to be effective in their work, they need to have a shared knowledge base. The knowledge base allows teams to more efficiently process and encode relevant information and then act upon it in a thoughtful and appropriate fashion. However, the shared knowledge base that governs a team is only as adequate as its communication system. Communication among team members is a collaborative effort. Natural biases in communication can play havoc with effective teamwork. The events of (and since) September 11, 2001, have led people to realize that effective communication is not merely a knowledge advantage, but is critical for security. It is the responsibility of team leaders to ensure that successful communication occurs among team members. The development of accurate team mental models and a transactive memory system (TMS) can partially combat the threat of the common information effect and hidden profiles.

# CHAPTER 6

# Team Decision Making:

## *Pitfalls and Solutions*

*On February 7, 1999, the audit committee of Enron Corporation's board of directors gathered in London to hear rather startling news. The company's auditors described Enron's accounting practices as "high risk." David B. Duncan, who headed up the Arthur Andersen LLP team at the company, informed the committee that Enron's accounting was "pushing the limits" and was "'at the edge' of acceptable practice" (Byrne, 2002a, p. 50). However, none of the directors "objected to the procedures described by the auditors, requested a second opinion, or demanded a more prudent approach. . . . In fact the sub-committee found that similar briefings by Andersen officials occurred once or twice each year from 1999 through 2001, with the same result: The auditors told board members that Enron was following high-risk accounting and no one drilled deep enough to learn the details or object. . . . Even worse, Enron's board members knew about and could have prevented many of the risky accounting practices, conflicts of interest, and hiding of debt that led to the company's implosion simply by asking some obvious questions" (Byrne, 2002a, p. 50). Arthur Andersen was aware as well. The previous CEO of Andersen, Joe Berardino, grouped their clients into four "risk" categories—maximum, high, moderate, and low risk. Enron was one of 50 clients labeled maximum risk. That alone should have been enough to put Enron front and center on Arthur Andersen's radar screen, but it did not happen. In fact, the system for airing conflicts at Andersen was designed to ensure that top executives never learned of them (Byrne, 2002b).*

It has become clear that the poor judgment and reckless, if not greedy, decision making in this case would repeat itself across the corporate world. Further, the decision-making debacles of Enron, Arthur Andersen, Worldcom, Qwest, Tyco, and Sotheby's square with most people's intuition that decisions made by committees can be of the worst caliber. However, good team decision making can be outstanding—far better than that attainable by any individual. The key, of course, is how to design the team so that decisions are made right, and doing it right is the topic of this chapter.

The Enron and Arthur Andersen debacles may have resulted, in part, from a poor team decision process. In hindsight, it seems ludicrous that well-trained, intelligent people (e.g., one-time Stanford University accounting professor Robert K. Jaedicke and others) could ignore such clear and present warning signs. However, as we know, this example does not stand apart from other examples of impaired decision making that have emerged in the corporate world. Because faulty team decisions can have disastrous consequences, not just for the company, but employees, shareholders, and the public at large, it is important to understand the processes and practices that lead to faulty team decision making.

# DECISION MAKING IN TEAMS

Decision making is a key activity that teams must do, no matter what their governance structure—self-managing, manager-led, or self-directing. This is true for tactical, problem solving, and creative teams. Decision making is an integrated sequence of activities that includes gathering, interpreting, and exchanging information; creating and identifying alternative courses of action; choosing among alternatives by integrating the often differing perspectives and opinions of team members; and implementing a choice and monitoring its consequences (Guzzo, Salas, & Associates, 1995). For a schematic diagram of an idealized set of activities involved in a decision-making process, see Figure 6-1. In teams, information is often distributed unequally among members and must be integrated, and the integration process may be complicated by uncertainty, status differences among members, failure of members to appreciate the significance of the information they hold or of the information not held by others, and so on.

There are a variety of well-documented decision-making biases that affect the ability of people to process information and weigh alternatives (for excellent reviews, see Bazerman, 2002; Murnighan & Mowen, 2001). Unfortunately, a number of group-related decision biases also crop up in teams.

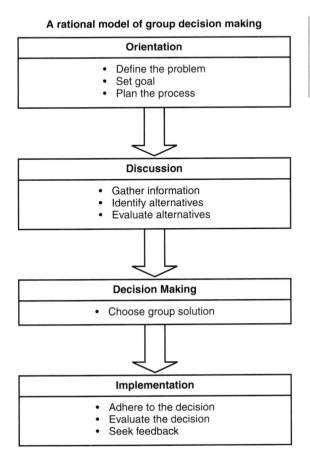

FIGURE 6-1  Anatomy of Group Decision Making
*Source:* Forsyth, D. 1990. *Group Dynamics* (2nd edition, p. 286). Pacific Grove, CA: Brooks/Cole.

We begin by discussing the key differences between individual versus group decision making. The rest of the chapter is problem focused, identifying five decision-making pitfalls that teams often encounter or experience. For each, we describe the problem and then provide preventative measures. The first problem that we focus on is groupthink, the tendency to conform to the consensus viewpoint in group decision making. We then discuss escalation of commitment, the Abilene paradox, group polarization, and unethical decision making.

## INDIVIDUAL VERSUS GROUP DECISION MAKING

A fundamental question for any leader considering whether to relegate a decision to a team is whether teams make better decisions than do individuals. And the data are in: Teams outperform the simple aggregation of individuals' decisions (or reviews, see Brown, 2000; Stasser & Dietz-Uhler, 2001). This supports a manager's use of a team for decision making. A more meaningful question for a manager considering staffing needs, however, concerns whether the "best team member" is superior to the team. Many studies clearly indicate that the "best" team member outperforms the team (see Hill, 1982, for a review), but "more realistic" studies of actual work teams indicate that teams outperform their "best" teammate 97 percent of the time (Michaelsen, Watson, & Black, 1989).

Perhaps it is the intrigue of this very question that has resulted in many management and executive education courses centered on this topic, wherein business people are challenged with simulations in which they find themselves stranded in inhospitable environments—Artic tundra, scorched desert, treacherous jungles—and together, they

### Sidebar 6-1. Team Building at 10,000 Feet

Tanna Oldfield's software company needed to establish rapport between the new hires and the company's old guard. The company wanted to step out of the box; therefore, the employees were asked to step out of a plane at 14,000 feet. The sky-high bonding exercise left the employees exhilarated and more confident—if they could conquer their fears about sky-diving, they could overcome work issues (Klein, 2001). Similarly, at Deer Hill Ranch in California, companies can send their team members 40 feet in the air wearing belay harnesses, and teams can work through their fears with the help of teammates on the ground (*PR Newswire,* August 2001). And in Gammons Gulch, a fabricated Western town 60 miles east of Tucson, Arizona, companies can pay $1,200 to $250,000 for a custom-scripted gunfight event (*Deseret News,* 2001).

In an extreme example, CEO Pat Burns of demandline.com told his five vice presidents that they might want to "think about getting in shape [and] be able to run six miles in less than 10-minute intervals," "be comfortable wearing backpacks," and "pack clothes for very cold weather" (Strasburg, 2000, p. B-1). But he did not tell them anything else before heading to the airport. Hours later, they found themselves in Anchorage, Alaska, donning 70-pound backbacks. Four unshaven, endurance-testing days later, the management team had climbed 4,500 vertical feet to the summit of ice-packed Matanuska Peak, waded through snow up to their waists, eaten dehydrated chicken, and dug ice pits for shelter and hygenic uses (Strasburg, 2000).

## Sidebar 6-2. Reality Television and Teamwork

Since the premiere of such successful shows as MTV's *The Real World* and CBS's *Survivor,* there has been a glut of reality-television shows featuring teams. These shows take a voyeuristic look at the lives of "real people" in high-stakes group survival situations. NBC's *Fear Factor* pits contestants against each other as they face lifelong phobias such as jumping out of planes or being immersed in a tank of spiders; in CBS's *The Amazing Race,* 16 teams of two travel around the world in a race to win half-a-million dollars. In another extreme example, three families signed up to spend five months living like 1883 Montana homesteaders—all filmed for PBS's *Frontier House.* The producers demanded that the show's participants be given nothing that was not available at the time (right down to their underwear) and no medications other than "moonshine"; even birth control was discouraged (but optional!). Some of the show's participating families became embroiled in conflict, much like the infamous Hatfields and McCoys (Pennington, 2002).

must plan and enact strategies to ensure their survival.[1] Some companies actually place people in such situations (see Sidebar 6-1), popular television shows are based on "survival" (see Sidebar 6-2), and some teams excel at adventure sports—but in the management laboratory and classroom, teammates are simply asked to rank (in order of importance) the usefulness of several objects (e.g., flashlight, canteen of water, knives, etc.). The team's rank order can then be benchmarked against that of an expert, and also, against the individual rankings made by each member of the team.

When this is done, an interesting phenomenon emerges: The performance of the team is nearly inevitably better than the simple, arithmetic average of the group members. Recall from Chapter 2 the team performance equation, wherein: Actual Productivity (AP) of a team = Potential Productivity (PP) + Synergy (S) − Performance Threats (T). In this particular case, the arithmetic average of the team represents the potential productivity of the group. If the actual productivity of the team exceeds this, it suggests that the group has experienced a synergistic process (i.e., something about working together has allowed the group to outperform how they could have performed by simply aggregating their own decisions). If the actual productivity of the team is worse, it suggests that the group process is flawed. In my management courses, I have repeatedly found that the actual productivity of the group exceeds that of the potential productivity; teams add a synergy of approximately 15 percent. However, the team leader is justified in asking whether the team's performance exceeds that of the best member of the team (for a review, see Michaelsen et al., 1989). This is an interesting question because it implicitly suggests that perhaps team decision making is best served by putting the trust of the group into one knowledgeable and competent group member. Michaelsen et al. (1989) studied individual versus group decision making in 222 project teams, ranging in size from three to eight members. In most instances, these groups outperformed their most proficient group member 97 percent of the time.

---

[1] One such simulation is *Desert Survival,* available from Human Synergistics International, 39819 Plymouth Road, C8020, Plymouth, MI 48170-8020; phone (800) 622-7584 or (734) 459-1030 (for international orders) or on-line at www.humansyn.com.

As a general principle, group performance increases over that of individual member performance as the demonstrability of the task increases. For example, groups perform at the level of the best individual on highly demonstrable mathematical, insight, and information-rich problems. Groups perform at the level of the second-best individual or group member on world knowledge problems, such as vocabulary, analogies, and ranking items for usefulness. And groups perform at the level of the average individual or group member on weakly demonstrable estimations of quantities (for a review, see Laughlin, Bonner, & Miner, 2002).

However, one problem is that groups are much more overconfident than are individuals, holding constant decision accuracy. For example, in one investigation, groups were asked to make stock price predictions (Fischhoff, Slovic, & Lichtenstein, 1977). The actual accuracy of the group was 47 percent, but their confidence level was 65 percent. Three days before the explosion of the Space Shuttle *Columbia* in 2003, NASA officials met to discuss ways to keep their shuttle fleet safe from space debris (one probable cause of *Columbia*'s breakdown), but concluded that repair work in flight—a possible solution—would be too costly, creating "more damage than what [they] were trying to repair" (*Associated Press,* February 14, 2003).

We are now ready to discuss the five key biases that threaten effective teamwork.

# DECISION-MAKING PITFALL 1: GROUPTHINK

**Groupthink** occurs when team members place consensus above all other priorities—including using good judgment when the consensus reflects poor judgment, improper or immoral actions, and so on. Groupthink, at its core, involves a deterioration of mental efficiency, reality testing, and moral judgments as a result of group pressures toward conformity of opinion. For a list of groupthink decisions in the political and corporate world, see Box 6-1. The desire to agree can become so dominant that it can override the realistic appraisal of alternative courses of action (Janis, 1972, 1982). The reasons for groupthink may range from group pressures to conform to a sincere desire to incorporate and reflect the views of all team members. Such pressure may also come from management if the directive is to reach a decision that all can agree to, such as in cross-functional teams.

Conformity pressures can lead decision makers to censor their misgivings, ignore outside information, feel too confident, and adopt an attitude of invulnerability. The pressure for unanimity is thought to be a recipe for ineffective group decision making and explains how a group of otherwise intelligent and thoughtful people can make serious miscalculations that result in disastrous outcomes.

Symptoms of groupthink cannot be easily assessed by outside observers. Rather, most groupthink symptoms represent private feelings or beliefs held by group members or behaviors performed in private. There are three key symptoms of groupthink that take root and blossom in groups that succumb to pressures of reaching unanimity:

- *Overestimation of the group:* Members of the group regard themselves as invulnerable and, at the same time, morally correct. This lethal combination can lead decision makers to believe they are above, and exempt from, standards.
- *Close-mindedness:* Members of the group engage in collective rationalization, often accompanied by stereotyping outgroup members, a topic we discuss further in Part III.

---

BOX 6-1

# Instances of Groupthink in Politics and the Corporate World

## EXAMPLES FROM POLITICS

- Neville Chamberlain's inner circle, whose members supported the policy of appeasement of Hitler during 1937 and 1938, despite repeated warnings and events that indicated it would have adverse consequences (Janis & Mann, 1977).

- President Truman's advisory group, whose members supported the decision to escalate the war in North Korea, despite firm warnings by the Chinese Communist government that U.S. entry into North Korea would be met with armed resistance from the Chinese (Janis & Mann, 1977).

- President Kennedy's inner circle, whose members supported the decision to launch the Bay of Pigs invasion of Cuba, despite the availability of information indicating that it would be an unsuccessful venture and would damage U.S. relations with other countries (Janis & Mann, 1977).

- President Johnson's close advisors, who supported the decision to escalate the war in Vietnam, despite intelligence reports and information indicating that this course of action would not defeat the Viet Cong or the North Vietnamese, and would generate unfavorable political consequences within the United States (Janis & Mann, 1977).

- The decision of the Reagan administration to exchange arms for hostages with Iran and to continue commitment to the Nicaraguan Contras in the face of several congressional amendments limiting or banning aid.

## EXAMPLES FROM THE CORPORATE WORLD

- Enron's board of directors was well informed about (and could therefore have prevented) the risky accounting practices, conflicts of interest, and hiding of debt that led to the company's downfall; likewise, Arthur Andersen (Enron's accounting firm) did nothing to halt the company's high-risk practices (Byrne, 2002a, 2002b).

- Gruenenthal Chemie's decision to market the drug thalidomide (Raven & Rubin, 1976).

- The price-fixing conspiracy involving the electrical manufacturing industry during the 1950s.

- The decision by Ford Motor Company to produce the Edsel (Huseman & Driver, 1979).

- The AMA's (American Medical Association's) decision to allow Sunbeam to use the AMA name as a product endorsement (Wolinsky, 1998).

- The selling of millions of jars of "phony" apple juice by Beech-Nut, the third largest baby food producer in the United States.

- The involvement of E. F. Hutton in "check kiting," wherein a money manager at a Hutton branch office would write a check on an account in Bank A for more money than Hutton had in the account. Because of the time lag in the check-collection system, these overdrafts sometimes went undetected, and Hutton could deposit funds to cover the overdraft in the following day. The deposited money would start earning interest immediately. The scheme allowed Hutton to earn a day's interest on Bank A's account without having to pay anything for it—resulting in $250 million in free loans every day (*ABA Banking Journal,* 1985; Goleman, 1988).

- The illegal purchases by Salomon Brothers at U.S. Treasury auctions in the early 1990s (Sims, 1992).

- *Pressures toward uniformity:* There is a strong intolerance in a groupthink situation for diversity of opinion. Dissenters are subject to enormous social pressure. This often leads group members to suppress their reservations. Thus, the group perceives itself to be unanimous.

Deficits arising from groupthink can lead to many shortcomings in the decision-making process. Consider, for example, the following lapses that often accompany groupthink:

- Incomplete survey of alternatives
- Incomplete survey of objectives
- Failure to reexamine alternatives
- Failure to examine preferred choices
- Selection bias
- Poor information search
- Failure to create contingency plans

Each of these behaviors thwarts the rational decision-making process we outlined at the beginning of this chapter.

## Learning from History

Consider two decisions made by the same U.S. presidential cabinet—the Kennedy administration. The Kennedy cabinet was responsible for the Bay of Pigs operation and the Cuban Missile Crisis. The Bay of Pigs was a military operation concocted by the United States in an attempt to overthrow Fidel Castro, the leader of Cuba. The Bay of Pigs is often seen as one of the worst foreign policy mistakes in U.S. history. The operation was regarded as a disaster of epic proportions, resulting in the loss of lives and the disruption of foreign policy. It is also a kind of puzzle because the invasion, in retrospect, seems to have been so poorly planned and so poorly implemented, yet it was led by people whose individual talents seemed to make them eminently qualified to carry out an operation of this sort. What led capable people who should have known better to proceed with such a disastrous plan? In contrast, Kennedy's response to the Cuban Missile Crisis was regarded as a great international policy success. These examples, from the same organizational context and team, make an important point: Even smart and highly motivated people can make disastrous decisions under certain conditions. Kennedy's cabinet fell prey to groupthink in the Bay of Pigs decision, but not in the Cuban Missile Crisis. Why was the same cabinet so successful in one instance, but such a miserable failure in another?

A number of detailed historical analyses have been performed (Kramer, 1999; Peterson, Owens, Tetlock, Fan, & Martorana, 1998) comparing these two historical examples, as well as several others. Some sharp differences distinguish between groupthink and effective groups.

Table 6-1 summarizes three kinds of critical evidence: (1) factors that may lead to groupthink; (2) factors that may promote sound decision making; and (3) factors that do not seem to induce groupthink. We focus on two types of behavior: that of the leader and that of the rest of the group.

A number of factors may lead to groupthink. Leader behavior that is associated with too much concern for political ramifications, or the analysis of alternatives in

**TABLE 6-1**    Precipitating and Preventative Conditions for the Development of Groupthink

| Conditions | Leader Behavior and Cognition | Team Behavior and Cognition |
|---|---|---|
| **Precipitous conditions** *(likely to lead to group-think)* | • Narrow, defective appraisal of options<br>• Analysis of options in terms of political repercussions<br>• Concern about image and reputation<br>• Loss-avoidance strategy | • Rigidity<br>• Conformity<br>• View roles in political terms (protecting political capital and status)<br>• Large team size<br>• High sense of collective efficacy<br>• Perceived threat to social identity |
| **Preventative conditions** *(likely to engender effective decision making)* | • Being explicit and direct about policy preferences allows the team to know immediately where the leader stands | • Task orientation<br>• Intellectual flexibility<br>• Less consciousness of crisis<br>• Less pessimism<br>• Less corruption (i.e., more concerned with observing correct rules and procedures)<br>• Less centralization<br>• Openness and candidness<br>• Adjustment to failing policies in timely fashion<br>• Genuine commitment to solving problems<br>• Encouraging dissent<br>• Acting decisively in emergencies<br>• Attuned to changes in environment<br>• Focus on shared goals<br>• Realization that trade-offs are necessary<br>• Ability to improvise solutions to unexpected events |
| **Inconclusive conditions** *(unlikely to make much of a difference)* | • Strong, opinionated leadership | • Risk taking<br>• Cohesion<br>• Internal debate |

terms of their political repercussions, is a key determinant of groupthink. The same is also true for group behavior; when groups are overly concerned with their political image, they may not make sound decisions.

In terms of preventative conditions, the behavior of the team has a greater impact on the development of groupthink than does leader behavior. Sound group decision making can be achieved through task orientation, flexibility, less centralization, norms of openness, encouraging dissent, focus on shared goals, and realizing that trade-offs are necessary.

## How to Avoid Groupthink

In this section, we identify some specific steps leaders can take to prevent groupthink. Prevention is predicated on two broad goals: The stimulation of constructive, intellectual conflict and the reduction of concerns about how the group is viewed by others—a kind of conformity pressure. We focus primarily on team design factors because those are the ones managers have the greatest control over. None of these can guarantee success, but they can be effective in encouraging vigilant decision making.

### Monitor Team Size

Team size is positively correlated with groupthink, with larger teams more likely to fall prey to groupthink (McCauley, 1998). People grow more intimidated and hesitant as team size increases. This is related to the principle of performance anxiety, which we discussed in Chapter 2. There is no magic number for team size, but with teams larger than 10 individual members may feel less personal responsibility for team outcomes and their behaviors may be too risky.

### Provide a Face-saving Mechanism for Teams

A small team that has the respect and support of their organization would seem to be in an ideal position to make effective decisions. Yet often, they fail to do so. One reason is that they are concerned with how their decision, and its fallout, will be viewed by others. Many teams are afraid of being blamed for poor decisions—even decisions for which it would have been impossible to predict the outcome. Often, face-saving concerns keep people from changing course, even when the current course is clearly doubtful. For this reason, it can be useful to provide teams with a face-saving mechanism or a reason for why outcomes might appear to be poor. This basically amounts to giving teams an external attribution for poor performance. Indeed, teams that are given an excuse for poor performance before knowing the outcome of their decision are less likely to succumb to groupthink than teams that do not have an excuse (Turner, Probasco, Pratkanis, & Leve, 1992).

### The Risk Technique

The risk technique is a structured discussion situation designed to reduce group members' fears about making decisions (Maier, 1952). The discussion is structured so that team members talk about the dangers or risks involved in a decision and delay discussion of any potential gains. Following this is a discussion of controls or mechanisms for dealing with the risks or dangers. This strategy may sound touchy-feely, but it basically amounts to creating an atmosphere in which team members can express doubts and raise criticisms without fear of rejection or hostility from the team. There are many ways to create such an atmosphere. One way is to have a facilitator play the role of devil's advocate for a particular decision. The mere expression of doubt about an idea or plan by one person may liberate others to raise doubts and concerns. A second method may be to have members privately convey their concerns or doubts and then post this information in an unidentifiable manner. Again, this liberates members to talk about their doubts.

### Invite Different Perspectives

In this technique, team members assume the perspective of other constituencies with a stake in the decision (Turner & Pratkanis, 1998). In 1986, the Space Shuttle *Challenger* exploded in space due to a major malfunction regarding the booster rockets and, in particular, O-ring failure. Roger Boisjoly, an engineer who tried to halt the flight in 1986 because he was aware of the likely trouble, said later, "I received cold stares . . . with looks as if to say, 'Go away and don't bother us with the facts.' No one in management wanted to discuss the facts; they just would not respond verbally to . . . me. I felt totally helpless and that further argument was fruitless, so I, too, stopped pressing my case" (Boisjoly, 1987, p. 7). In the *Challenger* incident, the federal government, local citizens, space crew families, astronomers, and so on all assumed the roles of "group members." Although the *Challenger* disaster happened in large part because of a disastrously poor understanding of how to interpret statistical data, the key point of adopting different perspectives is to create a mechanism that will instigate thinking more carefully about problems, which could prompt these groups to reconsider evidence.

The absence of different perspectives has also been identified as the root cause of the corporate, political, and managerial disasters that swept through Switzerland in 2001–2002, specifically, the grounding of Swissair in the fall of 2001; corporate-governance battles at Zurich Financial Services Group and Credit Suisse Group in spring of 2002; the July 11, 2002 arrest of the ambassador to Luxembourg on charges of money-laundering; and the air traffic failures that contributed to the July 1, 2002 Uberlingen crash. As it turns out, the boards of most Swiss companies were often "little more than rubber stamps, made up of members of the country's small, conservative, smug establishment" (Fairlamb, 2002, p. 57). Everyone knew everyone else and sat on each other's boards. Therefore, Nestlé CEO Peter Brabeck-Letmathe was a vice-chairman of Credit Suisse's board, while Credit Suisse honorary chairman Rainer E. Gut was a chairman of Nestlé. With a system like this, there are no opportunities for different, unbiased perspectives (Fairlamb, 2002).

When it comes to different perspectives, those persons offering up the counterpoint should prepare as they would if they were working on a court case—in other words, they should assemble data and evidence, as opposed to personal opinions (Kirsner, 2002). Professor Chip Heath adds that the naysayers should not point fingers or say that someone has "screwed up." Rather, it is better to take the "we have a problem" approach (Kirsner, 2002, p. 56).

### Appoint a Devil's Advocate

By the time that upper management is wedded to a particular plan or point of view, they are often impervious to evidence that is questionable or even downright contradictory. To make matters worse, those around them—often subordinates—don't want to challenge management's beliefs. This is why some teams institute a special "devil's advocate" responsibility to members of the team. For example, consider the case of Cisco Systems, which suffered a remarkable comedown in the spring of 2001, losing 88 percent of its value in one year. As it turns out, Cisco's upper management, enamored of their IT system, never modeled what would happen if a key assumption (namely, growth) disappeared from the equation (Charan & Useem, 2002). The Catholic Church used to appoint someone to the position of devil's advocate, a person who would review all of the people who were proposed as saints and try to spot flaws in arguments for sainthood. "They got rid of [the devil's advocate position] in 1983," jokes Michael Roberto, a professor at Harvard University, "and look what happened there" (Kirsner, 2002, p. 56). In contrast, Winston Churchill knew how to combat groupthink and yes-men. Worried that his own larger-than-life image would deter subordinates from bringing him the truth, he instituted a unit outside his chain of command, called the "statistical office," whose key job was to bring him the bleakest, most gut-wrenching facts. Similarly, Richard J. Schroth and A. Larry Elliott, authors of the book *How Companies Lie* (2002) suggest that "counterpointers" be appointed in teams, whose chief function is to ask the rudest possible questions.

Whereas a devil's advocate procedure can be effective, it is contrived dissent. It is better for a team to have genuine dissent (Schulz-Hardt, Jochims, & Frey, 2002). For example, in one study, when business people made investment decisions, genuine dissent was more effective than contrived dissent in avoiding confirmatory decision making (Schulz-Hardt et al., 2002).

### Structure Discussion Principles

The goal of structured discussion principles is to delay solution selection and to increase the problem-solving phase. This prevents premature closure on a solution and extends problem analysis and evaluation. For example, teams may be given guidelines that emphasize continued solicitations of solutions, protection of individuals from criticism, keeping the discussion problem centered, and listing all solutions before evaluating them (Maier, 1952).

### Establish Procedures for Protecting Alternative Viewpoints

Although teams can generate high-quality decision alternatives, they frequently fail to adopt them as preferred solutions (Janis, 1982; Turner et al., 1992). This means that most problems that teams face are not simple, "eureka" types of decisions, in which the correct answer is obvious once it is put on the table. Rather, team members must convince others about the correctness of their views. This is a difficult task when things like conformity pressure are operating and especially after team members have publicly committed to a particular course of action. For these reasons, it can be useful to instruct members to keep a log of all alternatives suggested during each meeting.

### Second Solution

This technique requires teams to identify a second solution or decision recommendation as an alternative to their first choice. This enhances the problem-solving and idea-generation phases, as well as performance quality (Hoffman & Maier, 1966).

### Beware of Time Pressure

Decisions involve idealistic considerations, such as moral principles and ideals, as well as practical considerations, such as difficulty, cost, or situational pressures. Therefore, it is undeniable that decision makers often make trade-offs. Moral principles are more likely to guide decisions for the distant future than for the immediate future, whereas difficulty, cost, and situational pressures are more likely to be important in near future decisions. In other words, managers are more likely to compromise their principles in decisions regarding near future actions compared with distant future actions (Liberman & Trope, 1998). At a more general level, time pressure acts as a stress on teams, and stress can impair the effectiveness of team decision making (see Morgan & Bowers, 1995, for a review).

# DECISION-MAKING PITFALL 2: ESCALATION OF COMMITMENT

It would seem that one remedy for groupthink would be clear feedback as to the effectiveness of the decision-making process. For example, the Coca-Cola Company's decision to introduce "New Coke" was eventually recognized as a mistake and reversed. Do such clear failures prompt teams to revisit their decision-making process and improve upon it? Not necessarily. In fact, under some conditions, teams will persist with a losing course of action, even in the face of clear evidence to the contrary. This type of situation is known as the **escalation of commitment** phenomenon.

Consider the decision-making problem in Box 6-2. Next, consider the following decision situations.

- A senior marketing manager at a major pet food corporation continues to promote a specific brand, despite clear evidence that the brand is losing market share to its competitors.
- A company continues to invest in a manager who is known to have handled many situations poorly and receives consistently subpar 360-degree evaluations.
- Quaker Oats continued to push Snapple, even though its market share dropped staggeringly.
- When the stock market tide is running, wildly enthusiastic investors will bid up companies' stock prices to levels known to be too high, in the certainty that they can "only go up." Two years later, they dump these companies at any price, believing with equal certainty that they are becoming worthless (Train, 1995).
- A company continues to drill for oil, despite being unable to turn a profit on drilling efforts in the past three years.
- John R. Silber, previous president of Boston University, decided to invest in Seragen, a biotechnology company with a promising cancer drug. After investing $1.7 million over six years, the value was $43,000 (Barboza, 1998).

In all these situations, individuals and teams committed further resources to what eventually proved to be a failing course of action. In most cases, the situation does not turn into a problem for a while. The situation becomes an escalation dilemma when the persons involved in the decision would make a different decision if they had not been

---

**BOX 6-2**

## New Product Investment Decision

As the president of an airline company, you have invested $10 million of the company's money into a research project. The purpose was to build a plane that would not be detected by conventional radar, in other words, a radar-blank plane. When the project is 90 percent completed, another company begins marketing a plane that cannot be detected by radar. Also, it is apparent that their plane is much faster and far more economical than the plane your company is building. The question is: Should you invest the last 10 percent of the research funds to finish your radar-blank plane?

❏ Yes, invest the money.
❏ No, drop the project.

involved up until that point, or when other objective persons would not choose that course of action. Often, in escalation situations, a decision is made to commit further resources to "turn the situation around." This process may repeat and escalate several times as additional resources are invested. The bigger the investment and the more severe the possible loss, the more prone people are to try to turn things around. Consider the situation faced by Lyndon Johnson during the early stage of the Vietnam War. Johnson received the following memo from George Ball, then undersecretary of state:

> The decision you face now is crucial. Once large numbers of U.S. troops are committed to direct combat, they will begin to take heavy casualties in a war they are ill-equipped to fight in a noncooperative if not downright hostile countryside. Once we suffer large casualties, we will have started a well-nigh irreversible process. Our involvement will be so great that we cannot—without national humiliation—stop short of achieving our complete objectives. Of the two possibilities I think humiliation will be more likely than the achievement of our objectives—even after we have paid terrible costs (Sheehan et al., 1971, p. 450).

The escalation of commitment process is illustrated in Figure 6-2. In the first stage of the escalation of commitment, a decision-making team is confronted with questionable or negative outcomes (e.g., a price drop, decreasing market share, poor performance evaluations, or a malfunction). This external event prompts a reexamination of the team's current course of action, in which the utility of continuing is weighed against the utility of withdrawing or changing course. This decision determines the team's com-

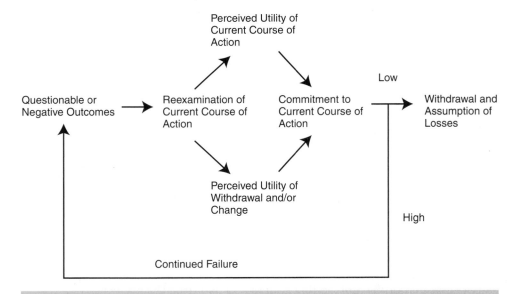

**FIGURE 6-2** Escalation of Commitment
*Source:* Ross, J., & Staw, B. M. 1993, August. "Organizational Escalation and Exit: Lessons from the Shoreham Nuclear Power Plant." *Academy of Management Journal,* 701–732.

mitment to its current course of action. If this commitment is low, the team may withdraw from the project and assume its losses. If this commitment is high, however, the team will continue commitment and continue to cycle through the decision stages. There are four key processes involved in the escalation of commitment cycle: project-related determinants, psychological determinants, social determinants, and structural determinants (Ross & Staw, 1993).

## Project Determinants

Project determinants are the objective features of the situation. Upon receiving negative feedback, team members ask whether the perceived setback is permanent or temporary (e.g., is reduced market share a meaningful trend or a simple perturbation in a noisy system?). If it is perceived to be temporary, there may appear to be little reason to reverse course. Then, when addressing questions like whether to increase investment in the project or to commit more time and energy to it, the team is essentially asking whether it wishes to escalate its commitment. Of course, this may often be the right choice, but it should be clear that such decisions also make it harder for the team to terminate that course of action if results continue to be poor.

## Psychological Determinants

Psychological determinants refer to the cognitive and motivational factors that propel people to continue with a chosen course of action. When managers or teams receive indication that the outcomes of a project may be negative, they should ask themselves the following questions regarding their own involvement in the process:

*What Are the Personal Rewards for Me in This Project?*
In many cases, the *process* of the project itself, rather than the outcome of the project, becomes the reason for continuing the project. This leads to a self-perpetuating reinforcement trap, wherein the rewards for continuing are not aligned with the actual objectives of the project. Ironically, people who have high, rather than low, self-esteem are more likely to become victimized by psychological forces—people with high self-esteem have much more invested in their ego and its maintenance than do those with low self-esteem.

It would seem to be in a project manager's best interest to invest in the product, rather than to benefit the company as a whole. However, managers or teams who fall prey to escalation of commitment will ultimately end up losing because their product won't be successful, and they will have suffered more than if they simply abandoned the project earlier on.

*Is My Ego and the Team's Reputation on the Line?*
"If I pull out of this project, would I feel stupid? Do I worry that other people would judge me to be stupid?" Ego protection often becomes a higher priority than the success of the project. When managers feel personally responsible for a decision, monetary allocations to the project increase at a much higher rate than when managers do not feel responsible for the initial decision (Staw, 1976).

In some sense, it does not seem too surprising that when managers personally oversee a project, they attempt to ensure that the project has every chance of success (e.g., by allocating more resources to it). After all, that is their job. A manager who works on a project from beginning to end is going to know more about it and may be in a better position to judge it. Furthermore, personal commitment is essential for the success of many projects. Whereas it is certainly good to nurture projects so that they have their best chance of survival, it is nearly impossible for most managers to be completely objective. This is where it is important to have clear, unbiased criteria by which to evaluate the success of a project.

### Am I Evaluating the Facts in an Unbiased Fashion?

The **confirmation bias** is the tendency for people to only see what they already believe to be true. When people are ego invested in a project, the confirmation bias will even be stronger. It is striking how even upon the receipt of what appears to be unsupportive data, people who have fallen prey to the confirmation bias will maintain, and in some cases increase, their resolve. For example, the confirmation bias is related to the costly protraction of strike activity—a form of escalation of commitment. As a quick demonstration of the confirmation bias, take the test in Box 6-3.

---

**BOX 6-3**

## Card Test

Imagine that the following four cards are placed in front of you and are printed with the following symbols on one side:

| Card 1 | Card 2 | Card 3 | Card 4 |
|--------|--------|--------|--------|
| E | K | 4 | 7 |

Now, imagine you are told that a letter appears on one side of each card and a number on the other. Your task is to judge the validity of the following rule, which refers only to these four cards: "If a card has a vowel on one side, then it has an even number on the other side." Your task is to turn over only those cards that have to be turned over for the correctness of the rule to be judged. Which cards do you want to turn over? *(Stop here and decide which cards to turn over before reading on.)*

Averaging over a large number of investigations (Oaksford & Chater, 1994), 89 percent of people select E, which is a logically correct choice because an odd number on the other side would disconfirm the rule. However, 62 percent also choose to turn over the 4, which is not logically informative because neither a vowel nor a consonant on the other side would falsify the rule. Only 25 percent of people elect to turn over the 7, which is a logically informative choice because a vowel behind the 7 would falsify the rule. Only 16 percent elect to turn over K, which would not be an informative choice.

Thus, people display two types of logical errors in the task. First, they often turn over the 4, an example of the confirmation bias. However, even more striking is the failure to take the step of attempting to disconfirm what they believe is true—in other words, turning over the 7 (Wason & Johnson-Laird, 1972).

*Is the Glass Half-Empty or Half-Full?*

If decision makers see themselves as trying to recover from a losing position, chances are they will engage in greater risk than if they see themselves as starting with a clean slate. Like the gambler in Las Vegas, decision makers who wait for their luck to change have fallen into the trap. For these reasons, decision makers who were initially responsible for the decision are likely to feel more compelled to continue to pursue the same course of action as compared with the successors of such managers. Escalation of commitment is partially responsible for some of the worst financial losses experienced by organizations. For example, from 1966 to 1989, the Long Island Lighting Company's investment in the Shoreham Nuclear Power Plant escalated from $65 million to $5 billion, despite a steady flow of negative feedback. The plant was never opened (Ross & Staw, 1993).

## Social Determinants

Most people want others to approve of them, accept them, and respect them. Consequently, they engage in actions and behaviors that they think will please most of the people most of the time, perhaps at the expense of doing the right thing, which may not be popular.

The need for approval and liking may be especially heightened among groups composed of friends. Indeed, groups of longtime friends are more likely to continue to invest in a losing course of action (41 percent) than groups composed of unacquainted persons (16 percent) when groups do not have buy-in from relevant organizational authorities. In contrast, when they are respected by their organization, groups of friends are extremely deft at extracting themselves from failing courses of action (Thompson et al., 1998). In fact, the greater the group's sense of social identity, or pride in the group, the more likely the group is to escalate commitment to an unreasonable course of action. For example, teams of people in a city council simulation, faced with an important budget allocation decision regarding a playground project, either wore team name tags (high social identity) or wore personal name tags (low social identity; Dietz-Uhler, 1996). Groups that were stronger in social identity showed greater escalation of commitment to the ill-fated playground project. Moreover, the use of group pronouns (*we, us, our*) rose as escalation rose!

## Structural Determinants

The same determinants that create groupthink on a team level also exist at the level of the institution. For instance, a project can itself become institutionalized, thereby removing it from critical evaluation. Instead, old-timers and newcomers learn to perceive the project as an integral part of the culture. It becomes impossible for these teams to consider removal or extinction of the project.

Often in organizations, political pressure can kill an otherwise viable project. Similarly, political support can keep a project alive that should be terminated. The escalation of commitment phenomenon implies that more often than not, teams will persevere with a losing course of action because of the psychological, social, and structural reinforcements in the situation. Teams become entrenched and committed to their positions and reluctant to move away from them.

## Avoiding the Escalation of Commitment Problem

Most teams do not realize that they are in an escalation dilemma until it is too late. Complicating matters is the fact that, in most escalation dilemmas, the team might have some early "wins" or good signs that reinforce the initial decision. How can a team best exit an escalation dilemma?

Unfortunately, there is no magical, overnight cure. The best advice is to adopt a policy of risk management: Be aware of the risks involved in the decision, learn how to best manage these risks, and set limits, effectively capping losses at a tolerable level. It is also important to find ways to get information and feedback on the project from a different perspective. More specifically:

### Set Limits

Ideally, a team should determine at the outset what criteria and performance standards will justify continued investment in the project or program in question. These should be unambiguously articulated and distributed to all relevant personnel.

### Avoid the Bystander Effect

In many situations, especially ambiguous ones, people quite frankly are not sure how to behave and, therefore, do nothing out of fear of acting foolishly. This dynamic explains the bystander effect, or the tendency to not help others who obviously need help in emergency situations (Latané & Darley, 1970). If team members have well-defined, predetermined limits, they need not try to interpret others' behavior; they can refer to their own judgment and act upon it.

### Avoid Tunnel Vision

Get several perspectives on the problem. Ask people who are not personally involved in the situation for their appraisal. Be careful not to bias their evaluation with your own views, hopes, expectations, or other details, such as the cost of extricating the team from the situation, because that will only predispose them toward the team's point of view. You don't want to hear your views parroted back to you—you want an honest, critical assessment.

### Recognize Sunk Costs

Probably the most powerful way to avoid escalation of commitment is to simply recognize and accept sunk costs. Sunk costs are basically water under the bridge: money (or other commitments) previously spent that cannot be recovered. It is often helpful for teams to have built into their agenda a period in which they consider removal of the project, product, or program. In this way, the situation is redefined as one in which a decision will be made immediately about whether to invest, that is, if you were making the initial decision today, would you make the investment currently under consideration (as a continuing investment), or would you choose another course of action? If the decision is not one that you would choose anew, you might want to start thinking about how to terminate the project and move on to the next one. Intel Founders Andy Grove and Gordon Moore correctly recognized sunk costs in 1985 when they sat down and asked themselves some tough questions: " 'If we got kicked out and the board brought in a new CEO,' Grove asked Moore, 'what do you think he would do?' 'Get out of memory chips was the answer' " (Charan & Useem, 2002). It was at that point that Intel decided to exit the memory business entirely and become a maker of microprocessors. However, most of the time, the recognition of sunk costs comes too late, if at all. For example, by the time Xerox President and CEO Anne Mulcahy admitted that the company had an "unsustainable business model," Xerox was on the verge of bankruptcy (Charan & Useem, 2002).

### Avoid Bad Mood

Unpleasant emotional states are often implicated in poor decision making (for a review, see Baumeister & Scher, 1988). According to Leith and Baumeister (1996), negative affect (such as bad mood, anger, embarrassment, etc.) leads to nonoptimal courses of action—holding out the hope for some highly positive but risky outcome. More precisely, when people are upset, they tend to choose high-risk, high-payoff options.

### External Review

In some cases, it is necessary to remove or replace the original decision makers from deliberations precisely because they are biased. One way to do this is with an external review of departments.

## DECISION-MAKING PITFALL 3: THE ABILENE PARADOX

In the case of groupthink and escalation of commitment, teams pursue a course of action largely because they are personally involved; a decision to discontinue might involve admission of a poor earlier choice. There is another kind of behavior that can lead teams to make undesirable choices—choices, in fact, that none of the individuals would have made on their own. Known as the **Abilene paradox** (Harvey, 1974), it is a kind of consensus seeking that has its roots in the avoidance of conflict. The Abilene paradox is basically a form of **pluralistic ignorance:** Group members adopt a position because they feel other members desire it; team members don't challenge one another because they want to avoid conflict or achieve consensus. Although this is a kind of "expectational bubble"—a set of expectations about other people's expectations that could be burst if even one person expressed a contrary view—it can have a dramatic impact on the actual decision-making behavior of the team. The story in Box 6-4 illustrates the dilemma.

To the extent that team members are more interested in consensus than debate, they may end up "in Abilene." Indeed, the mismanagement of agreement can be more problematic than the management of disagreement (Harvey, 1974). This may seem counterintuitive, but the consequences are very real.

It may seem strange to think that intelligent people who are in private agreement may somehow fail to realize the commonality of their beliefs and end up in Abilene. However, it is easy to see how this can happen if members fail to communicate their beliefs to each other.

Quandaries like the Abilene paradox may seem absurd, but they are easy to fall into. Strategies to avoid the situation include playing devil's advocate, careful questioning, and a commitment on the part of all team members to both fully air their opinions as well as respectfully listen to others. Note that none of these requires team members to abandon consensus seeking as a goal—if that is indeed their goal. However, it does require that consensus actually reflect the true beliefs of the team.

BOX 6-4

## The Abilene Paradox

The July afternoon in Coleman, Texas (population 5,607), was particularly hot— 104 degrees as measured by the Walgreen's Rexall Ex-Lax temperature gauge. In addition, the wind was blowing fine-grained West Texas topsoil through the house. But the afternoon was still tolerable—even potentially enjoyable. There was a fan going on the back porch; there was cold lemonade; and, finally, there was entertainment. Dominoes. Perfect for the conditions. The game required little more physical exertion than an occasional mumbled comment, "Shuffle 'em," and an unhurried movement of the arm to place the spots in the appropriate perspective on the table. All in all, it had the markings of an agreeable Sunday afternoon in Coleman—that is, it was until my father-in-law suddenly said, "Let's get in the car and go to Abilene and have dinner at the cafeteria."

I thought, "What, go to Abilene? Fifty-three miles? In this dust storm and heat? And in an un-air-conditioned 1958 Buick?"

But my wife chimed in with "Sounds like a great idea. I'd like to go. How about you, Jerry?" Since my own preferences were obviously out of step with the rest I replied, "Sounds good to me," and added, "I just hope your mother wants to go."

"Of course I want to go," said my mother-in-law. "I haven't been to Abilene in a long time."

So into the car and off to Abilene we went. My predictions were fulfilled. The heat was brutal. We were coated with a fine layer of dust that was cemented with perspiration by the time we arrived. The food at the cafeteria provided first-rate testimonial material for antacid commercials.

Some four hours and 106 miles later we returned to Coleman, hot and exhausted. We sat in front of the fan for a long time in silence. Then, both to be sociable and to break the silence, I said, "It was a great trip, wasn't it?"

No one spoke. Finally my mother-in-law said, with some irritation, "Well, to tell the truth, I really didn't enjoy it much and would rather have stayed here. I just went along because the three of you were so enthusiastic about going. I wouldn't have gone if you all hadn't pressured me into it."

I couldn't believe it. "What do you mean 'you all'?" I said. "Don't put me in the 'you all' group. I was delighted to be doing what we were doing. I didn't want to go. I only went to satisfy the rest of you. You're the culprits."

My wife looked shocked. "Don't call me a culprit. You and Daddy and Mama were the ones who wanted to go. I just went along to be sociable and to keep you happy. I would have had to be crazy to want to go out in heat like that."

Her father entered the conversation abruptly. "Hell!" he said.

He proceeded to expand on what was already absolutely clear. "Listen, I never wanted to go to Abilene. I just thought you might be bored. You visit so seldom I wanted to be sure you enjoyed it. I would have preferred to play another game of dominoes and eat the leftovers in the icebox."

After the outburst of recrimination we all sat back in silence. Here we were, four reasonably sensible people who, of our own volition, had just taken a 106-mile trip across a godforsaken desert in a furnacelike temperature through a cloudlike dust storm to eat unpalatable food at a hole-in-the-wall cafeteria in Abilene, when none of us had really wanted to go. In fact, to be more accurate, we'd done just the opposite of what we wanted to do. The whole situation simply didn't make sense (Harvey, 1974).

What factors lead to problems like the Abilene paradox? In general, if individual team members are intimidated or feel that their efforts will not be worthwhile, then they are less likely to air or defend their viewpoints. This is called *self-limiting behavior.* According to a survey of 569 managers by Mulvey, Veiga, & Elsass (1996), there are six key causes of self-limiting behavior in teams:

- *The presence of someone with expertise:* When team members perceive that another member of the team has expertise or is highly qualified to make a decision, they will self-limit. Members' perceptions of other teammates' competence play a key role, and these evaluations are formed quickly—often before a team meets for the first time.

- *The presentation of a compelling argument:* Frequently, the timing of a coherent argument influences decision making, such as when the decision is made after a lot of fruitless discussion.

- *A lack of confidence in one's ability to contribute:* If team members feel unsure about their ability to meaningfully contribute to the decision, they will be inclined to self-limit.

- *An unimportant or meaningless decision:* Unless the decision is seen as vital or important to the individual's well-being, there is a powerful tendency to adopt a "who cares" attitude.

- *Pressure from others to conform to the team's decision:* Roger Boisjoly reported that he felt incredible pressures to conform exerted by the NASA management team.

- *A dysfunctional decision-making climate:* When team members believe that others are frustrated, indifferent, disorganized, or generally unwilling to commit themselves to making an effective decision, they are likely to self-limit. Such a climate can be created in the early stages of a decision by inadvertent remarks such as, "this is a ridiculous task," "nothing's going to change, so why bother," and so on.

## How to Avoid the Abilene Paradox

The following suggestions are taken from Harvey (1974) and Mulvey et al. (1996).

*Confront the Issue in a Team Setting*
The most straightforward approach involves meeting with the organization members who are key figures in the problem and its solution. The first step is for the individual who proposes a solution to state it and then be open to any and all feedback. For example:

> I want to talk with you about the research project. Although I have previously said things to the contrary, I frankly don't think it will work and I am very anxious about it. I suspect that others may feel the same, but I don't know. Anyway, I am concerned that we may end up misleading one another, and if we aren't careful, we may continue to work on a problem that none of us wants and that might even bankrupt us. That's why I need to know where the rest of you stand. I would appreciate any of your thoughts about the project. Do you think it can succeed? (Harvey, 1974, p. 32).

*Conduct a Private Vote*
People often go along with what they think the team wants to do. Dissenting opinions are easier to express privately—distribute blank cards and ask team members to privately write their opinions. Guarantee them anonymity and then share the overall outcomes with the team.

*Minimize Status Differences*

High-status members are often at the center of communication, and lower status members are likely to feel pressures to conform more quickly. Although this can be difficult to avoid, reassurances by senior members about the importance of frank and honest discussion reinforced by the elimination of status symbols, like dress, meeting place, title, and so on, may be helpful. For example, when Samsung Chairman Lee Kun Hee decided to take Samsung into the auto business in 1997, most of Samsung's top managers silently opposed the $13B investment. But Lee was a powerful chairman and car fanatic. So when Samsung Motors collapsed just after a year, forcing Lee to spend $2B of his own money, he expressed the following sentiment: *Why didn't anybody come to me and tell me about their reservations?* (Charan & Useem, 2002).

*Frame the Task as a Decision to Be Made*

Framing the task as a decision to be made, rather than a judgment (which suggests personal opinion), helps cast a tone of somber decision making, absent of the trappings of power or personal prestige. When team members are given a decision-making responsibility, they approach the problem differently when the decision that needs to be made is framed as a *problem to be solved*. The typical approach is to view decisions as judgments, not problems. People typically view a problem as needing more analysis, such as pros and cons, and less opinion. Telling your team that you believe in "fact-based decision making" is a potentially helpful way of framing the decision.

*Provide a Formal Forum for Controversial Views*

This may be achieved by segmenting the discussion into pros and cons. Debate must be legitimized. Members should not have to worry about whether it is appropriate to bring up contrary views; it should be expected and encouraged. For example, Lucent CEO Rich McGinn did not do this in the late 1990s, even when the controversial views came from his own company. Lucent's scientists pleaded in vain with McGinn to develop OC-192, an optical technology that could transmit voice and data faster. McGinn did not listen, and shortly thereafter, competitor Nortel rolled out OC-192 instead. Moreover, McGinn did not listen to Lucent salespeople who were trying to tell him that his growth targets were unrealistic.

*Take Responsibility for Failure*

It is important to create a climate where teams can make mistakes, own up to them, and then move on without fear of recrimination. Consider what happened to a three-man forge team, called the "Grumpy Old Men," at Eaton Corporation in the Forge Division plant. Through an assumption at the start of their shift, they made an error that resulted in about 1,200 pieces of scrap. It was not an inexpensive mistake, but it was not one that would close the plant. The team had jeopardized the plant's output to customers. The team came forward to the plant leadership, admitted their error, described its potential impact, and demanded to be allowed to take corrective action so that the problem could never occur again. They even took it a step further and demanded to be allowed to go before the entire workforce at the start of each of the three shifts and admit their error and describe what they were doing to make sure it would not happen again (Bergstrom, 1997).

## DECISION-MAKING PITFALL 4: GROUP POLARIZATION

Consider the case in Box 6-5. Most people independently evaluating the problem state that the new company would need to have nearly a two-thirds probability of success before they would advise Mr. A to leave his current job and accept a new position (Stoner, 1961). What do you think happens when the same people discuss Mr. A's situation and are instructed to reach consensus?

You might expect the outcome of the team to be the same as the average of the individuals considered separately. However, this is not what happens. The group advises Mr. A to take the new job, even if it only has slightly better than a 50–50 chance of success! In other words, groups show a **risky shift.**

Now consider a situation in which a company is deciding the highest odds of an engine malfunction that could be tolerated on the release of a new vehicle. In this case, individual advisors are cautious, but when the same people are in a group, they collectively insist on even lower odds. Thus, they exhibit a **cautious shift.** According to Henry Miller, a former FDA reviewer, the FDA (as a team of bureaucrats) regularly falls prey to cautious shifts. Miller points out that public health suffers from the FDA's excessive cautiousness far more than from its risky behavior. For example, in the 1980s, some 10,000 Americans "unncessarily contracted hepatitis B when the FDA opted to require long, needlessly comprehensive trials of a new vaccine" (Stipp, 2002, p. 113).

Why are teams both more risky and more cautious than are individuals, considering the identical situation? The reason for this apparent disparity has to do with some of the peculiarities of group dynamics. Teams are not inherently more risky or cautious than individuals; rather they are more *extreme* than individuals. **Group polarization** is the tendency for group discussion to intensify group opinion, producing more extreme judgment than might be obtained by pooling the individuals' views separately (see Figure 6-3).

---

**BOX 6-5**

### Advice Question

*Mr. A, an electrical engineer who is married and has one child, has been working for a large electronics corporation since graduating from college five years ago. He is assured of a lifetime job with a modest, though adequate, salary and liberal pension benefits upon retirement. On the other hand, it is very unlikely that his salary will increase much before he retires. While attending a convention, Mr. A is offered a job with a small, newly founded company that has a highly uncertain future. The new job would pay more to start and would offer the possibility of a share in the ownership if the company survived the competition with larger firms.*

Imagine that you are advising Mr. A. What is the *lowest* probability or odds of the new company proving financially sound that you would consider acceptable to make it worthwhile for Mr. A to take the new job? Before reading on, indicate your response on a probability scale from zero to 100 percent.

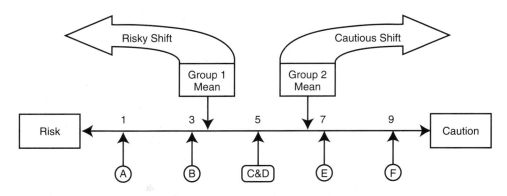

**FIGURE 6-3** Group Polarization Process. Imagine that Group 1 includes Person A (who chose 1), Person B (who chose 3), and Persons C and D (who both chose 5); the average of pregroup choices would be $(1 + 3 + 5 + 5)/4$, or 3.5. Because this mean is less than 5, a risky shift would probably occur in Group 1. If, in contrast, Group 2 contained persons C, D, E, and F, their pregroup average would be $(5 + 5 + 7 + 9)/4$ or 6.5. Because this mean in closer to the caution pole, a conservative shift would probably occur in the group.
*Source:* Adapted from Janis, I. L. 1982. *Victims of Groupthink* (2nd ed.). Boston: Houghton Mifflin.

Group polarization is not simply a case of social compliance or a bandwagon effect. The same individuals display the polarization effect when queried privately after group discussion. This means that people really believe the group's decision—they have conformed inwardly! The polarization effect does not happen in nominal groups. The polarization effect grows stronger with time, meaning that the same person who was in a group discussion two weeks earlier will be even more extreme in his or her judgment.

There are two psychological explanations for group polarization: the need to be right and the need to be liked.

### The Need to Be Right

Groups are presumed to have access to a broader range of decision-making resources and, hence, to be better equipped to make high-quality decisions than any person can alone. By pooling their different backgrounds, training, and experience, group members have at least the potential for working in a more informed fashion than would be the case were the decision left to any single individual. The implication of these two assertions is that individuals are **information dependent**—that is, they often lack information that another member has. Consequently, individuals look to the team to provide information that they do not know. This is an adaptive response. However, it can lead to problems when people treat others' opinions as facts and fail to question their validity. The need to be right, therefore, is the tendency to look to the group to define what reality is—and the more people who hold a particular opinion, the more right an answer appears to be. Whereas this information-seeking tendency would seem to be contradictory to the common information effect that we discussed in the previous chapter, the two processes are not inconsistent. The common information effect (and all of its undesirable consequences) are driven by a biased search for information. Conformity, or the adoption of group-level beliefs, is strongest when individuals feel unsure about their own position.

## The Need to Be Liked

Most people have a fundamental need to be accepted and approved of by others. Conformity is often a ticket to group acceptance. There is good reason for this: Teams provide valuable resources. One of the most straightforward ways to gain immediate acceptance in a group is to express attitudes consistent with those of the group members. Stated another way, most people like others who conform to their own beliefs. This means that people in groups will become more extreme in the direction of the group's general opinion, because attitudes that are sympathetic toward the group are most likely to be positively rewarded. The need to be liked refers to the tendency for people to agree with a group so that they can feel more like a part of that group.

Simply stated, people want to make the right decision and they want to be approved of by their team. Take the case concerning Mr. A, the electrical engineer. Most people are positively inclined when they agree to recommend to Mr. A that he seriously consider a job change. However, they vary greatly in their reasons for why Mr. A should change jobs. Someone in the group may feel that Mr. A should leave the secure job because it does not represent a sufficient challenge; others may think that Mr. A should leave the company because he should increase his standard of living. Thus, people feel that Mr. A should consider a move, but they have different (yet complementary) reasons supporting their belief. This is the rational type of conformity we discussed earlier. At the same time, members of the team want to be accepted—part of the socialization process we outlined in Chapter 4.

## Conformity Pressures

The group polarization effect is related to conformity pressure. **Conformity** occurs when people bring their behavior into alignment with a group's expectations and beliefs. Although many people think their beliefs and behavior are based on their own free will, social behavior is strongly influenced by others. For a clear and surprising demonstration of the power of conformity pressure, see Box 6-6.

Conformity is greater when the judgment or opinion issue is difficult and when people are uncertain. People are especially likely to conform if they face an otherwise unanimous group consensus (Asch, 1956; Wilder & Allen, 1977). Conformity is greater when people value and admire their team—rejection from a desirable group is very threatening (Back, 1951). For example, when people are aware that another member of their team advocated an inferior solution to a problem, they are less likely to intervene if they are motivated to be *compatible* than if they are motivated to be *accurate* (Quinn & Schlenker, 2002). However, we do not want to paint the picture that managers lack integrity. People are more willing to take a stand when they feel confident about their expertise, have high social status (Harvey & Consalvi, 1960), are strongly committed to their initial view (Deutsch & Gerard, 1955), and do not like or respect the people trying to influence them (Hogg & Turner, 1987).

Coupled with the need to be liked is the desire not to be ostracized from one's team. There is good reason for concern, because individuals who deviate from their

---

BOX 6-6

## Conformity Pressure

Suppose that you are meeting with your team. The question facing your team is a simple one: Which of the three lines in panel 2 of Figure 6-4 is equal in length to the line in panel 1? The team leader seeks a group consensus. She begins by asking the colleague sitting to your left for his opinion. To your shock, your colleague chooses line 1; then, each of the other four team members selects line 1—even though line 2 is clearly correct. You begin to wonder whether you are losing your mind. Finally, it's your turn to decide. What do you do?

Most people who read this example find it nearly impossible to imagine that they would choose line 1, even if everyone else had. Yet 76 percent make an erroneous, conforming judgment (e.g., choose line 1) on at least one question; on average, people conform one-third of the time when others give the obviously incorrect answer (Asch, 1956).

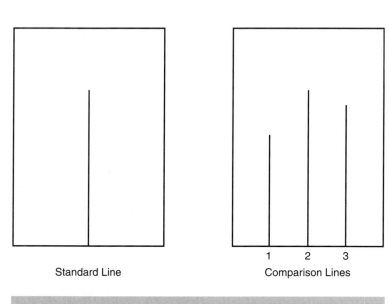

Standard Line

1  2  3
Comparison Lines

**FIGURE 6-4** Conformity Pressure

---

team's opinion are more harshly evaluated than are those who conform (Levine, 1989). A group may reject a deviant person even when they are not under pressure to reach complete consensus (Miller, Jackson, Mueller, & Schersching, 1987). Apparently, holding a different opinion is enough to trigger dislike even when it does not directly block the group's goals. For this reason, people are more likely to conform to the majority when they respond publicly (e.g., Deutsch & Gerard, 1955), anticipate future interaction with other group members (e.g., Lewis, Langan, & Hollander, 1972), are less confident

(Allen, 1965), find the question under consideration to be ambiguous or difficult (Tajfel, 1978), and are interdependent concerning rewards (e.g., Deutsch & Gerard, 1955).

Most managers dramatically underestimate the conformity pressures that operate in groups. Perhaps this is because people like to think of themselves as individualists who are not afraid to speak their own minds. However, conformity pressures in groups are real and they affect the quality of team decision making. The key message for the manager is to anticipate conformity pressures in groups, to understand what drives it (i.e., the need to be liked and the desire to be right), and then to put into place group structures that will not allow conformity pressures to endanger the quality of group decision making.

## DECISION-MAKING PITFALL 5: UNETHICAL DECISION MAKING

Unethical decision making is another type of bias that can affect even the most pristine people and companies. Unethical decision making can be small scale or affect the lives and welfare of hundreds of thousands of people. For example, the scandals that occurred at Sunbeam, Enron, Global Crossing, Qwest, and Worldcom cost investors more than $300B and put tens of thousands of people out of work (Byrne, 2002b). Unethical decision making shares many of the same dynamics involved in the other concepts we have discussed in this chapter, such as groupthink. According to Sims (1992), groupthink can lead to a culture of unethical behavior within a company. Whereas groupthink situations often center on a particular decision in a particular circumstance (e.g., the launch of the Shuttle *Challenger* in 1986), unethical decision making is more effusive and metastasizes through the organization. There is no one moment when executives sit down and conspire to commit wrongdoing. Rather, there is an "incremental descent into poor judgment" (Charan & Useem, 2002). Below, we consider some of the situational triggers of unethical decision making. We resist the urge to explain all such occurrences of unethical decision making as a simple manifestation of evil personalities. Rather, we believe that certain conditions may act as enabling conditions for unethical behavior.

### Rational Man Model

Undergirding virtually all economic theory and practice is the rational expectations model, also known as the *rational man model*. According to this model, people are fundamentally motivated to maximize their own utility, which has become equivalent to maximizing self-interest. So entrenched is this model in modern business analysis that to make any other assumption about human behavior is irrational, illogical, and flawed. However, the lay perception of the economic model has become somewhat of a caricature of the actual model in two important ways. First, people assume that others are more self-interested than they actually are. Second, people begin to view their own motivations as more driven by self-interest than is actually the case. Psychologist Dale Miller calls this "norm of self interest" (Miller, 1999). Miller provides evidence that the norm of self-interest is so pervasive that people often "invent" self-interested explanations of why they perform non-self-serving (or altruistic) acts, such as giving money to charity. Even more disconcerting, economist Robert Frank and his colleagues find that people who take business courses are significantly more likely to engage in questionable and potentially unethical behaviors—for example, failing to return money that they find in the street, behaving competitively in a prisoner's dilemma game, and so on—than people who don't take business courses (Frank, Gilovich, & Regan, 1993).

## Pluralistic Ignorance

Pluralistic ignorance, as discussed earlier in the Abilene paradox section, is the widely held belief that everyone else knows or believes something that we do not. The classic example of pluralistic ignorance is Hans Christian Andersen's story of the emperor's new clothes (1837/1959). In this story, a naked emperor walks through the town while everyone admires his "clothes"—each person sees a naked man, but believes that others do not. A major reason that unethical behavior might be promulgated is the belief that "everyone else is doing it." Said one young Enron control person, "If your boss was [fudging], and you have never worked anywhere else, you just assume that everybody fudges earnings" (Byrne, France, & Zellner, 2002, p. 118).

## Desensitization

Another problem concerns desensitization of behavior. When someone first crosses the line of appropriate behavior, that person is extremely sensitized. However, once the line is crossed, the individual is desensitized, and the normal system of internal checks and balances is turned off. One employee at Enron said, "The more people pushed the envelope with aggressive accounting, the harder they would have to push the next year. It's like being a heroin junkie. How do you go cold turkey?" (Byrne, France, & Zellner, 2002, p. 118).

The question, of course, is how to remedy or, ideally, prevent this situation. Consider the five steps below.

## Accountability for Behavior

One of the most shocking revelations of the fall of Enron and Arthur Andersen was the fact that the people involved assumed little or no formal accountability for their own behavior. For example, the committee on governmental affairs of the U.S. Senate discovered that there were almost no consequences for company directors who fail on the job. Their liability insurance is paid for by shareholders, but they are not held responsible for any damages. Perhaps this is why Byrne (2002a) writes, "Shareholders have a right to expect directors, who at Enron were paid as much as $350,000 a year in cash, stock options, and phantom stock, to be engaged and active. They should be assured that directors will place investors' interests above those of executives" (pp. 50–51). Perhaps the lack of accountability explains why the directors, in the Enron case, never asked the tough, obvious questions. For example, former Enron CEO Kenneth L. Lay had an approved credit line from the board that eventually totaled $7.5M, and the board allowed him to repay it with stock instead of cash. The chairman of the compensation committee, Charles A. LeMaistre, told the Senate investigators that he did not think it was the committee's responsibility to monitor Lay's credit line (Byrne, 2002a).

At an even more basic level, most leaders want to take credit and responsibility for good news but pawn off bad news. It's a way of protecting the ego. For example, former CEO of Mattel, Jill E. Barad, never assumed responsibility for the earnings surprises at

Mattel or adverse announcements. Instead, she blamed her subordinates and fired them (Byrne & Grover, 2000).

**Accountability** is the implicit or explicit expectation that one may be called on to justify one's beliefs, feelings, and actions to others (Lerner & Tetlock, 1999). Accountability implies that people who do not provide a satisfactory justification for their actions will suffer negative consequences. However, there are multiple forms and types of accountability, each with their own beneficial as well as detrimental effects on decision making (for a review, see Lerner & Tetlock, 1999). Lerner and Tetlock distinguish the following as considerations regarding accountability in organizational decision making:

- *Accountability to an audience with known versus unknown views:* People who know what the ultimate audience wants conform to their opinions. Consider, for example, that only financial-aid agents who do not know their audience's preferences match awards to needs effectively (Adelberg & Batson, 1978).
- *Pre- versus postdecisional accountability:* After people irrevocably commit themselves to a decision, they will attempt to justify their decisions. For example, people form less complex thoughts and hold more rigid and defensive views when they are accountable and have reported their attitudes (Tetlock, Skitka, & Boettger, 1989).
- *Outcome accountability versus process accountability:* In general, accountability for outcomes leads to greater escalation behavior, whereas accountability for process increases decision-making effectiveness (Doney & Armstrong, 1996).
- *Legitimate versus illegitimate accountability:* If accountability is perceived as illegitimate—for example, intrusive and insulting—any beneficial effects of accountability may fail or backfire (Lerner & Tetlock, 1999).

## Reward Model

Hand-in-hand with accountability is the system for reward and promotion. As we noted in Chapter 3, reward systems shape behavior in organizations. Several problems existed at Enron, with an unabashed emphasis on self-interest, even if it meant abusing evaluation systems. For example, several Enron executives commented that Andrew S. Fastow, the ex-chief financial officer, had a reputation for exploiting the review system to get back at people who expressed disagreement or criticism. And, although managers were supposed to be graded on teamwork, it paid to be individualistic. Another insider said, "You've got someone at the top saying the stock price is the most important thing, which is driven by earnings. Whoever could provide earnings quickly would be promoted" (Byrne, France, & Zellner, 2002).

## Appropriate Role Models

One of the likely problems for the fall of Enron was the reorganization of the company instigated by former CEO Jeffrey Skilling, beginning in 1997. Layers of management were eliminated, hundreds of outsiders were recruited and encouraged to bring new thinking, and senior-based salaries were abolished in favor of highly leveraged compensation that offered huge cash bonuses and stock options to top performers. Young people, many with their degrees just in hand, were given extraordinary authority, able to make $5M decisions without approval. Yet the "parents" weren't around. James O'Toole, professor at the Center for Effective Organizations at USC, says, "In larger companies like IBM and GE, even though there is a movement toward youth, there are still enough older people around to mentor them. At Enron, you had a bunch of kids running loose without adult supervision" (Byrne, France, & Zellner, 2002).

## Eliminate Conflicts of Interest

Analysis of the telecom industry scandal in the summer of 2002 revealed deep-seated conflicts of interest. Salomon Smith Barney's (SSB) telecom analyst, Jack B. Grubman, was actively involved with the companies he covered, making it impossible for him to be objective about those companies' prospects. For example, he helped former nonexecutive chairman Phillip Anschutz recruit Joseph Nacchio as Qwest's chief executive in 1997, and he aided founder and chairman of Global Crossing, Gary Winnick, in his $11B acquisition of Frontier Communication in 1999. Thus, when providing critical assessments about Qwest and Global Crossing for investors, he was conflicted, but did so anyway (Rosebush, Timmons, Crockett, Palmeri, & Haddad, 2002). Perhaps this is why Michael E. Capuano, House Democrat on the House Committee on Financial Services to examine the WorldCom accounting scale, said of Grubman, "We have an independent analyst who is neither independent and apparently can't analyze" (Rosebush et al., 2002, p. 37). It is a disturbing realization that most boards create conflicts of interest by offering board members a panoply of perks. For example, John Wakeham, a member of Enron's audit committtee, received $72,000 a year to consult on European operations. Tyco International paid director Frank Walsh $10M for his help on a merger; WorldCom Chairman Bert C. Roberts Jr. and other WorldCom employees got to fly on private aircraft—the list goes on and on (Lavelle, 2002).

## Create Cultures of Integrity

As we noted in Chapter 2, the culture of a team and organization is not under the direct control of upper management. Rather, it emerges as a result of design factors in the organization and the team. Even in the most tightly controlled, bureaucratic organizations, it is impossible to monitor the actions of every employee. This is where the implicit cultural code, or norms, are supposed to guide every team member to make the right decisions without supervision. However, in many instances, the cultures are rotten because no one is living (much less espousing) to do anything else. The failure to discipline transgressions can be just as damaging as the failure to reward excellent behavior in teams. For example, when SSB Chairperson John Gutfreund learned of the overbid in auctions of U.S. Treasury bonds by Paul Mozer, a trader, he failed to discipline him. Mozer evidently interpreted the lack of discipline as an endorsement of his behavior, and continued to overbid (Charan & Useem, 2002).

Business cultures that lack the ability to take swift and decisive action run the risk of unethical behavior by default. For example, Andersen was unable to respond swiftly to crises in the firm or govern itself decisively. It took Andersen five months to hire ex-CEO Joe Berardino; once in office, he was unable to fire a partner without a two-thirds vote of Andersen's 1,700 partners around the world. Even as the firm was engulfed in turmoil, the partners fought unproductively about who should speak publicly (Byrne, 2002a).

# CONCLUSIONS

Teams make important decisions and some of them will not be good ones, despite the very best of intentions. It is unrealistic to suggest that poor decision making, or for that matter even disastrous decision making, is avoidable. The key message hearkens back to a point we made early in Chapter 1, which has to do with creating an organization that can optimally learn from failure. Learning from failure is difficult when people suffer—especially innocent ones. The key for decision-making teams within organizations is to develop and use decision-making procedures, such as veto policies and preestablished criteria to guide decision making. All these decisions involve a certain level of risk, but that risk can be minimized. There is a clear difference between principled risk taking and unethical risk taking. Creating cultures of integrity involves ethical leadership from the top down and making sure that incentives for behavior do not encourage or reward unethical behavior.

# CHAPTER

7

# Conflict in Teams:

## Leveraging Differences to Create Opportunity

*"Each afternoon, in a tiny workroom on the 12th floor of the Mayo Clinic, the battle against cancer begins with an argument" (Roberts, 1999a, p. 148). The walls of the room are plastered with X-rays, CT scans, and data. A group of cancer specialists, surgeons, residents, and nurses debates how to diagnose, and ultimately treat, the day's patients. On one particular day, Dr. Lynn Hartmann, a medical oncologist, suggests a surgical procedure for a 65-year-old man with a possible kidney tumor. However, when she asks teammates John Edmonson and Harry Long for their opinions, they challenge her in a direct, point-counterpoint debate. Whereas this open debate might seem strange, it is precisely the vision that founder William Worrall Mayo established when he first opened the clinic in 1859. Mayo, an ambitious perfectionist and strong believer of the whole being greater than the sum of the parts, regularly preached, "No one is big enough to be independent of others." In the Mayo clinic, physicians are referred to as "consultants" to emphasize the fact that anyone, at any time, is expected to be called upon to discuss a patient. The open debates are part of the team culture at Mayo; consultants know that their recommendations will be rigorously questioned by team members and that this kind of careful scrutiny will lead to more accurate diagnoses and more effective treatments (Roberts, 1999a).*

A s we will see in this chapter, conflict is a lot like cholesterol: There's a good kind and a bad kind. Most people try to go on special diets so they can lower their bad cholesterol, hoping to avoid a heart attack. In teams, the bad kind of conflict is what we fear most—back-stabbing, character assassination, angry words, denial, gossip, and brush-offs. The good type of conflict—principled debate, challenging questions in search of the truth—is the type of conflict that characterizes high-performance teams such as the Mayo Clinic teams. This style of conflict is one that is often not present in teams. Indeed, most teams either actively avoid conflict and risk making "trips to Abilene" (as discussed in Chapter 6), or they engage in a type of conflict that is personal, rather than principled. Some team leaders, in fact, pride themselves on the fact that they never have conflict in their teams. We think these leaders do their teams a great disservice.

Our survey of executives and managers, presented in Chapter 1 of this book, revealed that team conflict is one of the top concerns of team management.[1] Conflict

---

[1]Survey of managers and executives in the Kellogg Leading High Impact Teams Program, 1997–2003.

that is not properly managed may lead to hostility, performance deficits, and, in extreme cases, dissolution of the team. Most people regard conflict to be detrimental to effective teamwork and believe that differences between team members should be immediately eliminated. However, differences in interests, perceptions, information, and preferences cannot be avoided, especially in teams that work together closely for extended periods of time. Moreover, conflict can be good for the team—when managed properly. The challenge for the leader is to transform conflict into opportunity. Conflict can have positive consequences, such as enhancing creativity or fostering integrative solutions reflecting many points of view.

This chapter begins by distinguishing among types of conflict and their relative and absolute levels within a team. We then discuss the team dilemma, which centers on the tension between one's own and the team's interests. Next, we describe voting and majority rule and when they are appropriate to use in teams. Finally, we discuss team negotiation and how to maximize mutual interests.

## TYPES OF CONFLICT

As we noted above, all conflict is not created equal. Many types of conflict can threaten teamwork. Before a manager launches into conflict management mode, it is important to accurately diagnose the type of conflict that plagues the team. According to Jehn (1995) there are three distinct types of conflict: relationship conflict, task conflict, and process conflict (see Table 7-1).

**TABLE 7-1**    Three Types of Conflict

| Type of Conflict | Definition | Example of items used to assess/ measure this type of conflict |
|---|---|---|
| **Relationship conflict** (also known as emotional conflict, A-type conflict, or affective conflict) | Involves disagreements based on personal and social issues that are not related to work | How often do people get angry while working in your team? How much relationship tension is there in your team? |
| **Task conflict** (also known as cognitive conflict or C-type conflict) | Involves disagreements about the work that is being done in a group | To what extent are there differences of opinion in your team? How much conflict is there about the work you do in your team? How often do people in your team disagree about opinions regarding the work to be done? How frequently are there conflicts about ideas in your team? |
| **Process conflict** | Centers on task strategy and delegation of duties and resources | How often do members of your team disagree about who should do what? How frequently do members of your team disagree about the way to complete a team task? How much disagreement about the delegation of tasks exists within your team? |

*Based on:* Jehn, K. 1995. "A Multimethod Examination of the Benefits and Detriments of Intragroup Conflict." *Administrative Science Quarterly, 40,* 256–282; Jehn, K.A., & Mannix, E.A. 2001. "The Dynamic Nature of Conflict: A Longitudinal Study of Intragroup Conflict and Group Performance." *Academy of Management Journal, 44*(2), 238–251.

**Relationship conflict** is personal, defensive, and resentful. Also known as **A-type conflict, emotional conflict,** or **affective conflict** (Guetzkow & Gyr, 1954), it is rooted in anger, personal friction, personality clashes, ego, and tension. Obviously, this is the type of conflict that most team leaders and team members try to avoid. Sometimes, however, they are not successful. For example, several former managers at Qwest, the telecommunications company that went under criminal investigation for its accounting practices, say that shouting matches among executives were not uncommon during CEO Joseph Nacchio's tenure with the company. At one meeting in 2000, one executive recalled, Nacchio flew into a rage, hurled a presentation folder across the room, and ordered everyone at the meeting to return to their offices (Hudson, 2002).

Relationship conflict is not always expressed via open shouting matches. In fact, some people, and some teams, go to great lengths to avoid any overt expression of conflict. For example, Argyris (1977b) describes a case in which lower-level managers had identified a number of serious production and marketing problems in their company. They told the middle managers. Once the middle managers were convinced that the situation described by the lower managers was actually true, they began to release some of the bad news, but they did so carefully, only in measured doses. They managed their communications carefully to make certain they were "covered" if upper management became upset. The result was that top management was never fully apprised of the problems—rather, they received a strangely edited view of the problem. Top management, therefore, continued to speak glowingly about the product, partially to ensure that it would get the financial backing it needed from within the company. Lower-level managers became confused and eventually depressed because they could not understand why top management continued to support the product. Their reaction was to reduce the frequency of their memos and the intensity of the alarm they expressed, while simultaneously turning the problem over to middle management.

**Task conflict,** or **cognitive conflict,** is largely depersonalized; also known as **C-type conflict**, it consists of argumentation about the merits of ideas, plans, and projects. Task conflict is often effective in stimulating creativity because it forces people to rethink problems and arrive at outcomes that everyone can live with. This is why having divergent views in a team is beneficial for creativity and innovation. For example, when a majority of members in a team is confronted by the differing opinions of minorities, the majority is forced to think about why the minority disagrees. This thought process can instigate novel ideas (Levine & Moreland, 1985; Nemeth, 1995).

**Process conflict** centers on disagreements that team members have about how to approach a task and, specifically, who should do what.

## Types of Conflict and Work Team Effectiveness

As a general rule, relationship conflict threatens team productivity, whereas task conflict benefits team functioning (Jehn, 1995; Shah & Jehn, 1993). Disagreement about a task is the most beneficial type of conflict.

Relationship conflict interferes with the effort people put into a task because members are preoccupied with reducing threats, increasing power, and attempting to build cohesion rather than working on the task. The anxiety produced by interpersonal animosity may inhibit cognitive functioning (Roseman, Wiest, & Swartz, 1994) and also distract team members from the task, causing them to work less effectively and produce suboptimal products (Wilson, Butler, Cray, Hickson, & Mallory, 1986).

In contrast, task conflict can improve decision-making outcomes and team productivity by increasing decision quality through incorporating devil's advocacy roles, constructive criticism, and stimulation of discussion.

Clear evidence for the advantages of task conflict over relationship conflict is found in observations of actual organizational work teams. According to Jehn (1997), who investigated everyday conflicts in six organizational work teams, relationship conflict is detrimental to performance and satisfaction (two major indices of team productivity); furthermore, emotionality reduces team effectiveness. Groups that accept task conflict but not relationship conflict are the most effective. Task conflict is associated with higher decision-making quality, greater understanding, higher commitment, and more acceptance. In contrast, relationship conflict significantly reduces decision quality, understanding, commitment, and acceptance. (For another illustration of the deleterious effects of relationship conflict, see Box 7-1.) Similarly, task conflict in teams composed of academics and practitioners is also conducive to productivity on a project, whereas relationship conflict is not (Amabile, Nasco, Mueller, Wojcik, Odomirok, Marsh, & Kramer, 2001).

Task conflict is productive because when people are in conflict about ideas, they are forced to consider the ideas of others. For example, consider a debate between two managers concerning how to market a company's product. Although they have their own individual ideas, when they try to persuade the other by presenting a rationale for their approach, each is forced, on some level, to integrate the other's point of view. Of

---

**BOX 7-1**

## The Effects of Relationship Conflict

Amason (1996) interviewed 48 top-management teams in small and midsize food processing firms across the United States and five top-management teams in furniture manufacturing firms in the southeastern United States. Both CEOs and managers were asked about strategic decisions and team behavior. Questions to assess relationship conflict included: How much anger was there among the group over this decision? How much personal friction was there in the group during this discussion? How much were personality clashes between group members evident during the decision? How much tension was there in the group during this decision? Questions to assess task conflict included: How many disagreements over different ideas about this decision were there? How many differences about the content of this decision did the group have to work through? How many differences of opinion were there within the group over this decision?

The results were striking: The presence of task conflict was associated with higher decision-making quality, greater understanding, higher commitment, and more acceptance. In contrast, the presence of relationship conflict significantly reduced decision quality, understanding, commitment, and affective acceptance.

course, it is possible to completely reject the other's arguments, but this is inappropriate in a healthy working relationship. It would also represent relationship rather than task conflict.

Jehn and Mannix (2001) investigated the evolution of conflict within teams over time. Teams performing well were characterized by low but increasing levels of process conflict, moderate levels of task conflict, and low levels of relationship conflict, with a rise near project deadlines. These teams had similar value systems, high levels of trust and respect, and norms that permitted open discussion.

## Proportional and Perceptual Conflict

### Proportional Conflict

Team members often have different ideas about the amount and type of conflict that exists in their group. In any team, for example, there may be differing actual levels of relationship, task, and process conflict. And the relative levels of such conflict are a crucial aspect for team leaders to understand as it affects task performance (Jehn & Chatman, 2000). **Proportional conflict composition** describes the relationship among the three types of conflict (task, relationship, and process) as the level of each type of conflict proportional to the other two and to the overall level of conflict within the group, rather than as an absolute level or amount of any one type. Consider the following example offered by Jehn and Chatman (2000): A team that experiences a moderate amount of constructive task conflict and no other conflict (no relationship or process conflict) will have a different experience than will members of another group with the same amount of task conflict but also a high proportional level of relationship conflict. In the former group, members should experience less stress, less distraction, and less anger, which are frequent consequences of relationship conflict (Amason, 1996; Jehn, 1994, 1995) as compared to members of the group containing more moderate levels of task and relationship conflict. Indeed, teams with a high proportion of task conflict experience a higher level of team member commitment, cohesiveness, individual performance, group performance, and member satisfaction. In contrast, a high proportion of relationship conflict is negatively related to member commitment, cohesiveness, individual performance, group performance, and member satisfaction.

### Perceptual Conflict

If proportional conflict refers to the relative amounts of task, relationship, and process conflict within a team, perceptual conflict refers to the extent to which there is agreement or lack thereof, in terms of whether team members perceive conflict. **Perceptual conflict composition** is the degree to which each person in a team perceives levels of conflict differently compared to other team members (Jehn & Chatman, 2000). Specifically, each members perceptions of conflict are compare to all other group members' perceptions of the group. Jehn and Chatman (2000) give the following example: Two team members in an eight-person team perceive arguments in the group pertaining to the task while the other six members do not detect such conflict. These two members have a larger "perceptual conflict" composition score than those members who believe that there is no task conflict. Importantly, disagreements as to whether and how much conflict exists in a team negatively influence team effectiveness.

## Transforming Relationship into Task Conflict

The key, of course, for the team leader is to learn how to transform relationship conflict into task conflict; or, ideally, design the team so that relationship conflict does not erupt and instead, only healthy task conflict exists. Usually, relationship conflict emerges when there is no other appropriate outlet for conflict. Cohesion and trust among team members allows cognitive conflict to productively emerge. Indeed, friends are better at applying effective conflict management strategies to suit the task at hand than are teams of strangers, whose conflict management approaches are less sophisticated (Shah & Jehn, 1993). Some specific strategies follow.

### Agree on a Common Goal or Shared Vision

The importance of a common goal is summed up in a quote by Steve Jobs, who is associated with two high-profile Silicon Valley companies—Apple Computers and Pixar, Inc. "It's okay to spend a lot of time arguing about which route to take to San Francisco when everyone wants to end up there, but a lot of time gets wasted in such arguments if one person wants to go to San Francisco and another secretly wants to go to San Diego" (Eisenhardt, Kahwajy, & Bourgeois, 1997, p. 80). Shared goals do not imply homogeneous thinking, but they do require everyone to share a vision. Steve Jobs is not alone in his thinking. Colin Sewell-Rutter, a director of The Results Partnership, a consultancy that specializes in improving board-level communications, concludes that "[t]he single most important source of problems within the boardroom is the lack of a shared vision, and shared corporate goals. . . . All the major difficulties ultimately stem from that" (Lynn, 1997, p. 31).

The 1993 departure of Ernest Mario as chief executive of pharmaceutical firm Glaxo (as it was then called) illustrates how conflicts can also mask the fact that teams never fundamentally agreed on what the company is about. Mario was thought to have been preparing a takeover of American rival Warner-Lambert, even though the then-chairman, Sir Paul Girolami, believed that the company should stick with its strategy of investing for organic growth. The result was a bitter conflict that culminated in Mario's departure with a $3M payoff (it was only after Girolami retired that Glaxo made its first takeover in decades when it bid for Wellcome).

### Create a Place for Task and Process Conflict and Get It Out in the Open

Most people, even seasoned managers and executives, feel uncomfortable about conflict. It is much easier to capitalize on constructive conflict by creating a time and place for it to occur, rather than expecting it to naturally erupt. Furthermore, discussing the potential for conflict before it erupts is a lot more effective than trying to deal with it after the fact. As an example of how companies create a forum for conflict, see Box 7-2.

### Training in Task Conflict

For many people, task conflict, or open debate, does not come naturally. They have lived their lives in repressed-conflict situations and have never had an opportunity to see healthy conflict in action. If task conflict is not in team members' repertoires, it will be impossible to cultivate conditions for it to thrive.

One step is to provide members with training in task conflict. Asking team members who have not been trained in task conflict to discuss their most sensitive issues is

---

**BOX 7-2**

### Creating a Forum for Conflict

Bovis Construction Corporation, which has worked on the renovation of Los Angeles City Hall and the construction of a football stadium in Nashville, deals with conflict in an open fashion. Prior to each project, Bovis construction teams hold a planning session in which team members openly address potential conflicts. These planning sessions are conducted by company facilitators who encourage the project owner, architects, contractors, and other players to map out processes they plan to follow to get the job done. During the session, participants draft and sign a "win-win agree-

ment," which includes a matrix that lays out what team members expect from one another. The first box in a matrix may detail the owner's responsibilities on the project, whereas the next box may look at the owner's expectations of the construction manager. Teams then use this matrix to review their progress on the project. Bovis managers agree that the process has not only decreased the adversity that is so prevalent on construction sites, but the firm has also saved millions of dollars and has completed projects on time (Oldham, 1998).

---

not the best starting point. Instead, training should begin with topics in which the stakes are low. Further, leaders and other team members can serve as "coaches" for one another (see Sidebar 7-1). Edmondson, Bohmer, and Pisano (2000) refer to the ability of teams to discuss tough issues as "psychological safety." A group that has a high level of psychological safety has interpersonal trust and mutual respect among members. Moreover, psychological safety leads to greater innovativeness, more openness, and comfort in raising difficult issues.

In their book, *Getting Disputes Resolved,* Ury, Brett, and Goldberg (1988) observed managers in many different types of companies—airlines, coal mines, and so on—discussing conflicts and in many cases, engaging in conflict. Ury et al. (1988) dis-

### Sidebar 7-1. Executive Coaches

It is not uncommon in business for people to have mentors, consultants, and even therapists—but the latest role is that of executive coach. Executive coaches address an extensive range of issues, from the inability to manage others or establish priorities to difficulties with hiring and promoting subordinates, giving clear assignments, and handling conflict. Coaches also help teams manage change arising from promotions, relocations, and mergers and acquisitions. Big companies believe in coaches—IBM, Sony, and Kodak all have hired them—and Ernst and Young spent $2M on coaches in 2001 (Johnston, 2002). Many teams are finding that the greatest benefit is to have an independent and objective third party to work with a team member to correct deficiencies or enhance strengths in a one-on-one format, rather than with a peer or supervisors. Individual coaching can cost $15K–$18K for a 6–18 month engagement, and team coaching can cost upwards of six figures (Johnston, 2002).

tinguished three ways that people talk to one another in such dispute situations, which they labeled: interests, rights, and power. Interests-based conflict is a lot like task conflict. It is not personal, and occurs when people attempt to learn about the other team members' underlying needs, desires, or concerns. The rights-based approach to conflict is heavily focused on standards of fairness, precedent, and legal issues. Finally, the power-based approach to conflict includes threats, attacks on character, and the use of rank or status.

As an example of the difference between interests-, rights-, and power-based approaches in teams, consider a team in which there has been a serious, long-standing conflict concerning the nature of the assignments given to team members. Some assignments are clearly regarded as more attractive and career-enhancing than others. However, for the organization to be successful, all assignments must be covered by the team. One of the members, Larry, begins a meeting by stating, "I am not at all happy with how the assignments for the project are handled. I am consistently having to do the least attractive part of the project and it is a lot of work. I want to be excused from that part of the project in the future." Three different team members might respond in the following ways, depending on which approach they take to the conflict at hand:

1. *Interests-based response:* "Larry, I've sensed that this is of great concern to you. We'd all like to hear more about your own views on this and what your proposals are. I will be honest in saying that I am not sure anything can change, at least for now, but I think that it is important that we all have a chance to understand exactly how each one of us perceives the workload and assignments on the project at this point."

2. *Rights-based response:* "Look, Larry, you agreed to cover that part of the project when we first took on the challenge four years ago. As a matter of fact, I believe that I have an e-mail from you indicating that you would agree to do that part of the work. As far as I am concerned, this is strictly a matter of precedent and what people have agreed to do. I am sure that our supervisor would reach the same conclusion as I would if she saw the e-mail I am referring to."

3. *Power-based response:* "I think you are completely out of line, Larry. It is not helping our team effort to have people like yourself acting like prima-donnas and demanding special treatment. We all have important things to do to meet the project goals. I am tired of having to walk on eggshells around this issue and I don't think that discussing unrealistic and selfish goals is a good use of our team time. We could simply follow a principle of rank in our team, but that would be bad for you. I am ready to continue our democratic process, but only on the condition that you start working with us as a team!"

The power-based team member in this example is using several techniques designed to threaten and intimidate. First, there are numerous unflattering character attacks—Larry is labeled as "out of line," "demanding," a "prima-donna," and "unrealistic and selfish." This comment also contains some thinly guised threats: If Larry does not shut up, this team member intends to pull rank. The rights-based team member, by focusing on the past, effectively says, "We cannot have this discussion." The interests-based team member clearly states that there may not be any room for movement, but she is open to understanding. In this way, the interests-based response models the double-loop style of communication (Argyris, 1977a). Most people, when faced with sensitive and important issues, find it far easier to launch into rights- or power-based arguments. However, nearly any rights- or power-based argument can be converted into an interests-based response without forcing team members to capitulate to others.

# TEAM DILEMMA: GROUP VERSUS INDIVIDUAL INTERESTS

In most teams, members have both cooperative and competitive motives (Deutsch, 1973). Team members share a common objective when they work together—this is the cooperative aspect. Yet in many teams, individual members have an incentive to further their own interests. Team efforts are often subverted when individual agendas lead to competition between members, and members become preoccupied with what others are getting, relative to what they themselves are getting. Sometimes the way teams are set up can lead to these kinds of conflict. For example, when individuals are compensated according to team rather than individual performance, conflict may arise to the detriment of the team if members' skills, abilities, or effort vary to a significant degree.

In many team situations, members face a choice between furthering team-level interests or their own personal interests. For example, consider project teams composed of various members within a company. Each employee may be, at any time, a member of four or more project teams. Consequently, the team members have other projects vying for their attention and have an incentive to work on pet projects, letting the rest of the team carry them on the other project. However, if everyone does this, each project suffers. The choice between individual and group interests is a **team dilemma**. The hallmark features of a team dilemma are when members are *interdependent* with regard to resources, and each person has an *incentive to free ride* on the group's efforts. The resources may be tangible outcomes, such as salaries, office space, or equipment, or intangible outcomes, such as information, services, or social support (Foa & Foa, 1975).

Team members in this case must choose between the team and self-interest. Consider the following team dilemmas:

- A group of MBA students is working on a class project that counts for 50 percent of their grade. Some take a higher course load than others; some are taking the course pass-fail; some are second-year students who already have jobs. How should the work be divided?
- Companies with significant R&D activities frequently use cross-functional teams. However, when the R&D is spread across different parts of the organization, members may want to retain control of the project in their own division, rather than collaborating with others across divisions, which might add substantial value.
- In large law firms, partners act as their own profit centers and, thus, have little incentive to provide knowledge to attorneys outside their group. Yet doing so improves the long-term viability of the firm in a competitive marketplace.

Team dilemmas pit individual incentives against group incentives in such a way that a poorer outcome for the organization is likely if each member acts in a self-interested way. The dilemma lies in the fact that members cannot simultaneously choose to cooperate and avoid exploitation by other members. Below, we expand upon strategies that effectively tip the balance in favor of team interest (versus individual interest; see also Table 7-2).

## Strategies to Enhance Cooperation and Minimize Competition

In Chapter 2, we offered some specific strategies to reduce free riding. Here, we add to the list.

**TABLE 7-2**   Tipping Points on the Team Dilemma

| These factors more likely to trigger self-interest | These factors more likely to trigger collective interest |
|---|---|
| Individually based reward structures (e.g., meritocracies) | Group-level reward structures |
| Existence of a hierarchy | Salient common identity |
| Resource scarcity | Shared threat |
| Stress and uncertainty | Cross-group friendships |
| Short-term relationships | Long-term relationships |
| Productivity goals | Harmony goals |
| Status differences | Equal status |

### Build Team Identity

The stronger a team's identity, the less sharply members distinguish between their self-interest and that of the group (Dawes, van de Kragt, & Orbell, 1990). There are several ways to increase team identity, such as linking individual outcomes (i.e., compensation) to team outcomes (i.e., performance). However, don't think that the price of building team identity is outside of your budget. For leaders like David Kelley, founder and former CEO of IDEO, and Steve Jobs, former CEO of Apple, Inc., T-shirts for each team member are the key. Recognition of individual efforts can also be effective. Sometimes, emphasizing team identity as being an integral part of a larger team effort, such as that of a plant, division, or firm, is effective, particularly when a conscious challenge is presented in which the team can either succeed or fail—for example, beating the competition to market with a new product. If the team has an identity or reputation of its own, that can also make members want to uphold their end of the work.

Certain things detract from team identity, the most important of which is whether members expect to work together in the future. If the cooperative effort is short-lived, individuals have less incentive to invest in the team. Hence, another way of enhancing team identity is to extend the length of time people expect to work as a team. Moreover, members who believe that other members will leave cooperate less than those who expect the team to remain intact (Mannix & Loewenstein, 1993). Therefore, preserving continuity in membership can also be important.

### Make Pledges

To the extent that team members make pledges, cooperation is greatly enhanced (Chen, 1996). Pledges or social contracts come in all shapes and forms, the most common being the business handshake, or the simple statement "You have my word." Social contracts are sometimes explicit ("You can count on me") and sometimes implicit (such as a wink, a nod, or a handshake). Social contracts capitalize on a basic psychological need for commitment and consistency. The power of pledges cannot be underestimated. In many instances, team members who make specific pledges or commitments to their team will act in ways that benefit the group, even at the expense of self-interest. For many of the teams we work with, we use team contracts. A team contract is a document that team members collectively write at the outset of their task work. The purpose of the team contract is to (1) clarify the team's goal and mission and (2) determine how the team can best work together to achieve their goals.

---

BOX 7-3

## Example of a Team Contract

### MISSION STATEMENT

Our mission is to be a high-performing team by:

- Focusing on learning as much as possible
- Participating fully
- Sharing our collective experiences
- Leveraging the diversity of our team
- Challenging one another's thinking
- Being innovative
- Having fun

### GUIDING PRINCIPLES/CONDITIONS FOR SUCCESS

- Share team leadership (self-governing)
- Rotate role of scribe
- Begin and end on time
- Attempt to minimize weekend work
- Debrief at the end of each work group session
- 100% attendance and active participation

---

There should be a clear understanding among all team members that this is a "living" document, meaning that it is subject to change and feedback from others. There should also be a clear understanding that this is indeed a "contract" for which members will hold themselves and other members accountable throughout the duration of teamwork. In short, teams who develop a team contract put themselves on the line. Ideally, team contract should be about one page long. (For an example of a team contract that was prepared by a team of consultants at the outset of an eight-week-long intensive learning project, see Box 7-3.)

## PERILS AND PITFALLS OF DEMOCRACY

In some teams, the choice facing members does not center upon a choice between the team and self-interest. Rather, members must agree on some course of action. This is particularly true when the decisions facing the team are complex. Consider, for example, team members who disagree about their weekly meeting time. This cannot be resolved by each member simply deciding the time that is best for him/her. Effective conflict resolution requires coordination and consensus among members. Voting is one method for reducing conflict, in which members agree to adopt the choice preferred by the majority. Voting is commonly used in organizational hiring, promotion, and firing decisions. Team members who vote among alternatives acknowledge that conflict exists, but agree to accept the outcome of the vote. The key issue becomes how to develop and utilize a suitable voting scheme.

### Voting Rules

There are several kinds of voting rules, and different rules are used in different situations. The objective of voting rules can be to find the alternative that the greatest number of team members prefer, the alternative the fewest members object to, or the choice that maximizes team welfare. Anything short of unanimity indicates disagreement or conflict within the team. In most cases, conflict will be reduced or eliminated following the conclusion of voting, although there are exceptions. For example, individuals who "lose" the vote may assert that the voting procedure was fraudulent or not carried out as agreed upon (Tyler & Smith, 1998).

Voting does not guarantee conflict resolution. First, members may not agree on a method for voting. For example, how is a winning choice to be determined? Some members may insist on unanimity, others on simple majority rule, and still others on a weighted majority rule. Second, even if a voting method is agreed on, it may not yield a decision (in the case of a tie, for instance) or may not yield a single decision. Finally, because voting does not eliminate conflicts of interest, but rather provides a way for members to live with conflict, such decisions may not be stable. In this sense, voting masks disagreement within teams, potentially threatening long-term group and organizational effectiveness.

### Majority Rule

Because team negotiation is so complex, members often use simplifying procedures to reach decisions (Bazerman, Mannix, & Thompson, 1988). For example, teams may use majority rule as a decision heuristic because of its ease and familiarity (Hastie, Penrod, & Pennington, 1983; Ordeshook, 1986). The most common voting procedure is majority rule. However, despite its demographic appeal, majority rule presents several problems in the attainment of consensus. First, majority rule ignores members' strength of preference for alternatives. The vote of a person who feels strongly about an issue counts only as much as the vote of a person who is virtually indifferent. Consequently, majority rule does not promote creative trade-offs among issues. For example, groups that use unanimous rule reach more win-win outcomes (i.e., profitable outcomes for everyone involved) compared with groups that use majority rule (Mannix, Thompson, & Bazerman, 1989; Thompson, Mannix, & Bazerman, 1988). When groups use voting in combination with strict agendas (in which the order of issues is discussed sequentially, rather than simultaneously), outcomes for the team as a whole plummet. Why? One of the successful keys to conflict management is the ability to make trade-offs among issues under discussion (i.e., "I will do this for you if you do such-and-such for me"; Mannix et al., 1989; Thompson et al., 1988). In short, when teams discuss only one issue at a time and vote on outcomes under consideration, this results in less profitable outcomes than when teams discuss issues simultaneously and seek consensus.

Second, teams that use majority rule are less likely to reach mutually beneficial, integrative outcomes than are teams requiring unanimity (Thompson et al., 1988). Majority rule inhibits the discovery of integrative agreements because it discourages information exchange about preferences (Castore & Murnighan, 1978).

### Unanimous Decision Making

Although unanimous decision making is time-consuming, it encourages team members to consider creative alternatives to expand the size of the pie and satisfy the interests of all members. On the other hand, unanimous rule can present formidable obstacles, such as when members refuse to compromise. By holding out, these members can force decisions their way when considerations like timeliness are important.

When a decision reached in these circumstances goes against what most members believe is right, it can lead to poor outcomes.

## Drawbacks to Voting

### Arrow Paradox

Consider the situation described in Box 7-4. The product development team members are victims of the **Arrow paradox,** in which the winners of majority rule elections change as a function of the order in which alternatives are proposed. In fact, any system of weighted voting (such as when members give three points to their first choice, two to their second, and one to their third) produces the same problem.

### Impossibility Theorem

The unstable voting outcomes of the product development team illustrate the **impossibility theorem** (Arrow, 1963), which states that the derivation of team preference from individual preference is indeterminate. Simply put, there is no method of combining group members' preferences that guarantees that group preference has been maximized when groups have three or more members and there are three or more options.

The context of voting often involves people explaining the reasons for their preferences. Sometimes they persuade others with their arguments; other times, the holes in their arguments become illuminated. Therefore, aside from the mathematical complexities involved in voting rules, voting serves an important function. The process itself can lead to buy-in, if not downright consensus, by the time the vote is through.

### Strategic Manipulation

Strategic manipulation further compounds the problem of indeterminacy of team choice (Chechile, 1984; Ordeshook, 1986; Plott, 1976; Plott & Levine, 1978). Consider a situation in which members do not vote for their first choice because by voting for

---

**BOX 7-4**

### When Voting Goes Awry

Suppose a three-person product development team (Raines, Warner, and Lassiter) is choosing among designs *A, B,* or *C.* Each manager's preference ordering is depicted below. As a way of resolving the conflict, Warner suggests voting between designs *A* and *B.* In that vote, *A* wins over *B.* Warner then proposes a vote between *A* and *C.* In that vote, *C* wins. Warner then declares design *C* the consensus choice—which Lassiter agrees to. However, Raines proposes a new vote, but this time starting with a contest between *B* and *C.* *B* wins this vote, eliminating *C.* Between *A* and *B, A* beats *B,* so Raines happily declares *A* the winner. Lassiter complains the whole voting process was fraudulent, but cannot explain why.

| MANAGER | DESIGN A | DESIGN B | DESIGN C |
|---------|---------|---------|---------|
| Raines | 1 | 2 | 3 |
| Warner | 2 | 3 | 1 |
| Lassiter | 3 | 1 | 2 |

*Note:* Numbers represent rank-ordered choices.

another choice, some other, undesirable option is sure to lose. This is an example of strategic manipulation—people do not vote in accord with their true preferences. Furthermore, members may manipulate the order in which alternatives are voted on, because when the alternatives are voted on sequentially in pairs, those voted on later are more likely to win (May, 1982).

### Coalitions

Coalitions are another way of asserting power in a group. A **coalition** is a group of two or more members who join together to affect the outcome of a decision involving at least three parties (Komorita & Parks, 1994). Coalitions involve both cooperation and competition: Members of coalitions cooperate with one another in competition against other coalitions but compete within the coalition regarding the allocation of rewards the coalition obtains. Power is intimately involved in both the formation of coalitions and the allocation of resources among coalition members. In some cases, members of an organizational coalition might be relatively equal in power (e.g., all may be of the same rank); however, in other cases, there might be extreme differences in power (e.g., a team of senior executives and junior hires). Although members of a coalition cooperate in joining resources (e.g., a team might rally together in an organization to gain a greater budget), eventually, they need to allocate the resources they attain among themselves (e.g., individual team members may think they deserve a higher percentage of the budget).

Power imbalance among coalition members can lead to a number of detrimental consequences, including more defecting coalitions (Mannix, 1993), fewer integrative agreements (Mannix, 1993; McAlister, Bazerman, & Fader, 1986), greater likelihood of bargaining impasse (Mannix, 1993), and more competitive behavior (McClintock, Messick, Kuhlman & Campos, 1973).

## TEAM NEGOTIATIONS

Some situations call for team members to discuss issues and build consensus—for example, when a team of professionals must divide responsibilities among themselves or members of a department must allocate funds. In both cases, members must arrive at a mutually satisfactory outcome although each may have different interests. This involves negotiation.

**Negotiation** occurs when interdependent parties make mutual decisions regarding the allocation of scarce resources (Bazerman et al., 1988). Negotiation is necessary when no one can dictate a solution. Furthermore, team members must agree for any decision to be binding. Failure to reach consensus can be costly for the team if, for example, it cannot move forward because it fails to reach agreement, if opportunities are missed due to protracted negotiations, if costs of negotiation increase over time (e.g., if lawyers or arbitrators must be paid), or if the rights to decision making are lost and must instead be sent to a higher level. An example of a lost opportunity due to impasse occurred at a prominent state university. A department had been granted special funds to create a badly needed additional wing of a new building. Unfortunately, department members could not agree on how to allocate the new space among themselves, preventing the drafting of final blueprints. Because no plans were forthcoming, the university withdrew the funding. This is an example of a **lose-lose outcome** (Thompson & Hrebec, 1996). When group members fail to reach consensus, it can be costly for everyone. In retrospect, the members of the department would have all been happier had the new wing been built, but at the time, they were absorbed in paralyzing conflict with one another.

What are some strategies that teams can use to avoid lose-lose outcomes and move toward mutual agreement? Most conflict situations contain the potential for joint gain, or integrative outcomes, although these may be obvious only after the fact. The following strategies are aimed at uncovering the win-win potential existing in most conflicts.

## The BATNA Principle

Team consensus is only feasible if it represents an improvement over each member's **best alternative to a negotiated agreement**, or **BATNA** (Fisher & Ury, 1981). If members have better options outside the team (such as with another team or different company), then group dissolution is inevitable. Thus, for consensus to be viable, the outcome must be at least as attractive as each person's best available outside option. Knowing the BATNAs of the parties involved greatly enhances the ability to achieve consensus.

## Avoid the Fixed-Pie Fallacy

The **fixed-pie fallacy** is the tendency of people in conflict to assume that their interests are completely opposed to those of others. The fixed-pie mentality can be extremely detrimental in negotiations (Thompson & Hastie, 1990). Although most negotiations contain potential for mutually beneficial agreements, the belief that the pie is fixed and the drive to grab the biggest slice is so pervasive that most people fail to recognize opportunities for win-win agreements.

For example, Thompson and Hrebec (1996) found that about 50 percent of people fail to realize when they have interests that are completely compatible with others, and about 20 percent fail to reach optimal agreements even when their interests are completely compatible. A key reason for such breakdowns is that people fail to exchange information about their interests, making it unlikely that faulty judgments will be challenged and corrected (Thompson, 1991). Furthermore, when people are provided with information about others' interests, they often overlook areas of common interest (Thompson & DeHarpport, 1994; Thompson & Hastie, 1990).

## Build Trust and Share Information

Rapport between members of the team makes mutually beneficial agreement more likely (Moore, Kurtzberg, Thompson, & Morris, 1999). Rapport is usually established when people find points of similarity. Surprisingly, it does not take much to find something in common with another person. For example, in one investigation (Nadler, Thompson, & Morris, 1999), students from two highly competitive rival MBA programs negotiated with one another via electronic mail. The bargaining zone was small and reputations were at stake. All buyer-seller pairs had exactly eight days to reach some kind of settlement. Some of the negotiators were randomly selected to have a "get acquainted" phone call with their opponent immediately before getting down to the business of negotiation. Others just immediately commenced negotiations. The results were dramatic: The impasse rate was cut nearly in half when negotiators spent a few minutes on the phone with the other person—a strong testament to the power of rapport in building trust in negotiations. Furthermore, those who had the phone call were convinced that their opponent had been especially selected for them on the basis of similarity, when in actual effect, the opponent was chosen at random.

These results may suggest that the better two persons know one another, the stronger their rapport should be and, consequently, the better they should be at finding common ground. However, this is not always the case. In fact, when friends negotiate, they often do worse than complete strangers (Fry, Firestone, & Williams, 1983; Thompson & DeHarpport, 1998). Friends are often uncomfortable negotiating with each other, and so may make premature concessions; as a result, they may overlook opportunities for expanding the pie in their hurry to reach a deal. Friends may also presume they know each other's interests, when this may not be the case. However, it can be awkward trying to explain your views to someone who knows you. Strangers, by contrast, do not need a pretense to clarify their point of view. The key take-away message goes back to our earlier point: it is important to create a forum for task conflict.

## Understand Underlying Interests

Integrative negotiation often requires that team members have information about each other's preferences (Pruitt & Lewis, 1975; Thompson, 1991). Most people neither provide nor seek the information necessary to reach such agreements. The most important question a team member can ask of another is: *What are your interests in this situation?* (Thompson, 1991).

## Share Information

The distinction between this strategy and building trust and providing information has to do with bilateral versus unilateral strategies. In the earlier strategy, it was assumed that teammates were mutually engaged in a process of information exchange. However, if that strategy fails, then we encourage some degree of unilateral (i.e., one-sided) information sharing. It would seem that teammates should always reveal their interests to fellow team members. However, they may hesitate to do so if they feel this will place them in a strategically disadvantageous position. Consider a team negotiating the allocation of scarce resources (research money, secretarial assistance, and travel support) among its members. One member may feel that, of these scarce resources, research support is most important, although secretarial and travel support are also valuable. This person may reason that a mutually beneficial agreement is possible by "trading" secretarial support for research support. However, he may hesitate to reveal his priorities, fearing that other members will demand large concessions on the secretarial and travel support issues in exchange for conceding research support. There are several advantages of revealing information: it builds trust, convinces others of your sincerity in achieving the priorities you do reveal, encourages others to incorporate your priorities in their proposals, and leads to faster agreements.

## Make Multiple Proposals Simultaneously

In some cases, team members are frustrated when their attempts to provide and seek information are not effective. This happens most commonly in the face of high distrust and less than amicable relations. The strategy of multiple offers can be effective even with the most uncooperative of team members. The strategy involves presenting the other team members with at least two (and preferably more) proposals of equal value to yourself. The other team members are asked to indicate which of the proposals they prefer. This should reveal information about how the other members value trade-offs between different issues. There are psychological benefits as well. When people believe they have more choices, they are more inclined to cooperate.

## Avoid Sequential Discussion of Issues

There is a pervasive tendency for teams to discuss issues sequentially. This usually stems from the belief that making progress on some issues will grease the wheels of cooperation for more difficult ones. However, sequential discussion inhibits joint discussion of sets of issues, reducing the likelihood that team members will identify potentially beneficial trade-offs between issues (Mannix et al., 1989; Thompson et al., 1988; Weingart, Bennett, & Brett, 1993). Just as we saw in the Arrow paradox, it may not be possible to find the best outcome if trade-offs are only considered pairwise.

Team members who discuss issues simultaneously exchange more information and have greater insight into other members' interests (Weingart et al., 1993). Teams following sequential agendas under majority rule are less likely to reach integrative agreements. This may stem from the fact that coalitions often form, preventing information exchange and discussion of members' underlying interests.

## Construct Contingency Contracts and Leverage Differences

Team members differ in their forecasts about what they think will happen in the future. These different expectations may make team negotiation difficult. For example, one member wants to protect against disaster stemming from a potentially bad investment; another may worry about how to spend the vast riches that are sure to follow. Each may have difficulty taking the other's position seriously, because each has very different expectations about what the consequences (and the value) of a decision may be. However, such differences in beliefs can actually improve the possibility of integrative agreements.

This is possible through the formation of **contingency contracts**. Consider the case of a cross-functional team in which a sales manager is more optimistic than the manufacturing manager about product sales. A contingent contract can be constructed, establishing that manufacturing will produce more products, but if sales fail to meet an agreed-upon level, the sales department will cover all manufacturing costs.

In other situations, team members may agree on the probability of future events, but feel differently about taking risks. For example, two colleagues may undertake a collaborative project, such as writing a novel, for which they both agree that the probability of success is only moderate. The colleague with an established career can afford to be risk seeking; the struggling young novelist may be risk averse. The two may capitalize on their different risk-taking profiles with a contingent contract. The more risk-averse colleague receives the entire advance on the book; the risk-seeking colleague receives the majority of royalties after publication of the novel.

People may value the same event quite differently depending on when it occurs. If one party is more impatient than the other, mechanisms for sharing the consequences over time may be devised. Two partners in a joint venture might allocate the initial profits to the partner who has high costs for time, whereas the partner who can wait will achieve greater profits over a longer, delayed period.

Capitalizing on differences often entails contingency contracts, in which team members make bets based upon different possible outcomes. For contingency contracts to be effective, they should be easy to evaluate and leave no room for ambiguity of interpretation. Conditions and measurement techniques should be spelled out in advance.

## Search for Postsettlement Settlements

Team members may decide to renegotiate after reaching a mutually agreeable settlement. It may seem counterintuitive or counterproductive to resume negotiations once an acceptable agreement has been reached, but the strategy of postsettlement settlements can be remarkably effective in improving the quality of negotiated agreements (Raiffa, 1982). In the postsettlement settlement, team members agree to explore other options with the goal of finding another that all members prefer more than the current one. The current settlement becomes the new BATNA. The postsettlement settlement strategy is effective because it allows team members to reveal their preferences without fear of exploitation; they can safely revert to their previous agreement if the postsettlement settlement discussion does not prove fruitful. If better terms are found, parties can be more confident they have reached a truly integrative agreement. If no better agreement is found, the team members may be more confident that the current agreement is really a win-win outcome.

## Invoke Norms of Justice

Team members in conflict who use objective appearing arguments are more effective than those who use subjective arguments. However, there are many different objective arguments. Consider the following:

- *Equity* (or contribution-based distribution) prescribes that benefits should be proportional to members' contributions (Adams, 1965).
- *Equality* (or blind justice) specifies that all team members should suffer or benefit equally (Messick, 1993).
- *Need* (or welfare-based justice) specifies that benefits should be proportional to members' needs (Deutsch, 1975).

The effectiveness of any given principle will be enhanced to the extent that it is simple, clear, justifiable, popular, and general. To be more specific, a fairness-based argument that has the following characteristics is more likely to win the support of team members and other relevant organizational actors (Messick, 1993):

- *Simplicity:* Team members should be able to articulate the procedure easily. This reduces the chances of misunderstanding and makes it easier to evaluate how accurately the procedure is being implemented.
- *Clarity:* The allocation procedure should be clear; if not, conflict may erupt concerning its interpretation.
- *Justifiability:* The procedure should be consistently applied across different individuals, time, and situations.
- *Consensus:* Team members should agree on the method of allocation. Team members often internalize effective social justice procedures, and such norms act as strong guidelines for decision making in teams. Because these norms often outlive current team members, new members are frequently indoctrinated with procedures the team found useful in the past (cf. Bettenhausen & Murnighan, 1985; Levine & Moreland, 1991, 1994).
- *Generality:* The procedure should be applicable to a wide variety of situations.

No matter how objective a fairness rule may appear, fairness is not an absolute construct. And people's uses of fairness are for the most part self-enhancing. We do not wish to evaluate here what is really fair, but rather to stress the importance of arriving at an outcome that is perceived as fair by everyone concerned.

Reputations for fairness can be extremely important in business and employment relationships and often set the background against which a negotiation takes place. Generally speaking, people with a reputation for fairness will be trusted more than those who are viewed differently. We are not saying that being "fair" or "not fair" is the right or moral thing to do in every circumstance, simply that a reputation for fairness can be beneficial in many negotiating contexts. Moreover, an expectation of fairness as a splitting rule is pervasive—despite the emphasis in virtually every business publication, textbook, and so on, for competitive behavior.

## WHAT TO DO WHEN CONFLICT ESCALATES?

Sometimes an organization will set up teams within the organizational structure to compete with one another. The idea is to create a healthy competition to spur motivation. However, this can lead to escalating conflict and destructive outcomes that need special interventions.

Conflict often escalates because people believe that coercion is effective in reducing the resolve of others. Paradoxically, most people believe that when others use coercion on them, it increases their resolve (Rothbart & Hallmark, 1988). The unfortunate consequence is that this perception encourages mutually aggressive behavior. (For an example of this in a military setting, see Sidebar 7-2.) What can be done to reduce the likelihood of strikes and get parties back to the bargaining table once a strike has begun?

### Sidebar 7-2. We, but Not They, Would Rather Fight Than Switch

During World War II, the American journalist Edward R. Murrow made a nightly broadcast from London, reporting on the psychological and physical consequences of the Nazi bombing of British cities (Rothbart & Hallmark, 1988). Contrary to Nazi intent, the bombing did not move the British toward surrender. In fact, it had the opposite effect: It strengthened the British resolve to resist German domination. Shortly after the United States entered World War II, the Americans joined the British in launching costly bombing raids over Germany. In part, the intent was to decrease the German people's will to resist. Later research reported by the Office of Strategic Services that compared the lightly and heavily bombed areas found only minimal differences in civilians' will to resist.

The likelihood of protracted conflict is intimately linked to the beliefs each party holds about what they regard to be a fair settlement (Thompson & Loewenstein, 1992). People in conflict have different ideas about what is fair, and the most difficult conflicts are ones in which the parties' ideas of fairness are highly discrepant. In fact, the length of costly strikes can be directly predicted by the discrepancy between what the parties involved regard to be a fair outcome: the greater the discrepancy, the longer the strike—and both parties ultimately lose. Thus, to reduce conflict, it is critical to understand how to get parties to move away from egocentric perceptions of fair outcomes to more reasonable ones. The key problem is that most people regard themselves to be uniquely immune to bias and benevolent in their own motivations (Farwell & Weiner, 1996); they regard bias to be something that afflicts the other party in conflict. Most people involved in really difficult conflicts hold the following perceptions: (1) they are fairer than others; (2) the other party's view is egocentrically motivated (and, hence, unfair); and (3) there is only one correct (and fair) way to view the situation. This trilogy of beliefs is a recipe for disaster, unless something can be done to move parties away from one (and hopefully more) of these views.

Most people are not aware that their own perceptions of fairness are egocentrically biased. For example, van Avermaet (1974) asked team members to complete several questionnaires. These took either 45 or 90 minutes. The questionnaires were constructed so that, for each duration, some participants completed six questionnaires, whereas others completed only three. When asked to allocate monetary rewards, participants emphasized the dimension that favored them in the allocation procedure (those who worked longer emphasized time; questionnaire completion was emphasized by those who worked on more questionnaires).

It is not surprising, then, that members who contribute less prefer to divide resources equally, whereas those who contribute more prefer the equity rule (Allison & Messick, 1990). In groups containing members having different power or status levels, those with low power want equality, whereas those with high power desire equity (Komorita & Chertkoff, 1973; Shaw, 1981).

As a way of dealing with how to minimize egocentric perceptions of conflict, it is probably most useful to first indicate which strategies seem like they would work, but usually don't. We are not saying that these strategies are doomed to failure, but rather that they have been tried and have not been shown to work, at least in simulated (yet realistic) conflict situations. It would seem that providing both parties with veridical information pertaining to the conflict situation (statistics on the labor supply, competitive analysis, etc.) would be helpful, at the very least serving as a reality check; however, this has not shown to be helpful. That is, when management and labor are provided with additional, unbiased information concerning disputes, this has the effect of further entrenching both parties more firmly in their own positions (Thompson & Loewenstein, 1992). To understand this backfire effect, it is important to recall our discussion of the confirmation bias. Parties interpret information in a way that is most favorable to their own position. Thus, they put their own spin on the facts in a way that gives them more confidence in their position.

It may seem that warning disputants about the existence of bias may be effective in reducing conflict and, at the very least, getting parties to perform a reality check of their own positions and beliefs supporting those positions. However, this does little to assuage biased perceptions (Babcock, Loewenstein, Issacharoff, & Camerer, 1995). Apparently, people regard bias as something that afflicts the "other guy"—not themselves. For similar reasons, taking the other person's point of view is generally not effective in reducing bias and conflict.

So much for what does *not* work. What *does* work to reduce egocentric perceptions of fairness? The key is to get parties to change their own perceptions about what is fair. Inducing parties to actively think about the weaknesses in their own position can be effective in reducing the length of costly strikes (Babcock et al., 1995). Furthermore, inviting a respected, neutral outsider to mediate can be effective (see Sidebar 7-3).

### Sidebar 7-3. Team Therapy

We've all heard of group therapy. What about team therapy? Like families, there is a tendency for companies to hide conflict from the view of outsiders, coupled with a stoic tendency to want to work things out on their own. However, there is a lot of sense in calling in informed and skilled outsiders to deal with conflict. Indeed, there has been a recent development of therapist teams to work directly with companies to deal with unproductive conflicts.

## CONCLUSIONS

Conflict in teams is unavoidable. However, it does not have to result in decreased productivity. Managed effectively, conflict can be key to leveraging differences of interest to arrive at creative solutions. However, many people intuitively respond to conflict in a defensive fashion, and this emotional type of conflict can threaten productivity. To the greatest extent possible, team members should depersonalize conflict. We have presented a variety of ways to achieve this. We have also cautioned against using majority rule, splitting the difference, and strict agendas, which might stifle the opportunity for team win-win gains.

# CHAPTER

# 8

# Creativity:

## *Mastering Strategies for High Performance*

*Tom Kelley, general manager of the design consulting company IDEO, recalls,*

> "One of the most painful brainstormers I ever went to was in this organization
> where they said [we were] going to do a brainstormer on . . . marketing oppor-
> tunities on this new project they were working on. And they went around the
> room . . . two minutes for each person. Really painful, because it violates all the
> rules of brainstorming. Well . . . I'm 15th and I really like what the second per-
> son said. [But] by the time you get to me, I've forgotten or the group has forgot-
> ten what that idea was. There's no building on the energy. . . . Never confuse a
> brainstormer with a regular meeting. In a regular meeting, the boss gets to frame
> the problem and probably have the last word. In a regular meeting, people cri-
> tique ideas that come up. In a regular meeting, you might go around the room
> and have people speak in turn; whereas none of those things would happen in a
> brainstormer. In a brainstormer, you would cover the walls with paper so that
> there's plenty of space to write. You'd have lots of colored marking pens and
> chocolate chip cookies and whatever it is that adds energy to the group. And
> people would build on the ideas of others. They'd have a bunch of wild ideas
> that no one would crtize [be]cause there's this rule called 'defer judgment.' And
> later, you do want to do some critique, but in the brainstomer you're going for
> what we call fluency and flexibility." (National Public Radio, February 8, 2001)

In his book, *The Art of Innovation* (2001), Tom Kelley talks about how companies, hell-bent on promoting creativity, effectively eliminate any chance of it through inef-fective group practices (such as the example above). Creativity is about breaking the rules and departing from tradition and what may seem to be the appropriate way of con-ducting business meetings. Why all the fuss about creativity? There is good reason to believe that creativity pays off. For example, a study done on the average rate of return for 17 products considered innovative by their industries showed a mean return of 56 percent, compared with an average return of 16 percent for all American businesses over a 30-year period (Horibe, 2001). Looking beyond products to companies, each 1 percent increase in spending on research and development produces a 4.3 percent increase in a company's market-to-book value ratio (Buchanan, 2002).

Just because the task facing a team is one that calls for creativity, however, is no guarantee that the team members will be creative. In fact, as we have seen in our discussion of decision-making biases, many factors inhibit the idea exchange process in groups. As we noted in Chapter 2, groups often suffer from motivation and coordination problems, all of which may lower performance standards.

Common wisdom holds that creativity in teams is lurking below the surface and that with the proper intervention or team design, it can be unleashed. This view of creativity as a latent or dormant force is not really accurate. In fact, if motivation and coordination losses are not managed carefully, individual creativity often exceeds that of most teams! However, if the situation is right, the combined efforts of team members exceed what is possible for each person to do independently. Unfortunately, this is rare; more often, the whole of team effort falls far short of the sum of the parts. The reasons have to do with the threats to performance that we discussed in Chapter 2.

In this chapter, we are interested in factors that can enhance creativity in teams. We call this **team creativity**. Team creativity is the opposite of threats to performance, which we discussed in Chapter 2. Team creativity refers to the synergistic gains that teams can, but certainly do not always, experience. It is what people mean when they say that the team's whole is greater than the sum of its parts: The group as a whole achieved something that would not have been possible by merely combining the individual efforts of members.

The creative process, as with all team endeavors, seeks to maximize synergies and minimize threats to performance. It refers to otherwise normal people doing incredible things in a team operating within a given external environment. Team creativity is the Holy Grail of teamwork: Everyone wants it, but very few people know where to look for it or how to set up the conditions to make it happen.

First, we discuss creative realism and describe how creativity can be measured. Next, we explain the differences between individual creativity and team creativity. Then, we describe several types of reasoning, including analogical reasoning and convergent and divergent thinking. Finally, we examine brainstorming techniques and discuss the advantages and disadvantages of each technique.

## CREATIVE REALISM

Most people think that creative ideas are wild ideas; on the contrary, creativity is the production of novel and useful ideas—the ability to form new concepts using existing knowledge. A creative act is original and valuable. Creativity is important for innovation. If creativity pertains to ideas, then innovation pertains to the services and products that result from creative ideas. Innovation is the implementation or adoption of new, useful ideas by people in organizations (Amabile, 1996). Creative thinking occurs when a problem solver invents a novel solution to a problem (Guilford, 1950). Figure 8-1 shows a $2 \times 2$ grid defining, on one continuum, creative and conservative ideas (Finke, 1995). According to the model, teams should strive to achieve creative ideas (i.e., highly original and novel ideas) as opposed to conservative, traditional ideas.

The second continuum is the one that is too often overlooked. It distinguishes ideas that are realistic (connected to current ideas and knowledge) from ideas that are idealistic (disconnected from current knowledge). If ideas are not connected to current ideas and knowledge, they are often not implementable.

The most desired outcome is for your ideas to fall into the upper left quadrant. This domain is called **creative realism,** because these ideas are highly imaginative and

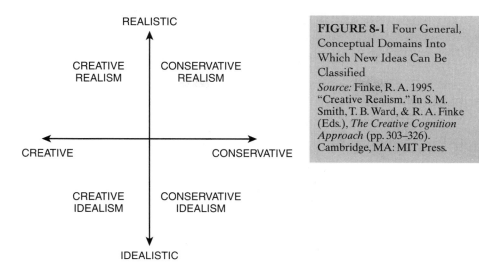

**FIGURE 8-1** Four General, Conceptual Domains Into Which New Ideas Can Be Classified
*Source:* Finke, R. A. 1995. "Creative Realism." In S. M. Smith, T. B. Ward, & R. A. Finke (Eds.), *The Creative Cognition Approach* (pp. 303–326). Cambridge, MA: MIT Press.

highly connected to current structures and ideas. An excellent example of creative realism was Thomas Edison's development of the electric light system. Many of Edison's inventions developed through continuity with earlier inventions (Weisberg, 1993; see Sidebar 8-1).

### Sidebar 8-1. Analogy in Edison's Development of an Electric Lighting System

After Edison invented the incandescent light, his next project was to develop an entire system whereby the invention could be made commercially successful. At the time, there were two in-place lighting systems (neither developed by Edison): gas lights and electrical arc lights. Gas lights could be directly controlled for brightness; gas fuel was produced offsite and sent through buried gas mains. Arc lighting was produced by an electrical spark between carbon rods, was very hot, and produced fumes. The generating plant was located directly by the user. Edison's electric lighting system was based on the principles of gas lighting. Edison wrote in his workbooks that he completely imitated the gas system, replacing the gas with electricity. In Edison's electric system, the source of power was remote from the user, and the wires that brought the power were underground. Furthermore, the individual lights were turned on and off by the user. The light bulb in Edison's system was called a burner and was designed to produce the same amount of light as a gas burner (Basalla, 1988; Weisberg, 1997).

As for the other quadrants, **conservative realism** represents ideas that are highly traditional and highly connected to current knowledge and practices. This creates little ambiguity and little uncertainty. **Conservative idealism** is perhaps the worst type of thinking for a team—an extension of a common idea that is unrealistic to begin with. These ideas exhibit little or no imagination and are not connected to existing knowledge. **Creative idealism** represents highly original, yet highly unrealistic, ideas.

The key question is how teams can maximize the probability of generating ideas that will eventually lead to products and services that represent creative realism. The ideas that flow from this type of thinking are highly original and very useful. The key, as we will see, is to not only permit but also to actively encourage team members to come up with ideas in the other quadrants. This way, it is possible for a great idea to emerge from a silly one. For example, when the team members at *BusinessWeek* were coming up with stories for a bonus issue, "25 Ideas for a Changing World" (August 26, 2002), they allowed each other to suggest silly ideas. Robert Barker, a columnist at *BusinessWeek,* said, "To suggest that each of the ideas explored in this bonus issue sprang forth perfectly formed, sharp, and irresistible, would be a handsome lie. The truth is that some of the early thinking was just bad" (Barker, 2002, p. 168).

David Kelley of IDEO design feels the same way about the creative process, and believes that enlightened trial and error beats the planning of the lone genius. According to IDEO, people should fail faster to succeed sooner. That is why suggesting silly or ridiculous ideas (creative idealism) actually helps pave the way towards truly innovative ideas. Scott Augustine, of Augustine Medical, reminds his teams clearly about the importance of creative idealism: "One thing that will get a senior manager in trouble fast is if I detect there's nothing new going on in their department. I ask people constantly, 'What experiments have you done lately?' It might be how to shuffle paper faster or how to eliminate a step in manufacturing—I'm not fussy. But if you can't tell me two or three things you've tried, that's a good way to get on my bad side" (Buchanan, 2002, p. 56). The theme of "think, build, test" is a common one across several companies.

## MEASURING CREATIVITY

As noted earlier, to be considered creative, an idea must be highly original and useful. The last part is the challenge—many people can come up with totally bizarre but useless ideas. The key is for these ideas to be valuable. One common way of evaluating the creativity of a team's ideas is via three indices: fluency, flexibility, and originality (Guilford, 1959, 1967).

- *Fluency* is a simple measure of how many different ideas a person (or team) generates. Alex Osborn, the father of modern brainstorming, was right: quantity often does breed quality (Dennis, Valacich, Connolly, & Wynne, 1996).
- *Flexibility* is a measure of how many different types of ideas a person (or team) generates.
- *Originality* is the ability to generate unusual solutions and unique answers to problems (Dennis et al., 1996).

As a way of thinking about these three indices of creativity, do the following exercise: See how many possible uses you can think of for a cardboard box. (Give yourself about 10 minutes to do this.)

Now let's score your creativity (or your team's creativity) on the cardboard box challenge. Suppose one person who completed this exercise, Geoff, generated three ideas: Using the box as a cage for a hamster, a container for a turtle, and as a kennel for a dog. Geoff would receive three points for fluency of ideas because these are three different ideas, but only one point for flexibility because the ideas are of the same category (i.e., a home for animals). It seems likely that creative people would generate more novel and unusual ways to use a cardboard box.

Suppose that another person, Avi, generated these unusual ideas for a cardboard box: Using it as a god, using it as a telephone (e.g., two boxes and some string), and trading it as currency.[1] Avi would get a score of three points for fluency (the same as Geoff) and three points for flexibility, because there are three separate categories of ideas for use, one involving religion, another communication, and yet another entirely different idea concerning economics. Think of flexibility as a kind of mental gymnastics—the ability to entertain different types of ideas, all in a short amount of time. Most people, and in particular, most teams, tend to get stuck in one of two types of categories of thought. This is a kind of cognitive arthritis. However, some of Avi's ideas clearly do not meet the requirements for structural connectedness, but as we will see, Avi and his team are in a much better position to set the stage for creative realism than is Geoff.

It is easy to see how flexibility in thought—that is, thinking about different categories of use—can influence originality. Thus, one simple key for enhancing creativity is to simply think of different categories, which can act as "primes" or "stimulants" of more ideas. By listing possible categories of use for a cardboard box (containers, shelter, building material, therapy, religion, politics, weaponry, communication, etc.), a person's score on these three dimensions could increase dramatically. Thus, a key strategy is to think in terms of categories of ideas, not just number of ideas. This can often help teams break out of a narrow perspective on a problem and open up new opportunities for creative solutions. For example, teams generate more diverse ideas when they are exposed to ideas from a wide range of categories (Nijstad, Stroebe, & Lodewijkx, 2002).

Originality refers to creativity on the conservative-creative continuum in Figure 8-1. Statistically, for an idea to be considered "original," less than 5 percent of a given population thinks of it. Thus, if there are 50 people in a company, an originality point is given to a particular idea only if two or fewer people come up with it.

There is usually a striking correlation among the three measures (fluency, flexibility, and originality). The people who get the highest scores on originality also get high scores on flexibility and fluency. And creative teams know that quantity is the best predictor of quality. For example, the creative team at University Games, a successful board game company, comes up with 2,000 ideas for toys every year; 75–100 of those are deemed promising enough to create prototypes. Of those, only 5–10 percent are licensed by companies and make it into kids' toy chests (Knight, 2001). Thus, there is a strong relationship between quantity, diversity, and novelty of ideas. According to Guilford (1950), flexibility is the driver. This runs counter to most business notions of creativity, in which diversity of ideas is often not rewarded, and quantity is interpreted as poor quality. Rather, in most companies and in most teams, quality is regarded as the single most important objective. Yet, if flexibility is indeed the driver, how do we set the stage for it?

## Convergent and Divergent Thinking

There are two key skills involved in creative thinking: divergent thinking and convergent thinking (Guilford, 1959, 1967). **Convergent thinking** is thinking that proceeds toward a single answer. For example, the expected value of a 70 percent chance of earning $1,000 is obtained by multiplying $1,000 by 0.7 to reach $700. **Divergent thinking**

---

[1]This example was suggested by Professor Terri Kurtzberg of NYU, whose dissertation focused on creativity; she has extensively used the cardboard box task.

moves outward from the problem in many possible directions and involves thinking without boundaries. It is related to flexibility and originality. Divergent thinking *is* out-of-the-box thinking.

Many of the factors that make up creative problem solving seem most closely related to divergent thinking. However, ideas eventually need to be evaluated and acted upon. This is where convergent thinking comes in. In convergent thinking, a team or person judges and evaluates the various ideas presented as to their feasibility, practicality, and overall merit.

Task conflict can stimulate the generation of divergent thinking in teams (Nemeth, 1994). For example, teams in which a single member proposes unusual or even incorrect solutions have outperformed teams in which no such "deviance" occurred. Cognitive deviance of this sort leads to a greater number of problem-solving strategies, original arguments, and associations compared with teams that lack a vocal minority (Nemeth & Kwan, 1987). Furthermore, once a team has experienced this type of activity, these performance advantages generalize to subsequent, unrelated tasks, even when the vocal, cognitively deviant member is not present (Smith, Tindale, & Dugoni, 1996).

People working independently excel at divergent thinking because there are no cognitive or social pressures to constrain their thought. In short, there are no conformity pressures. In contrast, teams are much less proficient at divergent thinking. The key reasons have to do with conformity pressures. To avoid social censure, people assess the norms of the teams and conform to them. These factors are exactly what produces the common information effect and groupthink. In contrast, teams excel compared with individuals when in comes to convergent thinking. Teams are better at judging the quality of ideas. This suggests that an effective team design for promoting creativity involves separating the generation of ideas—leaving this to individual team members—and then evaluating and discussing the ideas as a team. Presumably, this is what Osborn had in mind when he developed the strategy of brainstorming.

Divergent thinking is somewhat like Janusian thinking. **Janusian thinking** refers to the Roman deity, Janus, who had two faces looking in opposite directions. In this context, Janusian thinking refers to the ability to cope with (and even welcome) conflicting ideas, paradoxes, ambiguity, and doubt. Teams stimulate Janusian thinking in different ways. Tom Verberne (1997) suggests asking, "What if the world turned into your worst nightmare or your nicest dream?" (p. 69). Open-ended questions stimulate divergent thinking. This kind of thinking can prevent people from jumping to the most obvious (and often the most expensive) solution.

To achieve divergent thinking in his teams, Gerald Hirshberg, president of Nissan Design International, hires people in pairs of opposites—for example, he'll hire a Bauhaus designer (someone rational and structured in her thinking) and then he will hire an artist obsessed with pure form, color, and rhythm. The pair of opposites don't agree on anything, which often sparks wonderful and creative conflicts (Muoio, 1997). Xerox PARC invites people from "alien cultures" onto their teams—for example, they recruit anthropologists to work with computer-science teams (Muoio, 1997).

Impossibilities can also stimulate divergent thinking. For example, participants are challenged to think of ideas that are impossible to execute (e.g., living on the moon, traveling by satellite, etc.) and then identify conditions that might lead to the idea's fruition.

Thus, many of the factors that facilitate creative problem solving are related to divergent thinking. However, this is not to say that teams do not require convergent thinking. They do. The problem is that teams tend to focus on convergent thinking at the expense of divergent thinking. Thus, one paradox for teams, when it comes to creativity, is that teams excel at convergent thinking, but individuals excel at divergent thinking. This is paradoxical because intuitively, most people strongly believe that teams are more creative than individuals when, in fact, they aren't.

## Exploration and Exploitation

James March (1991) distinguished two different types of processes that companies pursue: exploration and exploitation. **Exploration** refers to activities such as search, variation, risk taking, experimentation, play, flexiblity, discovery, and innovation. For example, teams at Honda like to experiment with offbeat engineering projects that have little to do with the company's core businesses (cars, motorcycles, and power products). The company spent 16 years and several hundred million dollars developing a four-foot tall humanoid robot called Asimo that climbs stairs, shakes hands, and once rang the opening bell at the New York Stock Exchange (Taylor, 2002). **Exploitation** refers to refinement, choice, production, efficiency, selection, implementation, and execution. Obviously, there is a balance between the two activities. For example, Advanced Tissue Sciences Inc. requires employees to devote 80 percent of their time to existing product lines; the remaining 20 percent of the time, they can work on anything that they find exciting (Singer & Buchanan, 2002).

Teams that engage in exploration to the exclusion of exploitation are likely to find that they suffer the costs of experimentation without gaining many of its benefits, and they will exhibit too many underdeveloped new ideas and too little distinctive competence. Conversely, teams and organizations that engage in exploitation to the exclusion of exploration are likely to find themselves trapped in suboptimal stable equilibria. Brand analyst Will Rodgers, cofounder of SHR Perceptual Management, comments on the exploitation-exploration trade-off when it comes to car manufacturers: "Either they protect their market share and play not to lose, like GM and Toyota, or they go all out, place some big bets and play to win. BMW is playing to win" (Breen, 2002, p. 128). Both exploration and exploitation are important for creative teamwork.

## Creativity and Context Dependence

Consider the *Mona Lisa,* Stephen Hawking's theory of the universe, and the development of the microcomputer. All these are tremendously creative acts that seem to go above and beyond the simple measures of fluency, flexibility, and originality. These achievements are not only unique, but they are also impressive because they were invented with limited resources and in the face of numerous obstacles. Furthermore, if someone today developed the microcomputer, it would not be regarded as a creative act—not just because it has already been done, but because of other advances in technology that already exist. Similarly, if an artist painted the *Mona Lisa* today—even if it had not already been done by Leonardo da Vinci—it probably would not be regarded as an especially creative act. Thus, surrounding all creative products is a context. Creative acts take place within a particular context and within a particular domain given a set of certain resources (Csikszentmihalyi, 1988). To a large extent, the timeliness of an idea is an index of its usefulness or value.

## CREATIVE PEOPLE OR CREATIVE TEAMS?

Is creativity a characteristic of individuals or groups? The answer is both. There is little doubt that some people are more creative than others. Creativity as a trait is highly correlated with intelligence, motivation, ambition, persistence, commitment, determination, education, and success in general. Usually, creative people are passionate about specific things. Perhaps this is why, when Professor Joseph Campbell selects postdoctoral students for his laboratory, he does not want people who've earned straight As or Bs. He searches for the student who made both As and Fs, because he believes these people are not just smart—they let their passions rule them (Muoio, 1997). According to Amabile (1997), the single, most important aspect of creativity is loving what you do. As a case in point, Amabile points to Michael Jordan, who, by the the mid-1990s, was the most financially successful basketball player in history. Jordan's love of the game ruled him—hallmarked by a "love of the game" clause in his contract, which secured him the right to play in "pick-up games" whenever he wished. Amabile's (1997) experimental evidence also reveals that evaluation, surveillance, and even offering rewards to people can undermine creativity.

Creative people also are in tune with their creativity, and they know how to reinvigorate themselves. For example, Partha Mitra of Bell Laboratories is a prolific young researcher, with seven patents and four others pending. When he hits a dry spell, his trick is to go see a movie: "It sort of jogs my emotions, shakes up my brain" (Barker, 2002, p. 168).

The creative person is able to select the relevant information and ignore irrelevant information. An extended period of preparation is involved in most creative products and ideas. Indeed, creative people work very hard. For example, creative scientists typically work 70 to 80 hours a week. Think of it this way: It typically takes people at least 10 years to develop expertise in their domain, no matter what it is—chess, tennis, astrophysics, or management. Skilled chess players undergo years of study before they become "masters" (DeGroot, 1966). And, no one composes outstanding music without at least 10 years of intensive musical preparation (Weisberg, 1986). Basically, if you have been working hard for years at something, think in terms of decades before you become truly great!

However, most companies and most teams do not attempt to select creative people—they look for people who are passionate and skilled in what they do, and then seek to bring those people together with others who are similar (in the sense of being passionate) but different (in terms of ways of thinking). This idea—creative combinations of people—can be more effective than trying to select creative people because creativity is much more a function of the right idea at the right time than a chronic disposition.

## BRAINSTORMING

Alex Osborn, an advertising executive in the 1950s, wanted to increase the creativity of organizations. He believed that one of the main blocks to organizational creativity was the premature evaluation of ideas. He was convinced that two heads were better than one when it came to generating ideas, but only if people could be trained to defer judgment of their own and others' ideas during the idea generation process. Therefore, Osborn developed the most widespread strategy used by organizations to encourage creative thought in teams: brainstorming.

In an influential book, *Applied Imagination,* Osborn (1957, 1963) suggested that brainstorming could considerably increase the quality and quantity of ideas produced by group members. In short, Osborn believed that the group product could be greater than the sum of the individual parts if certain conditions were met. Hence, he developed rules to govern the conduct of brainstorming. Contrary to popular corporate lore that brainstorming sessions are wild and crazy free-for-alls where anything goes, Osborn's (1957, 1963) rules were specific and simple: (1) criticism is ruled out, (2) free-wheeling is welcome, (3) quantity is desired, and (4) combination and improvement of ideas are encouraged (see Table 8-1).

Brainstorming caught on like wildfire in corporations and is a technique that is still ever popular (Kayser, 1995). The goal of brainstorming is to maximize the quantity and quality of ideas. Osborn aptly noted that quantity is a good predictor of quality. A team is more likely to discover a really good idea if it has a lot of ideas to choose from. But there is even more to brainstorming than mere quantity. Osborn believed that the ideas generated by one person in a team could stimulate ideas in other people in a synergistic fashion, also known as cognitive stimulation.

Many companies use the original brainstorming rules suggested by Osborn over 45 years ago. Some companies, like Silicon Valley's IDEO, live by these rules. Douglas Dayton of IDEO says that five rules govern every brainstorming session at IDEO: "Have one conversation at a time. Build upon the ideas of others. Defer judgment. Encourage wild ideas (not wild behavior). Stay focused on the subject" (Gendron, 1998, p. 9).

Osborn believed, as did others, that the four rules had the effect of enhancing motivation among team members by stimulating them to higher levels of productivity via establishment of a benchmark or via competitive rivalry to see who could generate the most ideas. Osborn also thought that the social reinforcement of fellow members increased motivation. Finally, Osborn believed in a "priming effect," namely, that members would make mutual associations upon hearing the ideas presented by others.

**TABLE 8-1**    Rules for Brainstorming

| | |
|---|---|
| **Expressiveness:** | Group members should express any idea that comes to mind, no matter how strange, weird, or fanciful. Group members are encouraged not to be constrained nor timid. They should freewheel whenever possible. |
| **Nonevaluation:** | Do not criticize ideas. Group members should not evaluate any of the ideas in any way during the generation phase; all ideas should be considered valuable. |
| **Quantity:** | Group members should generate as many ideas as possible. Groups should strive for quantity, as the more ideas, the better. Quantity of ideas increases the probability of finding excellent solutions. |
| **Building:** | Because all of the ideas belong to the group, members should try to modify and extend the ideas suggested by other members whenever possible. |

*Source:* Adapted from Osborn, A.F. 1957. *Applied Imagination* (rev. ed.). New York: Scribner.

## Brainstorming on Trial

Osborn claimed to have (but did not provide) research evidence that a team who adopted these rules could generate twice as many ideas as a similar number of people working independently. Consequently, the question that organizational psychologists and management theorists asked of the brainstorming technique was, "Is it effective?" Controlled, scientific studies supported Osborn's intuition. Brainstorming instructions enhance the generation of ideas within a team, in comparison to teams working without those instructions (Parnes & Meadow, 1959). Thus, following the brainstorming guidelines can help increase team creativity.

However, Osborn's most controversial claim was that group brainstorming would be more effective—"twice as productive," in his words—than **individual brainstorming**, where group members work independently (Osborn, 1957). The research evidence testing this assertion has found that the opposite is true. Nearly all controlled investigations have found that *group brainstorming leads to the generation of fewer ideas than comparable numbers of solitary brainstormers in both laboratory and organizational settings* (Diehl & Stroebe, 1987; Jablin, 1981; Mullen, Johnson, & Salas, 1991; Paulus & Dzindolet, 1993; Paulus, Larey, & Ortega, 1995; Taylor, Berry, & Block, 1958). And most studies have found that *solitary brainstorming is much more productive than group brainstorming,* in terms of both quality and quantity of ideas (Diehl & Stroebe, 1987; Mullen et al., 1991). In fact, virtually all of the empirical studies on group brainstorming are strongly (not just mildly) negative (Diehl & Stroebe, 1987; Mullen et al., 1991) in regard to its effectiveness compared with solitary brainstorming. Thus, 45 years of research on brainstorming has found that brainstorming is significantly worse in terms of fostering creativity than having the same number of people work independently on a given task. As a typical example, look at the statistics in Table 8-2, which are actual performance data of brainstorming groups and solitary groups in terms of quantity and quality of ideas.

These results have been replicated several hundred times with a variety of teams brainstorming about all kinds of things, and the same pattern emerges again and again. "It appears particularly difficult to justify brainstorming techniques in terms of any performance outcomes, and the long-lived popularity of brainstorming techniques is unequivocally and substantially misguided" (Mullen et al., 1991, p. 18).

**TABLE 8-2**  Performance Data of Brainstorming and Solitary Groups

| | Face-to-Face Brainstorming Group | Same Number of People Working Independently (Solitary Brainstorming) |
|---|---|---|
| **Quantity:** The number of ideas generated | 28 | 74.5 |
| **Quality:** Percentage of "Good ideas" as judged by independent experts who did not know whose ideas they were evaluating | 8.9% | 12.7% |

*Source:* Adapted from Diehl, M., & Stroebe, W. 1987. "Productivity Loss in Brainstorming Groups: Toward a Solution of a Riddle." *Journal of Personality and Social Psychology, 53,* 497–509.

Thus, official rules of brainstorming, when followed, do enhance team performance, but brainstorming teams still generate fewer ideas than similar numbers of solitary brainstormers (nominal groups).

However, teams that use brainstorming don't like to hear this. Despite the empirical evidence attesting to the ineffectiveness of brainstorming, it remains a popular practice in business and industry (Hackman, 1990; Sutton & Hargadon, 1996; Swezey & Salas, 1992; Woodman, Sawyer, & Griffin, 1993). The obvious questions are, Why are brainstorming groups less effective than brainstorming individuals? And how could the intuition of so many companies and managers be so wrong?

## MAJOR THREATS TO TEAM CREATIVITY

There are four major problems that stifle the effectiveness of team brainstorming. The problem is not teamwork itself, but rather, the social and cognitive processes that operate in teams and how teams are managed. We refer to these problems as social loafing, conformity, production blocking, and downward norm setting.

### Social Loafing

**Social loafing** is the tendency for people to slack off—for example, not work as hard (either mentally or physically) in a group as they would alone. Indeed, as the number of team members increases, each person is more likely to free ride (Karau & Williams, 1993; Shepperd, 1993). It is as if members say to themselves, "I don't need to work really hard when thinking of ideas, because everyone else is working too." This free-riding tendency may be especially true when members' outcomes cannot be individually identified or evaluated. Moreover, when team members perceive their own contributions to be unidentifiable and dispensable, they are likely to loaf (Bouchard, 1972; Diehl & Stroebe, 1987; Harkins & Petty, 1982; Shepperd, 1993). Contrary to intuition, the degree to which a brainstorming topic is regarded as "enjoyable" does not affect persistence (Nijstad, Stroebe, & Lodewijkx, 1999).

### Conformity

A basic human principle is the desire to be liked and accepted by others (in particular, groups). People identify with groups and will sometimes engage in bizarre behaviors to gain acceptance by the group (Tajfel, 1978). People on a team may be somewhat apprehensive about expressing their ideas because they are concerned about others judging and evaluating them (Mullen et al., 1991). This is the need to be liked, which we discussed in Chapter 6 (decision making). Most people desire to be viewed positively by others (Leary, 1995). This concern for "what others will think of me" may inhibit idea generation in teams (Camacho & Paulus, 1995). **Conformity** can occur even when group members are concerned that others in the group will be critical of their suggestions, despite instructions designed to minimize such concerns (Collaros & Anderson, 1969; Diehl & Stroebe, 1987; Harari & Graham, 1975). In particular, team members may suggest "appropriate," traditional, conservative, and highly similar ideas—exactly the kind of behavior that most teams want to avoid. Many social conventions, even those in companies, suggest that in most settings, people should stay "on topic" and not present ideas that diverge greatly from the ones being discussed. Indeed, in interactive teams, there is much more of a tendency to stay on topic than with individual brainstorming. This convergent pattern limits the exchange of ideas that are relatively novel to the team and possibly have the most stimulation value. As a case in point, word association studies reveal that people make more conventional and clichéd responses when they are in a group than when they are alone. Some companies have liberated teams by using free-association exercises. For example, at Campbell's Soup Company, a group of product developers began brainstorming by randomly selecting the word "handle" from a dictionary. Through free association, someone suggested the word "utensil." This led to "fork." One participant joked about a soup that could be eaten with a fork. This group reasoned (in a convergent fashion) that soup could not be eaten with a fork unless it was thick with vegetables and meat—and Campbell's Chunky Soups, an extraordinarily successful product line, was born (Higgins, 1994).

## Production Blocking

**Coordination problems** arise when team members have to take turns presenting their ideas. In contrast, individual brainstormers have the entire allotted time for themselves. A person who is working alone on a problem can enjoy an uninterrupted flow of thought. In contrast, participants in a face-to-face brainstorming group must not only think of ideas, but also listen to others' ideas, and they have to wait for their turn to speak and remember to use conventional floor-taking and floor-yielding signals. It is cognitively difficult to maintain a train of thought or remember ideas generated while others are talking (Diehl & Stroebe, 1987). Members of teams may be prevented from generating new ideas during a team discussion because they are distracted by hearing the contributions of other members while waiting for their turn to participate. During the waiting period, members may listen to others' contributions and, in the process, forget to rehearse the ideas they want to mention. Consequently, people may forget their ideas or decide not to present them during the waiting period (Diehl & Stroebe, 1987, 1991; Stroebe & Diehl, 1994). Furthermore, the inability to express ideas or get floor time may be frustrating and depress motivation. Whereas Osborn theorized that groups could "build on" the ideas suggested by others, there is no evidence for any stimulating impact of unique or rare ideas in brainstorming (Connolly, Routhieaux, & Schneider, 1993). Production blocking interferes with idea generation in two distinct ways: (1) it disrupts the organization of idea generation when delays are relatively long; and (2) it reduces the flexibility of idea generation when delays are unpredictable (Nijstad, Stroebe, & Lodewijkx, in press).

## Downward Norm Setting

It is commonly observed that the performance of people working within a group tends to converge over time. Social comparison processes may lead team members to converge their performance levels into one another (Jackson & Harkins, 1985). For example, at Computer Discount Warehouse (CDW), salespeople working in the same physical location in the building report monthly sales figures more similar to one another than those working in other buildings and areas.[2] However, there is a pervasive tendency for the lowest performers in a group to pull down the team average. Indeed, people working in brainstorming groups tend to match their per-

---

[2]This observation was shared by a manager in the company.

formance to that of the least productive members, also known as **downward norm setting** (Camacho & Paulus, 1995; Paulus & Dzindolet, 1993). Downward norm setting is most likely to occur when there are no strong internal or external incentives for high performance in teams (Shepperd, 1993). For example, the initial performance level of the two lowest-performing members predict the performance of a group of four toward the end of the session (Paulus & Dzindolet, 1993). This performance level may set the benchmark for a team, in that it is seen as an appropriate or typical level of performance. Because groups start their brainstorming by performing at a relatively low level, high performers may feel like "deviants." As a result, they may move their performance in the direction of the low group standard. For example, participants in interactive dyads or groups of four tend to be more similar in their rate of idea generation than noninteracting groups (Camacho & Paulus, 1995; Paulus & Dzindolet, 1993). Unfortunately, the least productive members of the team are often more influential in determining overall team performance than the high performers.

## What Goes on During a Typical Group Brainstorming Session?

What exactly could we expect to observe in a typical team brainstorming session? Video- and tape-recorded interactions reveal an interesting set of events. The four problems noted above conspire to cause people in most brainstorming groups to:

- Fail to follow, or abide by, the rules of brainstorming
- Experience inhibitions, anxiety, and self-presentational concerns
- Slack off production
- Participate in social rituals, such as telling stories, repeating ideas, and giving positive feedback (a natural pattern of conversation that works well at cocktail parties, but kills creativity)
- Set their performance benchmarks too low
- Conform in terms of ideas
- Conform in terms of rate of idea generation

Perhaps the most disturbing news is that most people on brainstorming teams have no idea that this is occurring, such that interactive brainstorming teams feel quite confident about their productivity. Thus, the group suffers from a faulty performance illusion. Brainstorming teams and the companies who use them are their own worst enemy. They fall prey to the illusion that they function very effectively. They suffer from illusions of invulnerability, collective rationalization, belief in the morality of the group, and stereotyping of outgroups. In fact, the illusion of performance is so self-serving that people often take credit for the ideas generated by others (Stroebe, Diehl, & Abakoumkin, 1992).

Brainstorming is simply not as effective as it was hoped to be. What can be done to restructure the design of brainstorming groups?

---

## ENHANCING TEAM CREATIVITY

Fortunately, there are actions that team leaders can take to ward off the typical problems that brainstorming produces. The suggestions outlined below all have a strong scientific research basis, yet they are practical as well. Furthermore, most of the techniques are not expensive.

## Trained Facilitators

A trained facilitator can better follow rules of brainstorming (which are often unwittingly violated), help create an organizational memory, and keep teams on track. Indeed, trained facilitators can bring the level of team performance up to that of nominal groups (Oxley, Dzindolet, & Paulus, 1996). Furthermore, there are long-term benefits to this investment. Teams that are given several sessions in which they are guided by facilitators into productive idea generation patterns demonstrate high levels of productivity in subsequent sessions without the facilitators (Paulus, Putman, Coskun, Leggett, & Roland, 1996). Apparently, teams can become accustomed to sharing ideas without extensive social interaction or "filler" talk. For example, at the IDEO design firm, group leaders are used to facilitate all brainstorming sessions. According to IDEO managers, the key qualification of the facilitators is that they are "good with groups," not because they are experts in the particular product area. Another skill trained facilitators have is the ability to eliminate filler talk; indeed, the highest levels of productivity are obtained when the most ideas are allowed to be shared (Dugosh, Paulus, Roland, & Yang, 2000). Yet another key skill of facilitators is the generation of different categories of ideas.

## High Benchmarks

Brainstorming groups often underperform because they don't have relevant benchmarks. Information about other members' activity levels may increase performance as long as the benchmark is not too discrepant (Seta, 1982). Providing brainstormers with high performance standards greatly increases the number of ideas generated (Paulus & Dzindolet, 1993). Even when members are working independently and announcing to others how many ideas they are generating every five minutes, the number of ideas generated by the team is enhanced (Paulus, Larey, Putman, Leggett, & Roland, 1996). Similarly, a facilitator can periodically call brainstormers' attention to a graph on the computer screen indicating how the team's performance compares with that of other teams—this significantly enhances the number of ideas generated by the group (Shepherd, Briggs, Reinig, Yen, & Nunamaker, 1995–1996). Even forewarning teams that they will see a display of all ideas at the end of the session increases the number of unique ideas generated (Roy, Gauvin, & Limayem, 1996). It is also helpful for members to record their own ideas after the brainstorm.

Another way of setting high benchmarks is through internal competition. For example, people working on a task perform better when they are paired with a partner who is slightly better (versus slightly worse or the same; Seta, 1982). And, just as BMW's design team competes externally against Mercedes-Benz and Audi, they battle each other within the team to create a winning car. Design chief of BMW Chris Bangle typically assigns as many as six teams to develop concepts for a single new BMW (Breen, 2002). The competition can be intense, but the company is able to leverage the different ideas put forth by the competing teams.

## Brainwriting

**Brainwriting** works like this: At key intervals during a brainstorming session, group members cease all talking and all interaction, and write their ideas silently and independently (Geschka, Schaude, & Schlicksupp, 1973; Paulus, 1998; Paulus & Yang, 2000).

Writing ideas instead of speaking them eliminates the problem of production blocking because group members do not have to "wait their turn" to generate ideas. It may also reduce conformity because the written format eliminates the need for public speaking and is typically more anonymous than verbal brainstorming. The written ideas can subsequently be shared by the group in a round-robin fashion and summarized on a blackboard or flip chart. For example, investigations of brainstorming groups of four people revealed that brainwriting, followed by round-robin exchange, eliminated production blocking and social loafing as compared with standard brainwriting (Paulus & Yang, 2000).

Most groups will not welcome the idea of brainwriting, claiming that it ruins the flow of the group process. But the proof is incontrovertible: Brainwriting groups consistently generate more and better ideas than groups that follow their natural instincts. Alternating between team ideation and individual ideation is desirable because it allows teams to circumvent production blocking (coordination problems) and it also sets the stage for divergent thinking (Osborn, 1957). This two-step technique requires a considerable number of conditions to be in place for optimal productivity in group brainstorming. Each member needs to take time out for solitary mediations. Similar benefits can be accomplished through preliminary writing sessions, quotas or deadlines, brief breaks, and the use of specific, simple, and subdivided problems. Thus, by working together, then alone, and then together, teams are more likely to achieve the best in creative thinking (Osborn, 1963).

Even if brainwriting is not used, at the very least, all talking should be stopped periodically to allow members to think silently; the more pauses and silences that occur during brainstorming, the higher the quality of the ideas. Giving members brief breaks, even if they don't write anything down, can help (Horn, 1993). Indeed, periods of "incubation" in which group members reflect on ideas can generate additional ideas (Dugosh, Paulus, Roland, & Yang, 2000).

## Nominal Group Technique

A much better method of group brainstorming is to prepare by having a prior session of solitary writing, known as the **nominal group technique** (Delbecq & Van de Ven, 1971). The nominal group technique, or NGT, is a variation of the standard brainwriting technique (Geschka, Schaude, & Schlicksupp, 1973; Van de Ven & Delbecq, 1974) and involves an initial session of brainwriting prior to interactive teamwork. Thus, NGT separates the idea generation phase from the idea evaluation phase. To use the NGT, it is useful to have a facilitator, but it is not necessary. The facilitator introduces a problem on the board or on a flip chart. Once members understand the topic or issue, they silently write ideas for 10 to 15 minutes. Members state their ideas in a round-robin fashion and each idea is given an identification number. Once ideas are all listed, the team discusses each item, focusing on clarification. Following this, members privately rank the five solutions or ideas they most prefer. The leader-facilitator collects the cards and averages the rating to yield a group decision (see also Box 8-1).

It is worth noting that the NGT technique was compared with an interactive brainstorming process and the NGT technique overwhelmingly outperformed the standard brainstorming group (Gustafson, Shukla, Delbecq, & Walster, 1973). Also, nominal groups that perform in the same room generate more ideas than those in separate rooms (Mullen et al., 1991). The advantage of the nominal group technique is that it

---

BOX 8-1

### Rotating Nominal Group Technique

A variation called the **rotating nominal group technique** involves members writing down their ideas on individual sheets of paper or note cards. The meeting facilitator collects the note cards, shuffles them, and redistributes them to individual group members who read the cards aloud or discuss in small groups. This variation creates greater acceptance of others' ideas and prevents individual members from championing their own ideas.

---

maximizes information gain, ensures a democratic representation of all members' ideas (i.e., avoids the lumpy participation effect), and avoids production blocking. Yet members still have an opportunity for face-to-face discussion of issues. Although it might seem that the NGT would run the risk of generating redundant ideas, they are no more common per number of total ideas than in real face-to-face groups. There are some disadvantages of the NGT; it is less spontaneous and may require a separate meeting for each topic.

### Anonymous Nominal Group Technique

One variant of the NGT is the **anonymous nominal group technique**. In the anonymous NGT, members write down their ideas on individual sheets of paper or note cards. The meeting facilitator (or a group member) collects the note cards, shuffles them, and redistributes them randomly to members, who read the cards aloud or discuss their contents in small groups. This variation creates greater acceptance of others' ideas because the ideas are semianonymous; it also prevents individual members from only championing their own ideas.

### Delphi Technique

Another variant of the nominal group technique is the **Delphi technique** (Helmer, 1966, 1967). In this technique, group members do not interact in a face-to-face fashion at any point. This technique is ideally suited for groups whose members are geographically dispersed (making meetings difficult to attend) and for teams whose members experience such great conflict that it is difficult to meet about sensitive issues. This technique requires a leader or facilitator who is trusted by the team members. The entire process proceeds through questionnaires, followed by feedback that can be computerized. The leader distributes a topic or question to members and asks for responses from each team member. The leader then aggregates the responses, sends them back to the team, and solicits feedback. The process is repeated until there is resolution on the issue in question. The Delphi technique provides maximum structures, ensures equal input, and avoids production blocking—it is pretty easy to avoid coordination loss when team members never interact directly. The technique is a good alternative for teams who are physically separated but nevertheless need to make decisions. Because members respond independently, conformity pressures and evaluation apprehension are limited. One problem associated with this technique, which is not associated with regular brainstorming or nominal brainstorming, is that it can be quite time-consuming. Sessions can last several days, even weeks.

## Diversify the Team

The benefits of diversity outlined in Chapter 4 extend to creativity. Team members that have different backgrounds, training, and perspectives are naturally going to have different ways of looking at a problem. The more heterogeneous the team is, the more likely it is that the team members will be creative. Indeed, teams in which members are diverse with regard to background and perspective outperform teams with homogeneous members on tasks requiring creative problem solving and innovation (Jackson, 1992). This occurs when coworkers experience cognitive conflict (i.e., task conflict) in the absence of conformity pressures and respond by revising fundamental assumptions and generating novel insights (Levine, Resnick, & Higgins, 1993; Nemeth, 1994). As a result, teams with heterogeneous members generate more arguments (Smith, Tindale, & Dugoni, 1996), apply a greater number of strategies (Nemeth & Wachtler, 1983), detect more novel solutions (Nemeth & Kwan, 1987), and are better at integrating multiple perspectives (Gruenfeld, 1994, 1995; Peterson & Nemeth, 1996) than teams without conflicting perspectives. For example, Scott Augustine, of Augustine Medical, employs not just engineers but also prop builders recruited from regional theater and opera companies (Buchanan, 2002).

At Toyota, the approach to creative diversity is called *oobeya* (ooh-bay-uh)—Japanese for "big open office" (Warner, 2002a). For Toyota, *oobeya* means bringing together people from all parts of the company—design, engineering, manufacturing, logistics, and sales—every month for the two years before a car goes into production. According to Takeshi Yoshida, chief engineer for the new 2003 Toyota Corolla, "There are no taboos in *oobeya*. Everyone in the room is an expert. They all have a part to play in building the car. With everyone being equally important to the process, we don't confine ourselves to just one way of thinking our way out of a problem" (Warner, 2002a, p. 38). For a wonderful working illustration of the diverse team concept in a microbiology lab, see Box 8-2.

## Analogical Reasoning

Analogical reasoning is the act of applying one concept or idea from a particular domain to another domain. The simplest analogy might be something like this: *Green* is to *go* as *red* is to *stop*. A much more complex analogy that indicates creative genius is Kepler's application of concepts from light to develop a theory of the orbital motion of planets (Gentner, Brem, Ferguson, & Wolff, 1997). Similarly, chemist Friedrich Kekulé discovered the closed hexagonal structure of the benzene ring by imagining a snake biting its own tail.

As we saw in the example of Dunbar's microbiology labs, creative teams often apply a concept, idea or process from one domain to a new domain. To the extent that teams can recognize when a particular concept might be useful for solving a new problem, creativity can be enhanced. The problem is that it is not easy to transfer relevant information from one domain to another—humans tend to solve problems based upon their surface similarity to other situations, rather than their deep, structural similarity.

---

### Diversity in Labs Predicts Patents

Dunbar (1997) undertook a massive study of microbiology laboratories for an extended period of time. Each laboratory was staffed with trained scientists, and the goal of each lab was to make new discoveries. He attended all meetings and painstakingly recorded all interactions, both formal and informal, in search of the conditions for creativity. Over time, some labs distinguished themselves in terms of having more breakthrough discoveries, as measured by the number of new patents. The laboratories that were more successful in terms of developing new ideas—as measured by the number of new patents—did not have a larger staff, nor were its scientists better paid or smarter. The key differences between the highly creative laboratories and the other labs were threefold: diversity in staff member training and experience, paying attention to inconsistencies and failures, and the use of analogical reasoning. Thus, teams that were more heterogeneous in composition, learned from their failures, and freely drew from other domains to address problems were more likely to make breakthrough discoveries (based on Dunbar, 1997).

---

*Surface versus Structural Analogies*

To see the difference between surface-level similarity and deep-level similarity, consider the problem presented in Box 8-3. The problem is how to use a ray to destroy a patient's tumor given that the ray at full strength will destroy the healthy tissue en route to the tumor. An elegant (but not obvious) solution involves using a series of low-intensity rays from different angles that all converge on the tumor site as their destination (Gick & Holyoak, 1980). Only about 10 percent of people solve this problem. It would stand to reason that performance might improve if people were given an analogous problem beforehand. Consider the problem in Box 8-4. In this problem, a general needs to capture a fortress but is prevented from making a frontal attack by the

---

### The Tumor Problem

Suppose you are a doctor faced with a patient who has a malignant tumor in his stomach. It is impossible to operate on the patient, but unless the tumor is destroyed, the patient will die. There is a kind of ray that can be used to destroy the tumor. If the rays reach the tumor all at once at a sufficiently high intensity, the tumor will be destroyed. Unfortunately, at this intensity, the healthy tissue that the rays pass through on the way to the tumor will also be destroyed. At lower intensities, the rays are harmless to healthy tissue, but they will not affect the tumor either. What type of procedure might be used to destroy the tumor with the rays and, at the same time, avoid destroying the healthy tissue? (Gick & Holyoak, 1980; adapted from Duncker, 1945).

---

### BOX 8-4

## The Fortress Problem

A small country fell under the iron rule of a dictator. The dictator ruled the country from a strong fortress. The fortress was situated in the middle of the country, surrounded by farms and villages. Many roads radiated outward from the fortress like spokes on a wheel. A great general arose, who raised a large army at the border and vowed to capture the fortress and free the country of the dictator. The general knew that if his entire army could attack the fortress at once, it could be captured. His troops were poised at the head of one of the roads leading to the fortress, ready to attack. However, a spy brought the general a disturbing report. The ruthless dictator had planted mines on each of the roads. The mines were set so that small bodies of men could pass over them safely, since the dictator needed to be able to move troops and workers to and from the fortress. However, any large force would detonate the mines.

Not only would this blow up the road and render it impassable, but the dictator would destroy many villages in retaliation. A full-scale direct attack on the fortress therefore appeared impossible.

The general, however, was undaunted. He divided his army up into small groups and dispatched each group to the head of a different road. When all was ready, he gave the signal, and each group charged down a different road. All of the small groups passed safely over the mines, and the army then attacked the fortress in full strength. In this way, the general was able to capture the fortress and overthrow the dictator (Gick & Holyoak, 1980; adapted from Duncker, 1945).

*Source:* Gick, M. L., & Holyoak, K. J. 1983. "Schema Induction and Analogical Transfer." *Cognitive Psychology, 15,* 1–38. Reprinted in Holyoak, K. J., & Thagard, P. 1995. *Mental Leaps: Analogy in Creative Thought.* Cambridge, MA: MIT Press.

---

entire army. An elegant (and analogous) solution is to divide the army into small ground troops that each approach the fortress from a different road at the same time. At a surface level, the problems seem to have little or nothing in common—one from the medical world and the other from a military context. However, at a deeper level, the problems are highly analogous, as can be seen in Figure 8-2. What do you think happens when people are given the tumor problem prior to reading the fortress problem?

Even when given the tumor problem, only 41 percent of people spontaneously apply the convergence solution to the radiation problem. Yet when simply told to "think about the earlier problem," solution rates rise to around 85 percent. If people are given a story about a doctor treating a brain tumor in a similar fashion, solution rates rise to 90 percent. This points up an important aspect of creativity and knowledge: *People usually have the knowledge they need to solve problems, but fail to access it because it comes from a different context.* Thus, a key limitation of managers is not that they are lacking information and knowledge, but that they do not have access to relevant aspects of their own experience when they need it. Thus, applying previously learned knowledge to new situations is surprisingly difficult for most managers.

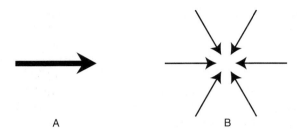

The single large arrow (A) can be mapped to a single
high-intensity ray; the multiple converging arrows (B) can
be mapped to multiple converging low-intensity rays.

**FIGURE 8-2** A Visual Analog of the Tumor Problem. The single large arrow (A) can be mapped to a single high-intensity ray; the multiple converging arrows (B) can be mapped to multiple converging low-intensity rays.
*Source:* Gick, M. L., & Holyoak, K. J. 1983. "Schema Induction and Analogical Transfer." *Cognitive Psychology, 15,* 1–38. Reprinted in Holyoak, K. J. & Thagard, P. 1995. *Mental Leaps: Analogy in Creative Thought.* Cambridge, MA: MIT Press.

### Inert Knowledge Problem

How many of us have experienced the frustration of seeing a connection after it was pointed out to us, but not before? This is known as the **inert knowledge problem**— it means that people's ability to take full advantage of their prior experience is highly limited. Even when they possess the relevant experience necessary to deal with a novel problem, they often fail to do so when their previous experience comes from a different context. In the research done in our laboratory, my colleagues and I have demonstrated a similar failure of transfer with managers and executives (Loewenstein & Thompson, 2000; Thompson, Loewenstein, & Gentner, 2000).

When people encounter a new situation or problem, they are reminded not of prior problems with the same underlying deep structure (such as how the tumor problem is similar to the fortress problem), but of problems with the same surface features (Gentner, Rattermann, & Forbus, 1993). In fact, they recall problems that have surface similarity about 55 percent of the time and problems that are deeply relevant about 12 percent of the time. This points to an important fact about managerial information processing: The knowledge people gain from their daily experience is often not accessed, despite the fact that once it is called to their attention, they regard it to be helpful (Forbus, Gentner, & Law, 1995; Gentner & Landers, 1985; Gentner et al., 1993; Gick & Holyoak, 1980, 1983; Holyoak & Koh, 1987; Reeves & Weisberg, 1994; Ross, 1987).

### How Companies Use Analogy for Creative Thinking

Many companies are recognizing the box-breaking potential of analogical reasoning as a way of using ideas that people have about other, seemingly unrelated things to solve pressing business problems. Alan Heeks, a Harvard MBA, uses an organic farm as a model for business life. Heeks goes so far as to run workshops at a 132-acre farm where analogies run rampant—participants think about harvesting for their future development, recycling, fertility, and sustainability. Heeks helps managers draw analogies between soil and a company's staff (Cox, 2000).

When NASA found it was necessary to design a satellite that would be tethered to a space station by a thin wire 60 miles long, designers realized that the motion of reeling in the satellite would cause it to act like a pendulum with an ever-widening arc. Stanford scientist Thomas Kane, using the analogy of a yo-yo, determined that a small electric motor on the satellite would allow it to crawl back up the tether to the space station (Higgins, 1994). Another use of analogy: A manufacturer of potato chips faced a frequently encountered problem—potato chips took up too much shelf space when they were packed loosely, but they crumbled when packed in smaller packages. The manufacturer found a solution by using a direct analogy: Dried leaves are highly similar to potato chips. They crumble very easily and they are bulky. Pressed leaves are flat. Could potato chips be shipped flat? As it turned out, they could not. However, the team realized that leaves are not pressed when they are dry, but when they are moist. So they packed potato chips in stacks, moist enough not to crumble, but dry enough to be nearly flat. The result was Pringles (Higgins, 1994). The Pennsylvania Chamber of Business in downtown Harrisburg chose the novel *River Horse* by William Least Heat-Moon as an analogy for the changes and transformation their organization was going through (Jaffe, 2000).

Barry Shuler, Marriott International's senior vice president of strategy and planning for information resources, has helped to technically season Marriott's executives by speaking in analogies. Shuler, a former racecar driver, sold the new network with the following analogy: "Bill Marriott Jr. [CEO and Chairman of the Board] owns several exotic cars. He loves talking about cars. I tell him the infrastructure—the hardware and the system software connecting the network—[is] like the road. Then I ask him, 'Why would you want a thousand roads coming to the same place when you can have one?' I compare our applications to trucks and cars driving on the road. And Information Resources people are the pit crew" (Radcliff, 2000). Analogical reasoning involves the application of diverse categories to a company's present problem or challenge. Another example: The D'Arcy advertising firm often holds "kidnappings" in which employees are suddenly whisked away to museums and then asked to think about a certain artist or exhibit as an analogy to their current product or service (Lee, 2002).

Hargadon (1998) calls the use of analogy in companies "knowledge brokering," and notes that the best innovators use old ideas as the raw material for new ideas. Moreover, the most dramatic impacts of new technologies often come from industries other than the ones in which they first emerged. For example, the steam engine, developed in the mining industry, revolutionized the railroad and shipping industries. Hargadon and Sutton (2000) outline four critical steps in the knowledge brokering cycle: (1) capturing good ideas, (2) keeping ideas alive, (3) imagining new uses for old ideas, and (4) putting promising concepts to the test.

### Creating an Organizational Memory

One of the biggest drains on performance is the repetition of ideas or forgetting of ideas in teams. Teams can create an organizational memory by recording ideas in full view. Group members repeat ideas more when they are not physically indexed. This wastes time. Thus, brainstorming sessions can be greatly improved by recording all ideas. For example, Buckman Laboratories Inc., a manufacturer of specialty chemicals for aqueous industrial systems based in Memphis, Tennessee, connects all of its associates worldwide with a proprietary knowledge network, K'Netix (Wah, 1999). Also, Sun

Microsystems's Java migration team created a shared-code library, which serves as a central communication hub from which they can check out whole pieces of software code rather than re-create them every time (Wah, 1999).

## Membership Change

Teams do not remain consistently intact. As we saw in Chapter 2, members enter and exit groups. My colleague, Hoon-Seok Choi, and I have extensively examined teams that either remain perfectly intact (i.e., do not experience any turnover) versus teams that experience at least one membership change (holding the total number of people in the team constant).[3] We find dramatic evidence that teams who experience membership change (i.e., an entry of a new member and an exit of an old member) generate more ideas (high fluency) and more different kinds of ideas (higher flexibility) than do groups who remain intact. Here is what we think happens: Teams that stay together, without any change in membership, develop a sort of cognitive arthritis—they get stuck in their same old ruts when it comes to idea generation. In contrast, teams that experience a change in membership are naturally exposed to more ideas due to a greater diversity in task-relevant skills and information. Moreover, when a group experiences a membership change, they are in a unique position to look at themselves more thoughtfully. That is, the presence of a newcomer can motivate old-timers to revisit their task strategy and develop new and improved methods for performing group tasks (Sutton & Louis, 1987). At that point, we think the team is in a better position not only to think about their working style but also to learn from others. Finally, groups that experience membership change are more task-oriented than are groups that remain intact in terms of their membership structure, due to the transitory nature of interaction among members (Ziller, 1965).

### *Stepladder Technique*

The **stepladder technique** (Rogelberg, Barnes-Farrell, & Lowe, 1992), a variant of the membership change technique, is a decision-making approach in which members are added one by one to a team. The first step of the technique involves the creation of a two-person subgroup (the core) that begins preliminary discussion of the group task. After a fixed time interval, another member joins the core group and presents his or her ideas concerning the task. The three-person group then discusses the task in a preliminary manner. The process continues in steps until all members have systematically joined the core group. When this occurs, the group arrives at a final solution. Each member must have sufficient time to think about the problem before entering into the core group. More important, the entering members must present their preliminary solutions before hearing the core group's preliminary solutions. A final decision cannot be reached until the group has formed in its entirety. Self-pacing stepladder groups (which proceed through the paces at a self-determined pace) produce significantly higher quality group decisions than conventional groups (Rogelberg & O'Connor, 1998). Members with the best individual decisions exert more influence in stepladder groups than in free interaction groups.

---

[3]This is based on research done by Hoon-Seok Choi and Leigh Thompson during 2001–2003. A paper that reviews this research can be obtained from either Leigh Thompson or Hoon-Seok Choi, Management and Organizations Department, Kellogg School of Management, Northwestern University, 2001 Sheridan Road, Evanston, Illinois 60208.

## Build a Playground

Dr. Ashley Montagu once said that your goal in life should be "to die young as late as possible." Similarly, creative people can honestly say, "I have worked every minute of my life" and "I never did a lick of work in my life." Some companies are creating the environments that engender this playful state of mind. And rightly so, given that work environments clearly affect creativity (Amabile, Conti, Coon, Lazenby, & Herron, 1996). According to Amabile et al., the degree of organizational encouragement, supervisory encouragement, freedom, and workload pressure all affect the ability of people to be creative in their organizations. According to Amabile, Hadley, and Kramer (2002), "creativity under the gun" almost never works, even despite our intuitions that working under pressure can force an insight.

One of the most popular approaches to stimulating creativity in the short term, as well as instilling long-term passion and motivation, is the creation of the work playground. There is no single blueprint for the playground. The basic idea is to break with old ideas about what it means to be at work—beige walls turn into tent-shaped fabric sails, "chat-zapping" elevators are replaced with conversation-instigating escalators, and the brainstorming areas (called "chill-out zones" at one office) are painted in funky technicolor hues (Long, 2002). Most important, functionality guides the fun playground.

Spaces that are designed to foster creativity involve a lot of fun elements. For example, Southern California's Foote, Cone, & Belding advertising agency reinvented the traditional workplace with 156 surfboards on the walls of its boardroom, removal of all doors from offices, and installed basketball and Italian bocce ball courts for creative brainstorming (*PR Newswire,* September 2001). In St. Louis, employees at the D'Arcy Masius Benton and Bowles advertising agency rock climb, visit art museums, and go to the movies on company time; executives at Aurora Foods encourage employees to write on the walls with markers and experiment with Play-Doh and Slinkys (Lee, 2002).

At the 3M Company, you won't find Nerf guns or beanbag chairs or even a cheerleader facilitator. However, 3M believes in the creative environment. The Innovation and Learning Center at 3M features books, videos, and technical training items geared to spark new thinking. 3M sums up their philosophy this way: "It doesn't work to urge people to think outside the box without giving them the tools to climb out" (Muoio, 1997).

### The Science of Play

According to theories of expertise and insight, great insights often come after a period of incubation (Dugosh et al., 2000). Often, the toughest problems are solved when the problem-solver is not directly attacking the problem. Perhaps that is why Tinker Hatfield of Nike admits that he does not know where his design ideas will come from (Muoio, 1997). The Air Jordan VI was inspired by the "Batboot" Tinker designed for Michael Keaton in the movie *Batman.* The inspiration for the Jordan VII was a poster for National Public Radio. Even the stodgiest of organizations are realizing the value of play and moving away from the "we've always done it this way" attitude, designing environments where people are free to express their ideas. For example, the U.S. Patent and Trademark Office realized that it was time to find new and different ways to manage the process of granting patents. Rather than create a top-down change program, they allowed more than 125 people to go "off the line" two days a week for several months (Muoio, 1997). This unprecedented commitment to innovation helped people lose their inhibitions. "Jacket-and-tie bureaucrats acted out skits to describe how a new patent process might work" (Muoio, 1997). The result was a radical redesign of the process that slashed patent-cycle times and reduced how many times a file is touched from 67 to eight.

### The Science of Mood

Whereas there is little or no research on whether bocce ball courts increase creativity, there is a powerful body of research suggesting that positive affect—whether it comes from reading a funny cartoon or seeing puppies play—increases creativity (Isen, Daubman, & Nowicki, 1987). The flip side is that negative mood decreases productivity. For example, Amabile and Conti (1999) studied the creativity of a large high-technology firm before, during, and after a major downsizing. Obviously, downsizings engender negative mood and, in this case, were accompanied by decreases in project team creativity.

### The Science of Space

Space and distance define how and whether people interact. The business of space is serious enough that British Petroleum has totally transformed the way it searches for oil, and ultra high-end fashion company Prada has revolutionized how it sells clothes to its customers, by using "creative space" designed by Steelcase (Brown, 2002). Augustine Medical has 15 conference rooms scattered about, each with several whiteboards, so that whenever a hallway conversation threatens to turn productive, it can instantly find a home. "An idea will go up on a whiteboard, and you'll see a parade of people from every part of the company going into that conference room for half an hour each" (Buchanan, 2002, p. 58). A separate space, called the Creative Room, is painted purple and gold and has variable mood lighting; a garish rabbit lamp adorns one wall; and toys such as Slinkys, modeling clay, building blocks, and gyroscopes sit invitingly on the conference table (Buchanan, 2002).

## ELECTRONIC BRAINSTORMING

Electronic brainstorming (EBS) has recently been introduced into organizations as a means of generating ideas; it makes use of computers to allow members to interact and to exchange ideas. In a typical EBS session, members are seated around a table that contains individual computer stations. A large screen projects all ideas generated by members. The ideas that are generated using EBS are anonymous and, thus, tend to be expressed more freely and in greater quantity.

EBS is used as part of a regular organizational meeting process. It gives organizations the opportunity to gather ideas efficiently, organize those ideas, and subsequently make decisions. It speeds up the meeting at which it is used, increases productivity, and allows the focus to remain on the ideas rather than on the people who spawned them. When members run out of ideas, they access the ideas produced by the team.

In EBS, people are usually not identified by their contributions. Typically, participants can view subsets of ideas generated by other team members on part of the screen at any time by using a keystroke. Ideas are projected on a large screen and people are asked to evaluate them. The team may eventually vote on the most preferred ideas. A facilitator guides both the idea generation and decision processes (Jessup & Valacich, 1993; Nunamaker, Briggs, & Mittleman, 1995).

## Advantages of Electronic Brainstorming

The key advantages of EBS are that it addresses all the blocks to productivity that occur in traditional brainstorming—that is, the threats to performance that occur because people have to compete for floor time; because only one person can talk at one time while others listen; because members may feel inhibited making suggestions, especially if there exist status differences among the team members; because people have a difficult time staying focused on idea generation, as opposed to repeating or evaluating someone else's idea; and because the organizational memory for ideas can be cumbersome or incomplete. EBS elegantly circumvents most of these problems.

### Parallel Entry of Ideas

Parallel entry of ideas, like brainwriting, means that all members of the team can generate ideas simultaneously. Although it might seem desirable to have members listen attentively to others' ideas, this, in fact, is highly inefficient (as the opening example of this chapter suggests). To be sure, EBS does not mean that members disregard or tune out the ideas of others; rather it means that they can both contribute and listen in a much more interactive and efficient fashion. The result is that most members regard the entire process to be more egalitarian and satisfying than a traditional brainstorming session, which can be dominated by one person or a subset of members and, consequently, highly frustrating for others.

### Anonymity

In addition to finessing the floor competition that can take place in traditional brainstorming sessions, EBS also has the attractive feature of reducing many people's inhibitions and concerns about what others think of them. As we saw in Chapter 2 (performance and productivity), performance pressure can lead to choking, and as we saw in Chapter 6 (decision making), conformity pressures are extremely strong in teams, even those whose members value independent thought. Because the ideas that are generated in EBS are anonymous, people can express themselves without having to worry about criticism, and the team, therefore, will be less conforming. This is especially true when teams are composed of members of differing status levels. K. C. Guinn, the CEO of Southwest Gas, commented on EBS, "Because the process is anonymous, the sky's the limit in terms of what you can say, and as a result it is more thought-provoking. As a CEO, you'll probably discover things you might not want to hear but need to be aware of" (Dennis, Nunamaker, Paranka, & Vogel, 1990, p. 38). In this sense, EBS can be a venue for the type of evaluations that we discussed in Chapter 3 (rewarding teamwork). That is, managers can get clear and full feedback on what others think of them or their ideas.

### Size

Traditional brainstorming groups suffer greatly from coordination and communication problems as the team grows. In contrast, EBS can easily handle large teams. This can be an advantage for the organization, putting more minds to work on the problem and involving several people in the creative process. It also has the potential for improving organizational memory.

### Proximity

An important way that EBS clearly dominates traditional brainstorming is that EBS groups can meet synchronously while being physically dispersed. The members do not have to be in the same place, or even in the same country, to interact.

### Memory

As noted, the creation and utilization of organizational memory is greatly facilitated with EBS. The members, whether or not they attended the EBS, have the option of viewing the session via computer disk. Mattel Media uses an interesting variation on electronic brainstorming in their team meetings. A self-proclaimed "technographer" records team members' new product ideas on a laptop, the entries appearing before the group either on a 35-inch color monitor or on the wall. Bernie DeKoven, whose title at Mattel was "Doctor Fun/Staff Design," did not allow anyone to write, in an attempt to minimize production blocking (based on the belief that if you are writing, you are not thinking). Thus, the note taker recorded everyone's ideas in front of the group. These ideas could be rated, evaluated, and eventually dumped. Furthermore, everyone left the meeting with a hard copy of the notes in hand—thus serving the organizational memory. In addition, DeKoven kept a "boneyard"—a file of ideas that were rejected in the meeting. Some of those dismissed notions became valuable later on in the context of another project. For example, when Andy Rifkin, former senior vice president of creative development for Mattel Media, was touring with toy buyers, he got repeated requests for activity-based toys for boys. Picking through the boneyard of a year-old meeting, he found a Hot Wheels CD-ROM concept for designing and decorating cars and printing licenses and tickets. The Hot Wheels Custom Car Designer became a best-selling item in stores (Grossmann, 1998).

### Refinement and Evaluation of Ideas

EBS allows the use of specialized software to help refine, organize, and evaluate ideas. Some software manufacturers have three types of components in their software: presession planning, in-session management, and postsession organization. Collectively, these tools finesse much of the task-management skills that are needed in meetings. Instead of delegating a person to perform these activities, they are automated.

### Equality

EBS places every participant on a level playing field. Practically, this means that no individual can dominate the meeting through rank, status, or raised voice. Thus, EBS ensures equality of input. Equality has many virtues in this type of teamwork. When members feel more equal, there is often more participation, which can increase productivity. For example, one company used traditional brainstorming to develop a one-year and a five-year plan (Dennis et al., 1990). The committee, composed of five members, spent two days trying to develop a mission statement. In the end, the statement was unacceptable to several key people in the company. When the same team used EBS, they developed a mission statement in two hours. Then they developed further objectives, goals, and strategies. This plan was accepted by the board, with no changes. The EBS session was more effective because each member of the team had input into the process.

## Disadvantages of Electronic Brainstorming

EBS does have disadvantages. As with most new technologies, the unrealistic expectation is that it will solve all known problems and not create any new ones. Technology cannot replace thinking: members must generate ideas and then evaluate them.

*Small Teams*

Smaller EBS groups do not generate as many ideas as do larger groups. For example, an 18-person EBS group generated more ideas than a three-person EBS group (Gallupe, 1992). This is not really a disadvantage, but rather an admonition to EBS managers that larger teams will be more productive—something that is not true in traditional brainstorming. However, this in no way implies that EBS with small teams is less effective than face-to-face brainstorming. Quite the contrary!

*Loss of Social Interaction*

Probably the most notable disadvantage is that EBS prevents members from interacting socially. Although we have seen that natural social interaction leads to inefficiencies in performance, social interaction does do other (positive) things for teams. Nonverbal communication, such as facial expressions, laughing, and intonation, is important for building feelings of rapport and trust between members. Furthermore, when people do not interact directly, greater misunderstanding and miscommunication can result. What's more, there is some concern that EBS may actually promote antisocial behavior, with people being more judgmental, pointed, and abrupt in their communications—something we discuss more in Chapter 12 on virtual teamwork. These drawbacks may leave team members less satisfied than when traditional brainstorming is used. There may be a dissociation between two measures of productivity: actual productivity (quantity and quality of ideas produced) and team satisfaction. The manager (and team) may have to make some hard choices about which objective to prioritize.

*Loss of Power*

Paralleling the greater equality that EBS creates in the organizations that use it is a resultant loss of power for individuals higher in status. Quite frankly, anonymity and equality of input may very well be regarded to be a disadvantage for managers accustomed to having their own ideas implemented. Thus, there could be a backlash of sorts, with organizational members accustomed to greater power attempting to return to traditional status hierarchies.

*No Credit*

The downside of the anonymity aspect of EBS is that members who generate ideas don't receive credit for them. As we saw in Chapter 3, recognition is often the most powerful form of reward. Because EBS is anonymous, this means that members are not accountable for generating and evaluating ideas. This means that some members may work hard and others may do nothing or free ride on the efforts of others (Diehl & Stroebe, 1987). Furthermore, EBS participants may feel that their contribution to the team will not make a difference. In contrast, people in traditional brainstorming groups are keenly aware of the contributions of others, which may promote high levels of participation.

It is important to note that EBS has not proven to be more successful than the nominal group technique. In summary, EBS is extraordinarily useful for managing the discussions of large, physically separated teams. EBS limits the demands of social synchronization—that is, coordination loss—and allows flexibility in accessing one's own, or others', ideas. It also creates a transactive memory system by using an external storage system that may limit the potentially debilitating effects of keeping track of ideas generated during the exchange of ideas (Nagasundaram & Dennis, 1993).

## Capstone on Brainstorming

There is no evidence that conventional brainstorming teams can exceed the performance of people working alone. The various inhibitory social and cognitive factors in teams simply outweigh the potential positive effects of social and cognitive stimulation (Paulus et al., 1998).

Why then, with all of its faults, is face-to-face group brainstorming so pervasive in companies? Part of the reason is that people falsely believe it is effective. Even upon discovering that there is virtually no research that supports its effectiveness, managers and executives refuse to give up the belief that brainstorming—in its traditional form—is effective. Most managers severely underestimate the process loss in teams—that is, the inhibitory cognitive and social factors such as social loafing, production blocking, coordination loss, task irrelevant behaviors, and filler talk—because they lack a relevant benchmark.

It is not uncommon for teams to cite advantages of brainstorming, such as increasing cohesion and building morale. They may suggest that productivity is a rather narrow basis for evaluating the effectiveness of idea-generating techniques such as group brainstorming (Kramer, Kuo, & Dailey, 1997; Sutton & Hargadon, 1996). They suggest that group brainstorming can have a number of positive side benefits, such as increased morale and a generally more effective work environment. Consider, for example, IDEO in Palo Alto, founded in 1978 by David Kelley. IDEO is the largest product design consulting firm in the United States and uses brainstorming on a regular basis. Convinced that IDEO was not just spinning its wheels when brainstorming, organizational psychologists performed an extensive case study of IDEO's brainstorming (Sutton & Hargadon, 1996). However, the productivity of the design engineers working in real groups was not compared with that of nominal groups—or any other variation on the process. Instead, the design engineers themselves were asked to speak to the benefits of brainstorming. One of the key benefits they cited was the development of an organizational memory of design solutions. For example, one brainstorming session at IDEO with 10 engineers present means that 20 percent of the engineers in Palo Alto are exposed to the ideas. IDEO is serious about creating organizational memory. Brainstormers are commonly videotaped and shown as reruns for stimulation. Other benefits cited by engineers included providing skill variety for designers and setting organizational norms regarding asking for help. Brainstorming at IDEO purportedly creates a status auction among designers, whose reputations are shaped during brainstorms. Finally, impressing clients and providing income for the firm were also cited as benefits of brainstorming.

We are not suggesting that companies and teams abandon brainstorming. Rather, we suggest they develop *hybrid* methods for creative work that capitalize on individuals' strengths and combine those with team strengths. For example, one manager told us that the simple act of asking team members to submit items *prior to* their weekly group meeting resulted in a tenfold increase in volume of ideas and higher quality of those ideas. With some simple changes, the productivity of teams can increase dramatically. The positive perspective on brainstorming stems from the validation that people receive when interacting in teams, especially those with cooperative goals, such as in brainstorming. For this reason, it is not at all surprising that brainstorming maintains a high degree of popularity in organizations (Grossman, Rodgers, & Moore, 1989; Rickards, 1993). The key is to use brainstorming at the *right time,* and in the *right way.*

## CONCLUSIONS

Creativity is the Holy Grail of teamwork. This is certainly true for creative teams, but also true for problem-solving and tactical teams. However, many of our intuitions about creativity are incorrect. We see this most clearly in the case of face-to-face brainstorming. The process of generating novel and useful ideas is often blocked in teams. Most creative ideas are applications or transfers of concepts, ideas, and processes from one domain to another. This may sound easy or straightforward, but most people under most conditions do not transfer ideas across domains, even when it would be useful. Johannes Kepler's analogy of the sun and planets as magnets; conceiving the heart as a pump; or even comparing potato chips to dried leaves may seem obvious in hindsight, but it is the getting there that is the hard part. The techniques described in this chapter—comparison and abstraction, maximizing flexibility of categorizing, brainwriting, and so on—are the keys to promoting creative teamwork.

# External Dynamics

# CHAPTER

# Networking, Social Capital, and Integrating across Teams

*"[P]ower is increasingly resident in the nodes, hidden in the networks. It's not at the top, at the mythical 'C level' in companies. It's not at the bottom, lurking in the depths of mass movements. It's somewhere in the middle of organizations, where all links come together. . . . Power today means being connected: The most powerful individual is the person who has the most links to others. The player with the most corporate board seats wins. So the most powerful man in America is not at the top of anything, but instead the most linked, the stickiest. That person is Vernon Jordan, deal-maker extraordinaire and Washington superlawyer. In 1998, he and his wife, Ann, sat on 17 boards combined. In 2002, he sat on 10, including American Express, Dow Jones, Revlon, and Xerox, making him 'the most central director of the corporate elite' "* (Rubin, 2002, p. 100).

There are 10,100 directorships in Fortune 1000 companies. They are held by 7,682 people. If each director were to serve on only one board, the network would not be connected. However, 14 percent of all directors serve on two boards and 7 percent on three or more boards. These overlapping directors create a unique network where each is 4.6 degrees (or 4.6 phone calls or handshakes) away from any other director. Jordan holds the singular position of being only three handshakes away from anyone in his network (Barabási, 2002).

What in the world do networks and links have to do with teamwork? Just about everything, if we consider the fact that teams are dependent on their leaders and members to plug them into the right people in the organization for their needed resources, contacts, and opportunities.

We saw in Part II that the manager must focus on internal team processes. However, there is more to creating and sustaining a successful team than supporting its internal activities. Team members interact with one another in the context of a larger environment. A team's environment includes the organization to which the team belongs and the clients they serve. This chapter focuses on the team's relationship to people outside of the team, who nevertheless affect the team's ability to achieve its goals. This is essential because, among other reasons, team productivity is often judged by those who consume the group's services; namely, its customers.

Defined in this way, the environment is both a cause and effect of team behavior: It influences internal team dynamics and is influenced by them. Managers often make the mistake of only focusing on internal team dynamics. However, to be effective, managers must also develop the external relationships of the team. These external relationships are increasingly important as companies diversify the traditional organizational structure of the company's activities. Organizations call upon teams to span traditional boundaries both inside companies, where they might provide a closer coupling between functional units, and outside companies, where they might provide links to customers, suppliers, or competitors (Clark & Fujimoto, 1987; von Hippel, 1988).

In this chapter, we first discuss what we mean by team boundaries. Then, we describe four prototypical teams in organizations in terms of how they manage their team boundaries and the trade-offs associated with each. Next, we focus on the external roles that team members play. We then discuss networking within the organization and contrast clique networks to entrepreneurial networks and strategies for increasing team effectiveness.

## TEAM BOUNDARIES

In the minds of the team members and the organization, an identifiable boundary exists between the team and the other parts of the organization. This, in fact, was one of the key defining characteristics of a team, as indicated in Chapter 1. In this chapter, we examine the in- and outflow of information, resources, and people across this border.

Team boundaries differentiate one work group from another and affect knowledge transfer and distribution of resources. In some cases, boundaries are well defined, but in other cases, boundaries are more ambiguous. If the boundary becomes too open or indistinct, the team risks becoming overwhelmed and losing its identity. If its boundary is too exclusive, the team might become isolated and lose touch with suppliers, managers, peers, or customers (Alderfer, 1977). Thus, teams can be **underbounded**—having many external ties but an inability to coalesce and motivate members to pull together—or **overbounded**—having high internal loyalty and a complex set of internal dynamics but an inability to integrate with others when needed. There is a trade-off between internal cohesion and external ties—more cohesive teams are less likely to engage in necessary external initiatives (Alderfer, 1976; Sherif, 1966). Although there is no perfect answer for how to deal with the tension between internal cohesion and the external environment, in this chapter we offer a combination of consciousness-raising about key issues and strategies for arranging the team environment so as to be maximally productive.

Leaders play an integral role in connecting a team with the external environment. Some leaders focus all their energies on the internal functioning of the team through classic coaching; other leaders spend most of their efforts on promoting the team within the organization. These are two extremes that are equally ineffective. In this section, we try to be more specific in pinpointing the choices leaders have in managing the interface between their team and the greater environment, and, most important, considering the effects on team productivity and performance.

The choices that a leader has, in terms of managing the interface, parallel the choices for control outlined in Chapter 1. Recall our analysis of manager-led, self-managing, self-designing, and self-governing teams. In the case of the leader managing the team within its environment, the relationship of interest is between the team and the environment. Table 9-1 outlines four types of teams in terms of their relationship to the environment: insulating teams, broadcasting teams, marketing teams, and surveying teams (see Ancona, 1990). Of course, these are four *pure* strategies, and *blends* may exist. It is useful to try to identify which style best characterizes a particular team.

**TABLE 9-1**    Prototypical Relationships Teams May Have with Their Environment

| Team's Relationship with Environment | Key Focus and Activities | Advantages | Disadvantages |
|---|---|---|---|
| **Insulating** | Team is isolated from other parts of organization or its customers; team concentrates solely on internal functioning; usually highly goal driven | • Less likely to compromise ideals and objectives<br>• Especially facilitative for creative teams | • Disconnected from rest of organization<br>• May develop groupthink or overconfidence |
| **Broadcasting** | Team concentrates on internal team processes until the team is ready to inform outsiders of its intentions | • Control over negative information<br>• Broadcasting is relatively inexpensive | • May fail to sense true needs of customers<br>• May fail to develop customer buy-in |
| **Marketing** | Team concentrates on getting buy-in from outsiders through advertising, self-promotion, lobbying | • High visibility often is helpful for team | • May fail to meet true needs of customers<br>• Marketing costs can be high |
| **Surveying** | Team concentrates on diagnosing needs of customers, experimenting with solutions, revising their knowledge, initiating programs, and collecting data | • Greatest potential customer satisfaction<br>• Understand outsiders' demands<br>• Rated by outsiders as higher performers | • Often extremely costly and time-consuming<br>• May surface latent conflict within the organization<br>• Possible low cohesion (due to divergent views created by surveying)<br>• Possible dissatisfaction |

*Source:* Based on Ancona, D.G. 1990. "Outward Bound: Strategies for Team Survival in an Organization." *Academy of Management Journal, 33*(2), 334–365.

## Insulating Teams

Insulating teams are, for the most part, sequestered from the environment. This may be a deliberate choice by the manager or leader; other times, the team may be ostracized by the organization. Managers often want to isolate their teams for security reasons (e.g., the Los Alamos team that developed the atomic bomb) or intellectual reasons (e.g., the Xerox PARC team that developed the computer). The greatest threat to the effectiveness of insulating teams is dissociation from the organization. Insulating teams may fail to develop a viable product or service because they are out of touch with the rest of the organization and industry, or they may have a great product but lack the support they need for success.

Insulating teams not only have to insulate themselves from others in the company so that they can focus on the work that needs to be done, but they also need to insulate themselves from outsiders, who have strategic reasons to learn their secrets. Competitors often want access to information so that they can decipher long-range business plans. And the increase in information technology has made insulation much more challenging. One company went to extreme lengths to preserve their project plans. They had scheduled a particularly important strategic-planning conference and had checked into the hotel. The conference room number and the name of their company was listed on the hotel's daily agenda sign, but no one showed up. At the appointed hour, without fanfare, they boarded a chartered bus designated for a nonexistent "tour group." From there, they departed to an unannounced locale and began their meeting far from the eyes of outsiders who wanted to infiltrate the meeting (Kaltenheuser, 2002).

### Broadcasting Teams

Broadcasting teams concentrate on their internal processes and simply inform others what they are doing. More often than not, the broadcasting team has little outside contact; it makes decisions about how to serve its customers from within. The team members let others outside the team know what they are doing after they have already made decisions.

### Marketing Teams

When we refer to *marketing teams,* we do not rely on the traditional, functional definition. Marketing teams promote their objectives, products, services, and culture actively within their organization. Often, their objective is to get buy-in from above and receive recognition. They differ from broadcasting teams in that they actively tailor their communication to suit the perceived needs, interests, and objectives of the organization. To use an analogy, the broadcasting team is like a news report; the marketing team is like an advertisement.

### Surveying Teams

Surveying teams try to put their finger on the pulse of the organization, their clients, and customers. For example, George Calhoun of ISCO International, a company that makes front-end systems and filters for wireless communications, sums up the source of his company's great ideas in one word: customers (Singer & Buchanan, 2002). The ideas that are captured during customer visits are submitted via a "trip report" so that no valuable information disappears. Gail Naughton, founder and vice-chairman of Advanced Tissue Sciences, believes in frequent exposure to customers, which, at Advanced Tissue Sciences, means patients. Says Naughton, "On a routine basis, we bring in burn victims and families of burn victims, or diabetic patients who have been spared an amputation because of our product, and we make sure that all of our associates understand how their work has touched these people's lives" (Singer & Buchanan, 2002, p. 65).

The downside of surveying, of course, is that the team may spend an undue amount of time and resources surveying clients and customers instead of engaging in the task at hand. In this sense, a surveying team is really a sort of task force. At some point, the surveying team has to make critical decisions about when to stop collecting and probing for information and develop a product or service for its customers.

It is rare for teams to be self-sufficient, and it is their dependence on others for economic, social, and political support that drives many of the strategies for interacting with the environment. Xerox PARC is an example wherein an insulated team used its insulation to advantage in developing essentially all the technology used in today's modern computer age. However, the team members were unsuccessful in selling their ideas to their own management (because virtually no broadcasting or marketing had been done). Therefore, Xerox did not obtain the benefits of its own special research group.

We have been looking at the team's relationship with its environment as a deliberate and purposeful decision made by the team's manager at the outset of team activity. However, this is rarely the case. The relationship a team has with its environment evolves—sometimes from direct managerial intervention, but more often from organizational norms, culture, and situational constraints. For example, if the physical facilities within an organization make interaction difficult between different units, teams will be more likely to adopt insulating or broadcasting strategies.

Our discussion of team management vis-à-vis the external environment may seem to be overly politicized. Indeed, there is a trade-off between the team members actually doing their work and their efforts at influencing management and other relevant external entities. In some sense, this is a hidden cost to the organization, similar to hiring lawyers or writing contracts—a form of team red tape. If so, the organization should try to find ways to avoid this. There are two messages here. One is for the team leader: If you fail to effectively manage the relationship between your team and the external environment, your team may be regarded as ineffective, regardless of its actual productivity. The other message is for the organization: By placing constraints and barriers upon the team's ability to control and gain access to resources, such as education, knowledge, and economic resources, team effectiveness may be hindered.

The interaction between a team and the organization is similar to the interaction between the members and the team itself in that there are struggles for power, status, and roles (Ancona, 1990). Just as members often spend time during the formation of a team to determine what role they will play and which members will have power, so, too, do teams play out these same issues with other organizational entities. For example, top management may set constraints and provide direction. Teams may react in a variety of ways; some welcome the direction, some try to shape the new directives, and others reject direction.

Just as people develop reputations and make impressions on others in the organization within the first few months of their arrival, so do teams. Early on, teams are labeled, and on the basis of this initial impression, a negative or positive escalating cycle in terms of both team reputation and team performance begins. Initial reputations may remain intact for quite some time, despite efforts to change them. Teams that do not overcome a negative initial evaluation may be perceived as failures—even if they eventually achieve their goals. "The inability to influence top management early on can be devastating to a team since they control resources and rewards. In short, labeling creates self-fulfilling prophecies" (Ancona, 1993, p. 233). Often, teams want to get down to work and not waste time navigating their external relationships. However, these very issues—if ignored early on—can haunt the team in the future. Therefore, even though teams must fulfill both internal and external activities, the point in time at which they undertake those activities is not trivial. Obtaining support from the environment is critical if a team is to enter a positive escalation cycle (Ancona, 1993).

## EXTERNAL ROLES OF TEAM MEMBERS

Just as members develop roles for the internal functioning of a team, they develop roles for the external functioning of a team (Ancona, 1990). Identifying and understanding the roles that team members play vis-à-vis the in- and outflow of information to the team is an important predictor of team productivity and performance.

Roles are not formally assigned; rather, through an implicit process of team negotiation, roles are taken on by members of the group. Members quickly size up others' abilities, and tasks are often delegated on the basis of demonstrated performance in these areas.

Although it would be impossible to list an exhaustive set of roles, Box 9-1 lists some of the most common and important roles that have been observed in work groups (see Ancona, 1990; Ancona & Caldwell, 1987, 1988, 1991, 1992).

Not all of these roles are identifiable in all teams. Because the boundary-spanning role has been studied in detail and can significantly affect the course of individuals' career paths within the organization (see Burt, 1999), we discuss it in more detail. Next, we consider how information that comes from outsiders (e.g., consultants) versus insiders (e.g., teammates) is differentially valued.

## KNOWLEDGE VALUATION

Rationally, managers should use knowledge that is of high quality, rather than focusing on apparently irrelevant considerations such as whether it comes from within the team or organization or from the outside. However, intuition and experience tell us that managers do not operate with this level of objectivity. One line of research, drawing from psychological theories of ingroup favoritism (Brewer, 1979), has determined that members of research groups are often subject to the **not-invented-here (NIH) syndrome,** where they overvalue knowledge that comes from ingroup members (Katz & Allen, 1982). However, whereas the NIH syndrome applies in some organizations, consider how managers in other organizations confer enormous authority to consultants and carefully monitor the ideas put forth by their competitors in the marketplace—all the while ignoring insiders and their ideas. According to Menon and Pfeffer (2002), managers, particularly those in competitive situations, sometimes place greater value on knowledge that comes from the outside (e.g., competitors, consultants), versus the same knowledge that might come from inside (e.g., colleagues, an internal task force). As a case in point, Menon and Pfeffer describe the curious acquisition of Zoopa by Fresh Choice. Fresh Choice and Zoopa, at least up until 1997, were competitors, both offering quick, cafeteria-style salad buffets and soups. Prior to and during the time of their acquisition of Zoopa, Fresh Choice scrupulously benchmarked and investigated Zoopa's best practices. However, after the acquisition, the value of the knowledge and information about Zoopa's best practices, which would now be quite easy to obtain, were seemingly not as valued. Similarly, managers at Xerox displayed very little interest in a new Internet technology that internal scientists at Xerox PARC had developed. However, several years later when an external firm developed a very similar techology,

---

BOX 9-1

## Common Roles in Work Groups

- The **boundary spanner** acts as a bridge between units or people in an organization who would not otherwise interact. Boundary spanners are exposed to more ideas than members who do not interact with other groups. Indeed, boundary spanners who spend time with different groups exhibit greater integrative complexity in their thinking (a form of creativity) than people who don't boundary span (Gruenfeld & Fan, 1999).

- The **bufferer** protects the team from bad or disappointing news that might cause morale to suffer and volunteers to absorb pressure or criticism from others.

- The **interpreter** shapes the collective understanding of the team. This is important because in many cases, the messages that teams receive from others are ambiguous and open to interpretation.

- The **advisor** informs the team about which options they should consider and what approach they should take in dealing with changing events.

- The **gatekeeper** controls the flow of information to and from a team.

- The **lobbyist** is an extremely critical role, especially for new-product groups. By providing meanings about what the team is doing and how successful it is to people outside the team, the lobbyist controls the interpretation of what the team is perceived to be doing. For example, Tom West, the leader of a team at IBM designing a computer, presented his computer differently to various groups (from Kidder, 1981). By presenting it as "insurance" (i.e., we will have it in case the other one designed by another team in the company does not work) to top management, he was allowed to set up a team that competed with another team in the company. By presenting it as a "technical challenge" to engineers, he was able to attract the best ones. By not saying anything at all to external competitors, he protected his company (Ancona, 1987).

- The **negotiator** or **mediator** is empowered by the team to negotiate on behalf of the group. This person has extraordinary power in terms of garnering resources, defining options, and so on. This person may act as a mediator in cases where the team is in conflict with others.

- The **spokesperson** is the voice of the team. This position is determined in two ways: By the group members themselves (for example, "Talk to Bob if you want to find out what happened in Lois's promotion decision"), and by the members of the external environment who have their choice in terms of contacting group members.

- The **strategist,** like the negotiator, plans how to approach management for resources and deal with threats and other negative information.

- The **coordinator** arranges formal or informal communication with other people or units outside the team.

---

Xerox responded favorably to the idea, and even sent their executives to investigate it as they contemplated acquiring the company.

Menon and Pfeffer offer two explanations for these kinds of biases in knowledge valuation. They contend that the availability or scarcity of internal versus external knowledge affects how it is valued. Internal knowledge is more readily available and hence subject to greater scrutiny, whereas external knowledge is more scarce, special, and unique. Thus, managers venerate competitors, whose ideas they see from a distance, while they reject internal ideas that are visible close up, warts and all. They value external ideas, which are seen as final products, while they are critical about internal ideas that they see in their earliest most unpolished state. And, finally, they value scarce, external ideas that are protected by patents and are nearly impossible to acquire, while they reject the internal knowledge that is so easily accessible to them.

Second, organizational incentives often punish managers by reducing their status when they learn from insiders (Blau, 1955), and reward them when they learn from outsiders. In support of this point, Menon and Pfeffer (2002) found that managers conducting a performance evaluation rewarded external learners more than they rewarded internal learners. Specifically, executives participated in a simulation in which they were a manager of a large hotel chain and were asked to evaluate the performance of two individuals who were described as hotel managers within their chain. The two managers had achieved identical performance, but one manager had learned from insiders within the chain while the other manager had learned from a competitor chain. The executives rated the external learner as more creative, competent, gaining more status, and were more likely to promote him and reward him with a higher bonus, as compared with the internal learner.

Menon and Blount (2002) developed a broader framework to explain how relationships between knowledge messengers and receivers might affect knowledge valuation. Rather than a rational perspective in which managers are expected to cull the best knowledge from their environments, or a random process in which receivers accept knowledge in the more arbitrary "garbage can model" (Cohen, March, & Olsen, 1972), they propose a relational perspective in which social relationships between knowledge messengers and receivers affect how a piece of knowledge comes to be evaluated. They identify several relational schemas (Baldwin, 1992) that represent the ways in which a receiver might perceive the messenger who delivers them knowledge. By determining the degree to which the messenger threatens the receiver's self or group, they generate six relational types, including colleagues, deviants, rivals, advisors, enemies, and intruders. Their analysis suggests that relationships evoke a variety of social psychological forces—including social comparison, status threats, and ingroup identification and favoritism—that shape the processes by which managers decide whether a piece of knowledge is valuable.

## NETWORKING: A KEY TO SUCCESSFUL TEAMWORK

The shift away from top-down management and bureaucratic structures means that more than ever, team members are in control of their own movement within the organization. This can bring opportunity for the team, the organization, and its members, but only if this task is handled optimally. The heart of this task involves management of relationships. In this section, we describe the key issues that managers should know when building the relationship between their team and the organization.

### Communication

In an ideal organizational environment, there would be perfect communication among the different functional and geographic units, and between individuals following the agreed-upon organizational chart. Among other things, such communication would have the advantage of quickly dispersing innovation, reducing unnecessary duplication of effort, moving toward the implementation of best practices, and a variety of other advantages. However, the reality of organizational communication is a far cry from the ideal. Communication among different functional and geographically dispersed units does not occur as frequently as it should. And who talks to whom is much more a function of informal, social networks than a bureaucrat's organizational chart might lead one to believe. In fact, a study from the Conference Board in New York suggests that the information technology (IT) approach isn't the most successful way to share knowledge or to transform knowledge into action. The study surveyed 200 executives at 158 large global companies and found that the most successful methods for turning knowledge into practical results come from informal employee networks (Hackett, 2000).

Thus, most organizations are composed of communication networks, in which communication is incomplete and information is not ubiquitously dispersed throughout the company. In a company, information may be controlled or held only by certain people, as opposed to being directly accessible to everyone in the organization.

## Human Capital and Social Capital

Why is it that some people are singled out and seem to advance faster through their organizations than other team members? Why is it that some teams are singled out and seem to win more approval from senior management than other teams? The typical explanation centers upon **human capital:** Inequalities result from differences in human individual ability. People who are more intelligent, educated, and experienced rise to the top of their organization; those who are less qualified do not.

However, there is another, perhaps more plausible, explanation that accounts for the existence of inequality. **Social capital** is the value managers add to their teams and organizations through their ties to other people (Coleman, 1988). Social capital refers to the resources available through social networks and elite institutional ties—such as club memberships—that a person can use to enhance his or her position. Social capital is the value that comes from knowing who, when, and how to coordinate through various contacts within and beyond the firm. Whereas human capital refers to individual ability, social capital refers to opportunity created through the interactions of people. Managers with more social capital get higher returns on their human capital because they are positioned to identify and develop more rewarding opportunities (Burt, 1992). Stated simply, certain managers are connected to certain others, trust certain others, feel obligated to support certain others, and are dependent on exchange and reciprocity with certain others, above and beyond those in their immediate functional unit.

To understand the value of social capital within the firm and how it affects team performance, it is necessary to consider the larger organizational environment. Organizational charts are rather crude depictions that reveal the chain of command and reporting relationships. However, as many managers can attest, the way that work gets done and information gets spread within an organization is a far cry from published organizational charts. Instead, informal systems of connections and relationships, developed over time, guide the flow of information between people and teams. Let's explore these informal networks in detail.

Consider Figure 9-1, which is a somewhat crude depiction of two organizational environments. The dots represent certain managers. The lines that connect the dots are the communication networks between people in the organization—simply, who talks

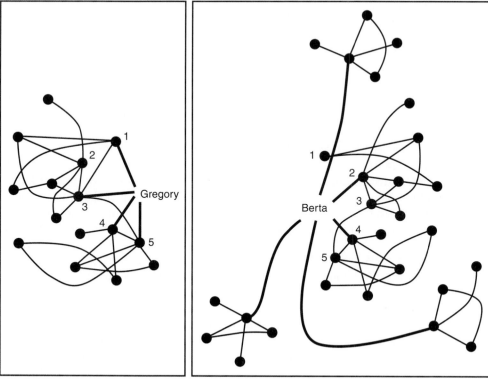

Panel A: Gregory                    Panel B: Berta

**FIGURE 9-1** Communication Networks of Two Managers within the Same Company
*Source:* Adapted from Burt, R. S. 1999. "Entrepreneurs, Distrust, and Third Parties: A Strategic Look at
the Dark Side of Dense Networks." In L. Thompson, J. Levine, & D. Messick (Eds.). *Shared Cognition in
Organizations: The Management of Knowledge.* Mahwah, NJ: Lawrence Erlbaum & Associates.

with whom. To be sure, members of a given department or functional unit are more
interconnected than are members of completely different functional units. However,
even within particular departments, there can be a high degree of variation in communication patterns. Moreover, there is high variation among organizational members in
terms of who reaches beyond the walls of the functional teams and communicates with
others.

Consider the two different panels in Figure 9-1. Panel A depicts the network (or
communication) structure of a manager, Gregory, who has a network of relatively close
colleagues—most likely from the same functional unit. This type of close-knit, self-con-
tained network is a **clique network,** and is reminiscent of the traditional family unit. In
the clique network, groups of people, all of whom know one another quite well, share
largely redundant communication structures. At the extreme, members of clique networks are only aware of others with whom they have direct contact.

When we contrast Gregory's communication network to Berta's in Panel B, we
notice some striking differences. First, Berta's network is much less tightly knit than is

Gregory's network. Second, Berta's network spans what appears to be more functional units than does Gregory's network. In a sense, Berta knows more people who don't know each other. Third, Berta's network is structurally more unique than is Gregory's network. Simply stated, Gregory's network is highly identical to all the other people in his clique. In contrast, Berta's network does not look like anyone else's, in terms of the connections she has. Before reading further, how do you think these differing network structures affect the performance of the team, the individuals involved, and the larger organization?

## The Importance of Boundary Spanning

Individuals (and teams) who span organizational divides and integrate the knowledge, innovation, and best practices from different areas of the organization (who otherwise have little incentive to do so) are extremely valuable for the organization. These people are known as **boundary spanners.** Boundary spanners bridge the functional gaps, or the **structural holes,** that exist in organizations. Structural holes are what separates nonredundant social contacts in the organization. A person who bridges or spans a structural hole fills a unique spot in the organizational network: bringing together people, knowledge, and information that would otherwise not be brought together. This, of course, is critical for maximizing diversity of ideas and setting the stage for creative thinking in the organization—not to mention avoiding duplication of effort and speeding along organizational innovations to relevant units. Indeed, teams whose members have access to different social networks, independent of their individual knowledge and skills, may be more likely to learn through relationships than teams whose members' social ties are redundant (Granovetter, 1973). The value of a boundary spanner is the ability to capitalize on the social structure of the organization which, as we have seen, is structurally imperfect.

When we again compare the networks of Gregory and Berta, we see that Gregory has a network that spans one structural hole (i.e., the relatively weak connection between a cluster reached through contacts 1, 2, and 3 versus the other cluster that is reached through contacts 4 and 5). In contrast, Berta preserves the connections with both clusters in Gregory's network, but expands the network to a more diverse set of contacts. Berta's network, adding three new clusters of people, spans 10 structural holes.

The structural holes that exist between people, functional units, and teams are *entrepreneurial* opportunities for teams and their leaders. Boundary spanners can broker the flow of information between people on opposite ends of a structural hole and control the form of projects that bring people together on opposite ends of the structural hole. For example, Eastman Chemical, the only chemical company to have received a Malcolm Baldrige National Quality Award, used "interlocking teams" to improve communication and break down the barriers between functions in the company (Milliken, 1996). In interlocking teams, the functional teams are networked to other teams in different functions via a supervisor who coordinates activities. Russel Justic, an Eastman technical associate in quality management, compares interlocking teams to conducting an orchestra: The conductor understands the part each performer plays in the whole and works to align the efforts of all performers to accomplish the composer's objectives. To symbolize the relationships between each team, photographs were taken of each team and linked geographically on a wall-size poster at headquarters. Eastman's interlocking teams spanned many of the company's structural holes and aided in dismantling the imperfect flow of information between different functions. Not only were the teams individually productive, but also their combined productivity separated the organization from others in the industry. In this way, the structure of a network is a competitive advantage for certain people and certain teams in the organization.

Quite frankly, managers with contact networks rich in structural holes are the people who know about, have a hand in, and exercise more control over rewarding opportunities. They have broader access to information because of their diverse contacts. This means that they are more often aware of new opportunities and have easier access to these opportunities than do their peers—even their peers of equivalent or greater human capital! For this reason, they are also more likely to be discussed as suitable candidates for inclusion in new opportunities. They are also likely to have sharpened and displayed their capabilities because they have more control over the substance of their work defined by relationships with subordinates, superiors, and colleagues.

## Cliques versus Boundary-Spanning Networks: Advantages and Disadvantages

Consider once again two people in a typical organization: Gregory and Berta. Gregory is in a tightly constructed, dense clique network. In contrast, Berta's network does not follow functional or organizational charts. It is much less dense, more unique, and more varied. Which person would a manager want to recruit for a team? Gregory or Berta? Let's consider their ability to add value.

Gregory is a member of a **clique network,** a tightly knit, exclusive, and cohesive group. Members of clique networks consider one another to be their closest contacts, and because they focus their efforts at primarily internal communications, they are often sequestered away from the larger organization. A closer look at the boards behind many top companies accused of fraudulent accounting, such as Enron and Arthur Andersen, reveal clique networks. For example, Jack Grubman of Salomon Smith Barney worked in a tight inner circle that included Worldcom, Winstart, McLeodUSA, Global Crossing, and Qwest—companies that all toppled during the accounting shakedown.

The loyalty and cohesiveness of inner circles can be both comforting to those situated securely in them and intimidating to those who stumble into them without a real ally. (As an example of this, see Box 9-2.)

In contrast, Berta's is an **entrepreneur network,** a less tightly knit group, with contacts in a variety of disparate organizational areas. In fact, Berta does not appear to be housed in any particular network. On the surface it might seem that Gregory would feel more secure, nestled in his cohesive group, and, hence, be more successful on the whole. Berta is a boundary spanner, a link between different subgroups and functional units that without her would not be connected. For this reason, Berta occupies a unique position in her network as she single-handedly bridges these separate groups. In this sense, Berta is an **information broker,** because she alone is at the critical junction between these networks and serves the important role of brokering information. Stated another way, the people in Berta's functional group are more information dependent on Berta than upon Gregory. In a very crude sense, Gregory is an organizational clone—expend-

---

BOX 9-2

### Understanding Dense Networks

Stumbling into a dense network can be a little alarming, if you are unsuspecting. After Sherron Watkins of Enron wrote her famous whistle-blower memo, former CEO Kenneth Lay sent her to talk to Elizabeth Tilney. Tilney had previously overseen Enron's communications and marketing and had worked on an internal employee "values" campaign. At the time Lay sent Watkins to see her, she was handling communications for a subsidiary, Enron Energy Services. Watkins wrote a second, two-page memo to Tilney, suggesting that she advise Lay to go public about Enron's wrongdoings, including the partnership with Enron Energy Services. Part of Watkins' memo read, "It's very hard to know who in the organization is giving us good answers and who's covering their prior work." What Watkins did not know was that Tilney was the wife of the investment banker who helped Merrill Lynch win the job to raise funds for the partnership and had a personal financial stake in it (Thornton & Zellner, 2002).

---

able—at least on a sociostructural level. In contrast, Berta is a critical player; remove her and the organization may suffer serious consequences and lost opportunities. Berta serves an important team and organizational function by garnering information that would otherwise be unavailable to the team or to the organization.

Is there anything *wrong* with Gregory's situation? He is in a highly cohesive group, which can be advantageous when it comes to managing the internal team environment. The problem is that Gregory does not really learn anything new by interacting with the members of his group. In contrast, because Berta's contacts do not know one another and, therefore, cannot apply social pressure on each other—as they can in clique networks—Berta is potentially privy to a greater amount of accurate and nonredundant information. Berta's position as a structural hole is an indicator that people on either side of the hole circulate in different flows of information. The structural hole between two clusters (or teams) does not mean that people in the two clusters are unaware of one another. Rather, people are so focused on their own activities that they have little time to attend to the activities of people in the other cluster.

In comparing Gregory's and Berta's networks, the information benefits in Berta's network are enhanced in several important ways that go a long way toward furthering individual, team, and organizational goals—the very things that we outlined in Chapter 2 to be critical measures of performance. First, from Berta's view, there is more benefit reaped because more contacts are included in the network. The diversity of contacts enhances the quality of benefits, because each cluster of contacts is an independent source of information. One cluster (e.g., a team), no matter how numerous its members, is only one source of information because people connected to one another know about the same things at approximately the same time. Because nonredundant contacts are only linked through the leader at the center of the network, the leader is assured of being the first to see new opportunities created by the need of one team that could be served by skills in another team. Berta has the opportunity of bringing together otherwise disconnected individuals where it will be rewarding. Furthermore, having more diverse contacts means that the manager is more likely to be among the people discussed as suitable candidates for inclusion in new opportunities. Because people communicate through Berta, she can adjust her image with each contact. Berta is able to monitor information more effectively than is possible with typical bureaucratic control; she is highly mobile relative to bureaucracy.

People like Berta also are advantageous from the perspective of the team and the larger organization. For example, teams in several plants operated by a Midwest manufacturing firm were evaluated in the early 1990s by the firm's quality control officers (Rosenthal, 1996). There was a striking association between team performance and team members' network structures: The more successful teams were composed of people with networks richer in structural holes. For a summary of the advantages and disadvantages of cliques and boundary-spanning networks, see Table 9-2 (see also Sidebar 9-1).

**TABLE 9-2**    Advantages and Disadvantages of Clique and Boundary-Spanning Networks

|  | **Clique Network** | **Boundary-Spanning Network** |
|---|---|---|
| **Advantages** | High cohesion | Leverages diversity |
|  | Loyalty and support | Capitalizes on opportunity |
|  | Increased efficiency of decision making | Greater innovation |
|  |  | Earlier promotions |
|  |  | Higher salaries |
| **Disadvantages** | Redundant communication | Greater conflict, both task |
|  | Biased communication | and relationship |
|  | Groupthink | Power struggles |
|  | Dispensable members |  |

## Advice for the Manager

In comparison with others who are equal in human capital, people like Berta have more successful careers. Managers with larger networks of more disconnected contacts get promoted earlier than comparable managers with smaller networks of more interconnected contacts (Burt, 1992; Podolny & Baron, 1997; Sparrowe & Popielarz, 1995). For example, in an investigation of 3,000 senior managers in a high-technology firm with over 100,000 employees, those promoted early had more social capital—as determined by their social network analysis (Burt, 1992). The benefits of social capital can

## Sidebar 9-1. Minority Managers

"Fast-track" minority managers develop networks that are well connected to both minority and white informal circles. In contrast, high-potential whites and non-fast-track minorities have few, if any, network ties with minorities. Ironically, many non-fast-track minorities feel that networking with members of their racial group is detrimental to their careers. Yet the more successful minorities consistently stress the value of same-race contacts in helping them to develop and implement strategies for career success (Ibarra, 1995). Minority fast-trackers develop networks that span a much broader set of social and corporate circles than the non-fast-trackers.

also affect CEO compensation. For example, a CEO's compensation is positively pre-dicted by the social capital of the chair of the compensation committee and the CEO's social capital relative to the chair (Belliveau, O'Reilly, & Wade, 1996). The network structure of team members affects how much information they share in common with others in a team. For this reason, boundary spanners are more cognitively central (i.e., aware of what other people know) than are nonboundary spanners. This affects their ability to influence the team. The more information team members share with others, the more cognitively central they are in the team. Also, cognitively central members acquire pivotal power in a team and exert more influence on consensus than members who are not cognitively central (Kameda, Ohtsubo, & Takezawa, 1997). Thus, those who are connected are more influential.

How can managers best try to expand their network and link their team within the organization? As the previous discussion argues, strategic network expansion involves connecting to people and teams in such a way that the manager (and the team) is fill-ing a structural hole. To see the difference between typical network expansion and strategic network expansion, see Figure 9-2.

## Structural Positioning

The reaction of many people to our analysis of social capital, structural holes, and entrepreneurial activity within organizations is that it seems very self-promotional, which, of course, is antithetical to traditional notions of teamwork. It is somehow discon-certing to believe that relationships among people within an organization hurt or facili-tate one's chances of advancing. We advocate a team-based view of structural positioning within the organization. That is, teams are more likely to achieve their goals and stay in touch with the needs of the organization if they have connections with others within the organization. Thus, the structural positioning of an entrepreneurial, as opposed to clique, network has benefits for individual team members, the team, and the organization.

From the point of view of the employee, organizational benefits are maximized in a large network of nonredundant contacts. It is better to know a lot of people who don't know one another. The opportunity is there because most people are too busy to keep in touch directly. Furthermore, people in organizations display a type of **functional ethnocentrism,** that is, believing that their own functional area is of key importance and that the other units do not matter as much. Entrepreneurs, such as Berta, take advantage of functional ethnocentrism and act as critical go-betweens to bring individuals, teams, and units together in ways that are profitable to themselves and the organization.

What are some practical steps that individuals, teams, and organizations can take to build more connections across functional groups? Consider the following strategies.

### Expand the Size of the Network
This does not mean increasing the size of the team but, rather, increasing the num-ber of people that the manager and the team come into contact with.

### Recognize the Limitations of Clique Networks
Clique networks contain a number of disadvantages for the organization and the team. People in clique networks fall prey to the homogeneity bias. For example, men in clique networks include significantly fewer women among their contacts (Burt, 1992). This can stifle creativity, propagate prejudice, and hinder the benefits of diversity.

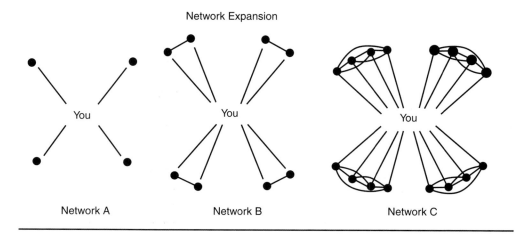

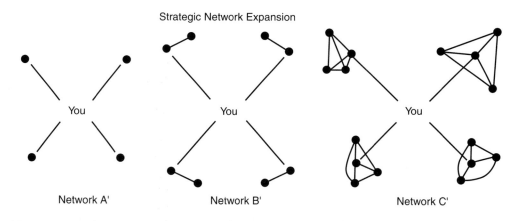

**FIGURE 9-2** Strategic Network Expansion
*Source:* Burt, R. S. 1992. *The Social Structure of Competition.* Cambridge, MA: Harvard University Press. Copyright © 1992 by the President and Fellows of Harvard College. Reprinted with permission.

### *Recognize Key Scripts*

Quite often, business opportunities are conducted in the context of social relationships (Uzzi, 1997). Many social relationships are common and therefore highly scripted or routinized, such as conducting a business meeting on the golf course. According to Uzzi and Gillespie (1999), these scripts are significant because they define the conditions under which networks are most effective. For this reason, it is difficult to form close relationships across gender lines if they are built through socializing activities such as playing golf, going to the theater, or evening dinner gatherings because these practices often have a different meaning between men and women than they do between persons of the same gender (Etzkowitz, Kemelgor, & Uzzi, 1999). (See Box 9-3 for an examination of women's and men's networks.)

---

**BOX 9-3**

### Social Capital and Gender

Etzkowitz, Kemelgor, and Uzzi (1999) investigated why women scientists with human capital equal to, or better than, their male counterparts do poorer in graduate school and are thereafter disadvantaged by a lack of contacts to the resources and tacit information important for identifying, developing, and following through on leading-edge research projects. The differential performance of women follows from their disadvantaged position in a social structure of relations, not their human capital endowments. By actively managing social networks, key barriers to the advancement of women in science can be overcome.

---

*Diversify Networks*

As we have seen, the homogeneity bias pulls people toward developing cliques of like-minded people—which is exactly the wrong type of network to foster. It may be more comfortable in the short run, but it will have negative, long-term consequences for the individual, the team, and the organization. A better alternative is to develop a diversified network, which means crossing organizational boundaries and functional areas. Uzzi (1997) distinguished embedded ties (social ties) from arm's-length (nonsocial, purely business) ties. According to Uzzi (1997), at the network level, the optimal composition of ties is achieved when a network has an integrated mix of embedded and arm's-length ties. This is because embedded ties and arm's-length ties can offer complementary benefits when combined, just as the overall value of a portfolio increases when it is composed of complementary assets that offset each other's inherent weaknesses and strengths. Networks dominated by one type of tie produce fewer benefits, which partly accounts for the negative effects of overly embedded (e.g., "old-boy") networks, or overly disembedded exchange networks (e.g., whipsawing of suppliers by large manufacturers; Uzzi, 1997).

*Build Hierarchical Networks*

In bureaucratic organizations, boundary spanners need to network not only laterally, but also hierarchically.

*Integrate across Teams*

Networking across structural holes is not limited to informal, individual activity. Teams can introduce structural strategies for integrating with other teams. Table 9-3 reviews seven structural solutions for integrating across teams within an organization. Three of the strategies focus on integrating between teams. Four of the strategies focus on integrating across multiple teams and components of a business unit.

None of these strategies is flawless. In fact, even though boundary spanning has the effect of increasing cognitive growth, teams often exhibit a cognitive territoriality in response to the presence of others. For example, old-timers in teams use a greater number of their own ideas after newcomers arrive than before (Gruenfeld & Fan, 1999; for more details, see Box 9-4).

**TABLE 9-3** Integrating across Teams: Formal Structural Solutions

| Integration between Teams | | | Integration across Multiple Teams and Components of a Business Unit (Tighter Integration) | | | |
|---|---|---|---|---|---|---|
| Liaison roles | Overlapping membership | Cross-team integrating teams | Management teams | Representative integrating teams | Individual integrating teams | Improvement teams |

| | |
|---|---|
| **Liaison roles** | One boundary spanner is formally a member of one team, but sits in on meetings of another team to share and gather information (e.g., a day shift worker sits in on night shift) |
| **Overlapping membership** | Several employees are members of two groups simultaneously or in sequence |
| **Cross-team integrating teams** | Team composed of several members from other teams with integration needs, responsible for documenting and communicating changes in a timely manner |
| **Management teams** | Forge strategy and direction for multiple teams in business unit; make resource trade-offs among teams that are consistent with strategy, manage team performance |
| **Representative integrating teams** | Nonmanagement team with authority to make decisions that affect system or context in which teams are embedded, composed of peers of team members |
| **Individual integrating roles** | Individuals in specific function provide integration with more flexibility than a team (e.g., a salesperson pulls together team for specific customer or project) |
| **Improvement teams** | Teams that initiate changes in how parts of business unit work together to improve business unit performance; must have legitimacy from the level of the organization at which their changes will be enacted; often not a full-time assignment but must be managed as an official project team |

*Sources:* Gruenfeld, D.H. 1997. "Integrating across Teams: Formal Structural Solutions." Presentation at Kellogg School of Management, May 1997, Evanston, IL; also based on Mohrman, S.A., Cohen, S.G., & Mohrman, A.M. 1995. *Designing Team-Based Organizations.* San Francisco: Jossey-Bass.

Greater integration is important to achieving the four major goals of productivity outlined in Chapter 2: achieving team goals, fostering team spirit, enhancing individual development, and furthering organizational objectives. In many cases, though, integration is not a choice—it is an absolute necessity for organizations. Consider, for example, the challenges that face Microsoft Corporation in managing large software development teams (Cusumano, 1997). Many software project managers prefer very small product teams of 12 or fewer programmers. This largely derives from a culture in the early days of programming, when two or three people built a new product. For example, initial versions of Microsoft's MS-DOS, Word, and Excel from the early 1980s had programming teams of six to 10 developers and consisted of just a few tens of thousands of lines of code. However, in the development of larger systems, with more memory-intensive graphical interfaces and complex functions, product development teams are forced to be larger. For example, the first version of Windows NT, introduced in 1993, consisted of 4.5 million lines of code and had a development team of about 450 people. Windows 95, introduced in 1995, consisted of 11 million lines of code. A team of about 300 people built the core components of Microsoft's Internet Explorer browser,

---

BOX 9-4

## An Investigation of Itinerant and Indigenous Team Members

Gruenfeld, Martorana, and Fan (2000) ingeniously investigated the consequences of temporary membership changes for itinerant members (i.e., members who leave their core group to visit a foreign work team and then, subsequently, return) and indigenous members of those foreign and origin groups. Although it would seem that itinerant members would learn new ideas that would transfer back to their core group once they returned, this was not always the case. In fact, members of all groups produced more unique ideas after itinerant members returned to their core group than before they left or during the temporary change period, but the ideas produced by the itinerant members were significantly less likely to be included in a group project designed to draw on knowledge of the work team than the ideas of indigenous members. After their return, itinerant members were perceived as highly involved in the group activity, but they were also perceived as more argumentative than they were before leaving, and although they produced more unique ideas than indigenous members, their contributions to the team project were perceived as less valuable. As a result, itinerant group members had less direct influence after their boundary-spanning stint than they did prior to it!

---

introduced in 1996, with more people involved in creating various modular features. Given that the complexity and magnitude of the task drives the teams to be larger and integrated, what is the best way to optimize integration among teams?

The teamwork integration process is especially difficult in software because it is so easy to change components and then extremely difficult to predict the effects on other components in the debugging and testing process. Software programmers do not work in an assembly line fashion, receiving work passed down to them. The parallel processing environment invites iteration or innovation constantly. Furthermore, there is also the problem of technical and management education. University computer science departments and management schools generally do not teach students how to design large-scale systems or manage large-scale products and work in teams of hundreds of people. For Microsoft, the key is to allow many small teams enough freedom to work in parallel, but to be able to function as one large team in terms of the overall picture. For example, at Microsoft, the core group for each team is generally one program manager and three to eight developers, including a development team leader. The extended team includes a parallel feature-testing team. Microsoft gives each team and each person within the team considerable autonomy and responsibility. Autonomy and responsibility allow each team to work relatively independently and "own" their features.

It is worth noting that this type of integration, which effectively allows small teams to work as one large team, may only work well when teams have been given responsibility. For example, Microsoft gives each team and each individual considerable autonomy and responsibility, which also allows teams to work relatively independently. Individual and feature teams set and maintain their own schedules, and relatively few rules are required for changes.

## RELATIONSHIPS OUTSIDE THE TEAM

Whereas it might seem somewhat like having an extramarital affair, having a relationship with someone outside the team is extremely valuable—especially for team leaders. We've seen that such connections may be strategically valuable, but they are also valuable at an emotional level. Teams, especially insulating ones, can often lack perspective. Therefore, it can be refreshing for members to have relationships with trusted others outside of the team, for the purposes of gaining perspective and balance. For many people whose work is their life (and whose life is their work), balancing ambition with personal health and work achievement with family and personal well-being is important—and often overlooked. Oftentimes, leaders don't feel that they have anyone to turn to for such perspective-taking (Maxwell & Hopkins, 2002). This is because it is difficult to have trusting relationships with people who so often want something from you. A recent analysis revealed that the five most common people that leaders turn to are business partners (23 percent), peer groups (19 percent), a fellow CEO (13 percent), a relative (12 percent), and former classmates and friends (10 percent) (Maxwell & Hopkins, 2002).

## DISTANCE

Even more encompassing than the social structure of an organization is its physical structure. Indeed, the physical layout of an organization can exert powerful effects on team productivity.

For better or for worse, teams operate within the physical constraints set by the organization. In terms of physical space, there is a direct, nearly perfect negative correlation between distance (as measured in feet) between employees' offices or workspaces and the interaction patterns between them. People form relationships, both personal and professional, to others who are close to them. Obviously, these processes feed on each other. Being physically close leads people to like and work with each other. People choose to be near those whom they like and want to work with. For example, even when students are seated alphabetically in a classroom, friendships are significantly more likely to form between those whose last names begin with the same or a nearby letter (Segal, 1974). This is what is called the **propinquity effect.** This may not seem important until you consider the fact that you may meet some of your closest colleagues, and perhaps even a future business partner, merely because of an instructor's seating chart! If an instructor changes seat assignments once or twice during the semester, each student becomes acquainted with additional colleagues (Byrne, 1961). To further see the power of the propinquity effect, consider the entering class of the Maryland State Police Training Academy (Segal, 1974). Trainees were assigned to their classroom seats and to their dormitory rooms by the alphabetical order of their last names. Some time thereafter, trainees were asked to name their three best friends in the group; their choices followed the rules of alphabetization almost exactly. Larsons were friends with Lees, not with Abromowitzes or Xiernickes, even though they were separated by only a few yards! (Byrne, 1961; Kipnis, 1957).

As another example, consider friendship formation among couples in apartment buildings. In this particular case, residents had been assigned to their apartments at random as vacancies opened up, and nearly all of them were strangers when they moved in. When asked to name their three closest friends in the entire housing project, 65 percent named friends in the same building. Of those living in the same building, the propinquity effect was in play: 41 percent of next-door neighbors indicated they were close friends, compared with only 22 percent who lived two doors apart, and only 10 percent who lived on the opposite ends of the hall.

The propinquity effect has an impact on **functional distance.** Certain aspects of architectural design make it more likely that some people will come into contact with each other more often than with others, even though physically, the distances might be the same. For example, more friendships were made with people on the same floor than on another floor, presumably because having to climb stairs to go visiting required more effort than just walking down the hall. People with a corner seat or office at the end of a corridor make fewer friends in organizations (Maisonneuve, Palmade, & Fourment, 1952). And teams that work in "war rooms" double their productivity, as compared with teams that don't (Teasley, Covi, Krishnan, & Olson, 2000). In a carefully controlled investigation, Allen (1977) examined the likelihood that team members would communicate at least once per week, solely as a function of the number of feet between their offices. The result was a near-perfect correlation: the less distance, the more likely the communication (see Figure 9-3).

The point is clear: What appear to be trivial aspects of the physical environment shape the pattern of communication and relationships in organizations and how the work gets done. Corporate responses to these issues have led to the development of more open work plans and flexible, project-based seating as ways to increase interaction, collegiality, and productivity in teams. For example, consider the Mars, Inc. company. There are no executive offices, only partitions in a large, open space. No one has a reserved parking spot, and executives' desks are out in the open. According to Mars's executives, this facilitates communication and cuts down on the need for many meetings. Similarly, McCaskey (1995) describes a company that created a special space for a new product development team on a separate floor from the rest of the company. The group was allocated a large space and was left on its own to arrange desks, common space, and so on. The result was an exceptionally high-functioning and productive team. A key reason for the success of the team was the fact that the spatial arrangement allowed team members to interact informally and frequently, yet at the same time, maintain some degree of personal space for independent thinking—exactly the same ingredients we discussed in Chapter 8 on creativity.

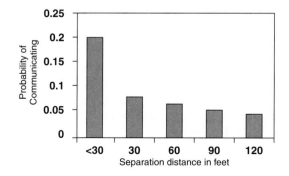

**FIGURE 9-3** Probability of Communicating at Least Once Per Week
*Source:* Adapted from Allen, T. J. 1977. *Managing the Flow of Technology: Technology Transfer and the Dissemination of Technological Information within the Research and Development Organization.* Cambridge, MA: MIT Press.

# TIME

Another contextual factor is time and the organization's norms of marking time—in particular, deadlines. How much time should a group devote to completing its work? A typical response might be "as long as it takes." This answer is neither good nor practical. When a work group is given a specific amount of time to do a job, its members adjust their behavior to "fit" whatever time is available. When time is scarce, team members work harder, worry less about the quality of their output, and focus on the task rather than social or emotional issues. However, if more time becomes available, these employees continue to work as though time was still scarce, rather than relaxing. It is important to properly manage how teams are initially introduced to their tasks.

Consider a telling example in which three groups were evaluated according to their ability to solve puzzles (McGrath, Kelly, & Machatka, 1984). Each group had a different task load (completing 20, 40, or 80 anagrams), time limit (5, 10, or 20 minutes), and group size (1, 2, or 4 persons). The situation was designed so that each group had three work periods. The task load remained the same for all periods for any given group, but the time interval either increased, decreased, or remained constant. Groups of any size, and over all possible time intervals, solved more anagrams per member-minute the *higher* the assigned task load; groups of any size and for any given task load solved more anagrams per member-minute the *shorter* the time limit; and for any given load and time limit, productivity was higher the *smaller* the size of the group. Thus, the more the work load per member-minute, the more work gets done. The point is clear: teams adapt themselves to the constraints presented to them, such as the amount of time they have to perform a task.

Not only is team performance susceptible to arbitrary "norming" cues, but team communication and interaction and some aspects of product quality are also affected by these factors (Kelly, Futoran, & McGrath, 1990; Kelly & McGrath, 1985). For example, short time limits on an initial task induce teams to spend more time on task-oriented behaviors and less time on interpersonal interaction, whereas teams with a longer time period engage in more interpersonal interactions.

Kelly et al. (1990) outlined two different kinds of problems related to this issue: capacity problems and capability problems. *Capacity* problems occur when there is not enough time to do all of the required tasks, although each task is easy. *Capability* problems occur when the task is difficult, even though there is plenty of time in which to do it. Capacity problems lead to a faster rate of task activity on subsequent trials, regardless of the actual time limits set for those later trials; capability problems lead to more extensive processing of information, hence a slower rate of production on subsequent trials, regardless of the actual time limits set for those trials.

# CONCLUSIONS

Teams are not independent entities within the organization. There is a critical tension between the internal relations among team members and the relationship the team shares with the rest of the organization. Both are necessary; neither is sufficient to ensure long-term survival of the team. Depending on the nature of the task that the team is working on, structural solutions should be put into place to ensure that the team is integrated with other individuals and teams within the organization. This activity itself requires that some members of the team act as boundary spanners and gate-keepers to bring needed information to the team, as well as distributing knowledge outside the team.

Managing the internal and external dynamics in a team is a difficult task, requiring constantly changing focus. The frequency of external communication may come at the expense of attention to internal processes (the ability to set goals, coordinate members' strategies, maintain cohesion, etc.; Ancona & Caldwell, 1991). Given that managing the internal team process and the external environment are somewhat opposing processes, how can leaders optimize the probability of successful teamwork? An important first step is to talk with team members about the importance of both internal functioning and external relationships. A second step is to assign roles or talk about how to manage the dual processes of internal dynamics and external relations. This can go a long way toward minimizing the diffusion of responsibility problem that often haunts teams. A third step is to identify goals and indices of team success at the outset; this largely avoids rationalizing behavior after the fact. A final step is to develop a team contract—a document written by all members that focuses on internal and external management issues.

# CHAPTER

# 10

# Leadership:

## *Managing the Paradox*

*" 'Nobody knows Reuben Mark,' marvels Andrew Shore, a Deutsche Bank analyst who has covered Colgate for 16 years. 'He just happens to be one of the most successful CEOs in the world.' . . . Famously indifferent to executive privilege, [Mark] places his own phone calls, occasionally answers his own phone (barking 'Hello, Colgate' into the receiver), and sometimes comes down from his 11th floor office to personally greet visitors in the lobby. Deutsche Bank's Shore calls him 'the most user-friendly chief executive I've ever known' " (Lardner, 2002, p. 106). Andrew McQuilling, an analyst who follows Colgate for UBS Warburg, says of Reuben Mark, "Many employees would take a bullet for him . . . for nearly 20 years, the guy has been walking what he's talking" (Lardner, 2002, p. 107). At Colgate's annual meeting, Mark saluted a few dozen employees from around the world for their innovations. He does not do interviews. Ever. He believes that CEOs should never be profiled in magazines, on talk shows, or otherwise implicitly take credit for the efforts of those who work for them.*

Most leaders will never have such praise bestowed on them. And, as we shall see, what makes the leader great is not the way she regards herself or what Wall Street thinks of her, but what the people who work for her think.

No one would dispute the fact that leadership is important for organizations. Similarly, very few would not argue that teamwork is important for organizational success. However, more people have trouble believing that leadership is essential for effective teamwork. In fact, teamwork and leadership often seem to be at odds with one another.

Teamwork, to those in power in command-and-control organizations, is not necessarily a good thing. A major investigation of first-line supervisors to employee involvement programs revealed that 72 percent of supervisors view participative management as good for their company and 60 percent view it as good for employees, but only 31 percent view it as beneficial for themselves (Klein, 1984). Yet companies often expect middle managers to metamorphose into stellar team leaders, ready to coach, motivate, and empower. The problem is that few people understand how to make this transformational process and many probably have an incentive to see it unravel. For example, in one plant, resistance to participative management programs took the form of supervisors keeping "hands off" as newly formed semiautonomous work teams attempted to solve problems. When questions arose that teams were unable to handle, supervisors replied, "That's not my job; it's the team's problem." In essence, the supervisors were undermining the teams so they could resume their traditional position of authority (Klein, 1984).

The flipside of the problem is that leaders want involvement, but everyone is too afraid to offer it. Scott Jessup, CEO of Marque, Inc., fears the idea that the CEO has to be the smartest person in the company: "If that is the case, I think we're all in trouble. I truly believe I'd rather have 10 smart people tackle a problem. . . . I would rather have that than have 10 people staring at me hoping like hell I make the right decision" (Strozniak, 2000).

Leaders who have successfully made the transformation comment that they learned something that they did not realize at the outset. For example, Eric Doremus, of Honeywell's defense avionics division in Albuquerque, reflects, "My most important task was not trying to figure out everybody else's job. It was to help this team feel as if they owned the project by getting them whatever information, financial or otherwise, they needed. I knew that if we could all charge up the hill together, we would be successful" (Caminiti, 1995, p. 94).

In the best of circumstances, teams are empowered groups of people who collaborate in a mutually beneficial fashion to enact positive change. Leadership—or one person taking the helm of the group's efforts—seems antithetical to teamwork. Yet, leaders are often necessary for effective teamwork—to shape goals, coordinate effort, and motivate members. We call this the **team paradox:** the fact that leaders often are necessary for teamwork, but that their very existence threatens teamwork, and vice versa. (For an example of the tension inherent in this paradox, see Box 10-1.)

Traditional notions of leadership—that is, top-down, command-and-control approaches—may be ineffective in the team-based organization. The question of how one leads others who are supposed to lead themselves is the essence of the leadership dilemma encountered by leaders of self-managing and self-directing teams (Stewart & Manz, 1995). Attempts to cope with this new leadership challenge often result in negative supervisor reactions, including resistance to change (Manz, Keating, & Donnellon, 1990), role conflict (Letize & Donovan, 1990), unwillingness to relinquish power (Verespej, 1990), fear of appearing incompetent (Manz et al., 1990), and fear of job termination (Verespej, 1990). These responses may cause leaders to engage in actions that thwart, rather than facilitate, team effectiveness.

---

**BOX 10-1**

### Example of Team Paradox

In 1989, J. D. Bryant was perfectly content overseeing a staff of 15 circuit-board assemblers at the Texas Instruments Forest Lane defense plant in Dallas. "Then one day I heard the company was moving to teams and that I was going to become a facilitator. I'm supposed to teach the teams everything I know and then let them make their own decisions." Not sure if something good or bad had happened, Bryant pressed his supervisor for more information: "'This is career enhancing?' He said, 'Oh yes. You won't have to do performance reviews any more. The team will take them on.'" Later the supervisor followed with, "Since you won't be a supervisor anymore, you'll have to take a 5 percent pay cut" (Caminiti, 1995, p. 93).

Leadership is perhaps easier to reconcile with effective teamwork when we realize that leadership comes in many forms. For example, a team may have a manager, administrator, supervisor, facilitator, director, coordinator, spokesperson, or chairperson. Leaders can also serve a vital role coordinating team members, resolving disputes or disagreements, motivating individuals, monitoring performance, and maintaining the goals and focus of the group.

This chapter addresses how people can be trained to become leaders and what techniques enable these leaders to be more effective. We describe two theories of leadership—the Great Person theory and the Great Opportunity theory—and explain why the Great Opportunity theory better describes how leadership is developed. We then describe several different leadership styles and present a model to help determine how much participation is appropriate for a leader to use in various situations. Warning: This chapter encourages quite a bit of self-reflection and analysis.

## LEADERS AND THE NATURE-NURTURE DEBATE: GREAT PERSON VERSUS GREAT OPPORTUNITY

Leadership is not the same as management. Management is a *function* that must be exercised in any business or team, whereas leadership is a *relationship* between the leader and the led that can energize a team or organization (Maccoby, 2000; see Table 10-1 for the difference between management and leadership).

There are two theories about what makes a leader effective. The *Great Person theory* asserts that leaders are born, not made; whereas the *Great Opportunity theory* claims that leadership can be learned as a skill. Strict proponents of the Great Person theory claim that people are either born leaders or born followers: They either have it or they don't. If they do have it, they dictate, command, and control. If they don't have it, they follow those who do have it. "The cowboy riding the range is the stereotypical American, and that has carried over into business" (Hequet, 1994, p. 7). This Great Person theory of leadership is unidirectional—from the top down, with leaders imparting truth, wisdom, and directives to those beneath them.

If the Great Person theory is true, we should be able to identify personality traits that make someone a great leader, or, at least, characteristics that predict the emergence of leadership. Psychologists, political scientists, and historians have studied the personality of leaders in governmental, business, and educational organizations to see what common threads can be found. However, decades of research have failed to yield

**TABLE 10-1**  Management versus Leadership

| Management | Leadership |
|---|---|
| A function | A relationship |
| Planning | Selecting talent |
| Budgeting | Motivating |
| Evaluating | Coaching |
| Facilitating | Building trust |

*Source:* Maccoby, M. 2000. "Understanding the Difference Between Management and Leadership." *Research & Technology Management,* Jan–Feb, pp. 57–59. Reprinted with permission.

an agreed upon list of key traits shared by all leaders (Yukl, 1981). It seems clear that there is little or no evidence to support connections between personality and leadership. For example, Simonton (1987) gathered information about 100 personal attributes of all U.S. presidents, such as their family backgrounds, educational experiences, occupations, and personalities. Only three of these variables—height, family size, and number of books published before taking office—correlated with how effective the presidents were in office. The other 97 characteristics, including personality traits, were not related to leadership effectiveness at all. By chance, 5 percent—five out of the 100—would be significant!

In contrast, there is overwhelming evidence that the *situation* can often make the leader. In fact, a great deal of evidence indicates that leadership has more to do with designing the environment than one's own personality. As a case in point, seemingly trivial situational factors, such as seating arrangements, can affect the emergence of leadership in groups. When a group sits at a table, the person at the head of the table has a greater probability of emerging as the leader, even when the seating is randomly determined (Nemeth & Wachtler, 1974; Riess, 1982; Riess & Rosenfeld, 1980). Consider a group of consultants who arranged for five-person groups to hold a discussion while seated at a rectangular table (Howells & Becker, 1962). They had two people sit on one side of the table and three on the other side. Although no one sat in the end seat, the consultants made specific predictions about who should emerge as the leader if eye contact and control of communication were important causal factors. Whereas those seated on the two-person side of the table could maintain easy eye contact with three of the group members, those on the three-person side could best focus their attention on only two members. Therefore, they predicted that those on the two-person side would be able to influence others more, and, hence, were more likely to become leaders. Indeed, 70 percent of the leaders came from the two-person side; only 30 percent from the three-person side!

Probably the most damning evidence to the Great Person theory are the studies of random selection of leaders. Organizations spend millions of dollars each year carefully selecting leaders, often using psychological tests to do so. However, evidence indicates that selected leaders may hinder effective team performance. In an investigation of team performance, teams with randomly selected leaders performed better on all organizational decision-making tasks than did teams whose leaders were systematically selected (Haslam, McGarty, Brown, Eggins, Morrison, & Reynolds, 1998). Moreover, teams with a random leader adhered more strongly to the team's decision. The key reason seems to be that systematically accepted leaders often undermine group goals because they assert their personal superiority at the expense of developing a sense of shared team identity.

Nevertheless, the Great Person theory is still used as a basis for recruitment and selection, and many companies and institutions routinely assess leadership potential with paper and pencil tests. Do these tests accurately predict leadership? The conclusion of decades of research is that there is no single test that can measure leadership. Even when leadership is measured, its relationship to the kinds of performance measures we would expect to see is largely inconclusive. It is rather fruitless to attempt to identify stable characteristics that will predict leadership. Even if it were possible (which we highly doubt), this kind of knowledge does not provide organizations or managers with much control over their own or another's behavior. Therefore, in a practical sense, trying to identify stable characteristics of leaders is ill-fated.

If the Great Person theory of leadership is flawed, then why do so many people believe that personality can predict leadership? There are two reasons. One has to do with the "romance" of leadership (Meindl, Ehrlich, & Dukerich, 1985). In short, the romanticized conception of leadership is that leaders have the ability to control and influence the fates of their organizations and people. Second, the **fundamental attribution error** is the tendency to overemphasize the impact of a stable personality and dispositional traits on a person's behavior and underemphasize the impact of the *situation* on people's behavior (Ross, 1977). In fact, more temporary, situational characteristics can usually explain a great deal of human behavior.

Why do people err on the side of attributing behavior to dispositions instead of more transient (and controllable) factors? The key reason is associated with our human need to predict and control. To the extent that people can predict the behavior of others, their chances for survival increase. For example, the ability to predict whether someone is trustworthy is highly adaptive. When people's behavior can be attributed to stable, dispositional characteristics, it is possible to more accurately predict their actions in various situations. Conversely, when people's behavior is attributed to temporary, environmental factors, it is more difficult to predict their behavior. Thus, the bias toward dispositional explanation is driven by our human need for control.

Just because we can't "select" leaders does not mean we cannot "develop" leaders. The Great Opportunity approach focuses on how leaders do two things vis-à-vis teamwork in their organizations. First, it focuses on how leaders directly interact with their teams. The second thing these leaders do is to structure the external environment so the team can best achieve its goals. In both of these tasks, leadership is bidirectional, with leaders learning from their team just as often as they provide direction for their team. These leaders maintain the relationship between the group and organization to ensure that organizational objectives are being pursued. Leaders also coordinate team members, resolve disputes or disagreements, motivate individuals, monitor performance, and establish the goals and focus of the group.

As we have seen in Chapters 4 and 9, leadership in a team-based organization requires leaders not just to lead the team, but to interface between the organization and the team. In this sense, the leader is an important boundary spanner. No manager has all of the requisite skills required for effective leadership, but the effective manager knows where to go to get these skills and resources.

Let's consider different leadership styles that leaders can develop and hone.

## LEADERSHIP STYLES

There is probably more written about leadership styles than any other subject in management. One trip to the bookstore, or one on-line search in the academic literature, can produce a dizzying array of enticing (yet poorly understood) leadership approaches. Often, these approaches are presented in the form of metaphor—leader as coach, leader as servant, leader as guide, leader as conductor, and so on. (For a look at how leaders use metaphors in their communication, see Box 10-2.) In a recent literature review of academic journals, we found more than 20 variations of leadership styles spanning a wide range, including visionary, charismatic, participatory, servant, contingent, transformational, and transactional. The corporate world and popular business press have coined even more varieties of leadership—often branding them with a particularly influential individual's name, such as the "Jack Welch lexicon of leadership" (Krames, 2001) or the "Warren Buffet CEO" (Miles & Osborne, 2001). Below, we consider a few of these styles. Our list is not exhaustive, and it does not include all the latest fads in leadership. The key point is that we don't want leaders to put themselves in the position of "diagnosing" themselves or, worse, "pigeonholing" themselves or others. Rather, the styles are presented as choices that the leader can make, or as skills to put in his or her repertoire.

### Task versus Person Leadership

As we noted in Chapter 4, the task-oriented leader focuses on accomplishing the objectives of the team; the relationship-oriented leader focuses on the process of getting there. (For an example of how leaders can examine their task-person approach, see Table 10-3.)

### Transactional versus Transformational Leadership

The transactional versus transformational paradigm views leadership as either a matter of contingent reinforcement of followers or the moving of followers beyond their self-interests for the good of the team, organization, or society (Bass, 1985; Burns, 1978; Hollander, 1964). Most notably, *transformational* leadership, as its name suggests, is developmental and usually begins with a transactional approach. At a basic level, leaders and their teams are in an exchange relationship that involves negotiation to establish outcomes and rewards (Hollander, 1986). Rousseau refers to this as the "psychological contract" (Rousseau & Tijoriwala, 1998). A psychological contract is a per-

---

**BOX 10-2**

### The Language of Leaders

My colleague, Ashleigh Rosette, and I reasoned that we could learn a lot about leaders by studying how they talked about their companies. Specifically, we were interested in the metaphors they used to discuss their companies. We identified *Fortune* magazine's top one hundred revenue companies for the year 2000 and retrieved the year 2000 Annual Report. (Each of these Annual Reports contains a Letter to the Shareholders written by the CEO—and/or chairman and/or president, hereafter "CEO"—of the company).

As we suspected, most CEOs use specific metaphors in their communications—specifically, our analysis revealed that 99 percent of the CEOs in our sample used analogies in their messages to the shareholders and, most importantly, 62 percent used analogical reasoning. The metaphors used by the CEOs fell into eight distinct categories: (1) sports, (2) biology/personification, (3) environment/nature, (4) war/heritage, (5) navigation, (6) arts, (7), structure, and (8) education/performance (see examples in Table 10-2). Some of the analogies did not fall into one of these categories and were included in a group we called "general" (13 percent). The most common type of analogical reasoning used by these CEOs was sports (see Table 10-2).

*Source:* Thompson, L., & Rosette, A. In press. "Leading by Analogy." In S. Chowdhury (Ed.), *Financial Times Next Generation Business Series.* London: Prentice Hall.

(*cont. on p. 238*)

**TABLE 10-2**   CEO's Analogies

| Type of Analogy | Example Quote, Company |
|---|---|
| Sports | "Parks and Resorts, which is responsible for our flagship theme park on three continents, **is like an athlete lettering in three sports**" (Michael Eisner, Disney). |
| Biology/Personification | "Better **jump with both feet into e-tailing** or get steam-rolled" (Lou Gerstner, IBM). |
| Environment and Nature | "While we have benefited from **the economic wind at our back** over the last several years, we all know what it's like to struggle against **a strong headwind**" (Harvey Golub & Kenneth Chenault, American Express). |
| War/Heritage | "We can **pierce the fog of the battlefield and enable our war fighters** to achieve information dominance in conflicts of the future" (Philip M. Condit & Harry C. Stonecipher, Boeing). |
| Navigation | ". . . I've had the good fortune to help a number of retailers **regain their footing and get back on course**" (Allen Questrom, JCPenney). |
| Arts | "When a business masterpiece has been created by a lifetime—or several lifetimes—of unstinting care and exceptional talent . . . how much better it is for **the 'painter' of a business Rembrandt** to personally select its permanent home than to have a trust officer or uninterested heirs auction it off" (Warren Buffett, Berkshire-Hathaway). |
| Structure/Buildings | "Our values are **the glue that binds our business together** and makes our company strong wherever we operate in the world" (Chad Holliday, Dupont). |
| Education/Performance | ". . . But it is on a short list because we are conscious that GM will **earn our grades every day** based on clearly measurable results in our core car-and-truck business." (John F. Smith, Jr., G. Richard Wagner Jr., & Harry J. Pearce, General Motors). |

*Source:* Thompson, L., & Rosette, A. In press. "Leading by Analogy." In S. Chowdhury (Ed.), *Financial Times Next Generation Business Series.* London: Prentice Hall.

son's belief in mutual obligations between that person and another party, such as an employer or leader. *Transactional* leadership depends on the leader's power to reinforce subordinates (team members) for their successful completion of the bargain (task). However, this type of leadership sets up a competitive relationship: "If you limit yourself to transactional leadership of a follower with rewards of carrots for compliance, or punishments with a stick for failure to comply with agreed-on work to be done by the follower, the follower will continue to feel like a jackass" (Levinson, 1980).

Transformational leaders, in contrast, motivate their teams to work toward goals that go beyond immediate self-interest. Transformational leaders motivate their teams to do more than they originally expected to do as they strive for higher-order outcomes (Burns, 1978). Because members of teams are interested in intrinsic aspects of their work, they expect their leader to be as well. Moreover, this affects peformance. People who are taught skills by an extrinsically motivated leader are less interested in learning and enjoy what they are doing less than people taught by an intrinsically motivated leader, even when the lessons and the learning are identical (Wild, Enzle, Nix, & Deci,

**TABLE 10-3**  Task-Person Leadership Questionnaire

*Directions:* The following items describe aspects of leadership behavior. Respond to each item according to the way you would most likely act if you were the leader of a work group. Circle whether you would most likely behave in the described way: always (A), frequently (F), occasionally (O), seldom (S), or never (N).

| A | F | O | S | N | 1. I would most likely act as the spokesperson of the group. |
|---|---|---|---|---|---|
| A | F | O | S | N | 2. I would encourage overtime work. |
| A | F | O | S | N | 3. I would allow members complete freedom in their work. |
| A | F | O | S | N | 4. I would encourage the use of uniform procedures. |
| A | F | O | S | N | 5. I would permit the members to use their own judgment in solving problems. |
| A | F | O | S | N | 6. I would stress being ahead of competing groups. |
| A | F | O | S | N | 7. I would speak as a representative of the group. |
| A | F | O | S | N | 8. I would needle members for greater effort. |
| A | F | O | S | N | 9. I would try out my ideas in the group. |
| A | F | O | S | N | 10. I would let the members do their work the way they think best. |
| A | F | O | S | N | 11. I would be working hard for a promotion. |
| A | F | O | S | N | 12. I would tolerate postponement and uncertainty. |
| A | F | O | S | N | 13. I would speak for the group if there were visitors present. |
| A | F | O | S | N | 14. I would keep the work moving at a rapid pace. |
| A | F | O | S | N | 15. I would turn the members loose on a job and let them go to it. |
| A | F | O | S | N | 16. I would settle conflicts when they occur in the group. |
| A | F | O | S | N | 17. I would get swamped by details. |
| A | F | O | S | N | 18. I would represent the group at outside meetings. |
| A | F | O | S | N | 19. I would be reluctant to allow the members any freedom of action. |
| A | F | O | S | N | 20. I would decide what should be done and how it should be done. |
| A | F | O | S | N | 21. I would push for increased production. |
| A | F | O | S | N | 22. I would let some members have authority that I could keep. |
| A | F | O | S | N | 23. Things would usually turn out as I had predicted. |
| A | F | O | S | N | 24. I would allow the group a high degree of initiative. |
| A | F | O | S | N | 25. I would assign group members to particular tasks. |
| A | F | O | S | N | 26. I would be willing to make changes. |
| A | F | O | S | N | 27. I would ask the members to work harder. |
| A | F | O | S | N | 28. I would trust the group members to exercise good judgment. |
| A | F | O | S | N | 29. I would schedule the work to be done. |
| A | F | O | S | N | 30. I would refuse to explain my actions. |
| A | F | O | S | N | 31. I would persuade others that my ideas are to their advantage. |
| A | F | O | S | N | 32. I would permit the group to set its own pace. |
| A | F | O | S | N | 33. I would urge the group to beat its previous record. |
| A | F | O | S | N | 34. I would act without consulting the group. |
| A | F | O | S | N | 35. I would ask that group members follow standard rules and regulations. |

T–P Leadership Style Scoring
Circle the item number for items 8, 12, 17, 18, 19, 30, 34, and 35.
Write the number 1 in front of a *circled item number* if you responded S (seldom) or N (never) to that item.
Also write a number 1 in front of *item numbers not circled* if you responded A (always) or F (frequently).
Circle the number 1s which you have written in front of the following items: 3, 5, 8, 10, 15, 18, 19, 22, 24, 26, 28, 30, 32, 34, and 35.
Count the circled number 1s. This is your score for concern for *people.*
Count the uncircled number 1s. This is your score for concern for *task.*
*Source:* Sergiovanni, T. J., Metzcus, R., & Burden, L. 1969. "Toward a Particularistic Approach to Leadership Style: Some Finds." *American Educational Research Journal, 6,* 62–69.

1997). Perhaps it is for this reason that leaders who are regarded to be most like team members are evaluated to be more effective than leaders who are seen as not very similar to their team (Hains, Hogg, & Duck, 1997).

Transformational leaders rely on three behaviors—charisma, intellectual stimulation, and individualized consideration—to produce change (Bass, 1985). Jamie Dimon, CEO of Bank One, has charisma. At a talk with employees, he strides up to the podium with Steppenwolf's "Born to be Wild" blaring. When he talks about competitors, he shouts, "I hate them! I want them to bleed!" (Tully, 2002, p. 88). His passionate, obsessive personality is not always nice—he is snappy, rude, and intrusive. Famous for his "one-minute meetings," he talks in a cascade of excited broken sentences. Says Linda Bammann, head of risk management for Bank One, "Talking to Jamie is like drinking from a fire hose" (Tully, 2002, p. 92). Transformational leaders have more satisfied subordinates (Hater & Bass, 1988; Ross & Offermann, 1997). However, as we noted in Chapter 2, satisfaction does not guarantee better objective performance (Iaffaldano & Muchinsky, 1985); and transformational leadership can have a dark side (Hogan, Raskin, & Fazzini, 1990). (For an example of the "dark side" of transformational leadership, see Box 10-3.)

### Active versus Passive Leadership

Leader activity can range from highly involved and active to laissez-faire (Bass, 1990). An active leader is highly involved in team activities and is highly visible to team members. In contrast, a passive leader is one who is usually not involved in the day-to-day activities of the team, and his or her influence is seldom directly felt by the team. Jim Lyons, of Consolidated Diesel, is a highly active leader. He takes one to two hours each day to walk around the shop floor, the offices, and the lab. To show that he is really present, he never wears a tie to work, and everyone calls him by his first name (Sittenfeld, 1999). Steve Ballmer, CEO of Microsoft, is an extremely active leader. Described by many as an "eats nails for breakfast" type of guy, he has balked at top-

---

**BOX 10-3**

### The Dark Side of Transformational Leadership

The People's Temple was a cultlike organization based in San Francisco that primarily attracted poor residents. In 1977, the Reverend Jim Jones, who was the group's political, social, and spiritual leader, moved the group with him to Jonestown, a jungle settlement in Guyana, South America. On November 18, 1978, Congressman Leo R. Ryan of California (who traveled to Guyana to investigate the cult), three members of Ryan's task force, and a cult defec-tor were murdered as they tried to leave Jonestown by plane. Convinced that he would be arrested and implicated in the murder, which would inevitably lead to the demise of the People's Temple, Jones gathered the entire community around him and issued a call for each person's death, to be achieved in a unified act of self-destruction. In November 1978, 910 people compliantly drank, and died from, a vat of poison-laced Kool-Aid.

down management and empowered a second tier of executives to run their businesses with less supervision. However, according to many colleagues, he is a "grade-A control freak" (Greene, Hamm, & Kerstetter, 2002, p. 69). He's obsessive about understanding every detail of a business—sales, costs, and marketing. Richard Belluzzo, ex-president of Microsoft, acknowledges that there were times when Ballmer knew Belluzzo's business better than Belluzzo did. To Ballmer—who believes that a business unit leader should be the expert on his or her business—that was a cardinal sin. Whereas Bill Gates had reclusive "think weeks" where he secluded himself at his family retreat, Ballmer holds "management sync weeks" every quarter, with day-after-day meetings involving executive staff and board. And, when Paul Gross stepped down as the leader of Microsoft's wireless-computing group, Ballmer took control of the division for nine months before handing of the job to Pieter Knook (Greene et al., 2002).

### Autocratic versus Democratic Leadership

Another view of leadership focuses on a continuum of behavior ranging from entirely autocratic to purely democratic (Bass, 1990). Also known as vertical leadership (emanating from the top down), this type of leadership stems from an appointed or formal leader of a team, whereas shared leadership is a group process in which leadership is distributed among, and stems from, team members. Autocratic leadership is displayed by leaders who seek sole possession of authority, power, and control, whereas democratic leadership is displayed by leaders who share authority, power and control with their team. In one investigation, the effectiveness of 71 change management teams in companies was examined as a function of vertical versus shared leadership (Pearce & Sims, 2002). Team effectiveness was measured six months after leadership was assessed and was also measured from the viewpoints of managers, internal customers, and team members. Shared leadership significantly predicted team effectiveness. For a summary of several different leadership styles and their representative behaviors, see Table 10-4.

---

## TEAM COACHING

Of all the different styles of leadership, coaching is one that most people embrace. Team coaching involves direct interaction with a team that is intended to help members use their collective resources to successfully accomplish their goals (Hackman, 2002). Examples of coaching include a "press" meeting before a new product is announced, giving the team feedback on their performance, or asking a team thoughtful questions about their recommendations for a new strategy. By contrast, a leader who personally coordinates the work of a team or who negotiates resources is, on the surface, doing things that are quite useful for the team, but is not coaching (Hackman, 2002). According to Hackman, "coaching is about building teamwork, not about doing the team's work" (2002, p. 167).

### Types of Coaching

The integrated model of teamwork, as laid out in Chapter 2, provides insight into three different types of coaching. Recall that essential conditions for team performance include ability (knowledge, skills, education, and information), motivation, and

**TABLE 10-4**    Representative Behavior of Five Types of Leaders

| Leader Type | Representative Behaviors |
| --- | --- |
| Aversive leadership | Engaging in intimidation |
| | Dispensing reprimands |
| Directive leadership | Issuing instructions and commands |
| | Assigning goals |
| Transactional leadership | Providing personal rewards |
| | Providing material rewards |
| | Managing by exception (active) |
| | Managing by exception (passive) |
| Transformational leadership | Providing vision |
| | Expressing idealism |
| | Using inspirational communication |
| | Having high performance expectations |
| Empowering leadership | Encouraging independent action |
| | Encouraging opportunity thinking |
| | Encouraging teamwork |
| | Encouraging self-development |
| | Participative goal setting |
| | Encouraging self-reward |

*Source:* Pearce, C. L., & Sims, H. P. 2002. "Vertical versus Shared Leadership as Predictors of the Effectiveness of Change Management Teams: An Examination of Aversive, Directive, Transactional, Transformational, and Empowering Leader Behaviors." *Group Dynamics: Theory, Research and Practice, 6*(2), 172–197.

strategy. Coaching can be educational, motivational, or strategic (Hackman, 2002). Coaching that focuses on ability, knowledge, and skill is *educational* in nature. For example, a coach might either provide or suggest that a person get training on particular skills, such as marketing or emotional intelligence. Coaching that focuses on how to reduce social loafing and enhance involvement is *motivational* in nature. For example, a coach might suggest that team members enhance their commitment to the team by outlining their goals and target dates for completing those goals. Finally, coaching that focuses on how to best integrate members' strengths and abilities is *strategic* in nature. For example, a coach might suggest that the team members practice performing a particular task with one another.

# LEADERSHIP AND POWER

As noted earlier, leadership, at its heart, involves a relationship between people. In any relationship, power operates as a key dynamic. Power is the ability of a person to control the outcomes of another person in a relationship (Kelley & Thibaut, 1978). Control over others' outcomes can be direct or indirect. And control can be unilateral or bilateral—with control being one-sided or two-sided. Leadership always involves power; even if a person is not a leader, he or she can still exercise power. Anyone in a leadership position needs to know about the use of power and how it affects others as well as themselves. The following is a lesson plan in sources of power and the use of power in teams.

## Sources of Power

There are many sources of power available to people in teams. French and Raven (1968) identified five key sources of power that people use in organizations and teams: expert, legitimate, reward, coercive, and referent power (see Table 10-5).

## Using Power

Whereas the common question is how effective each type of power is in terms of achieving the power-wielder's objectives, it is also important to know how power affects the wielder of power. Research evidence reveals some surprising findings about the effects of power on those who use it.

First, power is desirable at a fundamental, preconscious level. That is, the use of power itself is rewarding and stimulating. Thus, people are attracted to power. Second, people who are in a position of power often have an egocentrically biased view of themselves, believing themselves to be more fair, generous, and trustworthy than others evaluate them to be. In a complementary fashion, those who lack power are highly distrustful of those who have power (Lind & Tyler, 1988). People regard power-seeking people to be unethical and question the motives of those who seek to enhance their control. Third, people who are dependent on leaders not only tend to evaluate and judge leaders quite often, but also they have particular expectations of leaders, or Implicit Leadership Theories (ILTs), about whether a leader is worthy of influence (or LWI) (Kenney, Schwartz-Kenney, & Blascovich, 1996). ILTs are preconceived ideas that specify what teams expect of their leaders (Lord & Maher, 1993). Consequently, if a leader is judged to be LWI, teams are more willing to be influenced by that leader. Thus, the LWI accorded by teams to their leaders in large part determines the effectiveness of the leader. Given that ILTs drive LWI, it behooves leaders to understand the ILTs that teams hold of them. An examination of the behaviors that people expect of leaders (the ILTs that drive LWI) are somewhat different for appointed versus elected leaders (Kenney, Schwartz-Kenney, & Blascovich, 1996). For appointed leaders, being sympathetic (i.e., humorous, caring, interested, truthful, and open to ideas) and taking charge (i.e., responsible, active, determined, influential, aggressive, and in com-

**TABLE 10-5**   Sources Of Power

| Source of Power | Definition |
| --- | --- |
| Legitimate power | Based on a person's holding of a formal position; other person complies because of belief in legitimacy of power holder |
| Reward power | Based on a person's access to rewards; other person complies because of desire to receive rewards |
| Coercive power | Based on a person's ability to punish; other person complies because of fear of punishment |
| Expert power | Based on personal expertise in a certain area; other person complies because of belief in power holder's knowledge |
| Referent power | Based on a person's attractiveness to others; other person complies because of respect and liking for power holder |

*Source:* French, J. R. P. Jr., & Raven, B. H. 1968. "The Bases of Social Power." In D. Cartwright and A.F. Zander (Eds.), *Group Dynamics* (pp. 259–270). New York: Harper & Row.

**TABLE 10-6**   Leader Behaviors That Determine Whether People Accord Influence to a Leader

| Appointed Leaders Are Expected to Have These Characteristics and Skills | Elected Leaders Are Expected to Have These Characteristics and Skills |
|---|---|
| Caring | Tall |
| Interested | Clean-cut |
| Sense of humor | Open to others' ideas |
| Truthful | Respect for team |
| Open to others' ideas | Friendly |
| Imaginative | Caring |
| Knowledgeable | Honest |
| Responsible | Enthusiastic |
| Speak well | Sense of humor |
| Active | Popular |
| Determined | Knowledgeable |
| Influential | Responsible |
| Aggressive | Speak well |
| In command | Independent |
|  | Influential |
|  | Determined |
|  | Risk-taker |
|  | Aggressive |
|  | In command |

*Source:* Kenney, R. A., Schwartz-Kenney, B. M. & Blascovich, J. 1996. "Implicit Leadership Theories: Defining Leaders Described as Worthy of Influence." *Personality and Social Psychology Bulletin, 22*(11), 1128–1143.

mand) are key. For elected leaders, being well dressed (i.e., clean-cut), kind, and authoritative are most important. (For a specific list of the characteristics, see Table 10-6.)

It would seem that leaders would be hypervigilant about their styles, seeking constant feedback as to the effectiveness of their approach. However, the opposite is true. People in positions of power are less motivated to scan their environment or to process information. From a rational point of view, they are less dependent on others and, therefore, are less motivated to pay attention to the actions of others. In contrast, people who are powerless (i.e., resource dependent on others) have an incentive to carefully attend to those who are in power. For example, Kramer (1996) found that graduate students (who are dependent on professors to obtain their degree) spend an inordinate amount of time recalling and processing behaviors and activities engaged in by faculty members. Similarly, those who have more power show more variability in their behaviors—in short, they engage in a broader array of behaviors (Guinote, Judd, & Brauer, 2002).

Studies have also suggested that power makes people see the world with "rose colored glasses"—that is, it makes people focus on more positive, rewarding information and less on negative, threatening information. For example, Anderson and his colleagues have shown that powerful people make more optimistic judgments regarding the risks they face in their lives (e.g., health risks) compared with powerless individuals (Anderson & Galinsky, 2002). Further, when powerful people interact with others, they are more likely to focus on how much others like them, and less likely to focus on others' negative feelings toward them (Anderson & Berdahl, 2002). This tendency to focus on rewards might help explain why powerful people sometimes choose risky strategies in the pursuit of their goals. When contemplating a potential high-risk merger, for example, powerful organizational leaders might focus more on the potential payoffs of the merger and less on the inherent dangers.

# DECISION ANALYSIS MODEL: HOW PARTICIPATIVE DO YOU WANT TO BE?

Leaders will be more effective if they understand that not every decision requires the input of their entire team. Similarly, leaders are more effective when they realize that they cannot be a demagogue. Thus, all leaders face decisions concerning how participative they want to be. The amount of team participation varies along a continuum from zero to total involvement. How much participation is ideal? It is simply not practical to consult the team on every organizational issue, but where to draw the line is unclear. The decision analysis model of Vroom and Yetton (1973) provides a useful mechanism for the leader to consider.

As can be seen in Figure 10-1, the key questions facing the leader concern the *quality* of the decision to be made (e.g., is it necessary to find the best outcome, given time and budget constraints, or are most outcomes basically sufficient?), the *acceptance* needed for the decision (e.g., how much does the ultimate outcome need to be accepted by the organization?), the length of *time* required to make the decision (efficiency), and the amount of *growth* or development of the team. The model prompts leaders to be more deliberate in the decision-making process. This has the effect of increasing the consistency of their behavior, and consistency is the key principle by which leaders are evaluated. This model of leadership focuses on matching the leader and the situational requirements (Vroom & Jago, 1988; Vroom & Yetton, 1973).

## Decision Styles

Vroom & Jago (1988) considered five different decision methods available to the leader (see top of Figure 10-1). The first is **autocratic,** in which the leader makes the decision with little or no involvement of other team members. The second method, **inquiry,** involves the leader asking for information from the team but ultimately making the decision independently. The third method, the **consultative approach,** involves different degrees of consultation with team members; however, the leader is still the final decision maker. The fourth method, **consensus building,** involves extensive consultation and consensus building with the team. Here, the leader shares a problem with team members, and, together, they try to reach consensus. The leader essentially is another member of the team, and has no more or less influence than any other member. The final method involves total **delegation** of decision making to the team. The team makes the decision without the leader. The leader gives the problem to the team and lets the team determine the best course of action with virtually no additional input.

## Problem Identification

The leader must also determine the right questions and the right order in which to ask them. This also influences the best decision style in a particular context. For example, consider a situation in which a high-quality decision is crucial (the stakes are high), the leader has enough information or expertise to make the decision alone, and accep-

| AI | Leader makes the decision alone. |
| AII | Leader asks for information from the team but makes the decision alone. The team may or may not be told what the problem is. |
| CI | Leader shares the problem with the team and asks for information and evaluations from them. Meetings take place with each member separately, not as a group, and the leader makes the decision. |
| CII | Leader and team meet as a group to discuss the problem, but the leader makes the decision. |
| GII | Leader and team meet as a group to discuss the problem, and the team as a whole makes the decision. |

Note: A = alone, C = consultation, G = group.

**QR** Quality requirement: How important is the technical quality of this decision?

**CR** Commitment requirement: How important is the subordinate commitment to this decision?

**LI** Leader's information: Do you have sufficient information to make a high-quality decision?

**ST** Problem structure: Is the problem well structured?

**CP** Commitment probability: If you were to make a decision by yourself, is it reasonably certain that your subordinate(s) would be committed to the decision?

**GC** Goal congruence: Do subordinates share the organizational goals to be attained in solving this problem?

**CO** Subordinate effect: Is conflict among subordinates over the preferred solution likely?

**SI** Subordinate information: Do subordinates have sufficient information to make a high-quality decision?

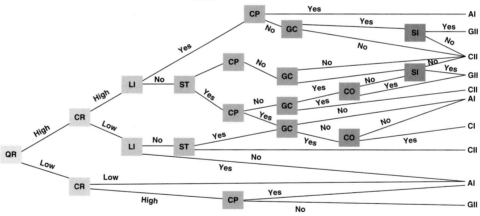

**FIGURE 10-1** Decision Analysis Model
*Source:* Vroom, V. H., & Jago, A. G. 1987. *The New Leadership: Cases and Manuals for Use in Leadership Training.* New Haven, CT: Authors.

tance by the team is not crucial—that is, the decision will work even without their support. In this case, a relatively autocratic style of decision making is ideal. It is efficient, and getting the decision implemented will cost very little. In contrast, consider a situation in which a high-quality decision is necessary and the leader has enough information to make the decision alone, but acceptance by subordinates is crucial—that is, the decision will not work without their active support. Here, a more participative style would be preferable. Indeed, leaders who adapt their style of decision making to existing conditions are generally more successful than those who are either uniformly autocratic or participative in style (Vroom & Jago, 1978). However, most team members prefer a participative approach by their leader, even under conditions where the decision model recommends an autocratic style (Heilman, Hornstein, Cage, & Herschlag, 1984). This means, of course, that the perceived effectiveness of decisions among leaders may very well differ from how the team feels (Field & House, 1990). Teams have strong aversion to autocratic decision-making strategies, even when these are predicted by the model to be most effective. Thus, the decision-making model is a useful device for helping the leader to be a consistent decision maker, but team members generally prefer participation.

### Decision Tree Model

The decision tree model is one in which all of these questions and alternatives are put together to formulate a sound decision, as illustrated in Figure 10-1. A fundamental assumption in this model is that consultation with teams and individuals is inefficient because it requires time; therefore, the model is conservative in that it tends to push the leader toward autocratic or independent decision making. However, in cases where the model recommends a relatively autocratic or individual control strategy, the leader must not let people think that they have control when they actually do not.

One question is whether the Vroom-Yetton model actually leads to better decisions. Many investigations have compared the effects of decisions made according to the model's prescriptions with effects of decisions made in a way inconsistent with the model (for a review, see Yukl, 2002). In general, results support the model. For example, Vroom and Jago (1988) computed the mean rate of success across five investigations and found that for decisions made in accordance with the model, the mean success rate was 62 percent, versus 37 percent for decisions made using a decision procedure outside of the feasible set.

## STRATEGIES FOR ENCOURAGING PARTICIPATIVE MANAGEMENT

Some managers believe that power and control should remain in the hands of a few high-level executives. This model of leadership assumes that the leader has all of the answers, knowledge, and ideas in the organization. This view, however, is being challenged by a model of leadership that delegates authority downward, toward individuals and groups. In this model, leadership is more equally shared by members as teams develop over time. Leadership style does make a difference. When teams have to learn a new task requiring coordination, leadership style (participative versus authoritative) makes a difference in the development and implementation of effective tactics. Teams led by a "coordinator," in which all team members share equal responsibility for determining the team strategy and directing its activities, implement better tactics than commander-led teams (Durham, Knight, & Locke, 1997).

Many managers claim that their team is empowered when, in fact, it is not. Just what does an "empowered" team do? Figure 10-2 depicts a continuum of team empowerment. Level 1 teams have the least power; they are often new teams, perhaps lacking the skills, experience, or training to implement more control. Perhaps this is why many successful self-directed organizations intentionally devote 20 percent of the team members' and leaders' time to training in the first year (Wellins, 1992). Job skill training is necessary to give team members the depth and breadth they need to effectively carry out the broadened range of activities that self-directed teams perform.

Understanding existing social and structural factors is critical to successfully forming empowered work teams. Probably the most regrettable state of affairs in the organization is when employees feel powerless. Feelings of powerlessness lead to depression and organizational decline. Part of effective team leadership should include a check on four factors, listed in Table 10-7, that can lead to a state of powerlessness in the organization: organizational factors, the leader's supervisory style, the organizational reward system, and job design. Furthermore, instead of the leader performing this check, the team members should do it themselves.

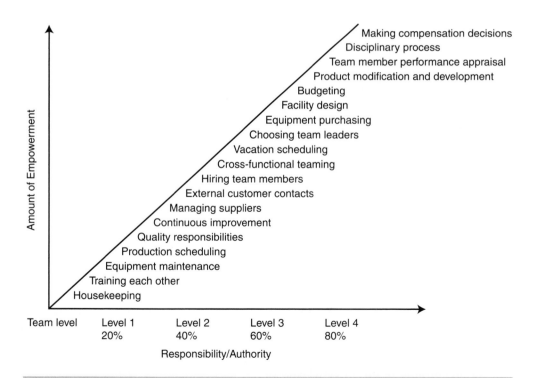

**FIGURE 10-2** Team Empowerment Continuum
*Source:* Wellins, R. S., Byham, W. C., & Wilson, J. M. 1991. *Empowered Teams* (p. 26). San Francisco: Jossey-Bass Inc., Publishers.

**TABLE 10-7**   Factors that Lead to a Potential State of Powerlessness

| Context Factor Leading to State of Powerlessness | Condition |
| --- | --- |
| Organizational factors | • Significant organizational change/transitions<br>• Start-up ventures<br>• Excessive, competitive pressures<br>• Impersonal, bureaucratic climate<br>• Poor communications and limited network-forming systems<br>• Highly centralized organizational resources |
| Supervisory style | • Authoritarian (high control)<br>• Negativism (emphasis on failures)<br>• Lack of reason for actions/consequences |
| Reward systems | • Noncontingency (arbitrary reward allocations)<br>• Low incentive value of rewards<br>• Lack of competence-based work<br>• Lack of innovation-based rewards |
| Job design | • Lack of role clarity<br>• Lack of training and technical support<br>• Unrealistic goals<br>• Lack of appropriate authority/discretion<br>• Low task variety<br>• Limited participation in programs, meetings, and decisions that have a direct impact on job performance<br>• Lack of appropriate/necessary resources<br>• Lack of network-forming opportunities<br>• Highly established work routines<br>• Too many rules and guidelines<br>• Low advancement opportunities<br>• Lack of meaningful goals/tasks<br>• Limited contact with senior management |

*Source:* Conger, J. 1989. "The Art of Empowering Others." *Academy of Management Executive, 3*(1), 17–24. Reprinted with permission.

Once management has considered the potential benefits of a more employee-empowering leadership style, management must determine how to best implement this new structure. In the following paragraphs, we provide several strategies to make a smooth transition from a bureaucratic to a commitment organization. *Empowerment, participative management*, and *self-managing teams* are popular buzzwords. However, they don't happen overnight—even when upper management has made a public commitment to creating an empowered workforce. Many companies that want to become more participatory in their management styles don't know how to begin. What are some down-to-earth, concrete steps for moving power downward in the organization—that is, into the hands of team members?

The variety of approaches to inviting participation in the workforce can be clustered into four types of approaches: task delegation, parallel suggestion involvement, job involvement, and organizational involvement (Lawler, 1988).

## Task Delegation

The idea behind task delegation is that leaders delegate meaningful tasks and responsibilities to others. **Delegation** is the handing over of the responsibility and authority required to accomplish a task without relinquishing final accountability. The spirit of task delegation is multifold: to invite others to have a share in the performance of work; to have leaders do other, more important things; and to mentor. This not only serves the interests of the employees, who presumably want to have a greater hand in the work and operations of the company, but it also serves the interests of the leader and the organization in creating more efficient uses of time. Many people have a somewhat old-fashioned view of leadership that holds that a leader is responsible not only for creating and defining the vision of the organization, but also must handle all of the details, manage all of the personal relationships, and determine the process. Many managers mistakenly think that every task requires their constant attention from beginning to end. These statements are supported by the experiences of two innovative leaders, Phil Carroll of Shell Oil and Rich Teerlink, former CEO of Harley-Davidson (Senge, 1996). Phil Carroll recalls: "When I first came in as CEO, everyone thought, 'Phil will tell us what he wants us to do.' But I didn't have a clue, and if I had, it would have been a disaster" (p. 43). Likewise, Rich Teerlink said, "Anyone who thinks the CEO can drive this kind of change is wrong. They succeeded by delegation" (p. 43).

Leadership, if it is to be effective, requires delegation, and leaders are still accountable for their delegates, as well as for themselves. Delegation is much easier said than done: There are right and wrong ways to delegate that depend on things such as team members' skill levels and the nature of the work. Box 10-4 outlines guidelines for successful delegation.

The inability to delegate effectively creates two negative consequences for the organization: overloaded executives and underutilized subordinates. Each of these conditions is associated with work-related stress and burnout—not to mention many different forms of underperformance. By giving meaningful responsibility to subordinates, managers give them the opportunity to perform their jobs well, demonstrate ability, experience success, be visible within the organization, develop skills, and experience new challenges.

## Parallel Suggestion Involvement

The idea behind parallel suggestion involvement is to invite employees and team members to make suggestions about organizational procedures and processes. Thus, employees are given opportunities and are actively encouraged to recommend different tactics for increasing sales, minimizing production costs, increasing customer satisfaction, and so on. The classic example of parallel suggestion involvement is the suggestion box, which is not even limited to employees—customers can be asked to make recommendations as well. Quality circles also invite workers to share ideas about improving production and products. The parallel suggestion strategy is cost-effective; providing a venue to solicit suggestions can be relatively inexpensive, but can potentially have huge payoffs in terms of improving organizational functioning. What's more, parallel suggestion involvement can significantly reduce turnover and absenteeism because employees who feel that their interests, concerns, and ideas are valued are more motivated. This was true for Delta Credit Union, which in early 1991 planned

---

BOX 10-4

## Key Guidelines for Successful Delegation (Hall, 1997)

**Use delegation to develop, not dump.** As people become more concerned about time management, there has been a tendency to think that this means getting rid of unwanted tasks. Be sure that you and your subordinates discuss the task in terms of what is in it for them. Don't just pass the buck. Pass on challenge, responsibility, and a chance to learn new skills or aspects of the organization.

**Set specific goals with subordinates.** This includes a review of the task, especially the results expected, and a timetable for getting things done and reviewing progress. Don't assume that they understand what you expect and/or need. Be specific and check for understanding.

**Discuss the meaning of the assignment** in terms of its value within the larger organizational picture.

**Provide for autonomy.** Make it clear that subordinates have the authority and resources and are free to "run with the ball," but reassure them that you will be there to provide support.

**Elicit questions from the subordinate.** Test for understanding of the talk.

**Get additional ideas** or other inputs from the subordinate.

**Provide feedback.** Your subordinates need to know how they are doing. This is helpful for taking corrective action before a deadline. It is especially reinforcing after a goal is accomplished.

**Provide times for follow-up.** Don't just delegate and expect the results to just happen. Plan to meet, review preliminary results, discuss problems, and so forth.

**Select the most motivated person.**

**Delegate only once,** and to only one person, group, or team. Nothing is more demoralizing for subordinates than to find out that other people are working on a project that they thought had been delegated solely to them.

---

to upgrade customer service by moving some of the eight branches to more expensive and larger locations (Clemmer, 1995). However, when managers shared some of their plans with customer focus groups, they learned they were completely off-target. Customers wanted improvements in existing branch services—reduced waiting and more of a family feeling. In short, by listening to their customers, Delta experienced asset growth of 25 percent in the following two years.

When using parallel suggestion involvement, it is important to differentially and accurately weigh staff input. Simply stated, team members differ in their ability to contribute to solving a problem. *Distributed expertise* refers to the fact that team members differ in the amount of knowledge and information that each bring to the problem (Hollenbeck, Ilgen, Sego, Hedlund, Major, & Phillips, 1995). Until leaders have had an opportunity to gather information they feel is relevant to their determination of each team member's ability to contribute, they may equally weight each person's input. Leaders have difficulty differentially weighting their staff as much as they should and tend to utilize an equal-weighting strategy (Brehmer & Hagafors, 1986). Once leaders have had experience with their team, some may have greater influence on the basis of their competence, ability, and willingness to accept extra-role responsibilities (Graen & Scandura, 1987). In one investigation, 84 leaders of four-person decision-making teams made 63 decisions. Both experience and providing leaders with accurate information about particular members led to greater differentiation and better accuracy in differentiation (Phillips, 1999).

## Job Involvement

Job involvement entails restructuring the tasks performed by employees to make them more rewarding, enriching, and, in the case of teams, more autonomous. When people are challenged with interesting tasks, they perform more effectively and creatively. There are a variety of ways by which this may be achieved, such as providing employees with feedback from customers, restructuring tasks so that employees complete a whole and meaningful piece of work, and training employees with new skills and knowledge so that their job scope increases. With job involvement, employees at the lowest levels get new information, power, and skills, and they may be rewarded differently. For example, individuals may be rewarded for team effort and group-level productivity. Unlike parallel suggestion involvement, job involvement affects the daily work activities of employees. For this reason, job involvement is considerably more costly than is parallel suggestion involvement because of the high start-up costs of reconfiguring job descriptions, training, and, in many cases, the physical reconfiguration of the workplace. A good example of greater job involvement comes from Microchip Technology in Arizona. According to Cathy Klevenger, who has been with Microchip Technology since it was founded, says, "You're not micromanaged, with people giving you the details of what to do. They give you the resources. And people expect you to come up with the solutions" (Trevison, 2002). However, it was not always this way: Employees who worked at the company when it was a money-losing division of General Instruments remember a place where fear and blame prevailed. Eventually, the company developed 11 guiding values that focused on employee empowerment. For example, at one morning meeting, a team was dealing with a machine that had lost power. Previously, people would have said, "It's your problem. I don't have any responsibility." Now, they take the responsibility: At that meeting, a facilities manager immediately began checking to see whether it was a problem in his building (Trevison, 2002).

Another example of job involvement can be found at Consolidated Diesel Co. in North Carolina, which relies on a team-based system (Sittenfeld, 1999). Employees are involved in designing solutions to problems in the plant. The teams design the work schedules, hire, and fire members. Does it work? It does. The plant's turnover rate is less than 2 percent, and the factory has never suffered a major layoff. Although most plants average one supervisor for every 25 employees, Consolidated Diesel has one for every 100 employees, a difference that yields $1M in savings per year. Additionally, the injury rate is one-fifth of the national average.

## Organizational Involvement

Just because leaders want to move in the direction of participation and empowerment, however, does not mean that this can be done by merely changing their own behavior and style independent of other organizational forces. Leadership style and strategy must be integrated into the organizational context (as indicated in Sidebar 10-

1). Consider, also, the results of a study of a government business enterprise in the communications industry. The key question concerned employees' willingness to support a participative management program. A key determinant of whether employees are committed is the "organizational grapevine"—the extent to which the organization and the key senior people have supported the program (Langan-Fox, Code, Gray, & Langfield-Smith, 2002).

---

### Sidebar 10-1. Organizational Culture and Commitment

"People hear senior management talk about empowerment, teamwork, and service. What they get are paternalistic pats on the head, motivation programs, and blame for not using the systems, processes, and technology dropped on them and their customers. The problem stems from the expanding gulf between rising expectations and the reality of the organization's traditional culture" (Clemmer, 1995, p. 62).

---

Consider two types of organizations: bureaucratic and commitment organizations. **Bureaucratic organizations** are the traditional, hierarchical style of leadership; information, rewards, knowledge, and power are concentrated at the top of the organization. In the classic bureaucratic organization, teams do not exist or at least are not acknowledged. Furthermore, when they do emerge, they are often ignored, suppressed, contained, or neglected (Walton & Hackman, 1986). **Commitment organizations** are the opposite extreme. Teams are expected and encouraged to form, power is not hierarchical, and the organization has a deliberate flat structure. For an example that illustrates the difference between bureaucratic and commitment organizations, see Box 10-5.

Organizational involvement, or the commitment approach, restructures the organization so that employees at the lowest level will have a sense of involvement (commitment) in not just how they do their own jobs (as in the job involvement approach) but in the performance of the entire organization. Organizational involvement strategies invite employees to contribute to higher order strategy decisions. The McGregor method and *Theory Y* (McGregor, 1960) are examples of high-involvement strategies in which employees make decisions about work activities, as well as organizational direction. Organizational involvement is based on the argument that if employees are going to care about the performance of their organization, they need to know about it, be able to influence it, be rewarded for it, and have the knowledge and skills to contribute to it.

A key difference between parallel suggestion involvement and organizational involvement is that employees not only make recommendations about how to improve organizational functioning, but also they implement their suggestions. Thus, employees and team members have **implementation power.** This disadvantage of the organizational involvement strategy is that it is very difficult to know which employee-suggested strategies are, in fact, worthwhile to implement. Moreover, there are very few company examples of high-involvement organizations. Dana Corporation, a manufacturer of products for the automobile and truck industry, is a good example of a high-involvement organization that is structured on a product basis—each of its relatively small divisions can serve customers autonomously, with substantial ownership over a product from beginning to end (Lawler, 1992).

---

BOX 10-5

### Going from Bureaucracy to Commitment

An example that illustrates the difference between bureaucratic and commitment organizations is the hierarchical leadership style of General Motors during the early 1980s (long lead time to react to market pressures, poor manufacturing quality, and dissatisfaction in the workforce) and the new Saturn division, where the guiding principle is focused on the empowerment of people (Keller & McGahan, 1994). General Motors was a bureaucratic corporation. It took the company twice as long as its Japanese counterparts to respond to outside market forces (i.e., introducing new models) and to build competitive cars. The company's executives blamed this inefficiency on high labor costs. According to

one supervisor, the way to regain competitiveness was "to go down the line and knock some heads off." This antagonism between management and the workers made the workers less willing to work with management to jointly solve problems and exacerbated the high labor costs. On the other hand, when GM launched the Saturn project, the company was able to share with its new hires the common vision of building an affordable and dependable car in a short time frame. They succeeded by delegating important decisions downward and by forming teams led by various charter team members. The Saturn plant does not suffer from long cycle times or abnormally high labor costs.

---

Another type of organizational involvement involves top management teams. It is precisely for reasons of greater empowerment and the benefits of creativity that many organizations turn to teams rather than a single individual for leadership at the top. Among other advantages, top-management teams, as opposed to individuals, are more likely to represent the wide range of interests of the people and groups in the organization and provide valuable development experiences for its members (Beer, Eisenstat, & Spector, 1990). Leadership via top-management teams challenges the traditional view of leadership because it moves away from the image of the leader as autonomous, prophetic, and omniscient, and toward the idea that leadership is a team process. It is unfortunate, however, that *top-management team (TMT)* is actually a misnomer for the teams that exist at the apex of many firms, because they have few "team" properties. Many TMTs are simply constellations of executive talent—individuals who rarely come together (and usually only for perfunctory information exchange), who rarely collaborate, and who focus almost entirely on their own pieces of the enterprise (Hambrick, 1997). For some suggestions on getting top executives to function like a real team, see Sidebar 10-2.

It would seem that empowerment and greater employee participation would be the preferred mode in most companies—certainly, at least, from the view of the employees. However, humans have a fundamental need for structure and order, and new employees are often uncomfortable in the absence of clear structures, guidelines, and constraints. For example, newly matriculated MBA students frequently lobby for instruc-

## Sidebar 10-2. Overcoming Senior Team Fragmentation

The potential advantages of TMTs are threatened by fragmentation, which is basically a lack of integration, vision, purpose, and coordination of effort and talent (Hambrick, 1997). There are five key steps that a CEO can take to deal with fragmentation and pull a TMT together (Hambrick, 1995, 1997):

- *Team identity:* The group should have a clear identity. Even simple things like identifying a team name, sharing a vision, or engaging in collaborative activities can build team identity.

- *Teamwork:* The team should do "real work" together, not just exchanging updates and reviewing others' work. Real work involves fact finding, analysis, and problem solving. On a practical level, this can be achieved by (a) convening the team together several times a year, including at least an in-depth, offsite meeting, and (b) establishing constructive norms, especially of openness, informality, and collegiality; even mundane matters such as attendance, punctuality, and preparation are critically important.

- *Team composition and roles:* Line executives should be given additional responsibilities for companywide endeavors. These "overlay" assignments can be temporary (such as leading a key task force) or more continuous (overseeing a staff or support unit). The team should strive for gradual, staggered turnover within the team, and attempt to avoid the extremes of uniformly long tenures and wholesale turnovers (which cause tumult and erratic relations). One strategy is to selectively rotate executives or, at least, appoint senior executives with multiunit experience in the company.

- *Team incentives:* At least one-third of every executive's target incentive compensation should be tied to overall company performance, and at least one-third of every executive's incentive reward should be paid out in restricted stock grants or stock options.

- *The CEO's team leadership:* The CEO must personally convey and reinforce openness and constructive candor; there can be no hidden agendas, no offline deals. The CEO must also convey and reinforce mutual trust; disagreement and minority views must not be penalized; and debate must stay on business issues, not on personal issues.

The opposite of fragmentation is organizational coherence. Even though most CEOs recognize the importance of coherence, few know how to carry this awareness into the design and process of their TMTs. Corporate coherence must emanate from the top of the firm, with the executive group thinking and acting as a team.

tor-assigned, rather than free-forming, study groups. What is the effect of empowerment and the ambiguity it brings to the individual, the team, and the organization?

When an organization removes existing structures to provide empowerment in a more democratic fashion, it may find the ambiguity associated with the new structure uncomfortable, and so respond by imposing a more controlling and bureaucratic structure than the one it sought to replace. This highly rational but powerfully oppressive bureaucracy is known as the **iron cage** (Weber, 1958). Out of a desire for order, people continually rationalize their bureaucratic relationships, making them less negotiated (i.e., less based upon commitment) and more structural (Weber, 1978). As a case in point, see Sidebar 10-3.

## Sidebar 10-3. Tightening the Iron Cage (from Barker, 1993)

ISE Communications is a small manufacturing company in a mountain state, located in a metropolitan area (Barker, 1993). ISE manufactures voice and data transmission circuit boards for the telecommunications industry. It employs a total of 150 employees, 90 of whom are in manufacturing. Originally, ISE was a division of a large telecommunications firm. The ISE management team bought it outright in 1984, although the large firm still remains ISE's largest customer. ISE has traditional manufacturing, engineering, sales, marketing, human resources, and executive staffs. ISE converted from traditional manufacturing into self-managing teams in 1988.

In 1988, the CEO of ISE made a commitment to restructure the organization into self-managing teams. Literally overnight he reconfigured the physical workspace and created several work teams called Red, Blue, Green, Orange, and so on. Before the change, the structure of ISE was such that three levels of managerial hierarchy existed between the vice president and the manufacturing workers. Line and shift supervisors formed the first managerial link. The assembly line in manufacturing organized the plant, with workers manufacturing circuit boards according to their place on the line. Workers had little input into work-related decisions (i.e., not even parallel suggestion involvement). Management disciplined all workers and interviewed and hired all new workers.

After the change, the managerial hierarchy extended directly from the new manufacturing teams to the vice president. Team work areas replaced the old assembly lines. Teams were responsible for all aspects of the product: complete fabrication, testing, packaging, and so on. Team members took on management issues within each team, electing someone to coordinate information, and to discipline, interview, hire, and terminate members. When workers reported to the plant on the next business day, there was mass confusion and chaos. What happened in the ensuing months was surprising.

ISE is an example of a company in which upper management moved from bureaucratic control to participative management. However, many of the effects were not intended. Three distinct phases were observed over a four-year period of change.

In the first phase, the challenge for the teams was to learn how to work together and supervise themselves functionally, that is, how to get a customer's order manufactured and out the door.

In the second phase, the teams had to deal with the socialization processes that had shaped the norms of the group. The company prospered and a large number of new workers had to be integrated into the teams; workers were unfamiliar with the existing teams' value consensus, and they posed an immediate challenge to the power relationships that the older employees had formed.

In the third phase, the company began to stabilize and turn a profit; teams' normative rules became more and more rationalized; and simple norms (e.g., we all need to be at work on time) became highly objective rules similar to ISE's old bureaucratic structure (e.g., if you are more than five minutes late, you're docked a day's pay). The social rules were more rigid. The senior group members took on the role of leader within each team. Not surprisingly, many employees were frustrated and confused. It is a bitter irony that some looked back fondly on the days in which there was greater bureaucratic control.

## CONCLUSIONS

Most of us have been socialized in bureaucratic organizations. In these organizations, participative management of the sort we have described seems like antimanagement or an admission of failure at one's own job. One senior-level banker from an international banking firm put it this way: "If I do the kind of things you are describing here—inviting other people who are supposed to be under me to make suggestions about how to accomplish my division's objectives—I am going to work myself out of a job." This investment banker was worried about others doing his job better than he could. This is perhaps the most often cited reason against participative management. The irony of this example is that the company would probably be better off if all of its employees invited participation. Traditional leadership may no longer be the right image of leadership in a corporate world placing an ever-heavier emphasis on team-based work units. A new image of leadership is necessary, one that is associated with being a leader among equals, rather than a leader of followers. Teams (or at least some teams) are often composed of talented individuals selected for their specific knowledge or skills to fit a particular role; in this case, the leader as director is not the right image. The leader as coordinator or assembler may be a better image. When this is true, the leader functions better, activities are performed better, teams work better, and the organization is more successful. The key idea is that it is in the interests of both leaders and organizations to move in this direction.

# CHAPTER

# 11

# Interteam Relations:

## *Competition and Cooperation*

*Cathy Filgas is cofounder and vice president of marketing and sales for Oregon-based Anthro Technology Furniture. Half of Anthro's employees operate forklifts and lasers on the late shift, and the other half pound on dial pads and keyboards from 9 A.M. to 5 P.M. Filgas tells of a time when a rather obnoxious warehouse employee came to her desk and complained about the customer-service team. "He had no idea what customer-service reps did all day, so he assumed they chatted on the phone and snacked on bonbons while he worked his heinie off. His comments hinted at a larger swell of animosity within the company—an us-versus-them mentality. As we began to grow from 20 to 100 people, I could see that battle intensifying" (Layne, 2000). Fortunately, Filgas took action and developed the "Shadow Program": Each week, one employee observes and develops a relationship with a fellow employee in an unfamilar department. The program assigns members of the manufacturing department to join the accounting team for a day, allows warehouse workers to sample marketing, and forces middle managers to recognize good ideas and winning strategies beyond their jurisdiction. Says Filgas, "You simply cannot spend an entire day with a person, eat lunch with them, and walk away with a sense of animosity" (Layne, 2000).*

Unfortunately, not all team leaders react the way Cathy Filgas did when they see conflict and competition among teams within the organization. Any given company houses several teams and they often (unwittingly) step on each other's toes. Moreover, in most companies, teams are needed to work collaboratively with other groups inside the organization, and as such, organizations rely on cross-functional teamwork. However, as was the case with Anthro Furniture, different groups and teams often view each other with disdain, making cross-team collaboration difficult. In this chapter, we examine how teams not only get work done, but also act as important sources of identity for people in organizations. People feel protective of their teams and at the same time can feel threatened even by the mere presence of other teams in the company. Often, unwitting executives can magnify these processes by fostering competition between teams. In this chapter, we begin by examining individual and team identity, interteam relationships, and biases associated with intergroup conflict. We conclude by outlining strategies for reducing the negative effects of intergroup conflict.

## PERSONAL AND TEAM IDENTITY

People define themselves in many ways by the organizations they belong to and the teams they are a member of. For this reason, people naturally seek group affiliations;

consequently, the reputation and accomplishments of their teams are a critical source of their self-identity and self-esteem. Indeed, feeling good about ourselves is often dependent upon feeling that our groups are adequate or superior to other groups (Tajfel & Turner, 1986). Moreover, teams provide people with a buffer against threats and setbacks: When our self-esteem is shaken by personal setbacks, our groups provide us with reassurance and identity (Meindl & Lerner, 1984). There is a potentially infinite number of group distinctions that people can use to define their identity. The following types of teams and groups are common to many people's identities:

- Gender groups
- Position, level, class (e.g., rank, how many people supervised)
- Functional unit (e.g., marketing, sales)
- Regional unit (e.g., midwestern, Northeastern)
- Ethnicity and race

The extent to which a given person identifies with a group occurs on three distinct levels: cognitive, emotional, and behavioral (Henry, Arrow, & Carini, 1999). In other words, people's affiliation with their teams affects how they think, feel, and act. To see how these three different aspects of group identity can be measured, see Table 11-1.

## Intrateam and Interteam Respect

Because teams are so important for people's identity, it is important for them to feel respected and accepted by their teams. The implications of respect extend far beyond the self-esteem of the members; people who don't feel respected by their team are not as loyal to their team and not as committed (Barreto & Ellemers, 2002). Conversely, respected members of "devalued" groups (organizational groups that have low status and prestige) are the most likely to donate their time to their team and work to improve its image, rather than their personal image (Branscombe, Spears, Ellemers,

**TABLE 11-1**   Three Sources of Group Identity: Emotional, Behavioral, and Cognitive

| Source of Identity | Items |
| --- | --- |
| Emotional (Affective) | I would prefer to be in a different group. (R) |
| | Members of this group like one another. |
| | I enjoy interacting with the members of this group. |
| | I don't like many of the other people in this group. (R) |
| Behavioral | In this group, members don't have to rely on one another. (R) |
| | All members need to contribute to achieve the group's goals. |
| | This group accomplishes things that no single member could achieve. |
| | In this group, members do not need to cooperate to complete group tasks. (R) |
| Cognitive | I think of this group as a part of who I am. |
| | I see myself as quite different from other members of this group. (R) |
| | I don't think of this group as part of who I am. (R) |
| | I see myself as quite similar to other members of this group. |

*Note:* Items with an (R) are reverse-scored.
*Source:* Henry, K. B., Arrow, H., & Carini, B. 1999. "A Tripartite Model of Group Identification: Theory and Measurement." *Small Group Research, 30*(5), 558–581.

& Doosje, 2002). In contrast, disrespected members of prestigious groups invest in group activity only if they might improve their personal image.

## Independence versus Interdependence

We noted in Chapter 1 that a defining characteristic of teamwork is interdependence. Gardner, Gabriel, and Lee (1999) distinguish two types of relational focus when it comes to teamwork: independence and interdependence. This distinction is also known as egocentric versus sociocentric (Schweder & Bourne, 1984) or individualism versus collectivism (Triandis, 1989). People with an independent outlook focus on the extent to which they are autonomous and unique; in contrast, people with an interdependent outlook focus on the extent to which they are embedded within a larger social network.

In one simple task, people were given a sheet of paper and asked to write 20 statements about themselves, each beginning with the words, "I am" (Gabriel & Gardner, 1999). People who are independent in their relational orientation tend to write statements that describe their inner values, attributes, and appearance (e.g., *ambitious, creative, slim*). People who are interdependent tend to write statements that describe themselves in relation to others and their social roles (e.g., *father, son, community member*).

Whether a team member views herself as independent or interdependent influences the motivations she has and how she achieves her goals (Markus & Kitayama, 1991; Morris, Podolny, & Ariel, 2000). As might be expected, our native cultural values influence our world outlook. It is not surprising that most North Americans value independence and autonomy, show a great disdain for conformity, and seek to be unique. In contrast, Asians value interdependence and, collectivity, show a disdain for uniqueness, and seek conformity (Kim & Markus, 1999). However, even within a culture, there is variation in individualism versus collectivism. For example, within the United States, people in the Deep South are more collectivistic, and people in the Mountain West and Great Plains are the most individualistic (Vandello & Cohen, 1999).

Perhaps even more striking is the fact that interdependence and independence can be activated within one person at any given time. For example, Gardner et al. (1999) instructed some people to read a paragraph that contained primarily independent prononouns (e.g., *I, me, mine*); in contrast, other people read identical paragraphs that contained collective pronouns (e.g., *we, us, ours*); then, she examined motivations and behaviors. European-Americans who read collectivist pronouns (*we, us, ours*) shifted toward collectivist values and judgments.

## Self-Interest versus Group-Interest

One of the most important challenges of effective teamwork is the fact that people often focus only on self-interest rather than team interests. In many groups, self- and team-interests are at odds. One deterrent of self-interest is the extent to which a person feels "identified" with his team (Turner, 1987). And strengthening group identity (rather than personal identity) increases the value that people attach to their team's welfare versus their personal welfare (De Cremer & Van Vugt, 1999). When groups receive performance feedback, as is often the case in organizations, teams that have strong group identities actually show an increase in group-level interest (De Cremer &

van Dijk, 2002). However, if personal, rather than team, identity is salient, members will act in a more self-interested fashion.

## Ingroups and Outgroups

The most basic categorization for teams is the classification of ingroups and out-groups (Jones, 1983; Wilder, 1986a, 1986b). In short: "Are you one of us or one of them?" People consider ingroups to be people who are like themselves or who belong to the same groups; outgroups are people who are not in their group or who are members of competitor groups. However, even ingroups and outgroups are subjective. Consider Figure 11-1, in which we see progressively more and more inclusive ways to categorize oneself. At the very basic level, a person might see him- or herself as an indi-vidual. At another level, a person might see him- or herself as a member of a particular team. At still another level, a person might see themselves as a member of a unit or functional area. Most of us have a chronic way of viewing our teams and organizations. Importantly, our chronic levels of perceiving ingroups and outgroups affects our behavior. Simply stated: A person who identifies with the company is going to engage in more cooperative behavior when interacting with a person from a different group because their self-identity is defined at the company level. In contrast is a person who sees himself primarily in terms of his team membership or his individual identity. For example, Brewer and Kramer (1986) told some people to think of themselves as indi-viduals and others to think of themselves as group members and found that the group orientation led to more generous, voluntary contributions of resources in a resource dilemma situation.

Thus, people's perceptions of themselves and their groups can expand and con-tract. Their behavior is influenced by how they categorize the system of social rela-tionships in their company: The more narrowly defined their groups are, the more

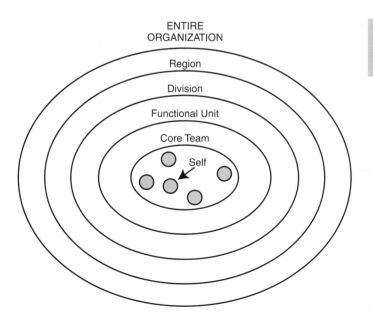

FIGURE 11-1 Levels of Identification in an Organization

competitive and self-serving their behavior is. Conversely, when they focus on the larger collective, they are more cooperative. The challenge for the team leader is to carefully balance "team spirit" with the competition that will naturally arise when the team sets itself apart from the rest of the company.

### Balancing the Need to Belong and the Need to Be Distinct

According to Brewer (1991), most people seek an optimal distinctiveness to their self-identities, such that they don't want to be too different or too similar to others. In short, people seek an optimal balance between their personal identities and their social identities. Personal identity is the individuated self—those characteristics that differentiate one person from others in a given team. Social identities are categorizations of the self into more inclusive social units that effectively depersonalize the self-concept, where *I* becomes *we*. For most people, the self-concept is expandable and contractable, such that some of the time, we want to be distinct from our team; other times, we want to be part of the group. Within an organization, the need to belong is often fulfilled through our primary team affiliations. The need for distinctiveness is often met through intergroup comparisons—in other words, teams may compare themselves with other teams within a company. One implication of the optimal distinctiveness model is that to secure loyalty, teams must not only satisfy members' needs for affiliation and belonging within a group, they must also maintain clear boundaries that differentiate them from other groups. The balance of individual versus social identities also affects people's behavior. For example, when faced with a conflict between making a profit for themselves and helping to preserve a collective resource, people who feel a need to belong are more likely to contribute to the greater good, whereas people who need to feel distinct act in a self-interested fashion (Caporael, Dawes, Orbell, & van de Kragt, 1989).

Although there is not a perfect negative correlation between group size and distinctivess, if the vast majority of people in an organization are not sufficiently differentiated, they will often mobilize into minority groups to meet their distinctiveness needs. Members of low-status groups are faced with a double conflict between positive social identity and distinctiveness in a way that is more difficult for them to resolve than in the case of high-status majority members (Brewer, 1991). On the one hand, members of minority groups can dissociate themselves from their group membership and seek positive identity elsewhere, but this threatens distinctiveness. On the other hand, they can embrace their distinctive group identity, but they may not enjoy the positive evaluations that come from the majority (Steele, 1990).

## INTERTEAM RELATIONSHIPS

We've made the point that people derive a part of their identity from their teams and that this identity is flexible—meaning that in some situations, they see themselves as part of the team, or even the larger organizations, but in other situations, they need to distinguish themselves and their team. Given that organizations are composed of multiple teams, each with their own identities, what might we expect in the way of interteam relationships?

## Social Comparison Processes

In most organizations, there is a significant focus on performance. And, as in most organizations, teams differ in their performance, which naturally leads to social comparison—simply put, *How does my team stack up against your team?* Consider a situation in which you are a member of a team that has little organizational support within your company. Your team competes with two other groups in your organization—one is a disadvantaged group (they don't have a lot of organizational support and resources); the other is an advantaged group (they have much organizational support and many resources; Rothgerber & Worchel, 1997). The performance of the disadvantaged team changes over time, so that it becomes either equal, worse, or better than your team's performance. How would you feel? **Social comparison theory** predicts that when another, comparable team in your organization performs similarly or better than your team, this threatens the identity of your team (Crocker & Major, 1989). Under such conditions, your team might be most likely to discriminate against (i.e., hurt) other disadvantaged teams that perform similarly or better than your own team. Conversely, your team is most helpful and supportive of other teams whose performance deteriorates over time—because such groups provide positive social comparison for your group (i.e., they make your team look good). In contrast, the "advantaged" outgroup is not as much of a threat to your team (because it is not easily comparable). Thus, teams are more likely to harm and discriminate against disadvantaged groups when their performance increases—thus threatening one's own team's performance (Rothgerber & Worchel, 1997).

## Post-merger Behavior

In most organizations, groups cannot always choose to maintain distinct identities. For better or for worse, they must undergo mergers and reorganizations. Some mergers occur internally and some occur through external means (e.g., acquisitions). Although mergers between groups are quite common, more than half have negative consequences, such as stress, turnover, and productivity loss (Mottola, Bachman, Gaertner, & Dovidio, 1997; Schweiger & Walsh, 1990). Moreover, the negative effects of ingroup bias may be heightened when companies merge (see Box 11-1). Anticipated mergers between groups can be viewed as the ultimate threat to group distinctiveness in that pre-merger boundaries are undermined and group members must lose their pre-merger identity (Terry, Carey, & Callan, 2001). However, the threat depends on the status of the group. For low-status organizational groups, a merger with a high-status group might provide opportunities to obtain higher status (Hornsey & Hogg, 2002). And, indeed, members of low-status groups are motivated to undermine boundaries with the high-status outgroup to improve the status of their group (Jetten, Spears, Hogg, & Manstead, 2000). On the other hand, low-status groups will resist mergers when the status differences remain salient between groups or when they expect not to be adequately represented in the merged group (van Knippenberg, van Knippenberg, Monden, & DeLima, 2002). High-status groups are accepting of mergers, except when they fear that mergers will undermine their group's superior position (Terry et al., 2001). There is some evidence that during an organizational merger, high-status groups feel less threatened than do low-status groups (Terry & O'Brien, 2001). Indeed, it is

## BOX 11-1

## Ingroup Bias in Response to an Organizational Merger

Employees from two hospitals were studied during the period of planning for a merger (Terry & Callan, 1998). One hospital was higher in status than the other hospital—a common issue that occurs when firms merge. How did the proposed merger affect intergroup relations between the two hospitals? A merger between two previously independent organizations made employees' pre-merger group membership more salient, and the unequal status issues meant an accentuation of intergroup status differences. There was clear evidence of an ingroup ("we are better than they are") bias, particularly among the low-status employees. Why? Employees of the lower-status organization may have been particularly threatened by the merger situation and, therefore, more likely to engage in a high level of ingroup bias—a form of identity protection. High-status employees rated the ingroup far better than the low-status hospital on status-relevant dimensions (high prestige in the community, challenging job opportunities, and high variety in patient type). In contrast, the low-status employees engaged in greater ingroup bias on the status-irrelevant dimensions (degree of industrial unrest, good relations between staff, good communication by management, relaxed work environment, and modern patient accommodations). The question is: Why? High-status employees were motivated to acknowledge their position of relatively high status. In contrast, the low-status employees, motivated by a desire to attain positive social identity, focused on dimensions that did not highlight the status differential that existed between the hospitals. Indeed, low-status employees recognized the superior status of the high-status hospital, and high-status employees were especially generous when evaluating the low-status group on dimensions that are irrelevant to status. Yet the amount of ingroup bias that the low-status employees exhibited on the status-irrelevant dimensions exceeded the extent to which the high-status employees were willing to acknowledge the strengths of the low-status employees on these dimensions.

low-status groups that feel most negative about mergers—as based on studies of airline companies (Terry et al., 2001) and scientific organizations (Terry & O'Brien, 2001).

Not surprisingly, leaders play an important role in defining the relationship between the pre-merger groups. And, as might be expected, group members prefer an ingroup leader over an outgroup leader, and the ingroup leader will favor the ingroup (Duck & Fielding, 1999). However, members of high-status groups do not show preference for an ingroup leader (Jetten, Duck, Terry, & O'Brien, 2001). According to Jetten, Duck, Terry and O'Brien (2002), leaders have four choices when it comes to balancing ingroups and outgroups: They can treat both groups equally, they can favor the ingroup, they can favor the outgroup, or they can behave in a complementary fashion, by favoring one group over the other on particular dimensions. Ingroup leaders are evaluated more favorably and are more likely to engender a common identity in the merged group when they behave in an ingroup-favoring fashion or in a complementary fashion (Jetten et al., 2002).

## Intergroup Conflict

Just as there can be conflict among members within a team, there can be conflict and competition between different teams or groups. Broadly speaking, there are two types of conflict between teams: **realistic** and **symbolic** (Bobo, 1983).

*Realistic Conflict*

Realistic conflict is conflict that erupts when different teams compete over scarce resources. For example, teams in one company might compete over different assignments, clients, space (i.e., real estate), ability to hire new personnel, and so on. Realistic group conflict involves competition between groups for the same resources (e.g., teams that compete over new hires, office space, assignments, territory, information, contacts, and, of course, remuneration). Naturally, groups in organizations prefer to be the "haves" rather than the "have nots," so they take steps to achieve two interrelated outcomes by: (1) attaining the desired resources and (2) preventing other groups from reaching their goals (Campbell, 1965; LeVine & Campbell, 1972). As competition persists, teams perceive one another in increasingly negative ways, and competition often leads to direct and open conflict.

As another example of conflict, consider the conflict between Andersen Consulting (now Accenture) and Arthur Andersen (now facing criminal charges). Prior to the schism between the companies, each group felt justified in claiming a greater share of the profit stream. Andersen Consulting, the smaller of the two groups, was highly profitable and felt justified in demanding more resources. Arthur Andersen, the founding company, saw the situation quite differently, arguing that the opportunities Arthur Andersen provided (e.g., clients, infrastructure, etc.) entitled them to a greater share of profits. The two firms split in 2000 after a bitter court case.

*Symbolic Conflict*

Symbolic conflict is conflict that exists independent of resource scarcity; it reflects fundamental differences in values. Much conflict in organizations does not seem to have its roots in resource scarcity; rather, it stems from fundamental differences in values or beliefs (e.g., team members in sales think marketing is dumb). Symbolic conflict involves differences of beliefs. (For an example of symbolic conflict and its independence from economic interests, see Box 11-2.)

*Mixed-Motive Conflict*

Most conflicts, whether they are realistic or symbolic, represent mixed-motive conflicts, particularly when they occur between different groups in the organization. **Mixed-motive conflicts** involve a combination of cooperation and competition. Simply said, teams have a desire to cooperate because they all work for the same company but simultaneously feel they are in competition with other teams.

*Interteam Conflict versus Interpersonal Conflict*

Conflict between groups is usually more intense and exaggerated than conflict between people (Carnevale, Pruitt, & Seilheimmer, 1981; Insko et al., 1987; McCallum et al., 1985; van Oostrum & Rabbie, 1995). For example, when people play against each other in prisoner's-dilemma-type games, they are not particularly competitive in a one-on-one fashion, averaging only 6.6 percent competitive responses over the course of the game. However, when a group plays against another group, competition rises to 53.5 percent over all the moves (Insko et al., 1987). This suggests that even though most

---

**BOX 11-2**

### Symbolic Conflict and Busing

Sears and Allen (1984) examined a controversial issue—busing. Busing is a shorthand term meant to refer to the transportation of children in a city to different schools so as to achieve racial balance. Whereas traditionally, children attend schools based on their housing district, busing attempts to even out the racial mix. Obviously, parents of children who are being bused could claim to have economic interests—their children's welfare is clearly affected in their eyes. People who don't have children, however, would most likely not have any economic interest in busing. However, Sears and Allen found that people whose lives were not affected by busing made strong protests against it. Thus, they concluded that busing does not represent an economic issue but rather a symbolic issue.

---

people may prefer to cooperate when they are in teams, a competitive orientation takes over.

*Extremism*

Inevitably, conflicts occur between groups, teams, and factions. Groups on opposite sides of a conflict tend to see the opposing side as being extremist. Members of teams exaggerate the degree of conflict they actually have with other teams and groups—opposing groups typically assume that the difference between the two sides' attitudes is 1.5 to 4 times greater than the actual difference. This means, of course, that escalation of interteam conflict is often more illusion than reality. As an example, consider the Western Canon debate—a factious dispute over the choice of books in introductory civilization and literature courses that has divided faculty and students within many universities, such as Stanford, Michigan, and Berkeley. There are two sides in the debate: traditionalists and revisionists. Traditionalists advocate preserving the prominence of the traditional canon; revisionists advocate teaching more works by female and minority authors.

To measure the degree of conflict between traditionalists and revisionists, English teachers in California were asked to select 15 books from a list of 50 for their own course and to indicate which books they believed the "other side" would want. Traditionalists predicted that they would have no books in common. In actuality, traditionalists and revisionists had almost 50 percent—or seven books—in common! (Robinson & Keltner, 1996).

Careful inspection of group members' perceptions, however, reveals a striking asymmetry in the accuracy of misperception: The status quo, or the group in power, is much less accurate than is a group that is not in power. Traditionalists predicted no overlap in book choices, whereas revisionists predicted a six-book overlap. Why is this?

Majority group members typically enjoy benefits of greater power. They are prone to exaggerate the views of their own and the other side. Minority group members are perceived by both sides to be more extremist than majority group members. For example, high-status social group members judge the personality and emotions of other members less accurately than do low-status group members (Gruenfeld, Keltner, & Anderson, 2003). In contrast, high-status members' emotions are more accurately judged by both low- and high-status members.

# WHEN AND WHY CONFLICT IS GOOD

We elaborated on the benefits of healthy, intellectual conflict in Chapter 7. Whereas intergroup or interteam conflict is usually more exaggerated and virulent than is interpersonal conflict, it can have some advantages. For example, with regard to leadership, people are more satisfied when conflict occurs at a superordinate level (i.e., involving the entire group) rather than at the intragroup level (involving competition between different subgroups within the team; Duck & Fielding, 1999).

## Cohesion

We noted in Chapters 2 and 4 that cohesion in groups is a positive quality. Interestingly, it is often the presence of an outside threat that can lead to greater feelings of cohesion and homogeneity within a group. For example, when group members believed that a team from a rival institution was biased against them, the members of the group saw themselves as being more similar than different—an important ingredient for cohesion (Rothgerber, 1997). Indeed, when a person's social identity is threatened, people will act to reduce the threat and restore a positive and distinct social identity (Tajfel & Turner, 1986). This cuts both ways, in terms of internal threat decreasing cohesion. For example, when group members believe that other team members think negatively of the team, they see the group members as dissimilar from one another (Doosje, Spears, & Koomen, 1995). Even thinking negative thoughts about one's own team leads to feelings of dissimilarity from the team. For example, when German team members were asked to list negative (as compared with positive) attributes of their group, they described themselves as being less similar to the team as a whole (Simon, Pantaleo, & Mummendey, 1995).

## How and Why Organizations Benefit from Minority Viewpoints

First, when we refer to a *minority viewpoint* we are not describing the views held by a demographic minority; rather, we are referring to the presence of a statistical minority. (However, the two may be correlated.) On the surface, it would appear that those who hold an opinion or view that is different from that of the rest of the team or organization are deviants or troublemakers. However, the mere presence of a minority opinion has beneficial effects in terms of propelling others to make sounder judgments and cause the team to have better discussions. Minority opinions can arise from one of two sources—from a member of one's own team (an ingroup member) or a member of another group (an outgroup member). Both can be effective; however, a minority opinion offered by an ingroup member is often more influential (David & Turner, 1996). Yet, people in an ingroup may be particularly unlikely to offer a different viewpoint because of the strong pressure to conform (see Chapter 6) and not express views that effectively threaten the group (Phillips, 2003). Indeed, when two people on the same team disagree with one another, there is more uncertainty, greater stress and anxiety, and more concern about social relationships (Moscovici, 1985a, 1985b). In short, people on the team may want to repair the relationships, rather than discuss the issues. Indeed, disagreement with outgroup members is more tolerable than disagreement with ingroup members (Phillips, 2003). Perhaps this is why ingroup minorities use the phrases "I don't know" and "I'm not sure" much more often when expressing a different view than do outgroup members (Phillips, 2003).

Intensive examinations of teams reveal that members in the majority exhibit greater integrative complexity than do members in the minority (Gruenfeld, 1995). For example, consider opinions rendered by the U.S. Supreme Court (Gruenfeld, 1995). The authors of majority opinions tend to concern themselves with specifying all imaginable contingencies under which the law should and should not apply to ensure the longevity of their precedent. In contrast, the authors of minority opinions often focus on arguments that could eventually facilitate the precedent's overruling. This suggests that people who are exposed to members who hold a majority view experience an increase in their own levels of integrative thought; in contrast, people exposed to minority opinions or unanimous groups actually experience a decrease in integrative thinking (Gruenfeld, Thomas-Hunt, & Kim, 1998).

## BIASES ASSOCIATED WITH INTERGROUP CONFLICT

Groups that are embroiled in interteam conflict do not always look at their situations objectively. In fact, they sometimes suffer from serious biases or misassumptions. Bias and prejudice are common in organizations and adversely affect the ability of teams and their organizations to accomplish their goals. Below are biases that should be identified and dealt with.

### Categorization: Us versus Them

Even when natural categories and teams don't exist in an organization, people will create them. The tendency to create ingroups and outgroups is known as the "need for categorization." In fact, from the first few microseconds of perception, people begin the categorization process. That means that when we meet a person for the first time, we immediately (and unconsciously) classify them according to gender, race, age, and so forth. Whereas this may seem harmless (as well as natural), it essentially means that we rely on stereotypes to guide our impression of someone. Consequently, we see others as conforming more to stereotypes than they actually do. Furthermore, even when given an opportunity to consider stereotypical and nonstereotypical information about someone, we preferentially attend to stereotype-confirming rather than disconfirming information. Additionally, when we can question a person directly, we usually seek to confirm our stereotypical beliefs (Snyder, 1984).

To see how readily people categorize others, consider the following investigations:

- *Case 1:* In a room of adults who do not know one another, a box is passed around containing two kinds of cards in it: One labeled "alphas," the other labeled "betas." Each person randomly draws a card from the box. Two groups are formed on the basis of an obviously arbitrary procedure. Members of each do not speak or communicate in any form with the members of the other group, nor do they talk among themselves. They are a group in name only. Nevertheless, in a subsequent evaluation period, members of each group rate the members of their own group as superior on a number of dimensions relative to members of the other group (Brewer, 1979; Tajfel, 1982; Tajfel & Turner, 1986).

- *Case 2:* In a room of adults who do not know one another, each person is presented with a page containing several dots and then asked to make an estimate of the total number of dots on the page. Two groups are then formed: those who allegedly underestimate the actual number of dots on the page and those who overestimate the dots (Bettencourt, Brewer, Croak, & Miller, 1992). When group members are subsequently asked to evaluate the competence, intelligence, creativity, and personal qualities of both groups, they favor their own group—even though they have not communicated with the other members of their group and dot estimation is nondiagnostic.
- *Case 3:* In simulated negotiations between Stanford and Cornell MBA students, each group awards the other significantly fewer stock options when given the opportunity (Thompson, Valley, & Kramer, 1995). Furthermore, group members reject options that would pay both teams extremely well; instead, team members seemed more intent on creating large payment differences, rather than maximizing their own welfare.

In all the preceding examples, when people categorize the world into two or more groups and then face the task of evaluating or judging these groups, they uniformly favor their own group. Ingroup bias, or the favorable treatment of one's own group and the subsequent harming of other groups, is rooted in feelings of threat. Specifically, when people or teams feel threatened by the presence or performance of another group, they are likely to show bias (Flippen, Hornstein, Siegal, & Weitzman, 1996).

There are a number of consequences of categorization. First the benefits: Categorization can clearly help groups achieve their goals and protect their interests. For example, in the competitive business of new product development, teams need to know who they are talking to. Second, categorizing people simply makes life easier because we can take their point of view. Thus, there are some clear benefits of categorization. However, there are some downsides that teams need to know about: First, we evaluate members of outgroups much more extremely. For example, in one investigation, 30 ethnic groups in Kenya, Uganda, and Tanzania rated one another on several evaluative dimensions. Overall, ratings of perceived "outgroups" tended to be more polarized—or extreme—than ratings of one's own group (see Brewer, 1986). Second, we use stereotypes to predict people's behavior.

## Ingroup Bias (or "We Are Better than Them")

People don't just segment the world into ingroup and outgroup members. Once they categorize others, they view members of their own group more favorably than members of the outgroup. The ingroup bias effect is so strong that members of groups systematically judge their group members to be better than the group average and above the median on a variety of social traits, even when all the members are judged consecutively! (Klar, 2002). When this occurs at a group level, it is called **ingroup bias;** when it occurs at the level of nations, regions, or ethic categories, it is called **ethnocentrism** (Sumner, 1906). Ingroup bias—the universal strong liking for one's own group and the simultaneous negative evaluation of outgroups—generates a set of stereotypes in which each group sees itself as good and the outgroup as bad, even when both groups engage in the same behaviors (Hastorf & Cantril, 1954). For example, the beliefs that "we are loyal; they are clannish" or "we are brave and willing to defend our rights; they are hostile and arrogant" are examples of the double standards that can often arise. In- and outgroup distinctions have implications for leadership as well. For example, when a leader is aligned with a perceived outgroup, people expect that leader to favor the outgroup (even if she actually does not; Duck & Fielding, 1999).

For example, in one investigation, teams were involved in an engaging task (making art posters; Moreland & McMinn, 1999). The teams then underwent various reorganizations in which new members were added or deleted from the same source group (ingroup exchange) or from a different source group (outgroup exchange). Posters were then evaluated for quality. Posters were evaluated much more generously when ingroup, rather than outgroup, reorganizations occurred, especially when team members identified strongly with their source group. Whereas every group received a (bogus) identical negative evaluation of its poster, the bogus criticism was more upsetting when ingroup rather than outgroup exchanges were made.

### Racism and Racial Discrimination

In his dissenting opinion in the *Wards Cove Packing Company* v. *Atonio* Supreme Court decision (1989), Justice Harry Blackmun stated, "[O]ne wonders whether the majority still believes that race discrimination—or more accurately, race discrimination against nonwhites—is a problem in our society, or even remembers that it ever was" (p. 2133–2136). To investigate the extent of race-based discrimination in hiring, the Urban Institute in Washington, D.C., selected and trained minority and majority group testers. Testers, matched on age, gender, physical strength and size, appearance, education, experience, demeanor, openness, observed energy level, and articulateness—all possible characteristics except for race (Turner, Fix, & Struyk, 1991)—applied for the same advertised low-skill, entry-level jobs. Four hundred and seventy-six audits conducted by 10 pairs of testers (one African-American and one Caucasian-American male) revealed clear differences in treatment by minority and majority job seekers. In 20 percent of the audits, Caucasians progressed further in the hiring process than their equally qualified African-American testing partners; and in 15 percent of the audits, the Caucasian received a job offer but his African-American counterpart did not. These findings suggest that Caucasian males continue to receive favorable treatment in the hiring process three times more frequently than their equally qualified African-American male counterparts (Turner et al., 1991). Moreover, government data agree with these field results: In 2001 alone, the Office of Federal Contract Compliance Programs obtained settlements worth nearly $30M, including back pay for nearly 7,000 victims of discrimination (U.S. Department of Labor, 2001c). Full-time working men in the United States earn 24 percent more than women, and the earnings of Caucasians exceeds that of African-Americans by 19 percent (U.S. Department of Labor, 2001b). Obviously, these statistics suggest that gender and racial discrimination continue to be a problem, and should be addressed.

### Denial

"In 1956, if a male coworker offered a female colleague a 'courtly' compliment on her appearance ('you sure look pretty today'), it would have been unlikely to be viewed as a demeaning or a discriminating action, and indeed, may well have been received with pleasure" (Inman & Baron, 1996, p. 727). However, nearly 50 years later, this same comment would not only be perceived as offensive and condescending, but it also might well put the perpetrator out of a job. In short, as our norms and awareness of roles and power change, so do our definitions of prejudice and discrimination. Noticing and correctly categorizing prejudice and discrimination is key in changing behavior.

Although evidence clearly indicates that the problems of racism, stereotyping, and discrimination are neither small, isolated, or problems of the past, many people do not believe they exist. In general, only the victims (and likely targets) of prejudice are more apt to perceive it. For example, women are more likely than men to perceive sexism and racism; moreover, African-Americans are more likely than Caucasians to perceive racism (Inman & Baron, 1996). This denial—the belief that "I have not seen it"—is an act of discrimination itself. One reason that people often don't see it is that the opposite of discrimination—privilege—is invisible (Rosette, 2003).

Yet the perception of discrimination is different than blaming one's lot on discrimination. Members of high-status groups are more likely than members of low-status groups to blame their failure on discrimination, and are less likely to blame it on themselves (Ruggiero & Marx, 1999). It is reasoned that Caucasian-Americans perceive less of a threat in the face of failure if they blame discrimination processes.

## "They All Look Alike": The Outgroup Homogeneity Bias

One unfortunate by-product of social categorization is the tendency to view outgroup members as interchangeable, faceless, stereotypical caricatures. For example, suppose that white managers watch a videotape of a discussion among members of a mixed-race group: three African-American men and three Caucasian men. After watching the videotape, the managers are presented with the actual text of the conversation and are asked to indicate who said what. They are told they will be evaluated based upon the accuracy of their memory. They are accurate at remembering whether a black or white person made a particular comment, and are fairly accurate in distinguishing among the three white males' comments, but their accuracy in terms of differentiating which African-American male said what is abysmal (Linville, Fischer, & Salovey, 1989). Thus, within-race errors are more prevalent than between-race errors, because people categorize members of outgroups not as individuals, but simply as "black men."

The faulty memory of the manager illustrates a pervasive tendency for people to assume much greater homogeneity of opinion, belief, expression, and interest among members of the outgroup than among members of their own group (Judd & Park, 1988; Katz & Braly, 1933; Park & Rothbart, 1982). This is another way of saying that most people believe that members of their own group are individuals and, consequently, should be evaluated upon their own merits, whereas members of outgroups are mere clones of one another, with no distinct identity.

The managerial implications of the "they all look alike" effect are very serious. Consider, for example, a police lineup in which a victim is asked to identify an assailant. A white victim is more likely to falsely identify a black perpetrator than a white one (Knight-Ridder Newspapers, 1991). Consider, also, the implications of a mixed-sex task force in a corporation. Moreover, when we fail to individuate members of other groups, we are more likely to behave in a punitive fashion (Rothgerber & Worchel, 1997). For example, Nazi guards behaved more leniently toward Jews who were individuated (i.e., the guards knew their names) than those who were deindividuated (Zimbardo, 1969).

# STRATEGIES FOR REDUCING NEGATIVE EFFECTS OF INTERGROUP CONFLICT

We have made the point that intergroup conflict, whether it occurs between groups that must deal with each other (such as with the case of different functional divisions, e.g., sales and marketing), or between groups that have undergone a merger, may lead to negative effects, often seriously hindering individual, group, and organizational effectiveness. It is a leader's job to deal effectively with these issues. Once intergroup hostility becomes established, it is no simple matter to reduce it. Some good faith efforts may even backfire. This section considers a number of strategies to effectively deal with the negative component of intergroup competition.

## Contact

The "mere contact" strategy is based on the principle that greater contact among members of different groups increases cooperation between group members. Unfortunately, contact in and of itself does not lead to better intergroup relations, and in some cases may even exacerbate negative relations between groups. For example, contact between African-Americans and Caucasians in desegregated schools does not reduce racial prejudice (Gerard, 1983; Schofield, 1986); there is little relationship between interdepartmental contact and conflict in organizations (Brown, Condor, Mathew, Wade, & Williams, 1986); and college students studying in foreign countries become increasingly negative toward their host countries the longer they remain in them (Stroebe, Lenkert, & Jonas, 1988).

Several conditions need to be in place before contact can have its desired effects of reducing prejudice:

- *Social and institutional support:* For contact to work, there should be a framework of social and institutional support. That is, people in positions of authority should be unambiguous in their endorsement of the goals of the integration policies. This fosters the development of a new social climate in which more tolerant norms can emerge.

- *Acquaintance potential:* A second condition for successful contact is that it be of sufficient frequency, duration, and closeness to permit the development of meaningful relationships between members of the groups concerned. Infrequent, short, and casual interaction will do little to foster more favorable attitudes and may even make them worse (Brewer & Brown, 1998). One of the keys to successful contact is self-disclosure, or the revealing of personal information about oneself (Ensari & Miller, 2002). This type of close interaction will lead to the discovery of similarities and disconfirm negative stereotypes.

- *Equal status:* The third condition necessary for contact to be successful is that participants have equal status. Many stereotypes of outgroups comprise beliefs about the inferior ability of outgroup members to perform various tasks. If the contact situation involves an unequal-status relationship between men and women, for example, with women in the subordinate role (e.g., taking notes, acting as secretaries), stereotypes are likely to be reinforced rather than weakened (Bradford & Cohen, 1984). If, however, the group members work on equal footing, prejudiced beliefs become hard to sustain in the face of repeated experience of task competence by the outgroup member.

- *Shared goal:* When members of different groups depend on each other for the achievement of a jointly desired objective, they have instrumental reasons to develop better relationships. The importance of an overriding, clear, shared group goal is a key determinant of intergroup relations. Sometimes a common enemy is a catalyst for bonding among diverse people and groups. For example, by "waging a war against cancer," members of different medical groups and laboratories can work together.

- *Cross-group friendships:* Sometimes it is not necessary for groups to have real contact with one another to improve intergroup relations. If group members know that another member of their own group has a friendship or relationship with a member of the outgroup, or a cross-group friendship, ingroup members have less negative attitudes toward the outgroup (Wright, Aron, McLaughlin-Volpe, & Ropp, 1997). It is not necessary that all members of a group have cross-group friendships; merely knowing that one member of the group does can go a long way toward reducing negative outgroup attitudes. For example, when team members are given cross-cut role assignments to other groups, this decreases bias not only of dominant, ingroup members but also of the minority, outgroup members (Bettencourt & Dorr, 1998). Moreover, members of groups don't even have to have prior interaction.

The contact hypothesis has received support in groups ranging from students at a multiethnic high school to banking executives involved in corporate mergers (Gaertner, Dovidio, & Bachman, 1996). The key appears to be that contact helps the people involved to develop a common shared identity. For example, when groups composed of Democrat and Republican party supporters are brought into a situation that involves a common fate and intergroup interaction, bias is reduced, even when measured in terms of the pleasantness of nonverbal facial reactions (Gaertner et al., 1999). It also helps for people to focus on their "emotions" rather than their "thoughts" when they think about interteam relations. People who focus on their emotions are more willing to interact with other groups (Esses & Dovidio, 2002). The opening example of Anthro Technology Furniture's shadow program is a clear application of contact (Layne, 2000). The Shadow Program boasts four distinct benefits: (1) bolstering empathy and cooperation among departments, (2) exposing company leaders to a variety of thought processes and perspectives, (3) allowing employees to investigate new positions within the company, and (4) forcing employees to articulate and explain their motivations, procedures, and thought processes so as to enact change.

### Cross-cut Role Assignmnents

When numerical representations of different groups are markedly different, cooperation alone is not sufficient for intergroup interaction (Rogers, Hennigan, Bowman, & Miller, 1984). In fact, being in a numerical minority prevents members' attitudes from benefitting from cooperative interaction (Bettencourt, Charlton, & Kernahan, 1997). Cross-cut role assignments are situations in which people are simultaneously members of more than one task group or team. Cross-cut role assignments decrease ingroup bias of both minority and majority groups (Bettencourt & Dorr, 1998).

## CONCLUSIONS

In this chapter we've made the point that it is natural and normal for people to identify with their teams and that conflict and competition between groups is a natural consequence of the process of establishing our social identity. We examined the positive consequences of interteam conflict, in terms of enhancing cohesion and stimulating creativity. We also looked at the dark side of interteam competition and the biased perceptions that can prevail. Leaders who witness their teams engaging in interteam competition should congratulate themselves—as this is an indication that the individuals in the team have identified strongly with their team. On the other hand, effective team leaders need to address the potential negative aspects of interteam conflict that may occur.

# 12
# Teamwork via Information Technology:

## *Challenges and Opportunities*

*On September 23, 1999, the Mars Climate Orbiter fired its main engine to go into orbit around the planet. All the information coming from the spacecraft leading up to that point looked normal. The engine burn began as planned, five minutes before the space-craft passed behind the planet as seen from Earth. However, flight controllers did not detect a signal when the spacecraft was expected to come out from behind the planet. "We had planned to approach the planet at an altitude of about 150 kilometers (93 miles)," said Richard Cook, a project manager for the Mars Surveyor Operations Project at NASA's Jet Propulsion Laboratory. "We thought we were doing that, but upon review of the last six to eight hours of data leading up to arrival, we saw indications that the actual approach altitude had been much lower. It appears that the actual altitude was about 60 kilometers (37 miles)" (Media Relations Office, NASA Jet Propulsion Laboratory, 1999). The spacecraft was over 56 miles off course and was ultimately lost in space—an avoidable human error that cost hundreds of millions of dollars. The key problem con-cerned a "failed translation of English units into metric units"—one team used English units (e.g., inches, feet, and pounds); the other used metric units for a key spacecraft oper-ation. The failure investigation board concluded the following: there were inconsistent communications, the operational navigation team was not fully informed on details, the communication channels were too informal, and the verification and validation process inadequate (Isbell, Hardin, & Underwood, 1999; Isbell & Savage, 1999).*

The failure of the Mars Climate Orbiter typifies the challenges of global team-work—failure to communicate despite the best of intentions and a passionately shared goal. In the rush to go global, corporations are requiring their managers to be effective across distances and cultures never before mastered. Teams of managers armed with laptop computers, fax modems, e-mail, voice mail, videoconferencing, inter-active databases, and frequent-flyer memberships are being charged with conducting business in the global arena. Virtual teams are expected to efficiently harness the knowl-edge of company employees regardless of their location, thereby enabling the company to respond faster to increased competition. The power of information technology is in bringing together teams of people who would otherwise not be able to interact. As we saw in our analysis of electronic brainstorming, information technology offers the potential for improving information access and information-processing capability.

Furthermore, information technology, in transcending time and place, offers the potential for members to participate without regard to temporal and spatial impediments.

However, as the Mars Climate Orbiter example illustrates, not all virtual teamwork proceeds seamlessly. Managers responsible for leading virtual teams have found that distance is a formidable obstacle, despite electronic media and jet travel. A decision made in one country is interpreted with reference to one's own cultural norms and standards or perhaps elicits an unexpected reaction from team members in another country. Remote offices fight for influence with the head office. Telephone conferences find distant members struggling to get onto the same page, literally and figuratively, in terms of shared viewpoint or strategy. Conflicts escalate strangely between distributed groups. Group members at sites separated by even a few kilometers begin to talk in the language of "us" and "them" (Armstrong & Cole, 1995). Thus, there is considerable debate among managers as to whether technology fosters or hinders teamwork in the workplace at the global, and even local, level.

This chapter examines the impact of information technology on teamwork at the global and local levels. We begin by describing a simple model of social interaction called the place-time model. This model will give us a framework through which we can evaluate the various forms of information technology and how they apply to team interaction. The model focuses on teams whose members either work in the same or a different physical *location* and at the same or a different *time*. For each of these cases, we describe what to expect and ways to deal with the limitations of that communication mode. Then, we move to a discussion of virtual teams, making the point that whenever teams must work together in a non-face-to-face fashion, this constitutes a virtual team. We describe strategies to help virtual teams do their work better. We then discuss transnational teams; we describe what transnational teams do and what it takes to get there. Obviously, transnational teams and global teamwork involve the diversity issues that we dealt with in Chapter 4. We follow this discussion with a section on how information technology affects human behavior. We do not attempt to provide a state-of-the-art review on types of information technology (which would be foolish to do in a book); our purpose is to identify the considerations that managers must wrestle with when attempting to bring together groups of people who are not in the same place.

## PLACE-TIME MODEL OF SOCIAL INTERACTION

The **place-time model** is based on the options that teams have when working across different locations and times. It is useful to conceptualize teams in terms of their geographic location (together versus separated) and in terms of their temporal relation-

**TABLE 12-1** Place-Time Model of Interaction

|  | **Same Place** | **Different Place** |
|---|---|---|
| *Same Time* | Face-to-face | Telephone Videoconference |
| *Different Time* | Single text editing Shift work | E-mail Voice mail |

*Source:* Thompson, L. 2001. *The Mind and Heart of the Negotiator* (2nd edition). Upper Saddle River, NJ: Prentice Hall.

ship (interacting in real time versus asynchronously). For any team meeting, there are four possibilities as depicted in the place-time model in Table 12-1. As might be suspected, communication and teamwork unfold differently face-to-face than they do via electronic media.

**Richness** is the potential information-carrying capacity of the communications medium. Communication media may be ordered on a continuum of richness, with face-to-face communication being at the relatively "rich" end, and formal written messages, such as memos, being at the relatively "lean" or modality-constricted end (Daft & Lengel, 1984; Daft, Lengel, & Trevino, 1987; see Figure 12-1). Face-to-face communication conveys the richest information because it allows the simultaneous observation of multiple cues, including body language, facial expression, and tone of voice, providing people with a greater awareness of context. In contrast, formal, numerical documentation conveys the least rich information, providing few clues about the context. Depending on the space and time relationships that characterize a team, groups are often constrained in their choice of communication medium.

Let's consider each of the four types of communication in the place-time model.

## Face-to-Face Communication

Face-to-face interaction is the clear preference of most managers and executives and rightly so. Face-to-face contact is crucial in the initiation of relationships and collaborations, and people are more cooperative when interacting face-to-face than via other forms of communication. Personal, face-to-face contact is the lubricant of the business engine. Without it, things don't move very well and relationships between businesspersons are often strained and contentious.

Face-to-face meetings are ideal when teams must wrestle with complex problems. For example, researchers need regular face-to-face contact to be confident that they accurately understand each other's work, particularly if it involves innovative ideas.

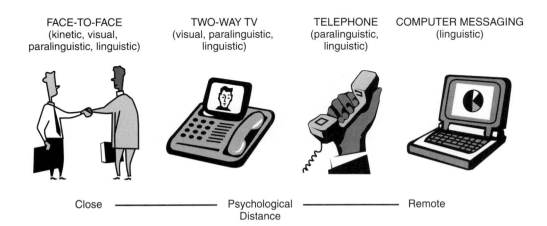

| FACE-TO-FACE (kinetic, visual, paralinguistic, linguistic) | TWO-WAY TV (visual, paralinguistic, linguistic) | TELEPHONE (paralinguistic, linguistic) | COMPUTER MESSAGING (linguistic) |

Close ——————— Psychological ——————— Remote
Distance

**FIGURE 12-1** Psychological Distancing Model
*Source:* Adapted from Wellens, A. R. 1989, September. "Effects of Telecommunication Media upon Information Sharing and Team Performance: Some Theoretical and Empirical Findings." *IEEE AES Magazine,* 14.

The half-life of confidence decays over time as researchers communicate through telephone and computer conferences; face-to-face contact is required to renew trust in their mutual comprehension (DeMeyer, 1991, 1993). Face-to-face team meetings are particularly important when a group forms, when commitments to key decisions are needed, and when major conflicts among members must be resolved (DeMeyer, 1991; Galegher, Kraut, & Egido, 1990; Sproull & Keisler, 1991). Work groups form more slowly, and perhaps never fully, when they don't have face-to-face contact (DeMeyer, 1991; Galegher et al., 1990).

In most companies, the incidence and frequency of face-to-face communication is almost perfectly predicted by how closely people are located to one another: Employees who work in the same office or on the same floor communicate much more frequently than those located on different floors or in different buildings. The incidence of communication literally comes down to feet—even a few steps can have a huge impact. For example, communication frequency between R&D researchers drops off logarithmically after only 5 to 10 meters of distance between offices (Allen, 1977). In a study of molecular biologists, MacKenzie, Cambrosio, and Keating (1988) found that critical techniques for producing monoclonal antibodies were not reported in journals, but were passed from scientist to scientist at the lab bench. And people in adjacent offices communicate twice as often as those in offices on the same floor, including via e-mail and telephone transmissions (Galegher et al., 1990).

Just what cues do people get out of face-to-face contact that makes it so important for interaction and productivity? Primarily, two things: First, *face-to-face communication is easier and, therefore, more likely to occur* than are other forms of communication. Simply stated, most people need a reason to walk up the stairs or to make a phone call. They underestimate how much information they get from chance encounters, which never happen in any mode but face-to-face because of this perceived effort. Second, although it is seldom consciously realized, *people primarily rely on nonverbal signals to help them conduct social interactions.* One estimate is that 93 percent of the meaning of messages is contained in the nonverbal part of communication, such as voice intonation (Meherabian, 1971). Perhaps this is why business executives endure the inconveniences of travel across thousands of miles and several time zones so that they can have face-to-face contact with others, even if it is only for a short period of time. (See Sidebar 12-1 for an example of the importance of face-to-face communication.)

The emphasis on the human factor is not just old-fashioned business superstition. Important behavioral, cognitive, and emotional processes are set into motion when people meet face-to-face. However, unless people are specially trained, they don't know what exactly it is about face-to-face interaction that facilitates teamwork—they just know that things go smoother.

Face-to-face interaction allows people to develop rapport—the feeling of being "in sync" or "on the same wavelength" with another person. Whether people feel rapport is a powerful determinant of whether they develop trust. The degree of rapport determines the efficiency and the quality of progress toward goal achievement, and whether the goal is ever achieved (Tickle-Degnen & Rosenthal, 1987).

Nonverbal (body orientation, gesture, eye contact, head-nodding) and paraverbal behavior (speech fluency, use of "uh-huhs," etc.) is the key to building rapport. When the person we are interacting with sits at a greater distance, with an indirect body orientation, backward lean, crossed arms, and low eye contact, we feel less rapport than

---

**Sidebar 12-1. The Importance of Face-to-Face Communication**

A group of top managers at a progressive Silicon Valley company hated their weekly meetings, but enjoyed e-mail because it is quick, direct, and to the point. They thought meetings were "gassy, bloated, and a waste of time." So they decided to cancel their regular meetings and meet only when confronted with problems just too tough to handle over the network. Three months later, the same people resumed their regularly scheduled face-to-face meetings. They discovered that they had created a "morale-busting, network-generated nightmare." When the managers did get together, the meetings were unpleasant and unproductive. Precisely because they could use e-mail to reach consensus on easy issues, arguing the thorny issues face-to-face turned their "big problem" meetings into combat zones. E-mail interaction had eliminated the opportunity for casual agreement and social niceties that make meetings enjoyable. Even the e-mail communication became more hostile as participants maneuvered themselves in anticipation of the big-problem meetings (Schrage, 1995).

---

when the same person sits with a forward lean, an open body posture, nods, and maintains steady eye contact. These nonverbal and paraverbal cues affect the way people work and the quality of their work as a team.

However, face-to-face communication is not the best modality for all teamwork. As a clear case in point, we saw in our discussion of creativity and brainstorming (Chapter 8) that face-to-face brainstorming is less productive compared with other, less rich forms of interaction.

### Same Time, Different Place

The same-time, different-place mode, in which people communicate in real time but are not physically in the same place, is often the alternative to face-to-face teamwork. The most common means is via telephone; videoconferencing is another example. Team members often rely on the telephone, but they do not always reach their party; up to 70 percent of initial telephone attempts fail to reach the intended party (Philip & Young, 1987). In telephone conversations, people lack facial cues; in videoconferencing, they lack real-time social cues, such as pauses, mutual gaze, and another person's immediate nonverbal response to what is being said (e.g., looking away or down). Yet at the same time, electronic interaction, such as in brainstorming groups, can greatly increase team productivity.

When technology tries to replace the dynamics of face-to-face interaction, it often falls short. The technology designed to make groups feel as though they are face-to-face does not lead to more and better communication. As a case in point, consider an engineering work group, located in two offices 1,000 kilometers apart, that experimented with an omnipresent video wall and cameras in all offices to link the sites together (Abel, 1990). Generally, the engineers interacted across the distance as one cohesive group, but there were some key exceptions: Video links were not very effective in generating new relationships or in resolving divisive differences, and miscommunication was treated as rudeness. Members of a design team were unable to listen to each other's ideas until they met face-to-face for three days, where they reached effective consensus. In a direct comparison of FtF (face-to-face) versus computer-mediated (CM) groups, group identity (i.e., cohesion and "we-feeling") was consistently lower in CM groups, especially when CM groups underwent membership change (i.e., reorganization; Bouas & Arrow, 1996).

What are the major ways in which group members who are physically distant from one another suffer because of their physical separation? There are several effects of physical separation of the team, some of which might not be immediately obvious (Armstrong & Cole, 1995).

### *Loss of Informal Communication*

Probably the most-felt impact is the inability to chat informally in the hall, inside offices, and so on. The impromptu and casual conversations that employees have by the water cooler and the coffee machine are often where the most difficult problems are solved, and the most important interpersonal issues are addressed. Beyond a very short distance, people miss the spontaneous exchanges that occur outside of formal meetings. Remote group members feel cut off from key conversations that occur over lunch and in the hall. Vince Anderson, director of environmental programs for Whirlpool Corp.'s North American Appliance Group in Evansville, Indiana, oversaw a two-year project using a virtual team that developed a chlorofluorocarbon-free refrigerator, involving the United States, Brazil, and Italy. The team met approximately every four months to discuss the project and it was these informal meetings—a backyard cookout and a volleyball game—that were the most valuable for the project (Geber, 1995).

### *Separation of Feedback*

Another negative impact of physical separation is feedback; greater distance tends to block the corrective feedback loops provided by chance encounters. One manager contrasted how employees who worked in his home office related to his decisions, compared with employees 15 kilometers away (Armstrong & Cole, 1995). Engineers in the home office would drop by and catch him in the hall or at lunch. "I heard you were planning to change project $X$," they would say. "Let me tell you why that would be stupid." The manager would listen to their points, clarify some details, and all would part better informed. In contrast, employees at the remote site would greet his weekly visits with formally prepared group objections, which took much longer to discuss and were rarely resolved as completely as the more informal hallway discussions. In short, groups working remotely do not get the coincidental chances to detect and correct problems on a casual basis. Managers tend to think of their home group as the people they sit beside at work. Geographic sites promote an informal, spontaneous group identity, reinforced by close physical proximity and the dense communication it promotes. Those working in an office all tend to have friends in nearby companies or groups, hear the same industry rumors, and share similar beliefs about technological trends. Thus, any distance—whether it be 15 miles or 15,000 miles—is problematic in this regard.

### *Loss of Informal Modeling*

Another impact is the loss of informal modeling and observational learning. Distance tends to block casual observation, which is often invaluable to monitoring and mentoring performance, especially for one-on-one team coaching. The inability of remote employees to watch successful project managers enact their roles, along with the inability to observe the learned employee, is a barrier to effective coaching of task and interpersonal-related skills.

### Out-of-the-Loop Employees

Another problem is that distant employees tend to be left out of discussions or forgotten. In a sense, they are "out of sight, out of mind." The default behavior is to ignore the person on the speakerphone. This is especially magnified when the person or group with less status is on the phone.

Time differences amplify the effects of physical distance. Distributed group members face the challenge of finding each other at the same time while they are living in different time zones. Furthermore, time differences sometimes highlight cultural differences. However, teams can try to overcome these cultural barriers. One group based in the United States and in Italy celebrated a project milestone in their weekly videoconference by sharing foods on the video screen and fax. The East Coast U.S. team, at 9 A.M., sent images of bagels and coffee. The Italian team, at 3 P.M. in their time zone, sent images of champagne and cookies.

Conflicts are expressed, recognized, and addressed more quickly if group members work in close proximity. A manager can spot a problem, "nip it in the bud," and solve the problem quickly. In geographically separated groups, the issues are more likely to just get dropped and go unresolved, contributing to a slow buildup in aggravation. People complain to their coworkers, reinforcing local perceptions of events, but do not complain to the distant leaders until feelings reach extremely high levels.

Although there are many disadvantages of distance, it is not always a liability for teams. The formality of a scheduled phone meeting can compel each party to better prepare for the meeting and to address the issues more efficiently. In addition, distance can reduce micromanagement. Some managers hinder their employees' performance by monitoring them too closely and demanding frequent updates. Distance can mitigate this problem. Most notably, groups can often be much more creative when interacting via information technology.

## Different Time, Same Place

In the different-time, same-place mode, team members interact asynchronously, but share the same work space. An example might be shift workers who pick up the task left for them by the previous shift or collaborators working on the same electronic document. After one partner finishes working on the document, it goes to the other partner, who will further edit and develop it.

Although people may not realize it, they rely a lot on their physical environments for important information and cues. Remember the concept of transactive memory systems that we introduced in Chapter 5: People often supplement their own memories and information-processing systems—which are fallible—with systems located in the environment. We discussed at length in Chapter 5 how people use other team members as information storage, retrieval, and processing devices. The same is true for the physical environment. A Post-it note on the back of a chair, or a report placed in a certain bin can symbolize an entire procedural system (e.g., how to make a long-distance conference call). Just as people become information dependent on other people, they also can become information dependent upon aspects of the physical environment in order to do their work. At the extreme, this type of dependence can be a limitation for groups that find it impossible to work outside the idiosyncratic confines of their workspace. Information and workspace dependence can negatively affect the productivity and motivation of a team.

The productivity of any team, and organizational effectiveness in general, is a joint function of the technical and the social system (Emery & Trist, 1973). The structure of a group, both internally and externally, and the technology the group works with are products of an active adaptation process, in which the technology is shaped by the organization or its subunits, as well as being a factor in shaping the organization. For example, consider the introduction of a new technology, CT scanners, in two hospitals (Barley, 1996). The introduction of the CT scanners increased uncertainty and upset the distribution of expertise and the division of labor in the hospital units. Both hospital units became more decentralized with the introduction of the CT scanners and the associated increase in uncertainty.

## Different Place, Different Time

In the different-place, different-time model, interactants communicate asynchronously in different places. The most pervasive means is e-mail. Asynchronous, distributed communication seems to be growing at a faster rate of popularity than are other forms of communication, such as the telephone and videoconferencing. The telephone has been around for 120 years, but less than half of the people on the planet have ever made a phone call. In contrast, the Internet is only about 30 years old, and in the year 2002, an estimated 580 million people used the Internet worldwide (Nua Internet Surveys, May 2002).

Yet e-mail changes the nature of behavior and team dynamics. In a June 21, 1999, *Wall Street Journal* article, Jack Welch, the former CEO of General Electric, said, "I just became an e-mail person. And one executive I e-mailed wrote back saying he couldn't stand my new skill. He said, 'How will I know without that big black scribble across the top of the page—with the width of the scribble determining the angst with which you are writing—how you feel?" (Blake, 1999, p. 12). The problem of conveying emotion via e-mail communication is a challenge for teams. Because it is easy to send a message, and social norms are not present when sending e-mail, people are often more risk taking. Furthermore, there is virtually no competition to attain and hold the floor, so people are at liberty to send frequent and long messages. Some people receive several hundred electronic messages each day.

There is an etiquette to sending e-mail. You can check your e-mail savvy by reviewing Box 12-1, which indicates keys to successful e-mail collaboration.

Is e-mail effective for learning? In the fall of 1996, an experiment was carried out in which 33 students enrolled in a social statistics course at California State University at Northridge. The students were randomly divided into two groups—one taught in a traditional classroom and the other taught virtually on the World Wide Web (Schutte, 1996). Text, lectures, and exams were standardized for both classes; the virtual class scored an average of 20 percent higher than the traditional class on examinations. Furthermore, the virtual class had significantly higher peer contact, more time spent on class work, a perception of more flexibility, better understanding of the material, and a greater liking for math than the traditional class. The virtual students seemed more frustrated, but not from the technology. Instead, their inability to ask questions of the professor in a face-to-face environment led paradoxically to greater involvement

BOX 12-1

## Keys to Successful E-Mail Collaboration

Given that you've got an international team that must communicate via information technology, how can you best achieve group goals? The following prescriptions are important (Thompson, 2000):

- *Make your messages concise and clear.* Most people overestimate the ability of others to make sense out of what they mean (Keysar, 1994). People have a hard enough time deciphering our messages in face-to-face interactions; accuracy decreases dramatically in e-mail exchanges. Many people assume that longer means clearer. It doesn't. People have a short attention span and often dislike long e-mail messages, or perhaps even stop reading them if they begin to fall off of the screen. Most people are capable of only retaining seven, plus-or-minus two, ideas in their head at any one time. As a general rule of thumb, most e-mail messages should fit on a single screen. **Screen loading,** or the tendency to write very long messages, can annoy the recipients, especially if they are busy. Teams perform better when they exchange a greater number of shorter e-mails, rather than fewer but longer e-mails. Increasing the rate of e-mail exchange prevents misunderstanding because misperceptions can be quickly rectified. This also builds reciprocity in exchange.

- *Responding to e-mail.* The asynchronous nature of e-mail provides people with the dubious luxury of not having to immediately receive or respond to e-mail messages. However, the sender of e-mail messages often expects a timely response. Not responding to e-mail may be perceived as rejection or disinterest. Newer forms of software allow senders to ascertain whether recipients have read their e-mail. Failure to provide a timely response to

e-mail is akin to giving the "silent treatment" to someone. Suspicion and hostility increase as the communication between parties diminishes.

- *Metacommunication.* **Metacommunication** is communication about communication. This boils down to people talking about how they should communicate. This is of critical importance in electronic interaction because the norms of turn-taking and conversation are not clear. In any electronic communication, it is important to let team members know how often you check your e-mail, whether you or someone else reads and responds to your e-mail, and whether you forward your e-mail to others.

- *Light of day test.* The golden rule of e-mail is the **light of day test**—is what you're saying in the e-mail suitable to be read by your mother, supervisor, or jury? Could it appear on the front page of the newspaper? If not, it's probably not a good idea to send it.

- *Watch your temper.* **Flaming** refers to the insults, criticisms, and character assassinations that people hurl over e-mail. Flaming remarks make fun of grammar, are patronizing (e.g., "I would recommend that you more closely read my first transmission prior to responding"), and include labeling and accusations (e.g., "That is completely ridiculous"; "Your idea is ludicrous"), character attacks, backhanded compliments ("I'm glad to see that you've come around to my point of view"), and blunt statements (e.g., "Why don't we stop treating each other as fools and start talking seriously?"). Flaming and other negative interpersonal behaviors that are found among computer-mediated communicaton system users stem from feelings of isolation (Keisler, Zubrow, Moses, & Gellar, 1985). In contrast, face-to-face groups have mechanisms and norms, such as conformity pressure, that largely prevent flaming (Rhoades & O'Connor, 1996).

People react to each other with less politeness, empathy, or inhibition if they cannot sense the other's social presence (Short, Williams, & Christie, 1976). People are much more likely to issue threats when communicating via information technology.

There is more uncertainty, doubt, and ambiguity in electronic mail exchanges. This stems from the asynchronous nature of communication. As a consequence, people become frustrated and seek to control the exchange by issuing threats (e.g., "I am not going to read my e-mail again"; "if I don't hear from you by 5 P.M., I will assume that the specifications are acceptable"). Along these lines, don't chastise or deliver negative feedback via e-mail; face-to-face (or telephone) communication is more appropriate.

among classmates, who formed study groups to "pick up the slack of not having a real classroom." Thus, the key performance differences here are most likely attributable to the collaboration among students instigated by the technology. It appears that the lack of rich communication in the virtual class led to the improved performance of students, who were sparked by the inadequacies of the virtual medium.

Information technology (in particular, the World Wide Web and the Internet) has led to the formation of new groups of people and communities. Nearly 84 percent of U.S. Internet users have contacted or belong to an on-line group (Pew Internet Project, 2001), and the Internet is the staging ground for a variety of communities and the "colonizing of cyberspace." Hagel and Armstrong (1997) suggest that on-line communities meet four types of consumer needs: (1) interest, (2) relationship building, (3) transaction, and (4) fantasy. Some even argue that these technologies are redefining individuals' identities as they explore the boundaries of their personalities, adopt multiple selves, and form on-line relationships that can be more intense than real ones (Turkle, 1995). Internet communities such as Motley Fool (personal investors), WebMD (health concerns), Wine.com (wine lovers), and TimeZone.com (timepiece aficionados) are composed of various "netizens" who find they are spending more and more of their existence communicating in a virtual, as opposed to real, fashion (Hof, Browder, & Elstrom, 1997; Rothaermel & Sugiyama, 2001).

It might seem that this type of community interaction is a far cry from the business world of information technology, but that is just the point. It is becoming harder to separate the personal lives of people and the communities to which they belong from their professional or business lives. The Internet does not make the clear distinction between work and home; the traditional distinction arises from physical separation, which is not the case on the Internet.

## INFORMATION TECHNOLOGY AND SOCIAL BEHAVIOR

Information technology has extremely powerful effects on social behavior (Keisler & Sproull, 1992). Many people are surprised at how they behave when communicating via e-mail. What are the key things to expect when interacting with teammates via information technology?

## Reduced Status Differences: The "Weak Get Strong" Effect

In face-to-face interactions, people do not contribute to conversation equally. One person or one clique usually dominates the discussion. In general, those with the higher status tend to talk more, even if they are not experts on the subject. Not surprisingly, managers speak more than subordinates and men speak more than women.

However, an odd thing happens on the way to the information technology forum: The traditional static cues are missing, and the dynamic cues are distinctly less impactive. This has a dramatic effect on social behavior: Power and status differences are weakened, and status differences are reduced. This means that high-status members (e.g., leaders) are less likely to dominate discussions in computer-mediated (CM) groups than in face-to-face (FtF) groups (Dubrovsky, Keisler, & Sethna, 1991); and a dominant member is less likely to emerge in CM groups than in FtF groups (Hiltz, Johnson, & Turoff, 1986).

Decision making occurs on the basis of task expertise, rather than status (Eveland & Bikson, 1989). People who are in weak positions in face-to-face encounters become more powerful because status cues are harder to read in non-face-to-face interaction (Sproull & Keisler, 1991). Traditional, static cues, like position and title, are not as obvious on e-mail. It is often impossible to tell whether you are communicating with a president or clerk because traditional e-mail simply lists the person's name, not a title. In most networks, when people send e-mail, the only signs of position and personal attributes are names and addresses. Addresses are often shortened and may be difficult to comprehend. Even when they can be deciphered, addresses identify the organization, but not the subunit, job title, social importance, or level in the organization of the sender. Dynamic status cues, such as dress, mannerisms, age, and gender, are also missing in e-mail. In this sense, e-mail acts as an equalizer because it is difficult for high-status people to dominate discussions (see Sidebar 12-2).

### Sidebar 12-2. Technology Can Be Empowering for Women

When a group of executives meet face-to-face, the men in these groups are five times more likely than the women to make the first decision proposal. When the same groups meet via computer, women make the first proposal as often as do men (McGuire, Keisler, & Siegel, 1987).

### Equalization of Team Members' Participation

The greater anonymity associated with virtual interaction reduces inhibitions and increases the likelihood that all members will contribute to the discussion (McGuire, Keisler, & Siegel, 1987; Siegel, Dubrovsky, Keisler, & McGuire, 1986; Weisband, 1992).

Additionally, when interacting via e-mail, an interesting dynamic happens: People respond more openly and conform less to social norms and other people. They focus more on the content of the task and less on the direction of high-status opinion leaders. E-mail and other forms of computer-mediated communication (CMC) are becoming increasingly prevalent. CMC is more democratic and less hierarchical in this way, with bad news conveyed upward to superiors with less delay (Sproull & Keisler, 1991). However, CMC does not appear to reduce gender differences. Postmes and Spears

(2002) examined the question of whether disguising individual and gender identity during group interaction would lead to more equal participation of men and women and the disappearance of gender differences (as compared with face-to-face groups). Surprisingly, gender differences in dominance were greatest when people were unable to individuate each other! At the same time, there is less awareness of the needs of the group or its members (McGrath, 1990). With more rudeness and less inhibition, conflicts in CMC are sharper and escalate more quickly. Consensus on complex, nontechnical issues is more difficult to reach (Hiltz, Johnson, & Turoff, 1986).

### Technology Can Lead to Face-to-Face Meetings

An important value of information technology may come from the ability to generate face-to-face meetings that simply would not have occurred otherwise. For example, Boeing used a high-level computer-aided engineering network to manage the development of its new 777 passenger jet. This software network has the ability to alert Boeing engineers whenever their proposed modifications in subassemblies interfere with other subassemblies—for example, when a hydraulic system modification might interfere with an electrical system. Boeing management discovered that its engineers were deliberately making modifications in the plans that interfered with other systems. What appeared to be a form of software sabotage was actually Boeing engineers taking advantage of the network to find out who was working on the other systems. That way, they could get together to talk about their designs. In other words, the network created the opportunity for productive collaboration around the 777 that Boeing's own management structure could not (Schrage, 1995).

### Increased Time to Make Decisions

CM groups have more difficulty reaching consensus than FtF groups (Dubrovsky et al., 1991; Hiltz et al., 1986; Siegel et al., 1986). The difficulty may be attributable in part to the diversity of opinions generated in CM interaction. CM groups take four to 10 times longer to reach a decision than face-to-face groups, with the greater differential occuring under no time constraints (Dubrovsky et al., 1991; Siegel et al., 1986). It takes longer to write than it does to speak; hence, communicating via information technology is slower. It takes four times as long for a three-person group to make a decision in a real-time computer conference as in a face-to-face meeting (Siegel et al., 1986). It takes as much as 10 times as long in a four-person computer-conference group that lacks time restrictions (Dubrovsky et al., 1991). This is especially true when the technology is new.

### Communication

It is useful to examine differences between traditional FtF teams and CM teams. Members of FtF teams engage in more communication than CM teams (for a review, see Hedlund, Ilgen, & Hollenbeck, 1998). The lower frequency of communication in CM groups is known as information supression (Hollingshead, 1996a, 1996b). CM groups may compensate for information suppression by enhancing more task-oriented messages as a proportion of their total messages (Hiltz, et al., 1986; Siegel et al., 1986), generating more diverse opinions or decision recommendations (Dubrovsky et al., 1991; Weisband, 1992) and having information more readily accessible (Hollingshead,

1996a). CM creates less inhibition and thus leads to greater expression of personal opinions, including the use of personal insults and profanity—the "flaming effect" (Dubrovsky et al., 1991; Siegel et al., 1986; Weisband, 1992). In one investigation, 64 four-person teams worked for three hours on a computer simulation interacting either face-to-face or via a computer-mediated network. Members of FtF teams were better informed and made recommendations that were more predictive of the correct team decision, but leaders of CM teams were better able to differentiate team members on the quality of their decisions (i.e., greater accountability).

## Risk Taking

CM groups make riskier decisions and exhibit greater polarization of judgment than FtF groups (McGuire et al., 1987; Siegel et al., 1986; Weisband, 1992). For example, in FtF groups, members' decision recommendations tended to conform to the prior recommendations of other members. In CM groups, the last decision recommendations were as divergent from the group's final decision as were the first (Weisband, 1992).

People intuitively perform cost-benefit analyses when considering different courses of action and, consequently, do not treat gains commensurately with losses. However, electronic interaction has an effect on risk-taking behavior. Consider the following choices:

**A.** Return of $20,000 over 2 years
**B.** 50 percent chance of gaining $40,000; 50 percent of gaining nothing

Option A is the safer investment; option B is riskier. However, these two options are mathematically identical, meaning that in an objective sense, people should not favor one option over the other. When posed with these choices, most managers are risk averse, meaning that they select the option that has the sure payoff as opposed to holding out for the chance to win big (or, equally as likely, not win at all). However, consider what happens when the following choice is proposed:

**C.** Sure loss of $20,000 over 2 years
**D.** 50 percent chance of losing $40,000; 50 percent of losing nothing

Most managers are risk seeking and choose option D. Why? According to the framing effect (Kahneman & Tversky, 1979), people are risk averse for gains and risk seeking for losses. This can lead to self-contradictory, quirky behavior. By manipulating the reference point, a person's fiscal policy choices can change.

We saw in Chapter 6 that groups tend to make riskier decisions than do individuals in the same situation. Thus, risk seeking is greatly exaggerated in groups that meet face-to-face. Paradoxically, groups that make decisions via electronic communication are risk seeking for both gains and losses (McGuire et al., 1987). Furthermore, executives are just as confident of their decisions whether they are made through electronic communication or face-to-face communication.

## Social Norms

As mentioned previously, when social context cues are missing or weak, people feel distant from others and somewhat anonymous. They are less concerned about making a good appearance, and humor tends to fall apart or to be misinterpreted. Additionally, the expression of negative emotion is no longer minimized because factors that keep people from acting out negative emotions are not in place when they communicate via information technology. Simply, in the absence of social norms that prescribe the expression of positive emotion, people are more likely to express negative emotion. When people communicate via e-mail, they are more likely to negatively confront others. Conventional behavior, such as politeness rituals and acknowledgment of others' views, decreases; rude, impulsive behavior, such as flaming, increases. People are eight times more likely to flame in electronic discussions than in face-to-face discussions (Dubrovsky et al., 1991).

### Task Performance and Quality of Group Decisions

Are people more effective when they communicate via information technology? The jury is still out. Hedlund et al. (1998) report that "studies addressing the quality of group decisions have either found no differences between the two communication modes or differences in favor of FtF groups" (p. 34). When the decision outcomes depend heavily on information exchange, FtF groups have an advantage over CM groups, but when other factors contribute to decision quality, CM groups may be better able to compensate for less information exchange (Hedlund et al., 1998).

All the team configurations discussed in this chapter, with the exception of the same-time, same-place teams, are virtual teams, and, as such, face special challenges. In the sections that follow, we consider strategies for enhancing rapport and teamwork in local teams and in remotely distributed teams.

## ENHANCING LOCAL TEAMWORK: REDESIGNING THE WORKPLACE

Telecommuting, or working from home, was the popular mantra of the late twentieth century. Telecommuting often calls to mind a bathrobe-clad "knowledge worker" throwing in her contribution from the comfort of a home office (Radigan, 2001). The number of workers telecommuting increased 20 percent per year during the 1990s. Over 16.5 million people work from home at least once a month, and 9.3 million do so at least once a week (Radigan, 2001). Managing virtual teams, making people accountable, and establishing clear goals are major challenges to telecommuting. Companies such as NetCom are investing in technologies that will allow them to monitor the status of every project at the end of each day.

Teams that must work together don't necessarily confine themselves to traditional space and time. The trend seems to be work anywhere, anytime—in your car, your home, your office, even your client's office. It means a radical disaggregation of work, going beyond the walls and confines of the traditional office (O'Hamilton, Baker, & Vlasic, 1996). For example, Jarlath MacNamara, founder of the Dublin, Ireland–based Cabs-on-Line, fitted a Ford Galaxy taxi with a laptop with e-mail and a browser, a cell phone, and a wireless modem and fax (Lyons, 1998). The traditional corporation exemplified by private offices, elevators, and cubicled workspaces is giving way to informal gatherings and chatting among employees in community spaces, such as lunchrooms and lounges. Corporate America is changing and the walls of the corporation are being replaced by mobile office systems that conform to the needs of the team, not the other way around.

For example, at the Aluminum Company of America (Alcoa), senior executives work in open cubicles and gather around "communications centers" replete with televisions, fax machines, newspapers, and tables that encourage impromptu meetings. CEO Paul H. O'Neill's favorite hangout is the kitchen, where he and his staff heat up take-out food and talk work (O'Hamilton et al., 1996). This type of change is radical, and it is at the heart of team redesign. By redesigning the environment that they work in, teams work more efficiently and effectively.

Indeed, technology that can boost employee efficiency and mobility is surpassing facilities and real estate as the second biggest corporate operating expense, after salaries and benefits (O'Hamilton et al., 1996). Increasingly, architects, interior designers, facilities managers, and furniture companies are assuming the new role of strategic design consultants not only with blueprints, but also with human behavior in the organization. This means that many of the old perks, such as large, private paneled offices and private lunchrooms, are disappearing. Instead, employees of every rank are out in the open. According to a 1995 survey by the International Facility Management Association, 83 percent of companies are embracing alternative office strategies. The following are some of the most promising options for maximizing team productivity in the new office space.

## Virtual or Flexible Space

Virtual or flexible space is physical space that is used on a temporary and changing basis to meet different needs. Instead of physical space setting limits on managerial behavior, such as how many people can be in a meeting at any one time and what information technology is or is not available, virtual space means that people determine their needs first and design the space to fit those needs. It is an entirely different way of thinking about space. Most important, virtual or flexible space does not mean open, fixed cubicles. For example, Allan Alley, vice president of Focus Systems Inc., a Wilsonville, Oregon, maker of computer-projection systems, states that open cubicles are the "worst of both worlds. . . . No impromptu meetings and a lot of wasted space" (O'Hamilton et al., 1996, p. 113).

A prime example of virtual or flexible space is the "cave and commons" design. The idea is to balance individual work and teamwork, as well as privacy and community. At Minneapolis-based advertising agency Fallon-McElligott, when it is time to brainstorm, art directors, space buyers, account managers, and copywriters wheel special desks (equipped with an employee's computer, files, and phone) into flexible space. The room may hold 30 employees on Monday, none on Tuesday, and 10 or so on Wednesday, depending on what needs to be done. At any given time, team members may be working independently in their own cubicles or meeting at a center table.

At Procter & Gamble, project groups were the central design theme in their Cincinnati building. Members of teams work in open cubicles grouped together, and can all see each other, regardless of rank. File cases are on wheels, and offices are designed out of "bricks" that can be reconfigured in a jiffy. P&G personnel travel between floors by escalator, instead of elevators, which tend to halt conversation. "Huddle rooms" are strategically placed where teams can come together to brainstorm, and electronic whiteboards, which can convert scribble to e-mail, are present in lunchrooms and lounges. Corridors are deliberately wide so employees can stop for a chat. Furthermore, P&G designed features to help dual-career families: A dry cleaner, shoe repair shop, and take-out cafeteria are all on site. The offices of the future are using space in creative ways that allow teams to overcome some of the disadvantages of distance teamwork.

### Flexible Furniture

Furniture for the new space is key for productivity. Consider the "personal harbor," a small, cylindrical booth made by Steelcase Inc., with a door that can be closed; because it is curved, it has the effect of increasing interior space. There is enough room inside for a flat work surface, computer setup, phones, file drawer, and other standard desk items. There's even a whiteboard and built-in CD player. The important design feature is that the harbors are grouped around a large puzzle-like table that can be broken into several pieces. When harbor doors are open, people move in and out of the group space to talk to colleagues and participate in meetings. Whereas most norms state that people should never leave a traditional meeting room, with the personal harbor, people stay in a meeting long enough to contribute and then go back to work.

Some companies are even turning to custom designers and artists to get what they want. For example, when Fallon-McElligott wanted to create its flexible space, interior designer Gary E. Wheeler created the award-winning "free address lockers" that resemble armoires on wheels. They hold a computer, files, phone, and a desktop, as well as a special universal plug to simplify "docking" all the electronics (O'Hamilton et al., 1996).

Inhale Therapeutic Systems, a small Palo Alto start-up working on novel drug-delivery technology, uses "bullpens"—large cubicles containing four people of various ranks and functions—with no walls or barriers of any kind between people (O'Hamilton et al., 1996). These bullpens enable the employees to communicate more frequently and informally.

### Hoteling

Employees are increasingly mobile, spending more of their work time on the road than in the office. This is why Richard Kalenka, managing partner of Pricewaterhouse-Coopers' San Diego office, says, "In our business, there's no real need for most of our workers to have their own offices or desks" (Kinsman, 2002). **Hoteling** is the office equivalent of a hotel room, wherein employees and teams don't have a permanent office, but instead have the use of an office when and wherever they need it. Hoteling is the provision of a building, office, or meeting rooms that can be reserved in advance, just like a hotel. Employees make reservations for workspace, check in for an afternoon, a day or a week, and then move along to make room for someone else. Hoteling can save large companies hundreds of thousands of dollars in office leases. The concept of hoteling has been embraced by consulting firms, accounting firms, and sales organizations such as Ernst & Young, KPMG, Accenture, IBM, and Deloitte & Touche, all of whose business depends heavily on regular contact with clients. For example, at Ernst & Young's Washington office, when employees call, they are asked for a personal ID and the dates they need "hotel" space. Within 30 seconds, the system confirms whether a workstation or a meeting room is available. Each "hotel" has a concierge to meet and help guests. When employees arrive, their name is on a door, and any files or supplies the employees have requested will be there too. Also, their phone numbers are forwarded. IBM has about

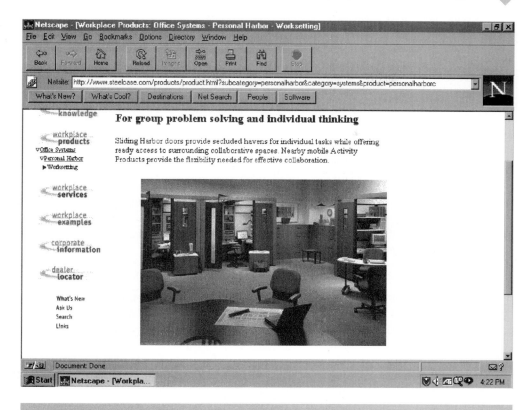

An office space using personal harbors designed by Steelcase, Inc.
*Source:* Steelcase, Inc.'s Web site at *www.steelcase.com.*

20,000 sales and service professionals nationwide using shared offices, which has cut about $1.4 billion from real-estate expenses (O'Hamilton et al., 1996). For hoteling to be effective, it must be hassle-free for the employee (Smith, 1997).

Hoteling can be extraordinarily cost-effective. It has allowed KPMG Peat Marwick LLP to hire new employees without leasing extra space. At Ernst & Young, staffers realize that the lack of individual offices shows up in the firm's profit margin, which, in turn, shows up in their bonuses (Smith, 1997).

However efficient, alternative forms of office space are not without problems. Advertising firm Chiat/Day abandoned hoteling in 1995 after attempting to create a virtual office for its Los Angeles employees. The company allowed employees to work from home or wherever else they chose, but found that people still came to the office on a daily basis. However, because the size of the office had been reduced, there wasn't sufficient work space or laptops to accommodate everyone. Also, the teams missed brainstorming and their creative environment (Kinsman, 2002). Implementing these types of alternative office spaces should be considered carefully (consider the lessons in Box 12-2).

The new design of offices and furniture indicates that most managers and executives regard face-to-face communication to be the ideal—and the more of it the better.

---

**BOX 12-2**

### Before Implementing Alternative Forms of Office Space . . .

**1.** The presence or absence of a strong champion is very important to the success/failure of the project.

**2.** Many issues that management may feel are barriers to implementing innovative ideas are perceived barriers.

**3.** A richer, more varied set of work settings that truly support the range of work activities must be provided.

**4.** A business approach to implementing innovations must be used instead of a cost approach.

**5.** User involvement is very critical to the success of the project.

**6.** Reinvesting a portion of the innovation cost savings is likely to result in a far higher level of employee satisfaction.

**7.** Using a pilot project to apply a standardized solution is ineffective.

**8.** The reassessment and data collection phase must not be eliminated.

**9.** Employees must be given time to adjust to the new work patterns.

*Source:* Becker, F., Quinn, K. L., Rappaport, A. J., & Sims, W. R. 1994. *Implementing Innovative Workplaces.* Ithaca: New York State College of Human Ecology, Department of Design and Environmental Analysis, Cornell University.

---

However, it is not always possible to bring team members together, especially those who are spread across the globe. The answer is the virtual team.

## VIRTUAL TEAMS

A **virtual team** is a task-focused group that meets without all members necessarily being physically present or even working at the same time. Virtual teams work closely together even though they may be separated by many miles or even continents. Virtual teams may meet through conference calls, videoconferences, e-mail, or other communications tools, such as application sharing. Teams may include employees only, or they may include outsiders, such as a customer's employees. Virtual teams work well for global companies, but they can also benefit small companies operating from a single location, especially if decision makers are often at job sites or on the road. They can be short-lived or permanent, such as operational teams that run their companies virtually. For example, British Petroleum company (BP) has developed a virtual team network that allows people to work cooperatively and share knowledge quickly, regardless of time, distance, and organizational boundaries (Prokesch, 1997). The company has reported benefits of the virtual team network in terms of improved interactions between land-based drilling engineers and offshore rig crews, the avoidance of a refinery shutdown because technical experts at another location could examine a corrosion problem remotely, and a reduction in reworking during construction projects. According to BP, the virtual team network saved at least $30M in its first year alone (Prokesch, 1997).

If a company has a need for virtual teams, the biggest challenge for productivity is *coordination of effort:* how to get people to work together compatibly and productively, even though face-to-face contact is limited and communication is confined to phone, fax, and e-mail. Jack Whalen, a research scientist in Xerox PARC's Scientific and Engineering Reasoning Area, acknowledges that even the best technologies can be rejected outright by teams or put to use in a totally unexpected way (Roberts, 1999b).

According to Griffith, Mannix, and Neale (2002), virtual teams need to consider three factors for their ultimate success: (1) their locations relative to one another, (2) the percentage of time they spend face to face, and (3) their level of technical support. Conflict is just as important for virtual teams as it is for colocated teams. An investigation by Griffith, Mannix, and Neale (2002) of a large software firm revealed that virtual teams have greater "process conflict" than do colocated teams.

## STRATEGIES FOR ENHANCING THE VIRTUAL TEAM

There are a variety of methods for creating rapport among team members. The trade-offs involve money and time. The following methods are used by various companies to address the rapport and trust problem that virtual teams encounter. Few of these methods have been tested in rigorous controlled research. We begin by discussing the most elaborate (and most expensive).

### Collaboratory

A **collaboratory** is the combination of technology, tools, and infrastructure that allows scientists to work with remote facilities and each other as if they were colocated (Finholt & Olson, 1997). It is a center without walls, in which scientists and technicians can perform research without regard to geographic location. Parallels in the business world include virtual corporations in the place of physical corporations (Davidow & Malone, 1992) and a global workplace instead of national or local workplaces (O'Hara-Devereaux & Johansen, 1994). Although the collaboratory requires no face-to-face contact, teams often need some degree of actual face-to-face contact to establish rapport. There are several types of interaction that will help develop rapport among team members and force them to work in a single geographic location. The length of the face-to-face interaction varies by method. Among them are initial face-to-face experience, temporary engagement, or the one-day videoconference.

### Virtual Team Technology

A surge of collaborative Web technology solutions for teaming have appeared in recent years. For example, the Documentum eRoom digital workplace helps teams fill the collaboration gap through enhanced dialogue, more and better communication, and efficient information sharing. Wilmington Trust Corporation Vice President Norma Closs says that with such technology, "[w]e are able to bring together management teams, lawyers, investment managers, and analysts in an online collaborative enviroment that supports the entire deal-making process, replacing the need for ongoing status meetings and significant executive travel" (*BusinessWire,* October 29, 2001). Other companies, such as Ford Motor, A. T. Kearney, Bausch & Lomb, and the BIC Group are careful to measure the savings of virtual team technologies—for example, A. T. Kearney saved five to seven hours per consultant per week through collaborative

**TABLE 12-2** Technologies That Support Groups

| Technology | Functional Role | Example |
|---|---|---|
| GCSS (Group Communication Support Systems) | Providing or modifying within-group communication | Video conference<br>Phone conference<br>Computer conference<br>Voice-mail<br>E-mail<br>Fax<br>Homepages<br>Web sites |
| GISS (Group Information Support Systems) | Supplementing information available to the group or its members by information drawn from databases | Quantitative databases (e.g., sales records, production and cost data)<br>Qualitative databases or archives (e.g., libraries, newspaper files) |
| GXSS (Group eXternal Support Sytems) | Providing or modifying external communication with those outside the group | Extranets (e.g., for obtaining upgrades) |
| GPSS (Group Performance Support Systems) | Channeling or modifying the group's task performance processes and task products | Tools for electronic brainstorming, evaluation and voting tools, etc. |

*Source:* Hollingshead, A. B. 2001. "Communication Technologies, the Internet, and Group Research." In M. Hogg and R.S. Tindale (Eds), *Blackwell Handbook of Social Psychology, Vol. 3: Group Processes* (pp. 557–573). Oxford, England: Blackwell.

technology (*Businesswire*, October 29, 2001). McGrath and Hollingshead (1994) classified group technologies into four major categories, based on the functional role that the technology plays in the work of a group (see Table 12-2).

### Initial Face-to-Face Experience

Bringing together team members for a short, face-to-face experience is often used by companies who want to lay a groundwork of trust and communication for later teamwork that will be conducted strictly electronically. The idea here is that it is much easier for people to work together if they have actually met in a face-to-face encounter. Face-to-face contact humanizes people and creates expectations for team members to use in their subsequent long-distance work together.

### Temporary Engagement

The idea here is to allow team members to work together in a sustained face-to-face fashion before separating them. For example, John Spencer, worldwide manager for the design and development of single-use cameras for Eastman Kodak Company in Rochester, New York, pulled together a project development team to design a new product that required the involvement of German design engineers. Spencer brought the German engineers to the United States for the initial six months of the project.

## One-Day Videoconference

Chris Newell, executive director of the Lotus Institute, the research and education arm of Lotus Development Corp. in Cambridge, Massachusetts, believes that introductions via videoconference are crucial to develop trust and relationships before doing teamwork electronically. Thus, if an initial, face-to-face meeting is out of the question, an alternative may be to at least get everyone on-line so that people can attach a name to a face. Depending on the size of the team and locations of different members, this alternative may be more feasible than a face-to-face meeting.

## Touching Base

If teams do not have an opportunity to work together at the outset of a project, then providing an opportunity for them to touch base at some later point can be helpful. This method is most useful for teams in which one or two members are remotely located. For example, Barbara Recchia, communications program manager at Hewlett Packard in Palo Alto, California, lives and works in Santa Rosa. In the early months of her remote work arrangement, she felt hopelessly out of touch with her colleagues (Geber, 1995). Eventually, she decided to drop in once a week instead of once a month to maintain her connection to her team. There are often special problems when just one member of the team is remotely located from the rest of the local team. Because much teamwork is done informally at the water cooler or at lunch, the remote person often feels lonely and disconnected from the rest of the team, and the rest of the team may leave that person out of the loop—if not deliberately, then just because it is cumbersome to bring the outsider up to date on all team actions.

Touching base can be done in microtime as well. For example, David Kelley of IDEO is adamant about the importance of informal, offline interaction—unscheduled conversations that traditional managers have long dismissed as time wasters. When an important Japanese client came to the IDEO studio for a design meeting, the parties discussed a project via translators for hours. Yet IDEO's people weren't clear on the client's expectations and concerns. "It took the equivalent of a commercial break to clear things up. When we had a break and everyone went to their own 'corners,' our Japanese-speaking people could tell us what was really going on with the client. Only in these informal spaces can you find out what people are really thinking" (Roberts, 1999b).

## Schmoozing

**Schmoozing** (as described in Chapter 4) is our name for superficial contact between people that has the psychological effect of having established a relationship with someone. There are a variety of non-face-to-face schmoozing strategies, such as exchanging pictures or biographical information or engaging in a simple get-acquainted e-mail exchange. The effectiveness of electronic schmoozing has been put to test, and the results are dramatic: schmoozing increases liking and rapport and results in more profitable business deals than when people just get down to business (Moore et al., 1999). Perhaps the most attractive aspect of schmoozing is that it is relatively low cost and efficient. Merely exchanging a few short e-mails describing yourself can lead to better business relations. However, you should not expect people to naturally schmooze—at least at the outset of a business relationship. Team members working remotely have a tendency to get down to business. As a start toward schmoozing, begin by telling the other person something about yourself that does not necessarily relate to the business at hand (e.g., "I really enjoy kayaking"); also, provide a context for your own work space (e.g., "It is very late in the day and there are 20 people at my door, so I don't have time to write a long message"). Furthermore, ask questions that show you are interested in the other party as a person; this is an excellent way to search for points of similarity. Finally, provide the link for the next e-mail or exchange (e.g., "I will look forward to hearing your reactions on the preliminary report and I will also send you the tapes you requested").

## TRANSNATIONAL TEAMS

Thus far, we have discussed teamwork via information technology as if it were strictly a burden or nuisance to be overcome. However, depending upon the goals of the company, it may be highly desirable to put together virtual teams, even when local teamwork is an alternative.

Many companies are international or multinational. A better goal might be to become a transnational company or team.[1] A *transnational team* is a work group composed of multinational members whose activities span multiple countries; transnational teams have successfully transcended the cultural, geographic, and managerial barriers to team effectiveness (Snow, Snell, Davison, & Hambrick, 1996). Global teamwork may be the best ticket going to becoming truly transnational. As cases in point, consider the following companies (Snow et al., 1996):

- In 1985, Fuji-Xerox sent 15 of its most experienced Tokyo engineers to a Xerox Corporation facility in Webster, New York. For the next five years, the Japanese engineers worked with a group of American engineers to develop the "world copier"—a huge success in the global marketplace.
- In 1991, Eastman Kodak formed a team to launch its latest consumer product, the photo CD. That group of experts, based in London, developed a strategy for the simultaneous introduction of the photo CD in several European countries. The photo CD has been Kodak's most successful multicountry product introduction in the 1990s.
- At IBM–Latin America, in 1990, a group of managers and technical specialists formed their own team to market, sell, and distribute personal computers in 11 Latin American countries. It took the team leader about a year to convince his boss that the team should be formally recognized and allowed to operate as an autonomous business unit.

In each of these cases, a transnational team was key to the company's efforts to globalize and extend the firm's products and operations into international markets. Global competitive strategies are complex and expensive, and they are often administered by a transnational team of managers and specialists.

Like the other types of teams we have discussed, transnational teams come into existence in one of two primary ways: from the top down or from the bottom up. Most transnational teams are formed from the top down, as in the case of manager-led or

---

[1]This section draws heavily upon the work of Snow, Snell, Davison, and Hambrick (1996).

self-managing teams. That is, senior managers see a competitive need, decide a transnational team should be formed, and put together a team with a particular mandate. For example, in 1991, Heineken formed the European Production task force, a 13-member team representing five countries. The task force wrestled with the issue of how many breweries the company should operate in Europe, what size and type they should be, and where they should be located. Eighteen months after it was formed, the task force presented its findings and recommendations to Heineken's board of directors, who enthusiastically accepted the recommendations.

In contrast, other transnational teams are emergent; like self-directing and self-governing teams, they evolve naturally from the existing network of individuals who depend on each other to accomplish their work objectives. These teams may cut across functions, business units, and countries and may even incorporate "outsiders" from other organizations, either temporarily or permanently. These teams may develop their own mandate and challenge higher managers to accept and support it. For example, the concept of one transnational team was instigated around a dinner table at an annual quality assurance convention held internally by Glaxo-Wellcome. They chose their own leader—a medical doctor—and she approached senior executives to obtain authorization and funding for the team.

Transnational teams are distinguished from other teams in terms of the complexity of their work and their multicultural membership. Transnational teams work on projects that are highly complex and have considerable impact on company objectives. It is imperative that transnational teams adeptly handle a variety of cross-cultural issues. In particular, transnational teams must take into account the degree of similarity among the cultural norms of the individuals on the team, language fluency, and leadership style (Snow et al., 1996). Here's where a clearly shared goal, well-articulated team member roles, shared values, and agreement upon performance criteria are critical. The more deliberate planning centered upon these factors that occurs on the front end of teamwork, the better.

Once formed, transnational teams can be used to accomplish a number of different objectives. Some companies use the teams primarily to help achieve global efficiency, to develop regional or worldwide cost advantages, and to standardize designs and operations (Ghoshal & Barlett, 1988). Other teams enable their companies to be locally responsive; they are expected to help their companies attend to the demands of different regions' market structures, consumer preferences, and political and legal systems. For example, local responsiveness was the main concern of Eastman Kodak's photo CD team as it sought to tailor the marketing strategy for the new product to each major country in the European market. A third use of transnational teams is for organizational learning, bringing together knowledge from various parts of the company, transferring technology, and spreading innovations throughout the company. For example, IBM has a global network of experts, led by a core team of six people headquartered outside of London, that consults around the world for clients in the airline industry. That team, the International Airlines Solution Centre, is composed of permanent and temporary members who fuse technical, consulting, and industry expertise to provide information technology to airlines and airport authorities. The team identifies knowledge located in one part of the world and applies it to problems that arise in another.

## CONCLUSIONS

Change is often disturbing for the corporate world, and technological change is often thought to be a "Frankenstein's monster." However, teams have been dealing with place and time issues for several decades. The older solution was to relocate employees; newer solutions are more varied, creative, (often) cheaper, and less permanent. There is a strong intuition in the business world that face-to-face communication is necessary for trust, understanding, and enjoyment. However, face-to-face communication in no way ensures higher team productivity—especially in the case of creative teams. Information technology can increase productivity of teams. The skilled manager knows when to use it, which obstacles are likely to crop up when using it, and how to address those obstacles.

# Appendices

# A P P E N D I X

# Managing Meetings:

1

## *A Toolkit*

*"A meeting is a gathering where people speak up, say nothing, and then all disagree."*
—KAYSER, 1990

The work of teams largely proceeds through meetings. Whether they are regularly scheduled or called out of need, effective meeting management is a key to success. Furthermore, people spend a lot of time in meetings. The average number of meetings jumped from seven to ten per week, based on surveys of business professionals between 1981 and 1995 by Mosvick and Nelson, authors of *We've Got to Start Meeting Like This!* (1996). Typical executives spend two-thirds of their time in scheduled meetings, and the amount of time managers spend in meetings increases with organizational level. Middle managers spend about 30 percent of their time in meetings; top management spends about 50 percent of their time in meetings. In addition to scheduled meetings, managers are involved in unscheduled and non-job-related meetings. In a study sponsored by the 3M Corporation, the number of meetings and conferences in industry nearly doubled during the previous decade and the cost of meetings nearly tripled. Most businesses spend 7 to 15 percent of their personnel budgets on meetings.

Perhaps meetings would not be a bad thing if they were economical and effective. Unfortunately, as much as 50 percent of meeting time is unproductive, and up to 25 percent of meeting time covers irrelevant issues. As one senior executive put it, "To waste your own time is unfortunate, but to waste the time of others is unforgivable." Companies are so overburdened with meetings that experts say it's a wonder any work gets done. Meetings also trigger stress. The 3M meeting network recently launched a World Wide Web site where workers describe their meeting horror stories. Not surprisingly, managers have resorted to using various tactics, which vary from the radical (removing all chairs to make people stand, locking the doors, requiring people to pay $0.25 before speaking, etc.) to the more tame (the example in Sidebar A1-1).

## THE 4P MEETING MANAGEMENT MODEL

The 4P model is a method for designing and implementing effective meetings (Whetton & Cameron, 1991). It has four key steps (see Table A1-1): (1) specify the **purpose** of the meeting, (2) invite the right **people,** (3) carefully **plan** the meeting content and format, and (4) effectively manage the meeting's **process.**

## Sidebar A1-1. Meeting Tactics

The Test and Metrology Services Department of the Collins Commercial Avionics Division of Rockwell International in Cedar Rapids, Iowa, operates as a self-directed team. The key to their effective meeting management is amazingly cheap: cards. The card system came about because even with an agenda, lengthy weekly meetings among its 20 members exceeded the allotted time. In the card system, two $8 \times 10$-inch cards are passed out to each member at the beginning of the meeting. Each side is color-coded and inscribed with words: red and green on one card; white and yellow on the other. When an issue is brought before the team, all members display the red "needs discussion" card. If someone wasn't there to talk about the issue, she shows a white "need to talk" card to the facilitator, who recognizes the cardholder. As the discussion progresses, team members change their cards to green "ready to vote" cards. The facilitator terminates the discussion only when no more red "needs discussion" cards are displayed. When voting, team members can agree (green card), be neutral (white card), support but not like it (yellow card), or disagree (red card). The team members can hold up a yellow ("to task team") card that indicates more information is required. Lab manager George Fluharty states that the card system has had a dramatic impact on reducing the length of meeting time and providing team members with a voice. Another advantage to the card system is that everyone votes; no issue is dropped until the facilitator views each member's card. The cards have gone a long way to reduce side discussions and disruptive noise during meetings. However, like any system, there are disadvantages to the card system: Team members may form opinions quickly and show their votes before discussion is completed; the system also lends itself to subtle, nonverbal communication, such as when a member lays her cards on the table to signal her opinion. To stop that from happening, team members suggested that cards remain in laps until action is requested and side discussions can be conducted only with cards (Pettit, 1997).

Skilled meeting managers do not just sit at the head of the table and call upon people to speak in a round-robin fashion. Nor do they run a "talk show" by simply airing ideas, conflicts, and concerns. Skilled meeting managers do not write down everything that is said; rather, they call out and punctuate key themes. Skilled meeting managers do not verbally paraphrase members' ideas; rather, they record them visually. Skilled meeting managers do not try to induce dominant members to yield the floor by saying, "keep it short" or "we need to hear from everyone"; rather, they use brainwriting at select times. They do not organize the meeting by who is there; rather, by what is to be done (see Sidebar A1-2). Munter and Netzley (2002) provide a full checklist for the meeting organizer and organize discussions around five key planning questions:

1. *Why meet?* (Define your purpose and choose your channel.)
2. *Who to include?* (Select and analyze the participants.)
3. *What to discuss?* (Orchestrate roles and set the agenda.)
4. *How to record ideas?* (Plan for graphic facilitation.)
5. *Where to meet?* (Plan for technology and logistics.)

**TABLE A1-1**    4P Meeting Management Model

| Key Skill | Questions to Ask |
|---|---|
| *Purpose*<br>• A complex problem needs to be resolved using the expertise of several people.<br>• Team members' commitment to a decision or to each other needs to be enhanced.<br>• Information needs to be shared simultaneously among several key people. | • What is the purpose of the meeting?<br>• Is the purpose clear to participants?<br>• Is a meeting the most appropriate means of accomplishing the goal?<br>• Are key people available to attend the meeting?<br>• Is the cost of the meeting in proportion to what will be accomplished? |
| *Participants*<br>• The size of the team should be compatible with the task.<br>• A balance between people with strong task orientations and those with strong interpersonal skills is desirable. | • Is the size of the meeting appropriate given the problem of coordination costs?<br>• What diversity of skills and backgrounds is important to have in the meeting? |
| *Plan*<br>• Provide for adequate physical space, etc.<br>• Establish priorities by sequencing agenda items and allotting time limits to each item.<br>• Prepare and distribute the agenda before or at the beginning of the meeting.<br>• Organize the agenda by content, not by who is there. Use a three-step approach: announcements, decisions, discussion (Tropman, 1996).<br>• Think about your visual aids: Visual aids are 43 percent more persuasive than no visuals (Armour, 1997).<br>• Choose the most appropriate decision-making structure (e.g., brainstorming, normal group technique). | • Has an agenda been created?<br>• Has the agenda for the meeting been distributed to members prior to the meeting?<br>• Have members been forewarned if they will be asked to report?<br>• Has the physical arrangement been considered (e.g., whiteboards, overheads, flipcharts)?<br>• Has key information been put into proper information displays?<br>• Has a note taker been assigned? |
| *Process*<br>• At the beginning, restate the overall purpose of the meeting and review the agenda and time constraints.<br>• Make note of the ground rules, such as how decisions will be made (e.g., raised hands, secret ballot).<br>• Use techniques to ensure equal participation from members.<br>• Conclude the meeting by summarizing key decisions, reviewing assignments, and determining objectives for the next meeting. | • If this is the first meeting of a team, has an icebreaker been included?<br>• Does the icebreaker get people involved in a behavioral or emotional way (at a minimum, a handshake or high-five)?<br>• Have the ground rules been determined and shared with members in advance of the meeting? |

*Sources:* Adapted from Whetton, D. A., & Cameron, K. S. 1991. *Developing Management Skills* (2nd ed.). Harper-Collins; Armour, S. 1997, December 8. "Business' Black Hole." *USA Today,* p. 1A.

## Sidebar A1-2. Announcements, Decisions, and Discussion

Most meetings are organized on the basis of who is there. Reports flow out person by person, department by department, often beginning with the most prestigious person and proceeding down. However, this type of round-robin format is inefficient. It is better to organize meetings by the content. Tropman, author of *Making Meetings Work* (1996), suggests that announcements should come first, then decisions, and finally discussion time, in that order.

Munter and Netzley (2002) argue that recording the comments in the meeting is a critical aspect of successful meeting management and present a variety of different ways to organize information on flip charts, and so on.

## DEALING WITH PROBLEM PEOPLE IN MEETINGS

There is no surefire way to deal with "problem people." As a general principle, having structure helps. It can also be helpful to give group members a list of desirable and undesirable role descriptions prior to the meeting. Table A1-2 is a list of typical group members. Although stated in jest, each description has a ring of truth to it.

## ADVICE FOR MEETING ATTENDEES

The burden of effective meeting management does not rest solely on the shoulders of the leader. Group members need to engage in the following proactive strategies (Whetton & Cameron, 1991):

- ***Determine if you need to attend the meeting.*** Don't attend merely because you have been invited. If you have doubts about whether the meeting's agenda applies to you, discuss with the leader why he or she feels your presence is important.

- ***Prepare.*** Acquaint yourself with the agenda, and prepare any reports or information that will facilitate others' understanding of the issues. Come prepared with questions that will help you understand the issues.

**TABLE A1-2**  Typical Group Members

| | |
|---|---|
| **Thelma Talk-a-Lot** | ("I just have to say this") |
| **Sam Stall** | ("Let's not rush into this") |
| **Don Domineering** | (talks 75% of the time about his own ideas) |
| **Nick Negative** | (explains that someone has to be the devil's advocate) |
| **Ted Theorizer** | ("It's really complex") |
| **Nancy Nuts-'n'-Bolts** | (always comes up with an impossible example to deal with) |
| **Jim Just-a-Little-Bit-More-Information-on-This-Topic-Please** | ("I don't feel we should decide until we know more") |
| **Herman Hypochondriacal** | (is convinced that any path makes vulnerabilities increase) |
| **Yolanda You're-Not-Going-to-Believe-What-Happened-to-Me** | (uses immediate, personal events rather than overarching views to analyze problems) |

*Source:* Tropman, J. E., & Morningstar, G. 1989. *Entrepreneurial Systems for the 1990s: Their Creation, Structure, and Management.* New York: Quorum Books. Reproduced with permission of Greenwood Publishing Group, Inc., Westport, CT.

- **Be on time.** Stragglers not only waste the time of other participants by delaying the meeting or by requiring summaries of what has happened, but they also hinder effective team building and hurt morale.

- **Ask for clarification on points that are unclear or ambiguous.** Most of the time, you will find that others in the room have the same question but are too timid to speak out.

- **When giving information, be precise and to the point.** Don't bore everyone with anecdotes and details that add little to your point.

- **Listen.** Keep eye contact with whoever is speaking, and try to ascertain the underlying ideas behind the comments. Be sensitive to the effect of your nonverbal behavior on speakers, such as slouching, doodling, or reading.

- **Be supportive of other group members.** Acknowledge and build on the comments of others (e.g., "As Jane was saying . . .").

- **Ensure equitable participation.** Take the lead in involving others so that everyone's talents are used. This is especially important if you know that some participants' points of view are not being included in the discussion. This can be accomplished by encouraging those who rarely participate (e.g., "Jim, your unit worked on something like this last year. What was your experience like?").

- **Make disagreements principle-based.** If it is necessary to disagree with, or challenge, the comments of others, follow the guidelines for collaborative conflict management (e.g., base your comments on commonly held principles or values; for example: "That's an interesting idea, Bill, but how does it square with the president's emphasis on cost-cutting?").

- **Act and react in a way that will enhance the group performance.** In other words, leave your personal agendas at the door and work toward the goals of the group.

## COMMON MEETING DISEASES AND FALLACIES

It is almost impossible to predict where most meetings will go awry. The following is a description of the most common meeting diseases and some ideas on how to combat them.

### The Overcommitment Phenomenon

*Symptoms:* Many people agree to perform tasks and accomplish goals that they cannot possibly do in the time allowed. In some cases, this problem is attributable to the pressures placed on managers to accomplish goals and say "yes." However, in many more instances, the overcommitment problem stems from a fundamental inability to estimate how long it will take to accomplish a task. In addition, people tend to make commitments in advance because their confidence in their ability to finish is higher when they are further away from the task (Gilovich, Kerr, & Medvec, 1993). Most people make subjective mental estimates of how long it will take to accomplish a task, such as writing a report, collecting information, or interviewing a recruit, by imagining the scenario and then estimating a time line based upon the running of the scenario. However, individuals' mental simulations fail to take into account the process losses that will inevitably thwart their efforts. For example, when they expect to spend two weeks writing a report, they fail to anticipate that their printer will break down and that they will have to spend a day offsite. Consequently, most managers are consistently behind schedule.

In many cases, managers and executives are asked to commit themselves to perform tasks and events at some time in the distant future. For example, a team leader might be asked to enroll in a three-day course next year, travel abroad to interview other team members, or attend a conference. Many people agree to these future invitations, but when the time approaches, regret that they have to do what they promised (Loewenstein & Prelic, 1991). People fail to adequately weigh the importance of their future opportunities and time constraints, so they commit to things in the future that they would most likely decline to do in the present.

*Treatment:* The easiest way to deal with the overcommitment problem is to simply double (or triple) the amount of time projected to accomplish a task. For example, publishers typically add six months to an author's projected completion time for a manuscript. Another way of combating the bias is to break the task down into its different elements and then estimate the time necessary to complete each part—people are more accurate at estimating the time necessary to accomplish smaller tasks. When someone asks you to do something, such as write a report, travel, or make a presentation, imagine that you are being asked to do this the next week, or even the next day. If you are disinclined, then it may not be a good idea to take it on.

## Calls for More Information

*Symptoms:* Often, teams are uncomfortable making decisions. This is particularly true when the decision matter is complex and value laden. Under such conditions, teams will do nearly anything to avoid making decisions. The manager faces an avoidance-avoidance conflict: Making a decision is difficult, but not making a decision makes one appear indecisive. Managers often respond to this avoidance-avoidance conflict by requesting more information. In theory, the amount of information relevant to any decision situation is boundless; however, at some point, decisions must be made. One way of avoiding decision making, but not appearing to be indecisive, is to request additional information. This makes people feel as though they are making progress, but actually, the additional information may not be diagnostic or useful. It is merely gathered so that the team members can better cognitively justify their decision. Decision avoidance is a particular concern when teams make negative decisions, such as downsizing.

Consider, for example, the following scenario (Savage, 1954):

> A businessman contemplates buying a certain piece of property. He considers the outcome of the next presidential election relevant to the attractiveness of the purchase. So, to clarify the matter for himself, he asks whether he would buy if he knew that the Republican candidate were going to win, and decides that he would do so. Similarly, he considers whether he would buy if he knew that the Democratic candidate were going to win, and again, finds that he would do so. Seeing that he would buy in either event, he decides that he should buy, even though he does not know which event obtains. (p. 21)

The preceding rationale is known as the **sure-thing principle** (Savage, 1954). It would seem irrational, or somewhat silly, if the businessperson in this case were to delay purchase until after the election, or to pay money to find out the election results ahead of time. Yet in organizations, decision makers often pursue noninstrumental information—information that appears relevant, but if available, would have no impact on choice. The problem does not end there. Once they pursue such information, people then use it to make their decision. Consequently, the pursuit of information that would have had no impact on choice leads people to make choices they otherwise would not have made (Bastardi & Shafir, 1998).

*Treatment:* The decision trap of calling for more information can best be dealt with by keeping a clear log that details the history of the decision. For example, a team member might say something like, "You know, this issue was first brought up two years ago, and it was agreed that a competitive analysis was necessary. This competitive analysis was performed and I brought you the results the following spring. Then, it was suggested that a task force be formed. We did this and came to some conclusions in a report circulated last fall. We agreed at that time that we would make a decision at this meeting. I realize that more information is always better, but I am beginning to wonder whether the costs of continuing to search for information are a way of avoiding a decision." This strategy is especially important in teams where membership changes (and, hence, organizational memory is lost) and in teams that must make tough decisions (e.g., employment terminations).

## Failed Memory and Reinventing the Wheel

*Symptoms:* Many teams face decisions that they make on a repeated basis. For example, merit review decisions, hiring decisions, admission decisions, funding decisions, and so on are all decisions that must be made repeatedly. However, teams often exhibit a memory loss of sorts, in terms of how they made previous decisions. As a result, they spend precious time arguing with one another as to how they made the decision in the past, and memories prove to be fallible. The failed memory problem is most likely to afflict teams that have not created a sufficient organizational memory. The failed memory problem also haunts teams that experience turnover. Under these situations, team members who take notes, or have some kind of record, have an enormous advantage.

*Treatment:* The key here is to make the process explicit and then to have it recorded in some fashion so that it can be later retrieved. The problem is that most people trust their memories at the time they are discussing the issue or making the decision; consequently, they don't bother to write down what they believe will be burned into their memory.

# APPENDIX

# Tips for Consultants and Facilitators

One of the most challenging consulting tasks is to facilitate a meeting for a company. Many companies think this is easy work to do and, consequently, expect miracles to happen. When the meeting does not accomplish what was hoped for, it is easy to blame the consultant or facilitator. There is also an information asymmetry. The consultant/facilitator is not privy to group norms and interpersonal dynamics. Many companies expect consultants to immediately dissect the motives of each member. Many mistakes are made prior to the beginning of the meeting. Often, teams that need outside facilitators are beseiged by thorny political and personnel issues. Even the issue of who hires the consultant can be a political one. Others may see the consultant as a hired gun.

What can an outside facilitator do to make the most out of meetings?

## DO YOUR HOMEWORK

Find out as much as you can about the group, the company, and the individual members before the meeting. Ideally, interview the members of the group individually, either by phone, in person, or via a short questionnaire to determine their views of the issues to be addressed in the meeting and their major concerns about the ability of the meeting to accomplish these objectives. Of course, you should guarantee each person that you will not reveal the particulars of what they have said. If you plan to provide a summary overview, then tell each person that. This is your first meeting with each team member, and trust is a key issue in getting the information that you need and securing your future relationship with the group. At the very least, get biographies of the group members and ask them how long they've been with the organization, their role in the team, and so on. I find it useful to ask them to draw pictures of the team's reporting relationships—it reveals how they think about the group.

## PLAN THE PHYSICAL ENVIRONMENT

Most people seriously underestimate the effect that the physical environment can have on the nature of interaction. Consequently, I am a stickler for this. In many cases, I will create explicit diagrams of where the chairs and tables should be put and fax this to the meeting coordinator several weeks in advance. It is usually too late to move furniture by the time you arrive for the meeting; people will want to talk to you, not rearrange the room. Your key materials for the meeting should include a room large enough for people to sit comfortably; movable chairs; conference-table seating for small groups;

half-rounds, or full-rounds for larger groups; a pad of paper or note cards for each member and a pencil or pen; two or three flip charts; and a whiteboard or a chalkboard. It is useful to also have an overhead projector. If you don't know the group, ask for name badges or nameplates that are computer printed. Usually, it is impossible to read handwriting on nametags unless you are standing only two feet away, and you will probably be about 15 to 20 feet away.

## EXPLAIN WHO YOU ARE AND WHY YOU ARE THERE

Begin the meeting by stating why you are there. You will be viewed as an outsider, or interloper, to the group. This creates tension. People will often feel defensive, paranoid, and suspicious of what is to come. You should immediately state that you are there to facilitate the process and to help the group make the best use of their time, and that you do not have a particular stake in the substantive issues. In most cases, you should be clear about who asked you to come in. Above all, don't assume that the reasons for hiring a meeting facilitator have been accurately communicated to the group. Even if a memo was sent out, it may not have been read. Some people may feel strongly opposed to an outside facilitator. Tell the group who you are, but don't try to impress them. You can also "normalize" the situation by giving them statistics that support the idea that making the best use of meetings is of quintessential importance and that even the best organizations are not experts at meeting management. The objective is to give them confidence that you are qualified to do this job. Often, the group will feel somewhat defensive that they need to hire someone to manage themselves.

## FIND OUT WHO THE GROUP IS

You know who the individual members are, but the group will have its own personality. This is extremely tricky. The group members, in most cases, will know one another intimately, but you will not know them.

If the group members do not know one another well, it is useful for everyone to introduce themselves. If the group members do know one another well, having members talk about themselves is boring for other people. In this case, a useful technique is the **next-in-line strategy,** in which members introduce others in the group. For example, each person introduces the person to their left. This is more interesting for group members because they hear, perhaps for the first time, how they are viewed by others. This also serves as an icebreaker, because members are often touched at the admiration given to them by others. (Often, people sit by others whom they like, so having someone introduce the person sitting next to them ensures a favorable introduction.)

## USE GROUND RULES

It is imperative to let the group know that you will be using and enforcing meeting ground rules. You may want to acknowledge that the ground rules may seem somewhat silly or reminiscent of their school days, but that companies that use these ground rules are more effective. If you have the time, it is best to have the group suggest some ground rules, so that they "own" them. If you don't have the time, you can write some rules quickly on a flip chart and briefly walk through it with the members. An example

**TABLE A2-1** Meeting Ground Rules

- Everyone stays for duration of meeting
- Form an agenda and stick to it
- Form a time line and stick to it
- No "new business"
- No semantic/philosophical discussions
- No "let's call for more information" (decision avoidance)
- No evaluation of ideas until evaluation period
- No more reports

list of ground rules is presented in Table A2-1. You may not want to use all of these, but they give you a starting point from which members can add their own rules (or modify the ones on the list).

The most difficult challenge facing the consultant is enforcing the ground rules. They will get broken, and the temptation will be to excuse or ignore rule-breaking behavior. However, it is imperative to demonstrate that you will enforce these ground rules. You should actually do this early on in the meeting (e.g., "Pat, I need to remind you that we agreed to not mention personal names when talking about the peer review," or "Stan, your five minutes are up.").

## CREATE AN AGENDA

You should ideally have an agenda that is distributed to members in advance of the meeting. Expect to be challenged on the agenda either directly (e.g., "If you don't mind, I want to bring up $x$, $y$, and $z$") or indirectly (e.g., "Don't you think we should talk about $x$, $y$, and $z$ before we do this?"). The best way of handling this is to create a post-discussion agenda and explain that there may be time for these issues after the scheduled meeting.

## CLOSING THE MEETING

It is important to bring the meeting to a close in a way that gives the members a sense of what has been accomplished and decided, what steps need to be taken before the next meeting, and what the goal of the next meeting will be (which should be scheduled with everyone present). Finally, you should close in a way that allows each member to "briefly and deeply" reflect on the meeting. Each one of the agenda items should be recapped, and homework or follow-up should be assigned to individual members. A summary of decision and action items should be distributed as soon as possible to the group. I like to spend the last five to 10 minutes going around and having each person say the one thing that happened today that they "did not expect" (otherwise everyone will state the obvious, like "we got a lot done" or "the time passed quickly").

## SOLICIT FEEDBACK FOR YOURSELF AND THE GROUP

This step is important, especially if you have not worked with the group in the past. Distribute a short questionnaire to each participant that asks the following three questions: (1) What in this meeting went well and should be kept? (2) What in this meeting did not go so well and should be eliminated? (3) What in this meeting did not happen and should be included? (Tropman, 1996). If you will be working with the group again, you should aggregate the list of responses and circulate it among group members.

# APPENDIX

# A Guide for Creating
# Effective Study Groups

Most students enrolled in MBA programs must work in groups to complete important projects and requirements en route to obtaining their degree. Some students work with the same group throughout their program; other students work with several different groups each semester. This is a guide for helping these groups to be as maximally effective as possible.

## VERY EARLY ON

In the beginning, when the group is first forming, it is helpful to do some kind of structured exercise that moves beyond usual chit-chat. For this reason, it is helpful to have a somewhat structured but fun exercise that moves people beyond superficial pleasantries and encourages people to talk about their expectations for the team, work styles, and so on. For great resources on team exercises, the following resources and books are very useful:

- The Kellogg Teams and Groups (KTAG) Center's cases on the Dispute Resolution Research Center's CD-ROM of cases and exercises[1]
- *Experiences in Management and Organizational Behavior* (4th edition; Bowen, Lewicki, Hall, & Hall, 1997)
- *Leadership Games* (Kaagan, 1999); *Principles of Human Relations* (Maier, 1952)
- *The Role-Play Technique: A Handbook for Management and Leadership Practice* (Maier, Solem, & Maier, 1975)
- *A Handbook of Structured Experiences for Human Relations Training* (Pfeiffer, 1974)

## SOMETIME DURING THE FIRST WEEK OR TWO

There are a host of tensions and dilemmas that can threaten the effectiveness of any study group. We suggest the team meet and complete a "Team Contract" (see KTAG cases and exercises, available at http://www.kellogg.nwu.edu/research/drrc/teams.htm).

We also suggest that groups that will work together for long periods of time discuss the following issues in the first week or two:

---

[1]The Kellogg Teams and Groups (KTAG) center cases and exercises cited in this appendix are are available through the Kellogg Teams and Groups Center (KTAG), Kellogg School of Management, Northwestern University, 2001 Sheridan Road, Evanston, Illinois 60208-2011. Phone: (847) 491-8068; e-mail: drrc@kellogg. northwestern.edu; order form is also available on-line at http://www.kellogg.nwu.edu/research/drrc/teams.htm.

## Team Goals

- *Learning:* "Are we here to learn and to help others learn or are we here to get a good grade?" There is not a right answer to this question, but differing goals in the group can hurt later performance.
- *Standards:* "Is perfectionism more important than being on time, or vice versa?"
- *Performance:* "Are we a high-pass (dean's list) group or a pass (survival) group?"

## Thought Questions

- What happens if the project leader has lower standards than some other members about writing a paper or report?
- What happens if one group member is not very skilled at some topic area (i.e., how do you utilize that member's input on group projects and incorporate ideas that do not appear to be adding value)?

## Person-Task Mapping

- Is it best to capitalize on the existing strengths of team members or to play to people's weaknesses?
- Suppose your team has a quantitative guru. Do you want to assign the "quant jock" to do all the math and econometrics problems, or use this as an opportunity to let other team members learn?

## Additional Questions

- *Member skills:* Do you want to use your study group meeting time to bring all group members up to speed or should those who need help get it on their own time?
- *Person-task focus:* Are people the group's first priority or is working the first priority?
- *Structure:* Should the team meeting be structured (e.g., agenda, timekeeper, assigned roles) or should it be free-form?
- *Interloper:* Are other people (outside the group) allowed to attend group meetings and have access to group notes, outlines, homework, and so on, or is group work considered confidential?
- *Communication standards:* Are group members expected to adapt to the most advanced methods of communication, or does group work happen at the lowest common denominator?
- *Project leader pacing:* There would seem to be an advantage for group members who volunteer early on for group projects because commitments and pressures build up later in the semester. How will the group meeting process adapt to increasing workloads?

# AFTER THE GROUP IS WELL UNDERWAY

After the group is well underway, it is a good idea to take stock of how the group is working together. We suggest the "Team Assessment," ideally administered by a coach, facilitator, or instructor acquainted with the study group (see KTAG cases and exercises).

Another useful idea is to do some version of a peer-feedback performance review, wherein individuals receive confidential feedback and ratings about how they are viewed by other team members. This can often be completely computerized (see Appendix 4).

## ON A REGULAR BASIS

It is important that study groups revisit the team contract. Are the expectations being met? What issues and topics should be talked about that are not currently in the contract? What issues are in the contract that do not seem relevant?

## SPECIAL TIPS FOR LONG-TERM STUDY GROUPS

Consider the actual advice from MBA students who were enrolled in an intensive two-year program. Their study groups were assigned to them and maintained throughout the two-year program. During the time they worked together, members were asked for their input on what did and did not work in their study groups in regard to maximizing learning and using time effectively. Box A3-1 summarizes the students' responses.

---

**BOX A3-1**

### Advice for Long-Term Study Groups

- An agenda should be distributed before each group meeting date so everyone can prepare properly. Decide upon the agenda for the next meeting before adjourning the current meeting.

- Define who is expected to do what for each project.

- A written outline or "straw man" is needed to focus the group discussion on any particular project. Several alternatives should be evaluated during the outline stage before selecting which alternative will be taken for any project.

- Each major group project has a project leader responsible for doing most of the writing (in some cases, all of the writing). Other group members provide input early in the project and after a draft has been written. Assignments can be done in parallel by using this method, which helps to meet deadlines.

- Some groups summarize class readings for the project leader during the weeks that they are busy completing the project.

- The workload is not divided equally on every project. Over a two-year period, everyone will get the chance to contribute.

- Rotate responsibilities with each module or semester. For example, one person in the group may be the agenda captain for an entire module. The agenda captain organizes the meeting agendas and runs the meetings for that entire module. Rotating responsibilities every week wastes time deciding who does what.

- Try to meet on the same day and time each week. This makes it easier to plan travel schedules in advance.

- At the end of each major assignment, review the effectiveness of the process used to fulfill requirements. Adjust the process to improve effectiveness.

- Improve communication within the group by using e-mail and standardized software.

- Focus on the goals of the meeting first, then socialize.

- Maintain a sense of humor!

*Source:* Taken from compiled lists from the Executive Masters Program, Kellogg School of Management, Northwestern University, Evanston, Illinois. Lists compiled by R. Weeks (1996) and K. Murnighan (1998).

# APPENDIX

# Example Items from Peer Evaluations and 360-Degree Performance Evaluations

Chapter 3 went into detail about the purpose and implementation of 360-degree evaluations. Some people, however, may be unfamiliar with 360-degree evaluations. The fact is, there are no standards. In this appendix, we present examples of two 360-degree evaluation tools. The first one is a peer evaluation system; it is brief and is designed for students enrolled in MBA programs. The second one is much more extensive and designed to provide senior managers with confidential feedback about their leadership abilities and potential.

## TEAMNET

**TeamNet** is Kellogg's Web-based peer evaluation system developed by students, faculty, and staff that enables students to give each other anonymous feedback on their team skills. The method is simple and completely automated. At the end of each academic quarter, students sign on to a Web page and provide anonymous feedback to their teammates by rating each other on 12 key criteria related to improving team-based outcomes. The computer then compiles mean and standard deviation scores for each student. After all responses are compiled, students automatically receive a private e-mail with their personal scores from each of their teams. To enable them to track their progress in building their team skills over time, students also receive their scores from prior quarters.

The system allows students to get direct and timely feedback on their team skills. They can track their skill development in particular areas (e.g., leadership) over time and across different teams and projects to focus on skill development. What's more, students learn how to use peer-based reviews. The automated process means that the information is collected and disseminated efficiently. The feedback is intended for personal growth and does not impact a student's grades nor is it transmitted to employers, and so on. TeamNet also enables managers-in-training to practice giving feedback to team members.

Figure A4-1 illustrates how students using the TeamNet Web site can select the specific team and teammates they want to evaluate; Figure A4-2 illustrates a sample matrix for evaluating a teammate and lists all 12 items on the TeamNET questionnaire; and Figure A4-3 illustrates a sample of an output feedback that a student might receive from the TeamNet system.

Note: The values for this demonstration have been selected below and are reflected in subsequent figures.

Please select the course for the team you will be evaluating, and complete the related information:

Course/Section: ACCT D30 Section 62 Tue–Fri 9:00–10:40 ▼

Number of Teammates (Do not count yourself) 4 ▼

Hours/week of Team Meeting (avg.) 3 ▼

Team Selection Method Assigned ▼

Did you use a team consultant? ○ Yes ⊙ No

**Please select the names of your Teammates.**

Have you been this person's teammate before?

|  |  | Yes | No |
|---|---|---|---|
| Teammate 1: | Joe Smith ▼ | ○ | ⊙ |
| Teammate 2: | Jan Smith ▼ | ○ | ⊙ |
| Teammate 3: | John Doe ▼ | ○ | ⊙ |
| Teammate 4: | Jane Doe ▼ | ○ | ⊙ |

**FIGURE A4-1** Selecting a Team to Evaluate Using TeamNet. Note: The values for this demonstration have been selected below and are reflected in subsequent figures.
*Source:* Uzzi (1997); TeamNet website at *http://www1.kellogg.nwu.edu/teamnet/teamnetcover.asp*

## INDUSTRIAL EXAMPLE OF 360-DEGREE EVALUATIONS

The questionnaire in Table A4-1 from RHR International Company is designed to assess leadership behavior among senior employees. These behaviors encompass critical success factors in the company. The leaders choose at least nine people (one or two line managers, four or five peers, four or five subordinates) to complete the questionnaire, which is processed confidentially.

**Each teammate receives feedback in the matrix below (one matrix per question; one question per website frame):**

| Teammate | Needs Serious Improvement (bottom 10%) 1 | Below Most 2 | Average 3 | Better Than Most 4 | Exception (top 10%) 5 |
|----------|---------|---------|---------|---------|---------|
| Jane Doe | ○ | ○ | ○ | ○ | ○ |
| John Doe | ○ | ○ | ○ | ○ | ○ |
| Jan Smith | ○ | ○ | ○ | ○ | ○ |
| John Smith | ○ | ○ | ○ | ○ | ○ |

**Items Rated:**
Consistently on time to meetings.
Flexible in setting meeting times.
Came to meetings prepared with work assignments.
Sufficiently contributed to the work load (e.g. writing papers, preparing slides, etc.)
Encouraged innovation among team members.
Maintained focus on team goals.
Maintained appropriate balance between talking and listening.
Changed his/her opinion when appropriate.
Communicated ideas effectively.
[Was] respectful of group members.
Provided feedback effectively.
[Was] receptive of feedback (non-defensive).

**FIGURE A4-2**  TeamNet Questionnaire Items and Rating System
*Source:* Uzzi (1997); TeamNet website at *http://www1.kellogg.nwu.edu/teamnet/teamnetcover.asp*

*Note: The values for this demonstration do not reflect student's actual scores.*

The **Mean** and Standard Deviation of the evaluations you received for each class are listed below.

The aggregate statistics combine all of the peer evaluations you received for all your classes last term, including classes that lacked sufficient respondents to report individually; however, stats for sections in which you did not complete a TeamNet evaluation are not included and are omitted in the aggregate stats

**John Doe**

| Scale: 1-needs serious improvement 5-exceptional | Logistics: On time | Logistics: Flexible | Logistics: Prepared | Logistics: Contributed | Discussion: Encouraged innovation | Discussion: Focused on goal | Discussion: Talking vs. listening | Discussion: Changed own opinion as needed | Discussion: Communicated efficiently | Discussion: Respectful | Feedback: Gave effective feedback | Feedback Receptive of feedback |
|---|---|---|---|---|---|---|---|---|---|---|---|---|
| Fall 2001–2002 | | | | | | | | | | | | |
| Accounting D30 | **9.3** 0.6 | **7.7** 2.3 | **9.3** 0.6 | **9.7** 0.6 | **9.7** 0.6 | **9.7** 0.6 | **9.3** 0.6 | **9.3** 0.6 | **9.7** 0.6 | **10** 0 | **9.7** 0.6 | **10** 0 |
| Economics D30 | *Sorry. Since you did not complete a TeamNet evaluation for this section, you are unable to receive scores for this section.* | | | | | | | | | | | |
| Management & Strategy D30 | **9** 1.7 | **8.7** 2.3 | **9** 1.7 | **8.7** 2.3 | **9** 1.7 | **9.3** 1.2 | **9** 1.7 | **9.3** 1.2 | **9** 1 | **9.3** 1.2 | **9** 1 | |
| Marketing D30 | *Fewer than 3 responses; insufficient number to report for this section.* | | | | | | | | | | | |
| Org. Behavior D30 | **9** 1.7 | **8.3** 2.1 | **8.7** 2.3 | **8.7** 2.3 | **9.3** 1.2 | **9.3** 1.2 | **9** 1.7 | **9.3** 1.2 | **9.3** 1.2 | **9.3** 1.2 | **9.3** 1.2 | **9.3** 1.2 |
| Aggregate | **9.1** 1.3 | **8.2** 2 | **9** 1.5 | **9** 1.7 | **9.3** 1.1 | **9.4** 0.9 | **9.1** 1.3 | **9.3** 0.9 | **9.3** 0.9 | **9.6** 0.9 | **9.3** 0.9 | **9.6** 0.9 |

Comments for this team: Great team player! Strong listening and communication skills; responsible and creative.

**FIGURE A4-3** Sample TeamNet Output Feedback Sheet
*Source:* Uzzi (1997); TeamNet website at *http://www1.kellogg.nwu.edu/teamnet/teamnetcover.asp*

**TABLE A4-1**    360-Degree Leadership

| Key Leadership Quality | Questions |
|---|---|
| *Provide Vision:* "Developing vision and demonstrating commitment to the company's strategies, and inspiring a sense of direction" | • Establishes initiatives that promote a global mindset in the organization<br>• Creates a compelling scenario of the future involvement with the team and inspires buy-in<br>• Identifies and applies models and processes that will stimulate behaviors in support of the company's vision<br>• Puts the vision in practice by adopting desired behaviors and corresponding values<br>• Actively gains information concerning markets and environment factors that can have an impact on strategies<br>• Ensures that team and individual objectives support the company's vision<br>• Creates a sense of team purpose according to vision and strategies<br>• Shares insights and facilitates understanding and open communication around vision<br>• Is able to imagine scenarios that are in discontinuity with the existing processes or products |
| *Show Entrepreneurship:* "Thinking ahead, seizing opportunities to develop new markets, products, or services and taking calculated risks to achieve growth" | • Demonstrates passion and energy to move forward<br>• Invents strategies using various sources of data and individual experiences<br>• Encourages proactive behaviors resulting in business growth<br>• Takes calculated risks, then decides<br>• Supports and rewards self-starting behaviors of collaborators<br>• Seeks solutions beyond current practices<br>• Demonstrates an action-oriented attitude<br>• Explores and optimizes the use of resources and expertise available within the team<br>• Communicates information and personal perceptions on new business opportunities for the company |
| *Influence and Convince:* "Persuading others to share a point of view, to adopt a specific position, or to take a course of action" | • Determines appropriate strategies to influence people<br>• Builds networks and uses the authority or power of others to convince<br>• Develops propositions tailored to the interest of the different parties involved<br>• Builds a climate of trust<br>• Expresses perspective with courage and integrity<br>• Listens to others' viewpoints or objections and tests their ideas<br>• Seeks to convince by underlining potential benefits of proposed solutions<br>• Negotiates proposals to determine common course of action<br>• Gains team adherence through effective communication |

*(cont.)*

**TABLE A4-1** *Continued*

| Key Leadership Quality | Questions |
|---|---|
| *Achieve Results:* "Directing the activity of others by setting challenging goals for personal and team accomplishment and by controlling their achievements" | • Sets the example by showing high performance<br>• Sets challenging goals that require a "step change"<br>• Develops strategies and facilitates actions to overcome barriers<br>• Initiates corrective actions to address performance<br>• Supports and works alongside others to help improve performance and results<br>• Introduces and applies new methods within the company<br>• Communicates performance expectations to others<br>• Creates a performance-oriented spirit within the team<br>• Provides regular feedback on achieved performance<br>• Puts in place performance measurement tools |
| *Focus on Customer:* "Managing proactively the various customer demands while maintaining a consistent level of effectiveness" | • Demonstrates a "customer first" attitude and meets with customers regularly<br>• Is involved in the customer's decision-making process<br>• Identifies customer needs and communicates relevant customer-related information<br>• Acts as an advocate by influencing the company on the customer's behalf<br>• Initiates actions that add value to the customer<br>• Ensures team priorities and cooperation are in line with customer service requirements<br>• Asks customers for feedback on service quality<br>• Ensures that performance matches the customer's needs<br>• Keeps close to customers' business evaluations<br>• Is responsive to customer complaints and keeps word |
| *Enhance Cooperation and Adaptation:* "Managing people and teams across businesses and cultures" | • Creates an environment that fosters and rewards cooperation among diverse work teams<br>• Identifies interdependencies and understands the dynamics of bringing different cultures together<br>• Has gained credibility in managing outside home country<br>• Challenges self and others to consider issues from a wider and more global perspective<br>• Is sensitive and adaptable to other cultures<br>• Understands the challenges and opportunities of doing business globally<br>• Shares best practices, solutions, and a wide array of management processes across businesses<br>• Explores diverse methods of learning and acting<br>• Encourages relationships between people to enhance trust and communication across distances and differences |
| *Empower:* "Allocating decision-making authority and creating sense of ownership of the job, missions, or project assignments" | • Sets the example in creating a collaborative team spirit to stimulate initiative<br>• Facilitates the free expression of ideas by showing tolerance such that others are willing to act<br>• Approves and facilitates decision-making among collaborators and is supportive in times of crisis |

*(cont.)*

**TABLE A4-1**  *Continued*

| Key Leadership Quality | Questions |
|---|---|
| | • Exposes staff to situations or challenges outside their area of responsibility<br>• Gives credit to others for what they have accomplished<br>• Builds trust and openness with others<br>• Recognizes creativity in others and allows them to experiment<br>• Shows the willingness to delegate authority to the lowest possible level<br>• Communicates standards or criteria by which team members can measure their progress |
| *Manage Change:*<br>"Fostering innovation and questioning the existing while maintaining constant effectiveness" | • Addresses the needs for change by anticipating and acting upon trends affecting markets and customers<br>• Determines and explains implications of change on the various components of the organization<br>• Creates an environment that encourages people through continuous improvement processes<br>• Recognizes own mistakes and uses these as a learning opportunity<br>• Thinks outside the box and does not hesitate to change habits<br>• Creates a sense of urgency in others to achieve change<br>• Questions self or solicits feedback to adapt to change requirements, and encourages others to do the same<br>• Maintains operational effectiveness while implementing agreed changes<br>• Ensures persistent follow-up of change strategies<br>• Allows new ideas to emerge and ensures their purposeful development through team effort |
| *Develop Talents:*<br>"Creating a learning and continuous improvement climate with an appropriate level of coaching and organizational support" | • Links business and individual development needs<br>• Identifies potentials and develops them<br>• Identifies areas of need and opportunities for self-development<br>• Actively deploys feedback, guidance, and coaching to support people development<br>• Creates opportunities for others to practice new behaviors and to develop skills for current and future role<br>• Measures progress and evaluates benefits of talent development<br>• Provides guidance, practical instructions, and directions in training activities<br>• Recognizes the achievements and development progress of others<br>• Takes charge of developing effective teams<br>• Supports the development of collaborators even for responsibilities outside the entity |

*Note:* All questions answered on 4-point scale: 1 = almost never; 2 = sometimes; 3 = usually; 4 = almost always; CS = can't say
*Source: 360 Degree Leadership.* RHR International Co., © 1998. Reprinted with permission from RHR International Co., Wood Dale, IL.

# References

*ABA Banking Journal*. 1985, July. "Hutton Aftermath: A Violation of Business Ethics or Downright Fraud?" Computers and Operations section, p. 30.

Abel, M. J. 1990. "Experiences in an Exploratory Distributed Organization." In J. Galegher, R. E. Kraut, & C. Egido (Eds.), *Intellectual Teamwork: Social and Technological Foundations of Cooperative Work* (pp. 489–510). Mahwah, NJ: Lawrence Erlbaum Associates.

Adams, S. 1965. "Inequity in Social Exchange." In L. Berkowitz (Ed.), *Advances in Experimental Social Psychology* (Vol. 2, pp. 267–299). New York: Academic Press.

Adelberg, S., & Batson, C. D. 1978. "Accountability and Helping: When Needs Exceed Resources." *Journal of Personality and Social Psychology, 36,* 343–350.

Alderfer, C. P. 1976. "Boundary Relations and Organizational Diagnosis." In M. Meltzer & F. Wickert (Eds.), *Humanizing Organizational Behavior* (pp. 142–175). Springfield, IL: Charles C. Thomas.

Alderfer, C. P. 1977. "Group and Intergroup Relations." In J. R. Hackman & J. L. Suttle (Eds.), *Improving Life at Work* (pp. 227–296). Palisades, CA: Goodyear.

Allen, T. J. 1977. *Managing the Flow of Technology: Technology Transfer and the Dissemination of Technological Information within the R&D Organization.* Cambridge, MA: MIT Press.

Allen, V. L. 1965. "Situational Factors in Conformity." In L. Berkowitz (Ed.), *Advances in Experimental Social Psychology* (Vol. 2, pp. 267–299). New York: Academic Press.

Allison, S., & Messick, D. 1990. "Social Decision Heuristics and the Use of Shared Resources." *Journal of Behavioral Decision Making, 3,* 195–204.

Amabile, T. M. 1996. *Creativity in Context: Update to the Social Psychology of Creativity.* Boulder, CO: Westview.

Amabile, T. M. 1997. "Motivating Creativity in Organizations: On Doing What You Love and Loving What You Do." *California Management Review, 40*(1), 39–58.

Amabile, T. M., & Conti, R. 1999. "Changes in the Work Environment for Creativity during Downsizing." *Academy of Management Journal, 42*(6), 630–640.

Amabile, T. M., Conti, R., Coon, H., Lazenby, J. & Herron, M. 1996. "Assessing the Work Environment for Creativity." *Academy of Management Journal, 39*(5), 1154–1184.

Amabile, T. M., Hadley, C. N., & Kramer, S. J. 2002, August. "Creativity under the Gun." *Harvard Business Review,* 52–61.

Amabile, T. M., Nasco, C. P., Mueller, J., Wojcik, T., Odomirok, P. W., Marsh, M., & Kramer, S. J. 2001. "Academic-Practitioner Collaboration in Management Research: A Case of Cross-Profession Collaboration." *Academy of Management Journal, 44*(2), 418–431.

Amason, A. 1996. "Distinguishing the Effects of Functional and Dysfunctional Conflict on Strategic Decision Making: Resolving a Paradox for Top Management Teams." *Academy of Management Journal, 39*(1), 123–148.

Ancona, D. G. 1987. "Groups in Organizations: Extending Laboratory Models." In C. Hendrick (Ed.), *Annual Review of Personality and Social Psychology: Group and Intergroup Processes* (pp. 207–231). Beverly Hills, CA: Sage.

Ancona, D. G. 1990. "Outward Bound: Strategies for Team Survival in an Organization." *Academy of Management Journal, 33*(2), 334–365.

Ancona, D. G. 1993. "The Classics and the Contemporary: A New Blend of Small Group Theory." In J. K. Murnighan (Ed.), *Social Psychology in Organizations: Advances in Theory and Research.* Upper Saddle River, NJ: Prentice Hall.

Ancona, D. G., & Caldwell, D. F. 1987. "Management Issues Facing New-Product Teams in

High Technology Companies." In D. Lewin, D. Lipsky, & D. Sokel (Eds.), *Advances in Industrial and Labor Relations* (Vol. 4, pp. 199–221). Greenwich, CT: JAI Press.

Ancona, D. G., & Caldwell, D. F. 1988. "Beyond Task and Maintenance: Defining External Functions in Groups." *Groups and Organizational Studies, 13,* 468–494.

Ancona, D. G., & Caldwell, D. F. 1991. *Bridging the Boundary: External Process and Performance in Organizational Teams.* Working paper 3305-91-BPS. Cambridge, MA: Sloan School of Management.

Ancona, D. G., & Caldwell, D. F. 1992. "Demography and Design: Predictors of New Product Team Performance." *Organization Science, 3*(3), 321–341.

Ancona, D. G., & Nadler, D. A. 1989. "Top Hats and Executive Tales: Designing the Senior Team." *Senior Management Review, 31*(1), 19–28.

Anderson, C., & Berdahl, J. L. 2002. "The Experience of Power: Examining the Effects of Power on Approach and Inhibition Tendencies." *Journal of Personality and Social Psychology. 83*(6), 1362–1377.

Anderson, C., & Galinsky, A. 2002. "Power, Risk, and Decision-Making." Manuscript in preparation, Kellogg School of Management, Northwestern University, Evanston, IL.

Anderson, H. C. (1837/1959). *The Emperor's New Clothes (Kejserens Nye Klæder).* Translated and illustrated by E. Blegvad. New York: Harcourt.

Anonymous. 1996. "Microsoft Teamwork." *Executive Excellence, 13*(7), 6–7.

Antonioni, D. 1994. "The Effects of Feedback Accountability on Upward Appraisal Ratings." *Personnel Psychology, 47,* 349–356.

AP/Canadian Press. 2002, July 28. "Miners Huddled Together for Warmth, Encouraged Each Other, Rescued Miner Says."

Argote, L. 1989. "Agreement about Norms and Work-Unit Effectiveness: Evidence from the Field." *Basic and Applied Social Psychology, 10*(2), 131–140.

Argote, L. 2002. "Organizational Learning." Presentation for the Kellogg School of Management/School of Education and Social Policy. Evanston, IL: Northwestern University.

Argote, L., Insko, C. A., Yovetich, N., & Romero, A. A. 1995. "Group Learning Curves: The Effects of Turnover and Task Complexity on Group Performance." *Journal of Applied Social Psychology, 25,* 512–529.

Argote, L., & Kane, A. (in press). "Learning from Direct and Indirect Organizations: The Effects of Experience Content, Timing, and Distribution." In P. Paulus and B. Nijstad (Eds.), *Group Creativity.* New York: Oxford University Press.

Argyris, C. 1977a. "Double Loop Learning." *Harvard Business Review, 55*(5), 115–125.

Argyris, C. 1977b. "Organizational Learning and Management Information Systems." *Harvard Business Review, 55*(5), 115–125.

Armour, S. 1997, December 8. "Business' Black Hole." *USA Today,* p. 1A.

Armstrong, D. J., & Cole, P. 1995. "Managing Distances and Differences in Geographically Distributed Work Groups." In S. E. Jackson & M. N. Ruderman (Eds.), *Diversity in Work Teams: Research Paradigms for a Changing Workplace* (pp. 187–215). Washington, DC: American Psychological Association.

Arnold, D. W., & Greenberg, C. I. 1980. "Deviate Rejection within Differentially Manned Groups." *Social Psychology Quarterly, 43*(4), 419–424.

Arrow, H. 1998. "Standing Out and Fitting In: Composition Effects on Newcomer Socialization." *Research on Managing Groups and Teams, 1,* 59–80.

Arrow, H., & McGrath, J. E. 1995. "Membership Dynamics in Groups at Work: A Theoretical Framework." In B. M. Staw & L. L. Cummings (Eds.), *Research in Organizational Behavior* (Vol. 17, pp. 373–411). Greenwich, CT: JAI Press.

Arrow, K. J. 1963. *Social Choice and Individual Values.* New York: John Wiley & Sons.

Asch, S. E. 1956. "Studies of Independence and Conformity: A Minority of One against a Unanimous Majority." *Psychological Monographs, 70*(9, Whole No. 416).

Ashford, S. J., & Cummings, L. L. 1983. "Feedback as an Individual Resource: Personal Strategies of Creating Information." *Organizational Behavior and Human Decision Processes, 32,* 370–398.

Associated Press. 1990, March 20. "Company: Miswiring Caused Satellite Deployment Failure."

Associated Press. 2003, February 14. "Before Columbia, NASA Mulled Space Repairs."

Attaran, M., & Nguyen, T. T. 1999, July 1. "Succeeding with Self-Managed Work Teams." *Industrial Management,* p. 24–28.

Austin, J. T., Villanova, P., & Hindman, H. D. 1996. "Legal Requirements and Technical Guidelines Involved in Implementing Performance Appraisal Systems." In G. Ferris & R. M. Buckley (Eds.), *Human Resources Management: Perspectives, Context, Function, and Outcomes.* (3d ed., p. 283). Upper Saddle River, NJ: Prentice Hall.

Babcock, L., Loewenstein, G., Issacharoff, S., & Camerer, C. 1995. "Biased Judgments of Fairness in Bargaining." *American Economic Review, 85*(5), 1337–1343.

Back, K. W. 1951. "Influence through Social Communication." *Journal of Abnormal Social Psychology, 46,* 9–23.

Baldwin, M. W. 1992. "Relational Schemas and the Processing of Social Information." *Psychological Bulletin, 112*(3), 461–484.

Bales, R. F. 1955. *How People Interact in Conferences.* New York: Scientific American.

Bales, T. 1958. "Task Roles and Social Roles in Problem-Solving Groups." In E. E. Maccoby, T. M. Newcomb, & E. I. Hartley (Eds.), *Readings in Social Psychology.* New York: Holt, Rinehart, & Winston.

Balf, T. 2000, September. "Let's Go Round Up the Best People." *Fastcompany, 38,* 84–86.

Barabási, A. 2002. *Linked: The New Science of Networks.* Cambridge, MA: Perseus Publishing.

Barboza, D. 1998, September 20. "Loving a Stock, Not Wisely, but Too Well." *New York Times,* section 3, p. 1.

Barchas, P. R., & Fisek, M. H. 1984. "Hierarchical Differentiation in Newly Formed Groups of Rhesus and Humans." In P. R. Barchas (Ed.), *Essays toward a Sociophysiological Perspective* (pp. 23–33). Westport, CT: Greenwood Press.

Barker, J. R. 1993. "Tightening the Iron Cage: Concertive Control in Self-Managing Teams." *Administrative Science Quarterly, 38,* 408–437.

Barker, R. 2002, August 26. "The Art of Brainstorming." *BusinessWeek, Bonus Issue: 25 Ideas for a Changing World,* pp. 168–169.

Barley, S. R. 1996. "Technicians in the Workplace: Ethnographic Evidence for Bringing Work into Organization Studies." *Administrative Science Quarterly, 41*(3), 404–441.

Barreto, M., & Ellemers, N. 2002. "The Impact of Respect versus Neglect of Self-Identities on Identification and Group Loyalty." *Personality and Social Psychology Bulletin, 28*(5), 629–639.

Barrick, M. R., Stewart, G. L., Neubert, M. J., & Mount, M. K. 1998. "Relating Member Ability and Personality to Work-Team Processes and Team Effectiveness." *Journal of Applied Psychology, 83,* 377–391.

Basalla, G. 1988. *The Evolution of Technology.* New York: Cambridge University Press.

Bass, B. M. 1985. *Leadership and Performance Beyond Expectations.* New York: Free Press.

Bass, B. M. 1990. *Bass & Stogdill's Handbook of Leadership: Theory, Research, & Management Applications* (3d ed.). New York: Free Press.

Bastardi, A., & Shafir, E. 1998. "On the Pursuit and Misuse of Useless Information." *Journal of Personality and Social Psychology, 75*(1), 19–32.

Baumeister, R. F. 1984. "Choking under Pressure: Self-Consciousness and Paradoxical Effects of Incentives on Skillful Performance." *Journal of Personality and Social Psychology, 46,* 610–620.

Baumeister, R. F., & Scher, S. J. 1988. "Self-Defeating Behavior Patterns among Normal Individuals." *Psychological Bulletin, 104,* 3–22.

Baumeister, R. F., & Steinhilber, A. 1984. "Paradoxical Effects of Supportive Audiences on Performance under Pressure: The Home Field Disadvantage in Sports Championships." *Journal of Personality and Social Psychology, 47*(1), 85–93.

Baumeister, R. F., Twenge, J. M., & Nuss, C. K. 2002. "Effects of Social Exclusion on Cognitive Processes: Anticipated Aloneness Reduces Intelligent Thought." *Journal of Personality and Social Psychology, 83*(4), 817–827.

Bazerman, M., Mannix, E., & Thompson, L. 1988. "Groups as Mixed-Motive Negotiations." In E. J. Lawler & B. Markovsky (Eds.), *Advances in Group Processes: A Research Annal.* (Vol. 5, pp. 195–216). Greenwich, CT: JAI Press.

Bazerman, M. H. 2002. *Judgments in Managerial Decision Making.* (5th edition). New York: Wiley.

Becker, F., Quinn, K. L., Rappaport, A. J., & Sims, W. R. 1994. *Implementing Innovative Workplaces.* New York State College of Human Ecology, Department of Design and Environmental Analysis. Ithaca: Cornell University.

Beer, M., Eisenstat, R. A., & Spector, B. 1990. *The Critical Path to Corporate Renewal.* Boston: Harvard Business School Press.

Bellinger, G. D., Castro, D., & Mills, A. 2000. "Data, Information, Knowledge, and Wisdom." Available at: *http://www.outsights. com/systems/dikw/dikw.htm.*

Belliveau, M. A., O'Reilly III, C. A., & Wade, J. B. 1996. "Social Capital: The Effects of Social Similarity and Status on CEO Compensation." *Academy of Management Journal, 39,* 1568–1593.

Benne, K. D., & Sheats, P. 1948. "Functional Roles of Group Members." *Journal of Social Issues, 4,* 41–49.

Bennis, W., & Nanus, B. 1985. *Leaders.* New York: Harper & Row.

Berger, J., Rosenholtz, S. J., & Zelditch, M. 1980. "Status Organizing Processes." *Annual Review of Sociology, 6,* 479–508.

Bergstrom, R. Y. 1997, February. "Be Prepared to Be Involved." *Automotive Manufacturing and Production, 109*(2), 66–69.

Bernardin, H. J., & Cascio, W. F. 1988. "Performance Appraisal and the Law." In R. S. Schuler, S. A. Youngblood, & V. L. Huber (Eds.), *Readings in Personnel and Human Resource Management.* (3d ed., p. 239). St. Paul, MN: West Publishing Company.

Bettencourt, B. A., Brewer, M. B., Croak, M. R., & Miller, N. 1992. "Cooperation and the Reduction of Intergroup Bias: The Role of Reward Structure and Social Orientation." *Journal of Experimental Social Psychology, 28*(4), 301–319.

Bettencourt, B. A., Charlton, K., & Kernahan, C. 1997. "Cooperative Interaction and Intergroup Bias: The Interaction Between Numerical Representation and Social Orientation." *Journal of Experimental Social Psychology, 33,* 630–659.

Bettencourt, B. A., & Dorr, N. 1998. "Cooperative Interaction and Intergroup Bias: Effects of Numerical Representation and Cross-Cut Role Assignment." *Personality and Social Psychology Bulletin, 24*(12), 1276–1293.

Bettenhausen, K., & Murnighan, J. K. 1985. "The Emergence of Norms in Competitive Decision-Making Groups." *Administrative Science Quarterly, 30,* 350–372.

Blake, G. 1999, November–December. "E-mail with Feeling." *Research • Technology Management,* pp. 12–13.

Blascovich, J., Mendes, W. B., Hunter, S. B., & Salomon, K. 1999. "Social 'Facilitation' as Challenge and Threat." *Journal of Personality and Social Psychology, 77*(1), 68–77.

Blau, P. M. 1955. *The Dynamics of Bureaucracy.* Chicago: University of Chicago Press.

Blinder, A. S. 1990. "Pay, Participation, and Productivity." *Brookings Review, 8*(1), 33–38.

Bloomfield, R., Libby, R., & Nelson, M. W. 1996. "Communication of Confidence as a Determinant of Group Judgment Accuracy." *Organizational Behavior and Human Decision Processes, 68*(3), 287–300.

Bobo, L. 1983. "Whites' Opposition to Busing: Symbolic Racism or Realistic Group Conflict?" *Journal of Personality and Social Psychology, 45*(6), 1196–1210.

Bohrnstedt, G. W., & Fisher, G. A. 1986. "The Effects of Recalled Childhood and Adolescent Relationships Compared to Current Role Performances on Young Adults' Affective Functioning." *Social Psychology Quarterly, 49*(1), 19–32.

Boisjoly, R. M. 1987, December 13–18. "Ethical Decisions—Morton Thiokol and the Space Shuttle Challenger Disaster." Speech presented at the American Society of Mechanical Engineers, Winter Annual Meeting, Boston, MA.

Bond, C. F., & Anderson, E. L. 1987. "The Reluctance to Transmit Bad News: Private Discomfort or Public Display?" *Journal of Experimental Psychology, 23,* 176–187.

Bouas, K. S., & Arrow, H. 1996. "The Development of Group Identity in Computer and Face to Face Groups with Membership Change." *Computer Supported Cooperative Work, 4,* 153–178.

Bouchard, T. J. 1972. "Training, Motivation, and Personality as Determinants of the Effectiveness of Brainstorming Groups and

Individuals." *Journal of Applied Psychology, 56*(4), 324–331.

Bowen, D. D., Lewicki, R. J., Hall, D. T., & Hall, F. S. 1997. *Experiences in Management and Organizational Behavior* (4th edition). New York: Wiley.

Bradford, D. L., & Cohen, A. R. 1984. *Managing for Excellence.* New York: John Wiley & Sons.

Branscombe, N. R., Spears, R., Ellemers, N., & Doosje, B. 2002. "Intragroup and Intergroup Evaluation Effects on Group Behavior." *Personality and Social Psychology Bulletin, 28*(6), 744–753.

Brawley, L. R., Carron, A. V., & Widmeyer, W. N. 1988. "Exploring the Relationship between Cohesion and Group Resistance to Disruption." *Journal of Sport and Exercise Psychology, 10*(2), 199–213.

Breen, B. 2002, September. "BMW: Driven by Design." *Fastcompany,* pp. 122–135.

Brehmer, B., & Hagafors, R. 1986. "Use of Experts in Complex Decision Making: A Paradigm for the Study of Staff Work." *Organizational Behavior and Human Decision Processes, 38,* 181–195.

Brewer, M. 1979. "Ingroup Bias in the Minimal Intergroup Situation: A Cognitive-Motivational Analysis." *Psychological Bulletin, 86,* 307–324.

Brewer, M. 1991. "The Social Self: On Being the Same and Different at the Same Time." *Personality and Social Psychology Bulletin, 17*(5), 475–482.

Brewer, M. B. 1986. "The Role of Ethnocentrism in Intergroup Conflict." In S. Worchel and W. G. Austin (Eds.), *The Psychology of Intergroup Relations.* Chicago, IL: Nelson-Hall.

Brewer, M. B., & Brown, R. J. 1998. "Intergroup Relations." In D. T. Gilbert, S. T. Fiske, & G. Lindzey (Eds.), *The Handbook of Social Psychology* (4th ed., Vol. 2, pp. 554–594). New York: McGraw-Hill.

Brewer, M. B., & Kramer, R. M. 1986. "Choice Behavior in Social Dilemmas: Effects of Social Identity, Group Size, and Decision Framing." *Journal of Personality and Social Psychology, 50*(3), 543–549.

Brickner, M. A., Harkins, S. G., & Ostrom, T. M. 1986. "Effects of Personal Involvement: Thought-Provoking Implications for Social Loafing." *Journal of Personality and Social Psychology, 51*(4), 763–770.

Brown, J. 2002, March 18. "Prada Gets Personal." *BusinessWeek,* p. EB8.

Brown, P., & Levinson, S. 1987. *Politeness: Some Universals in Language Use.* Cambridge, England: Cambridge University Press.

Brown, R. 2000. *Group Processes* (2nd edition). Oxford, England: Blackwell.

Brown, R. J., Condor, F., Mathew, A., Wade, G., & Williams, J. A. 1986. "Explaining Intergroup Differentiation in an Industrial Organization." *Journal of Occupational Psychology, 59,* 273–286.

Brown, S. F. 2002, July 22. "Building America's Anti-Terror Machine: How Infotech Can Combat Homeland Insecurity." *Fortune,* pp. 99–104.

Buchanan, L. 2002, August 1. "The Innovation Factor: Inside the Idea Mill." *Inc. Magazine.*

Buckingham, M., & Coffman, C. 1999. *First, Break All the Rules: What the World's Greatest Managers Do Differently.* New York: Simon & Schuster.

Burke, P. J. 1967. "The Development of Task and Social-Emotional Role Differentiation." *Sociometry, 30,* 379–392.

Burns, J. M. 1978. *Leadership.* New York: Harper & Row.

Burt, R. S. 1992. *The Social Structure of Competition.* Cambridge, MA: Harvard University Press.

Burt, R. S. 1999. "Entrepreneurs, Distrust, and Third Parties: A Strategic Look at the Dark Side of Dense Networks." In L. Thompson, J. Levine, & D. Messick (Eds.), *Shared Cognition in Organizations: The Management of Knowledge.* Mahwah, NJ: Lawrence Erlbaum & Associates.

Bushe, G. R. 1984. "Quality Circles in Quality of Work Life Projects: Problems and Prospects for Increasing Employee Participation." *Canadian Journal of Community Mental Health, 3*(2), 101–113.

BusinessWire, 2001, October 29. "Workplace Transformation Initiatives Address Changing Business Climate; Enable eRoom Technology Customers to Respond to New-World Challenges." Cambridge, MA.

Byrne, D. 1961. "Interpersonal Attraction and Attitude Similarity." *Journal of Abnormal and Social Psychology, 62,* 713–715.

Byrne, J. A. 1998, August 31. "The Corporation of the Future." *BusinessWeek,* p. 102.

Byrne, J. A. 2002a, July 29. "No Excuses for Enron's Board." *BusinessWeek,* pp. 50–51.

Byrne, J. A. 2002b, August 12. "Fall from Grace." *BusinessWeek,* pp. 51–56.

Byrne, J. A., France, M., & Zellner, W. 2002, February 25. " 'The Environment Was Ripe for Abuse': Enron's Unrelenting Stress on Growth and its Absence of Controls Helped Push Execs into Unethical Behavior." *BusinessWeek,* pp. 118–120.

Byrne, J. A., & Grover, G. 2000, February 21. "Mattel's Lack-of-Action Figures." *BusinessWeek,* p. 50.

Camacho, L. M., & Paulus, P. B. 1995. "The Role of Social Anxiousness in Group Brainstorming." *Journal of Personality and Social Psychology, 68,* 1071–1080.

Camerer, C. F., Loewenstein, G., & Weber, M. 1989. "The Curse of Knowledge in Economic Settings: An Experimental Analysis." *Journal of Political Economy, 97,* 1232–1254.

Caminiti, S. 1995. "What Team Leaders Need to Know." *Fortune, 131*(3), 93–100.

Campbell, D. T. 1965. "Ethnocentric and Other Altruistic Motives." In D. Levine (Ed.), *Nebraska Symposium on Motivation* (pp. 283–311). Lincoln: University of Nebraska Press.

Cannon-Bowers, J. A., Salas, E., & Converse, S. A. 1993. "Shared Mental Models in Expert Team Decision Making." In N. J. Castellan (Ed.), *Individual and Group Decision Making* (pp. 221–246). Mahwah, NJ: Lawrence Erlbaum & Associates.

Cannon-Bowers, J. A., Tannenbaum, S. I., Salas, E., & Converse, S. A. 1991. "Toward an Integration of Training Theory and Technique." *Human Factors, 33*(3), 281–292.

Caporael, L. R., Dawes, R. M., Orbell, J. M., & van de Kragt, A. J. C. 1989. "Selfishness Examined: Cooperation in the Absence of Egoistic Incentives." *Behavioral and Brain Sciences, 12,* 683–739.

Carder, S., & Gunter, L. 2001, October 1. "Can You Hear Me? Corporate America's Communication with Dissatisfied Customers." *Journal of American Culture,* pp. 109–112.

Carnevale, P. J., Pruitt, D., & Seilheimmer, S. 1981. "Looking and Competing: Accountability and Visual Access in Integrative Bargaining." *Journal of Personality and Social Psychology, 40,* 111–120.

Carron, A. V., Widmeyer, W. N., & Brawley, L. R. 1988. "Group Cohesion and Individual Adherence to Physical Activity." *Journal of Sport and Exercise Psychology, 10*(2), 127–138.

Castore, C. H., & Murnighan, J. K. 1978. "Determinants of Support for Group Decisions." *Organizational Behavior and Human Performance, 22,* 75–92.

Caudron, S. 1996. "How Pay Launched Performance." *Personnel Journal* (now known as *Workforce*), *75*(9), 70–76. Reprinted with permission.

Ceron, G. F. 2001, July 25. "New York Stock Exchange to Cut 150 Jobs, or 10% Staff." Dow Jones News Service, *www.djnewswires.com.*

Charan, R., & Useem, J. 2002, May 27. "Why Companies Fail." *Fortune,* 145(11), 50–62.

Chatman, J. A., Polzer, J. T., Barsade, S. G., & Neale, M. A. 1998. "Being Different yet Feeling Similar: The Influence of Demographic Composition and Organizational Culture on Work Processes and Outcomes." *Administrative Science Quarterly, 43,* 749–780.

Chechile, R. 1984. "Logical Foundations for a Fair and Rational Method of Voting." In W. Swapp (Ed.), *Group Decision Making* (pp. 97–114). Beverly Hills, CA: Sage.

Chen, X. P. 1996. "The Group-Based Binding Pledge as a Solution to Public Goods Problems." *Organizational Behavior and Human Decision Processes, 66*(2), 192–202.

Christensen, C., Larson, J. R., Abbott, A., Ardolino, A., Franz, T., & Pfeiffer, C. 1998. "Decision Making of Clinical Teams: Communication Patterns and Diagnostic Error." Manuscript under review.

Cialdini, R. B. 1989. *Indirect Tactics of Image Management: Beyond Basking.* Mahwah, NJ: Lawrence Erlbaum & Associates.

Cini, M., Moreland, R. L., & Levine, J. M. 1993. "Group Staffing Levels and Responses to Prospective and New Members." *Journal of Personality and Social Psychology, 65,* 723–734.

Clark, K. B., & Fujimoto, T. 1987. "Overlapping Problem Solving in Product Development." Working paper 87-048. Cambridge, MA: Harvard University Graduate School of Business Administration.

Clemmer, J. 1995. *Pathways to Performance: A Guide to Transforming Yourself, Your Team, and Your Organization.* Rocklin, CA: Macmillan Canada and Prima Publishing.

Cohen, G. L., Steele, C. M., & Ross, L. D. 1999. "The Mentor's Dilemma: Providing Critical Feedback across the Racial Divide." *Personality and Social Psychology Bulletin, 25*(10), 1302–1318.

Cohen, M. D., March, J. P., & Olsen, J. P. 1972. "A Garbage Can Model of Organizational Choice." *Administrative Science Quarterly, 17,* 1–25.

Cole, R. E. 1982. "Diffusion of Participating Work Structures in Japan, Sweden and the United States." In P. S. Goodman et al. (Eds.), *Change in Organizations* (pp. 166–225). San Francisco, CA: Jossey-Bass.

Coleman, J. S. 1988. "Social Capital in the Creation of Human Capital." *American Journal of Sociology, 94,* S95–S120.

Collaros, P. A., & Anderson, L. R. 1969. "Effect of Perceived Expertness upon Creativity of Members of Brainstorming Groups." *Journal of Applied Psychology, 53*(2, Pt. 1), 159–163.

Collins, E. G., & Guetzkow, H. 1964. *A Social Psychology of Group Processes for Decision Making.* New York: Wiley.

Conger, J. 1989. "The Art of Empowering Others." *Academy of Management Executive, 3*(1), 17–24. Reprinted with permission.

Connolly, T., Routhieaux, R. L., & Schneider, S. K. 1993. "On the Effectiveness of Group Brainstorming: Test of One Underlying Cognitive Mechanism." *Small Group Research, 24,* 490–503.

Cox, A. 2000, August. "Where There's Muck There's Brass: Can a Few Days on The Farm Really Improve Your Performance at Work?" *Guardian* (London).

Crocker, J., & Major, B. 1989. "Social Stigma and Self-Esteem: The Self-Protective Properties of Stigma." *Psychological Review, 96,* 608–630.

Crocker, J., Voelkl, K., Testa, M., & Major, B. 1991. "Social Stigma: The Affective Consequences of Attributional Ambiguity." *Journal of Personality and Social Psychology, 60,* 218–228.

Csikszentmihalyi, M. 1988. "Society, Culture and Person: A Systems View of Creativity." In R. Sternberg (Ed.), *The Nature of Productivity: Contemporary Psychological Perspectives.* New York: Cambridge University Press.

Csikszentmihalyi, M. 1997. *Finding Flow: The Psychology of Engagement with Everyday Life.* New York: Basicbooks.

Cummings, T. G., & Mohrman, S. A. 1987. "Self-Designing Organizations: Towards Implementing Quality-of-Work-Life Innovations." In R. W. Woodman & W. A. Pasmore (Eds.), *Research in Organizational Change and Development* (Vol. 1, pp. 275–310). Greenwich, CT: JAI Press.

Cusumano, M. A. 1997. "How Microsoft Makes Large Teams Work Like Small Teams." *Sloan Management Review, 39*(1), 9–20.

Daft, R. L., & Lengel, R. H. 1984. "Information Richness: A New Approach to Managerial Behavior and Organization Design." *Research in Organization Behavior, 6,* 191–223.

Daft, R. L., Lengel, R. H., & Trevino, L. K. 1987. "Message Equivocality, Media Selection, and Manager Performance: Implications for Information Systems." *MIS Quarterly, 11*(3), 355–366.

Dahle, C. 1999, November. "Xtreme Teams." *Fastcompany, 29,* 310.

David, B., & Turner, J. C. 1996. "Studies in Self-Categorization and Minority Conversion: Is Being a Member of the Out-Group an Advantage?" *British Journal of Social Psychology, 35,* 179–199.

Davidow, W. H., & Malone, M. S. 1992. *The Virtual Corporation: Structuring and Revitalizing the Corporation for the 21st Century.* New York: HarperCollins.

Davis, J. 1969. *Group Performance.* Reading, MA: Addison-Wesley.

Dawes, R., Orbell, J., & van de Kragt, A. 1988. "Not Me or Thee but We: The Importance of Group Identity in Eliciting Cooperation in Dilemma Situations." *Acta Psychologica, 68,* 83–97.

Dawes, R., van de Kragt, A., & Orbell, J. 1990. "Cooperation for the Benefit of Us—Not Me, or My Conscience." In J. Mansbridge (Ed.), *Beyond Self Interest* (pp. 97–110). Chicago: University of Chicago Press.

De Cremer, D. 2002. "Respect and Cooperation in Social Dilemmas: The Importance of Feeling Included." *Personality and Social Psychology Bulletin, 28*(10), 1335–1341.

De Cremer, D., & van Dijk, E. 2002. "Reactions to Group Success and Failure as a Function of Identification Levels: A Test of the Goal-Transformation Hypothesis In Social Dilemmas." *Journal of Experimental Social Psychology, 38,* 435–442.

De Cremer, D., & Van Vugt, M. 1999. "Social Identification Effects in Social Dilemmas: A Transformation of Motives." *Journal of Experimental Social Psychology, 29,* 871–893.

DeGroot, A. 1966. "Perception and Memory versus Thought. Some Old Ideas and Recent Findings." In B. Kleinmuntz (Ed.), *Problem Solving: Research, Method, and Theory* (pp. 19–50). New York: John Wiley & Sons.

Delbecq, A. L., & Van de Ven, A. H. 1971. "A Group Process Model for Identification and Program Planning." *Journal of Applied Behavioral Sciences, 7,* 466–492.

DeMatteo, J. S., Eby, L. T., & Sundstrom, E. 1998. "Team-Based Rewards: Current Empirical Evidence and Directions for Future Research." *Research on Organization Behavior, 20,* 141–183.

DeMeyer, A. 1991. "Tech Talk: How Managers Are Stimulating Global R&D Communication." *Sloan Management Review, 32*(3), 49–58.

DeMeyer, A. 1993. "Internationalizing R&D Improves a Firm's Technical Learning." *Research-Technical Management, 36*(4), 42–49.

Dennis, A. R., Nunamaker, J. F. Jr., Paranka, D., & Vogel, D. R. A. 1990. "A New Role for Computers in Strategic Management." *Journal of Business Strategy, 11*(5), 38–42.

Dennis, A. R., Valacich, J. S., Connolly, T., & Wynne, B. E. 1996. "Process Structuring in Electronic Brainstorming." *Information Systems Research, 7,* 268–277.

*Deseret News.* 2001, July 1. "Wild West Corralling Corporate Getaway Action." P. M06.

Deutsch, M. 1973. *The Resolution of Conflict.* New Haven, CT: Yale University Press.

Deutsch, M. 1975. "Equity, Equality, and Need: What Determines Which Value Will Be Used as the Basis of Distributive Justice?" *Journal of Social Issues, 31,* 137–149.

Deutsch, M., & Gerard, H. B. 1955. "A Study of Normative and Informational Social Influence upon Individual Judgment." *Journal of Abnormal and Social Psychology, 51,* 629–636.

Devadas, R., & Argote, L. 1995. "Organizational Learning Curves: The Effects of Turnover and Work Group Structure." Invited paper presented at the annual meeting of the Midwestern Psychological Association, Chicago, IL.

Diehl, M., & Stroebe, W. 1987. "Productivity Loss in Brainstorming Groups: Toward a Solution of a Riddle." *Journal of Personality and Social Psychology, 53*(3), 497–509.

Diehl, M., & Stroebe, W. 1991. "Productivity Loss in Idea-Generating Groups: Tracking Down the Blocking Effect." *Journal of Personality and Social Psychology, 61*(3), 392–403.

Dietz-Uhler, B. 1996. "The Escalation of Commitment in Political Decision Making Groups: A Social Identity Approach." *European Journal of Social Psychology, 26,* 611–629.

Dion, K. 2000. "Group Cohesion: From 'Field of Forces' to Multidimensional Construct." *Group Dynamics: Theory, Research, and Practice, 4*(1), 7–26.

Dion, K. L., & Evans, C. R. 1992. "On Cohesiveness: Reply to Keyton and Other Critics of the Construct." *Small Group Research, 23*(2), 242–250.

Doney, P. M., & Armstrong, G. M. 1996. "Effects of Accountability on Symbolic Information Search and Information Analysis by Organizational Buyers." *Journal of the Academy of Marketing Science, 24,* 57–65.

Doosje, B., Spears, R., & Koomen, W. 1995. "When Bad Isn't All Bad: Strategic Use of Sample Information in Generalization and Stereotyping." *Journal of Personality and Social Psychology, 69,* 642–655.

*Dow Jones News Service.* 1998, April 14. "Japan's LTCB Asks Workers to Grade Executives."

Drach-Zahavy, A., & Erez, M. 2002. "Challenge versus Threat Effects on the Goal-Performance Relationship." *Organizational Behavior and Human Decision Processes, 88,* 667–682.

Drolet, A., Larrick, R., & Morris, M. W. 1998. "Thinking of Others: How Perspective-Taking Changes Negotiators' Aspirations and Fairness Perceptions as a Function of Negotiator Relationships." *Basic and Applied Social Psychology, 20*(1), 23–31.

Dubrovsky, V. J., Keisler, S., & Sethna, B. N. 1991. "The Equalization Phenomenon: Status Effects in Computer-Mediated and Face-to-

Face Decision-Making Groups." *Human-Computer Interaction, 6*(2), 119–146.

Duck, J. M., & Fielding, K. S. 1999. "Leaders and Subgroups: One of Us or One of Them?" *Group Processes and Intergroup Relations, 2*(3), 203–230.

Dugosh, K. L., Paulus, P. B., Roland, E. J., & Yang, H-C. 2000. "Cognitive Stimulation in Brainstorming." *Journal of Personality of Social Psychology, 79*(5), 722–735.

Dunbar, K. 1997. "How Scientists Think: On-Line Creativity and Conceptual Change in Science." In T. B. Ward, S. M. Smith, & J. Vaid (Eds.), *Creative Thought: An Investigation of Conceptual Structures and Processes.* Washington, DC: American Psychological Association.

Durham, C., Knight, D., & Locke, E. A. 1997. "Effects of Leader Role, Team-Set Goal Difficulty, Efficacy, and Tactics on Team Effectiveness." *Organizational Behavior and Human Decision Processes, 72*(2), 203–231.

Edmondson, A., Bohmer, R., & Pisano, G. 2000. "Collaborating to Learn: Effects of Organizational and Team Characteristics on Successful Adoption of New Medical Technology in Hospital-Based Surgical Teams." In M. A. Neale, E. A. Mannix, and T. L. Griffith (Eds.), *Research on Managing Groups and Teams: Technology* (Vol. 3, pp. 29–51). Stamford, CT: JAI.

Eisenberger, R., & Selbst, M. 1994. "Does Reward Increase or Decrease Creativity?" *Journal of Personality and Social Psychology, 49,* 520–528.

Eisenhardt, K. M., Kahwajy, J. L., & Bourgeois, L. J., III. 1997, July 1. "How Management Teams Can Have a Good Fight." *Harvard Business Review, 75*(4), 77–85.

Emery, F. E., & Trist, E. L. 1973. *Towards a Social Ecology: Contextual Appreciation of the Future in the Present.* New York: Plenum Press.

Ensari, N., & Miller, N. 2002. "The Out-Group Must Not Be So Bad After All: The Effects of Disclosure, Typicality, and Salience on Intergroup Bias." *Journal of Personality of Social Psychology, 82*(2), 313–329.

Esses, V. M., & Dovidio, J. F. 2002. "The Role of Emotions in Determining Willingness to Engage in Intergroup Contact." *Personality and Social Psychology Bulletin, 28*(9), 1202–1214.

Etzkowitz, H., Kemelgor, C., & Uzzi, B. 1999. *Social Capital and Career Dynamics in Hard Science: Gender, Networks, and Advancement.* New York: Cambridge University Press.

Eveland, J. D., & Bikson, T. K. 1989. *Workgroup Structures and Computer Support: A Field Experiment.* Santa Monica, CA: Rand Corp.

Fairlamb, D. 2002, July 29. "Trouble in Paradise." *BusinessWeek,* pp. 56–57.

Fan, E. T., & Gruenfeld, D. H. 1998. "When Needs Outweigh Desires: The Effects of Resource Interdependence and Reward Interdependence on Group Problem Solving." *Basic and Applied Social Psychology, 20*(1), 45–56.

Faraj, S., & Sproull, L. 2000. "Coordinating Expertise in Software Development Teams." *Management Science, 46*(12), 1554–1568.

Farwell, L., & Weiner, B. 1996. "Self-Perceptions of Fairness in Individual and Group Contexts." *Personality and Social Psychology Bulletin, 22*(9), 867–881.

Feldman, D. C. 1977. "The Role of Initiation Activities in Socialization." *Human Relations, 30,* 977–990.

Fenn, D. 1996, May 1. "Teams: A Formula for Success." *Fastcompany.*

Field, R. H. G., & House, R. J. 1990. "A Test of the Vroom-Yetton Model Using Manager and Subordinate Reports." *Journal of Applied Psychology, 75*(3), 362–366.

Finholt, T. A., & Olson, G. M. 1997. "From Laboratories to Collaboratories: A New Organizational Form for Scientific Collaboration." *Psychological Science, 8*(1), 28–36.

Finke, R. A. 1995. "Creative Realism." In S. M. Smith, T. B. Ward, & R. A. Finke (Eds.), *The Creative Cognition Approach* (pp. 303–326). Cambridge, MA: MIT Press.

Fischhoff, B. 1975. "Hindsight Does Not Equal Foresight: The Effect of Outcome Knowledge on Judgment under Uncertainty." *Journal of Experimental Psychology: Human Perception and Performance, 1,* 288–299.

Fischhoff, B., Slovic, P., & Lichtenstein, S. 1977. "Knowing with Certainty: The Appropriateness of Extreme Confidence." *Journal of Experimental Psychology: Human Perception and Performance, 3*(4), 552–564.

Fisher, R., & Ury, W. 1981. *Getting to Yes: Negotiating Agreement without Giving In.* Boston: Houghton Mifflin.

Fishman, C. 1996. "Whole Foods Is All Teams." *Fastcompany, 2,* 103.

Fishman, C. 1999. "How Teamwork Took Flight." *Fastcompany, 28,* 188.

Fleming, J. H., & Darley, J. M. 1991. "Mixed Messages: The Multiple Audience Problem and Strategic Communication." *Social Cognition, 9,* 25–46.

Flippen, A. R., Hornstein, H. A., Siegal, W. E., & Weitzman, E. A. 1996. "A Comparison of Similarity and Interdependence as Triggers for In-Group Formation." *Personality and Social Psychology Bulletin, 22*(9), 882–893.

Foa, U., & Foa, E. 1975. *Resource Theory of Social Exchange.* Morristown, NJ: General Learning Press.

Forbus, K. D., Gentner, D., & Law, K. 1995. "MAC/FAC: A Model of Similarity-Based Retrieval." *Cognitive Science, 19*(2), 141–205.

Forsyth, D. 1990. *Group Dynamics* (2nd Edition). Pacific Grove, CA: Brooks/Cole.

Foushee, H. C., Lauber, J. K., Baetge, M. M., & Comb, D. B. 1986. *Crew Factors in Flight Operations: III. The Operational Significance of Exposure to Short-Haul Air Transport Operations* (NASA TM 88322). Moffett Field, CA: NASA Ames Research Center.

Frank, R. H., & Cook, P. J. 1995. *The Winner-Take-All Society.* New York: Penguin.

Frank, R. H., Gilovich, T., & Regan, D. T. 1993. "Does Studying Economics Prohibit Cooperation?" *Journal of Economic Perspectives, 7*(2), 159–171.

Freedman, J. L., Cunningham, J. A., & Krismer, K. 1992. "Inferred Values and the Reverse Incentive Effect in Induced Compliance." *Journal of Personality and Social Psychology, 62,* 357–368.

French, J. R. P., & Raven, B. 1968. "The Bases of Social Power." In D. Cartwright and A. F. Zander (Eds.), *Group Dynamics* (pp. 259–270). New York: Harper & Row.

Friedlander, F. 1987. "The Design of Work Teams." In J. W. Lorsch (Ed.), *Handbook of Organizational Behavior.* Upper Saddle River, NJ: Prentice Hall.

Fry, W. R., Firestone, I., & Williams, D. L. 1983. "Negotiation Process and Outcome of Stranger Dyads and Dating Couples: Do Lovers Lose?" *Basic and Applied Social Psychology, 4,* 1–16.

Fuegen, K., & Biernat, M. 2002. "Reexamining the Effects of Solo Status for Women And Men." *Personality and Social Psychology Bulletin, 28*(7), 913–925.

Gabrenya, W. K., Latané, B., & Wang, Y. 1983. "Social Loafing in Cross-Cultural Perspective: Chinese on Taiwan." *Journal of Cross-Cultural Psychology, 14*(3), 368–384.

Gabriel, S., & Gardner, W. L. 1999. "Are There 'His' and 'Hers' Types of Interdependence? The Implications of Gender Differences in Collective versus Relational Interdependence for Affect, Behavior, and Cognition." *Journal of Personality and Social Psychology, 77,* 642–655.

Gaertner, S. L., Dovidio, J. F., & Bachman, B. A. 1996. "Revisiting the Contact Hypothesis: The Induction of a Common Ingroup Identity." *International Journal of Intercultural Relations, 20*(3 & 4), 271–290.

Gaertner, S. L., Dovidio, J. F., Rust, M. C., Nier, J. A., Banker, B. S., Ward, C. M., Mottola, G. R., & Houlette, M. 1999. "Reducing Intergroup Bias: Elements of Intergroup Cooperation." *Journal of Personality and Social Psychology, 76*(3), 388–402.

Galagan, P. 1986. "Work Teams That Work." *Training & Development Journal, 40*(11), 33–35.

Galegher, J., Kraut, R. E., & Egido, C. (Eds.). 1990. *Intellectual Teamwork: Social and Technological Foundations of Cooperative Work.* Hillsdale, NJ: Erlbaum.

Gallupe, R. B. 1992. "Electronic Brainstorming and Group Size." *Academy of Management Journal, 35,* 351–353.

Gardner, W. L. 1992. "Lessons in Organizational Dramaturgy: The Art of Impression Management." *Organizational Dynamics, 21*(1), 33–46.

Gardner, W. L., Gabriel, S., & Lee, A. Y. 1999. " 'I' Value Freedom, but 'We' Value Relationships: Self-Construal Priming Mirrors Cultural Differences in Judgment." *Psychological Science, 10*(4), 321–326.

Garfield, C. 1992. *Second to None* (p. 252). New York: Avon.

Gauron, E. F., & Rawlings, E. I. 1975. "A Procedure for Orienting New Members to Group Psychotherapy." *Small Group Behavior, 6,* 293–307.

Geber, B. 1995, April. "Virtual Teams." *Training Magazine, 32*(4), 36–40.

Gendron, G. 1998, May. "FYI: Growing by Design." *Inc., 20*(6), 9.

Gentner, D., Brem, S., Ferguson, R., & Wolff, P. 1997. "Analogy and Creativity in the Works of Johannes Kepler." In T. B. Ward, S. M. Smith et al. (Eds.), *Creative Thought: An Investigation of Conceptual Structures and Processes* (pp. 403–459). Washington, DC: American Psychological Association.

Gentner, D., & Gentner, D. R. 1983. "Flowing Waters or Teeming Crowds: Mental Models of Electricity." In D. Gentner & A. Stevens (Eds.), *Mental Models.* Mahwah, NJ: Lawrence Erlbaum & Associates.

Gentner, D., & Landers, R. 1985. "Analogical Reminding: A Good Match Is Hard to Find." *Proceedings of the International Conference on Cybernetics and Society* (pp. 607–613), Tucson, AZ. New York: Institute of Electrical and Electronics Engineers.

Gentner, D., Rattermann, M. J., & Forbus, K. D. 1993. "The Roles of Similarity in Transfer: Separating Retrievability from Inferential Soundness." *Cognitive Psychology, 25*(4), 524–575.

Gerard, H. 1983. "School Desegregation: The Social Science Role." *American Psychologist, 38,* 869–878.

Gersick, C. J. C. 1988. "Time and Transition in Work Teams: Toward a New Model of Group Development." *Academy of Management Journal, 31,* 9–41.

Geschka, H., Schaude, G. R., & Schlicksupp, H. 1973, August. "Modern Techniques for Solving Problems." *Chemical Engineering,* 91–97.

Ghoshal, S., & Barlett, C. A. 1988. "Innovation Processes in Multinational Corporations." In M. L. Tushman & W. L. Moore (Eds.), *Readings in the Management of Innovation* (2d edition). Cambridge, MA: Harper & Row.

Gibb, J. R. 1951. *Dynamics of Participative Groups.* Boulder: University of Colorado.

Gick, M. L., & Holyoak, K. J. 1980. "Analogical Problem-Solving." *Cognitive Psychology, 12,* 306–355. Adapted from Duncker, K. 1945. "On Problem Solving." *Psychological Monographs 58,* no. 270.

Gick, M. L., & Holyoak, K. J. 1983. "Schema Induction and Analogical Transfer." *Cognitive Psychology, 15,* 1–38. Reprinted in Holyoak, K.J., & Thagard, P. 1995. *Mental Leaps: Analogy in Creative Thought.* Cambridge, MA: MIT Press.

Gigone, D., & Hastie, R. 1993. "The Common Knowledge Effect: Information Sharing and Group Judgment." *Journal of Personality and Social Psychology, 65*(5), 959–974.

Gigone, D., & Hastie, R. 1997. "The Impact of Information on Small Group Choice." *Journal of Personality and Social Psychology, 72*(1), 132–140.

Gillespie, D. F., & Birnbaum-More, P. H. 1980. "Status Concordance, Coordination and Success in Interdisciplinary Research Teams." *Human Relations, 33*(1), 41–56.

Gilovich, T. 1987. "Secondhand Information and Social Judgment." *Journal of Experimental Social Psychology, 23*(1), 59–74.

Gilovich, T., Kerr, M., & Medvec, V. H. 1993. "The Effect of Temporal Perspective on Subjective Confidence." *Journal of Personality and Social Psychology, 64*(4), 552–560.

Gilovich, T., Savitsky, K., & Medvec, V. H. 1998. "The Illusion of Transparency: Biased Assessments of Others' Ability to Read One's Emotional States." *Journal of Personality and Social Psychology, 75*(2), 332–346.

Gladstein, D. L. 1984, December. "Groups in Context: A Model of Task Group Effectiveness." *Administrative Science Quarterly, 29,* 499–517.

Glickman, A. S., Zimmer, S., Montero, R. C., Guerette, P. J. et al. 1987. "The Evolution of Teamwork Skills: An Empirical Assessment with Implications for Training." *US Naval Training Systems Center Technical Reports,* No. 87-016.

Gold, M., & Yanof, D. S. 1985. "Mothers, Daughters, and Girlfriends." *Journal of Personality and Social Psychology, 49*(3), 654–659.

Goldstein, I. L. 1989. "Critical Training Issues: Past, Present, and Future." In I. L. Goldstein et al., *Training and Development in Organizations.* San Francisco, CA: Jossey-Bass.

Goleman, D. 1988, June. "Recent Studies Explain Why Some Meetings Fail." *New York Times,* p. C1.

Goleman, D. 1995. *Emotional Intelligence: Why It Can Matter More Than I.Q.* New York: Bantam.

Goodman, P. S., & Garber, S. 1988. "Absenteeism and Accidents in a Dangerous Environment: Empirical Analysis of Underground Coal Mines." *Journal of Applied Psychology, 73*(1), 81–86.

Goodman, P. S., & Leyden, D. P. 1991. "Familiarity and Group Productivity." *Journal of Applied Psychology, 76*(4), 578–586.

Graen, G., & Scandura, T. A. 1987. "Toward a Psychology of Dyadic Organizing." In B. Staw & L. L. Cummings (Eds.), *Research in Organizational Behavior* (Vol. 9, pp. 175–208). Greenwich, CT: JAI Press.

Granovetter, M. 1973. "The Strength of Weak Ties." *American Journal of Sociology, 78,* 1360–1379.

Greek, D. 1997. "Steel Rewrites the Rules." *Professional Engineering, 10*(13), 19–20.

Greenberg, J. 1988. "Equity and Workplace Status: A Field Experiment." *Journal of Applied Psychology, 75,* 561–568.

Greenberg, J. 1996. *Managing Behavior in Organizations.* Upper Saddle River, NJ: Prentice Hall. P. 189.

Greene, C. N. 1989. "Cohesion and Productivity in Work Groups." *Small Group Behavior, 20,* 70–86.

Greene, J., Hamm, S., & Kerstetter, J. 2002, June 17. "Ballmer's Microsoft." *BusinessWeek,* pp. 66–74.

Greenwald, A. G., & Banaji, M. 1995. "Implicit Social Cognition: Attitudes, Self-Esteem, and Stereotypes." *Psychological Review, 102*(1), 4–27.

Griffin, D. W., & Ross, L. 1991. "Subjective Construal, Social Inference, and Human Misunderstanding." In M. P. Zanna (Ed.), *Advances in Experimental Social Psychology* (Vol. 24, pp. 319–359). San Diego, CA: Academic Press.

Griffith, J. 1989. "The Army's New Unit Personnel Replacement System and Its Relationship to Unit Cohesion and Social Support." *Military Psychology, 1,* 17–34.

Griffith, T. L., Mannix, E. A., Neale, M. A. 2002. "Conflict and Virtual Teams." In S. G. Cohen and C. B. Gibson (Eds.), *Creating Conditions for Effective Virtual Teams.* San Francisco, CA: Jossey-Bass.

Griffith, V. 1997, July 18. "Teamwork's Own Goals." *Financial Times,* p. 12.

Gross, S. E. 1995. *Compensation for Teams: How to Design and Implement Team-Based Reward Programs.* New York: AMACOM.

Grossman, J. 1998, April. "We've Got to Start Meeting Like This." *Inc. Magazine, 20*(5), 70.

Grossman, S. R., Rodgers, B. E., & Moore, B. R. 1989, December. "Turn Group Input into Stellar Output." *Working Woman,* 36–38.

Gruenfeld, D. H. 1994. "Status and Integrative Complexity in Decision-Making Groups: Evidence from the United States Supreme Court and a Laboratory Experiment." *Dissertation Abstracts International, Section B: The Sciences & Engineering, 55*(2-B), 630.

Gruenfeld, D. H. 1995. "Status, Ideology and Integrative Complexity on the U.S. Supreme Court: Rethinking the Politics of Political Decision Making." *Journal of Personality and Social Psychology, 68*(1), 5–20.

Gruenfeld, D. H. 1997, May. "Integrating across Teams: Formal Structural Solutions." Presentation at J. L. Kellogg School, Evanston, IL.

Gruenfeld, D. H. (Ed.) 1988. *Composition.* Stamford, CT: JAI Press.

Gruenfeld, D. H., & Fan, E. T. 1999. "What Newcomers See and What Oldtimers Say: Discontinuities in Knowledge Exchange." In L. Thompson, J. Levine, & D. Messick (Eds.), *Shared Cognition in Organizations: The Management of Knowledge.* Mahwah, NJ: Lawrence Erlbaum & Associates.

Gruenfeld, D. H., Keltner, D. J., & Anderson, C. 2003. "The Effects of Power on Those Who Possess It: An Interpersonal Perspective on Social Cognition." In Bodenhausen, G. & Lambert, A. (Eds.), *Foundations of Social Cognition: A Festschrift in Honor of Robert S. Wyer, Jr.* Mahwah, NJ: Erlbaum.

Gruenfeld, D. H., Mannix, E. A., Williams, K. Y., & Neale, M. A. 1996. "Group Composition and Decision Making: How Member Familiarity and Information Distribution Affect Process and Performance." *Organizational Behavior and Human Decision Processes, 67*(1), 1–15.

Gruenfeld, D. H., Martorana, P., & Fan, E. T. 2000. "What Do Groups Learn from Their Worldiest Members?: Direct and Indirect Influence in Dynamic Teams." *Organizational Behavior and Human Decision Processes, 82,* 45–59.

Gruenfeld, D. H., Thomas-Hunt, M. C., & Kim, P. 1998. "Cognitive Flexibility, Communication Strategy, and Integrative Complexity in Groups: Public Versus Private Reactions to Majority and Minority Status." *Journal of Experimental Social Psychology, 34,* 202–226.

Guetzkow, H., & Gyr, J. 1954. "An Analysis of Conflict in Decision-Making Groups." *Human Relations, 7,* 367–381.

Guilford, J. P. 1950. "Creativity." *American Psychologist, 5,* 444–454.

Guilford, J. P. 1959. *Personality.* New York: McGraw-Hill.

Guilford, J. P. 1967. *The Nature of Human Intelligence.* New York: McGraw-Hill.

Guinote, A., Judd, C. M., & Brauer, M. 2002. "Effects of Power on Perceived and Objective Group Variability: Evidence That More Powerful Groups Are More Variable." *Journal of Personality and Social Psychology, 82*(5), 708–721.

Gustafson, D. H., Shukla, R. K., Delbecq, A. L., & Walster, G. W. 1973. "A Comparative Study of Differences in Subjective Likelihood Estimates Made By Individuals, Interacting Groups, Delphi Groups, and Nominal Groups." *Organizational Behavior and Human Performance, 9,* 280–291.

Guzzo, R. A., Salas, E., & Associates. 1995. *Team Effectiveness and Decision Making in Organizations.* San Francisco, CA: Jossey-Bass.

Hackett, B. 2000. "Beyond Knowledge Management: New Ways to Work." Research Report R-1262-00-RR. New York: The Conference Board.

Hackman, J. R. 1987. "The Design of Work Teams." In J. W. Lorsch (Ed.), *Handbook of Organizational Behavior.* Upper Saddle River, NJ: Prentice Hall.

Hackman, J. R. 1990. "Introduction: Work Teams in Organizations: An Oriented Framework." In J. Hackman (Ed.), *Groups That Work and Those That Don't.* San Francisco, CA: Jossey-Bass.

Hackman, J. R. 2002. *Leading Teams: Setting the Stage For Great Performances.* Boston, MA: Harvard Business School Press.

Hackman, J. R., Brousseau, K. R., & Weiss, J. A. 1976. "The Interaction of Task Design and Group Performance Strategies in Determining Group Effectiveness." *Organizational Behavior and Human Performance, 16,* 350–365.

Hackman, J. R., & Morris, C. G. 1975. "Group Tasks, Group Interaction Process and Group Performance Effectiveness. A Review and Proposed Integration." In L. Berkowitz (Ed.), *Advances in Experimental Social Psychology* (Vol. 8, pp. 45–99). New York: Academic Press.

Hackman, J. R., & Oldham, G. R. 1980. *Work Redesign.* Menlo Park, CA: Addison-Wesley Publishing Company.

Hackman, R. 1996, April. Presentation on group behavior. Evanston, IL: J. L. Kellogg School of Management.

Hagel, J., & Armstrong, A. G. 1997. *Net Gain: Expanding Markets through Virtual Communities.* Boston, MA: Harvard Business School Press.

Hains, S. C., Hogg, M. A., & Duck, J. M. 1997. "Self-Categorization and Leadership: Effects of Group Prototypicality and Leader Stereotypicality." *Personality and Social Psychology Bulletin, 23*(10), 1087–1099.

Hall, F. 1997. "Effective Delegation." In D. D. Brown, R. J. Lewicki, D. T. Hall, & F. S. Hall (Eds.), *Experiences in Management and Organizational Behavior* (4th edition). New York: John Wiley & Sons. Reprinted with permission.

Hambrick, D. C. 1995. "Fragmentation and the Other Problems CEOs Have with Their TMT's." *California Management Review, 37*(3), 110–127.

Hambrick, D. C. 1997. "Corporate Coherence and the TMT." *Planning Review, 25*(5), 24–29.

Hammonds, J. 2002, August 1. "Handle with Care: How UPS Handles Packages Starts with How It Handles Its People." *Fastcompany,* pp. 102–103.

Hanks, M., & Eckland, B. K. 1978. "Adult Voluntary Association and Adolescent Socialization." *Sociological Quarterly, 19*(3), 481–490.

Harari, O., & Graham, W. K. 1975. "Tasks and Task Consequences as Factors in Individual and Group Brainstorming." *Journal of Social Psychology, 95*(1), 61–65.

Harber, K. D. 1998. "Feedback to Minorities: Evidence of a Positive Bias." *Journal of Personality and Social Psychology, 74*(3), 622–628.

Hargadon, A. B. 1998. "Firms as Knowledge Brokers: Lessons in Pursuing Continuous Innovation." *California Management Review, 40*(3), 209–227.

Hargadon, A. B., & Sutton, R. I. 2000, May/June. "Building an Innovation Factory." *Harvard Business Review,* 157–166.

Harkins, S. G., & Jackson, J. M. 1985. "The Role of Evaluation in Eliminating Social Loafing." *Personality and Social Psychology Bulletin, 11,* 457–465.

Harkins, S. G., & Petty, R. E. 1982. "Effects of Task Difficulty and Task Uniqueness on Social Loafing." *Journal of Personality and Social Psychology, 43*(6), 1214–1229

Harkins, S. G., & Szymanski, K. 1987. *Social Loafing and Social Facilitation: New Wine in Old Bottles.* Beverly Hills, CA: Sage.

Harvey, J. 1974. "The Abilene Paradox: The Management of Agreement." *Organizational Dynamics, 3*(1), 63–80. © American Management Association International. Reprinted with permission.

Harvey, O. J., & Consalvi, C. 1960. "Status and Conformity to Pressure in Informal Groups." *Journal of Abnormal and Social Psychology, 60,* 182–187.

Haslam, S. A., McGarty, C., Brown, P. M., Eggins, R. A., Morrison, B. E., & Reynolds, K. J. 1998. "Inspecting the Emperor's Clothes: Evidence That Random Selection of Leaders Can Enhance Group Performance." *Group Dynamics: Theory, Research, and Practice, 2*(3), 168–184.

Hastie, R., Penrod, S., & Pennington, N. 1983. *Inside the Jury.* Cambridge, MA: Harvard University Press.

Hastorf, A. H., & Cantril, H. 1954. "They Saw a Game: A Case Study." *Journal of Abnormal Social Psychology, 49,* 129–134.

Hastorf, A. H., Northcraft, G. B., & Picciotto, S. R. 1979. "Helping the Handicapped: How Realistic Is the Performance Feedback Received by the Physically Handicapped?" *Personality and Social Psychology Bulletin, 5,* 373–376.

Hater, J. J., & Bass, B. M. 1988. "Supervisors' Evaluations and Subordinates' Perceptions of Transformational and Transactional Leadership." *Journal of Applied Psychology, 73,* 695–702.

Heath, C. 1999. "On the Social Psychology of Agency Relationships: Lay Theories of Motivation Overemphasize Extrinsic Rewards." *Organizational Behavior and Human Decision Processes, 78*(1), 25–62.

Hecht, T. D., Allen, N. J., Klammer, J. D., & Kelly, E. C. 2002. "Group Beliefs, Ability and Performance: The Potency of Group Potency." *Group Dynamics: Theory, Research and Practice, 6*(2), 143–152.

Hedlund, J., Ilgen, D. R., & Hollenbeck, J. R. 1998. "Decision Accuracy in Computer-Mediated versus Face-to-Face Decision Making Teams." *Organizational Behavior and Human Decision Processes, 76*(1), 30–47.

Heilman, M. E., Hornstein, H. A., Cage, J. H., & Herschlag, J. K. 1984. "Reactions to Prescribed Leader Behavior as a Function of Role Perspective: The Case of the Vroom-Yetton Model." *Journal of Applied Psychology, 69*(1), 50–60.

Helmer, O. 1966. *Social Technology.* New York: Basic Books.

Helmer, O. 1967. *Analysis of the Future: The Delphi Method.* Santa Monica, CA: Rand Corporation.

Henry, K. B., Arrow, H., & Carini, B. 1999. "A Tripartite Model of Group Identification: Theory and Measurement." *Small Group Research, 30*(5), 558–581.

Hequet, M. 1994, April. "Teams at the Top." *Training,* pp. 7–9.

Hertel, G., Kerr, N. L., & Messe, L. A. 2000. "Motivation Gains in Performance Groups: Paradigmatic and Theoretical Developments on the Köhler Effect." *Journal of Personality and Social Psychology, 79*(4), 580–601.

Higgins, E. T. 1999. " 'Saying Is Believing' Effects: When Sharing Reality about Something Biases Knowledge and Evaluations." In L. Thompson, J. M. Levine, & D. M. Messick (Eds.), *Shared Cognition in Organizations: The Management of Knowledge.* Mahwah, NJ: Lawrence Erlbaum & Associates.

Higgins, J. 1994. "Creating Creativity." *Training and Development, 48*(11), 11–15.

Hill, M. 1982. "Group versus Individual Performance: Are N+1 Heads Better Than One?" *Psychological Bulletin, 91,* 517–539.

Hill, S. 1995. "The Social Organization of Boards of Directors." *British Journal of Sociology, 46*(2), 245–278.

Hillkirk, J. 1993, July 26. "Tearing Down Walls Builds GE." *USA Today,* p. 5B.

Hiltz, S. R., Johnson, K., & Turoff, M. 1986. "Experiments in Group Decision Making: Communication Process and Outcome in Face-to-Face versus Computerized Conferences." *Human Communication Research, 13*(2), 225–252.

Hinds, P., Carley, K. M., Krackhardt, D., & Wholey, D. 2000. "Choosing Workgroup Members: The Balance of Similarity, Competence, and Familiarity." *Organizational Behavior and Human Decision Making Processes, 81*(2), 226–251.

Hof, R. D., Browder, S., & Elstrom, P. 1997, May 5. "Internet Communities." *BusinessWeek,* no. 3525, pp. 64–80.

Hoffman, L. R., & Maier, N. R. F. 1966. "An Experimental Reexamination of the Similarity-Attraction Hypothesis." *Journal of Personality and Social Psychology, 3,* 145–152.

Hoffman, R. 1995, April. "Ten Reasons You Should Be Using 360-Degree Feedback." *HR Magazine, 40*(4), 82–85.

Hogan, R., Raskin, R., & Fazzini, D. 1990. "The Dark Side of Charisma." In K. E. Clark & M. B. Clark (Eds.), *Measures of Leadership* (pp. 343–354). West Orange, NJ: Leadership Library of America.

Hogg, M., & Turner, J. C. 1987. "Intergroup Behaviour, Self-Stereotyping and the Salience of Social Categories." *British Journal of Social Psychology, 26,* 325–340.

Hogg, M. A. 1987. "Social Identity and Group Cohesiveness." In J. C. Turner, M. A. Hogg, P. J. Oakes, S. D. Reicher, & M. Wetherell (Eds.), *Rediscovering the Social Group: A Self-Categorization Theory* (pp. 89–116). Oxford, England: Basil Blackwell.

Holland, K. 1996. "Sexual Healing at Mitsubishi?" *BusinessWeek,* no. 3477, p. 48.

Hollander, E. P. 1964. *Leaders, Groups, and Influence.* New York: Oxford University Press.

Hollander, E. P. 1986. "On the Central Role of Leadership Processes." *International Review of Applied Psychology, 35,* 39–52.

Hollenbeck, J. R., Ilgen, D. R., LePine, J. A., Colquitt, J. A., & Hedlund, J. 1998. "Extending the Multilevel Theory of Team Decision Making: Effects of Feedback and Experience in Hierarchical Teams." *Academy of Management Journal, 41,* 269–282.

Hollenbeck, J. R., Ilgen, D. R., Sego, D. J., Hedlund, J., Major, D. A., & Phillips, J. 1995. "Multilevel Theory of Team Decision Making: Decision Performance in Teams Incorporating Distributed Expertise." *Journal of Applied Psychology, 80,* 292–316.

Hollingshead, A. B. 1996a. "Information Suppression and Status Persistence in Group Decision Making: The Effects of Communication Media." *Human Communication Research, 23,* 193–219.

Hollingshead, A. B. 1996b. "The Rank-Order Effect in Group Decision Making." *Organizational Behavior and Human Decision Processes, 68*(3), 181–193.

Hollingshead, A. B. 1998. "Group and Individual Training." *Small Group Research, 29*(2), 254–280.

Hollingshead, A. B. 2000. "Perceptions of Expertise and Transactive Memory in Work Relationships." *Group Processes and Intergroup Relations, 3*(3), 257–267.

Hollingshead, A. B. 2001. "Communication Technologies, the Internet, and Group Research." In M. Hogg and R. S. Tindale (Eds.), *Blackwell Handbook of Social Psychology,* Vol. 3: *Group Processes* (pp. 557–573). Oxford, England: Blackwell.

Holyoak, K. J., & Koh, K. 1987. "Surface and Structural Similarity in Analogical Transfer." *Memory and Cognition, 15*(4), 332–340.

Homans, G. 1950. *The Human Group.* New York: Harcourt Brace.

Hopkins, K. R., Nestleroth, S. L., & Bolick, C. 1991. *Help Wanted: How Companies Can Survive and Thrive in the Coming Worker Shortage.* New York: McGraw-Hill.

Horibe, F. 2001. *Creating the Innovation Culture: Leveraging Visionaries, Dissenters and Other Useful Troublemakers in Your Organization.* New York: Wiley.

Horn, E. M. 1993. "The Influence of Modality Order and Break Period on a Brainstorming Task." Unpublished honors thesis, University of Texas at Arlington.

Hornsey, M. J., & Hogg, M. A. 2002. "The Effects of Status on Subgroup Relations." *British Journal of Social Psychology, 41,* 203–218.

Howells, L. T., & Becker, S. W. 1962. "Seating Arrangements and Leadership Emergence." *Journal of Abnormal and Social Psychology, 64,* 148–150.

*HR Focus.* 2002, May. "Training Investments Climb Despite Recession and Layoffs." P. 9.

Huber, V. L., Neale, M. A., & Northcraft, G. B. 1987. "Judgment by Heuristics: Effects of Ratee and Rater Characteristics and Performance Standards on Performance-Related Judgments." *Organizational Behavior and Human Decision Processes, 40,* 149–169.

Hudepohl, D. 2001, March 1. "Face Your Fears." *Sports Illustrated for Women,* p. 53.

Hudson, K. 2002, September 2. "Notebaert Abides by Service Credo: New Qwest CEO Creates Noticeably Different Climate." *Denver Post,* p. C01.

Huguet, P., Charbonnier, E., & Monteil, J. 1999. "Productivity Loss in Performance Groups: People Who See Themselves as Average Do Not Engage in Social Loafing." *Group Dynamics: Theory, Research, and Practice, 3*(2), 118–131.

Huseman, R. C., & Driver, R. W. 1979. "Groupthink: Implications for Small Group Decision Making in Business." In R. Huseman & A. Carroll (Eds.), *Readings in Organizational Behavior* (pp. 100–110). Boston, MA: Allyn & Bacon.

Iaffaldano, M. T., & Muchinsky, P. M. 1985. "Job Satisfaction and Job Performance: A Meta-Analysis." *Psychological Bulletin, 97,* 251–273.

Ibarra, H. 1995. "Race, Opportunity, and Diversity of Social Circles in Managerial Networks." *Academy of Management Journal, 38*(3), 673–703.

Ickes, W. 1983. "A Basic Paradigm for the Study of Unstructured Dyadic Interaction." *New Directions for Methodology of Social and Behavioral Science, 15,* 5–21.

Ickes, W., & Turner, M. 1983. "On the Social Advantages of Having an Older, Opposite-Sex Sibling: Birth Order Influences in Mixed-Sex Dyads." *Journal of Personality and Social Psychology, 45*(1), 210–222.

Ilgen, D. R., & Feldman, J. M. 1983. "Performance Appraisal: A Process Focus." In L. L. Cummings & B. M. Staw (Eds.), *Research in Organizational Behavior* (Vol. 5, pp. 141–197). Greenwich, CT: JAI Press.

Imperato, G. 1997. "Harley Shifts Gears." *Fastcompany, 9,* 104.

Inman, M. L., & Baron, R. S. 1996. "Influence of Prototypes on Perceptions of Prejudice." *Journal of Personality and Social Psychology, 70*(4), 727–739.

Insko, C., Pinkley, R., Hoyle, R., Dalton, B., Hong, G., Slim, R., Landry, P., Holton, B., Ruffin, P., & Thibaut, J. 1987. "Individual Versus Group Discontinuity: The Role of a Consensus Rule." *Journal of Experimental Social Psychology, 23,* 250–267.

International Labour Organization (ILO). 1997, December 11. "Women's Progress in Workforce Improving Worldwide, But Occupational Segregation Still Rife." *www.ilo.org.*

Isbell, D., Hardin, M., & Underwood. J. 1999, September 30. "Mars Climate Orbiter Team Finds Likely Cause of Loss." Washington, DC: Jet Propulsion Laboratory for NASA's Office of Space Science. Release No. 99–113.

Isbell, D., & Savage, D. 1999, November 10. "Mars Climate Orbiter Failure Board Releases Report, Numerous NASA Actions Underway In Response." Washington, DC: Jet Propulsion Laboratory for NASA's Office of Space Science. Release No. 99–134.

Isen, A. M., Daubman, K. A., & Nowicki, G. P. 1987. "Positive Affect Facilitates Creative Problem Solving." *Journal of Personality and Social Psychology, 47,* 1206–1217.

Jablin, F. M. 1981. Cultivating Imagination: Factors That Enhance and Inhibit Creativity in Brainstorming Groups. *Human Communication Research, 7*(3), 245–258.

Jackson, J. M., & Harkins, S. G. 1985. "Equity in Effort: An Explanation of the Social Loafing Effect." *Journal of Personality and Social Psychology, 49,* 1199–1206.

Jackson, S. E. 1992. "Team Composition in Organizational Settings: Issues in Managing an Increasingly Diverse Work Force." In S. Worchel, W. Wood, & J. A. Simpson (Eds.), *Group Process and Productivity* (pp. 138–173). Newbury Park, CA: Sage.

Jackson, S. E., Brett, J. F., Sessa, V. I., Cooper, D. M., Julin, J. A., & Peyronnin, K. 1991. "Some Differences Make a Difference: Individual

Dissimilarities and Group Heterogeneity as Correlates of Recruitment, Promotions, and Turnover." *Journal of Applied Psychology, 76*(5), 675–689.

Jacobs, R. C., & Campbell, D. T. 1961. "The Perpetuation of an Arbitrary Tradition through Several Generations of a Laboratory Microculture." *Journal of Abnormal and Social Psychology, 62,* 649–658.

Jaffe, A. 2000, November. "Chamber Gleans Words of Wisdom from Novel's Plot." *Sunday Patriot News* (Harrisburg, PA), p. D01.

Janis, I. L. 1972. *Victims of Groupthink.* Boston: Houghton Mifflin.

Janis, I. L. 1982. *Victims of Groupthink* (2nd edition). Boston: Houghton Mifflin.

Janis, I. L., & Mann, L. 1977. *Decision Making: A Psychological Analysis of Conflict, Choice, and Commitment* (p. 130). New York: Free Press. Reprinted with permission.

Jarman, M. 1998, April 19. "Complete Turnaround: 360-degree Evaluations Gaining Favor with Workers, Management." *Arizona Republic,* p. D1.

Jehn, K. A. 1995. "A Multimethod Examination of the Benefits and Detriments of Intragroup Conflict." *Administrative Science Quarterly, 40,* 256–282.

Jehn, K. A. 1997. "A Qualitative Analysis of Conflict Types and Dimensions in Organizational Groups." *Administrative Science Quarterly, 42,* 530–557.

Jehn, K. A. 1999. "Diversity, Conflict, and Team Performance: Summary of Program of Research." *Performance Improvement Quarterly, 12*(1), 6–19.

Jehn, K., & Chatman, J. A. (2000). "Reconceptualizing Conflict: Proportional and Relational Conflict." *International Journal of Conflict Management, 11*(1), 51–69.

Jehn, K. A. & Mannix, E. A. 2001. "The Dynamic Nature of Conflict: A Longitudinal Study of Intragroup Conflict and Group Performance." *Academy of Management Journal, 44*(2), 238–251.

Jehn, K. A., Northcraft, G. B., & Neale, M. A. 1999. "Why Differences Make a Difference: A Field Study of Diversity, Conflict and Performance In Workgroups." *Administrative Science Quarterly, 44*(4), 741–763.

Jessup, L. M., & Valacich, J. S., (Eds.). 1993. *Group Support Systems.* New York: Macmillan.

Jetten, J., Duck, J., Terry, D. J., & O'Brien, A. 2001. "When Groups Merge: Low- and High-Status Groups' Responses to Aligned Leaders." Unpublished raw data, University of Exeter.

Jetten, J., Duck, J., Terry, D. J., & O'Brien, A. 2002. "Being Attuned to Intergroup Differences in Mergers: The Role of Aligned Leaders for Low-Status Groups." *Personality and Social Psychology Bulletin, 28*(9), 1194–1201.

Jetten, J., Spears, R., Hogg, M. A., & Manstead, A. S. R. 2000. "Discrimination Constrained and Justified: The Variable Effects of Group Variability and Ingroup Identification. *Journal of Experimental Social Psychology, 36,* 329–356.

Johnson-Laird, P. N. 1980. "Mental Models in Cognitive Science." *Cognitive Science, 4*(1), 71–115.

Johnston, C. 2002, January 1. "Put Me In, Coach." *Inside Business,* p. 28.

Jones, E. E., Farina, A., Hastorf, A. H., Markus, H., Miller, D. T., & Scott, R. A. 1984. *Social Stigma: The Psychology of Marked Relationships.* New York: W.H. Freeman.

Jones, E. E., Stires, L. K., Shaver, K. G., & Harris, V. A. 1968. "Evaluation of an Ingratiator by Target Persons and Bystanders." *Journal of Personality, 36*(3), 349–385.

Jones, J. M. 1983. "The Concept of Race in Social Psychology: From Color to Culture." In L. Wheeler & P. Shaver (Eds.), *Review of Personality and Social Psychology* (Vol. 4). Newbury Park, CA: Sage.

Judd, C. M., & Park, B. 1988. "Out-Group Homogeneity: Judgments of Variability at the Individual and Group Levels." *Journal of Personality and Social Psychology, 54*(5), 778–788.

Kaagan, S. S. 1999. *Leadership Games: Experiential Learning for Organizational Development.* Thousand Oaks, CA: Sage.

Kahneman, D., & Tversky, A. 1979. "Prospect Theory: An Analysis of Decision under Risk." *Econometrica, 47,* 263–291.

Kaltenheuser, S. 2002, July 1. "Working the Crowd." *Across the Board,* pp. 50–55.

Kameda, T., Ohtsubo, Y., & Takezawa, M. 1997. "Centrality in Sociocognitive Networks and

Social Influence: An Illustration in a Group Decision-Making Context." *Journal of Personality and Social Psychology, 73*(2), 296–309.

Kaminoff, L. 2002, April 24. "AKAM Associates Forms 'Superintendent's Club.'" *Real Estate Weekly,* S14.

Kane, A., & Argote, L. 2002. "Social Identity and Knowledge Transfer between Groups." Paper presented at the Annual Meeting of the Academy of Management, Denver, CO.

Kanter, R. M. 1977. "Some Effects of Proportions on Group Life: Skewed Sex Ratios and Responses to Token Women." *American Journal of Sociology, 82,* 465–490.

Karau, S. J., & Williams, K. D. 1993. "Social Loafing: A Meta-Analytic Review and Theoretical Integration." *Journal of Personality and Social Psychology, 65,* 681–706.

Katz, D., & Braly, K. 1933. "Racial Stereotypes of 100 College Students." *Journal of Abnormal and Social Psychology, 28,* 280–290.

Katz, D., & Kahn, R. L. 1978. *The Social Psychology of Organizations* (2nd edition). New York: John Wiley & Sons.

Katz, R. 1982. "The Effects of Group Longevity on Project Communication and Performance." *Administrative Science Quarterly, 27,* 81–104.

Katz, R., & Allen, T. J. 1982. "Investigating the Not Invented Here (NIH) Syndrome: A Look at the Performance, Tenure, and Communication Patterns of 50 R&D Project Groups." *R&D Management, 121,* 7–19.

Katzenbach, J. R., & Smith, D. K. 1993, March–April. "The Discipline of Teams." *Harvard Business Review, 71*(2), 111–120.

Kayser, T. A. 1995. *Mining Group Gold: How to Cash in on the Collaborative Genius of Work Teams.* Chicago: Irwin.

Keisler, S., & Sproull, L. 1992. "Group Decision Making and Communication Technology." *Organizational Behavior and Human Decision Processes, 52,* 96–123.

Keisler, S., Zubrow, D., Moses, A., & Gellar, V. 1985. "Affect in Computer-Mediated Communication: An Experiment in Synchronous Terminal-to-Terminal Discussion." *Human Computer Interaction, 1*(1), 77–104.

Keller, G., & McGahan, A. 1994. "Saturn: A Different Kind of Car Company." Harvard Business School Case No. 9-795-010.

Prepared by G. Keller, under the supervision of A. M. McGahan and in consultation with A. Hax. Boston: Harvard Business School Publishing.

Keller, R. T. 1986. "Predictors of the Performance of Project Groups in R&D Organizations." *Academy of Management Journal, 29,* 715–725.

Kelley, D., & Lavandara, E. 2001, September 23. "Whole Foods Market Using Team Strategy with Good Results." *CNN: Live Today.* © eMediaMillWorks, Inc.

Kelley, H. H. 1962. *The Development of Cooperation in the "Minimal Social Situation."* Washington, DC: American Psychological Association.

Kelley, H. H. 1983. "The Situational Origins of Human Tendencies: A Further Reason for the Formal Analysis of Structures," *Personality and Social Psychology Bulletin, 9*(1), 8–36.

Kelley, H. H., & Thibaut, J. 1978. *Interpersonal Relations: A Theory of Interdependence.* New York: Wiley.

Kelley, T. 2001. *The Art of Innovation: Lessons in Creativity from IDEO, America's Leading Design Firm.* New York: Doubleday.

Kelly, J. R., & Karau, S. J. 1999. "Group Decision Making: The Effects of Initial Preferences and Time Pressure." *Personality and Social Psychology Bulletin, 25*(11), 1342–1354.

Kelly, J. R., & McGrath, J. E. 1985. "Effects of Time Limits and Task Types on Task Performance and Interaction of Four-Person Groups." *Journal of Personality and Social Psychology, 49*(2), 395–407.

Kelly, J. R., Futoran, G. C., & McGrath, J. E. 1990. "Capacity and Capability: Seven Studies of Entrainment of Task Performance Rates." *Small Group Research, 21*(3), 283–314.

Kempton, W. 1986. "Two Theories of Home Heat Control." *Cognitive Science, 10,* 75–90.

Kempton, W. 1987. *Two Theories of Home Heat Control.* New York: Cambridge University Press.

Kenney, R. A., Schwartz-Kenney, B. M., & Blascovich, J. 1996. "Implicit Leadership Theories: Defining Leaders Described as Worthy of Influence." *Personality and Social Psychology Bulletin, 22*(11), 1128–1143.

Kerr, N. L. 1983. "Motivation Losses in Small Groups: A Social Dilemma Analysis." *Journal of Personality and Social Psychology, 45,* 819–828.

Kerr, N. L. 1989. "Illusions of Efficacy: The Effects of Group Size on Perceived Efficacy in Social Dilemmas." *Journal of Experimental Social Psychology, 25,* 287–313.

Kerr, N. L., & Bruun, S. 1981. "Ringelmann Revisited: Alternative Explanations for the Social Loafing Effect." *Journal of Personality and Social Psychology, 37,* 224–231.

Keysar, B. 1994. "The Illusory Transparency of Intention: Linguistic Perspective-Taking in Text." *Cognitive Psychology, 26*(2), 165–208.

Keysar, B. 1998. "Language Users as Problem Solvers: Just What Ambiguity Problem Do They Solve?" In S. R. Fussell & R. J. Kreuz (Eds.), *Social and Cognitive Approaches to Interpersonal Communication* (pp. 175–200). Mahwah, NJ: Lawrence Erlbaum & Associates.

Keysar, B., & Henly, A. 2002. "Speakers' Overestimation of their Effectiveness." *Psychological Science, 13*(3), 207–212.

Kidder, T. 1981. *Soul of a New Machine.* New York: Avon.

Kim, H., & Markus, H. R. 1999. "Deviance or Uniqueness, Harmony or Conformity? A Cultural Analysis." *Journal of Personality and Social Psychology, 77*(4), 785–800.

Kim, P. 1997. "When What You Know Can Hurt You: A Study of Experiential Effects on Group Discussion and Performance." *Organizational Behavior and Human Decision Processes, 69*(2), 165–177.

King, R. T. Jr. 1998, May 20. "Levi's Factory Workers Are Assigned to Teams, and Morale Takes a Hit." *Wall Street Journal,* p. 1.

Kinsman, M. 2002, April 17. "Consulting Firms Abandon Traditional Offices, Use Short-Term Space Concept." *Knight-Ridder Tribune Business News.*

Kipnis, D. 1957. "The Effects of Style of Leadership and Incentives upon the Inducement of an Attitude Change." Thesis, New York University.

Kirsner, S. 2002, September. "How to Get Bad News to the Top." *Fastcompany,* p. 56.

Klar, Y. 2002. "Way beyond Compare: Nonselective Superiority and Inferiority Biases in Judging Randomly Assigned Group Members Relative to Their Peers." *Journal of Experimental Social Psychology, 38,* 331–351.

Klein, D. 2001, April 16. "Out of the Cubicle." *Newsweek,* p. 61.

Klein, J. A. 1984, September–October. "Why Supervisors Resist Employee Involvement." *Harvard Business Review,* 87–95.

Klimoski, R., & Inks, L. 1990, April. "Accountability Forces in Performance Appraisal." *Organizational Behavior and Human Decision Processes, 45*(2), 194–208.

Klimoski, R., & Mohammed, S. 1997. "Team Mental Model: Construct or Metaphor?" *Journal of Management, 20*(2), 403–437.

Knight, H. 2001, December 14. "Fun Factories: A Top-Secret Visit to Toymaking Shops Reveals Latest Creations." *San Francisco Chronicle,* p. 1.

Knight-Ridder Newspapers. 1991, October 13. "Whites' IDs of Blacks in Crime Cases Often Wrong, Studies Show." *Columbus Dispatch.*

Kohn, A. 1993, September–October. "Why Incentive Plans Cannot Work." *Harvard Business Review, 71,* 54–63.

Komorita, S., & Chertkoff, J. 1973. "A Bargaining Theory of Coalition Formation." *Psychological Review, 80,* 149–162.

Komorita, S., & Parks, C. 1994. *Social Dilemmas.* Madison, WI: Brown & Benchmark.

Kraiger, K., & Ford, J. K. 1985, February. "A Meta-Analysis of Ratee Race Effects in Performance Ratings." *Journal of Applied Psychology, 70*(1), 56–65.

Kramer, M. W., Kuo, C. L., & Dailey, J. C. 1997. "The Impact of Brainstorming Techniques on Subsequent Group Processes: Beyond Generating Ideas." *Small Group Research, 28*(2), 218–242.

Kramer, R. M. 1996. "Divergent Realities, Convergent Disappointments in the Hierarchic Relation: Trust and the Intuitive Auditor at Work." In R. M. Kramer & T. R. Tyler (Eds.), *Trust in Organizations* (pp. 216–245). Thousand Oaks, CA: Sage.

Kramer, R. M. 1999. "Social Uncertainty and Collective Paranoia in Knowledge Communities: Thinking and Acting in the Shadow of Doubt." In L. Thompson, J. Levine, & D. Messick (Eds.), *Social Cognition in Organizations: The Management of Knowledge.* Mahwah, NJ: Lawrence Erlbaum Associates.

Krames, J. A. 2001. *The Jack Welch Lexicon of Leadership: Over 250 Terms, Concepts, Strategies & Initiatives of the Legendary Leader.* New York: McGraw-Hill.

Krauss, R. M., & Fussell, S. R. 1991. "Perspective-Taking in Communication: Representations of Others' Knowledge in Reference." *Social Cognition, 9,* 2–24.

Krauss, R. M., & Fussell, S. R. 1996. "Social Psychological Models of Interpersonal Communication." In E. T. Higgins & A. W. Kruglanski, (Eds.), *Social Psychology: Handbook of Basic Principles* (pp. 655–701). New York: Guilford.

Kravitz, D. A., & Martin, B. 1986. "Ringelmann Rediscovered: The Original Article." *Journal of Personality and Social Psychology, 50*(5), 936–941.

Kresa, K. 1991. "Aerospace Leadership in a Vortex of Change." *Financier, 15*(1), 25–28.

"Labor Letter: Training Holds." 1992, July 14. *Wall Street Journal,* p. A-1.

LaFasto, F. M. J., & Larson, C. E. 2001. *When Teams Work Best: 6,000 Team Members and Leaders Tell What It Takes to Succeed.* Newbury Park, CA: Sage.

Langan-Fox, J., Code, S., Gray, R., & Langfield-Smith, K. 2002. "Supporting Employee Participation: Attitudes and Perceptions in Trainees, Employees, and Teams." *Group Processes and Intergroup Relations, 5*(1), 53–82.

Lardner, J. 2002, September. "In Praise of the Anonymous CEO." *Business 2.0,* pp. 104–108.

Larson, C. E., Foster-Fishman, P. G., & Keys, C. B. 1994. "Discussion of Shared and Unshared Information in Decision-Making Groups." *Journal of Personality and Social Psychology, 67*(3), 446–461.

Larson, C. E., & LaFasto, F. M. J. 1989. *Teamwork: What Must Go Right/What Can Go Wrong.* Newbury Park, CA: Sage.

Larson, J. R., & Christensen, C. 1993. "Groups as Problem-Solving Units: Toward a New Meaning of Social Cognition." *British Journal of Social Psychology, Special Issue: Social Processes in Small Groups I: Theoretical Perspectives, 32*(1), 5–30.

Larson, J. R., Christensen, C., Franz, T. M., & Abbott, A. S. 1998. "Diagnosing Groups: The Pooling, Management, and Impact of Shared and Unshared Case Information in Team-Based Medical Decision Making." *Journal of Personality and Social Psychology, 75*(1), 93–108.

Larson, J. R., Foster-Fishman, P. G., & Franz, T. M. 1998. "Leadership Style and the Discussion of Shared and Unshared Information in Decision-Making Groups." *Personality and Social Psychology Bulletin, 24*(5), 482–495.

Latané, B. 1981. "The Psychology of Social Impact." *American Psychologist, 36,* 343–356.

Latané, B., & Darley, J. M. 1968. "Group Inhibition of Bystander Intervention in Emergencies." *Journal of Personality and Social Psychology, 10,* 215–221.

Latané, B., & Darley, J. M. 1970. *The Unresponsive Bystander: Why Doesn't He Help?* New York: Appleton-Century-Crofts.

Laughlin, P. R. 1980. "Social Combination Processes of Cooperative Problem-Solving Groups on Verbal Interactive Tasks." In M. Fishbein (Ed.), *Progress in Social Psychology* (Vol. 1). Mahwah, NJ: Lawrence Erlbaum & Associates.

Laughlin, P. R., Bonner, B. L., & Miner, A. G. 2002. "Groups Perform Better Than the Best Individuals on Letters-to-Numbers Problems." *Organizational Behavior and Human Decision Processes, 88,* 605–620.

Lavelle, L. 2002, June 17. "When Directors Join CEOs at the Trough." *BusinessWeek,* p. 57.

Lawler, E. E. 1988. "Choosing an Involvement Strategy." *Academy of Management Executive, 11*(3), 197–204.

Lawler, E. E. 1992. *The Ultimate Advantage: Creating the High-Involvement Organization.* San Francisco, CA: Jossey-Bass.

Lawler, E. E. 2000. *Rewarding Excellence: Pay Strategies for the New Economy.* San Francisco, CA: Jossey-Bass.

Lawler, E. E., Mohrman, S. A., & Ledford, G. E. Jr. 1995. *Creating High Performance Organizations: Practices and Results of Employee Involvement and Total Quality Management in Fortune 1000 Companies.* San Francisco, CA: Jossey-Bass.

Layne, A. 2000, September. "Walk a Mile in My Shadow." *Fastcompany, 38.*

Leary, M. 1995. *Self-Presentation: Impression Management and Behavior.* Dubuque, IA: Brown & Benchmark.

Lee, T. 2002, January 7. "Get Those Creative Juices Flowing." *St. Louis Post-Dispatch,* Business Plus section, p. 8B.

Leith, K. P., & Baumeister, R. F. 1996. "Why Do Bad Moods Increase Self-Defeating Behavior?: Emotion, Risk-Taking, and Self-Regulation." *Journal of Personality and Social Psychology, 71*(6), 1250–1267.

LeJeune, M. 1997, December. "Beat, Meter Latest Team Building Ideas." *Colder County Business Report.*

LePine, J., Hollenbeck, J. R., Ilgen, D. R., Colquitt, J. A., & Ellis, A. 2002. "Gender Composition, Situational Strength, and Team Decision-Making Accuracy: A Criterion Decomposition Approach." *Organizational Behavior and Human Decision Processes, 88*(1), 445–475.

Lerner, J. S., & Tetlock, P. E. 1999. "Accounting for the Effects of Accountability." *Psychological Bulletin, 125*(2), 255–275.

Letize, L., & Donovan, M. 1990, March. "The Supervisor's Changing Role in High Involvement Organizations." *Journal for Quality and Participation,* pp. 62–65.

Levine, J. M. 1989. "Reaction to Opinion Deviance in Small Groups." In P. Paulus (Ed.), *Psychology of Group Influence* (2nd edition, pp. 187–231). Mahwah, NJ: Lawrence Erlbaum & Associates.

Levine, J. M., & Choi, H. (in press). "Impact of Personnel Turnover on Team Performance and Cognition." In E. Salas & S. M. Fiore (Eds.), *Team Cognition: Process and Performance at the Inter/Intra Individual Level.* Washington, DC: American Psychological Association.

Levine, J. M., Choi, H., & Moreland, R. L. (2003). "Newcomer Innovation in Work Teams." In P. Paulus & B. Nijstad (Eds.), *Group Creativity.* New York: Oxford University Press.

Levine, J. M., & Moreland, R. L. 1985. "Innovation and Socialization in Small Groups." In S. Moscovici, G. Mugny, & E. van Avermaet (Eds.), *Perspectives on Minority Influence* (pp. 143–169). Cambridge, England: Cambridge University Press.

Levine, J. M., & Moreland, R. L. 1991. "Culture and Socialization in Work Groups." In L. B. Resnick, J. M. Levine, & S. D. Teasley (Eds.),

*Perspectives on Socially Shared Cognition* (pp. 585–634). Washington, DC: American Psychological Association.

Levine, J. M., & Moreland, R. L. 1994. "Group Socialization: Theory and Research." In W. Stroebe & M. Hewstone (Eds.), *The European Review of Social Psychology* (Vol. 5, pp. 305–336). Chichester, England: Wiley.

Levine, J. M., Resnick, L. B., & Higgins, E. T. 1993. "Social Foundations of Cognition." *Annual Review of Psychology, 44,* 585–612.

LeVine, R. A., & Campbell, D. T. 1972. *Ethnocentrism: Theories of Conflict, Ethnic Attitudes and Group Behavior.* New York: John Wiley & Sons.

Levinson, H. 1980. "Power, Leadership, and the Management of Stress." *Professional Psychology, 11,* 497–508.

Levinson, S. C. 1983. *Pragmatics* (p. 264). Cambridge, England: Cambridge University Press.

Lewin, K. 1943. "Forces behind Food Habits and Methods of Change." *Bulletin of the National Research Council, 108,* 35–65.

Lewin, K. 1947. "Frontiers in Group Dynamics: Concept, Method, and Reality in Social Science." *Human Relations, 1,* 5–42.

Lewis, B. P., & Linder, D. E. 1997. "Thinking about Choking? Attentional Processes and Paradoxical Performance." *Personality and Social Psychology Bulletin, 23*(9), 937–944.

Lewis, S. A., Langan, C. J., & Hollander, E. P. 1972. "Expectation of Future Interaction and the Choice of Less Desirable Alternatives in Conformity." *Sociometry, 35,* 440–447.

Liang, D. W., Moreland, R. L., & Argote, L. 1995. "Group versus Individual Training and Group Performance: The Mediating Role of Transactive Memory." *Personality and Social Psychology Bulletin, 21*(4), 384–393.

Libby, R., Trotman, K. T., & Zimmer, I. 1987. "Member Variation, Recognition of Expertise, and Group Performance." *Journal of Applied Psychology, 72*(1), 81–87.

Liberman, N., & Trope, Y. 1998. "The Role of Feasibility and Desirability Considerations in Near and Distant Future Decisions: A Test of Temporal Construal Theory." *Journal of Personality and Social Psychology, 75*(1), 5–18.

Liden, R. C., & Graen, G. 1980. "Generalizability of the Vertical Dyad Linkage Model of

Leadership." *Academy of Management Journal, 23*(3), 451–465.

Lind, E. A., & Tyler, T. R. 1988. *The Social Psychology of Procedural Justice.* New York: Plenum.

Lindquist, D. 2002, March 1. "There's No 'I' In This Team." *Chief Executive* (U.S.), pp. 56–60.

Linville, P. W., Fischer, G. W., & Salovey, P. 1989. "Perceived Distributions of the Characteristics of In-Group and Out-Group Members: Empirical Evidence and a Computer Simulation." *Journal of Personality and Social Psychology, 57,* 165–188.

Lipman-Blumen, J., & Leavitt, H. J. 1999. *Hot Groups: Seeding Them, Feeding Them, and Using Them to Ignite your Organization.* New York: Oxford University Press.

Littlepage, G., Robison, W., & Reddington, K. 1997. "Effects of Task Experience and Group Experience on Group Performance, Member Ability, and Recognition of Expertise." *Organizational Behavior and Human Decision Processes, 69*(2), 133–147.

Loewenstein, J., & Prelic, D. 1991. "Negative Time Preference." *AEA Papers and Proceedings, 81*(2), 347–352.

Loewenstein, J., & Thompson, L. 2000, October. "The Challenge of Learning." *Negotiation Journal,* 399–408.

Long, S. 2002, April 12. "This CEO Handles Complaints Himself." *Straits Times* (Singapore).

Longnecker, C. O., Sims, H. P., & Gioia, D. A. 1987. "Behind the Mask: The Politics of Employee Appraisal." *Academy of Management Executive, 1,* 183–193.

Lord, R. G., & Maher, K. J. 1993. *Leadership and Information Processing: Linking Perceptions and Performance.* New York: Routledge.

*Los Angeles Times* 1992, May 18. "Coming Renaissance of the LAPD; the Importance of Police Reform—and Willie L. Williams," p. B4.

Louis, M. R. 1980. "Surprise and Sense Making: What Newcomers Experience in Entering Unfamiliar Organizational Settings." *Administrative Science Quarterly, 25,* 226–251.

Lynn, M. 1997. "Board Games: Those Who Make It to the Top Are Not Usually Shy, Retiring Types, and Cadbury Only Increases the Likelihood of Conflict." *Management Today,* 30–34.

Lyons, M. 1998, April 8. "Taxi a High-Tech Office on Wheels." *Irish Times,* p. 16.

Maccoby, M. 2000, January/February. "Understanding the Difference between Management and Leadership." *Research • Technology Management,* pp. 57–59.

MacKenzie, M., Cambrosio, A., & Keating, P. 1988. "The Commercial Application of a Scientific Discovery: The Case of the Hybridoma Technique." *Research and Policy, 17*(3), 155–170.

Maier, N. R. F. 1952. *Principles of Human Relations, Applications to Management.* New York: John Wiley & Sons.

Maier, N. R. F., Solem, A. R., & Maier, A. A. 1975. *The Role-Play Technique: A Handbook for Management and Leadership Practice.* La Jolla, CA: University Associates.

Maisonneuve, J., Palmade, G., & Fourment, C. 1952. "Selective Choices and Propinquity." *Sociometry, 15,* 135–140.

Makiney, J. D., & Levy, P. E. 1998. "The Influence of Self-Ratings versus Peer Ratings on Supervisors' Performance Judgments." *Organizational Behavior and Human Decision Processes, 74*(3), 212–228.

Manning, J. F., & Fullerton, T. D. 1988. "Health and Well-Being in Highly Cohesive Units of the U.S. Army." *Journal of Applied Social Psychology, 18,* 503–519.

Mannix, E. 1993. "Organizations as Resource Dilemmas: The Effects of Power Balance on Coalition Formation in Small Groups." *Organizational Behavior and Human Decision Processes, 55,* 1–22.

Mannix, E., & Loewenstein, G. 1993. "Managerial Time Horizons and Inter-Firm Mobility: An Experimental Investigation." *Organizational Behavior and Human Decision Processes, 56,* 266–284.

Mannix, E., Thompson, L., & Bazerman, M. H. 1989. "Negotiation in Small Groups." *Journal of Applied Psychology, 74,* 508–517.

Manz, C. C., Keating, D. E., & Donnellon, A. 1990. "Preparing for an Organizational Change to Employee Self-Management: The Management Transition." *Organizational Dynamics, 19*(2), 15–26.

March, J. G. 1991. "Exploration and Exploitation in Organizational Learning." *Organization Science, 2*(1), 71–87.

Markham, S. E., Dansereau, F., & Alutto, J. A. 1982. "Group Size and Absenteeism Rates: A Longitudinal Analysis." *Academy of Management Journal, 25*(4), 921–927.

Markus, H. R., & Kitayama, S. 1991, April. "Culture and the Self: Implications for Cognition, Emotion, and Motivation." *Psychological Review, 98*(2), 224–253.

Massey, G. C., Scott, M. V., & Dornbusch, S. M. 1975. "Racism without Racists: Institutional Racism in Urban Schools." *Black Scholar, 7*(3), 2–11.

Maxwell, J. H., & Hopkins, M. 2002, September. "Who Do You Call When No One Has the Answers?" *Inc.,* 38–46.

May, K. 1982. "A Set of Independent, Necessary and Sufficient Conditions for Simple Majority Decisions." In B. Barry & R. Hardin (Eds.), *Rational Man and Irrational Society* (pp. 299–303). Beverly Hills, CA: Sage.

Mazur, A. 1985. "A Biosocial Model of Status in Face-to-Face Groups." *Social Forces,* 64, 377–402.

McAlister, L., Bazerman, M. H. & Fader, R. 1986. "Power and Goal Setting in Channel Negotiations." *Journal of Marketing Research,* 23, 238–263.

McCallum, D., Harring, K., Gilmore, R., Drenan, S., Chase, J., Insko, C., & Thibaut, J. 1985. "Competition and Cooperation between Groups and between Individuals." *Journal of Experimental Social Psychology, 21,* 301–320.

McCaskey, M. B. 1995. "Framework for Analyzing Work Groups." Harvard Business School Case No. 9-480-009. Boston, MA: Harvard Business School Publishing.

McCauley, C. 1998. "Groupthink Dynamics in Janis's Theory of Groupthink: Backward and Forward." *Organizational Behavior and Human Decision Processes, 73*(2–3), 142–162.

McClintock, C., Messick, D., Kuhlman, D., & Campos, F. 1973. "Motivational Bases of Choice in Three-Choice Decomposed Games." *Journal of Experimental Social Psychology, 57,* 250–260.

McGrath, J. E. 1984. *Groups: Interaction and Performance.* Upper Saddle River, NJ: Prentice Hall.

McGrath, J. E. 1990. "Time Matters in Groups." In J. Galegher, R. E. Kraut, & C. Egido (Eds.), *Intellectual Teamwork: Social and Tech-nological Foundations of Cooperative Work.* Mahwah, NJ: Lawrence Erlbaum & Associates.

McGrath, J. E., & Hollingshead, A. B. 1994. *Groups Interacting with Technology.* Newbury Park, CA: Sage.

McGrath, J. E., Kelly, J. R., & Machatka, D. E. 1984. "The Social Psychology of Time: Entrainment of Behavior in Social and Organizational Settings." *Applied Social Psychology Annual, 5,* 21–44.

McGregor, D. 1960. *The Human Side of Enterprise.* New York: McGraw-Hill.

McGuire, T., Keisler, S., & Siegel, J. 1987. "Group and Computer-Mediated Discussion Effect in Risk Decision-Making." *Journal of Personality and Social Psychology, 52*(5), 917–930.

Media Relations Office, NASA Jet Propulsion Laboratory. 1999, September 23. "NASA's Mars Climate Orbiter Believed to Be Lost." Pasadena, CA: California Institute of Technology, National Aeronautics and Space Administration. Release No. 99-080.

Meherabian, A. 1971. *Silent Messages.* Belmont, CA: Wadsworth.

Meindl, J. R., Ehrlich, S. B., & Dukerich, J. M. 1985. "The Romance of Leadership." *Administrative Science Quarterly, 30,* 78–102.

Meindl, J. R., & Lerner, M. O. 1984. "Exacerbation of Extreme Responses to an Out-Group." *Journal of Personality and Social Psychology, 47*(1), 71–84.

Menon, T., & Blount, S. 2002. "Shedding Some Light on the Organizational Garbage Can: How Social Relationships Affect the Valuation of Knowledge." Working paper. Chicago: University of Chicago Graduate School of Business.

Menon, T., & Pfeffer, J. 2002. "Valuing Internal vs. External Knowledge: Explaining the Preference for Outsiders." Working paper. Chicago: University of Chicago Graduate School of Business.

Messick, D. 1993. "Equality as a Decision Heuristic." In B. A. Mellers & J. Baron (Eds.), *Psychological Perspectives on Justice* (pp. 11–31). New York: Cambridge University Press.

Meyer, C. 1994, May–June. "How the Right Measures Help Teams Excel." *Harvard Business Review,* pp. 95–103.

Michaels, S. W., Brommel, J. M., Brocato, R. M., Linkous, R. A., & Rowe, J. S. 1982. "Social Facilitation in a Natural Setting." *Replication in Social Psychology, 4*(2), 21–24.

Michaelsen, L. K., Watson, W. E., & Black, R. H. 1989. "A Realistic Test of Individual versus Group Consensus Decision Making." *Journal of Applied Psychology, 74*(5), 834–839.

Michel, J. G., & Hambrick, D. C. 1992. "Diversification Posture and Top Management Team Characteristics." *Academy of Management Journal, 35*(1), 9–37.

Miles, R. P., & Osborne, T. 2001. *The Warren Buffett CEO: Secrets of the Berkshire Hathaway Managers.* New York: Wiley.

Miller, C. E., Jackson, P., Mueller, J., & Schersching, C. 1987. "Some Social Psychological Effects of Group Decision Rules." *Journal of Personality and Social Psychology, 52,* 325–332.

Miller, D. T. 1999. "The Norm of Self-Interest." *American Psychologist, 54*(12), 1053–1060.

Miller, D. T., & Ratner, R. 1998. "The Disparity between the Actual and Assumed Power of Self-Interest." *Journal of Personality and Social Psychology, 74*(1), 53–62.

Milliken, W. F. 1996. "The Eastman Way." *Quality Progress, 29*(10), 57–62.

Milliman, J. F., Zawacki, R. F., Norman, C., Powell, L., & Kirksey, J. 1994, November. "Companies Evaluate Employees from All Perspectives." *Personnel Journal, 73*(11), 99–103.

Mintzberg, H. 1973. *The Nature of Managerial Work.* New York: Harper & Row.

Misra, M., & Misra, P. 2002, March 3. "Innovations That Make a Difference." *Business Today,* p. 54.

Mohrman, S. A., Cohen, S. G., & Mohrman, A. M. 1995. *Designing Team-Based Organizations.* San Francisco, CA: Jossey-Bass.

Mohrman, S. A., Lawler, E. E., & Mohrman, A. M. 1992. "Applying Employee Involvement in Schools." *Educational Evaluation and Policy Analysis, 14*(4), 347–360.

Moore, D., Kurtzberg, T., Thompson, L., & Morris, M. 1999. "Long and Short Routes to Success in Electronically-Mediated Negotiations: Group Affiliations and Good Vibrations." *Organizational Behavior and Human Decision Processes, 77*(1), 22–43.

Moreland, R. L., Argote, L., & Krishnan, R. 1996. "Socially Shared Cognition at Work." In J. L. Nye & A. M. Brower (Eds.), *What's Social about Social Cognition?* Thousand Oaks, CA: Sage.

Moreland, R. L., Argote, L., & Krishnan, R. 1998. "Training People to Work in Groups." In R. S. Tindale et al. (Eds.), *Theory and Research on Small Groups.* New York: Plenum Press.

Moreland, R. L., & Levine, J. M. 1982. "Socialization in Small Groups: Temporal Changes in Individual-Group Relations." In L. Berkowitz (Ed.), *Advances in Experimental Social Psychology* (Vol. 15, pp. 137–192). New York: Academic Press.

Moreland, R. L., & Levine, J. M. 1989. "Newcomers and Oldtimers in Small Groups." In P. Paulus (Ed.), *Psychology or Group Influence* (2nd edition, pp. 143–186). Mahwah, NJ: Lawrence Erlbaum & Associates.

Moreland, R. L., & Levine, J. M. 1992. "The Composition of Small Groups." In E. J. Lawler, B. Markovsky, C. Ridgeway, & H. A. Walker (Eds.), *Advances in Group Processes* (Vol. 9, pp. 237–280). Greenwich, CT: JAI Press.

Moreland, R. L., & Levine, J. M. 2000a. "Socialization in Organizations and Work Groups." In M. Turner (Ed.), *Groups at Work: Theory and Research* (pp. 69–112). Mahwah, NJ: Erlbaum.

Moreland, R. L., & Levine, J. M. 2002b. "Socialization and Trust in Work Groups." *Group Processes and Interpersonal Relations, 5*(3), 185–201.

Moreland, R. L., & McMinn, J. G. 1999. "Gone but Not Forgotten: Loyalty and Betrayal Among Ex-Members of Small Groups." *Personality and Social Psychology Bulletin, 25*(12), 1476–1486.

Morgan, B. B., & Bowers, C. A. 1995. "Teamwork Stress: Implications for Team Decision Making." In R. A. Guzzo & E. Salas (Eds.), *Team Effectiveness and Decision Making in Organizations* (pp. 262–290). San Francisco: Jossey-Bass.

Morris, M. W., Podolny, J. M., & Ariel, S. 2000. "Missing Relations: Incorporating Relational Constructs into Models of Culture." In P. C. Earley & H. Singh (Eds.), *Innovations in International and Cross-Cultural Management* (pp. 52–90). Thousand Oaks, CA: Sage Publications.

Moscovici, S. 1985a. "Innovation and Minority Influence." In S. Moscovici, G. Mugny, & E. Van Avermaet (Eds.), *Perspectives on Minority Influence* (pp. 9–52). Cambridge, England: Cambridge University Press.

Moscovici, S. 1985b. "Social Influence and Conformity." In G. Lindzey & E. Aronson (Eds.), *Handbook of Social Psychology* (3rd edition, Vol. 2, pp. 347–412). New York: Random House.

Mosvick, R., & Nelson, R. B. 1996. *We've Got to Start Meeting Like This!: A Guide to Successful Meeting Management* (rev. ed.). Indianapolis, IN: Park Avenue.

Mottola, G. R., Bachman, B. A., Gaertner, S. L., & Dovidio, J. F. 1997. "How Groups Merge: The Effects of Merger Integration Patterns on Anticipated Commitment to the Merged Organization." *Journal of Applied Social Psychology, 27,* 1335–1358.

Mullen, B., Johnson, C., & Salas, E. 1991. "Productivity Loss in Brainstorming Groups: A Meta-Analytic Integration." *Basic and Applied Social Psychology, 12,* 3–23.

Mulvey, P. W., Veiga, J. F., & Elsass, P. M. 1996. "When Teammates Raise a White Flag." *Academy of Management Executive, 10*(1), 40–49.

Munter, M., & Netzley, M. 2002. *Guide to Meetings.* Upper Saddle River, NJ: Prentice Hall.

Muoio, A. 1997, August. "They Have a Better Idea . . . Do You?" *Fastcompany, 10,* 73–79.

Murnighan, J. K. 1992. *Bargaining Games.* New York: William Morrow and Co. Reprinted with permission.

Murnighan, J. K., & Mowen, J. C. 2001. *The Art of High-Stakes Decision-Making: Tough Calls in a Speed-Driven World.* New York: Wiley.

Nadler, J., Thompson, L., & Morris, M. 1999, August. "Schmooze or Lose: The Efforts of Rapport and Gender in E-mail Negotiations." Paper presented at the Academy of Management Annual conference, Chicago IL.

Nagasundaram, M., & Dennis, A. R. 1993. "When a Group Is Not a Group: The Cognitive Foundation of Group Idea Generation." *Small Group Research, 24,* 463–489.

Nahavandi, A., & Aranda, E. 1994. "Restructuring Teams for the Re-engineered Organ-

ization." *Academy of Management Review, 8*(4), 58–68.

National Public Radio, 2001, February 8. "Fresh Air."

Naylor, J. C., & Briggs, G. E. 1965. "Team-training Effectiveness Under Various Conditions." *Journal of Applied Psychology, 49*(4), 223–229.

Nelson, B. 1994. *1001 Ways to Reward Employees.* New York: Workman Publishing Co. Reprinted with permission.

Nemeth, C. J. 1994. "The Value of Minority Dissent." In S. Moscovici, A. Mucchi-Faina, et al. (Eds.), *Minority Influence: Nelson-Hall Series in Psychology* (pp. 3–15). Chicago: Nelson-Hall Publishers.

Nemeth, C. J. 1995. "Dissent as Driving Cognition, Attitudes, and Judgments." *Social Cognition, 13,* 273–291.

Nemeth, C. J., & Kwan, J. L. 1987. "Minority Influence, Divergent Thinking and Detection of Correct Solutions." *Journal of Applied Social Psychology, 17*(9), 788–799.

Nemeth, C. J., & Wachtler, J. 1974. "Creating the Perceptions of Consistency and Confidence: A Necessary Condition for Minority Influence." *Sociometry, 37*(4), 529–540.

Nemeth, C. J., & Wachtler, J. 1983. "Creative Problem Solving as a Result of Majority vs. Minority Influence." *European Journal of Social Psychology, 13*(1), 45–55.

Neuman, G. A., Wagner, S. H., & Christiansen, N. D. 1999. "The Relationship between Work-team Personality Composition and the Job Performance of Teams." *Groups and Organization Management, 24,* 28–45.

Neuman, G. A., & Wright, J. 1999. "Team Effectiveness: Beyond Skills and Cognitive Ability." *Journal of Applied Psychology, 84*(3), 376–389.

Nieva, V. F., Myers, D., & Glickman, A. S. 1979, July. "An Exploratory Investigation of the Skill Qualification Testing System." *U.S. Army Research Institute for the Behavioral and Social Sciences,* TR 390.

Nijstad, B. A., Stroebe, W., & Lodewijkx, H. F. M. (in press). "Production Blocking and Idea Generation." *Journal of Experimental Social Psychology.*

Nijstad, B. A., Stroebe, W., & Lodewijkx, H. F. M. 1999. "Persistence of Brainstorming Groups:

How Do People Know When to Stop?" *Journal of Experimental Social Psychology, 35,* 165–185.

Nijstad, B. A., Stroebe, W., & Lodewijkx, H. F. M. 2002. "Cognitive Stimulation and Interference in Groups: Exposure Effects in Idea Generation." *Journal of Experimental Social Psychology, 38*(6), 535–544.

Novak, C. J. 1997, April. "Proceed with Caution When Paying Teams." *HR Magazine, 42*(4), 73–78.

Nua Internet Surveys. 2002, May. "How Many Online?" Dublin, Ireland: ComputerScope, Ltd. URL: *http://www.nua.ie.*

Nunamaker, J. F. Jr., Briggs, R. O., & Mittleman, D. D. 1995. "Electronic Meeting Systems: Ten Years of Lessons Learned." In D. Coleman & R. Khanna (Eds.), *Groupware: Technology and Applications* (pp. 149–193). Upper Saddle River, NJ: Prentice Hall.

Nunamaker, J. F. Jr., Romano, N. C., & Briggs, R. O. 2002. "Increasing Intellectual Bandwidth: Generating Value from Intellectual Capital with Information Technology." *Group Decision and Negotiation, 11,* 69–86.

Oaksford, M., & Chater, N. 1994. "A Rational Analysis of the Selection Task as Optimal Data Selection." *Psychological Review, 101,* 608–631.

Oberle, J. 1990. "Teamwork in the Cockpit." *Training, 27*(2), 34–38.

Oddou, G. 1987. "Rock Climbing, Rappelling, and Sailing: Effective Management and Organization Development Tools?" *Consultation: An International Journal, 6*(3), 145–157.

O'Hamilton, J., Baker, S., & Vlasic, B. 1996, April. "The New Workplace." *BusinessWeek, 3473,* 106–117.

O'Hara-Devereaux, M., & Johansen, R. 1994. *Global Work: Bridging Distance, Culture and Time.* San Francisco, CA: Jossey-Bass.

Oldham, J. 1998, May 18. "Conflict and Cookies: Companies Coax Problems Out into the Open and Use Them to Make Working Groups More Effective." *Los Angeles Times,* p. 22.

Olson, M. 1965. *The Logic of Collective Action.* Cambridge, MA: Harvard University Press.

Ordeshook, P. 1986. *Game Theory and Political Theory: An Introduction.* Cambridge, England: Cambridge University Press.

O'Reilly, C. A., & Caldwell, D. F. 1985. "The Impact of Normative Social Influence and Cohesiveness on Task Perceptions and Attitudes: A Social-Information Processing Approach." *Journal of Occupational Psychology, 58,* 193–206.

Orsburn, J. D., Moran, L., Musselwhite, E., & Zenger, J. H. 1990. *Self-Directed Work Teams: The New American Challenge.* Chicago: Irwin.

Osborn, A. F. 1957. *Applied Imagination* (rev. ed.). New York: Scribner.

Osborn, A. F. 1963. *Applied Imagination* (3rd edition). New York: Scribner.

Osgood, C. E. 1979. *GRIT 1.* Dundas, Ontario: Peace Research Reviews (Vol. 8, no. 1, 0553-4283).

Oxley, N. L., Dzindolet, M. T., & Paulus, P. B. 1996. "The Effects of Facilitators on the Performance of Brainstorming Groups." *Journal of Social Behavior and Personality, 11*(4), 633–646.

Park, B., & Rothbart, M. 1982. "Perception of Outgroup Homogeneity and Levels of Social Categorization: Memory for Subordinate Attitudes of Ingroup and Outgroup Members." *Journal of Personality and Social Psychology, 42,* 1050–1068.

Parks, C. D., & Cowlin, R. A. 1996. "Acceptance of Uncommon Information into Group Discussion When That Information Is or Is Not Demonstrable." *Organizational Behavior and Human Decision Processes, 66*(3), 307–315.

Parnell, C. 1998. "Teamwork: Not a New Idea, but It's Transforming the Workplace." *Executive Speeches, 12*(3), 35–40.

Parnes, S. J., & Meadow, A. 1959. "Effect of 'Brain-storming' Instructions on Creative Problem-Solving by Trained and Untrained Subjects." *Journal of Educational Psychology, 50,* 171–176.

Parsons, T., Bales, R. F., & Shils, E. 1953. *Working Paper in the Theory of Action.* Glencoe, IL: Free Press.

Pascale, R. 1998. "Grassroots Leadership—Royal Dutch/Shell." *Fastcompany, 14,* 110.

Pascarella, P. 1997. "Compensating Teams." *Across the Board, 34*(2), 16–22.

Paulus, P. B. 1998. "Developing Consensus about Groupthink after All These Years." *Organizational Behavior and Human Decision Processes, 73*(2–3), 362–374.

Paulus, P. B., & Dzindolet, M. T. 1993. "Social Influence Processes in Group Brainstorming." *Journal of Personality and Social Psychology,* 64, 575–586.

Paulus, P. B., Larey, T. S., & Ortega, A. H. 1995. "Performance and Perceptions of Brainstormers in an Organizational Setting." *Basic and Applied Social Psychology, 17,* 249–265.

Paulus, P. B., Larey, T. S., Putman, V. L., Leggett, K. L., & Roland, E. J. 1996. "Social Influence Process in Computer Brainstorming." *Basic and Applied Social Psychology, 18,* 3–14.

Paulus, P. B., Putman, V. L., Coskun, H., Leggett, K. L., & Roland, E. J. 1996. "Training Groups for Effective Brainstorming." Presented at the Fourth Annual Advanced Concepts Conference on Work Teams—Team Implementation Issues, Dallas, TX.

Paulus, P. B., Larey, T. S., Brown, V., Dzindolet, M. T., Roland, E. J., Leggett, K. L., Putman, V. L., & Coskun, H. 1998, June. "Group and Electronic Brainstorming: Understanding Production Losses and Gains in Idea Generating Groups." Paper presented at Learning in Organizations Conference, Carnegie-Mellon University, Pittsburgh, PA.

Paulus, P. B., & Yang, H. 2000. "Idea Generation in Groups: A Basis for Creativity in Organizations." *Organizational Behavior and Human Decision Processes, 82*(1), 76–87.

Pearce, C. L., & Sims H. P. Jr. 2002. "Vertical Versus Shared Leadership as Predictors of the Effectiveness of Change Management Teams: An Examination of Aversive, Directive, Transactional, Transformational and Empowering Leader Behaviors." *Group Dynamics: Theory, Research, and Practice, 6*(2), 172–197.

Pelled, L. H., Eisenhardt, K. M., & Xin, K. R. 1999. "Exploring the Black Box: An Analysis of Work Group Diversity, Conflict, and Performance." *Administrative Science Quarterly, 44,* 1–28.

Pennington, G. 2002, April 30. "Three Families Learn Survival Skills of 1880s Pioneers in 'Frontier House.'" *St. Louis Post-Dispatch,* Everyday Magazine, p. F-1.

Perkins, D. V. 1982. "Individual Differences and Task Structure in the Performance of a Behavior Setting: An Experimental Evaluation of Barker's Manning Theory." *American Journal of Community Psychology, 10*(6), 617–634.

Perrow, C. 1984. *Normal Accidents: Living with High-Risk Technologies.* New York: Basic Books.

Peterson, R. S., & Nemeth, C. J. 1996. "Focus versus Flexibility: Majority and Minority Influence Can Both Improve Performance." *Personality and Social Psychology Bulletin, 22*(1), 14–23.

Peterson, R. S., Owens, P. D., Tetlock, P. E., Fan, E. T., & Martorana, P. 1998. "Group Dynamics in Top Management Teams: Groupthink, Vigilance, and Alternative Models of Organizational Failure and Success." *Organizational Behavior and Human Decision Processes, 73,* 272–305.

Pettit, J. 1997, January. "Team Communication: It's in the Cards." *Training and Development, 15*(1), 12–14.

Petty, R. E., Cacioppo, J. T., & Kasmer, J. 1985. "Effects of Need for Cognition on Social Loafing." Paper presented at the Midwestern Psychology Association Meeting, Chicago, IL.

Petty, R. M., & Wicker, A. W. 1974. "Degree of Manning and Degree of Success of a Group as Determinants of Members' Subjective Experiences and Their Acceptance of a New Group Member." *Catalog of Selected Documents in Psychology, 4,* 43.

Pew Internet Project. 2001, November 1. "Most US Internet Users Visit Online Groups." Pew Internet and American Life Project, Washington, DC. URL *http://www.pewinternet.org/index.asp.*

Pfeffer, J. 1983. "Organizational Demography." In B. M. Staw & L. L. Cummings (Eds.), *Research in Organizational Behavior* (Vol. 5, pp. 299–359). Greenwich, CT: JAI Press.

Pfeiffer, J. W. 1974. *A Handbook of Structured Experiences for Human Relations Training* (Vols. 1–10). La Jolla, CA: University Associates.

Phelps, R. 1996, September. "Cadbury Trusts in Teamwork." *Management Today,* p. 110.

Philip, G., & Young, E. S. 1987. "Man-Machine Interaction by Voice: Developments in Speech Technology. Part I: The State-of-the-Art." *Journal of Information Science Principles and Practice, 13*(1), 3–14.

Phillips, J. M. 1999. "Antecedents of Leader Utilization of Staff Input in Decision-Making Teams." *Organizational Behavior and Human Decision Processes, 77*(3), 215–242.

Phillips, K. W. 2003. "The Effects of Categorically Based Expectations on Minority Influence: The Importance of Congruence." *Personality and Social Psychology Bulletin, 29*(1), 3–13.

Plott, C. 1976. "Axiomatic Social Choice Theory: An Overview and Interpretation." *American Journal of Political Science, 20,* 511–596.

Plott, C., & Levine, M. 1978. "A Model of Agenda Influence on Committee Decisions." *American Economic Review, 68,* 146–160.

Podolny, J. M., & Baron, J. N. 1997. "Resources and Relationships: Social Networks and Mobility in the Workplace." *American Sociological Review, 62*(5), 673–693.

Polzer, J. T., Milton, L. P., & Swann, W. B. 2002. "Capitalizing on Diversity: Interpersonal Congruence in Small Work Groups." *Administrative Science Quarterly, 47,* 296–324.

Pope, S. 1996. "The Power of Guidelines, Structure, and Clear Goals." *Journal for Quality and Participation, 19*(7), 56–60.

Postmes, T., & Spears, R. 2002. "Behavior Online: Does Anonymous Computer Communication Reduce Gender Inequality?" *Personality and Social Psychology Bulletin, 28*(8), 1073–1083.

Poza, E. J., & Marcus, M. 1980, Winter. "Success Story: The Team Approach to Work Restructuring." *Organizational Dynamics, 8*(3), 3–25.

Prentice, D. A., Miller, D. T., & Lightdale, J. R. 1994. "Asymmetries in Attachments to Groups and to Their Members: Distinguishing between Common-Identity and Common-Bond Groups." *Personality and Social Psychology Bulletin, 20,* 484–493.

Prentice-Dunn, S., & Rogers, R. W. 1989. "Deindividuation and the Self-Regulation of Behavior." In P. B. Paulus (Ed.), *Psychology of Group Influence* (2nd edition), Mahwah, NJ: Lawrence Erlbaum & Associates.

*PR Newswire* 1998, February 26. "RSA's Secret-Key Challenge Solved by Distributed Team in Record Time; Team of Computer Enthusiasts Cracks Government-Endorsed DES Algorithm in Less Than Half the Time of Previous Challenge."

*PR Newswire* 2001, August 9. "Workforce Productivity Enhanced by Getting Back to the Business of Nature."

*PR Newswire* 2001, September 25. " Surfboards in the Boardroom and Bocce Ball Out Back."

Prokesch, S. E. 1997. "Unleashing the Power of Learning: An Interview with British Petroleum's John Browne." *Harvard Business Review, 75*(5), 146–168.

Pruitt, D. G., & Lewis, S. A. 1975. "Development of Integrative Solutions in Bilateral Negotiation." *Journal of Personality and Social Psychology, 31,* 621–630.

Quinn, A., & Schlenker, B. 2002. "Can Accountability Produce Independence? Goals as Determinants of the Impact of Accountability and Conformity." *Personality and Social Psychology Bulletin, 28*(4), 472–483.

Radcliff, D. 2000, April 1. "Marriott: Want to See the Benefits of IT and Business Alignment?" *ComputerWorld,* p. 58.

Radigan, J. 2001, December 1. "Remote Possibilities: Companies Are More Interested Than Ever in a Far-Flung Workforce." *CFO,* p. S5.

Raiffa, H. 1982. *The Art and Science of Negotiation.* Cambridge, MA: Belknap.

Rampton, S., & Stauber, J. 2000. *Trust Us, We're Experts: How Industry Manipulates Science and Gambles with Your Future.* New York: J. P. Tarcher/Putnam.

Raven, B. H., & Rubin, J. Z. 1976. *Social Psychology: People in Groups.* New York: John Wiley & Sons.

Reeves, L., & Weisberg, R. W. 1994. "The Role of Content and Abstract Information in Analogical Transfer." *Psychological Bulletin, 115*(3), 381–400.

Rhoades, J. A., & O'Connor, K. M. 1996. "Affect in Computer-Mediated and Face-to-Face Work Groups: The Construction and Testing of a General Model." *Computer Supported Cooperative Work, 4,* 203–228.

Rickards, T. 1993. "Creative Leadership: Messages from the Front Line and the Back Room." *Journal of Creative Behavior, 27,* 46–56.

Riess, M. 1982. "Seating Preferences as Impression Management: A Literature Review and Theoretical Integration." *Communication, 11,* 85–113.

Riess, M., & Rosenfeld, P. 1980. "Seating Preferences as Nonverbal Communication: A

Self-Presentational Analysis." *Journal of Applied Communications Research, 8,* 22–30.

Ringelmann, M. 1913. *Aménagement des fumiers et des purins.* Paris: Librarie agricole de la Maison rustique.

Roberts, P. 1999a, April. "The Agenda: Total Teamwork." *Fastcompany, 23,* 148.

Roberts, P. 1999b, October 1. "Live From Your Office! It's . . . The Company Talk Show!" *Fastcompany, 28,* 150.

Robinson, D. 2001, February 19. "Keeping Workers Happy Is More Important Than Ever." *Knight-Ridder Tribune Business News.*

Robinson, R. J., & Keltner, D. 1996. "Much Ado about Nothing? Revisionists and Traditionalists Choose an Introductory English Syllabus." *Psychological Science, 7*(1), 18–24.

Rogelberg, S. G., Barnes-Farrell, J. L., & Lowe, C. A. 1992. "The Stepladder Technique: An Alternative Group Structure Facilitating Effective Group Decision Making." *Journal of Applied Psychology, 77*(5), 730–737.

Rogelberg, S. G., & O'Connor, M. S. 1998. "Extending the Stepladder Technique: An Examination of Self-Paced Stepladder Groups." *Group Dynamics: Theory, Research, and Practice, 2*(2), 82–91.

Rogers, M., Hennigan, K., Bowman, C., & Miller, N. 1984. "Intergroup Acceptance in Classroom and Playground Settings." In N. Miller & M. B. Brewer (Eds.), *Groups in Contact: The Psychology of Desegregation* (pp. 187–212). Orlando, FL: Academic Press.

Rosebush, S., Timmons, H., Crockett, R. O., Palmeri, C., & Haddad, C. 2002, August 5. "Inside the Telecom." *BusinessWeek,* pp. 34–40.

Roseman, I., Wiest, C., & Swartz, T. 1994. "Phenomenology, Behaviors, and Goals Differentiate Emotions." *Journal of Personality and Social Psychology, 67,* 206–221.

Rosenfeld, J. 2000, September. "Built In Sub Time." *Fastcompany, 38,* 274–286.

Rosenthal, E. A. 1996. *Social Networks and Team Performance.* Unpublished Ph.D. dissertation, University of Chicago.

Rosette, A. 2003. *Privileged and Unaware: A Recipe for Discrimination and Prejudice.* Unpublished Ph.D. dissertation, Kellogg School of Management. Evanston, IL: Northwestern University.

Ross, B. H. 1987. "This Is Like That: The Use of Earlier Problems and the Separation of Similarity Effects." *Journal of Experimental Psychology: Learning, Memory and Cognition, 13*(4), 629–639.

Ross, J., & Staw, B. M. 1993, August. "Organizational Escalation and Exit: Lessons from the Shoreham Nuclear Power Plant." *Academy of Management Journal, 36*(4), 701–732.

Ross, L. 1977. "The Intuitive Psychologist and His Shortcomings: Distortions in the Attribution Process." In L. Berkowitz (Ed.), *Advances in Experimental Social Psychology* (Vol. 10, pp. 173–220). Orlando, FL: Academic Press.

Ross, S. M., & Offermann, L. R. 1997. "Transformational Leaders: Measurement of Personality Attributes and Work Group Performance." *Personality and Social Psychology Bulletin, 23*(10), 1078–1086.

Rothaermel, F. T., & Sugiyama, S. 2001. "Virtual Internet Communities and Commercial Success: Individual and Community-Level Theory Grounded in the Atypical Case of TimeZone.com." *Journal of Management, 27*(3), 297–312.

Rothbart, M., & Hallmark, W. 1988. "In-Group and Out-Group Differences in the Perceived Efficacy of Coercion and Conciliation in Resolving Social Conflict." *Journal of Personality and Social Psychology, 55,* 248–257.

Rothgerber, H. 1997. "External Intergroup Threat as an Antecedent to Perceptions of In-Group and Out-Group Homogeneity." *Journal of Personality and Social Psychology, 73*(6), 1206–1212.

Rothgerber, H., & Worchel, S. 1997. "The View from Below: Intergroup Relations from the Perspective of the Disadvantaged Group." *Journal of Personality and Social Psychology, 73*(6), 1191–1205.

Rouse, W., & Morris, N. 1986. "On Looking into the Black Box: Prospects and Limits in the Search for Mental Models." *Psychological Bulletin, 100,* 359–363.

Rousseau, D. M., & Tijoriwala, S. A. 1998. "Assessing Psychological Contracts: Issues, Alternatives, and Measures." *Journal of Organizational Behavior, 19,* 679–695.

Roy, M. C., Gauvin, S., & Limayem, M. 1996. "Electronic Group Brainstorming: The Role of Feedback on Productivity." *Small Group Research, 27,* 215–247.

Rubin, H. 2002, August. "Desperately Seeking Vernon." *Fastcompany,* p. 100.

Ruder, M. K., & Gill, D. L. 1982. "Immediate Effects of Win-Loss on Perceptions of Cohesion in Intramural and Intercollegiate Volleyball Teams." *Journal of Sport Psychology, 4*(3), 227–234.

Ruggiero, K. M., & Marx, D. M. 1999. "Less Pain and More to Gain: Why High-Status Group Members Blame Their Failure on Discrimination." *Journal of Personality and Social Psychology, 77*(4), 774–784.

Rutkowski, G. K., Gruder, C. L., & Romer, D. 1983. "Group Cohesiveness, Social Norms, and Bystander Intervention." *Journal of Personality and Social Psychology, 44*(3), 545–552.

Saavedra, R., & Kwun, S. K. 1993. "Peer Evaluation in Self-Managing Work Groups." *Journal of Applied Psychology, 78*(3), 450–462.

Sackett, P. R., DuBois, C. I. Z., & Wiggins-Noe, A. 1991. "Tokenism in Performance Evaluation: The Effects of Work Group Representation on Male-Female and White-Black Differences in Performance Ratings." *Journal of Applied Psychology, 76,* 263–267.

Salter, C. 2002, September. "Diversity Without the Excuses." *Fastcompany,* p. 44.

Savage, L. J. 1954. *The Foundations of Statistics.* New York: John Wiley & Sons.

Sawyer, J. E., Houlette, M., & Muzzy, E. L. 2002. "Decision Performance in Racially Diverse Cross-Functional Teams: The Effect of Convergent versus Crosscut Diversity Structure." Working Paper, Newark, DE: University of Delaware.

Schein, E. H. 1988. *Process Consultation: Its Role in Organization Development* (Vol. 1). Reading, MA: Addison-Wesley.

Schofield, J. W. 1986. "Black and White Contact in Desegregated Schools." In M. Hewstone & R. J. Brown (Eds.), *Contact and Conflict in Intergroup Encounters* (pp. 79–92). Oxford, England: Blackwell.

Schrage, M. 1995. *No More Teams!: Mastering the Dynamics of Creative Collaboration.* New York: Currency Doubleday.

Schrage, M. 1998, October 5. "Why Your Department Needs to Implement 360s." *Computerworld,* p. 33.

Schroth, R. J., and Elliott, A. L. 2002. *How Companies Lie: Why Enron Is Just the Tip of the Iceberg.* New York: Crown Business.

Schulz-Hardt, S., Frey, D., Lüthgens, C., & Moscovici, S. 2000. "Biased Information Search in Group Decision Making." *Journal of Personality and Social Psychology, 78*(4), 655–669.

Schulz-Hardt, S., Jochims, M., & Frey, D. 2002. "Productive Conflict in Group Decision Making: Genuine and Contrived Dissent as Strategies to Counteract Biased Decision Making." *Organizational Behavior and Human Decision Processes, 88,* 563–586.

Schutte, J. G. 1996. "Virtual Teaching in Higher Education: The New Intellectual Superhighway or Just Another Traffic Jam?" Working paper. Northridge, CA: California State University.

Schwartz, B. 1986. *The Battle for Human Nature: Science, Morality, and Modern Life.* New York: Norton.

Schweder, R. A., & Bourne, E. J. 1984. "Does the Concept of the Person Vary Cross-Culturally?" In R. A. Schweder & R. A. LeVine (Eds.), *Culture Theory: Essays on Mind, Self and Emotion* (pp. 158–199). New York/Cambridge, MA: Cambridge University Press.

Schweiger, D. M., & Walsh, J. P. 1990. "Mergers and Acquisitions: An Interdisciplinary View." In K. M. Rowland & G. R. Ferris (Eds.), *Research in Personnel and Human Resource Management* (Vol. 8, pp. 41–107). Greenwich, CT: JAI.

Sears, D. O., & Allen, H. M. Jr. 1984. "The Trajectory of Local Desegregation Controversies and Whites' Opposition to Busing." In N. Miller & M. Brewer (Eds.), *Groups in Contact: The Psychology of Desegregation* (pp. 123–151). New York: Academic Press.

Sears, D. O., & Funk, C. L. 1990. "The Limited Effect of Economic Self-Interest on the Political Attitudes of the Mass Public." *Journal of Behavioral Economics, 19*(3), 247–271.

Sears, D. O., & Funk, C. L. 1991. "Graduate Education in Political Psychology. Annual Meeting of International Society of Political Psychology, Washington, DC." *Political Psychology, 12*(2), 345–362.

Sedekides, C., Campbell, W. K., Reeder, G. D., & Elliot, A. J. 1998. "The Self-Serving Bias in Relational Context." *Journal of Personality and Social Psychology, 74*(2), 378–386.

Segal, M. W. 1974. "Alphabet and Attraction: An Unobtrusive Measure of the Effect of Propinquity in a Field Setting." *Journal of Personality and Social Psychology, 30*(5), 654–657.

Seifter, H., & Economy, P. 2001. *Leadership Ensemble: Lessons in Collaborative Management from the World's Only Conductorless Orchestra.* New York: Henry Holt & Company, Inc.

Sekaquaptewa, D., & Thompson, M. 2002. "The Differential Effects of Solo Status on Members of High- and Low-Status Groups." *Personality and Social Psychology Bulletin, 28*(5), 694–707.

Selbert, R. 1987, November. "Women at Work." *Future Scan, 554,* 1–3.

Senge, P. M. 1996. "Leading Learning Organizations: The Bold, the Powerful, and the Invisible." In F. Hesselbein, M. Goldsmith, & R. Beckhard (Eds.), *The Leader of the Future: New Visions, Strategies, and Practices for the Next Era* (pp. 41–57). San Francisco, CA: Jossey-Bass.

Sergiovanni, T. J., Metzcus, R., & Burden, L. 1969. "Toward a Particularistic Approach to Leadership Style: Some Finds." *American Educational Research Journal, 6,* 62–69.

Seta, J. J. 1982. "The Impact of Comparison Processes on Coactors' Task Performance." *Journal of Personality and Social Psychology, 42,* 281–291.

Shah, P. P., & Jehn, K. A. 1993. "Do Friends Perform Better Than Acquaintances? The Interaction of Friendship, Conflict, and Task." *Group Decision and Negotiation, 2*(2), 149–165.

Shaw, M. E. 1981. *Group Dynamics: The Psychology of Small Group Behavior* (3d edition). New York: McGraw-Hill.

Shea, G. P., & Guzzo, R. A. 1987, Spring. "Group Effectiveness: What Really Matters?" *Sloan Management Review, 28*(3), 25–31.

Sheehan, N., et al. 1971. *The Pentagon Papers: As Published by The New York Times, Based on the Investigative Reporting by Neil Sheehan, Written by Neil Sheehan [and others].* Articles and documents edited by G. Gold, A. M. Siegal, & S. Abt. New York: Bantam.

Shepherd, M. M., Briggs, R. O., Reinig, B. A., Yen, J., & Nunamaker, J. F. Jr. 1995–1996. "Invoking Social Comparison to Improve Electronic Brainstorming: Beyond Anonymity." *Journal of Management Information Systems, 12,* 155–170.

Shepperd, J. A. 1993. "Productivity Loss in Performance Groups: A Motivation Analysis." *Psychological Bulletin, 113,* 67–81.

Sherif, M. 1966. *In Common Predicament: Social Psychology of Intergroup Conflict and Cooperation.* Boston: Addison-Wesley.

Short, J., Williams, E., & Christie, B. 1976. *The Social Psychology of Telecommunications.* New York: John Wiley & Sons.

Shure, G. H., Rogers, M. S., Larsen, I. M., & Tasson, J. 1962. "Group Planning and Task Effectiveness." *Sociometry, 25,* 263–282.

Siegel, J., Dubrovsky, V., Keisler, S., & McGuire, T. 1986. "Group Processes in Computer-Mediated Communication." *Organizational Behavior, 37,* 157–187.

Silberman, M. 1990. *Active Training: A Handbook of Techniques, Designs, Case Examples, and Tips.* San Diego, CA: University Associates, Inc., Lexington Books/D. C. Heath and Company.

Simon, B., Pantaleo, G., & Mummendey, A. 1995. "Unique Individual or Interchangeable Group Member? The Accentuation of Intragroup Differences versus Similarities as an Indicator of the Individual Self versus the Collective Self." *Journal of Personality and Social Psychology, 69,* 106–119.

Simon, H. 1973. "The Structure of Ill Structured Problems." *Artificial Intelligence, 4*(1), 181–201.

Simonton, D. K. 1987. *Why Presidents Succeed: A Political Psychology of Leadership.* New Haven, CT: Yale University Press.

Sims, R. R. 1992. "Linking Groupthink to Unethical Behavior in Organizations." *Journal of Business Ethics, 11*(9), 651–662.

Singer, T., & Buchanan, L. 2002, August 1. "The Innovation Factor: A Field Guide to Innovation." *Inc.,* pp. 63–70.

Sittenfeld, C. 1999, July–August. "Powered By the People." *Fastcompany, 26,* 178.

Smith, C. M., Tindale, R. S., & Dugoni, B. L. 1996. "Minority and Majority Influence in Freely

Interacting Groups: Qualitative vs. Quantitative Differences." *British Journal of Social Psychology, 35,* 137–149.

Smith, S. 1997, February 24. "Accountants Adopt Hoteling Idea without Reservations." *San Francisco Business Times.*

Snow, C. C., Snell, S. A., Davison, S. C., & Hambrick, D. C. 1996. "Use Transnational Teams to Globalize Your Company." *Organizational Dynamics, 24*(4), 50–67.

Snyder, M. 1984. "When Belief Creates Reality." In L. Berkowitz (Ed.), *Advances in Experimental Social Psychology* (Vol. 18, pp. 248–306). New York: Academic Press.

Sommers, N. 1982. "Responding to Student Writing." *College Composition and Communication, 33,* 148–156.

Sparrowe, R. T., & Popielarz, P. A. 1995. "Weak Ties and Structural Holes: The Effects of Network Structure on Careers." Paper presented at the annual meetings of the Academy of Management, Vancouver, BC.

Sproull, L., & Keisler, S. 1991. *Connections: New Ways of Working in the Networked Organization.* Cambridge, MA: MIT Press.

Stafford, D. 2002, June 11. "Team-based Decision-making Works at Edwardsville, Kan., Auto Products Plant." *Knight-Ridder Tribune Business News: Kansas City Star.*

Stasser, G. 1988. "Computer Simulation as a Research Tool: The DISCUSS Model of Group Decision Making." *Journal of Experimental Social Psychology, 24*(5), 393–422.

Stasser, G. 1992. "Information Salience and the Discovery of Hidden Profiles by Decision-Making Groups: A 'Thought' Experiment." *Organizational Behavior and Human Decision Processes, 52,* 156–181.

Stasser, G., & Dietz-Uhler, B. 2001. "Collective Choice, Judgment, and Problem-Solving, Vol. 3: Group Processes." In M.A. Hogg and S. Tindale (Eds.), *Blackwell Handbook of Social Psychology* (pp. 31–55). Oxford, England: Blackwell.

Stasser, G., & Stewart, D. D. 1992. "Discovery of Hidden Profiles by Decision-Making Groups: Solving a Problem versus Making a Judgment." *Journal of Personality and Social Psychology, 63,* 426–434.

Stasser, G., Stewart, D. D., & Wittenbaum, G. M. 1995. "Expert Roles and Information Exchange during Discussion: The Importance of Knowing Who Knows What." *Journal of Experimental Social Psychology, 31,* 244–265.

Stasser, G., Taylor, L. A., & Hanna, C. 1989. "Information Sampling in Structured and Unstructured Discussions of Three- and Six-Person Groups." *Journal of Personality and Social Psychology, 57,* 67–78.

Stasser, G., & Titus, W. 1985. "Pooling of Unshared Information in Group Decision Making: Biased Information Sampling During Discussion." *Journal of Personality and Social Psychology, 48,* 1467–1478.

Stasser, G., & Titus, W. 1987. "Effects of Information Load and Percentage of Shared Information on the Dissemination of Unshared Information in Group Discussion." *Journal of Personality and Social Psychology, 53,* 81–93.

Staw, B. H. 1976. "Knee-Deep in the Big Muddy: A Study of Escalating Commitment to a Chosen Course of Action." *Organizational Behavior and Human Decision Processes, 16*(1), 27–44.

Steele, S. 1990. *The Content of Our Character: A New Vision of Race in America* (pp. 111–125). New York: St. Martin's Press.

Steiner, I. 1972. *Group Process and Productivity.* New York: Academic Press.

Stewart, D. D., Billings, R. S., & Stasser, G. 1998. "Accountability and the Discussion of Unshared, Critical Information in Decision Making Groups." *Group Dynamics: Theory, Research, and Practice, 2*(1), 18–23.

Stewart, G. I., & Manz, C. C. 1995. "Leadership and Self-managing Work Teams: A Typology and Integrative Model." *Human Relations, 48*(7), 747–770.

Stipp, D. 2002, July 22. "The Big Gap at the FDA." *Fortune,* pp. 113–116.

Stogdill, R. M. 1972. "Group Productivity, Drive, and Cohesiveness." *Organizational Behavior and Human Performance, 8*(1), 26–43.

Stokes, J. P. 1983. "Components of Group Cohesion: Inter-Member Attraction, Instrumental Value, and Risk Taking." *Small Group Behavior, 14,* 163–173.

Stoner, J. A. F. 1961. "A Comparison of Individual and Group Decisions Involving Risk." Thesis, Massachusetts Institute of Technology.

Strasburg, J. 2000, August 27. "Companies Take to the Great Outdoors." *San Francisco Examiner,* p. B-1.

Stroebe, W., & Diehl, M. 1994. "Why Are Groups Less Effective Than Their Members? On Productivity Losses in Idea Generating Groups." *European Review of Social Psychology, 5,* 271–301.

Stroebe, W., Diehl, M., & Abakoumkin, G. 1992. "The Illusion of Group Effectivity." *Personality and Social Psychology Bulletin, 18*(5), 643–650.

Stroebe, W., Lenkert, A., & Jonas, K. 1988. "Familiarity May Breed Contempt: The Impact of Student Exchange on National Stereotypes and Attitudes." In W. Stroebe, A. W. Kruglanski, D. Bar-Tal, & M. Hewstone (Eds.), *The Social Psychology of Intergroup Conflict* (pp. 167–187). New York: Springer-Verlag.

Strozniak, P. 2000, September 18. "Teams at Work: Team Culture at Small Manufacturers." *Industry Week,* 47–50.

Sumner, W. 1906. *Folkways.* New York: Ginn.

*Sunday Times–London,* 2002, March 24. "The Firm that Lets Staff Breathe." News International, Features Section, *100 Best Companies to Work For 2002.*

Sundstrom, E. D., DeMeuse, K. P., & Futrell, D. 1990. Work Teams: Applications and Effectiveness. *American Psychologist, 45*(2), 120–133.

Sundstrom, E. D., & Sundstrom, M. G. 1986. *Work Places: The Psychology of the Physical Environment in Offices and Factories.* Cambridge, England: Cambridge University Press.

Sundstrom, E. D., McIntyre, M., Halfhill, T., & Richards, H. 2000. "Work Groups: From the Hawthorne Studies to Work Teams of the 1990s and Beyond." *Group Dynamics, 4,* 44–67.

Sutton, R. I., & Hargadon, A. 1996. "Brainstorming Groups in Context: Effectiveness in a Product Design Firm." *Administrative Science Quarterly, 41,* 685–718.

Sutton, R. L., & Louis, M. R. 1987. "How Selecting and Socializing Newcomers Influences Insiders." *Human Resource Management, 26,* 347–361.

Svenson, O. 1981. "Are We All Less Risky and More Skillful Than Our Fellow Drivers?" *Acta Psychologica, 47,* 143–148.

Swann, W. B., Milton, L. P., & Polzer, J. T. 2000. "Should We Create a Niche or Fall in Line? Identity Negotiation and Small Group Effectiveness." *Journal of Personality and Social Psychology, 79*(2), 238–250.

Swezey, R. W., & Salas, E. (Eds.). 1992. *Teams: Their Training and Performance.* Norwood, NJ: Ablex Publishing Corp.

Tajfel, H., (Ed.). 1978. *Differentiation between Social Groups: Studies in the Social Psychology of Intergroup Relations.* New York: Academic Press.

Tajfel, H. 1982. "Social Psychology of Intergroup Relations." *Annual Review of Psychology, 33,* 1–39.

Tajfel, H., & Turner, J. C. 1986. "The Social Identity Theory of Intergroup Behavior." In S. Worchel & W. G. Austin (Eds.), *Psychology of Intergroup Relations* (pp. 7–24). Chicago: Nelson-Hall.

Taylor, A. 2002, July 22. "Honda Goes Its Own Way." *Fortune,* pp. 146–152.

Taylor, D. W., Berry, P. C., & Block, C. H. 1958. "Does Group Participation When Using Brainstorming Facilitate or Inhibit Creative Thinking?" *Administrative Science Quarterly, 3,* 23–47.

Taylor, D. W., & Faust, W. L. 1952. "Twenty Questions: Efficiency of Problem-Solving as a Function of the Size of the Group." *Journal of Experimental Social Psychology, 44,* 360–363.

Taylor, F. W. 1911. *Shop Management.* New York: Harper & Brothers.

Taylor, S. E., & Brown, J. D. 1988. "Illusion of Well-Being: A Social Psychological Perspective on Mental Health." *Psychological Bulletin, 103,* 193–210.

Teasley, S., Covi, L., Krishnan, M. S., & Olson, J. S. 2000. "How Does Radical Collocation Help a Team Succeed?" In *Proceedings of ACM 2000 Conference on Computer Supported Cooperative Work* (pp. 339–347), Philadelphia, PA.

Terry, D. J., & Callan, V. J. 1998. "In-Group Bias in Response to an Organizational Merger." *Group Dynamics: Theory, Research, and Practice, 2*(2), 67–81.

Terry, D. J., Carey, C. J., & Callan, V. J. 2001. "Employee Adjustment to an Organizational Merger." *Personality and Social Psychology Bulletin, 27*(3), pp. 267–280.

Terry, D. J., & O'Brien, A. T. 2001. "Status, Legitimacy, and Ingroup Bias in the Context of an Organizational Merger." *Group Processes and Intergroup Relations, 4,* 271–289.

Tesser, A., & Rosen, S. 1975. "The Reluctance to Transmit Bad News." In L. Berkowitz (Ed.), *Advances in Experimental Social Psychology* (Vol. 8). New York: Academic Press.

Tetrault, L. A., Schriescheim, C. A., & Neider, L. L. 1988. "Leadership Training Interventions: A Review." *Organizational Development Journal, 6*(3), 77–83.

Tetlock, P. E., Skitka, L., & Boettger, R. 1989. "Social and Cognitive Strategies for Coping with Accountability: Conformity, Complexity and Bolstering." *Journal of Personality and Social Psychology, 57,* 632–640.

Thibaut, J., & Kelley, H. 1959. *The Social Psychology of Groups.* New York: John Wiley & Sons.

Thompson, J. 1967. *Organizations in Action.* New York: McGraw-Hill.

Thompson, L. 1991. "Information Exchange in Negotiation." *Journal of Experimental Social Psychology, 27,* 161–179.

Thompson, L. 2001. *The Mind and Heart of the Negotiator* (2nd edition). Upper Saddle River, NJ: Prentice Hall.

Thompson, L., & DeHarpport, T. 1994. "Social Judgment, Feedback, and Interpersonal Learning in Negotiation." *Organizational Behavior and Human Decision Processes, 58,* 327–345.

Thompson, L., & DeHarpport, T. 1998. "Relationships, Good Incompatibility, and Communal Orientation in Negotiations." *Basic and Applied Social Psychology, 20*(1), 33–43.

Thompson, L., & Hastie, R. 1990. "Social Perception in Negotiation." *Organizational Behavior and Human Decision Processes, 47,* 98–123.

Thompson, L., & Hrebec, D. 1996. "Lose-Lose Agreements in Interdependent Decision Making." *Psychological Bulletin, 120*(3), 396–409.

Thompson, L., Kray, L., & Lind, A. 1998. "Cohesion and Respect: An Examination of Group Decision Making in Social and Escalation Dilemmas." *Journal of Experimental Social Psychology, 34,* 289–311.

Thompson, L., & Loewenstein, J. 1992. "Egocentric Interpretations of Fairness and Negotiation." *Organizational Behavior and Human Decision Processes, 51,* 176–197.

Thompson, L., Loewenstein, J., & Gentner, D. 2000. "Avoiding Missed Opportunities in Managerial Life: Analogical Training More Powerful Than Individual Case Training." *Organizational Behavior and Human Decision Processes, 82*(1), 60–75.

Thompson, L., Mannix, E., & Bazerman, M. 1988. "Group Negotiation: Effects of Decision Rule, Agenda, and Aspiration." *Journal of Personality and Social Psychology, 54,* 86–95.

Thompson, L., & Rosette, A. In press. "Leading by Analogy." In S. Chowdhury (Ed.), *Financial Times Next Generation Business Series,* Prentice Hall: London.

Thompson, L., Valley, K. L., & Kramer, R. M. 1995. "The Bittersweet Feeling of Success: An Examination of Social Perception in Negotiation." *Journal of Experimental Social Psychology, 31*(6), 467–492.

Thornton, E., & Zellner, W. 2002, August 12. "The Real Story of the Watkins Memo." *BusinessWeek,* p. 8.

Tickle-Degnen, L., & Rosenthal, R. 1987. "Group Rapport and Nonverbal Behavior." In *Review of Personality and Social Psychology* (Vol. 9, pp. 113–136). Beverly Hills, CA: Sage.

Tippett, D. D., & Peters, J. F. 1995. "Team Building and Project Management: How Are We Doing?" *Project Management Journal, 26*(4), 29–37.

Toffler, A. 1991. *Powershift: Knowledge, Wealth, and Violence at the Edge of the 21st Century.* New York: Bantam Books.

Train, J. 1995, June 24. "Learning from Financial Disaster." *Financial Times* (Weekend Money Markets), p. II.

Trevison, C. 2002, August 22. "Microchip Bringing Magic to Gresham." *Oregonian, East Zoner,* p. 01.

Triandis, H. C. 1989. "Cross-Cultural Studies of Individualism and Collectivism." In J. J. Berman (Ed.), *Cross-Cultural Perspectives: Nebraska Symposium on Motivation* (Vol. 37, pp. 41–133). Lincoln: University of Nebraska Press.

Tropman, J. E. 1996. *Making Meetings Work: Achieving High Quality Group Decisions.* Thousand Oaks, CA: Sage.

Tropman, J. E., & Morningstar, G. 1989. *Entrepreneurial Systems of the 1990s: Their Creation, Structure, and Management.* New York: Quorum Books. Reproduced with permission of Greenwood Publishing Group, Inc., Westport, CT.

"The Trouble With Teams: Management Focus." *Economist,* 1995, January 14, p. 61.

Tuch, S. A., & Martin, J. K. 1991. "Race in the Workplace: Black and White Differences in the Sources of Job Satisfaction." *Sociological Quarterly, 32*(1), 103–116.

Tully, S. 2002, August 19. "The Jamie Dimon Show." *Fortune,* pp. 88–96.

Turkle, S. 1995. *Life on the Screen: Identity in the Age of the Internet.* New York: Simon & Schuster.

Turner, J. C. 1987. "A Self-Categorization Theory." In J. C. Turner, M. A. Hogg, P. J. Oakes, S. D. Reicher, & M. Witherell (Eds.), *Rediscovering the Social Group: A Self-Categorization Theory* (pp. 42–67). Oxford, England: Basil Blackwell.

Turner, M. A., Fix, M., & Struyk, R. J. 1991. *Opportunities Denied, Opportunities Diminished: Racial Discrimination in Hiring.* Washington, DC: Urban Institute Press.

Turner, M. E., & Pratkanis, A. R. 1998. "A Social Identity Maintenance Model of Groupthink." *Organizational Behavior and Human Decision Processes, 73*(2–3), 210–235.

Turner, M. E., Probasco, P., Pratkanis, A. R., & Leve, C. 1992. "Threat, Cohesion, and Group Effectiveness: Testing a Social Identity Maintenance Perspective on Groupthink." *Journal of Personality and Social Psychology, 63,* 781–796.

Tyler, T. R. 1990. *Why People Obey the Law.* New Haven, CT: Yale University Press.

Tyler, T. R., & Smith, H. J. 1998. "Social Justice and Social Movements." In D. Gilbert, S. T. Fiske, & G. Lindzey (Eds.), *Handbook of Social Psychology* (4th edition). New York: McGraw-Hill.

Tziner, A., & Eden, D. 1985. "Effects of Crew Composition on Crew Performance: Does the Whole Equal the Sum of Its Parts?" *Journal of Applied Psychology, 70,* 85–93.

Ury, W. L., Brett, J. M., & Goldberg, S. B. 1988. *Getting Disputes Resolved: Designing Systems to Cut the Costs of Conflict.* San Francisco: Jossey-Bass.

U.S. Department of Labor 2001a. *Labor Force Statistics from the Current Population Survey.* Washington, DC: U.S. Bureau of Labor Statistics and the Bureau of Census.

U.S. Department of Labor 2001b. *Median Weekly Earnings of Full-Time Wage and Salary Workers By Selected Characteristics* (D-20). Washington, DC: Bureau of Labor Statistics.

U.S. Department of Labor 2001c. *Office of Federal Contract Compliance Programs Accomplishment Data for Fiscal Years 1990–2001.* Washington, DC: Employment Standards Administration.

Uzzi, B. 1997. "Social Structure and Competition in Interfirm Networks: The Paradox of Embeddedness." *Administrative Science Quarterly, 42,* 35–67.

Uzzi, B., & Gillespie, J. J. 1999. "Access and Governance Benefits of Social Relationships and Networks: The Case of Collateral, Availability, and Bank Spreads." In H. Rosenblum (Ed.), *Business Access to Capital and Credit.* Washington, DC: Federal Reserve Bank.

van Avermaet, E. 1974. "Equity: A Theoretical and Experimental Analysis." Unpublished doctoral dissertation, University of California, Santa Barbara.

van Boven, L., Kruger, J., Savitsky, K., & Gilovich, T. 2000. "When Social Worlds Collide: Overconfidence in the Multiple Audience Problem." *Personality and Social Psychology Bulletin, 26*(5), 619–628.

Vandello, J. A., & Cohen, D. 1999. "Patterns of Individualism and Collectivism Across the United States." *Journal of Personality and Social Psychology, 77*(2), 279–292.

Van de Ven, A. H., & Delbecq, A. L. 1974. "The Effectiveness of Nominal, Delphi, and Interacting Group Decision Making Processes." *Academy of Management Journal, 17*(4), 605–621.

Van Knippenberg, D., Van Knippenberg, B., Monden, L., & De Lima, F. 2002. "Organizational Identification After a Merger: A Social Identity Perspective." *British Journal of Social Psychology, 44,* 233–262.

Van Maanen, J. 1977. "Experiencing Organization: Notes on the Meaning of Careers and Socialization." In J. Van Maanen (Ed.), *Organizational Careers: Some New Perspectives* (pp. 15–45). New York: John Wiley & Sons.

van Oostrum, J., & Rabbie, J. M. 1995. "Intergroup Competition and Cooperation within Autocratic and Democratic Management Regimes." *Small Group Research, 26*(2), 269–295.

Verberne, T. 1997. "Creative Fitness." *Training and Development, 51*(8), 68–71.

Verespej, M. A. 1990, December 3. "When You Put the Team in Charge." *Industry Week,* pp. 30–31.

von Hippel, E. A. 1988. "Task Partitioning: An Innovation Process Variable" (Working Paper No. 2030-88). Cambridge, MA: Sloan School of Management.

Vroom, V. H., & Jago, A. G. 1978. "The Validity of the Vroom-Yetton Model." *Journal of Applied Psychology, 63*(2), 151–162.

Vroom, V. H., & Jago, A. G. 1988. *The New Leadership: Managing Participation in Organizations.* Upper Saddle River, NJ: Prentice Hall.

Vroom, V. H., & Jago, A. G. 1987. *The New Leadership: Cases and Manuals for Use in Leadership Training.* New Haven, CT: Authors.

Vroom, V.H., & Yetton, P.W. 1973. *Leadership and Decision-Making.* Pittsburgh, PA: University of Pittsburgh Press.

Wageman, R. 1995. "Interdependence and Group Effectiveness." *Administrative Science Quarterly, 40*(1), 145–180.

Wageman, R. 1997. "Case Study: Critical Success Factors for Creating Superb Self-Managing Teams at Xerox." *Compensation & Benefits Review, 29*(5), 31–41.

Wagner, G., Pfeffer, J., & O'Reilly, C. 1984. "Organizational Demography and Turnover in Top Management Groups." *Administrative Science Quarterly, 29,* 74–92.

Wah, L. 1999, May 1. "Making Knowledge Stick." *Management Review,* pp. 24–29.

Walker, R. 2002, August. "Hook, Line, Sinker." *Inc.,* pp. 85–88.

Walton, R. E. 1977. "Work Innovations at Topeka: After Six Years." *Journal of Applied Psychology, 63,* 81–88.

Walton, R. E., & Hackman, J. R. 1986. "Groups under Contrasting Management Strategies." In P. S. Goodman et al. (Eds.), *Designing Effective Workgroups.* San Francisco, CA: Jossey-Bass.

Wanous, J. P. 1980. *Organizational Entry: Recruitment, Selection, and Socialization of Newcomers.* Reading, MA: Addison-Wesley.

*Wards Cove Packing Company, Inc.* v. *Atonio,* 109 S. Ct. 2115 (1989).

Warner, F. 2002a, August. "In a Word, Toyota Drives for Innovation." *Fastcompany,* pp. 36–38.

Warner, F. 2002b, September. "Microsoft Eats the Dog Food." *Fastcompany,* pp. 46–48.

Wason, P. C., & Johnson-Laird, P. N. 1972. *Psychology of Reasoning: Structure and Content.* Cambridge, MA: Harvard University Press.

Watson, T., & Leinwand, D. 2002, July 30. "Miners Tell of Days in the Dark." *USA Today,* p. 3A.

Watson, W. E., Kumar, K., & Michaelsen, L. K. 1993. "Cultural Diversity's Impact on Interaction Process and Performance: Comparing Homogeneous and Diverse Task Groups." *Academy of Management Journal, 36*(3), 590–602.

Waung, M., & Highhouse, S. 1997. "Fear of Conflict and Empathic Buffering: Two Explanations for the Inflation of Performance Feedback." *Organizational Behavior and Human Decision Processes, 71*(1), 37–54.

Webb, S., & Smith, A. 1991. "IS Training Survey: Manufacturing Training Holds Up as Recession Continues." *Industrial Society,* pp. 13–15.

Weber, M. 1958. *The Protestant Ethic and the Spirit of Capitalism.* Translated by T. Parsons. New York: Scribner's.

Weber, M. 1978. *Economy and Society: An Outline of Interpretive Sociology.* Translated by G. Roth & C. Wittich. Berkeley: University of California Press.

Wegner, D. M. 1986. "Transactive Memory: A Contemporary Analysis of the Group Mind." In B. Mullen & G. Goethals (Eds.), *Theories of Group Behavior* (pp.185–208). New York: Springer-Verlag.

Wegner, D. M., Giuliano, T., & Hertel, P. 1995. "Cognitive Interdependence in Close Relationships." In W. J. Ickes (Ed.), *Compatible and Incompatible Relationships* (pp. 253–276). New York: Springer-Verlag.

Weick, K. E., & Gilfillan, D. P. 1971. "Fate of Arbitrary Traditions in a Laboratory Microculture." *Journal of Personality and Social Psychology, 17,* 179–191.

Weingart, L. R. 1992. "Impact of Group Goals, Task Component Complexity, Effort, and Planning on Group Performance." *Journal of Applied Psychology, 77,* 682–693.

Weingart, L. R., Bennett, R., & Brett, J. F. 1993. "The Impact of Consideration of Issues and Motivational Orientation on Group Negotiation Process and Outcome." *Journal of Applied Psychology, 78,* 504–517.

Weisband, S. P. 1992. "Group Discussion and First Advocacy Effects in Computer-Mediated and Face-to-Face Decision Making Groups." *Organizational Behavior and Human Decision Processes, 53,* 352–380.

Weisberg, R. W. 1986. *Creativity, Genius and Other Myths.* New York: Freeman.

Weisberg, R. W. 1993. *Creativity: Beyond the Myth of Genius.* San Francisco: Freeman.

Weisberg, R. W. 1997. "Case Studies of Creative Thinking." In S. M. Smith, T. B. Ward, & R. A. Finke (Eds.), *The Creative Cognition Approach.* Cambridge, MA: MIT Press.

Weitzman, M. 1984. *The Share Economy.* Cambridge, MA: Harvard University Press.

Wellens, A. R. 1989, September. "Effects of Telecommunication Media upon Information Sharing and Team Performance: Some Theoretical and Empirical Findings." *IEEE AES Magazine, 4,* 14.

Wellins, R. S. 1992. "Building a Self-Directed Work Team." *Training and Development, 46*(12), 24–28.

Wellins, R. S., Byham, W. C., & Wilson, J. M. 1991. *Empowered Teams* (p. 26). San Francisco, CA: Jossey-Bass, Inc.

Werner, D., Ember, C. R., & Ember, M. 1981. *Anthropology: Study Guide and Workbook.* Upper Saddle River, NJ: Prentice Hall.

Whetton, D. A., & Cameron, K. S. 1991. *Developing Management Skills* (2nd edition). New York: HarperCollins.

Whitehead, A. N. 1929. *The Aims of Education.* New York: MacMillan.

Wicker, A. W., Kermeyer, S. L., Hanson, L., & Alexander, D. 1976. "Effects of Manning Levels on Subjective Experiences, Performance, and Verbal Interaction in Groups." *Organizational Behavior and Human Performance, 17,* 251–274.

Wicker, A. W., & Mehler, A. 1971. "Assimilation of New Members in a Large and a Small Church." *Journal of Applied Psychology, 55,* 151–156.

Wild, T. C., Enzle, M. E., Nix, G., & Deci, E. L. 1997. "Perceiving Others as Intrinsically or Extrinsically Motivated: Effects on Expectancy Formation and Task Engagement." *Personality and Social Psychology Bulletin, 23*(8), 837–848.

Wilder, D. A. 1986a. "Social Categorization: Implications for Creation and Reduction of Intergroup Bias." In L. Berkowitz (Ed.), *Advances in Experimental Social Psychology* (Vol. 19, pp. 291–355). Orlando, FL: Academic Press.

Wilder, D. A. 1986b. "Cognitive Factors Affecting the Success of Intergroup Contact." In S. Worchel & W. Austin (Eds.), *Psychology of Intergroup Relations* (pp. 49–66). Chicago: Nelson-Hall.

Wilder, D. A., & Allen, V. L. 1977. "Veridical Social Support, Extreme Social Support, and Conformity." *Representative Research in Social Psychology, 8,* 33–41.

Williams, C. L. 1992. "The Glass Escalator: Hidden Advantages for Men in 'Female' Professions." *Social Forces, 39,* 253–267.

Williams, K. D. 1981. "The Effects of Group Cohesiveness on Social Loafing in Simulated Word-Processing Pools." *Dissertation Abstracts International, 42*(2-B), 838.

Williams, K. D. 1997. "Social Ostracism." In R. Kowalski (Ed.), *Aversive Interpersonal Behaviors* (pp. 133–170). New York: Plenum Publishers.

Williams, K. D., Harkins, S. G., & Latané, B. 1981. "Identifiability as a Deterrent to Social Loafing: Two Cheering Experiments." *Journal of Personality and Social Psychology, 40*(2), 303–311.

Williams, K. D., & Williams, K. B. 1984. "Social Loafing in Japan: A Cross-Cultural Development Study." Paper presented at the Midwestern Psychological Association Meeting, Chicago.

Wilson, D. C., Butler, R. J., Cray, D., Hickson, D. J., & Mallory, G. R. 1986. "Breaking the Bounds of Organization in Strategic Decision Making." *Human Relations, 39,* 309–332.

Wittenbaum, G. M. 1998. "Information Sampling in Decision-Making Groups: The Impact of Members' Task-Relevant Status." *Small Group Research, 29,* 57–84.

Wolinsky, H. 1998, November 11. "Report Calls AMA a House Divided." *Chicago Sun-Times,* p. 72.

Woodman, R. W., Sawyer, J. E., & Griffin, R. W. 1993. "Toward a Theory of Organizational Creativity." *Academy of Management Review, 18*(2), 293–321.

Worringham, C. J., & Messick, D. M. 1983. "Social Facilitation of Running: An Unobtrusive Study." *Journal of Social Psychology, 121,* 23–29.

Wright, S. C., Aron, A., McLaughlin-Volpe, T., & Ropp, S. A. 1997. "The Extended Contact Effect: Knowledge of Cross-Group Friendships and Prejudice." *Journal of Personality and Social Psychology, 73*(1), 73–90.

Yukl, G. A. 1981. *Leadership in Organizations.* London: Prentice-Hall International.

Yukl, G. A. 2002. *Leadership in Organizations* (5th edition). Upper Saddle River, NJ: Prentice Hall.

Zaccaro, S. J. 1984. "Social Loafing: The Role of Task Attractiveness." *Personality and Social Psychology Bulletin, 10,* 99–106.

Zajonc, R. 1968. "Attitudinal Effects of Mere Exposure." *Journal of Personality and Social Psychology, 9* (monograph supplement, No. 2, Part 2).

Ziller, R. C. 1957. "Four Techniques of Group Decision-Making under Uncertainty." *Journal of Applied Psychology, 41,* 384–388.

Ziller, R. C. 1965. "Toward a Theory of Open and Closed Groups." *Psychological Bulletin, 64,* 164–182.

Zimbardo, P. G. 1969. "The Human Choice: Individuation, Reason, and Order versus Deindividuation, Impulse, and Chaos." In W. Arnold & D. Levine (Eds.), *Nebraska Symposium on Motivation, 1969* (Vol. 17, pp. 237–307). Lincoln: University of Nebraska Press.

Zurcher, L. A. 1965. "The Sailor Aboard Ship: A Study of Role Behavior in a Total Institution." *Social Forces, 43,* 389–400.

Zurcher, L. A. 1970. "The 'Friendly' Poker Game: A Study of an Ephemeral Role." *Social Forces, 49,* 173–186.

# Author Index

# Subject Index